BOTTOM LINE'S
SUPER HEALING
UNLIMITED

1,739 REMARKABLE SECRETS FROM THE WORLD'S GREATEST HEALTH EXPERTS

Bottom Line
Books

www.BottomLineSecrets.com

Bottom Line's Super Healing Unlimited
1,739 Remarkable Secrets from the World's Greatest Health Experts

Copyright © 2008 by Boardroom® Inc.

First Edition

10 9 8 7 6 5 4 3 2 1

ISBN 0-88723-483-6

Bottom Line Books® is a registered trademark of
Boardroom® Inc.
281 Tresser Boulevard, Stamford, CT 06901

Printed in the United States of America

Contents

1 • HEALTH ROUNDUP

Easy Ways to Ward Off Winter Colds and Flu…
    And Boost Your Immunity 1
Feed a Cold, Starve a Fever 3
Moderate Wine Drinking May
    Prevent the Common Cold 3
The Common Cold Need Not Be So Common 3
Exercise Helps to Defend Against Colds 5
Cold Sore Remedy 5
How to Stop Sinus Misery and Keep
    It from Coming Back 5
How to Get Sinus Relief 7
Faster-Acting Sinus Infection Treatment 9
Hum to Help Your Sinuses 9
Allergy Attack Self-Help 9
Hay Fever Self-Defense…
    How to Stop the Misery 9
Breakthrough for Asthma Patients 11
Breathing Problems Are Not Always
    Asthma Related 11
Singing Silences Snoring 11
Stop Feeling Tired: Hidden Causes of
    Chronic Fatigue 11
Foods that Help Chronic Fatigue 13
You Don't Have to Put Up with
    Fatigue Anymore 13
Feel More Energetic! It's Easy! 14
Eight Ways to Feel More Energetic 16

Is Adrenal Fatigue Making You Sick? 17
Favorite Natural Sleep Remedies 18
How to Get to Sleep…and Stay Asleep 18
Curb Insomnia with a Bedtime Snack 20
How to Get a Good Night's Sleep 20
Sweet Sleep Aid from the Grocer 22
When to Get the Best Sleep 22
What to Take When You Can't Sleep 22
Minimize Sleep Interference 24
How to Prevent Nighttime Visits
    To the Bathroom 24
Restless Legs Relief 24
Relief for Nighttime Leg Cramps 24
Tonic Water Fights Leg Cramps 25
Quick Varicose Vein Treatment 25
Quick Fixes for Problem Feet 25
Amazing Nail Remedy 27
Easy Wart Treatment 27
Better Cut Care 27
Ulcer Preventative 28
Little-Known Causes of Stomach Upset 28
Gallstone Prevention 28
What to Do If You Feel Faint 28
How to Minimize Mosquito and
    Tick Annoyances 29
Another Reason to Beware of Ticks 29
Acupressure Cure for Hiccups 30
Dandruff Magic 30

2 • SKIN, EYES, EARS, NOSE & TEETH

Smart and Simple Skin Care Solutions 31
Skin Strategies for Looking Younger 33
Treatment for Rosacea 34
Natural Sun Protection...34
Throw Out Old Sunscreen.......................................35
Better Protection Against Sun Damage 35
Skin Care Self-Defense 35
Quick Action Helps Stop Outbreaks of
   Poison Ivy 35
Good News for Psoriasis Sufferers 36
Tanning Beds Can Fight Psoriasis.............................37
Better Vision with Bifocals, Trifocals
   Or Progressive Lenses 37
Is Vision-Correcting Laser Eye Surgery for You? 38
Secrets of Cataract Prevention…and Reversal 39
Cataract Control 40
Glaucoma Facts 40
Eye Self-Defense 41
An Herb for Your Eyes 41
Common Eye Problems 41
How to Treat Eye Problems 42
What to Do If You Have Eye Floaters.........................42
Stem-Cell Transplants for Blindness 42
Obesity Can Lead to Blindness.................................42
Can Earwax Removal Help Hearing Loss?...................43
How to Reverse Hearing Loss 43
Stop the Noise of Tinnitus 43
A Natural Treatment for Tinnitus..............................44
Avoid Sinus Infections…Naturally............................44
Blow Your Nose Gently to Help Your Ears 46
Breakfast in Bed Fights Allergies.............................46
Shocking Dangers of Gum Disease...........................46
Protecting Your Gums Can Save Your Life 48
The Truth About Fluoridated Water 49
Fight Cavities in Your Sleep 50
Extra-Special Protection for Teeth and Gums 50
Should You Have Your Fillings Removed? 50
Best Ways to Whiten Teeth 50
How to Relax at the Dentist's Office 51
Soothe Sensitive Teeth 52
Sugar-Free Soda Warning 52
Dental Problems May Be an
   Early Sign of Osteoporosis 52

3 • SYMPTOMS & SOLUTIONS

Medical Red Flags: Seven Symptoms
   Never to Ignore..53
How to Stay Out of the Doctor's Office 55
Immunity Boosters: How to Be Illness-Free 56
If You Have a Persistent Cough… 58
Hidden Health Trap: Your Gender Matters 58
Hormones Can Cause Hidden Health Problems........60
What You Should Know About
   Adult-Onset Diabetes 61
Diabetes Indicators 63
How to Get the Best Diabetes Treatment...................63
Help for Diabetes...65

New Pain Relief for Diabetics 65
Vinegar May Fight Diabetes....................................65
Coffee Cure to Prevent Diabetes 65
The Dangerous Health Problem Most
   Doctors Miss 66
Thyroid Disease Could Be the
   Cause of Your Symptoms 67
Screening for Osteoporosis 69
Bone Loss Warning..69
How to Build Strong Bones the Natural Way.............69
Eating Prunes May Help Prevent Bone Loss 71
How to Beat Osteoporosis.......................................71
Osteoporosis Drug Warning 73
How to Keep Your Hips Healthy 73
Are You at Risk for Hip Problems?...........................74
What You Must Know About Inflammation 75
Taking a Break May Save Your Life 77
Love Your Liver—How to Care for
   Your Second-Largest Organ.................................77
The Deadly Disease Most People
   Don't Know They Have.......................................78
Protect Your Pancreas 80
Kidney Stones: How to Prevent and Treat Them.......82
Gout Treatments that Really Work............................84
Simple Cures for Gout 85
How to Soothe Those Aching Feet............................86
Self-Test for Foot Problems.....................................88

4 • TAKE CONTROL OF YOUR HEALTH

The Ultimate Medical Checkup 89
Important Medical Tests Doctors
   Don't Tell You About 91
Beware of "Normal" Test Results..............................92
How to Survive a Medical Emergency
   Without a Doctor 93
How Doctors Stay Well with Sickness
   All Around All Day Long 94
How to Stay Healthy: Recommendations from
   Six Prominent Doctors..96
How to Stay in Touch with Your Doctor 98
Female Doctors Have Better Bedside Manners
   Than Male Doctors 99
How to See a Specialist Faster 99
How to Guard Against Medical Misinformation 99
Do Your Own Medical Research 101
How Much Do You Know About Your Doctor? 102
How to Protect Your Full Rights as a Patient............103
How to Keep Your Medical Information Private......105
Don't Become a Victim of Medical Error.................106
How to Avoid Becoming a
   Medical-Error Statistic......................................106
Your Responsibilities for Your Health 107
How to Get the Most Out of Your
   Annual Physical 108
What to Do When Your Doctors Disagree 109
How to Make Sure Your Mammogram
   Is Read Accurately...110
Biopsy Alert 110

What You Need to Know About All
The Scary Errors in Medical Tests 111
Do You Really Need That Diagnostic Test? 113
Full-Body CT Scan Hype 115
Best Home Medical Tests...115
What You Need to Know Before You
Get a Blood Test 117
These Genetic Tests Could Save Your Life 117
Why You Must Know Your Family's
Medical History...119
Better Emergency Medical Care 120
Self-Defense Against Prescription Mistakes.............120
Has Your Medication Been Switched?.......................121
How to Shrink Your Medical Bills by 25% or More.....121
The Most Dangerous Scams Can Cost You Your
Health…or Your Life—Not Just Your Money 123
Internet Fraud Warning..125
Beware of These Health Scams................................125

5 • MEDICATIONS, DRUGS, VITAMINS & SUPPLEMENTS

Protect Yourself and Your Family from
Medication Mishaps 126
How Dangerous Medication Mistakes
Can Be Avoided 128
Pill Dosage Danger..129
The Very Simple Secret of Stopping Side Effects
From Medications..129
Don't Take Antidepressants with Aspirin 131
Antidepressant Alert..131
Medications that Cause Weight Gain 131
Drug Side Effects and Women 132
Drug Patches: Healing with Fewer Side Effects 132
Emergency Warning: Know Your Medications.........133
How to Get Drugs Not Yet FDA Approved 133
Older Drugs May Be Better than Newer Versions 133
New-Drug Dangers..134
Do Drug Companies Call the Shots? 134
Are Cholesterol-Lowering Medications Safe?...........135
Avoid Expensive Combo Drugs................................135
Are You Taking Medications Properly? 136
Is Your Medication Depleting Your
Body of Nutrients?..136
Don't Mix Culinary Herbs and These Drugs.............136
Timing Your Medications for Maximum Benefit 136
Best Time to Take Heart Pills 138
Blood Pressure Trap...138
Over-the-Counter Drugs: Some Are Much Safer
And More Effective than Others 138
Aspirin Isn't Just for Headaches 140
Aspirin Therapy Alert...141
Protect Your Stomach If You Take Aspirin Daily 141
When to Take Your Daily Aspirin 141
Beware of Accidental Acetaminophen Overdose 141
Acetaminophen/Alcohol Alert 142
Are You Taking the Wrong Pain Pill? 142
Six Dangerous Myths About Antibiotics 144
Antibiotics and Calcium Don't Mix 145

Many Herbal Supplements and Drugs
Shouldn't Be Combined...145
Drugs and Sun Don't Always Mix 147
Peanut Alert..147
Secrets to Living Longer: Miraculous Supplements.....147
Supplements Adults Should Take Daily....................149
Use Melatonin Wisely...149
Best Supplements for Boosting Energy,
Strength and Stamina 149
Glucomannan: A Wonder Supplement.....................150
Get the Most from Vitamin and
Mineral Supplements 150
Look for the USP on the Label 151
The Omega-3 Solution: Fatty Acids Fight
Heart Disease, Arthritis and Obesity 151
Unexpected Benefits of Vitamin D 153
Vitamin D Boosts Calcium Absorption 154
Tired? Forgetful? You May Need More B Vitamins 154
Too Much of a Good Thing?.....................................156
Get More Vitamin C from Orange Juice....................156
Vitamin C and Stress..156
Antioxidant Therapy 156
Antioxidant Supplement Warning.............................158
Vitamins and Colon Polyps 158
Vitamin Danger 158
Does St. John's Wort Interfere with Cancer Drugs? ..159
Vitamin A Danger 159
Men Need Calcium, Too...159
Potassium Warning 160
Zinc Alert 160
Hidden Ephedra 160
Does Cookware Boost Your Intake of Iron? 160
Fish Oil Supplements Are Harmful for Some 161
Beware of Chromium Picolinate 161

6 • DIET & NUTRITION SOLUTIONS

Prevent Asthma, Cataracts, Gallstones, Heart
Failure and IBS by Eating the Right Foods............162
How Nutritionists Shop for Groceries.......................164
Don't Be Fooled by Food Labels 165
Smart Food Choices Boost Brainpower....................165
Three Foods that Are No Longer Taboo 166
Beware! Six Healthy Foods that Can Be
Very Dangerous…to You.......................................167
Time Bombs—Hidden Salt, Sugar and Fat in
Everyday Foods...168
The Truth About Fats and Oils 169
Breaking the Sugar Habit 170
Sweet Treat Lengthens Life 171
Amazing Miracle Drug: Your Morning Coffee 172
Cinnamon for Diabetes 173
Drink Your Cocoa..174
Cranberries Protect Against Disease 174
Apples Really Do Keep the Doctor Away.................174
Let Oregano Help Keep You Healthy 174
Cooked Carrots Are More Nutritious
Than Raw Ones...174
Choose Rye Bread Over Wheat 175

Cook Your Pasta al Dente 175
Grape Juice and Aspirin 175
Soy Milk and Calcium.............................175
Nondairy Ways to Get Calcium 175
Tea Drinking Builds Strong Bones............176
Black Tea Boosts Immunity 176
The Simple Drink that Fights Cancer, Heart
    Disease, Colds and Cavities 176
Nuts vs. Cholesterol.................................177
Organic Food Trap...................................177
Produce with High and Low Pesticide Levels 177
Separate Your Produce.............................178
Does Washing Produce with Water Remove
    All Bacteria? 178
Keep Mercury Levels Down.......................178
Make Sure Your Water Is Safe to Drink.....178
Foods that Relax You................................179
Yogurt Eases Allergies 181
Foods that Trigger Hay Fever.....................181
Beans—the Perfect Food 181
Better Bean Digestion 183
Secrets of Avoiding Digestive Problems 183
Avoid Heartburn When Eating Out............184
How Long to Keep Foods 185
Is Microwaving in Plastic Safe?.................185

7 • EXERCISE & WEIGHT LOSS

Secrets of the Diet Masters 186
Outsmart Your Fat Triggers to Lose Weight
    And Keep It Off 188
Almonds for Weight Loss 189
Weight-Loss Secrets That Really Work 189
Feel-Full Snacks That Are Only About
    150 Calories Each 191
Asian Weight-Loss Secret..........................191
Lose Belly Fat and Save Your Life 191
Six Ways to Lose That Too-Big Potbelly 193
A Harvard MD Weighs In on the Eating Debate.......194
High-Protein Diet Danger 196
The Calcium Diet: Lose Weight Faster with
    This Vital Mineral 196
When It's OK to Use Diet Drugs.................197
How to Recognize a Dangerous Diet 197
Hidden Causes—Why You May Be Gaining
    Weight 198
Stop Food Cravings and Lose Weight 199
Simple Ways to Stop Uncontrolled Eating...............200
Most People Don't Realize When They're Full 202
Reduced-Fat Foods Could Cause Weight Gain 202
Healthier Peanut Butter 202
Eating Out with America's Top Food Cop.....202
Easy Way to Increase Fat Burning 204
Six Ways to Trigger Your Natural Fat Burners 204
How to Exercise to Burn More Fat 206
How Hollywood Stars Shape Up—Fast!.....206
Be Your Own Personal Trainer 207
Exercise Opportunities: Use Anything…
    Anywhere...209

Painless Ways to Build Exercise into
    Your Daily Routine 209
Can Fat Be Fit? 211
How to Exercise Anytime, Anywhere.........211
Best Time to Exercise 213
How to Avoid Injury When Working Out.............213
Injuries: When to Use Heat…or Cold 215
Raisins Before a Workout 215
A Stronger Body in Only 30 Minutes a Week 215
Revised Exercise Guidelines 217
Exercise as Medicine 217
Exercise Fights Ulcers..............................219
Heartburn and Weight Lifting 220
Muscle Loss Prevention 220
Yoga Is for Everyone 220
The Stretch Cure 222
Walk and Live Longer 223
Walking Boosts Brainpower 223
Fitness Walking to Cure Disease................223
Better Fitness Walking 225

8 • HEADACHES, ARTHRITIS & CHRONIC PAIN

Little-Known Headache Triggers 226
Caffeine and Ibuprofen............................228
Anti-Headache Diet Keeps You Pain-Free 228
Get to the Root of the Headache 229
Faster Pain Relief....................................229
Quick Headache Relief 229
Foot Massage Helps Headaches 229
Natural Remedies for Headache Pain.........229
How to Stop Migraine Pain.......................231
Breakthroughs for Headache Relief 233
Treatment Options for Migraine Relief.......234
Acid Reflux May Cause Migraines 236
Arthritis Relief..236
Relieve Arthritis Pain…Naturally 238
Water Helps to Fight Osteoarthritis 239
Use Ginger to Ease Arthritic Knee Pain.....240
Knee Surgery May Not Help Arthritis 240
Stop Knee Pain—Without Surgery 240
Is It Serious?..242
Amazing Advances in Joint-Replacement
    Surgery 242
If You Think Osteoarthritis is Inevitable,
    You're Wrong! 244
Breakthrough Treatments for Arthritis......246
Arthritis Pain Relief Strategies 248
Arthritis Food Cures................................248
Amazing New Ways to Control Rheumatoid
    Arthritis..248
Rheumatoid Arthritis/Heart Attack Link 249
Ten-Step Program for Chronic Pain Works
    Very, Very Well 250
Stop Pain Fast with Self-Hypnosis 251
Unraveling the Mysteries of Fibromyalgia..............253
Getting Relief from Mysterious Muscle Pain 253
Get Pain Relief from Natural Remedies 254

Seven Myths About Multiple Sclerosis.......................255
Surprising Secret to Stopping Back Pain 257
You Can Beat Chronic Back Pain 259
Back Attack—When to See the Doctor 260
How to Manage Back Pain 261
Should You See a Chiropractor?.............................262

9 • HEART DISEASE & STROKE

Heart Attack Prevention Secrets:
   Low-Tech Strategies Are Effective 265
#1 Heart Attack Trigger 267
If You're Having a Heart Attack… 267
Chill Therapy for Cardiac Arrest Victims 267
How to Help Heal Yourself.....................................267
How to Recover from a Cardiac Crisis.....................269
Heart Attack Self-Defense......................................270
Triglycerides: Too-Often Overlooked Culprit
   In Heart Disease 272
Syndrome X…the Little-Known Cause of
   Many Heart Attacks..273
What's Your Risk for Heart Disease?........................275
The Ultimate Cholesterol-Lowering Diet..................275
OJ for Your Cholesterol..277
Cranberry Juice Fights Heart Disease 277
Trans Fatty Acids Are Worse than Butter..................277
Easier Cholesterol Control 278
The Miracle Heart Drugs Millions of
   Americans Take 278
Lower Your Cholesterol Without Drugs 279
Beyond Cholesterol: Six Threats to Your Heart
   Doctors Often Overlook...................................281
Have Your Homocysteine Levels Been Tested?........282
Better Test to Predict Heart Attack Risk...................283
Self-Defense Against ER Misdiagnosis.....................283
Bypass Surgery Danger for Women.........................283
Heart-Bypass Surgery Side Effect 284
Baldness Linked to Heart Trouble 284
Good News About Nutraceuticals 284
Chocolate Is Good for the Heart 286
Eat Citrus to Reduce Heart Disease 286
Consume Split Peas for a Healthier Heart 286
Drinking Beer Combats Blood Clots 286
New Strategies for Controlling High
   Blood Pressure..287
Eat Your Way to Lower Blood Pressure....................288
Better Blood Pressure Reduction............................289
Falling Blood Pressure Alert 289
How to Avoid a Stroke…and Get the Right
   Life-Saving Help If It Strikes.............................289
One-Minute Stroke Diagnosis.................................290
Better Stroke Detection..291
Do You Know the Symptoms of a Ministroke?........291
Surprising Stroke Risks Even
   Doctors Overlook 291
The Migraine–Stroke Link......................................293
Stents May Help Prevent Stroke—Safely..................293
Potential Risk of Artery Surgery 293

10 • CANCER PREVENTION & TREATMENT

Proven Ways to Reduce Your Risk
   Of 12 Common Cancers....................................294
Beware of Hidden Carcinogens 297
Acrylamide: A Tasty Risk.......................................299
Take a Nutritional Approach to Cancer
   Prevention..299
Warning for Women Smokers.................................300
Up to 70% of Cancers Can Be Avoided…
   Improve Your Odds 301
If the Doctor Says Cancer… 302
Cancer Survival Secrets 303
Surprising Strategies for Coping with Cancer 304
A New Way to Look at Cancer Statistics 306
Cancer Fighter on a Sandwich................................306
Cancer Cure? 306
Coping with Chemo 306
Out-of-Body Cancer Therapy 308
What You Must Know About Lymphoma..................308
Best Therapies for Prostate Cancer 310
Better Prostate Cancer Detection 312
When a High PSA Reading Is Not a Problem 312
Prostate Biopsy Self-Defense 312
Treating Prostate Cancer 312
The Very Latest Thinking on Hormone Therapy......314
Better Breast Cancer Detection...............................316
Foods that Prevent Breast Cancer 316
Carrots Combat Ovarian Cancer 316
New Pap Smear Testing..316
Proper Screening for Colon Cancer 316
Dietary Iron Increases Colon Cancer Risk 318
Skin Cancer: Debunking the Myths 318
Melanoma Is on the Rise.......................................320
More Effective Melanoma Screening.......................321
Most Common Sites for Melanoma.........................322
Aspirin May Reduce Pancreatic Cancer Risk...........322

11 • SURGERY & HOSPITALS

Medical Mistakes Can Be Very, Very Costly 323
How to Get Much Better Hospital Care....................325
How to Make Your Hospital Stay Briefer, Safer
   And Less Expensive...326
What Hospitals Don't Want You to Know 327
How to Choose the Right Surgeon 328
Better Nursing Care...329
How to Pick a Hospital..329
Hospital Overcharge Self-Defense…
   Keep Records…Keep Track…Keep at It...............330
Don't Be Afraid to Visit a Hospital Patient 331
Simple Way to Avoid Infectious Diseases 331
Take Aspirin in the Hospital 331
How to Survive a Trip to the ER 332
Emergency Room Self-Defense 333
Don't Have Surgery Until You Read This 334
Important Presurgery Test.......................................335
Should You Forgo Surgery?.....................................335
Secrets of Successful Surgery 337
Goof-Proof Surgery 338

Smoking and Surgery 338
Children and Surgery 339
Secrets of Safe, Pain-Free Surgery 339
Safer Surgery 340
How to Reduce the Hidden Risk of
    Any Surgery—Anesthesia 341
Avoid the Risk of Surgical Infection 342
In-Office Surgery: Eight Questions that Could
    Save Your Life 342
Secrets of Speedy Rehabilitation After Stroke,
    Surgery or Injury 343
How to Recover from Surgery Faster 344
Protect Yourself from Hospital Staph 346

12 • HEALTH INSURANCE

How to Outsmart Your Managed Care
    Organization 347
How to Get the Most Out of Managed Care ...349
Get More from Your HMO 350
911 Danger? 351
How to Fight Your Insurer…and Win 351
How to Get Your HMO to Pay Your
    Claims Fast 352
When You Can't Resolve a Health Insurance
    Problem… 353
Advice About Appeals 354
Short-Term Health Insurance 354
If You Must Buy Your Own Health Insurance…
    Choose Wisely 354
How to Escape Common Health
    Insurance Traps 356
How to Get All the Medical Insurance
    You Are Due 358
Cutting Medication Costs 358
Patient and Doctor Confidentiality 358
If Your Income Stopped Today…Would You
    Be Able to Pay Your Bills? 358
How to Know If Long-Term-Care Insurance
    Is for You 359
Shrewder Long-Term-Care Insurance Buying ...360
What to Do if You Lose Your Health Insurance ...360
Latest Medicare Scam: Old Bills 361

**13 • ALTERNATIVE & NATURAL
    SOLUTIONS**

Important Therapies That Are
    Too Often Overlooked 362
Powerful Herbal Medicines People Rarely
    Hear About 364
Supercharge Your Immunity with Herbs 365
Herbal Remedies: Secrets of Greater
    Effectiveness and Safer Use 367
Little-Known Risks from Popular
    Herbal Remedies 368
Age-Old Remedies Are the Best Cures 369
Remedies for Summer Ills 371
Proven Home Remedies for Common Aches
    And Pains 372

Simple Remedies that Really Work 373
Uncommon Cures for Asthma, Depression,
    Headaches and More 374
All-Natural Ways to Help Arthritis,
    High Blood Pressure and More 376
Use Cold-Water Therapy for Relief 378
Oils that Improve Health 379
Healing Teas 379
Use Vinegar to Treat Common Ailments 380
How to Strengthen Your Immune System Easily ...381
Strengthen Your Body's Ability to Heal Itself ...382
How to Create Your Own Medical Miracle 384
Hypnosis Heals 385
Controlling Chronic Pain with
    Magnetic Therapy 385
Magnet Dangers 387
Hand Reflexology 387
Drug-Free Strategies for Irritable Bowel
    Problems 388
Natural Relief for Crohn's Disease and IBS ...390
Natural Way to Treat Constipation 390
Anti-Diarrhea Root 390
How to Cure Stomach Ailments Naturally 391
Quick Herbal Relief for Indigestion 392
Natural Treatment for Indigestion 393
Breathing Your Way to Better Health 393
Aromatherapy…For Much More than Just
    Pleasant Smells 394
Scents to Boost Energy, Mood, Memory
    And More 396
Natural Decongestant 396

14 • AGING & LONGEVITY

Secrets of Maximum Longevity 397
Are You Aging Too Fast? 399
Antiaging Strategies for Your Body and Mind ...399
Longevity Boosters from the World's
    Longest-Lived People 401
Exercise at Any Age 403
Self-Defense Strategies for Older Patients ...403
What You Can Do Now to Stay Healthy and
    Keep Out of a Nursing Home 404
Sexual Problems of Older People and
    How to Solve Them 406
Can Testosterone Make You Younger? 407
Don't Believe the Hype About hGH 408
How to Age-Proof Your Body…Naturally 408
New Rules for Living Longer 410
Think Positively and Live Longer 411
Age-Proof Your Brain 411
Brain-Boosting Pills: What Really Works…and
    What Doesn't 413
Simple Strategies to Improve Your Memory ...414
How to Keep Your Brain Strong and
    Memory Working 416
Memory-Boosting Marvel 417
Protect Yourself from Dementia 418
Early Sign of Dementia 419

Olive Oil Helps Keep Your Brain Healthy, Too........419
What You Can Do to Keep Your Brain Healthy 420
Common Drugs Fight Alzheimer's 421
Possible Cause of Alzheimer's 421
Natural Helper for Alzheimer's.................................421
Surprising Reasons Why People Fall 421
Test Your Mobility 423
Protect Your Bones Against Fracture 423
Home Remedies for Common Conditions 425
Hidden Threat to Older Adults 427
Do You Have an Alcohol or Drug Problem? 428
The Fountain of Youth Is in the Foods You Eat 428
The Ultimate Antiaging Diet 430
Chocolate Boosts Longevity 431
Eating Fish May Lower Risk of Blindness................431
The Wrinkle-Cure Diet—What to Eat to Look
    Much Younger..432
Acne Medication for Facial Wrinkles.......................433
"Senior" Vitamins Are Not Worth the Cost 433
How to Keep Your Bladder Very Healthy 434

15 • EMOTIONAL HEALTH

How to Get Unstuck in Work, Life
    And Relationships..436
Controlling Anxiety Without Drugs..........................437
Drug-Free Ways to Fight Depression 439
Let the Sun In 440
If Your Antidepressant Causes Impotence… 441
Alternative Treatment for Depression 441
Feeling Fatigued or Depressed?................................441
Cures for Common Phobias......................................441
How to Keep Upbeat and Stay Healthy 443
Self-Hypnosis…The Edge You Need to
    Overcome Bad Habits 444
Essential Secret of Kicking Addictions 445
You Know the Dangers of Smoking…
    Here's How to Quit!..446
How to Overcome Addictions You May Not
    Even Know You Have...446
Be Happy with Your Body Image at Any Age........448
Lower Stress in Five Minutes or Less 449
Quick and Easy Stress-Busters................................450
Better Breathing for a Much Healthier You 451
The Incredible Healing Power of Prayer..................451
Proof that Prayer Heals 452
Cultivate the Power of Patience 453
Proven Patience Boosters 454
Forgive Your Way to Better Health 455

16 • HEALTHY TRAVEL

Medical Emergencies Overseas—
    It Pays to Be Prepared 457
When in Europe… 459
Basic Travel-Medicine Kit 459

Protect Your Health While Traveling 459
Stock Up Before You Go...460
Don't Get Sick on Your Vacation 460
Stay Away from These Cities If You
    Have Health Problems..461
Tropical Travel Ahead?...461
How to Stay Healthy While Traveling by Air 461
Avoid Stomach Trouble When You Fly 463
What's Even Worse than Airline Food?.....................463
When You Shouldn't Get on a Plane 463
First Aid for Air Travelers 463
How to Avoid Jet Lag..464
New Treatment for Traveler's Diarrhea 465
Natural Relief for Traveler's Diarrhea 465
Cayenne Prevents Dysentery....................................466
Self-Defense Against Viral Illness on Cruises 466
How to Handle Illness After a Trip 466

17 • VERY, VERY PERSONAL

Why We Love: The Science of
    Sexual Attraction...467
Sex Makes You Look Younger 469
Best Ways to Boost Your Sexual Fitness...................469
When Was the Last Time You Had Sex? 471
Make Time for Sex 473
How to Make Sex Exciting…Again 473
Ten Foods that Boost Sex Drive 474
Sex Boost from Soy..475
Natural Aphrodisiacs..475
Nutrients that Boost Libido......................................476
Sex Too Soon After Childbirth Can Be Deadly........476
Nature's Rx for Women's Health Problems 477
Hysterectomy Is Rarely the Only Solution 478
Most Uterine Fibroids Can Be Left Alone 479
Beware of Diagnosing Your Own
    Yeast Infection..479
Oral Sex Trap 479
New Treatment for Incontinence..............................480
Try Kegel Exercises for Incontinence......................480
Managing Menopause Without Drugs......................480
Alternatives to Hormone Replacement 481
Natural Alternative to HRT 482
Fighting Hot Flashes in Women…and Men 482
Latest Ways to Prevent and Treat Impotence 482
Top Doctor Answers Tough Questions
    About Viagra 484
Natural Treatment for Impotence 485
Help for Premature Ejaculation 485
Vasectomies Do Not Affect Sex 486
Natural Treatment for Prostate Enlargement 486
Getting Help for Embarrassing Medical
    Problems 486
Help for Those Persistent and Annoying
    Problems 488

1

Health Roundup

Easy Ways to Ward Off Winter Colds and Flu... And Boost Your Immunity

Some people get laid low by every ailment that is making the rounds, while others sail through the winter season with nary a sniffle. The strength of your immune system is the critical factor. This biological army of cells and chemicals guards your intestinal tract and mucous membranes and patrols your bloodstream.

Overwork, stress and insufficient sleep can sap the vitality of these disease fighters. Regular exercise is known to improve immune function. But above all, your defending troops must be well fed to stay strong.

FEEDING YOUR IMMUNE SYSTEM

The number-one cause of immune weakness is *micronutrient starvation,* a shortage of vitamins, minerals and protective plant-based substances called *phytochemicals*.

These micronutrients are abundant in fruits and vegetables, but only about 25% of Americans consume the full number of daily servings recommended by the National Institutes of Health. (Visit *www.5aday.gov* for details.)

To maximize your intake of the key micronutrients, eat for color. Choose deep-colored fruits and vegetables whenever you can. These are filled with natural disease-fighting phytochemicals, such as carotenoids and flavonoids.

Best fruits, in order: Blueberries, blackberries, strawberries, raspberries, plums, oranges, red grapes, cherries, kiwis, pink grapefruit.

Best vegetables, in order: Kale, spinach, brussels sprouts, alfalfa sprouts, broccoli florets, beets, red bell peppers, onions, corn, eggplant.

Choose organically grown fruits and vegetables. Preliminary research suggests that organic

Robert Rountree, MD, medical director, Boulder Well-Care, a family practice, Boulder, CO. He is also a member of the adjunct faculty, Institute for Functional Medicine, Gig Harbor, WA. He has been researching immunity for more than 20 years and is coauthor of *Immunotics: A Revolutionary Way to Fight Infection, Beat Chronic Illness, and Stay Well* (Putnam).

1

produce may have more phytochemicals than conventionally grown plant foods.

If you choose to use nonorganic fruits and vegetables, scrub them thoroughly with a cleanser, such as Fit Fruit & Vegetable Wash, to help remove pesticide residues that can poison the immune system.

In addition to upping your intake of fruits and vegetables, eat fish at least twice a week. Fish contains omega-3 fatty acids, a type of polyunsaturated fat that boosts health and protects against some cancers.

I recommend wild salmon because it has very little mercury. Avoid large fish that are high in mercury, such as swordfish, shark, king mackerel and tilefish. Canned tuna is better than fresh because it comes from smaller fish.

If you don't like fish, you can take fish oil or flaxseed oil supplements. Be sure to follow instructions on the label.

Foods to avoid: Sugar-filled candies, cakes, cookies, jams and refined carbohydrates, such as white bread and pasta. These elevate blood sugar and interfere with the enzymes and cells of the immune system.

Foods that are heavy in saturated fat (such as red meat and whole-milk products) and trans fats (margarine and many commercially prepared desserts) weaken cell membranes and sabotage immune function.

SUPERCHARGERS

Everyone should take a daily multivitamin/mineral supplement that includes vitamin C, 2,000 milligrams (mg)...vitamin E in the form of tocopherol complex, 200 to 400 international units (IU)*...magnesium, 200 to 300 mg...and selenium, 100 to 200 micrograms (mcg). If you're still getting sick, you may need to boost your immune system with additional supplements. This is particularly important if you are under stress, work in a school or hospital or travel extensively—all of which put you at high risk of infection. *You can take all of the following every day if you wish...*

•**NAC,** short for *N-acetyl-cysteine,* a type of amino acid. It boosts levels of *glutathione,* a keystone of the body's armor against the toxic

*Check with your doctor for the proper amount—high amounts of vitamin E may be dangerous for some people.

free radicals. It thins mucus, making the respiratory system less prone to infection. NAC is particularly protective against colds, flu and sore throats.

Dose: 500 to 600 mg/day.

•**Grape seed extract,** which is rich in concentrated *proanthrocyanidins,* highly potent forms of the health-boosting bioflavonoids that are found in berries, citrus fruits and onions. These fortify the body against infection, help soothe inflammation, stimulate germ-fighting natural killer cells and increase the production of *interleukin-2,* a messenger chemical that activates other immune cells.

Dose: 150 to 300 mg/day.

•**Astragalus.** For thousands of years, traditional Chinese medicine has used this herb to strengthen the body's *we'i ch'i* ("defensive energy"). It is a general immune-system tonic that also can help fight a cold or flu if you're already sick. It stimulates the activity of *macrophages,* which swallow bacteria and viruses whole, and other disease-fighting cells.

Dose: 1,000 to 2,000 mg/day.

•**Probiotics.** The lower intestinal tract is host to colonies of bacteria, mostly friendly species that keep destructive germs at bay by crowding them out, stimulating production and activity of white blood cells and producing natural germicidal substances. Poor diet and exposure to antibiotics (including those that have entered the food chain in chicken and beef cattle) can deplete the body of its micro helpers.

Dose: 10 to 20 billion organisms daily of *L. acidophilus* in capsule or powder form. Follow package directions.

•**Green tea.** It is particularly helpful in the digestive tract, where it kills harmful bacteria. The antioxidants in green tea are more powerful immune boosters than vitamin C or E.

Dose: Two cups daily, or 1,000 mg of extract.

AN IMMUNE-FRIENDLY LIFESTYLE

Other ways to boost immunity...

•**Sufficient rest.** Sleep deprivation robs your body of the downtime it needs for self-repair. A single sleepless night markedly lowers immune activity. If you have trouble sleeping, try taking at bedtime L-theanine (100 to 400 mg)...or valerian (200 to 800 mg)…or melatonin (1 to 5 mg). If you are pregnant or taking medication, check with your physician.

• **Moderate exercise.** Physical activity invigorates your immune system, but exercising to exhaustion creates damaging stress. Don't try to make up for a whole week of inactivity on the weekend.

• **Home hygiene.** Drink only filtered water, and use unbleached paper goods and nontoxic cleaning supplies.

• **Workplace protection.** Keep your keyboard, phone and desk clean. Don't use the pens, keyboards or phones of coworkers who are often sick. Be wary of bathroom doorknobs—push the door open with your arm or grasp the knob with a paper towel.

Feed a Cold, Starve a Fever

It really does make sense to feed a cold and starve a fever.

In a unique study that tested the effectiveness of Mom's favorite adage, researchers found that eating boosted the immune system's ability to fight rhinoviruses—the type that cause the common cold. And fasting quadrupled the levels of *interleukin-4,* a chemical messenger involved in the immune response that helps ward off fevers.

Ask your doctor for recommendations on your specific illness.

Gijs R. van den Brink, MD, researcher, laboratory for experimental internal medicine, Academic Medical Center, Amsterdam.

Moderate Wine Drinking May Prevent The Common Cold

In one study, people who drank eight to 14 glasses of wine per week were half as likely to come down with a cold as the nondrinkers.

Red wine was more protective than white. Beer and hard liquor had no effect.

Caution: More than one alcoholic beverage daily has been shown to increase breast cancer risk and may cause other health problems.

Miguel A. Hernan, MD, DrPH, assistant professor of epidemiology, Harvard School of Public Health, Boston. His one-year study of 4,287 men and women was published in the *American Journal of Epidemiology.*

The Common Cold Need Not Be So Common

Bennett Lorber, MD, DSc, professor of medicine and microbiology and chief of the section of infectious diseases, Temple University School of Medicine, Philadelphia.

The average person gets two colds a year, and the average cold lasts seven days. Bennett Lorber, MD, a leading expert on the common cold, offered some practical advice on how to beat these averages. *Here's how to improve your chances of staying well…*

WHAT CAUSES COLDS?

A cold is not a single disease. It's a set of related symptoms caused by a viral infection of the upper respiratory tract. Colds can be caused by any of more than 150 different viruses.

A cold begins when a virus particle binds to chemical receptors found on cells in the upper part of the nose.

Each time you touch someone who has virus particles on his/her skin and then transfer the virus to your nose or eyes, you're likely to catch the cold.

Trap: Cold viruses can survive for three to four hours on the skin surface. Thus, you can shake someone's hand in the morning, then rub your eyes at lunch…and still become infected.

Viruses can also be transferred from drinking glasses, door handles, pens and other inanimate objects for about three hours after being handled by an infected person.

Occasionally, colds are caught by inhaling virus particles put into the air after a cold sufferer has sneezed or coughed.

Studies show that the common cold is almost never transmitted by kissing. High temperatures inside the mouth seem to inhibit the reproduction of the viruses that cause colds, keeping the virus population down.

WHO GETS COLDS?

Anyone can catch a cold—especially someone who spends lots of time around children.

Because they haven't yet developed immunity to many cold viruses, children under age 12 typically get five to seven colds per year—twice that number if they're in day care. When these kids get sick, they tend to pass the illness along to their families.

Another factor that can raise the risk of catching a cold is psychological and/or physical stress, such as that associated with the loss of a loved one…or running a marathon or another form of extremely vigorous exercise.

MINIMIZING YOUR RISK

There's no foolproof way to avoid colds. But adopting these strategies—especially during cold season—should help…

●**Avoid shaking hands with someone who obviously has a cold.** If someone is sneezing or sniffling, offer a smile—but not your hand.

A cold sufferer is most infectious two to three days after the onset of symptoms. Five days or so after symptoms appear, the person is no longer infectious.

●**Wash your hands often.** Any soap is capable of killing cold viruses. Don't worry about using antibacterial soap.

Until you wash your hands, keep your hands away from your nose and eyes.

●**Keep your home clean.** The cleaner your household, the less likely countertops, telephones, cooking utensils, etc., are to spread cold viruses.

Make liberal use of household disinfectant. To make your own disinfectant, mix one part bleach with nine parts water.

GETTING RELIEF FROM SYMPTOMS

Despite its reputation as a cold fighter, vitamin C is of no value for the prevention or treatment of colds. That's been demonstrated by several good studies.

Nor is there any solid evidence that echinacea, goldenseal or any other herbal remedy is of value against colds. The same is true for homeopathic remedies.

Antibiotics are effective only against bacterial infections—not against viral infections like the common cold.

What about zinc? In recent years, this purported cold remedy has become so popular that drugstores have had trouble keeping their shelves stocked with it.

Several studies have shown that sucking on lozenges of zinc gluconate does reduce the severity and duration of cold symptoms. But other studies have found just the opposite.

Since zinc lozenges are of unproven effectiveness—and since zinc gluconate can cause nausea—it's best to stick to cold remedies of proven effectiveness. *These include…*

●**Over-the-counter (OTC) antihistamines.** *Clemastine fumarate* (Tavist) and *brompheniramine maleate* (Dimetapp) can reduce nasal discharge by up to 25%, sneezing by up to 50% and coughing by up to 40%.

●**Pseudoephedrine.** This drying agent, found in Sudafed and other OTC cold remedies, is effective against a range of symptoms, including congestion and runny nose.

In one study, 60 milligrams (mg) given four times a day for four days improved overall symptoms by nearly 50%.

●**Naproxen.** This nonsteroidal anti-inflammatory drug (NSAID)—the main ingredient in Aleve and other OTC painkillers—is effective in fighting headache, body aches, malaise and cough.

Caution: Aspirin and acetaminophen have been shown to prolong "shedding" of cold viruses, thereby making colds last longer.

●**Nasal spray.** Medicated sprays or drops such as *oxymetazoline* (Afrin) provide temporary relief of congestion. However, Afrin is off limits to people with high blood pressure.

Caution: Such sprays should be used for no more than three days. Used longer than that, the sprays can cause "rebound" congestion, in which stuffiness becomes worse than it was before treatment.

Some studies suggest that the asthma drug *ipratropium bromate* (Atrovent) may be effective against colds. In one study, use of an ipratropium inhaler reduced nasal discharge by 25%.

If nothing else works for your cold, ask your doctor about trying ipratropium.

HEAT vs. COLDS

A study published in the *British Medical Journal* found that breathing humid air (heated to 109.4° Fahrenheit) for 20 minutes at the first sign of a cold decreased symptoms by 40%. But other studies found no such benefit.

Given the conflicting findings, what is a cold sufferer to do? Consider breathing steam from a boiling kettle several times a day. It won't hurt—and could help.

Exercise Helps to Defend Against Colds

Avoid colds by being physically active. A study of middle-aged adults found that those who were most active throughout the day had fewer colds.

Men with the highest levels of physical activity accumulated at work, at home and in regular exercise experienced a 35% reduction in risk of colds compared with less active men. Highly active women experienced a 20% reduction in risk.

Any kind of activity, as long as it was at least moderately intense and performed for a total of two to three hours per day, provided cold-reducing benefits—from structured exercise to gardening and yardwork to brisk walking.

Chuck Matthews, PhD, research assistant professor, department of epidemiology and biostatistics, University of South Carolina, Columbia.

Cold Sore Remedy

Cold sores heal faster and cause less pain when treated topically with Pepto-Bismol or another bismuth-containing antacid.

What to do: Once every four hours, use a cotton ball to dab the liquid onto the sore.

Other potentially effective remedies for cold sores include the over-the-counter amino acid supplement *lysine* and the prescription ointment *acyclovir* (Zovirax).

Matthew Lozano, MD, family physician in private practice, Fresno, CA.

How to Stop Sinus Misery and Keep It From Coming Back

M. Lee Williams, MD, associate professor emeritus of otolaryngology and head & neck surgery, Johns Hopkins University School of Medicine, Baltimore. He is author of *The Sinusitis Help Book: A Comprehensive Guide to a Common Problem* (John Wiley & Sons).

More than 50 million Americans a year experience sinus trouble. Common as it is, sinusitis is very poorly understood. Even many physicians are in the dark about causes and effective treatments.

WHY SINUSES HURT

There are more than 40 different sinuses (hollow spaces) located in the head. The eight sinuses located next to and above the nose tend to cause the most trouble.

When these *paranasal* sinuses are healthy, mucus continually drains from them into the nose. The mucus helps protect delicate nasal membranes from irritation and infection.

Sinus trouble arises when the tiny drainage holes through which this mucus flows become blocked. Mucus backs up into the sinuses, and bacteria flourish in this accumulating mucus. Sinus membranes become inflamed and/or infected, causing pain and a sensation of pressure.

Sinusitis (inflammation of the sinuses) typically occurs in the aftermath of a cold or flu. These respiratory illnesses cause nasal membranes to swell, blocking sinus openings.

Nasal congestion caused by allergies to pollen, dust, animal dander, etc., can also set the stage for sinus infection. The same goes for exposure to airborne irritants such as soot, paint fumes and car exhaust.

Most cases of sinusitis last only a week or two. But severe, prolonged or recurrent sinus infections can cause scar tissue to form within the sinuses or their drainage openings.

The scar tissue can block sinuses permanently. Permanent blockage can also be caused by a cyst or polyp in the sinus…or by a malformation of the cartilage or bone within the nose.

Whatever the cause, obstruction that is allowed to persist inevitably leads to sinusitis.

SINUS SYMPTOMS

Sinusitis is often accompanied by a milky or greenish-yellow nasal discharge as well as postnasal drip, bad breath, sore throat and dull head pain.

The pain usually occurs around or between the eyes…in the forehead…at the base of the nose…or in the cheeks. Occasionally, it's felt along the top, sides or back of the head. Sinusitis pain usually disappears at night, only to return the following day.

PREVENTION—THE BEST CURE

Especially if you're prone to sinusitis, take steps to prevent the sinus blockage that leads to infection and scarring…

•**Reduce your chances of catching colds and flu.** Avoid close contact with anyone who is obviously infected. Wash your hands frequently during the cold/flu season.

Each fall, ask your doctor whether you should consider getting a flu shot.

•**Minimize your exposure to air that is too dry or humid.** Breathing dry air thickens mucus and inhibits its flow.

Conversely, excessive humidity can cause nasal and sinus membranes to swell, leading to sinus blockage.

There's little you can do about being exposed to humidity extremes while outside. But try to keep the humidity inside your home at 45% to 65%. Use a humidifier or dehumidifier if necessary.

Don't sit or sleep near a drafty window, radiator or heating or air-conditioning vent.

Steer clear of saunas and steam baths if you're prone to sinus trouble.

•**Avoid exposure to allergens and irritants.** Take steps to avoid contact with pollen, dust, dust mites, animal dander and any other allergens that have bothered you in the past.

Don't smoke. Limit your contact with secondhand smoke, too.

Avoid swimming pools in winter. Chlorine can irritate already-dry sinus membranes, making them vulnerable to infection.

Limit your consumption of alcohol to one drink per day. Drinking can cause sinus and nasal membranes to swell.

SELF-CARE FOR SINUSITIS

If you have sinus symptoms, you can usually ease the discomfort on your own…

•**Take an over-the-counter decongestant that contains *pseudoephedrine,*** such as Sudafed. This will open your sinus passages and allow mucus to flow.

Decongestant pills work a bit better than sprays, which frequently don't penetrate deeply enough. And unlike sprays, pills do not cause "rebound" congestion, in which the nasal swelling goes away briefly only to come back worse than before.

Caution: Avoid decongestant pills if you have high blood pressure or urinary problems. If you take any prescription drug, ask your doctor or pharmacist if it could interact with pseudoephedrine.

•**Apply hot compresses to the painful area for five minutes every few hours—** especially after being out in cold weather.

In addition to relieving pain, compresses will improve circulation in the region, helping your body fight the sinus infection.

•**Sleep with your head and shoulders elevated.** This promotes drainage of mucus from your sinuses. Try sleeping on three pillows or—better yet—on a foam sleeping "wedge" with a pillow on top of that.

If you sleep on your side: Keep your head turned so that the more painful side faces up.

●**Avoid air travel.** Pressure changes that occur during descent can force infected matter deeper into the sinuses. That makes the infection harder to treat.

If you *must* fly with a cold or sinus infection, take a decongestant just before departure. Ask your doctor if you should be taking an oral antibiotic as well.

WHEN TO SEE THE DOCTOR

If sinusitis persists for 10 days or longer—or if your symptoms are severe and/or getting worse—you may need antibiotic therapy.

Treated promptly, even severe sinusitis generally clears up with a couple of weeks of antibiotic therapy. If you ignore the symptoms for weeks or months before seeking treatment, however, several *months* of antibiotic therapy may be necessary.

DO YOU NEED AN OPERATION?

Sinus surgery may be necessary if the pain and congestion persist despite prolonged treatment with decongestants and/or antibiotics. *It may also be necessary if…*

…the sinuses are filled with mucus, pus and cannot drain.

…the infection has extended to the eyes or surrounding bones.

…the sinuses are blocked by a polyp, cyst, scar tissue or some anatomical defect.

The simplest form of surgery is *puncture and irrigation.* In this procedure, the surgeon flushes out the infected sinus by injecting a salt-containing solution through the nose.

This outpatient procedure is performed under local anesthesia. Complications are rare. Recovery is usually immediate.

Another commonly used surgical technique is *functional endoscopic sinus surgery.* In this procedure, the surgeon uses a small, lighted "telescope" inserted through the nose to remove diseased tissue, open clogged drainage openings and restore sinus function.

Endoscopic surgery typically requires several weeks of healing. The most common complications after the procedure include swelling and infection.

How to Get Sinus Relief

Harvey M. Plasse, MD, clinical associate professor of otolaryngology, New York University School of Medicine, and director of otolaryngology, NYU Downtown Hospital, both in New York City. He is coauthor of *Sinusitis Relief* (Henry Holt).

Don't assume that sinus inflammation is harmless. Left untreated, this annoying condition eventually causes permanent scarring of the sinuses—and may, in rare cases, even lead to blindness or brain abscess.

AN ACCURATE DIAGNOSIS

Because sinusitis often begins as a common cold, the condition frequently goes undiagnosed and untreated.

Anyone who experiences a cold for more than 10 days should be checked for the presence of sinus infection.

Other symptoms…

●**Thick or discolored nasal discharge** (yellow or green).

●**Fever.**

●**Bad breath.**

●**Facial pain or pressure in the forehead and over the eyes,** between the cheek and nose, in upper teeth or between the eyes.

●**Reduced or absent sense of smell.**

●**Ear pain.**

Symptoms that subside within four weeks are diagnosed as *acute sinusitis…subacute sinusitis* lasts for four to 12 weeks. If not treated effectively, this condition can turn into *chronic sinusitis,* in which symptoms persist for more than 12 weeks.

ACUTE SINUSITIS

Antibiotics are the primary treatment for acute sinusitis. The main goal is to eradicate the infection and prevent the development of chronic sinusitis.

The effective antibiotics include *amoxicillin* (Amoxil)…*amoxicillin* and *clavulanate* (Augmentin)…*cefpodoxime* (Vantin)…and *cefuroxime* (Ceftin).

Important: Many people make the mistake of discontinuing the antibiotic once symptoms begin to subside. But the drug should always be taken for the full course—typically 10 days—to ensure that the bacteria are eliminated. If symptoms are unchanged after three days, your doctor should reevaluate your condition and possibly switch antibiotics.

In addition to taking antibiotics, sinusitis sufferers should drink at least eight 8-ounce glasses of water daily. It's also important to avoid alcohol, sugary drinks and caffeinated beverages. *Other strategies to consider...*

●**Fill a bowl to one-third full with hot water,** drape a towel over your head and the bowl and inhale the steam for several minutes. The warm moisture helps loosen secretions in the nose, throat and lungs, making them easier to clear.

●**Use an over-the-counter (OTC) mucus thinner,** such as *guaifenesin* (Robitussin or Mucinex), to loosen phlegm.

●**Take an OTC oral decongestant,** such as *pseudoephedrine* (Sudafed).

●**Try an OTC nasal spray decongestant,** such as *naphazoline* (Privine) or *oxymetazoline* (Afrin).

Caution: Never use a spray decongestant for more than three consecutive days. Doing so often triggers rebound swelling of the nose.

The saline nasal sprays are also very helpful. They clear the nose of secretions and irritants. Saline sprays can be used as frequently as every two hours.

CHRONIC SINUSITIS

If chronic sinusitis develops, a longer course of antibiotics—typically prescribed for three to six weeks—should be taken.

Reason: Chronic sinusitis has been linked to anaerobic bacteria, especially hardy microorganisms that can survive without oxygen.

The condition is also more likely to involve multiple types of bacteria. A long-term course of antibiotics is the most effective treatment against these bacteria.

Inflammation and swelling can be reduced by using a nasal steroid spray, such as *beclomethasone* (Beconase)...or an oral steroid, such as *prednisone* (Deltasone) or *dexamethasone* (Decadron).

Oral or spray decongestants eliminate congestion. Mucus thinners promote drainage. Anticholinergic nasal sprays, such as *ipratropium bromide* (Atrovent), may help with dry secretions.

To determine if allergies are involved, your doctor should conduct a skin or blood test that will measure your reaction to a variety of different allergens.

Nasal fungus is also being identified in an increasing number of chronic sinusitis cases. Newer, less toxic antifungal medications, itraconazole and amphotericin B, have improved prognosis in the treatment of sinus fungal infections.

WHEN TO SEE A SPECIALIST

If sinusitis symptoms persist longer than four weeks or if you suffer recurrent bouts of acute sinusitis, see an *otolaryngologist* (ear, nose and throat specialist) for a thorough exam.

The exam should include a nasal endoscopy, in which an endoscope is passed through the nose into the sinuses to check for blockages and to collect a sample of mucus.

A *computed tomography* (CT) scan of the sinuses should also be performed to check for nasal polyps, thickening of the mucous membrane, changes in bone structure or increased bone thickness.

SINUS SURGERY

If drug treatment doesn't help, sinus surgery may be your best option. New, less-invasive techniques have made sinus surgery easier and safer than ever before.

The surgical method of choice is *functional endoscopic sinus surgery* (FESS), in which an endoscope inserted through the nose into the sinuses is used to clean and drain the sinuses... remove an obstructive growth, such as a polyp, tumor or cyst...or to reopen or enlarge the natural openings of the sinuses to allow drainage and ventilation.

But surgery should always be a last resort, so if your doctor thinks you should go under the knife, be sure to get a second—or even third—opinion before proceeding.

Faster-Acting Sinus Infection Treatment

When taken with antibiotics, the supplement *bromelain,* made from pineapple enzymes, breaks down mucus and helps clear up a sinus infection faster than using antibiotics alone. Take 500 milligrams (mg) three times a day in addition to a doctor-prescribed antibiotic. Available in health food stores.

Benjamin F. Asher, MD, chairman, alternative medicine committee, American Academy of Otolaryngology, Alexandria, VA, and an instructor in surgery/otolaryngology, Dartmouth Medical School, Hanover, NH.

Hum to Help Your Sinuses

Humming can help relieve sinus infections. In one study, *nitric oxide,* a gas that is lethal to bacteria, increased 15-fold in the nose during humming. An increase in nitric oxide indicates improved sinus air exchange, whereby fresh air enters the sinuses and replaces "old air." Poor ventilation of the sinuses is a risk factor for sinus infections.

Self-defense: To ventilate your sinuses, hum for one minute every one to two hours.

Jon O. Lundberg, MD, PhD, professor of physiology and pharmacology, Karolinska Institute, Stockholm, Sweden.

Allergy Attack Self-Help

During an allergy attack, apply pressure to the center of the web between the thumb and index finger of one hand. Angle the pressure toward the bone that connects to the index finger. Maintain pressure for two minutes. Take slow, deep breaths. Repeat with the other hand. This stimulates the acupressure points that relieve allergic reactions.

Michael Reed Gach, PhD, director, Acupressure Institute, Berkeley, CA, *www.acupressure.com.*

Hay Fever Self-Defense... How to Stop The Misery

Stuart H. Young, MD, clinical associate professor of pediatrics and internal medicine, Mount Sinai School of Medicine, and allergist in private practice, both in New York City. He is coauthor of *Allergies: The Complete Guide to Diagnosis, Treatment and Daily Management* (Consumer Reports Books).

If you're among the 20 million Americans who suffer from sneezing, congestion, runny nose and itchy eyes—perhaps also headaches, earaches, fatigue and moodiness—the first thing you need is a diagnosis.

Your doctor should start by ruling out other causes of your symptoms, such as nasal polyps or sinus infection. After that, he/she can usually diagnose hay fever based on your medical history—when your symptoms typically appear and disappear.

Note: Hay fever doesn't normally cause fever. Hay fever symptoms plus fever could mean a sinus infection or another infection.

If you have hay fever, these proven strategies will help eliminate your symptoms...

REDUCE POLLEN EXPOSURE

The most common cause of hay fever is an allergy to ragweed pollen. But pollen from cocklebur, lamb's-quarters, pigweed and other weeds that bloom in summer and fall causes comparable symptoms. West of the Rockies, hay fever symptoms stem mainly from sagebrush, saltbush and sheep sorrel pollen.

Best defenses...

●**Keep windows closed at home—**and also in your car.

●**Use an air conditioner to filter out pollen.** Change the filter as often as the manufacturer suggests...or when it looks dirty.

●**Since pollen levels peak in early morning,** save your outdoor activities for after 10 am. Listen for pollen counts on the news.

●**Have someone else do outdoor chores.** Even if offending plants don't grow in your vicinity, pollen can travel up to 500 miles.

●**Eliminate pollen-carrying plants from your yard.**

●**If you are extremely allergic and are outdoors for long periods,** shower and shampoo when you go back in. Put clothes directly into the washing machine or hamper. Washing helps keep pollen out of your house.

●**If you have severe hay fever,** consider wearing a simple filter mask while outdoors. The masks are sold at home-improvement and hardware stores. They must fit snugly over your nose and mouth.

AVOID OTHER IRRITANTS

You can also help curb hay fever by avoiding three other respiratory irritants…

●**Alcohol.** Alcoholic beverages increase nasal congestion in hay fever sufferers. During hay fever season, keep alcohol consumption to a minimum. Better yet—avoid alcohol altogether.

●**Diesel exhaust.** It contains compounds that exacerbate hay fever. Diesel exhaust plus pollen can produce an allergic response that is significantly greater than the response to ragweed alone.

Also—give trucks and buses a wide berth when you're walking on the street. Many have diesel engines.

●**Ozone.** If the air quality index—which forecasts ozone pollution—is poor, stay inside as much as possible. Ozone exacerbates hay fever.

TAKE MEDICATION

If symptoms persist despite your taking these precautions, medication may be helpful…

●**Antihistamines are usually the first choice.** But over-the-counter (OTC) allergy medications make some people sleepy.

Best: *Loratadine* (Claritin) and *fexofenadine* (Allegra). They relieve all allergy symptoms except congestion—without causing drowsiness.

Caution: Women who are of childbearing age should take loratadine. Recent studies have shown that it may be safer than fexofenadine during pregnancy.

For mild, intermittent symptoms, take these medicines as needed. For daily symptoms, take the medicine regularly throughout hay fever season. Check with your doctor for dosage instructions.

If you also suffer from runny nose and congestion, Claritin-D and Allegra-D may be the best choice. They both contain the decongestant *pseudoephedrine.*

●**Steroid nasal sprays** such as *fluticasone* (Flonase) or *budesonide* (Rhinocort) are best if your only symptom is nasal congestion.

They are sometimes used in conjunction with decongestants.

Bonus: Steroid sprays are safer than cortisone pills because they work directly on affected nasal membranes. Oral steroids cause many side effects, including high blood pressure, cataracts, ulcers and osteoporosis. They are used only in severe cases when other treatments have failed.

Downside: Irritation of nasal membranes. Point the nozzle slightly away from the delicate septum of the nose.

●**Nasal saline sprays** rinse the nose and help to reduce sinus inflammation. All brands are about equal.

ALLERGY SHOTS

Most hay fever sufferers don't need to get allergy shots. But shots may be helpful if your symptoms are so severe that you require cortisone medication regularly during the season …if your allergies last beyond ragweed season…or if you also have asthma or allergies other than hay fever that give you year-round symptoms.

Sensitivity tests generally reveal which allergens are causing the problem. The doctor applies a small drop of several different allergens to the skin, scratches the skin under each drop with a tiny needle, then waits 20 minutes for a mosquito bite–like reaction.

The tests help determine appropriate treatment. You could receive small injections of an *allergen* (allergy-triggering substance) in gradually increasing doses weekly for up to two years. This method works to eventually desensitize you to that allergen.

Breakthrough for Asthma Patients

A new medication may help to reduce asthma attacks by more than 50%.

Omalizumab (Xolair) also allows patients to reduce use of inhaled corticosteroids, which can cause side effects. The drug, which is injected once or twice a month, is for patients with moderate to severe allergic asthma that can't be adequately controlled by other drugs.

Caution: Patients who were given omalizumab in clinical trials had slightly higher cancer rates than placebo patients, but the difference was not statistically significant. Patients with a personal or family history of cancer should discuss the potential risks of this medication with their doctors.

Thomas Casale, MD, chief of allergy and immunology and director of clinical research, Creighton University, Omaha.

Breathing Problems Are Not Always Asthma Related

Breathing problems thought to be caused by asthma are sometimes caused by exercise-induced *vocal cord dysfunction* (VCD). Many of the symptoms of the two disorders are similar—difficulty speaking and breathing, chest tightness and panic.

Self-defense: If you suffer asthma attacks only when exercising, ask your doctor about undergoing *spirometry* (breathing into a breath-measuring device) and other tests to distinguish VCD from asthma.

Patients diagnosed with VCD often benefit from a few weeks of speech therapy.

Susan M. Brugman, MD, pediatric pulmonologist, National Jewish Medical and Research Center, Denver.

Singing Silences Snoring

Even those people who can't carry a tune snored less after performing vocal exercises 20 minutes a day for three months.

Theory: Singing tones flabby throat muscles that cause snoring.

If you snore: Before trying singing, ask your doctor about *sleep apnea,* a potentially dangerous airway disorder that causes sufferers to stop breathing repeatedly during the night. This is a serious condition that may require surgery or other treatment.

Edzard Ernst, MD, PhD, director and professor, Peninsula Medical School, department of complementary medicine, run jointly by the Universities of Exeter and Plymouth, Exeter, England.

Stop Feeling Tired: Hidden Causes of Chronic Fatigue

Benjamin Natelson, MD, professor of neurosciences, University of Medicine and Dentistry—New Jersey Medical School, and director, New Jersey Chronic Fatigue Syndrome Center, both in Newark. He is author of *Facing and Fighting Fatigue—A Practical Approach* (Yale University Press).

Fatigue is one of the leading reasons why Americans see their doctors. Unfortunately, it is also one of the most undertreated ailments in the US.

Problem: If doctors cannot diagnose a specific illness as the cause of fatigue—a virus, for example—they frequently dismiss their patients' complaints.

Good news: Fatigue is typically caused by a treatable condition, such as sleep deprivation, ongoing psychological stress or depression. In rare cases, it can be caused by *chronic fatigue syndrome* (CFS).

If you eat a nutritious, balanced diet and are in otherwise good health—but still feel sapped of energy for more than six weeks—here's what to do...

IS DISEASE TO BLAME?

The first step is to rule out any underlying illness. To do this, your doctor should order blood tests for anemia…diabetes…hepatitis and other liver disorders…infectious mononucleosis…lupus…Lyme disease…rheumatoid arthritis…and thyroid deficiency.

You should also undergo a *creatine phosphokinase* (CPK) test of muscle chemistry…a test for low magnesium…and a "sed rate" (sedimentation rate) analysis to check for general inflammation of body tissues.

If the results are normal, your doctor should perform a test of *dehydroepiandrosterone* (DHEA)—a hormone that is produced in the adrenal glands.

Chronic sinusitis—an ongoing sinus infection that causes facial pain, nasal discharge and recurring sinus headaches—is another cause of fatigue. If you have these symptoms, ask your doctor for a CT scan of the sinuses.

COMMON CULPRITS

If no specific illness is detected, you and your doctor should focus on three key areas…

• **Sleep habits.** If you snore—or sleep lightly for much of the night—you may have a breathing disorder known as *sleep apnea*. This condition causes repeated awakenings and prevents deep, restful sleep.

If you suspect snoring is the problem, ask your doctor about breathing aids, including adhesive strips such as BreatheRight, medications and nasal sprays. If the more serious diagnosis of sleep apnea is possible, consider consulting a sleep clinic.

If you have trouble falling—or staying—asleep, you may have poor "sleep hygiene." Avoid caffeine after lunchtime and try to wake up at the same time each morning.

• **Stress.** Even minor stress—such as getting stuck at a red light when you're late—can drain your energy. If your daily activities include such stresses, you may be exhausted at the end of the day.

Your doctor should also analyze your lifestyle to detect a stress pattern. A stress-management program can help you cope.

• **Depression.** This is the most overlooked cause of persistent fatigue. Unless symptoms are severe, many people who are depressed never realize what's wrong with them.

Good news: Depression usually subsides when treated with psychotherapy and antidepressants—such as *selective serotonin reuptake inhibitors* (SSRIs), including *fluoxetine* (Prozac) and *sertraline* (Zoloft).

If both depression and insomnia are present, a sedating antidepressant, such as *amitriptyline* (Elavil), may be preferable.

DIAGNOSING CHRONIC FATIGUE

If these measures do not help, you may have CFS. This disorder, which affects approximately 2% of Americans, is suspected when a lack of energy interferes with personal, professional or social activities.

CFS is typically diagnosed if you have four or more of the following symptoms for at least six months…

Fatigue that lasts more than 24 hours following physical activity…impaired short-term memory…muscle or joint pain…recurring headaches…sore throat…tender lymph glands …waking up tired in the morning, even after a full night's sleep.

Although medical experts have not identified the causes of CFS, possible triggers include…

• **Fibromyalgia.** This illness is marked by chronic muscle and joint pain, but some fibromyalgia patients also experience severe, chronic fatigue.

Treatment: Pain management with *gabapentin* (Neurontin), *hydromorphone* (Dilaudid) or another medication.

• **Infection.** Many cases of CFS begin with fever, sore throat or swollen or tender lymph glands—all of which suggest an infection.

Treatment: Antibiotics if the infection is bacterial.

• **Premenstrual syndrome (PMS).** Eighty-five percent of CFS sufferers are female. Because PMS exacerbates fatigue, some experts believe it may contribute to CFS.

Treatment: SSRI antidepressants, such as *paroxetine* (Paxil) and *sertraline* (Zoloft).

TREATING CHRONIC FATIGUE

Regardless of what's triggering your CFS, a specialist* is likely to focus on two aspects of treatment that may surprise you…

●**Aerobic exercise.** It can enhance sleep, increase metabolic activity, reduce stress and relieve depression. Begin with easy walking—no faster than a slow stroll—three times a week for five minutes at a time. Build up to at least 20 minutes of walking every day.

●**Cognitive-behavioral therapy.** Dwelling on how tired you are actually increases stress and fatigue.

A trained cognitive-behavioral therapist can help you reduce CFS symptoms. It often takes just one or two sessions to identify "catastrophic" thinking—*My life is terrible. I can't do anything.*

This therapy helps you focus on a more positive appraisal—*I can handle this. My fatigue lessens from time to time.*

Other treatments include…

●**Drug therapy.** There is no drug treatment for CFS. But *ondansetron* (Zofran), an anti-nausea drug that boosts levels of the neurotransmitter serotonin, is undergoing clinical trials. Some reports suggest it may help ease CFS.

●**Supplements.** Magnesium and/or DHEA supplements may also help if patients are deficient in them.

Foods that Help Chronic Fatigue

Chronic fatigue syndrome (CFS), a condition characterized by fatigue and musculo-skeletal pain, is linked to an imbalance of *phospholipids,* a type of fat, in the brain. *Eicosapentaenoic acid* (EPA), a fat found in fish, restores that balance by inhibiting the

*To locate a chronic fatigue specialist, contact a university-affiliated medical center in your area to find an internist or infectious-disease physician who sees CFS patients in his/her practice. Or contact the Chronic Fatigue Immune Dysfunction Syndrome Association of America, 704-365-2343, *www.cfids.org.*

breakdown of phospholipids, and helping form new ones.

Eating more salmon, white albacore tuna and other fatty fish rich in EPA may ease the fatigue and depression often associated with this condition. Consult your doctor about the best way to incorporate this dietary strategy into your treatment plan.

Basant K. Puri, MD, PhD, consultant and senior lecturer, Imperial College, University of London. His research was published in Acta Psychiatrica Scandinavica.

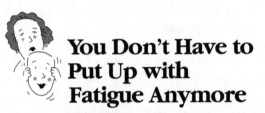

You Don't Have to Put Up with Fatigue Anymore

Erika T. Schwartz, MD, internist in private practice, Armonk, NY. She is author of Natural Energy: From Tired to Terrific in 10 Days *(Putnam).*

You've tried getting more sleep. You've tried exercising and taking other steps to control psychological stress. Yet you're still feeling tired and run down.

You know it's unwise to prop yourself up with caffeine. But what else can you do to boost your energy levels?

Once anemia, heart disease, thyroid disease, hepatitis, mononucleosis and other medical causes of fatigue have been ruled out, the average physician is at a loss as to what to do next.

"You'll just have to learn to live with it," he might say. Or, "Well, you are getting older."

This is not necessarily the only explanation. *These nutrition-based strategies can be very effective in giving you more energy…*

DRINK MORE WATER

Many cases of fatigue can be traced to the *mitochondria,* the microscopic "power plants" inside each cell of the body.

Mitochondria synthesize *adenosine triphosphate* (ATP), a high-energy molecule that's used throughout the body as a source of energy. But the chemical reactions that yield ATP also make free radicals and other toxins as by-products.

To flush out these toxins, the body needs at least 64 ounces of water a day. Less than that, and mitochondria are apt to become "clogged" with toxins, becoming inefficient at pumping out ATP.

RECONSIDER SALT

For many people with high blood pressure, salt deserves its status as a dietary no-no. But in healthy individuals, moderate salt intake boosts energy levels.

Salt helps the body hold onto the water it takes in. By boosting water retention, salt helps keep mitochondria free of toxins and functioning properly.

As long as your blood pressure is normal, it's safe to boost your intake of chicken stock, miso soup, salted nuts and other unprocessed sources of salt whenever you feel fatigued.

EAT SMALL, EAT OFTEN

Eating three big meals a day puts your blood sugar (glucose) levels on a roller coaster. Low glucose can cause fatigue.

Eating every three hours helps keep your energy up by steadying your glucose levels.

You should aim to consume a healthy, balanced mix of protein and fiber at each meal. Because fiber- and protein-rich foods are digested slowly, they provide a steady, reliable source of energy.

Eat plenty of vegetables, brown rice, multigrain bread, grilled chicken or fish, nuts and dried fruits.

ENERGY-BOOSTING SUPPLEMENTS

Three nutrients are of proven value in the treatment of chronic fatigue...

•**L-carnitine.** This amino acid helps transport fatty acids into the mitochondria, where they're used to make ATP.

L-carnitine is found in lamb, beef and other meats, but you'd have to consume impossibly large amounts of these natural food sources to get the 1,000 milligrams (mg) of L-carnitine needed each day to boost your energy.

Ask your doctor about taking the prescription L-carnitine supplement *Carnitor*. The typical dosage is three or four 330-mg tablets a day.

•**Coenzyme Q10.** This antioxidant enzyme acts as a catalyst to "spark" synthesis of ATP.

Organ meats are the best source of co-enzyme Q10, but you'd have to eat far too much to get the recommended 100 mg of coenzyme Q10 per day.

Coenzyme Q10 is sold over-the-counter in powder or gel form. The gel is more easily absorbed. The typical dosage is two 50-mg gel-caps a day.

•**Magnesium.** This mineral is needed for ATP synthesis. Unfortunately, chocolate, caffeine, soft drinks and highly processed foods tend to deplete the body of magnesium. As a result, magnesium deficiency is common in the US, and fatigue is a symptom of magnesium deficiency.

At special risk: Diabetics, people who consume lots of caffeine and people who take diuretic drugs.

Good sources of magnesium include wheat bran...brown rice...spinach...kale...chicken...turkey...pork...apricots...and curry powder.

Ask your doctor about taking a magnesium supplement, too.

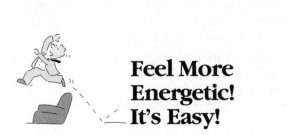

Feel More Energetic! It's Easy!

Richard N. Podell, MD, MPH, medical director, The Podell and King Medical Practice, with locations in Somerset and Springfield, NJ, *www. drpodell.org*. Dr. Podell is one of several doctors nationwide who are conducting studies on Ampligen, an experimental drug for chronic fatigue syndrome. He is author of several books, including *Doctor, Why Am I So Tired?* (Fawcett).

Among older people, chronic fatigue is often symptomatic of diabetes, thyroid disease, anemia, hepatitis or another underlying illness.

In young people, it's more likely to be the result of psychological stress, anxiety or depression...or poor sleep, poor nutrition and/or a lack of exercise.

Up to 1% of American adults have *chronic fatigue syndrome* (CFS), a debilitating and as-yet incurable condition that's believed to be triggered by one or more viruses.

Whenever fatigue lasts for three weeks or longer—or interferes with your work or your enjoyment of life—see a physician. Simple blood tests can detect most of the common physical causes of fatigue.

Good news: For most fatigue sufferers, these changes in diet and lifestyle provide a substantial energy boost...

•**Eliminate sugar and cut back on carbohydrates.** In some people, the body responds to sugar and carbohydrates by releasing too much insulin. This causes glucose levels to plummet, resulting in fatigue.

I often ask my patients suffering from fatigue to stop eating sugar and cut their daily consumption of carbohydrates to two slices of bread or one serving of pasta. These changes often trigger a dramatic rise in energy. You'll know within three weeks if the changes are going to make a difference for you.

•**Exercise four times a week.** Regular exercise causes the body to release energizing compounds called *endorphins*. It also boosts the flow of oxygen to the brain...and reduces stress and anxiety.

Start at a low level of exercise. Then increase the distance or pace by about 10% each week, as long as you don't feel worse.

While many people feel energized after each exercise session, others require several months of reconditioning before their fatigue dissipates.

•**Eliminate caffeine from your diet.** Despite its reputation as a stimulant, the caffeine in cola, coffee and black tea tends to exacerbate fatigue. *There are two reasons for this...*

•Caffeine is addictive. You need increasing amounts to feel "normal." When you fail to get your usual "dose" of caffeine, you feel tired.

•Too much caffeine causes anxiety, which can interfere with restful sleep.

If you regularly drink caffeinated beverages, give them up for a week. See if you feel more energetic. Reduce your intake by one cup a day. This will help you avoid caffeine-withdrawal headaches.

•**Consume alcohol in moderation**—and *never* late at night. Alcohol disrupts sleep,

especially when consumed after 7 pm. It also exacerbates the low blood sugar condition *hypoglycemia.*

If you're trying to boost your energy, one drink a day is the limit. Total abstinence is better.

•**Eat fruits and vegetables daily.** Green beans, broccoli, spinach, carrots, summer squash and certain other vegetables—and most fruits—are rich sources of potassium, magnesium and other key nutrients.

Having five servings each of vegetables and fruits every day helps ensure you're getting everything needed for optimal metabolism.

•**Have a daily "energy cocktail."** Most Americans are deficient in at least one essential nutrient. Such deficiencies interfere with energy production, causing fatigue.

Many of us would benefit from taking a multivitamin/multimineral supplement, along with daily supplements containing...

•Fish oil or primrose oil (1 gram). These oils contain essential fatty acids that help the body produce beneficial prostaglandins.

•N-acetylcysteine (600 milligrams [mg]). This supplement supplies the body with a key antioxidant called *glutathione.*

•Bilberry or grape-seed extract (60 mg). These increase energy, speed up metabolism and improve circulation.

•B-complex (25 to 50 mg of each B vitamin). B vitamins are water-soluble, so they're depleted more quickly than other nutrients.

Women of childbearing age should also take an iron supplement to replace iron lost during menstruation.

•**Take ginseng.** This stimulant herb, often taken in capsule form, isn't addictive the way caffeine is. For best results, ask your doctor about using ginseng intermittently for up to two weeks at a time. Follow label directions carefully.

•**Take naps.** Americans today sleep about an hour less than they did just 90 years ago. Sleeping an extra 45 minutes each night can bring big improvements in energy levels.

If you can't find the extra 45 minutes, take a 10- or 20-minute nap whenever you feel tired.

Trap: Excessive daytime napping interferes with nighttime sleep.

•**Discuss medications with your doctor.** Fatigue is a common side effect of *hundreds* of prescription and over-the-counter drugs.

Show your doctor or pharmacist a list of every drug you take. In many cases, switching to a slightly different drug will eliminate fatigue.

Caution: Never change medications without first consulting your doctor.

•**Take frequent mental breaks.** Set aside five to 20 minutes at least once a day for quiet time. Use the time to practice deep breathing.

What to do: Sit comfortably. Inhale slowly through your nostrils until your lungs fill. Gently contract your stomach muscles and hold for a few seconds. Exhale slowly. Repeat the cycle until your quiet time is up.

A single deep breathing session can provide a surge of energy that lasts one hour or more.

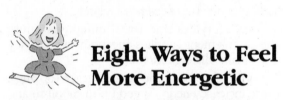

Eight Ways to Feel More Energetic

Jamison Starbuck, ND, naturopathic physician in family practice and lecturer, University of Montana, both in Missoula. She is past president of the American Association of Naturopathic Physicians and a contributing editor to *The Alternative Advisor: The Complete Guide to Natural Therapies and Alternative Treatments* (Time-Life).

If you are over age 40, fatigue is likely to be a frequent complaint. And if you're like many people, your doctor has checked you over and proclaimed that you're fine. "You are just getting older" is the typical refrain.

The obvious solution is to get more sleep. To be productive, most middle-aged adults need at least seven hours each night. But some people get adequate sleep—and still feel tired. If that's the case, don't head for the rocker. *Try these strategies to get more pep...*

•**Drink more water.** It's an old saw, but true. Most folks just don't drink enough water. That's too bad because dehydration makes us sluggish. To determine how many ounces of water you should drink each day, divide your weight in pounds by two. Add an extra eight ounces for every 30 minutes of aerobic exercise you perform, plus an additional eight ounces for every cup of caffeinated coffee, black tea or soda that you consume.

•**Take a daily B-complex vitamin supplement.** The B vitamins provide energy and help maintain healthy muscle and nerve cells. Aging and stress increase our need for these vitamins, while alcohol and caffeine deplete them from our bodies. Take a B supplement daily with breakfast. Make sure it contains at least 50 milligrams (mg) each of B-1, B-3, B-5 and B-6...and 400 micrograms (mcg) each of B-12 and folic acid.

•**Try licorice.** This herb improves immune health, so it's a great tonic for people with fatigue. Be sure to use the herb, not the candy. Take one-half teaspoon of tincture daily for up to two months.

Caution: Check with your doctor before trying this—or any—herbal remedy. Licorice is not safe for people with high blood pressure or liver or kidney disease.

If you dislike the taste of licorice: Try schisandra. Like licorice, this herb helps the body to overcome exhaustion by enhancing immune function. Take one-half teaspoon of the tincture daily for up to two months.

•**Exercise.** Starting an exercise program can be very overwhelming if you suffer from fatigue. That's why I recommend some gentle stretching exercises combined with walking. For specific exercises, get a copy of the book *Stretching,* written by Bob Anderson and published by Shelter.

•**Lose weight.** Even a small weight gain is enough to make some people feel tired. Hard to believe? Imagine strapping a 10-pound bag of sugar to your back and taking it with you everywhere you go. You'll have more energy if you drop unnecessary body weight.

•**Declutter.** Living in a mess—and feeling guilty about it—is tiring. Clutter also distracts the mind, making it more difficult to concentrate. Get just one room—or even one area—organized. You'll get a boost.

•**Pare down your schedule.** Doing less is not easy. But overscheduling is a primary cause of fatigue. If you're often tired, keep a journal of your daily activities for one week. You'll probably find that you are doing more than you think. Is all of it necessary? Is it enjoyable? If not, eliminate some activities and make time for rest and pleasure.

•**Have fun.** We all know that laughter is essential to physical well-being. But, sadly, merriment is a foreign concept for some people. Finding delight in life is energizing. Whether it's mountain climbing or reading in a hammock, find the things that give you a lift and indulge.

More from Jamison Starbuck...

Is Adrenal Fatigue Making You Sick?

My office is often filled with people complaining of fatigue. Many of these patients have already been told by a medical doctor that nothing is wrong with them—or that their weariness is symptomatic of depression. Dissatisfied with this advice, they turn to naturopathic medicine, hoping that I have an answer. In many cases, I do.

The answer often lies with their adrenals, two strawberry-sized glands situated just above the kidneys. Through the secretion of numerous hormones, including cortisol, DHEA and aldosterone, the adrenals control the metabolism of fat, carbohydrate and protein...regulate inflammation...and influence mood, sleep, blood pressure and digestion.

Complete failure of the adrenals is rare. Lots of people, however, are troubled by what naturopathic physicians call "adrenal fatigue." Typically, this condition results from prolonged physical or psychological stress. Like the batteries of a car whose headlights are left on all night, the adrenals simply run down.

In addition to exhaustion, symptoms of adrenal fatigue include poor sleep, insomnia between 2 am and 4 am and increased susceptibility to infection and allergic reactions. Cholesterol is the primary building block for adrenal hormones, so a total blood cholesterol level below 160 is often a warning sign of adrenal fatigue.

Fortunately, the adrenals are pretty forgiving. Many of my patients find that they feel much better after devoting a month to stress reduction and improved nutrition. *Here's what I typically recommend...*

•**Don't skip meals...**and don't substitute sweets for "real" foods. Each meal should include protein—a cup of lowfat or fat-free yogurt, cottage cheese, a glass of soy milk or several ounces of beans, tuna or meat. Protein reduces adrenal stress by stabilizing blood sugar levels.

•**Take vitamin B-5.** Also known as *pantothenic acid*, vitamin B-5 is critical for proper adrenal function. You can get B-5 from fish, milk, beans, peas, whole grains, broccoli, cauliflower and kale. But people who suffer from adrenal fatigue usually benefit from taking a B-5 supplement. I typically recommend 50 milligrams (mg) per day.

•**Spend more time relaxing.** I often recommend yoga, qi gong, deep breathing exercises or simply walking quietly in a natural setting. As much as possible, avoid situations or activities that rev you up—noisy, busy restaurants, bars or gyms, scary movies, tense family or work settings.

•**Try acupressure.** Once or twice a day, press firmly on the fibrous spot between the thumb and first finger, about one inch in from the edge of the web. Known in traditional Chinese medicine as LI4 (large intestine 4), this acupuncture point is used in a variety of treatments. Pressing on this spot is said to "tonify" the adrenals by "quieting the spirit."

•**Consider herbal medicine.** Ashwaganda is traditionally used in India to treat nervous exhaustion and stress-induced ailments. The typical daily dose is 500 mg three times per day. Licorice root helps reverse adrenal fatigue by slowing the excretion of cortisol. The typical daily dose is 500 mg. Take one or both herbs for up to three months.

Caution: People with high blood pressure should not take licorice. And women who are pregnant or nursing should take herbs only with a doctor's supervision.

Also from Jamison Starbuck...

Favorite Natural Sleep Remedies

A good night's sleep is one of life's blessings. But, unfortunately, one out of three adults suffers from insomnia, which impacts their emotional well-being, immune health and vulnerability to infectious disease.

Medical doctors use prescription sedatives, such as *zolpidem* (Ambien), or antidepressants, such as *trazodone* (Desyrel), to treat insomnia. These drugs will generally work for short-term treatment, but their safety may diminish if they are used for more than 30 consecutive days. Both types of drugs cause side effects, such as constipation and drowsiness.

The chief triggers of insomnia are emotional stress, pain and hormone irregularity. Determine which of these fits your situation, and select one or more of the natural remedies listed.* Unlike the prescription drugs, which simply knock you out, natural medicine treats the cause of your insomnia. *Here's my approach...*

EMOTIONAL STRESS

If your sleeplessness is caused by emotional anxiety, my favorite homeopathic treatment is Calms Forté (Hylands). This formula has all the key ingredients, such as passionflower, oat and chamomile, and is found at health food stores. Two pellets, dissolved under the tongue at bedtime, quell both mild anxiety and the tendency to overthink. If you awaken frequently, you can repeat this dose up to three times throughout the night. I also recommend the herbs valerian and hops for stress-related insomnia. Take 60 drops of each herb together, in tincture form, in four ounces of hot water at bedtime. Both herbs are mildly sedating, generally safe and can be combined with Calms Forté.

*Some of these remedies may be inappropriate for women who are pregnant or nursing, or some people with chronic health conditions. Consult your doctor.

PHYSICAL PAIN

Insomniacs who suffer from joint and back pain can improve their sleep by relaxing their muscles at bedtime. Start with a warm Epsom salts bath just before bed (use at least two cups of Epsom salt per tub). For even greater relaxation, also take 300 milligrams (mg) of magnesium along with a homeopathic preparation of magnesium known as Mag. Phos 6X (four pellets under the tongue). Take both at bedtime immediately after the Epsom bath.

HORMONE IRREGULARITY

Menopause, premenstrual syndrome, thyroid hyperactivity or a surge in stress hormones precipitated by life changes or excessive exercise can all cause insomnia. Hormone-related insomnia should be evaluated and treated by your medical doctor or naturopathic physician.

One hormone-related insomnia which most people can treat themselves is connected to *seasonal affective disorder* (SAD), a condition that causes mild to moderate depression from autumn to spring. One dose of 0.5 to 2 mg of the hormone *melatonin,* taken at bedtime, may well correct the insomnia linked to SAD. Melatonin is available at health food stores and pharmacies. Start with the 0.5 mg dose and increase after five days, if needed. I recommend discontinuing melatonin for SAD-related insomnia by the end of March.

How to Get to Sleep...and Stay Asleep

Karl Doghramji, MD, director, Sleep Disorders Center, Thomas Jefferson University Hospital, and professor of psychiatry, Jefferson Medical College, both in Philadelphia, *www.jeffersonhospital.org/sleep.*

An occasional night without sleep is an annoyance, but persistent insomnia—and the crushing fatigue that usually results—can threaten your health and the health of others.

The National Highway Traffic Safety Administration (NHTSA) reports that insufficient sleep contributes to more than 100,000 traffic accidents in the US each year. People with chronic insomnia often underperform at work …have family problems…and are four times more likely to suffer from depression than those who sleep soundly.

WHAT CAUSES INSOMNIA?

Some people are born with a neurological "hardwiring" that causes *hyperarousal*—meaning that the brain stays alert when it is time to sleep. *Other causes…*

●**Negative life experiences,** such as a stressful family life or childhood abuse. Stress and anxiety inhibit sleep by causing the brain to remain "on guard."

●**Medical problems,** such as *restless legs syndrome* (RLS), which causes leg pain or discomfort at night…and *sleep apnea,* a condition in which breathing periodically stops—sometimes hundreds of times each night.

Restless legs syndrome is usually treated with medication, vitamins and other preventive measures. Sleep apnea may require surgery, respiratory devices and/or exercise.

●**Menopause.** About one in four women experiencing menopause has insomnia. Hormonal changes and the resulting hot flashes and night sweats can disrupt sleep.

●**Disruptions of the body's internal clock.** Individuals with *advanced sleep phase syndrome* fall asleep very early in the evening and wake up very early in the morning. People who have *delayed sleep phase syndrome* tend to fall asleep very late and wake up late the following day.

BEST TREATMENTS

Insomnia that is caused by a medical problem or hormonal change will generally clear up when the underlying condition is treated. Other cases usually require a combination of drug and behavioral treatments. Drugs will provide immediate relief. Behavioral therapy has long-term benefits that may make medication unnecessary. Psychotherapy may also be necessary to relieve anxiety.

Nearly everyone with insomnia sleeps better when they develop better lifestyle habits. *Some behavioral approaches…*

●**Relax during the hour before bedtime.** Read, listen to music, take a hot bath. Or try yoga, meditation or deep breathing. Avoid activities that bring on anxiety, such as paying bills or watching the news.

●**After 12 noon, avoid caffeine**—coffee, cola, black or green tea, chocolate and some pain medications, such as Excedrin. Even in small amounts, caffeine can disrupt sleep in vulnerable individuals. Foods containing *L-tryptophan,* such as milk and turkey, may promote sleep, but studies in this area are unclear.

●**Don't drink alcohol at night.** It makes sleep less restful.

●**Go to bed and get up at the same time every day,** even on weekends. Avoid naps, even short ones. They make it harder to fall asleep at night.

●**Exercise for at least 30 minutes daily.** Weight lifting, aerobic workouts and other forms of exercise may promote sleep. But don't exercise within three hours of bedtime because it temporarily raises alertness. I recommend *outdoor* morning exercise—exposure to light helps regulate the body clock.

●**Listen to relaxation tapes.** Some people sleep better when they listen to recordings of whale songs or forest or ocean sounds before going to bed. When sleep is disturbed by traffic or other noise, sound generators that produce "white noise" can help, as can earplugs.

OTHER TECHNIQUES

For patients with more severe sleep problems, I sometimes suggest that they chart their sleep for about two weeks. They write down when they go to bed, wake in the night, get up in the morning, etc., so they can estimate how much time they actually spend sleeping. I then have them limit themselves to that amount of time in bed each night. This eliminates the frustration of tossing and turning.

Example: Suppose a patient normally spends eight hours in bed but sleeps for about five. I might suggest he/she go to bed at midnight and set the alarm for 5 am. If he is sleeping soundly, I might increase the time in bed by about 15 minutes every few days, as long as he continues to sleep soundly.

I also sometimes recommend light therapy. Patients sit in front of a light box for 30 minutes daily to reset their body clocks. They do this first thing in the morning if they have trouble falling asleep and in the afternoon or evening if they wake up too early. Middle-of-the-night awakenings usually aren't caused by body clock disturbances and aren't likely to respond to light therapy.

Light boxes and lamps that produce 10,000 lux—the recommended amount of light—are available from Light Therapy Products (800-486-6723 or *www.lighttherapyproducts.com*).

DRUGS

The most commonly prescribed drugs for insomnia, *zolpidem* (Ambien) and *zaleplon* (Sonata), are relatively safe and effective when taken under a physician's supervision. They provide rapid relief for many insomniacs. This can diminish the fear of further sleeplessness, which can be a strong force behind the perpetuation and escalation of insomnia.

Doctors generally advise these medications be used for short periods of time, usually two weeks. However, some chronic insomniacs need them for longer periods. Ambien, taken at bedtime, works for seven to eight hours. It helps people get to sleep and eliminates any middle-of-the-night awakenings. Sonata wears off in four hours. It can be taken at bedtime if you have trouble falling asleep or in the middle of the night if you wake up.

Long-acting *benzodiazepines* (Dalmane Doral and Valium) are effective but may cause a daytime "hangover effect." The shorter-acting benzodiazepine, Halcion, causes less of a hangover effect, but a decrease in the drug's effectiveness over time can necessitate increasing the dose. It has also been linked to rebound insomnia, which can be even worse than the original insomnia.

Over-the-counter products that contain the antihistamine *diphenhydramine*—Benadryl, Tylenol PM, etc.—may work well for some individuals. But the effects of diphenhydramine are unpredictable. Some people don't get the necessary sedation to help them sleep. Others experience next-day drowsiness.

HERBS AND SUPPLEMENTS

The herb valerian, as a supplement or a tea, may help. Studies are needed before its use can be endorsed. There is little evidence that kava or melatonin supplements work—and they may be harmful. Melatonin supplements have been linked to infertility and heart damage. Kava may cause liver damage.

To find a doctor who specializes in sleep disorders, contact the American Academy of Sleep Medicine at 708-492-0930 or *www.aasm net.org*.

Curb Insomnia with a Bedtime Snack

To fall asleep faster, try snacking on cheese and crackers before bedtime.

Like milk—a well-known sleep inducer—cheese is loaded with *tryptophan*. This amino acid induces the body to make the neurotransmitter *serotonin,* which has sedative properties.

To keep fat and calories to a minimum: Choose a low-fat cheese.

If insomnia persists: Consult your doctor.

Peter Hauri, PhD, emeritus professor of psychology, Mayo Clinic College of Medicine, and director, Mayo Clinic Insomnia Program, both in Rochester, MN.

How to Get a Good Night's Sleep

James B. Maas, PhD, professor of psychology, Cornell University, Ithaca, NY. He is author of *Power Sleep* (Villard).

If you're having trouble sleeping, you are probably well acquainted with the basic recommendations for sound sleep…

●**Avoid caffeine and alcohol** near bedtime.

●**Avoid nicotine.** If you smoke, quit.

●**Take a warm bath or shower** just before turning in.

•**Get regular exercise** (such as brisk walking or biking) and eat a wholesome diet.

•**Avoid sources of stress** and anxiety late in the evening.

But if insomnia persists despite your best efforts to follow these strategies, the culprit could be your bedroom. *Here's how to set up your "sleep environment" for a restful night of sleep…*

•**Make sure your home is safe and secure.** You will sleep better knowing that your family is protected against fires, burglary and other threats.

In addition to smoke detectors and good door and window locks, consider investing in a burglar alarm.

•**Choose bedroom decor carefully.** Sky blue, forest green and other "colors of nature" are especially conducive to sleep. So are paintings of landscapes…or family photos taken on a favorite trip.

Bedroom office trap: Looking at stacks of bills or other paperwork makes it hard to fall asleep. If your home lacks a den or study, find a hallway or another place in your home to set up your office.

•**Eliminate light "pollution."** The easiest way to keep light from disturbing your sleep is to wear light-blocking eyeshades. You can pick up a pair at a drugstore.

If you find eyeshades uncomfortable, rid your bedroom of illuminated clocks, night-lights and other sources of light.

If streetlamps or other light sources shine in through your bedroom windows, fit your windows with light-blocking "blackout" curtains.

•**Silence environmental noise.** Any sound louder than 70 decibels (the equivalent of a dripping faucet) is disruptive to sleep. *If you cannot eliminate a particular sound, block it using these strategies…*

•Furnish your bedroom with heavy drapes and thick carpeting. If you're building a new home, make sure the walls and ceilings have good sound insulation.

•Wear sound-blocking earplugs. Several types are available at drugstores. They cost only a dollar or two a pair.

•Use a "white noise" generator. White noise is high-frequency sound like that produced by rainfall, surf, rustling leaves, etc. It masks other, more intrusive sounds…and helps lull you to sleep.

Low-cost white-noise generator: A bedside FM radio tuned between stations to static. Alternatively, you can play compact discs containing recorded nature sounds…or use an electronic sound-masking device like those sold by The Sharper Image and other retailers.

•**Keep your bedroom cool.** An overheated bedroom can set off the body's wake-up call in the middle of the night. It can trigger nightmares, too.

Best temperature for restful sleep: 65°F.

•**Maintain ideal humidity.** Most people sleep best when relative humidity stays between 60% and 70%. Check it occasionally using a humidity indicator. This simple gauge is available at hardware stores for about $5.

If humidity regularly falls outside this range, a humidifier or dehumidifier can help. These devices are sold at department and hardware stores. They cost from $50 to $200.

•**Buy the best mattress you can afford.** If you like innerspring mattresses, spring count is crucial. A mattress for a full-size bed should have more than 300 coils…a queen, more than 375…a king, more than 450.

If you prefer the feel of a foam mattress, make sure the foam density is at least two pounds per cubic foot.

Whatever kind of mattress you pick, be sure to "test-drive" it at the store. You and your partner should have at least six extra inches of leg room.

Mattress maintenance: Once a month, rotate the mattress so that the head becomes the foot. Flip the mattress, too.

For more information on mattresses, contact the Better Sleep Council, 501 Wythe St., Alexandria, Virginia 22314. *www.bettersleep.org.*

•**Pick good sheets and bedclothes.** If you wear pajamas or a nightgown to bed, be sure the garment is soft to the touch—and roomy. Cotton and silk are more comfortable than synthetics.

When purchasing sheets, opt for cotton, silk or—best of all—linen. It feels smooth against the skin and absorbs moisture better than other fabrics. Also, sheets with a high thread count (700 is the highest) tend to be the softest.

●**Avoid overly soft pillows.** People often pick pillows that are too soft to provide proper support for the head and neck.

Down makes the best pillow filling. If you're allergic to down, polyester microfiber is a good second choice.

Some people troubled by insomnia find that a pillow filled with buckwheat hulls is particularly comfortable. These pillows are sold in most department stores.

●**Don't be a clock-watcher.** The last thing you want during the wee hours is a visible reminder of how much sleep you're losing.

If you wake up in the middle of the night, don't even glance at the clock. If necessary, get rid of the clock…or turn it to face away from you before you turn in for the night.

●**Keep a writing pad on your nightstand.** To avoid ruminating on fears or "to do" lists as you try to fall asleep, jot them down as soon as they arise. Vow to deal with any problems or obligations the following day.

If worries keep you awake anyway, read or watch television until you feel drowsy. If you sleep with a partner, get a lamp designed for reading in bed—ideally one with a gooseneck and a dimmer switch.

Sweet Sleep Aid from The Grocer

Eat a handful of cherries one hour before bedtime. They contain lots of *melatonin,* the naturally occurring sleep agent.

Better: Juice made from cherry concentrate contains 10 times more melatonin than the whole fruit.

University of Texas Health Science Center, San Antonio, www.uthscsa.edu.

When to Get The Best Sleep

Early morning sleep is really the most restful sleep you can get.

Recent study: Men sent to bed at 2:15 am and awakened at 6:15 am slept more soundly than ones sent to bed at 10:30 pm and awakened at 2:30 am.

So, if you can get only four hours of sleep, stay up as late as possible to get the most benefit from your limited sleep.

Caution: This does not replace a full night's sleep. Resume a normal sleep pattern as quickly as possible.

Christian Guilleminault, MD, professor of psychiatry and behavioral science, Stanford University School of Medicine, and associate director, Sleep Disorders Center, both in Palo Alto, CA.

What to Take When You Can't Sleep

Robert E. Hales, MD, professor and chair, department of psychiatry, University of California, Davis, School of Medicine. A past president of the Association for Academic Psychiatry, Dr. Hales has coauthored or coedited many books on mental health, including The Mind/Mood Pill Book (Bantam).

If you're among the 40 million Americans who are troubled by insomnia, you probably already know about the importance of keeping regular bedtime and wake-up hours …avoiding late-afternoon or evening caffeine and alcohol…and forsaking reading or TV viewing while in bed.

Perhaps you have gone so far as to try over-the-counter sedatives. Unfortunately, these nonprescription drugs are seldom of much benefit. And they can cause unpleasant side effects, including dry mouth, blurred vision and constipation.

In most cases, herbal and/or prescription sleep aids help you fall asleep faster and stay asleep longer. And when used appropriately, they're quite safe.

Important: Before trying any sleep aid, you should be checked for an underlying cause of your sleeplessness, such as a prescribed medication, depression, anxiety or primary sleep disorder, such as *obstructive sleep apnea*—a potentially serious condition that causes you to wake up repeatedly.

If you have sleep apnea, *benzodiazepine* drugs or other sleep-inducing medications may further interfere with your breathing, and that can be life-threatening.

OCCASIONAL MILD INSOMNIA

The herbal remedies valerian and kava kava are often highly effective at curbing mild insomnia, which is defined as transient periods of disturbed sleep due to a major life event, such as a wedding, a relocation or a new job.

Unlike sedative hypnotic agents, such as the benzodiazepine *temazepam* (Restoril), valerian does not cause morning-after drowsiness or stomach upset. It can, however, cause headaches and restlessness.

Kava kava* can cause grogginess the following morning, but it is often the best choice if you prefer a mild, sleep-enhancing over-the-counter sleep preparation. Neither remedy is habit-forming.

Capsules and tea bags of valerian and kava kava are sold in health food stores.

Caution: The US Food and Drug Administration (FDA) does not regulate herbal remedies. So it's best to stick with brands found effective by friends or recommended by your pharmacist or doctor.

TROUBLE FALLING ASLEEP

If you frequently have trouble *falling* asleep, your best bet may be the nonbenzodiazepine drug *zolpidem* (Ambien). It typically works within 15 minutes. Zolpidem doesn't cause next-day grogginess, although it can cause diarrhea, nausea and dizziness.

Zolpidem is not habit-forming, but it may become less effective after several weeks of use and require a larger dose.

*Long-term use may cause liver damage.

TROUBLE STAYING ASLEEP

The benzodiazepines *temazepam* (Restoril), *lorazepam* (Ativan) and *clonazepam* (Klonopin) are highly effective against early-morning awakenings. Compared to zolpidem, they stay in the body longer, approximately eight to 12 hours.

Like all benzodiazepines, these three drugs are addictive. They should be used for no more than two to three consecutive weeks, and then sporadically—only when you need help with your sleep. They are off-limits to current and former substance abusers.

Benzodiazepines also can cause rebound insomnia. If you go off one of the drugs abruptly after taking it for several weeks, you may experience one or two nights in which you have trouble falling asleep, wake up frequently and have nightmares.

To avoid this, gradually reduce your dose over the course of a week or two. This should be done in consultation with your doctor.

Side effects of benzodiazepines include next-day grogginess, nausea and dizziness.

CHRONIC SLEEP PROBLEMS

Chronic sleep problems often accompany depression. Doctors have found that the prescription antidepressant *trazodone* (Desyrel)—taken at a small dosage—often helps both conditions.

Trazodone is generally not habit-forming, although it can cause headaches, nausea and stomach upset.

Trazodone can increase the blood levels of the heart drug *digoxin* (Lanoxin) and the anti-seizure drug *phenytoin* (Dilantin). It can also reduce the effectiveness of the anticoagulant *warfarin* (Coumadin).

If you take one of these drugs: Alert your doctor before considering trazodone.

Two related drugs—*nefazodone* (Serzone) and *mirtazapine* (Remeron)—may be better options for older people or for those taking blood pressure medication.

USING SLEEP AIDS SAFELY

Avoid alcohol for at least several hours before taking a sleep-inducing remedy or drug. Otherwise, you can become confused and/or experience problems with breathing and coordination.

Especially hazardous: Mixing a benzodiazepine drug with alcohol. The combination can be deadly.

Older people tend to metabolize drugs more slowly than younger people. For this reason, a sleeping pill dosage that would be safe and effective in a younger person might cause dizziness and other side effects in older people.

If you're age 60 or older, ask your doctor about taking half of the usual recommended dosage of the sleep aid.

Minimize Sleep Interference

Turning on the bedroom or bathroom light during the night can interfere with your ability to get back to sleep.

Problem: Even brief exposure to light causes the body to stop producing the sleep-inducing hormone *melatonin.*

To minimize sleep disturbance when you get out of bed during the night, keep a low-light flashlight at your bedside…and/or install a night-light in your bathroom.

David C. Klein, PhD, laboratory of developmental neurobiology, National Institute of Child Health and Human Development, Bethesda, MD.

How to Prevent Nighttime Visits To the Bathroom

Put an end to nighttime bathroom visits by avoiding bladder irritants, such as citrus fruits, spicy foods and nicotine…and diuretic drinks, including anything that contains caffeine or alcohol, for several hours before bedtime.

Also, drink your last fluids of the day no later than three hours before bedtime. Most fluids will be in your bladder by the time you are ready for sleep, so you should be able to use the bathroom and then sleep through the night.

Gary Lemack, MD, associate professor of urology, University of Texas Southwestern Medical Center, Dallas.

Restless Legs Relief

An unpleasant tingling sensation in the legs, *restless legs syndrome* (RLS) can make it difficult to fall asleep and stay asleep. *To help ease symptoms…*

- **Massage legs before bed.**
- **Take a warm bath.**
- **Apply a heating pad.**
- **Avoid caffeine, nicotine and alcohol.**
- **Exercise regularly.**
- **Try a relaxation technique,** such as meditation or yoga.

If these approaches don't work, see your doctor about medication.

Barbara Phillips, MD, director, sleep apnea center, Samaritan Hospital, Lexington, KY. For more on RLS, send a self-addressed, stamped, business-sized envelope to the RLS Foundation, 1610 14th St. NW, Suite 300, Rochester, MN 55901, *www.rls.org.*

Relief for Nighttime Leg Cramps

To alleviate a leg cramp at night, flex your foot up. Point toes at the ceiling and hold until the cramping stops. Or stand up, bend your knee and place your weight on the affected leg for a few minutes—this stretches out the calf muscle. A heating pad or ice pack may provide some relief.

To prevent cramps: Drink six to eight glasses of water daily so you do not become dehydrated. Loosen bed covers so toes do not point downward while you sleep. Stretch your calf muscles regularly during the day. Riding a stationary bike before bed and regular aquatic exercise may also help.

Mary McGrae McDermott, MD, associate professor of medicine, Feinberg School of Medicine, Northwestern University, Chicago.

Tonic Water Fights Leg Cramps

If you get leg cramps during the day, try drinking tonic water before bedtime. It contains *quinine*—a muscle relaxant that can be effective against leg cramps.

An eight-ounce glass of tonic water contains 27 milligrams (mg) of quinine—enough to relieve cramps in many people. Add orange juice or lemon to tonic water to make it taste less bitter.

Paul Davidson, MD, associate clinical professor of medicine, University of California, San Francisco.

Quick Varicose Vein Treatment

Large varicose veins in the legs can be removed without surgery. A brief outpatient procedure—known as *endovenous radiofrequency vein closure*—takes about 20 minutes and involves only a one-quarter-inch incision in the thigh. A catheter tipped with a radiotransmitter is threaded through this incision and into the problem vein. High-intensity radio waves emitted by the catheter tip seal off the vein.

Patients can resume normal activity the next day. With conventional surgery, recovery takes up to seven days.

Mitchel P. Goldman, MD, associate clinical professor of dermatology, University of California, San Diego, School of Medicine.

 # Quick Fixes for Problem Feet

Suzanne M. Levine, DPM, podiatrist in private practice, 885 Park Avenue, New York City. She is author of *Your Feet Don't Have to Hurt* (St. Martin's Press) and coauthor of *The Botox Book* (M. Evans and Company). For more on foot problems, go to Dr. Levine's Web site, *www.institutebeaute.com.*

Anyone who has ever suffered from athlete's foot knows that antifungal creams usually clear up the condition in about two weeks. What most people don't know is that the medication must be used for a full month to eradicate the fungus.

Like athlete's foot, most foot problems are either caused—or worsened—by the sufferers themselves. *Here are five painful foot ailments and the mistakes that cause them...*

BUNIONS

Millions of American adults undergo surgery each year to remove bunions—bony protrusions that usually appear on the outside of the big toe. Many of these operations could be prevented with proper self-care.

Common mistake: Wearing high heels or shoes with tight toes. This can cause inflammation and swelling, which irritate and worsen the bunions.

To avoid this problem, it's important to buy shoes that are not too tight in the toe box. If you are unsure of size, have your feet measured. Many people are wearing shoes that are up to one full size too small.

If you already suffer from bunions, you can reduce the pressure with over-the-counter (OTC) orthotic inserts that support the arch.

If OTC orthotic inserts don't help, you may need to get prescription orthotics from a podiatrist. They work by correcting a person's abnormal gait.

Typical cost: $250 to $500.

Wearing snug socks also helps to reduce the friction on bunions.

To relieve painful bunion attacks: Mix up one cup of vinegar in one gallon of warm water, and soak the foot for 15 minutes daily.

Also, wrap ice or a package of frozen peas in a thin towel and apply to the bunion twice a day for 15 minutes. These treatments will reduce swelling and pain.

CALLUSES

Calluses are thick layers of dead skin cells that accumulate in areas of the foot exposed to frequent pressure. High heels or flat shoes can make calluses worse by shifting body weight to the forefoot. Shoes with one-inch heels are preferable because they put less pressure on this part of the foot.

Common mistake: Using the OTC callus-removal products. They don't always work very well—and the active ingredient (*salicylic acid*) can damage healthy skin.

It is often more effective to remove calluses after taking a warm bath or shower.

What to do: Very gently abrade the callus with a pumice stone. Before going to bed, apply a moisturizer that contains copper, a softening agent that will make calluses easier to remove.

A good choice: Copper Complex.

If this process doesn't help, ask your doctor about *microdermabrasion.* This 15- to 30-minute, painless outpatient procedure eliminates the need for surgery.

During microdermabrasion, a podiatrist uses aluminum oxide crystals to exfoliate the callus.

Typical cost: $125 to $200.

CORNS

These kernel-shaped areas of thickened tissue are similar to calluses but usually form at the tips of—or between—toes.

Common mistake: Cutting or roughly abrading corns. This causes more pain and often results in infection.

It's more effective to soak the corn in an Epsom salt solution for 10 minutes. Then gently rub the corn with a pumice stone. Repeat the treatment daily until the corn is gone.

FALLEN ARCHES

People develop fallen arches when the feet flatten over time. This happens when aging, weight gain, excess impact from running or walking and/or hormonal changes cause loosening of the *plantar fascia* ligaments at the bottom of the feet.

Other people may have inherited a low arch. The condition causes arch pain—often accompanied by heel or ankle pain.

Common mistake: Forgoing physical activity. Inactivity usually worsens the condition.

Arch pain can usually be reduced or eliminated with exercises that stretch the Achilles tendons and the plantar fascia ligaments.

Do each of the following stretches six times, twice daily. Hold each stretch for 30 seconds.

• **Place your right foot on a chair or step.** Keep both heels flat. Lean forward over the chair or step until you feel a stretch in the right calf. Repeat with the left foot.

• **Stand on a step facing the stairs with your feet together.** Move your right foot back until the heel hangs over the edge. Lower the heel until you feel a stretch in the right calf. Repeat with the left foot.

• **Sit in a chair.** Rest your right ankle on your left knee. Gently pull the toes of your right foot upward toward your chest, until you feel a stretch in the arch of the foot. Repeat with the left foot.

People with fallen arches should wear dress shoes with one-inch heels or athletic shoes with built-in arches. Slip-in orthotic inserts (either prescription or OTC) are helpful for restoring proper arch and support.

To determine if you have fallen arches: Walk in wet sand, and look at your footprints. The print of a normal foot has a gap between the heel and the forefoot. However, a fallen arch will have little or no gap.

INGROWN NAILS

Ingrown toenails curve and push into the flesh instead of growing straight over the toe. The condition causes pain, redness and/or swelling at the ends or sides of the toes.

Common mistake: Trimming nails on a curve. That increases the risk for ingrown nails.

To reduce this risk, soak your feet in warm water, wash thoroughly with soap and trim the nails straight across.

If there is redness or other signs of infection, apply an OTC antibiotic ointment, such as bacitracin or Neosporin.

If pain and redness don't go away after two days: Your doctor may need to remove the portion of nail beneath the skin. This can be done in a 15-minute outpatient procedure.

Amazing Nail Remedy

Howard Garrett, known as "The Dirt Doctor," *www.dirtdoctor.com*. He has devoted his career to educating the public about organic gardening. Mr. Garrett hosts the Texas radio show *The Natural Way* on K-SKY. He is also author of *The Dirt Doctor's Guide to Organic Gardening* (University of Texas).

Ed Dillard was listening to my regional radio talk show on gardening and heard a caller ask how to get rid of fungus on roses. I answered, "Use cornmeal."

For 27 years, Dillard had been plagued by toenail fungus. He had thick, ugly yellow nails and wondered if cornmeal would work.

Dillard soaked his feet for one hour in cornmeal and warm water. There was no change in his nails. But about a month later, he noticed healthy pink nail tissue at the base of his big toenail, though he had only soaked one time. He repeated the cornmeal soak weekly and about a year later, he was fungus free.

He called me and told of his success on the air. Since then, I have heard from thousands of people who have used cornmeal to treat nail fungus, athlete's foot, ringworm and other fungal problems. Some physicians speculate that the microorganisms in cornmeal, activated by warm water, literally eat the microscopic fungi.

Cornmeal Rx: Put one inch of cornmeal, yellow or white, in a pan, and add just enough warm, not hot, water to cover it. Let this sit for 30 minutes. Then add enough warm water to cover up your feet. Soak for at least one hour once per week until the fungus is gone. For other fungal problems that require soaking in a bath, add two cups of cornmeal to the water.

Easy Wart Treatment

Put duct tape over a wart, and leave it on for seven days. Then uncover the area for 12 hours. Repeat the cycle until the wart falls off.

Duct tape keeps moisture in and helps break down wart tissue.

Daniel M. Siegel, MD, clinical professor of dermatology, Mohs College, State University of New York, Stony Brook.

Better Cut Care

Common wound cleaners can do more harm than good. For example, *mercurochrome* and *merthiolate* contain mercury, which is toxic. Rubbing alcohol damages and dries out skin. Hydrogen peroxide and iodine damage the skin and slow healing.

Betadine in a concentration of 1% or less is safe for cleaning wounds, but it could cause iodine poisoning if used on large open wounds. Antibiotic ointments may help prevent infection in minor wounds, but they can cause skin irritation and allergic reactions.

What to do: Clean the wound under cool running water, or swab it with a clean, wet cloth. Use soap on the surrounding skin—not on the wound itself.

Apply an adhesive bandage to keep the wound clean and moist to reduce scarring. Don't pick at scabs—these are the body's natural bandages.

University of California, Berkeley *Wellness Letter, www.wellnessletter.com*.

Ulcer Preventative

To prevent stomach ulcers, eat more *polyunsaturated fats*. Corn oil, sunflower oil, safflower oil and fish oil, all polyunsaturated fats, stopped the growth of the bacterium responsible for most stomach ulcers. However, *saturated fats* (coconut oil, butter) and *monounsaturated fats* (such as olive oil) did not.

This result is consistent with the fact that people whose diets are high in polyunsaturated fats have a lower risk of stomach ulcers. Research suggests that substituting foods containing these oils for ones containing saturated fats may reduce the likelihood of developing ulcers, and possibly also cut the risk of stomach cancer.

Duane Smoot, MD, chairman and associate professor of medicine, Howard University College of Medicine, Washington, DC.

Little-Known Causes of Stomach Upset

Charlene Prather, MD, associate professor of internal medicine and gastroenterology, Saint Louis University School of Medicine.

If you suffer from stomach upset—such as gas, bloating, cramps, nausea and even diarrhea or constipation—there are several possible culprits...

●**Antacids.** Some brands contain magnesium, which causes diarrhea by shunting water into the intestines. Other brands contain aluminum, which causes constipation.

Self-defense: Take just enough antacid to ease stomach upset. Alternate between magnesium- and aluminum-based brands.

●**Fatty foods.** Fats slow the passage of food through the stomach and intestines. This can cause nausea and cramps.

Self-defense: Avoid fatty foods...chew cardamom seeds, a folk remedy for relieving an upset stomach.

●**Fruit.** Apples, mangoes, oranges, peaches, pears, etc., contain fructose, a sugar that can lead to bloating.

Self-defense: Spread your five fruit servings throughout the day—so you won't get all of your fructose at once.

●**Politeness.** Stifling a belch can cause painful gas buildup.

Self-defense: Belch when you must—quietly and away from others. Limit gas by avoiding carbonated beverages and the use of straws, which can cause you to swallow air.

●**Sugarless gum.** Many brands contain *sorbitol, xylitol* or *mannitol,* artificial sweeteners that may promote the growth of gas-causing colon bacteria.

Self-defense: Have no more than three sticks of gum per day.

●**Whole grains.** Too much fiber can cause constipation, intestinal gas and bloating.

Self-defense: When increasing fiber intake, do so slowly to give your body time to adjust. Drink eight to 10 glasses of water daily.

Gallstone Prevention

Exercise prevents gallstones. Men who exercised for 30 minutes five times a week were 34% less likely than sedentary men to develop stones.

Under study: Whether exercise prevents gallstones in women.

Another risk reducer: Weight loss.

Michael F. Leitzmann, MD, MPH, epidemiological investigator, National Cancer Institute, Bethesda, MD. His eight-year study of 45,813 men 40 to 75 years of age was published in the Annals of Internal Medicine.

What to Do If You Feel Faint

Feeling light-headed or seeing black spots? You can temporarily prevent yourself from passing out by crossing your legs at the ankles and contracting the muscles in your legs, abdomen and buttocks.

People prone to fainting who practiced this technique either avoided fainting altogether or delayed it for an average of two-and-a-half minutes, which is often enough time to find a safe place to sit or lie down. If you still feel yourself losing consciousness, lower yourself to the ground to reduce the chances of injuring yourself when you fall.

Fainting can be triggered by blood pooling in the legs and abdomen, which causes a drop in blood pressure.

C.T. Paul Krediet, researcher, department of internal medicine, Academic Medical Center, Amsterdam.

How to Minimize Mosquito and Tick Annoyances

Richard Pollack, PhD, public health entomologist, Harvard School of Public Health, Boston.

Spending time outdoors on a warm summer day can be very enjoyable, but fighting insects can ruin your good time. *To avoid ticks and mosquitoes, it's best to...*

●**Choose a lotion/cream bug repellent that contains no more than 35% DEET.** Apply sparingly. DEET can cause adverse reactions—particularly skin rashes—when it has higher concentrations. It is, however, the most effective repellent available—and it can be used safely.

Recommended: Use the lowest effective concentration possible—generally no more than 35% for adults...and no more than 15% for children. Apply the repellent sparingly. Wash with soap and water when the protection is no longer needed. Treat clothes, rather than skin, whenever possible.

Important: The repellent you choose should be registered by the US Environmental Protection Agency (EPA). Look for one that has an EPA registration number on the label. These repellents are under strict regulation.

●**Apply a permethrin spray to the outside of clothing.** Especially effective at killing ticks, these sprays may also work with mosquitoes and other biting flies. Spray only enough to moisten the material. Let clothes dry before wearing. Hardware and garden-supply stores sometimes carry brands such as *Duranone* and *Permanone.* These sprays can also be obtained through SCS Ltd., 800-749-8425.

●**Don't assume that the "natural" formulas are better.** Many of the so-called "natural," non-DEET formulas on the market don't specifically claim to repel insects, and may not be registered with the EPA. Consumers have no idea what's in them—or how safe and effective they are.

Other ways to reduce exposure to biting insects and ticks and the pathogens they may transmit: Wear long sleeves and pants when possible...perform a tick check at the end of each day...get proper medical attention if you have been bitten by a tick.

Another Reason to Beware of Ticks

The tickborne disease *ehrlichiosis* is on the rise. Most cases occur in the East, Upper Midwest and along the Pacific Coast.

Symptoms: Abrupt onset of fever, chills, headache and malaise—sometimes accompanied by gastrointestinal upset—a week or two after being bitten by an infected tick.

Like Lyme disease, ehrlichiosis usually is treated with antibiotics.

Double whammy: You can contract both illnesses from a single tick bite.

Peter J. Krause, MD, professor of pediatrics, University of Connecticut Health Center, Farmington, and director of infectious disease, Connecticut Children's Medical Center, Hartford.

Acupressure Cure For Hiccups

To put an end to persistent hiccups, simply place both your index and middle fingers behind your jawbone on the soft area under each earlobe. Press inward with your fingers until the spots feel sore, then hold for two minutes while breathing deeply. This should stop the involuntary diaphragm contractions that cause hiccups.

Michael Reed Gach, PhD, director, Acupressure Institute of America, Berkeley, CA, and author of *Acupressure's Potent Points* (Bantam Doubleday Dell).

Dandruff Magic

Dandruff can often be controlled simply by shampooing in cool water.

Reason: Washing your hair with hot water strips the skin of natural oils that help control flaking. So do alcohol-based styling products like mousse or gel.

Individuals with severe dandruff often benefit from rotating dandruff shampoos with different active ingredients—tar, selenium, zinc and salicylic acid.

Dee Anna Glaser, MD, professor and vice chairman of dermatology, Saint Louis University School of Medicine.

2

Skin, Eyes, Ears, Nose & Teeth

Smart and Simple Skin Care Solutions

The secret of looking younger than your age begins with skin care. But the countless new products and procedures in advertising and magazines have left many people unsure about how to treat common skin problems.

Noted dermatologist Barney Kenet, MD, cleared up the confusion about skin care…

•**Is there any way to reverse skin aging once wrinkles and age spots start to appear?** Skin that has been overexposed to the sun's ultraviolet rays can be improved.

The first step is to limit further damage by using a sunscreen every day—in summer and winter, rain and shine—even if you are only outside intermittently during the day.

Reason: Ultraviolet exposure is cumulative. You may be in sunlight for only five minutes a day. But that small amount totals 35 minutes by the end of the week.

•Use a sunscreen with a *sun protection factor* (SPF) of 15 on your face and any exposed parts of your body every morning. Sunscreens not only protect your skin from harmful ultraviolet radiation, they also allow sun-damaged skin to repair itself.

Apply sunscreen-based moisturizer after washing your face, while your skin is still damp.

If you must be in the sun for an extended period of time, wear a broad-brimmed hat, long sleeves, slacks and sunglasses. Try to avoid the sun's peak hours between 11 am and 4 pm.

•Apply creams that contain *alpha hydroxy acid* (AHA) every evening. AHA is in many over-the-counter skin creams. The compound can have a positive effect on skin that has been overexposed to the sun.

Researchers have not yet proven how or why AHA works. But research shows that when

Barney J. Kenet, MD, dermatologic surgeon, NewYork-Presbyterian Hospital/Cornell Medical Center, New York City. He is cofounder of the American Melanoma Foundation (*www.melanomafoundation.org*) and coauthor of *How to Wash Your Face: America's Leading Dermatologist Reveals the Essential Secrets to Youthful, Radiant Skin* (Simon & Schuster).

31

AHA products are used regularly, the skin's outer layers take on a more youthful fullness.

●Use Retin-A or Renova daily to improve wrinkling, skin texture and uneven pigment. Apply at night. Either skin product requires a prescription. Results take four to 12 months.

Side effects may include redness and irritation...but both can be reduced by adjusting the frequency and amount of the application. Discuss the application of these creams with your dermatologist.

●**What can be done about cellulite—that dimply skin on thighs, hips and buttocks?** At the moment, there is no cure for cellulite. Many products promise to reduce or eliminate these ripples—but they don't actually deliver.

Anticellulite creams and lotions were the rage a few years ago, but they never lived up to their promises.

Endermologie—the process of rolling or kneading the skin with a massage machine—has no scientific data to prove effectiveness. Yet there are reports that some people find it beneficial.

If your skin is dry, massaging it with a lotion can make it look smoother for a while—but the effect doesn't last. Not even liposuction has much impact on cellulite.

Exercise and losing weight can provide some benefit—especially if the weight is lost in the areas where cellulite typically appears. But weight loss and exercise aren't the complete answers to making cellulite disappear.

●**What can be done for adults who have pimples?** First determine your skin type by monitoring which factors contribute to your breakouts. *Your skin may be...*

●Environmentally sensitive.

●Hormonally reactive.

●Stress reactive.

Men and women with occasional breakouts may be reacting to excessive stress. Constantly touching the face makes it worse.

When blemishes appear, use over-the-counter products that contain salicylic acid or benzoyl peroxide. Prevent breakouts during menstruation by applying AHA or salicylic products one week prior to menstruation.

Avoid caffeine, alcohol and spicy foods. They can make breakouts redder.

●**How does diet affect the skin?** Eating right is critical for healthy-looking skin. A diet rich in vitamins and fiber can restore your body and even help correct the ravages of sun, dehydration and time. The most important nutrients for good skin are vitamins A, C and E.

The best way to get these nutrients is through foods—especially leafy or dark-colored vegetables, such as tomatoes and peppers. You can also get these vitamins in supplements—but they need to be taken throughout the day rather than all at once in order to be effective.

Topical creams containing these vitamins are of little benefit. In fact, applying vitamin E to a wound or scar has been shown to *slow* the healing process.

Drinking lots of water helps your skin. However, too much water *on* your skin can actually be drying.

Reduce your shower time to five minutes. Use medium-warm water, not hot. You may even want to skip your daily shower once or twice a week.

●**What is the best way to wash your face?** The most important skin-care advice is *don't overwash*. Most adults over age 30 wash too often and too long, and the result is itchy, irritated skin.

Avoid deodorant soaps. They irritate your skin. I prefer soap-free cleansers in liquid form. Massage gently with your fingertips, and don't scrub with a washcloth. Rinse your face with tepid water—and gently pat dry.

●**What can be done about dandruff?** Those itchy flakes are signs of an inflammatory condition called *seborrheic dermatitis*. Dandruff results from the overproduction of cells on the outer layer of the scalp. The cause is unknown, but you can treat it with shampoos that contain zinc pyrithione.

If you have a more oily scalp and hair, use tar-based shampoos.

Like all your skin, the scalp can become dry, especially during winter. Too much hair washing and showering, low humidity and wearing hats can contribute to scalp problems. Warm oil treatments once a week can help—drugstore products or homemade ones, using two table-spoons of olive oil.

Using shampoos that contain AHA once or twice a week also helps to remove grime and retain moisture.

Skin Strategies For Looking Younger

Nicholas Lowe, MD, clinical professor of dermatology, UCLA School of Medicine, and senior lecturer in dermatology, University College, London, England. He is coauthor of *Skin Secrets—The Medical Facts Versus the Beauty Fiction* (Sterling).

Antiaging creams for the skin are virtually becoming a reality, as the fine line between cosmetics and skin medications continues to blur. There are several ways to keep your skin young and supple, whether you're male or female, and no matter what your age. *For example...*

●**Apply full-spectrum sunscreen every morning.** While some skin types are more prone to wrinkles than others, the way your skin ages has less to do with your genes than with the amount of sunlight your skin is exposed to.

Up to 80% of skin damage is ascribed to the ultraviolet rays of the sun—both *ultraviolet B* (UVB) rays, which are the primary cause of sunburn and skin cancer, and *ultraviolet A* (UVA) rays, which are largely responsible for the damage that is associated with aging.

Unlike UVB rays, UVA rays can penetrate the skin even on cloudy days. That's why the most important way to keep your skin young is to apply full-spectrum sunscreen (which absorbs both UVA and UVB rays) with a sun-protection factor (SPF) of 15 or higher every morning.

Women should apply sunscreen right after bathing, then let it dry before putting on makeup. Men should apply sunscreen right after bathing and shaving.

This sunscreen rule holds even if you don't plan to be outdoors for very long.

Reason: Sun damage can occur even while driving your car—UV rays go right through your vehicle's windows.

Breakthrough: It's never too late to start this regimen. Researchers have found that by protecting your skin this way on a daily basis, you can actually begin to *reverse* sun damage that has already occurred.

●**Apply topical antioxidant cream.** Most skin damage is caused by the toxic effect of *free radicals*—rogue molecules created during the natural cell oxidation process. These molecules are missing a crucial electron, and so they try to grab an electron from wherever they can, often tearing apart healthy cells in the process. When exposed to sunlight or some other toxin, such as secondhand cigarette smoke, the production of free radicals accelerates.

To fight off these vicious free radicals, your body comes equipped with its own all-natural antioxidants, which have extra electrons that can be given up to neutralize the rogue molecules. You can get added protection by taking supplements of the antioxidant vitamins A, C and E (be sure to consult your doctor for the dosages that are right for you). However, while a daily multivitamin pill provides antioxidant protection to much of your body, unfortunately only about 1% of dietary vitamins make it through to your skin.

Better solution: Apply a topical antioxidant cream to your skin about 10 minutes before your sunscreen.

Example: SkinCeuticals Topical Vitamin-C Skin Firming Cream.

●**Try using a retinoid cream.** I advise my patients not to waste their money on the expensive skin creams sold in better department stores. They do not provide any special benefits to their skin.

On the other hand, the topical retinoid *tretinoin* (a vitamin A derivative)—available by prescription under the brand names Retin-A, Renova and Avita—can reverse many signs of sun damage, including finely crisscrossing lines, areas of whitish pebbling, spider veins in the cheeks and rough, dull, uneven or yellowish skin tone. It can also generate new *collagen,* a fibrous tissue protein, making the *dermis* (the layer beneath your epidermis, or outer skin) plumper and firmer.

I recommend using either a 0.05% formulation of tretinoin or an even milder cream containing 0.025%. Apply the cream either every other night or every third night. It should be applied to your face and any other body parts you're concerned about, preferably about 30 minutes after washing.

Within four to six months, you'll start to see significant improvement in your fine wrinkles, along with a clearer, smooth skin surface and a generally brighter, rosier complexion.

Tretinoin is best used at night—because it's degraded by sunlight and it makes your skin more sensitive to ultraviolet light.

Warning: Tretinoin can be irritating to the skin, although after two to six weeks, your skin should develop resistance to the worst signs of irritation, such as becoming red, flaky or itchy.

●**To moisturize your face, use a glycolic acid cream.** A cream containing glycolic acid in the range of 5%—such as NeoStrata Ultra Moisturizing Face Cream—will moisturize and protect your skin, and will also help reverse the drying effects of retinoid creams. Glycolic acid stimulates the synthesis of new skin tissue and inhibits the effect of free radicals.

I recommend applying one of these skin moisturizers every morning, and—if you're also applying a tretinoin cream—again in the evening, on those nights when you're not using the tretinoin. Follow the same rule of applying it to a clean face, about 30 minutes after washing.

Note: If your doctor prescribes a stronger glycolic acid cream, he/she will probably recommend using it only at night.

●**Use as few different makeup products as possible**—to minimize your chances of developing *contact dermatitis,* a skin condition marked by inflammation, redness, itching or broken skin. This condition, sometimes called *allergic dermatitis,* is actually caused by chemical irritation, rather than an allergic reaction. The more chemicals your skin is exposed to, the greater chance irritation will occur.

●**Drink alcohol in moderation.** Heavy consumption of alcohol (more than one drink a day for women and two drinks a day for men)

dilates the blood vessels, leading to spider veins in your cheeks. It can also exacerbate *rosacea*—a skin condition marked by flushing, lumpiness, red lines and a swollen, red nose.

●**Avoid cigarette smoke.** Smoking cigarettes will cause widespread free-radical damage to your skin, causing it to age prematurely. The act of smoking also causes fine lines to develop around the lips. However, even exposure to someone else's cigarette smoke will accelerate the activity of toxic free radicals in your skin, leading to skin damage.

Treatment for Rosacea

A topical medication called *azelaic acid* (Finacea) is effective in treating *rosacea,* a chronic skin condition that causes redness, tiny pimples and broken blood vessels on the face.

Applied twice daily directly to the skin, the gel clears the *papules* (small, red lesions similar to acne) and *pustules* (bacterially infected papules) that characterize mild to moderate forms of rosacea.

Since rosacea is a chronic condition, azelaic acid must be used indefinitely to prevent flare-ups, but application frequency can be reduced. Side effects are minor but include transient stinging, burning or tingling sensations.

Alan B. Fleischer Jr., MD, professor and chair, department of dermatology, Wake Forest University School of Medicine, Winston-Salem, NC.

Natural Sun Protection

G et additional sun protection by eating all the right foods. Five daily servings of carrots, sweet potatoes, mangoes, tomatoes and other carotenoid-rich foods can make your skin twice as resistant to the sun's rays.

Beta-carotene and lycopene, the carotenoids that give these foods their deep, rich color, will build up in your skin over time and help protect you from sunburn and wrinkles. Protection against skin cancer hasn't been proven yet.

Important: You should always wear sunscreen while outdoors.

Wilhelm Stahl, PhD, professor of chemistry, Heinrich-Heine-University, Düsseldorf, Germany.

Throw Out Old Sunscreen

Sunscreen that is three years old or older—or past its expiration date—should be discarded. The active ingredients lose effectiveness over time, and do so more quickly if stored in a warm environment. So sunscreen left over from prior years may not provide the degree of protection described on its label.

David J. Leffell, MD, professor of dermatology and surgery, Yale University School of Medicine, New Haven, CT.

Better Protection Against Sun Damage

Wear protective clothing as well as sunscreen to protect yourself against skin cancer and skin damage.

Dangerous ultraviolet rays from a strong summer and/or southern sun can penetrate clothes to reach areas where you might not apply sunscreen.

Safety: Wear tightly woven clothes to minimize openings the sun can penetrate.

Thick fabrics block more sun. Polyester, wool, silk and unbleached cotton are more protective than bleached cotton, polyamide and polyacryl (synthetic materials) clothing. Dyes help block the ultraviolet rays. Loose-fitting garments that cover as much skin as possible are preferable. New clothes tend to be more protective than old, since stretching, moisture, shrinking, washing and fading reduce protection.

Robert Sheeler, MD, medical editor, *Mayo Clinic Health Letter,* 200 First St. SW, Rochester, MN 55905.

Skin Care Self-Defense

Some nonmedical technicians are performing procedures that until recently were performed only by doctors.

Many skin care salons and so-called wellness centers are offering laser treatments, chemical peels, micro-dermabrasion and cosmetic treatments for hair and blood vessel removal.

But the people handling the equipment may have attended only a one-day training course. When used incorrectly, lasers can cause burns, scars and other injuries.

Self-defense: Make sure there is a doctor on-site. Ask for a test patch...and call for medical attention if a problem occurs.

Harold J. Brody, MD, clinical professor of dermatology, Emory University Medical School, Atlanta.

Quick Action Helps Stop Outbreaks of Poison Ivy

To prevent an outbreak *after* exposure to the poisonous plant poison ivy...

●**Immediately cleanse exposed skin** with rubbing alcohol and rinse with water.

●**As soon as possible,** shower with soap and water.

Poison ivy contains an allergy-causing resin called *urushiol.* This resin can be removed from clothes, shoes, tools, etc., by cleaning them with a mixture of alcohol and water. Be sure to wear rubber gloves.

A climbing plant, poison ivy grows in three-leaf groupings. The leaves are green during the summer and red in the fall.

The late William L. Epstein, MD, professor of dermatology, University of California, San Francisco.

Good News for Psoriasis Sufferers

Michael Zanolli, MD, associate clinical professor of medicine, Vanderbilt University, and a dermatologist in private practice, both in Nashville.

If you have psoriasis, chances are your doctor has recommended an over-the-counter (OTC) lotion and/or powerful prescription medication. As most sufferers know, however, these strategies are *not* always effective.

Now: An arsenal of treatments brings relief more quickly and completely to the six million Americans afflicted.

WHAT IS PSORIASIS?

Psoriasis results from an abnormality of the immune system. When signals go awry in cells that protect the body from infection, skin cell growth speeds up and produces skin lesions.

The condition produces raised red patches covered by silvery scales. It occurs most often on the knees, elbows, scalp, feet—and even the genitals. Severe psoriasis can cover a person's entire body.

Psoriasis tends to run in families. Triggers, such as stress, injury to the skin, infections and drug reactions, can precipitate attacks.

TREATMENT OPTIONS

Because there is no cure for psoriasis, treatment has traditionally focused on reducing the symptoms. *Doctors recommend trying one or more of the following approaches...*

•**Topical treatments.** OTC or prescription preparations are the first line of defense. Applied directly to the skin, they reduce or eliminate redness, flakiness and itching. They may suffice for mild psoriasis that affects limited areas of the body. Steroid creams, ointments and lotions are most commonly used.

Drawback: Topical treatments can be messy and must be applied daily.

Latest development: Topical agents—such as *calcipotriene* (Dovonex), a synthetic form of vitamin D, and *tazarotene* (Tazorac), a vitamin A derivative—help to normalize cell growth. Especially when used with steroid creams, these treatments provide results within four weeks with few side effects.

•**Phototherapy.** This treatment, which involves exposure to ultraviolet light, typically is used when topical treatment isn't enough or when the psoriasis rash covers more than 10% of the body. Your doctor may also prescribe the drug *methoxsalen* (Oxsoralen), which sensitizes the skin to the effects of light. This combination therapy is known as *photochemotherapy.*

Drawback: When more than 200 treatments are given, phototherapy may increase skin cancer risk.

Latest development: Narrow-band ultraviolet B phototherapy, restricted to the wavelengths of light that are most beneficial for psoriasis. It works as well as medication-boosted phototherapy, with as few as 20 treatments and less risk for skin cancer.

•**Systemic medications.** These drugs, taken by pill or injection, are usually reserved for psoriasis that remains severe despite other treatment. They are the most powerful weapons against psoriasis.

Drawback: The most potent systemic drugs, *methotrexate* (Rheumatrex) and *cyclosporine* (Neoral), can damage the liver. These drugs also can make you vulnerable to infection because they inhibit immune function.

Latest development: New drugs that target the problem more precisely than the older systemic medications and may be safer.

Instead of first trying topicals and phototherapy, a patient with troublesome psoriasis can start treatment with these medications. The only real drawback is cost—up to $15,000 for a course of treatment.

These drugs are known as *biologics* (because they consist of proteins derived from living cells) and *immunomodulators* (because they alter immune function). *Examples...*

•**Alefacept (Amevive).** This is the first biologic drug to be approved by the US Food and Drug Administration (FDA) specifically for psoriasis. It blocks the activation of disease-fighting

T-cells, the lymphocytes that signal skin cells to multiply. It is given by injection every week for 12 consecutive weeks.

In more than one-third of patients treated with alefacept, psoriasis clears almost entirely. They need little additional treatment besides moisturizers for up to six months. Another one-half to one-third improve substantially.

• **Etanercept (Enbrel).** This immunomodulator was the first drug to be approved by the FDA specifically for psoriatic arthritis, a chronic inflammatory disease that causes joint pain and swelling of the hands, feet, back and hips. It appears to work well for the skin lesions, too.

It blocks an immune system messenger chemical called *tumor-necrosis factor* (TNF) that causes joint inflammation and fuels the development of the psoriasis rash. Etanercept is injected subcutaneously (just under the skin) twice a week, so patients can administer it themselves, like insulin for people with diabetes.

• **Infliximab (Remicade).** Like etanercept, this immunomodulator targets TNF. Although it was developed to treat Crohn's disease and rheumatoid arthritis, it also seems to be effective against psoriasis. In a clinical trial, nearly 90% of psoriasis patients showed dramatic improvement after just five intravenous infusions.

• **Efalizumab (Raptiva).** This biologic drug was recently approved by the FDA. It targets the psoriasis process most precisely of all, preventing T-cells from migrating to the skin. Like etanercept, psoriasis patients can inject it themselves at home, just under the skin.

Tanning Beds Can Fight Psoriasis

Phototherapy for psoriasis involves treatment with ultraviolet B (UVB) light. If UVB treatment is not available at the dermatologist's office, a tanning bed, which emits some UVB light, may provide some relief.

Caution: Tanning-salon staff are not trained in phototherapy, and potency of UVB light may vary. You should try this only if your doctor recommends it, and use only a facility that he/she chooses. Most insurance companies cover this form of phototherapy, but you might need preapproval by your carrier.

Christopher S. Carlin, MD, former research fellow, department of dermatology, University of Utah Health Sciences Center, Salt Lake City, dermatologist in private practice with West Dermatology in California, and leader of a study of 26 psoriasis patients, presented at an annual meeting of the American Academy of Dermatology.

Better Vision with Bifocals, Trifocals or Progressive Lenses

If bifocals, trifocals or progressive lenses are designed poorly, they may encroach on the wearer's distance vision. If he wasn't given proper instruction in how to wear them, he also may have difficulty.

When walking down stairs or over a curb, lower your head to look through the top (distance) portion of the lenses. If you don't, you will be looking through the bottom part of the lens, which corrects for near vision and makes things seem closer. This will impair your depth perception and may cause you to fall. If the bottom part, for near vision, is too low, you will have to raise your neck uncomfortably to read or see nearby items.

Also: Progressive lenses, which don't have lines, must be designed precisely for your eyes and frames. If the lens centers are not where your pupils are, all the optics will be distorted.

Melvin Schrier, OD, vision consultant and optometrist, New York City.

Is Vision-Correcting Laser Eye Surgery For You?

Douglas D. Koch, MD, professor of ophthalmology, Baylor College of Medicine, Houston. He is editor of *The Journal of Cataract & Refractive Surgery,* 4000 Legato Rd., Suite 850, Fairfax, VA 22033.

If your eyesight is less than perfect, you may be wondering whether you should have vision-correcting eye surgery.

Hundreds of thousands of Americans have undergone the most popular form of the surgery, known as *laser in situ keratomileusis* (LASIK). That number will certainly continue to grow in the coming years.

A 15-minute outpatient procedure, LASIK has proven highly effective at correcting nearsightedness (*myopia*) and certain other vision problems. But it's not without drawbacks. *Some of the most common questions...*

●**How effective is LASIK?** It's very effective for people with mild to moderate myopia, farsightedness (*hyperopia*) or astigmatism. Among people with one of these problems, 90% of those who undergo LASIK wind up with vision of 20/40 or better. About 50% to 60% achieve perfect 20/20 vision.

LASIK cannot correct cataracts, glaucoma or macular degeneration. However, it may correct *presbyopia,* the aging-related vision problem that necessitates the use of reading glasses.

●**How safe is it?** As with any invasive procedure, there is a slight risk for infection. Ordinarily, infection caused by LASIK can be eradicated with antibiotics. But in rare cases, the infection leaves the patient with mild vision loss.

In extremely rare cases—fewer than one in 10,000—someone whose vision had been correctable with eyeglasses winds up legally blind after LASIK.

Altogether, about 1% of people who undergo LASIK experience complications either during surgery or afterward.

●**Who is a candidate for LASIK?** Anyone with mild to moderate myopia, hyperopia or astigmatism who would prefer not to wear contact lenses or eyeglasses.*

The main consideration is this—*would it dramatically enhance your life to be able to see clearly without corrective lenses?* If not, it makes no sense to assume even the tiny risk that your eyesight could be harmed.

●**Who is not a candidate?** Anyone with dry eyes, severe diabetes, an immune system disorder, glaucoma or another ailment that might affect the healing process.

LASIK is also off-limits to people who have had previous eye surgery...who have unusually thin corneas...or who have *keratoconus.* That's a condition in which the cornea develops a conical shape.

Federal regulations require that LASIK patients be at least 18. There is no upper age limit.

●**Exactly what does LASIK involve?** The patient, who might be given a mild sedative like *diazepam* (Valium), reclines on a chair or gurney. The eyelashes are taped back, and a speculum is used to hold the eye open.

Using a special cutting device known as a *microkeratome,* the ophthalmologist slices a thin flap of cornea. That's the transparent "window" at the front of the eye. This flap is folded, hinge-like, back from the eye.

Next, the ophthalmologist uses an excimer laser to vaporize portions of the cornea, reshaping it to alter its refractive power. That's the extent to which it bends light rays that enter the eye.

The corneal flap is then folded back into its original position, and the eye is treated with antibiotic drops.

Some patients recover within 24 hours. Others take several weeks. Typically, an eye patch is worn for several hours after surgery, and then at night for a few days.

●**Is LASIK performed on both eyes at once?** Most patients like to take care of both

*Vision problems are measured in diopters. In general, LASIK should not be used for myopia of more than 12 diopters...hyperopia of more than six diopters...or astigmatism of more than six diopters. With advances in technology, it may soon be possible to treat more severe vision problems.

eyes at once. But I sometimes prefer to do one eye and then the other eye a week or so later—to make sure that the patient is recovering well from the first surgery.

●**What's the best way to pick a LASIK surgeon?** Get a referral from your ophthalmologist or family doctor...or from the head of the ophthalmology department at a local teaching hospital or medical school.

You'll want to select a board-certified ophthalmologist who has performed at least 100 LASIK procedures.

Secrets of Cataract Prevention... And Reversal

Robert Abel, Jr., MD, opthalmologist in private practice, Wilmington, DE. He is author of *The Eye Care Revolution* (Kensington Health).

Cataracts are a leading cause of vision loss in the US, affecting nearly half of adults age 65 or over. But it's a mistake to think of cataracts as affecting only older people. The physical changes that cause them begin almost at birth.

Background: The transparent lens of the eye consists of proteins densely interwoven in a crystalline structure. When these proteins are damaged by free radicals—harmful oxygen molecules produced in the body, especially upon exposure to sunlight and cigarette smoke —the lens becomes cloudy or opaque.

Eventually this leads to vision loss, from reduced nighttime vision to blindness.

Good news: People who have already begun to form cataracts can often preserve their sight and forestall cataract surgery by blocking the effects of free radicals. It even may be possible to reverse damage that's already been done. *A few things that help...*

●**Protect the eyes from ultraviolet radiation.** Along with visible light, sunlight contains invisible *ultraviolet* (UV) light. Since the lenses of the eyes are transparent, UV light has no trouble getting in and sparking production of free radicals.

Everyone, children included, should wear sunglasses outside—even on cloudy days.

Most quality sunglasses block UV light. If you are not sure that yours do, you should have them tested by an optometrist.

If you wear prescription glasses, spend a little more for the anti-UV coating.

●**Take eye-protecting supplements.** The liver produces antioxidants that help block the action of free radicals. Taking antioxidant supplements—and eating antioxidant-rich foods— confer extra protection.

The main antioxidant for preventing lens damage is *glutathione*. The liver produces glutathione when you eat sulfur-containing foods, such as onions, garlic, asparagus and eggs. But this may not be enough to guard against cataracts.

Ask your doctor about taking a daily glutathione booster, such as *N-acetylcysteine* (NAC). NAC is converted into glutathione in the body.

NAC supplements—sold over-the-counter in drug stores and health food stores—help prevent and even reverse cataracts.

Other eye-protecting antioxidants include...

●Vitamin C. Data from a Tufts University study suggest that taking 400 milligrams (mg) of vitamin C a day can reduce the risk for severe cataracts by 77%.

Other research has shown that people who eat lots of fruits and vegetables, which are high in vitamin C and other antioxidants, have a significantly lower risk.

Ask your doctor about taking 2,000 mg of vitamin C a day, divided into two doses.

Vitamin C supplementation is especially important for people who smoke. Cigarette smoke, including second-hand smoke, vastly increases levels of free radicals within the eyes. And each cigarette smoked destroys about 25 mg of vitamin C in the body.

●Vitamin E. This is another powerful antioxidant, one that's difficult to get from food sources. High doses may be dangerous for some people, so ask your doctor about taking 400 international units (IU) of vitamin E in the form of mixed tocopherols once a day.

● Quercetin. This bioflavonoid antioxidant blocks the action of *aldose reductase,* an enzyme in the body that boosts the risk for cataracts. Ask your doctor about taking 1,000 mg a day.

● Magnesium. This mineral helps dilate blood vessels in the eyes, helping the body flush out free radicals. Take 400 to 500 mg on an empty stomach at bedtime to increase blood flow to the eyes during sleep.

● Carotenoids. Take a daily vitamin that contains about 5,000 IU of vitamin A and 12 mg of lutein. These compounds have been shown to protect eye lenses from damage.

● **Drink six eight-ounce glasses of water a day.** Unlike most other tissues in the body, the lenses themselves have no blood vessels to regulate fluid levels. They depend on water that you consume to remove lactic acid and other protein-damaging toxins.

● **Eat less saturated fat.** People who are obese are at above-average risk for cataracts. That's because obesity tends to go hand in hand with consumption of saturated fat, which triggers formation of free radicals.

Read food labels carefully. Polyunsaturated and monounsaturated fats are okay in moderation. But over time, eating lots of saturated fat —along with hydrogenated or partially hydrogenated fat—will cause trouble for your eyes.

Good news: Eating less red meat, baked goods and full-fat dairy foods will automatically reduce the amount of saturated fat in your diet.

● **Ask your doctor about eucalyptus honey.** Preliminary research involving dogs suggests that eucalyptus-honey eye drops can help reverse cataracts.

Also promising: MSM (*methylsulfonylmethane*) eye drops, which may prevent cataracts by increasing levels of sulfur in the lens.

IF SURGERY BECOMES NECESSARY

If you do wind up needing cataract surgery, rest assured that it's among the safest, most effective operations being done.

Typically, just a few minutes are needed to remove the damaged lens and replace it with an artificial lens. It's not uncommon for people to have cataract surgery and return to work the same day.

The standard technique for removing cataracts is called *phacoemulsification.* The surgeon uses ultrasound to break up the damaged proteins in the lens. At this point, the proteins can be flushed with saline solution and removed from the eye. Then the surgeon inserts the artificial lens.

Some replacement lenses are *multifocal*— that is, they're designed to correct both near and distance vision.

It may sound like a great idea, but people with this type of artificial lens tend to have problems with glare at night. Most people prefer a single-vision implant.

Picking a surgeon: Make sure he has experience performing phacoemulsification. The more often a surgeon has performed the procedure, the more successful it is likely to be.

You'll want someone who does at least four cataract operations a week.

Cataract Control

Vitamin C may prevent cataracts. At least 10 studies show that taking 300 milligrams (mg) of vitamin C daily decreases the risk of age-related cataracts—but the recommended dietary allowance is only 60 mg per day.

Good food sources of vitamin C are fresh fruits and vegetables, including all citrus fruits, tomatoes, brussels sprouts and spinach. People over the age of 50 should consider taking supplements to be sure they get enough vitamin C and other important nutrients.

Vitamin C supplements are especially important for smokers (and those who live with smokers) because they tend to develop cataracts 10 years earlier than others.

Stuart Richer, OD, PhD, chief of optometry, DVA Medical Center, North Chicago, IL.

Glaucoma Facts

Glaucoma is an eye disorder that can strike at any age. It is a leading cause of blindness and is most common in people over age 65, but congenital glaucoma may be diagnosed much earlier—even at birth.

Risk factors: Family history of the disease, African-American or Caribbean heritage, elevated intraocular pressure.

Self-defense: Frequent, thorough eye exams starting at age 30...or even earlier if you have personal risk factors.

Louis Cantor, MD, professor of ophthalmology, Indiana University School of Medicine, Indianapolis.

Eye Self-Defense

The risk of macular degeneration is higher in individuals whose diets are low in the carotenoids *lutein* and *zeaxanthin*.

Foods that are rich in these substances include eggs, grits, corn bread, orange juice, spinach, broccoli, orange peppers, squash, pumpkin, kiwi fruit and red grapes.

A breakdown of cells in the retina, macular degeneration is a leading cause of blindness in individuals age 40 or older.

Alan C. Bird, MD, professor of clinical ophthalmology, University College, London. His study of the carotenoid content of foods was published in the *British Journal of Ophthalmology*.

An Herb for Your Eyes

David Winston, herbalist and ethnobotanist certified by the American Herbalists Guild, and dean, Herbal Therapeutics School of Botanical Medicine, Broadway, NJ.

During World War II, British pilots observed that night vision was better among those who regularly ate bilberry jam. Subsequent research showed that bilberry, a cousin of the American blueberry, benefits a variety of vision disorders.

Besides boosting night vision, bilberry can be used to slow the progression of a condition called *retinitis pigmentosa* (RP). This hereditary eye disorder begins with night blindness and leads eventually to total blindness.

Bilberry also strengthens capillary walls within the retina. That's good news for people with diabetic retinopathy or macular degeneration.

Important: Bilberry is most useful in preventing and slowing visual degeneration. It won't restore vision already lost.

Bilberry is rich in potent antioxidants called *anthocyanosides*. These compounds speed production of a retinal pigment called *visual purple*. Bilberry extract is standardized to contain 25% anthocyanosides.

Diabetics and others who wish to take bilberry as a preventive measure can take one 160-milligram capsule daily. The capsules are sold at health food stores.

If you've been diagnosed with diabetic retinopathy, RP or macular degeneration, ask your doctor about taking two or three bilberry capsules. At these doses, no adverse effects have been reported.

Or you can eat fresh blueberries—cooked enough to break down the skin. That allows the active components to be absorbed. Eat a cup of berries daily—in pancakes...or as syrup or sauce.

Common Eye Problems

Even minor eye conditions can be irritating. *Here are a few of the most common...*

●**Red eyes.** May come from fatigue, eye strain or allergies. If there is any discharge, see a doctor—you may have *conjunctivitis* (pink eye).

●**Scratchy, dry sensation.** Your tear gland may not be producing enough tears—try artificial tears or a humidifier.

●**Sudden pain followed by tears,** blurry vision, redness and sensitivity to light. See an ophthalmologist immediately.

●**Small bump on the edge of the lid.** This is probably a stye, which is an infected tear gland—use a warm compress and ask your doctor about taking an antibiotic.

James J. Salz, MD, clinical professor of ophthalmology, Los Angeles County University of Southern California Medical Center, Los Angeles.

How to Treat Eye Problems

If your eyes itch, it is most likely allergies. If they burn, it's probably dry eye. If they are sticky and crusty and you wake up with thick mucus in the eye, it's bacterial conjunctivitis.

See your doctor for the most effective treatments for each of these eye conditions. Prescription anti-allergy eyedrops typically last longer and are more effective than over-the-counter (OTC) anti-allergy drops.

The treatment of choice for dry eye is an OTC artificial tear product, such as Systane. The only prescription medication available, which was recently approved by the US Food and Drug Administration (FDA), is the anti-inflammatory drug *cyclosporine* (Restasis). This may be useful in severe cases where inflammation is a problem. Bacterial conjunctivitis is treated with fluoroquinolone antibiotics, such as *gatifloxacin* (Zymar) or *moxifloxacin* (Vigamox).

Mark Abelson, MD, associate clinical professor of ophthalmology, Harvard Medical School, and senior clinical scientist, Schepens Eye Research Institute, both in Boston.

What to Do If You Have Eye Floaters

Eye floaters usually are nothing to worry about. These black specks, which move when you adjust your gaze, usually don't affect vision, and there is no treatment.

Floaters often are permanent, but some eventually may disappear on their own. They occur when the vitreous gel that fills the eye partially liquifies. This happens naturally with age, but it can occur sooner in nearsighted people or because of injury.

Caution: If many floaters suddenly appear or they are accompanied by flashes, see your doctor immediately. This can indicate that the eye's vitreous gel has collapsed suddenly, which may result in retinal detachment or other significant eye damage. Surgery may be recommended in select cases.

Thomas J. Liesegang, MD, ophthalmologist, Mayo Clinic, Jacksonville, FL.

Stem-Cell Transplants For Blindness

Stem-cell transplants for eyes can cure some cases of blindness. If blindness is the result of corneal damage—by certain diseases or chemical or heat burns—and a relative has compatible tissue, surgeons can remove tissue containing stem cells from the donor eye...remove damaged tissue in the patient's blind eye...then attach the donor tissue.

The new tissue should grow over the blind eye's cornea and restore sight. See an eye surgeon for more information.

Richard S. Fisher, PhD, director, corneal disease program, National Eye Institute, National Institutes of Health, Bethesda, MD.

Obesity Can Lead to Blindness

People with a *body mass index* (BMI) of 30 or higher are 68% more likely to develop potentially blinding cataracts than those who are leaner.

BMI is calculated by multiplying your weight in pounds by 704.5, and dividing that number by your height in inches squared. For an electronic calculator, go to the National Heart, Lung and Blood Institute's Web site at *http://nhlbisupport.com/bmi*.

Theory: Obesity is linked to reduced blood sugar control and inflammation, both of which may also contribute to cataract formation.

June M. Weintraub, ScD, epidemiologist, environmental health section, San Francisco Department of Public Health.

Can Earwax Removal Help Hearing Loss?

Removing earwax via a syringe can improve hearing—but not always.

In a study of more than 100 patients who visited a doctor for earwax removal, two-thirds did *not* experience better hearing after the procedure. However, in patients who did benefit, hearing improved significantly—by up to 35 decibels.

Patients who do not benefit from earwax removal may be hearing impaired. They should see an audiologist for testing.

David Memel, MD, senior teaching associate, division of primary health care, University of Bristol, England.

How to Reverse Hearing Loss

Partial hearing loss can often be reversed by eliminating dairy products from the diet. Anecdotal evidence shows that some patients who stop eating dairy products and foods that are rich in whey—such as many breads and pastries—may experience significant improvements in hearing.

Theory: Age-related hearing loss may be caused by an allergic response to a protein in dairy and whey products.

If you suffer from age-related hearing loss: As a three-week trial, eliminate from your diet all dairy products as well as manufactured foods containing whey or milk protein, and see if your hearing improves.

In addition, see a doctor who is an ear and hearing specialist (otologist) for a thorough examination.

Robert A. Anderson, MD, founder and executive director, American Board of Holistic Medicine, East Wenatchee, WA.

Stop the Noise of Tinnitus

Natan Bauman, EdD, director, New England Tinnitus and Hyperacusis Clinic, and the Hearing, Balance, & Speech Center, both in Hamden, CT. He invented Solace, a fully digital, programmable broadband noise generator, used in the treatment of tinnitus. www.hearingbalance.com.

Approximately 17% of Americans and up to one-third of adults age 65 and older experience some degree of *tinnitus* (pronounced tin-EYE-tus or TIN-uh-tus). People with tinnitus hear sounds—ringing, buzzing, roaring and chirping—inside their own heads.

For most sufferers, the sounds are mainly an annoyance, but they can be so loud and persistent that it's impossible for some sufferers to concentrate or carry on a conversation.

CAUSES

Tinnitus isn't a disease—it's a symptom of an underlying medical problem. *The most common causes...*

●**Damage to hairs on auditory cells in the inner ear**—a result of aging and/or life-long exposure to loud sounds. The damaged hairs emit abnormal electrical signals that the brain interprets as sounds.

●**Heavy, long-term use of aspirin or other anti-inflammatory drugs.** Some antibiotics and quinine (a drug used to treat malaria and nighttime leg cramps) also can cause tinnitus.

●**Atherosclerosis, the buildup of cholesterol and other fatty substances in arteries,** can cause noisy blood turbulence in blood vessels in the ears.

Excessive accumulation of earwax can partially block external sounds and make internal sounds louder and more distracting.

TREATMENTS

Tinnitus sometimes can be eliminated by treating the underlying problem—removing excess earwax or reducing the dose of anti-inflammatory drugs.

For the majority of sufferers, the noise won't go away, but it can be made less bothersome. *The best approaches...*

●**Limit salt intake to less than 2,000 milligrams daily.** Excessive sodium can cause noise-producing fluid accumulations in the inner ear—especially in people who have Ménière's disease, a condition marked by a buildup of fluid in the inner ear.

• **Restrict caffeine and alcohol.** Caffeine causes blood vessels to constrict...alcohol causes them to dilate—both of which can increase tinnitus sounds by increasing blood turbulence.

• **Keep auditory cells busy with background noise.** This can make it easier to ignore tinnitus. You might try a portable fountain in the living room or soft music in the bedroom. A sound generator, available from audiologists, fills ears with a "static-y" sound. Setting a TV or radio in between stations creates similar static.

• **Retrain the ears with a tinnitus retraining instrument (TRI).** About 80% of tinnitus patients get significant and permanent relief within 16 months. This hearing aid–like device generates sounds that are almost as loud as the tinnitus. Used under an audiologist's supervision and worn for eight hours daily, it trains the central nervous system to perceive tinnitus as background noise rather than as a distracting "main" sound.

Tinnitus often is accompanied by stress and frustration. Treatment with TRI always is combined with counseling—usually cognitive therapy, which helps people gain control over their tinnitus.

• **Wear a hearing aid to amplify external sounds.** It's often the best approach for those with age-related hearing loss as well as tinnitus. The improvement in hearing makes internal noises less distracting. Consult an audiologist.

 ## A Natural Treatment For Tinnitus

Ginkgo biloba may quiet chronic tinnitus. In four of five studies reviewed, a daily dose of 120 to 160 milligrams (mg), taken as tablets or in liquid form, had significant benefit for those with ringing in the ears.

Theory: Ginkgo biloba increases blood supply to the inner ear, which may help to relieve chronic tinnitus.

If you suffer from tinnitus: Ask your doctor if ginkgo biloba would be a helpful treatment for you.

Caution: Ginkgo can cause excessive bleeding if you take a blood-thinning drug, such as *warfarin* (Coumadin).

Edzard Ernst, MD, PhD, director, Complementary Medicine Unit, Universities of Exeter and Plymouth, England.

Avoid Sinus Infections... Naturally

Murray Grossan, MD, otolaryngologist, Tower Ear, Nose and Throat Clinic, Cedars-Sinai Medical Center, Los Angeles. He is coauthor of *The Sinus Cure—7 Simple Steps to Relieve Sinusitis and Other Ear, Nose and Throat Conditions* (Ballantine).

Believe it or not, sinus infection, which affects 37 million Americans each year, is more prevalent today than it was in the preantibiotic age!

That's not to say that antibiotics aren't effective. When *sinusitis* (the technical name for a sinus infection) occurs, treatment with a full course of antibiotics is often essential to kill off the infectious bacteria.

Decongestants can help to relieve sinusitis symptoms. So can oral or topical steroids (to combat sinus inflammation) and antihistamines, if underlying allergies are involved.

Increasingly, doctors are realizing that to successfully fight off sinus infection and prevent it from recurring, *medication alone isn't enough*. You also have to ensure that the mucous membranes lining your nasal and sinus passages are healthy and functioning properly.

SYMPTOMS

Sinusitis occurs whenever the mucous membranes in your nose and sinuses become irritated by a cold, allergy, pollutants or exposure to dry or cold air. This irritation causes the membranes to become inflamed. When this happens, the motion of the *cilia* (the tiny hairs that coat all the mucous membranes and are responsible for moving mucus over their surfaces) slows down. At the same time, the irritation stimulates your mucous glands to secrete more mucus than usual to dilute the bacteria.

Result: Mucus gets trapped in the sinuses, where it can easily become infected because the swelling meant to dilute the bacteria now blocks the sinus openings, and prevents the body from washing away the bacteria. *Symptoms of sinus infection include...*

- **Facial pressure around the eyes,** cheeks and forehead.
- **Cold symptoms** lasting more than 10 days.
- **Thick, green/yellow mucus.**
- **Postnasal drip,** which occurs when excess mucus drips down the back of the throat.
- **Pain in the upper molars.**
- **Fatigue and a flu-like achiness.**

TREATMENT

The following natural treatments will help to keep your cilia healthy and functioning and prevent mucus from building in your sinuses. When a sinus infection does occur, these same treatments will help to increase the effectiveness of antibiotics and other medications—speeding healing and making a recurrence less likely.

1. Drink hot liquids. One of the best ways to unclog sinuses is to drink hot tea—black, green, herbal or decaffeinated, it doesn't matter—or hot chicken soup throughout the day. Drink enough so that your urine turns light in color. These hot liquids help moisturize your mucus membranes, speeding up the movement of your cilia and thus washing mucus out of your sinuses more quickly. (Sorry, coffee lovers, but hot coffee isn't nearly as effective.)

Note to travelers: The dry air on jetliners is particularly rough on the sinuses—so when flying, carry tea bags with you and ask your flight attendant for hot water to make tea.

2. Apply warm compresses to your face. Do this three times a day for five minutes. A small towel soaked in warm water, then placed over your face below and between the eyes, will help increase the circulation in your sinuses, which will also help speed up the movement of your cilia.

3. Irrigate your sinuses. For over 3,000 years, yoga practitioners have kept their sinuses healthy through the practice of sniffing a saltwater solution rapidly in and out of their noses at low pressure.

Caution: Don't try this unless you have been taught how to do it.

Fortunately, for those of us who aren't yogis, a device called the Hydro Pulse Nasal and Sinus Irrigator will do this for you. The pulsating flow from the Hydro Pulse is very gentle.

An even simpler alternative is a Lavage irrigation bottle. Ideally, irrigation should be done using Ringer's solution, the solution used in hospitals for intravenous treatment, and sold over the counter in drugstores.

Or you can use an isotonic saline solution (not too salty, just right) that does not contain any *benzalkonium.* Benzalkonium is a preservative that can impair nasal function, and some people complain that it burns. To make up your own preservative-free saline solution, add one teaspoon of table salt to one pint of water.

If you're prone to sinus infections, I recommend irrigating your sinuses twice a day, especially during the cold winter months.

Ringer's solution, designed for irrigation use, is sold under the name Breathe-ease XL (it's also available as a nasal spray). To order the Hydro Pulse Nasal and Sinus Irrigator, a Lavage irrigation bottle or Breathe-ease products, visit the Web site *www.sinus-allergies.com.*

4. Clear your sinuses with aromatherapy. To help open up congested nasal passages and sinuses, drop some eucalyptus or menthol oil into a bowl of hot water, then breathe in the vapors—or simply open up a jar of either oil and inhale the fumes directly.

Vicks VapoRub is also effective. Simply dab a bit on the skin underneath your nose.

Other aromatherapy decongestants include horseradish (grate it and put it on a sandwich) and, if you're really brave, Japanese wasabi mustard. All of these therapies work best if used a couple of times a day, especially during the winter months.

5. Take breakfast in bed. When you sleep at night, your body temperature drops and your cilia movement slows down. By taking breakfast in bed along with a cup of hot tea, you'll give your cilia a chance to warm up and clear out the night's accumulated mucus before you start placing demands on your respiratory system.

6. Elevate your head when sleeping. Elevating your head with one or two pillows will help your sinuses and nasal passages stay open while you sleep. The more your head is elevated, the better the effect.

7. Dustproof your bedroom. Dust and dust mites can wreak havoc on your mucus membranes, especially when you're asleep and your cilia are at rest.

In your bedroom, avoid all heavy draperies and wall-to-wall carpeting (which is a notorious dust-collector). Use throw rugs instead, and toss them in the washing machine at least every six weeks. Overall, make your bedroom as bare as possible, and dust all surfaces and behind furniture weekly. To further reduce dust in your bedroom, I recommend using a HEPA air purifier, and running it throughout the day. (Most people find the filter too noisy for nighttime use.)

8. Get plenty of rest. If your sinuses are acting up, you will be amazed at how much improvement you'll see after taking the weekend off and spending it in bed. Be sure to get some mental rest at the same time. Turn off the phone and avoid the news. Instead, rent some funny videos, find a good book, lie back and enjoy. Relaxation can help the body heal.

More from Murray Grossan...

Blow Your Nose Gently to Help Your Ears

If you blow your nose hard, you can rupture an eardrum. However, that's not the most serious consequence that could occur. You also can cause a sinus or ear infection by blowing too hard. Nose-blowing can force bacteria from the nasal chamber into your sinuses and the middle ear. The excessive pressure also could blow a hole in the inner ear, which could result in permanent hearing loss, tinnitus and dizziness.

Self-defense: Always blow your nose gently.

Also from Murray Grossan...

Breakfast in Bed Fights Allergies

You can alleviate allergy symptoms by having breakfast in bed. Allergy sufferers tend to be sensitive to temperature changes, which is why they cough and sneeze when they leave a warm bed. Drinking hot tea in bed warms the body and prevents this reaction.

Caffeinated or decaffeinated tea increases the speed of nasal cilia, tiny hairs in the mucous membranes, to rid the nose of allergy-triggering dust that has accumulated during sleep.

Helpful: Keep a thermos of hot tea at your bedside and drink a cup in the morning.

Shocking Dangers of Gum Disease

Michael P. Bonner, DDS, dentist in group practice, Rockdale, TX, and a member of the Academy of General Dentistry and the American Academy of Anti-Aging Medicine. He is coauthor of *The Oral Health Bible* (Basic Health).

You already know that gum disease can cause cavities, bad breath and tooth loss. You also may know that infected gums increase the risk for heart damage.

What you may not know—and what dentists are just now finding out—is that gum disease also can drastically increase a person's odds of suffering very serious ailments, such as stroke and some types of pneumonia.

THE PROBLEM

Gum disease is caused by plaque, a sticky film of bacteria that coats the teeth. Mild inflammation along the gum line is known as *gingivitis*. More serious *periodontal disease* occurs when plaque migrates underneath the gums and causes pockets of infection.

Gum disease isn't just a dental problem. The infection triggers the production of inflammatory *cytokines*, immune chemicals that are converted in the liver to *C-reactive protein* (CRP).

Some doctors believe that elevated CRP is a more accurate marker for heart attack and stroke than high cholesterol levels.

A normal CRP level is 0.8 milligrams (mg) or less per liter of blood. The level increases by 500 to 1,000 times in people who have more advanced gum disease.

Result: Gum disease increases the risk for heart attack by 200% to 400% and can double the risk for stroke. Gum disease and elevated levels of CRP also have been linked to life-threatening blood clots in the legs (*deep vein thrombosis*) or in the lungs (*pulmonary embolism*).

DO YOU HAVE GUM DISEASE?

If you have any of the following symptoms, you probably have gum disease and should see a dentist right away.

- **Puffy, red or swollen gums...**or gums that bleed after brushing or flossing.
- **Shiny gums.**
- **Teeth that have loosened.**
- **Persistent bad breath.**
- **An elevated CRP level** (above 0.8 mg per liter of blood).

HOW TO PROTECT YOURSELF

Daily flossing, brushing and the use of mouthwash help, but they don't *eliminate* gum disease. That's because these methods don't reach the microorganisms that collect beneath the gums to cause disease.

To improve your dental regimen, follow this five-step program...

- **Step 1.** Use a power brush. A manual toothbrush with soft, rounded bristles removes most surface plaque, but ultrasonic toothbrushes are more effective. They pulsate about 31,000 times a minute, generating waves of fluid that remove plaque from the microscopic pits found in the teeth. Brush with a power brush two to three times a day.

My favorite: Sonicare, available at most pharmacies.

Typical cost: $120.

In combination with flossing, daily power brushing greatly decreases the risk for systemic infection, which occurs when a break in gum tissue allows germs to enter the bloodstream.

Important: Use nontoxic toothpastes and mouthwashes. If you read the labels on commercial products, you will find warnings, such as "do not swallow" or "in case of accidental misuse, contact a poison control center." That is because these products can be toxic.

Certain toothpastes contain *propylene glycol,* the key ingredient in many antifreezes. Some mouthwashes contain ethyl alcohol, which dries oral tissues.

Better: All-natural products that clean the teeth and inhibit harmful organisms without the concern of toxicity.

- **Step 2.** Floss your teeth thoroughly, yet gently, at least once a day. You can use waxed or unwaxed floss. If your teeth are close together, use flat dental tape, such as Glide, which is available at most pharmacies.

- **Step 3.** Scrape your tongue. The large surface of the tongue harbors tremendous quantities of disease-causing organisms and inflammatory chemicals.

Even if you floss and brush several times daily, microorganisms from the tongue can constantly reinfect gum tissue and increase risk for systemic infection.

Tongue scrapers, sold in pharmacies, are inexpensive and available as plastic strips with serrated edges or as single-handled metal or plastic devices with a scraping edge at one end. Both types are equally effective.

When scraping the tongue, reach as far back as possible. A few passes is usually enough. Perform once or twice daily.

- **Step 4.** Irrigate your gums. The narrow space (sulcus) between a tooth and surrounding gum tissue harbors up to 100 trillion microorganisms.

Infection in the sulcular spaces generates enormous quantities of inflammatory chemicals, which should be removed daily to prevent chronic infection.

Home irrigation devices shoot water into the mouth and flush out accumulated buildup (cellular debris and infectious microorganisms) that brushing and flossing don't reach.

My favorite: Hydro Floss, 800-635-3594, *www.oralcaretech.com*.

Typical cost: $86 to $130.

•**Step 5.** Supplement your diet. Several nutrients play a crucial role in gum health and can help reduce or eliminate systemic inflammation and infection. Take these amounts daily in two divided doses, with meals. Tablets are fine unless otherwise noted. *Key supplements to ask your doctor about...*

•**Vitamin C** can reduce gum bleeding and tenderness. As an antioxidant, it also may improve the immune system's ability to control harmful organisms.

Typical daily dose: 500 to 1,000 mg.

Smart: Take 1,500 mg of vitamin C tablets in *chewable* form about 15 minutes before going to the dentist. It quickly suppresses inflammation that may occur when oral procedures push infectious organisms into the bloodstream.

Warning: You may need to take antibiotics before you have any kind of oral procedure performed, including a routine cleaning, if you have had joint-replacement surgery within the past year, or if you have a heart murmur. Dental procedures may allow bacteria to enter the bloodstream, which can infect artificial joints or heart valves in people with heart murmurs. Consult your physician for details.

•**Bioflavonoids** are derived from citrus fruits. They strengthen gums and help prevent germs from entering the bloodstream. Bioflavonoids also help to boost immunity and reduce infection.

Typical daily dose: 500 mg.

•**Coenzyme Q-10** is required for collagen formation. Take only in soft capsule form.

Typical daily dose: 60 to 120 mg.

•**Grape seed extract** contains *proanthocyanidins*, antioxidant compounds that inhibit the release of inflammatory compounds.

Typical daily dose: 100 to 200 mg.

•**Methylsulfonylmethane (MSM)** is a form of organic sulfur that builds healthy gum tissue. MSM is absorbed better when taken with 500 to 1,000 mg of vitamin C.

Typical daily dose: 1,000 to 3,000 mg.

Protecting Your Gums Can Save Your Life

Alan Winter, DDS, periodontist and partner, Park Avenue Periodontal Associates, 532 Park Ave., New York City 10021.

Tooth decay is fast becoming a thing of the past, thanks mostly to access to fluoridated water. But people keep losing their teeth—to periodontal disease.

Sooner or later, 80% of adults develop this disease, also known simply as gum disease. It's caused by *Porphyromonas gingivalis* and other plaque-forming bacteria that work their way below the gum line.

Good dental hygiene helps keep these bacteria in check. If allowed to flourish, however, these nasty microbes attack gum tissue.

Once this tissue erodes, teeth slowly loosen and ultimately may need to be extracted.

Extra danger: The same bacteria that cause gum disease are now thought to contribute to heart disease and pregnancy complications.

DO YOU HAVE GUM DISEASE?

Early gum disease is characterized by chronic bad breath and red, swollen gums that bleed when teeth are brushed. Or—spaces may form between teeth and teeth may become loose.

Caution: Some people develop severe gum disease *without* obvious symptoms. For this reason, it's essential to have your gums professionally examined—and your teeth professionally cleaned—*at least twice a year.*

Gum disease progresses slowly in some people, rapidly in others. Psychological stress can aggravate the condition by releasing hormones that bacteria feed on.

Gum disease can also be aggravated by smoking...by systemic diseases like diabetes... and by eating sugary foods. The gums can also be affected by calcium channel blockers, *phenytoin* (Dilantin) and certain other drugs.

REGULAR EXAMS ARE KEY

While semiannual dental exams are sufficient for most people, those with existing gum trouble should have their teeth examined and cleaned four times a year.

Reason: Bacteria carve out tiny pockets between gums and teeth. When these pockets exceed three millimeters (about one-eighth inch) in depth, the bacteria change from a comparatively harmless form to a virulent form.

This transition occurs after the bacteria have been growing for eight to 12 weeks.

If you have your teeth professionally cleaned every three months, the bacteria will be disrupted before they cause significant damage to your gums.

PROPER BRUSHING TECHNIQUE

Brush your teeth twice a day for at least 60 seconds. Use an old-fashioned manual brush with soft nylon bristles and a small head.

Hard bristles—especially those of horsehair or another natural fiber—are too abrasive.

What about electric toothbrushes? They don't really clean any better, although they can add an element of fun, motivating some people to brush more frequently.

Irrigating devices that clean using pressurized water generally do not remove bacterial plaque—only food particles.

THE IMPORTANCE OF FLOSSING

Flossing is even more important than brushing. Most periodontal disease starts *between* teeth, in areas that are out of the reach of toothbrush bristles.

Best approach: Floss once a day with unwaxed dental floss. Slide the floss into the space between teeth, then move it gently under the gum line.

Once bacteria have established themselves in deep pockets, the only way to get rid of them is to have your teeth professionally cleaned.

DENTAL SCALING

If professional cleaning isn't doing the trick, you may need dental scaling. In this process, a dentist or dental hygienist uses a special instrument to go farther below the gum line than is possible in a regular cleaning, scraping away bacterial plaque and mineral deposits (tartar) from the roots of the teeth.

Scaling renders teeth less hospitable to bacteria. It also causes the pockets in which they live to shrink.

Three or four 60-minute visits are required.

Total cost: $400 to $1,000.

GUM SURGERY

If gum disease is advanced—or if it persists after scaling—surgery may be necessary.

In the typical procedure, diseased areas of gum are peeled back in flaps, exposing the roots of the teeth so that they can be thoroughly cleaned.

Once the tooth roots are smoothed and free of plaque, the pockets should shrink.

Two to four 60- to 90-minute procedures are required.

Total cost: $3,000 to $6,000.

ANTIBIOTICS

Although antibiotics are often helpful for controlling bacterial growth during or after surgery, they're no substitute for gum surgery when it is necessary.

Trap: If tooth roots aren't smoothed and the pockets corrected, the bacteria—and the gum disease—recur quickly once antibiotics are discontinued.

Remember, gum disease is a chronic condition. Even if you have surgery, you must remain extremely vigilant.

More from Alan Winter...

The Truth About Fluoridated Water

The rewards of fluoridated water seem to outweigh the risks. The addition of fluoride to the public water supplies has reduced tooth decay by as much as 70%, according to the National Institutes of Health. Fluoride strengthens the enamel in children's tooth buds—the developing teeth that have not yet erupted—and this helps prevent decay.

Caution: Too much fluoride can cause mottling or discoloration of teeth, but this rarely happens. The levels of fluoride found in US drinking water—one part per million gallons—are generally safe.

Many very young children don't drink enough fluoridated water or drink nonfluoridated bottled or well water. If this is the case in your family, talk to your pediatrician about giving your child supplements.

Also: Ingesting fluoride has no real benefit for adults because their teeth and enamel are already fully formed.

Fight Cavities in Your Sleep

To fight cavities while you're sleeping, use your finger or toothbrush to rub a dab of fluoride toothpaste along the gumline before bed. Overnight, teeth will absorb the enamel-strengthening fluoride.

Luke Matranga, DDS, associate professor of general dentistry, Creighton University School of Dentistry, Omaha.

Extra-Special Protection for Teeth and Gums

Nonsurgical treatment for periodontal disease can save teeth and make extractions unnecessary.

Recent study: Aggressive cleaning, known as *root planing and scaling,* plus antibiotic treatment for two weeks made 87% of surgeries and extractions unnecessary. The benefits lasted for five years.

If you have periodontal disease, ask your dentist about alternatives to surgery.

Walter J. Loesche, DMD, PhD, Marcus Ward Professor of Dentistry Emeritus, University of Michigan School of Dentistry, Ann Arbor, and leader of a study of 90 patients with periodontal disease, published in The Journal of the American Dental Association.

Should You Have Your Fillings Removed?

Some people have been concerned that the silver-colored, mercury-containing amalgam fillings may cause serious conditions, such as multiple sclerosis and Alzheimer's disease.

But there's no proof to support these fears. The mercury the fillings contain is mixed with other metals, such as silver, to form a stable alloy. Removing fillings can weaken teeth, since the replacement filling must be made larger.

If a dentist wants to remove an amalgam filling, ask if there are other options.

Frederick C. Eichmiller, DDS, director, Paffenbarger Research Center, Gaithersburg, MD.

Best Ways to Whiten Teeth

Paul J. Berson, DDS, clinical assistant professor of restorative dentistry, University of Pennsylvania School of Dental Medicine, Philadelphia.

You would like whiter teeth, but those whitening toothpastes haven't worked. The reality is that whitening toothpastes can make teeth less bright because they abrade the enamel.

So what *does* work? Drug stores stock dozens of tooth-whitening products, and nearly all dentists perform whitening procedures. *Here's what you need to know…*

IN-OFFICE WHITENING

The fastest and most precise whitening technique is performed by a dentist. A whitening agent—usually carbamide peroxide or hydrogen peroxide—is applied to teeth, then exposed to ultraviolet light to accelerate the chemical reaction. Teeth get significantly lighter in a single, one-hour treatment. One or two additional treatments may be needed if teeth are deeply stained.

Gums are covered with rubber to protect them from the chemical. Some people experience tooth sensitivity after the treatment. This usually disappears within 24 hours.

Cost: $500 to $650.*

People who have had the procedure should treat their teeth at home once a month or so to keep them white. Your dentist can provide a custom-fitted mouthpiece (tray) that holds the whitening solution.

Cost for mouthpiece and home bleaching chemicals: $100 to $150.

Stains from tobacco, coffee and tea are the easiest to eliminate. Age-related yellowing that occurs when tooth enamel gets thinner and reveals the yellowish *dentin* (the inner part of the tooth) takes more work, but it also can be lightened in most cases.

Dentin that is deeply stained—due to childhood use of *tetracycline*, for example, or root canals that have caused the interior of the tooth to darken—may require veneers or other restorative dental techniques. Whitening treatments won't work on dental restoration—crowns, veneers, bonding or bridgework.

HOME WHITENING KITS

These kits, available at drug stores, contain the same whitening agents dentists use—but they aren't as concentrated. It can take several months to see a difference.

Home whitening systems come with mouth trays that fit over your teeth. The kits contain enough whitening gel for about one month. Fill the trays with whitening agent, then slip them over your teeth for 30 minutes twice daily until you achieve desired whiteness.

Kits cost $70 to $100. In the long run, however, home whitening may cost *more* than in-office procedures.

Also, the trays don't fit teeth as well as dentist-made trays. The whitening agent may leak out and burn the gums...or it might not coat teeth evenly, resulting in uneven whitening.

WHITENING GELS

These over-the counter gels contain a mild concentration of hydrogen peroxide. They cost about $15 and are applied twice daily for two weeks.

*Tooth whitening generally is not covered by insurance.

They are unlikely to irritate gums but whiten teeth only slightly. You may have mild tooth sensitivity until you stop using them.

WHITENING STRIPS

Available over-the-counter, these contain a mild concentration of hydrogen peroxide. They're applied to teeth and left in place for 30 minutes once or twice a day. You might experience temporary tooth sensitivity but little or no gum irritation.

A box of 84 strips costs $30 to $45. Generally, you have to use them for a few months to see a significant degree of improvement.

ULTRASONIC BRUSHES

Sound waves from ultrasonic brushes, such as Sonicare and Ultima, travel inside the pores and cause stain deposits to vibrate and shake loose. Ultrasonic brushes won't eliminate stains, but they can help maintain brightness once teeth are whitened.

Cost: $80 to $120.

How to Relax at The Dentist's Office

Many people feel apprehensive when going to the dentist. *To help alleviate stress, follow this advice...*

●**To feel more in control,** have the dentist explain the procedure in advance.

●**Take an active role in decisions** about your treatment.

●**Communicate your fears** to the dentist so he/she can help you cope with them.

●**Agree on a signal,** such as raising your hand, to indicate that you need a short break during treatment.

●**Find a distraction**—many dentists now offer TV, headsets with music, etc.

●**Review pain-control options,** such as premedication with something to help you relax or local or general anesthesia.

D. Scott Navarro, DDS, vice president, professional services, Delta Dental Plans Association, Oak Brook, IL.

Soothe Sensitive Teeth

Use a cotton ball to apply warm olive oil at the gum line. This creates a lasting seal that protects sensitive roots that have become exposed as a result of gum recession.

Helpful: Heat the oil in a pan until it begins to smoke. Dry your teeth with a cotton ball. Use another to dab the oil onto your teeth.

See your dentist if sensitivity persists.

Danny Bui, DDS, dentist in private practice, Bethesda, MD.

Sugar-Free Soda Warning

Sugar-free diet soda can harm your teeth. Diet soda is highly acidic and can eat away tooth enamel over time. People who sip sugar-free soft drinks all day can damage their teeth to the point where they need significant repair.

More damaging: When people sip drinks without eating any food, or have an otherwise dry mouth.

Reason: Acid residue from the soda stays on the teeth longer.

Antidote: Rinse your mouth with water after drinking any soda.

Sheldon Nadler, DMD, dentist in private practice, New York City.

Dental Problems May Be an Early Sign Of Osteoporosis

Since teeth are embedded in the jawbone, the early warning signs of bone loss may include severe gum disease, bone loss around teeth, tooth loss and/or loosened dentures.

Self-defense: Ask your dentist if any of your dental problems could be due to bone loss.

To help prevent osteoporosis: Consume at least 1,200 milligrams (mg) of calcium along with 400 to 800 international units (IU) of vitamin D...perform weight-bearing and muscle-strengthening exercises...and don't smoke or abuse alcohol.

Barbara J. Steinberg, DDS, clinical professor of surgery, Drexel University College of Medicine, Philadelphia.

3

Symptoms & Solutions

Medical Red Flags: Seven Symptoms Never to Ignore

Most of us will see a doctor if we detect a suspicious lump or changes in a mole. And if severe chest pain occurs, even the most stoic among us will head to the nearest emergency room.

Other symptoms are easier to miss—or *dismiss*. But prompt diagnosis and treatment will safeguard your health...and possibly save your life—or that of a loved one.

Here are seven red flags that may signal a medical emergency...

ABDOMINAL DISTRESS

Persistent cramps, bloating, vomiting or a change in appetite or bowel habits can indicate a variety of problems.

Best-case scenario: Spastic colon...viral infection...lactose intolerance...or indigestion.

Worst-case scenario: An ulcer...tumor... ruptured appendix...ovarian cyst...intestinal obstruction...inflammatory bowel disease...or inflammation of the digestive tract, gallbladder or pancreas.

Seek emergency treatment: If you're vomiting and haven't moved your bowels or passed gas in 24 hours—or if you have sudden, acute abdominal pain accompanied by fever—you may require emergency surgery.

Note: If your condition is serious enough to warrant emergency treatment, it's probably best to avoid driving. Call 911 or ask a friend or neighbor to take you to the nearest hospital as quickly as possible.

For milder discomfort, eliminate possible culprits, including aspirin, caffeine, alcohol, dairy products and artificial sweeteners. Try easing any symptoms with an over-the-counter (OTC) product, like Maalox or Pepto-Bismol.

Marie Savard, MD, an internationally-recognized internal medicine physician, expert on wellness and champion for patient rights. She is author of *How to Save Your Own Life* (Warner Books). *www.drsavard.com.*

See your doctor: If symptoms persist for one week or longer, get a checkup.

COUGH

A dry, nonproductive cough that lasts for more than two weeks requires medical attention.

Best-case scenario: Post-nasal drip...acid reflux...or continuing irritation from coughing.

Worst-case scenario: Infection...severe asthma...lung cancer...malignancy of the lymphatic system (lymphoma)...or congestive heart failure.

See your doctor: Get a physical exam and chest X-ray within one week.

HEADACHE

If you are experiencing the worst headache of your life—especially if accompanied by vomiting—it should not be ignored.

Best-case scenario: Acute viral infection... or migraine.

Worst-case scenario: A leaking aneurysm ...infection of the lining covering the brain and spinal cord (bacterial meningitis) if accompanied by fever and stiff neck...or brain tumor.

Seek emergency treatment: You will need to undergo a CT scan or *magnetic resonance imaging* (MRI) scan to determine the cause. If it's an aneurysm, you may require emergency surgery. For bacterial meningitis, intravenous antibiotics should be given as soon as possible.

MENTAL CHANGES

Watch for confusion, memory lapses or odd or impaired thinking.

Best-case scenario: Mild depression... stress...low blood sugar...or a deficiency in vitamin B-12.

Worst-case scenario: Severe depression... brain tumor...encephalitis...or an adverse drug reaction. Many drug combinations can cause this reaction, but antihistamines and sedatives are particularly suspect.

Important: Discuss possible drug interactions with your doctor and pharmacist before taking any new medication.

Seek emergency treatment: If disorientation is sudden and acute, mental changes could reflect a serious problem with the central nervous system. Therefore, it is critical to receive a prompt evaluation.

See your doctor: For mild or gradual symptoms, get a checkup within 24 hours.

RECTAL BLEEDING

Be concerned if you pass a dark black or maroon stool...or see bright red blood on toilet paper or in the bowl.

Best-case scenario: Hemorrhoids or a tear in the lining of the anus (fissure) can cause bright red blood...iron supplements or Pepto-Bismol can cause black stool.

Worst-case scenario: Rectal cancer if blood is bright red...or colon cancer, bleeding ulcer or *diverticulosis* (outpouchings, or sacs, usually in the large intestine) if stool is black or maroon.

Seek emergency treatment: If stool is black or maroon and accompanied by dizziness or lightheadedness, you could be suffering from internal bleeding caused by a stomach ulcer or diverticulosis. Treatment includes blood transfusions and surgery.

See your doctor: For black stool not attributable to iron supplements or Pepto-Bismol, get evaluated as soon as possible. For bright red blood, get a checkup within two weeks. Don't assume hemorrhoids.

UNEXPLAINED WEIGHT LOSS

If you lose your appetite or drop more than 5% of your body weight, despite normal eating, something is wrong.

Best-case scenario: Mild depression... diabetes...overactive thyroid (*hyperthyroidism*) ...or intestinal parasites.

Worst-case scenario: Severe depression... cancer...hepatitis or other liver disease...tuberculosis...or chronic inflammation of the intestinal wall (Crohn's disease).

See your doctor: Get a complete physical, including a thorough blood workup, within two weeks.

VISION DISTURBANCES

Don't shrug it off if you experience blurred or cloudy vision, wavy lines, redness, intense pain or itching in the eye.

Best-case scenario: Allergies...diabetes... pink eye (*conjunctivitis*)...or even outdated corrective lenses.

Worst-case scenario: Retinal tear or detachment…glaucoma…inflammation of the muscular lining of the eye (*uveitis*)…or foreign matter in the eye.

See your doctor: Have a checkup from an ophthalmologist within 24 hours.

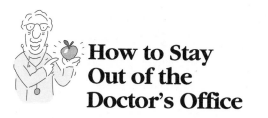

How to Stay Out of the Doctor's Office

Edward T. Creagan, MD, cancer specialist and professor of clinical oncology, Mayo Clinic Medical School, Rochester, MN. He is author of *How Not to Be My Patient: A Physician's Secrets for Staying Healthy and Surviving Any Diagnosis* (Health Communications).

In my 30-year career as a cancer specialist, I have cared for approximately 55,000 patients. And more than half of these people could have avoided a trip to my examining room. That's because their cancers (or, in some cases, heart disease and diabetes) developed as the result of unhealthy lifestyles, rather than a genetic roll of the dice.

Because I see the devastating effects of such lifestyles each day, I have made it a point to develop personal habits that give me the best possible odds for staying healthy. *My secrets…*

PREVENTION AND EARLY DETECTION

An annual physical is important for everyone over age 50. If you are younger than 50 and are generally healthy, ask your doctor how often you should be examined. I'm 59 and I see my internist every spring for regular screenings. These exams are absolutely essential.

My advice: In addition to annual physicals and any other screening tests your doctor may recommend for you, be sure to schedule colonoscopies (one every five years after age 50). Women should have mammograms (annually after age 40) and Pap tests every one to three years if they're sexually active. Men should have *prostate-specific antigen* (PSA) blood tests and digital rectal exams annually starting at age 50. If a first-degree relative (parent or sibling) had cancer, begin monitoring with these tests 10 years before the age that family member developed the cancer.

HEALTHFUL EATING

My wife, Peggy, and I are vegetarians who eat fish. This means we don't eat animal-based saturated fats, which boost the risk for cardiovascular disease. We get protein from beans, nuts and fish.

I never eat fried or calorie-dense foods, such as butter. We use olive oil, even on toast. The only thing I ever order at a fast-food restaurant is low-fat ice cream.

I carry my own lunch when I work at the hospital. It typically includes a peanut butter and jelly sandwich on high-fiber (at least 2 grams per slice) whole-wheat bread, pretzels, carrots and low-fat yogurt. I drink six to eight six-ounce glasses of water a day.

My advice: Plan at least one meatless dinner a week, such as spaghetti with marinara sauce…black beans and brown rice with salad …or tofu with stir-fried vegetables.

SUPPLEMENTS

Nutritional supplements are not the same as the good stuff nature puts in leaves or berries. However, it can be difficult to get all your vitamins through food. I take a daily multivitamin that contains 18 milligrams (mg) of iron, because, as a vegetarian, I don't eat iron-rich meats. I also supplement daily with 400 international units (IU) of vitamin E and 500 mg of vitamin C. These vitamins are good antioxidants. They also enhance muscle recovery after exercise.

I have a family history of heart disease, so I add an 81-mg baby aspirin each day to decrease my risk for heart attack and stroke.

My advice: If you take supplements, understand what you are taking and why. Most people take whatever is advertised. Consult your physician, pharmacist or a registered dietician for guidance. A health-food store employee rarely has the proper training.

PHYSICAL ACTIVITY

I run eight to 12 miles, five days a week. If I can't run, I swim and use aerobic machines, such as the treadmill and stair climber.

On alternate days, I also lift weights (one set of 12 repetitions per major muscle group). I opt for free weights over weight machines because they work both the core muscles, such as the abdominals, and the supporting muscles, such as the *paraspinals* (muscles next to the spine), which help my posture.

My advice: Get at least 30 minutes of physical activity every day. It can be performed in intervals of 10 minutes at a time. For example, walk hard enough to make your heart beat faster. Also, lift weights every other day or at least twice a week.

STRESS MANAGEMENT

Every year, I take a personal, silent three-day retreat in a monastery, which helps me focus and put my life into perspective. A few times a year, I also go to a cabin on a lake in northern Wisconsin, and leave my laptop at home.

Each day, I make a to-do list of what's important. This way, I don't let other people's agendas drive mine. I also take a 15- to 20-minute walk around the block daily at noon to clear my head and renew my energy for the afternoon.

My advice: Leave the laptop and cell phone at home when you take a vacation. Take a daily "retreat" by practicing meditation or deep breathing, going for a walk or even watching a funny movie.

SOCIAL CONNECTEDNESS

Connections with our family, friends and even pets give us reasons for getting up in the morning.

To stay connected to my three sons who are scattered across the country, I write them each a letter, in longhand, every Monday, no matter where I am or how hectic my schedule might be. The act itself is my "therapy," and I don't expect a response. I also attend church to promote my spiritual connectedness.

My advice: Form stable long-term relationships. This is your buffer against stress and a great way to boost your immune system. Spend time in nature, a house of worship or with a spiritual community to foster a faith in some type of "higher power." If your work does not provide you with a sense of meaning and purpose in life, find a hobby or outside interest that does. This will give you a reason to push on even in the face of illness or adversity.

Immunity Boosters: How to Be Illness-Free

Leo Galland, MD, director, Foundation for Integrated Medicine, New York City. His latest book is *The Fat Resistance Diet* (Broadway). *www.fatresistancediet.com.* Dr. Gallard is a recipient of the Linus Pauling award.

Making it through the winter without a cold or the flu feels like winning the good-health lottery. You can increase your chances of being a winner by choosing the right foods, exercises, habits and attitudes.

PROTEIN POWER

When it comes to winterizing your immune system, you think of oranges, grapefruit and other vitamin C–rich foods. But there's an even more important food—protein. To have strong immunity, you must eat about 50 to 60 grams (g) of protein a day.

You can comfortably get about 15 to 20 g of protein through grains and other plant-based foods, but you'll need to add another 30 to 40 g from meats, fish and poultry, eggs, dairy products and beans.

As a guide, there are six to seven grams of protein in…

- **One egg.**
- **One ounce of lean meat,** fish or chicken.
- **One ounce of hard cheese.**
- **Four ounces of milk.**

Note: A three-ounce serving of meat, fish or chicken is about the size of a deck of cards.

HEALTHY FATS

Another way to boost immunity is to consume omega-3 fatty acids. You'll get enough for this purpose by eating oily fish, such as salmon, halibut and sardines, two or three times a week, especially if you accompany it with leafy green vegetables, which also contain omega-3 fatty acids.

Other sources: Fish oil supplements (1,000 to 2,000 milligrams [mg] daily), ground flaxseed (one tablespoon daily) and flax oil (one teaspoon daily).

VITAMIN A FOR VITALITY

Vitamin A helps maintain the health of mucous linings, the first line of defense against colds and infections. The body converts vitamin A from animal-based *retinol* or plant-based *beta-carotene,* the plant compound that makes vegetables yellow, red or orange. But vitamin A is tricky—too much can be toxic. Scientists have recently discovered that high (but not high enough to be considered toxic) amounts, when derived from retinol, may be associated with osteoporosis. (We often think of osteoporosis as a woman's problem, but men over 65 are vulnerable to bone loss, too.)

I advise patients to eat lots of foods that contain beta-carotene—carrots, spinach, squash and red peppers—but not to take vitamin A or beta-carotene in supplement form except in a multivitamin. Even then, be sure your multivitamin has no more than 5,000 international units (IU), unless there is a specific reason to take more.

OTHER SUPPLEMENT CONSIDERATIONS

Your multivitamin should also contain zinc and selenium, both great immunity boosters.

You'll be getting vitamins C and E in a supplement as well, but you might wonder about taking higher amounts. This has become controversial, especially as it concerns immunity in older people.

In one study, supplemental E reversed immune weaknesses. In a second, equally credible study, the participants who took E and C had more winter infections than those who were taking a placebo.

People taking fish or flax oil to obtain omega-3 fatty acids seem to benefit from taking daily dosages of 200 to 400 IU of E and from 200 to 1,000 mg of C (total including the amount in your multivitamin). If you are not taking fish or flax oil, don't take additional E or C.

Medical warning: Vitamins E and C may interfere with the effectiveness of statin (cholesterol-lowering) drugs. If you are taking a statin, do not take additional supplements of E or C without discussing this with your doctor.

MORE ON MEDS

Get a flu shot every year—the best time is around October. Studies show that people who were vaccinated have fewer cases of respiratory illnesses and the flu.

Cortisone-based drugs are often prescribed for arthritis, allergies and other conditions. However, these medications impair the immune function. If you need something for arthritis, studies have shown that glucosamine helps some arthritis sufferers. There is no reason to take the combination pill glucosamine/chondroitin, though. Chondroitin increases the price and it does nothing for arthritis.

Antibiotics may be bad for immunity, too, especially when they are taken long term or intermittently but frequently.

SPEEDING UP AND SLOWING DOWN

Exercise benefits the immune system, but don't do anything too strenuous. If you aren't used to exercise, 30 minutes a day of brisk walking is plenty to start with. Don't push yourself so hard that you can't comfortably carry on a conversation at the same time. An adequate amount of sleep is also important, especially uninterrupted sleep.

Unfortunately, as people get older they tend to wake up more often during the night and sleep less overall. It's important to overcome this. Try putting yourself on a nighttime schedule that allows for eight hours of sleep. Even though you may not get that much sleep, you'll improve your chances.

BEATING STRESS

Studies have confirmed that stress—whether from a serious, significant life event or simply from everyday hassles—has a negative effect on the immune system.

Self-awareness is the basis for changing your response to stressful situations, or at least managing stress better. Each evening, review the level of stress that you experienced that day. Ask yourself what stressed you and what it was about the situation that upset you.

Most people get stressed because of the way they think. Their brains amplify situations, making them much more drama-filled than they actually were. Once you recognize how your thoughts contribute to stress, you can begin to adjust your thinking. There are many books, such as *Don't Sweat the Small Stuff* by Richard Carlson, PhD (Hyperion), that can help you change your thought pattern.

To lower stress in an emergency: Move slowly, breathe deeply, meditate or pray. In a few minutes, you'll find yourself relaxed and able to focus positively.

If You Have a Persistent Cough...

Persistent cough or shortness of breath can be symptomatic of *chronic obstructive pulmonary disease* (COPD). A potentially deadly inflammation of the lungs, COPD reduces airflow and makes breathing difficult.

If you smoke, have a persistent cough, phlegm or shortness of breath: Ask your doctor about receiving lung spirometry testing, which measures air volume during inhalation and exhalation.

Bartolome Celli, MD, professor of medicine, Tufts University School of Medicine, Boston.

Hidden Health Trap: Your Gender Matters

Marianne J. Legato, MD, internist, founder and director, Partnership for Gender-Specific Medicine, Columbia University, and professor of clinical medicine, Columbia's College of Physicians and Surgeons, both in New York City. She is author of *Eve's Rib: The New Science of Gender-Specific Medicine and How It Can Save Your Life* (Harmony).

Until recently, medical researchers assumed that men and women were physiologically identical, with the exception of their reproductive organs. But scientists have uncovered vital differences in the ways in which men's and women's bodies function, experience illness and respond to treatments.

Much remains to be explored in the emerging field of gender-specific medicine. However, new findings already show that common conditions can be treated much more effectively when gender is taken into consideration. *For example...*

PAIN IN WOMEN

Men and women have different physiological responses to intense pain.

For example, a man's blood pressure rises during intense pain. A woman's blood pressure remains stable or declines, but her heart rate accelerates. This difference has important implications after surgery, when anesthesiologists typically monitor blood pressure to assess a patient's need for painkilling analgesics.

Self-defense: A female surgical patient should request that heart rate be monitored along with blood pressure. If her heart rate increases, more pain medication needs to be administered.

SKIN CANCER IN MEN

More than one million adult Americans are diagnosed with skin cancer each year. Among these cases, white men age 45 or older are twice as prone as women to the most common skin cancers (basal and squamous cell carcinoma). Men are also more vulnerable to deadly melanoma, accounting for nearly two-thirds of the 7,000 deaths caused by this type of cancer each year.

Given that men just naturally have more protective melanin, or skin pigmentation, than women, their greater susceptibility to skin cancer is likely due to the fact that they typically spend more work and leisure time outdoors and are less inclined to wear sunscreen.

Self-defense: All adults age 40 or older should have a dermatologist perform a total-body examination annually to check for signs of skin cancer. The exam should include the scalp, toes, soles, even genitalia. Men's skin cancers occur most frequently on the ears and neck, two spots that are typically vulnerable due to their shorter hair. Women's skin cancers tend to appear on the legs and hips. But malignancies can strike even in unexposed areas. Both men and women should perform monthly self-exams and wear sunscreen with a sun-protection factor (SPF) of at least 15 daily.

HEART DISEASE IN WOMEN

Long considered a man's problem, heart disease kills one in two women. Although male heart attack victims typically have chest pain, 20% of female heart attack sufferers do not experience this symptom. Instead, women feel pain or discomfort in the upper abdomen or back, and have shortness of breath, nausea or profuse sweating. Consequently, their condition is frequently misdiagnosed as indigestion or anxiety.

Other important facts…

• **Standard stress tests are inadequate for detecting *coronary artery disease* (CAD) in women.** This screening tool involves monitoring a patient on a treadmill for changes in blood pressure or cardiac electrical activity (measured with an *electrocardiogram,* or ECG).

These measurements are accurate indicators of heart disease in men. But an ECG is less valid in women because their cardiac electrical activity is likely to change during a treadmill test even with normal heart function.

Self-defense: Instead of a stress test, female heart patients should request a stress echocardiogram. This test uses an ultrasound probe to view your heart's motion at rest and during peak exercise.

• **Women with low levels of "good" HDL cholesterol are at increased risk for heart disease**—regardless of their "bad" LDL cholesterol levels. While both men and women should have HDL levels above 45, a level below 45 is especially dangerous in women.

Self-defense: Ask your doctor about boosting low HDL with cholesterol drugs (statins), *hormone-replacement therapy* (HRT) or niacin (a B vitamin).

OSTEOPOROSIS IN MEN

Before the age of 60, women lose bone mass faster than men. After this age, men and women lose bone at approximately the same rate. In fact, men account for one-quarter of the diagnosed osteoporosis cases in the US.

While the "male" hormone *testosterone* helps maintain bone, particularly in the arms and legs, it's the "female" hormone *estrogen* that is key to a man's—and a woman's—bone density.

Self-defense: Excluding estrogen therapy (which men cannot take due to its feminizing effects), the best weapons against osteoporosis are bisphosphonate drugs, such as *alendronate* (Fosamax) and *risedronate* (Actonel). These drugs increase bone mass and reduce risk for fractures. Adequate calcium intake (1,500 milligrams [mg] daily for all adults over age 50…1,000 mg to 1,200 mg for those who are under age 50) and weight-bearing exercises are also vital for bone density.

COLON CANCER IN WOMEN

Some people just assume that colon cancer affects far fewer women than men. That's false. Colon cancer afflicts the sexes nearly equally and is the third-leading cause of cancer deaths among women.

Caught early, colon cancer is highly treatable. But most colon malignancies are asymptomatic until the late stages. That makes regular screening essential.

Colon cancer tends to occur up to 20% higher in a woman's colon than it does in a man's colon. This makes malignancies undetectable with a sigmoidoscope—a device used to examine the beginning, or left side, of the colon.

Caution: Because the sigmoidoscopes don't access the right side, or ascending, colon, this test is of questionable value for both sexes. This is especially important because cancers are inexplicably occurring with greater frequency in this location.

Self-defense: All adults age 50 or older should have an annual occult blood test of stool to detect blood not visible to the naked eye. A confirmed positive finding should be followed with a colonoscopy, an outpatient procedure in which a long, flexible viewing tube is inserted through the rectum, to examine the entire colon. A routine colonoscopy every 10 years is recommended.

Studies also show that gallbladder removal (a surgery more common in women because they are more prone to gallstones) increases colon cancer risk.

If you've had colon polyps or gallbladder surgery or have a first-degree relative (parent or sibling) with colon cancer, consult your doctor. Although recent evidence has called into question the safety of HRT, postmenopausal women on HRT are 37% less likely to develop colon cancer than those not on HRT.

To decrease the risk of colon cancer, every adult should exercise regularly and eat a high-fiber, low-fat diet consisting of at least four vegetables and two fruits daily and 30% or less of calories from fat.

Hormones Can Cause Hidden Health Problems

Glenn D. Braunstein, MD, chairman, department of medicine, Cedars-Sinai Medical Center, and professor of medicine, University of California, both in Los Angeles. He is past chair of the Food and Drug Administration's Endocrinologic and Metabolic Drugs Advisory Committee.

Scientific research has linked hormones to high blood pressure, sexual dysfunction and other troubling conditions.

"HIDDEN" HYPERTENSION

High blood pressure (*hypertension*) is a leading cause of stroke, heart attack and kidney failure. It's especially dangerous because it often causes no symptoms.

One cause of hypertension is *primary aldosteronism* (PAL), a condition that often goes undiagnosed. PAL occurs when one—or occasionally both—adrenal glands produce too much *aldosterone,* a hormone that balances sodium and potassium in the body.

Doctors used to think that low potassium was the telltale sign of PAL. And, as a result, patients with normal potassium levels were rarely tested for it.

Recent study: For two years, Australian researchers looked for PAL in patients with hypertension. Of 54 patients diagnosed with PAL,

only seven had low potassium. Doctors now estimate that this condition is about 10 times more common than previously believed.

Implication: All patients with hypertension should ask their doctors to perform a blood test for PAL, even if potassium levels are normal. Surgical removal of the affected adrenal gland will cure or improve hypertension in nearly all PAL patients.

SAFER STEROID USE

The steroid hormones *prednisone* and *cortisone* are often prescribed to control asthma, rheumatoid arthritis, inflammatory bowel disease and other conditions.

However, long-term use of these drugs can lead to osteoporosis, as well as obesity and high blood pressure—both of which are risk factors for heart disease. Doctors have long known that taking steroids increases the potential for heart damage—but they didn't realize to what extent.

Recent study: Researchers in the United Kingdom and the Netherlands collected information on prescriptions, hospitalizations and causes of death for more than 164,000 adults over a four-year period.

Nearly half of the patients were given steroids at some point. Overall, those patients had a 32% chance of suffering a cardiovascular event, such as heart attack, over the next 10 years. The risk was only 19% in people who didn't take steroids.

Implication: Steroids are useful drugs that are unlikely to cause side effects when taken in low doses for short periods of time—a few weeks during an arthritis flare-up, for example. People who take them for chronic conditions need to be checked at least every three months for cardiovascular risk factors, such as high blood pressure, glucose intolerance and elevated cholesterol.

Important: Talk to your doctor about lifestyle measures that can reduce your risk for heart disease while taking these drugs.

Best choices: Do not smoke...exercise for at least 30 minutes most days of the week... and eat a healthful, balanced diet that's low in fat and high in legumes, whole grains and fruits and vegetables.

IMPROVED SEXUAL FUNCTION

About 5 million American men have low levels of testosterone, a condition called *hypogonadism.* One of the main symptoms is an inability to have erections. The drug *sildenafil* (Viagra), which typically is prescribed to treat erectile dysfunction, often doesn't work when testosterone levels are below normal.

Recent study: Italian researchers divided men with sexual dysfunction and low/normal testosterone levels into two groups. Those in one group were given testosterone patches, while those in the second group were given a placebo. All of the men used Viagra.

After one month, men in the testosterone group had better erectile function than those using the placebo patches—probably because testosterone directly improves blood flow to the penis and also stimulates libido.

Implication: Men with erectile dysfunction who aren't helped by Viagra (and other impotence drugs) should request a blood test to measure their testosterone levels.

Important: Schedule the test for 10 am or earlier. Testosterone levels are generally at their highest early in the day.

Also: Research suggests that women who are taking *hormone replacement therapy* (HRT) to offset menopausal discomfort may benefit from adding testosterone to the mix. The hormone appears to block some of the estrogen-related breast changes that increase a woman's risk for breast cancer.

Caution: Men with prostate cancer should not use testosterone supplements.

ATHEROSCLEROSIS PREVENTION

Atherosclerosis occurs when deposits of fat, cholesterol and other substances adhere to artery walls and impede blood flow to the heart.

Healthy habits—not smoking, eating a low-fat diet, exercising regularly, etc.—lower atherosclerosis risk. But these strategies don't directly affect existing fatty buildups in the coronary arteries.

A new family of experimental drugs known as *growth hormone–releasing peptides* (GHRPs) appears to prevent atherosclerosis and may reverse buildups that have already formed.

Recent study: Researchers fed laboratory mice high-fat, high-cholesterol diets. Half received GHRP injections. After 18 weeks, those given the drugs had decreased fat in the arteries.

Implication: If GHRPs prove safe and effective in humans, they could potentially be used alone or with cholesterol-lowering statins to treat or prevent atherosclerosis.

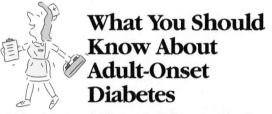

What You Should Know About Adult-Onset Diabetes

Richard Jackson, MD, medical director, outpatient intensive treatment program, Joslin Diabetes Center, and assistant professor of medicine, Harvard Medical School, both in Boston.

Diabetes can lead to heart disease, stroke and blindness. It can also interfere with blood flow to the extremities, a problem that sometimes necessitates the amputation of fingers and toes.

Good news: With proper treatment, these problems can almost always be avoided.

Unfortunately, only half of the estimated 12 million Americans who have the more common, adult-onset (type 2) form of the disease know that they're ill.*

Of those who know they have diabetes, only a tiny fraction are getting aggressive treatment.

UNCONTROLLED BLOOD SUGAR

In a healthy person, insulin keeps the level of glucose (blood sugar) within the normal range —60 to 140 milligrams per deciliter (mg/dl).

In individuals with type 1 diabetes, the pancreas fails to produce enough insulin to keep glucose levels in check.

In most cases of type 2 diabetes, the problem is not that the patient's production of insulin declines. It's that cells become resistant to the glucose-lowering effects of insulin.

*Approximately 1 million Americans have the other form of diabetes, type 1 (juvenile-onset). It occurs when the pancreas fails to produce any insulin at all.

The more resistant the cells become, the higher glucose levels rise. The higher the glucose levels, the greater the risk for long-term complications.

What's the secret to avoiding long-term complications of diabetes? Keeping glucose levels under control *at all times*.

WARNING SIGNS

Type 2 diabetes usually strikes people after the age of 40. *It causes...*

- **Excessive thirst.**
- **Frequent urination.**
- **Blurry vision.**
- **Increased hunger.**
- **Unexplained weight loss.**
- **Skin infections.**
- **Fatigue.**
- **Vaginal infections.**

These symptoms are often extremely mild. The only way to be sure you don't have diabetes is via a blood sugar test. Insist on having this test as part of each annual checkup.

If your blood sugar is ordinarily above 140 mg/dl—or your blood sugar after fasting is above 120 mg/dl—your doctor should perform additional tests.

Especially helpful: The glucose tolerance test. This involves fasting overnight, then having your blood sugar checked before and after drinking a glucose mixture.

HEMOGLOBIN A1-C TEST

If you have diabetes, it's important to monitor your blood sugar levels closely.

Many diabetics continue to believe that daily do-it-yourself blood-sugar tests are all that are needed. They're wrong. These daily finger-prick tests reveal only what your blood sugar level is at that particular moment. The only way to know whether your blood sugar has *consistently* been within safe levels is to have a doctor test your blood for *hemoglobin A1-C*.

This simple test reveals the average blood-sugar level over the preceding eight weeks. The test should be used every three months.

Cost: About $45 per test.

In a National Institutes of Health study of 1,400 diabetics, half of the participants received standard diabetes care—dietary planning, drug therapy and exercise combined with daily blood-sugar testing. The other half received more intensive care aimed at lowering the hemoglobin A1-C level.

Result: Diabetics who lowered their hemoglobin A1-C had 70% fewer complications than those who didn't.

DIET AND EXERCISE

Mild cases of type 2 diabetes can usually be controlled via careful eating habits and regular exercise—and, of course, carefully monitoring blood sugar and hemoglobin A1-C levels.

Since the body uses bread, pasta and other carbohydrates to make glucose, some doctors urge diabetics to severely limit their intake of refined carbohydrates.

Yet many diabetics do fine on a high-fiber, moderate-carbohydrate diet—as long as they space their meals carefully. It's essential to check blood sugar to follow the effects of your diet.

Aim: To spot any increases in glucose levels.

If you drink alcohol, do so in moderation—and only when your diabetes is under control. Diabetics should *never* drink alcohol on an empty stomach.

Best: Work with a doctor *and* a nutritionist to develop a workable meal-planning strategy ...and an appropriate regimen of walking or another aerobic exercise.

Getting aerobic exercise for 20 to 45 minutes, four days a week, is usually very effective at controlling glucose levels.

Best time to exercise: About 60 to 90 minutes after eating a meal, when blood sugar levels are at their highest.

ANTIDIABETIC MEDICATION

Even if they're diligent about eating right and exercising regularly, about one-third of all type 2 diabetics need medication to help control their glucose levels.

Several classes of medication are available...

- **Sulfonylureas.** These drugs squeeze a little extra insulin out of the pancreas...and boost the body's sensitivity to insulin.

Common sulfonylureas include *glyburide* (Micronase), *glipizide* (Glucotrol) and *glimepiride* (Amaryl).

•*Metformin* (**Glucophage**). Like sulfonylureas, this drug boosts the body's sensitivity to insulin. Since it also triggers weight loss, metformin is often a good choice for overweight diabetics.

•*Acarbose* (**Precose**). This drug works by slowing the digestion of carbohydrates.

If glucose levels remain elevated despite the use of one or more of these drugs—or if the drugs lose their effectiveness—insulin injections may be necessary.

CHECKUPS TO PREVENT TROUBLE

As insurance against complications, diabetics should have regular checkups. The goal is to catch complications as early as possible.

Daily: Check feet for redness, swelling or sores that aren't healing. Diabetes-related circulation problems render the feet unusually vulnerable to infection.

Yearly: A doctor should test your blood pressure and cholesterol levels...and your microalbumin level (to test kidney function). Also—an ophthalmologist should check your eyes for signs of *diabetic retinopathy*, a condition that can lead to blindness.

Diabetes Indicators

Bad breath and bleeding gums may be signs of diabetes. Because people with diabetes have decreased salivary flow and reduced ability to fight infection, bacteria grow more rapidly in the pockets around teeth. This makes them more susceptible to receding gums, oral infections and periodontal disease. Bad breath is the result of fermented bacteria in the mouth, sinuses or pharynx.

Self-defense: If you notice bleeding gums, bad breath or any other symptoms of diabetes, such as increased thirst, fatigue or frequent urination (especially at night), see your doctor for a complete evaluation.

Craig W. Valentine, DMD, dentist in private practice, Lakeland, FL, and spokesperson, Academy of General Dentistry, Chicago.

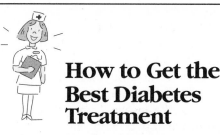

How to Get the Best Diabetes Treatment

Irl B. Hirsch, MD, endocrinologist and medical director, Diabetes Care Center, University of Washington Medical Center, Seattle. He is author of *12 Things You Must Know About Diabetes Care Right Now!* (McGraw-Hill).

Dramatic improvements in diabetes treatment are becoming available for the 12 million Americans who are diagnosed with the condition each year.

The US Food and Drug Administration (FDA) approved *insulin glargine* (Lantus), a more effective, longer-lasting drug that is injected once a day instead of the standard once- or twice-daily insulins.

The FDA has also given its approval to a fast-acting insulin powder that can be administered via an inhaler—not injections.

In the meantime, diabetes treatment remains tricky. For 90% of cases—people with adult-onset (type 2) diabetes—treatment means careful control of their blood sugar (glucose) levels through diet, exercise and sometimes oral or injected medication.

For the remaining 10% of the cases—people who have juvenile-onset (type 1) diabetes—a complicated regimen of daily insulin injections is required.

Problem: When treating patients with diabetes, few physicians adhere to the professional guidelines set forth by the American Diabetes Association (ADA).

Some fail to perform thorough physical exams or order vital tests. Others don't prescribe necessary medications, such as cholesterol-lowering drugs. That puts people with diabetes at risk for blindness, kidney problems, heart disease, nerve damage and other complications.

Diabetes specialist Irl B. Hirsch, MD, offered answers about effective diabetes care...

•**How often should the necessary tests be performed?** People with diabetes should measure their own blood glucose levels with a blood glucose meter. All meters sold today have met FDA criteria for accuracy.

If you take insulin, check your glucose levels four times a day—before meals and at bedtime. If you don't take insulin, do it twice daily, varying the time of day.

Whether you take insulin or not, measuring glucose levels one to two hours after meals can also be helpful in identifying glucose "spikes."

Blood glucose levels should measure 80 to 120 milligrams per deciliter (mg/dl) before a meal...and 100 to 140 mg/dl at bedtime.

Blood pressure should also be monitored. If you are being treated for hypertension, take your own blood pressure with a cuff at least once a week. If your blood pressure is 130/85 or below, you can have your blood pressure taken at your usual doctor's visits.

Diabetics also need the *glycated hemoglobin* (hemoglobin A1c) blood test to measure blood glucose control over the previous 12 to 16 weeks. The reading should be below 7%. If you take insulin, have the test quarterly. If you treat diabetes with oral medication or through diet alone, have the test performed twice a year.

A foot exam should be performed twice a year to check for calluses and sores that could lead to infection or even amputation.

All diabetes patients also need an annual dilated eye exam...a urine protein test...and a cholesterol and fasting triglycerides profile, measured by a blood test.

Levels of HDL ("good") cholesterol should be above 45...LDL ("bad") cholesterol below 100...and triglycerides below 200.

●**When is it appropriate to consult a specialist?** If you have problems controlling your blood glucose, cholesterol and/or blood pressure, see an endocrinologist. That's a medical doctor specializing in diseases of the endocrine system, including diabetes.

In addition, an ophthalmologist (a physician specializing in eye disease) or optometrist (a nonphysician who checks for common eye problems) should perform your eye exam to monitor for damaged blood vessels.

A podiatrist should custom-fit orthotics—shoe inserts—if your feet become swollen and red from ill-fitting shoes.

And a nephrologist (a physician specializing in the kidneys) should treat you if you suffer from kidney disease.

If you see a specialist or take medication prescribed by another physician, be sure to tell your primary care doctor.

●**Are diabetes patients at higher risk for heart disease?** Yes. About two-thirds of them die as a result of heart disease—three times more than people without diabetes.

Additional risk factors include smoking...an LDL cholesterol level that is above 160...a total cholesterol level above 240...blood pressure above 140/90...obesity...protein in the urine...family history of high cholesterol or premature heart attack.

More serious risk factors include an abnormal *electrocardiogram* (ECG)...*atherosclerosis* (hardening of the arteries)...or chest pain on exertion. If you have two or more of these three risk factors, ask your doctor about undergoing a *nuclear stress test*.

During this procedure, a radioactive material is injected and the heart is viewed, often while you are exercising.

To lower your risk, it's important to lose weight, if necessary...follow a low-fat, low-calorie, high-fiber diet...and exercise.

Many cholesterol-lowering drugs, such as *pravastatin* (Pravachol), *simvastatin* (Zocor) and *atorvastatin* (Lipitor), may help. The ADA also recommends one baby or adult aspirin taken daily to thin the blood and lower heart attack risk.

●**Why is high blood pressure so dangerous for people with diabetes?** High blood pressure is common in type 2 diabetes patients. Type 1 patients, especially before age 40, generally have hypertension only if they also have kidney disease.

Hypertension increases your risk for kidney disease, eye problems, heart attack and stroke.

To lower your risk, lose weight, if necessary...don't add salt to your food...stop smoking...limit daily alcohol intake to two ounces of hard liquor, two glasses of wine or two beers...and exercise regularly.

If diet and lifestyle changes do not lower your blood pressure, your doctor may prescribe an *angiotensin-converting enzyme* (ACE) inhibitor, such as *ramipril* (Altace).

This class of drugs—which also protects the kidney and heart—is the first line of defense against hypertension.

●**What's the best exercise for people with diabetes?** It depends on your age and health. Aerobic activities, such as walking, biking and swimming, are good choices for most people.

Exercise 20 to 45 minutes at a time—or spread throughout the day—three times a week. Avoid weight lifting. It requires "bearing-down" movements that may cause retinal damage.

Help for Diabetes

Diabetes can be helped with cholesterol-lowering statin drugs. Daily use of statins can cut risk of heart disease and stroke by about one-third for people with diabetes.

If you have diabetes, ask your doctor about taking statins routinely—even if your cholesterol level is fine—in addition to treatment to control blood sugar and blood pressure.

Rory Collins, MD, codirector, Clinical Trial Service Unit, and professor of medicine and epidemiology, Oxford University, England.

New Pain Relief for Diabetics

Pain relief for diabetics and others with damaged nerves in legs or feet is available. In *anodyne therapy,* near-infrared light-emitting "paddles" are placed over damaged areas to improve circulation and reduce pain. Ninety-five percent of patients get relief.

Standard treatment: 12 sessions that take 40 minutes each.

Results last one year. The therapy also can treat chronic inflammation and foot ulcers. It is not for pregnant women or people with cancer.

Information: 800-521-6664, *www.anodyne therapy.com.*

Joseph Prendergast, MD, medical director, Endocrine Metabolic Medical Center, Redwood City, CA.

Vinegar May Fight Diabetes

In one study, healthy patients and patients with a prediabetic condition known as *insulin resistance* drank a vinegar drink (⅛ cup of vinegar, diluted with ¼ cup of water and sweetened with saccharine) or a placebo drink before a high-carbohydrate meal. The vinegar treatment improved insulin sensitivity by up to 40% in both groups.

Theory: Vinegar inhibits the breakdown of carbohydrates, thereby decreasing the blood glucose spikes that tend to occur in people who have diabetes.

If you are diabetic or insulin resistant: Talk to your doctor about drinking diluted vinegar before meals.

Carol S. Johnston, PhD, professor of nutrition, Arizona State University East, Mesa.

Coffee Cure to Prevent Diabetes

Four to five cups of caffeinated coffee a day can cut diabetes risk by 30%. Drinking more has no added benefit. Decaffeinated coffee has only a slight effect. Tea has none. Other caffeinated beverages, such as cola, were not studied.

Caution: Additional study is required before researchers can recommend coffee specifically to protect against diabetes.

Frank B. Hu, MD, PhD, associate professor of nutrition and epidemiology, Harvard School of Public Health, Boston, and the leader of a study of more than 100,000 people that was presented at a meeting of the American Diabetes Association.

The Dangerous Health Problem Most Doctors Miss

Daniel Einhorn, MD, endocrinologist and medical director, Scripps Whittier Institute for Diabetes, La Jolla, CA. He is chairman of the National Task Force on Insulin Resistance Syndrome, American College of Endocrinology.

About one in five Americans has a condition that increases his/her risk of developing significant health problems like diabetes, heart disease, even some cancers—and most doctors miss the diagnosis.

These people have *insulin resistance syndrome,* also known as metabolic syndrome or, previously, Syndrome X. It's not a disease but a group of risk factors that often occurs in people who are overweight and don't exercise enough.

The majority of patients with insulin resistance syndrome winds up with heart disease. About 90% of patients with type 2 diabetes have it. Despite this, doctors rarely talk about it with their patients—or make the connection between individual risk factors and the syndrome as a whole.

To explain more about the causes and treatments of insulin resistance syndrome, noted authority Daniel Einhorn, MD, answered some questions…

•**What are the signs of insulin resistance syndrome?** There are five related problems doctors need to look for. *You have the syndrome if you have at least three of them…*

•Obesity, especially in the abdomen—a waist that measures more than 40 inches in men and 35 inches in women.

•Fasting blood sugar level of 110 milligrams per deciliter of blood (mg/dl) or higher.

•Triglycerides, a type of fat in your blood, higher than 150 mg/dl.

•HDL ("good") cholesterol below 40 mg/dl in men and 45 mg/dl in women.

•Blood pressure of 130/85 or higher.

•**What is insulin resistance—and why is it a problem?** Glucose, a blood sugar that cells need for energy, only can be utilized in the presence of the hormone insulin. *Insulin resistance* means that cells have become less sensitive to insulin's effects. Glucose then stays in the blood rather than getting transported inside cells. High levels of blood glucose can damage cells in blood vessels, nerves and organs.

Insulin resistance frequently increases over time. The pancreas has to produce ever-larger amounts of insulin to overcome the cells' resistance. Type 2 diabetes occurs when the pancreas no longer can supply enough insulin.

There is strong evidence that the cells' resistance to insulin is a contributing factor to the other ailments that also are signs of the syndrome—hypertension (high blood pressure), low HDL and high triglycerides.

•**What causes the syndrome?** Obesity, lack of exercise and advancing age are contributing factors. Genetics plays a major role, too. People with a family history of diabetes and cardiovascular disease have about a 50% higher risk of getting the syndrome.

•**Is there a test for the syndrome?** No—and that is a major problem in diagnosing it. If someone has risk factors for the syndrome, he/she may be given an oral glucose challenge test. In this test, a fasting patient is given 75 grams of glucose solution. Blood sugar levels are checked two hours later. A reading above 140 mg/dl suggests insulin resistance.

•**Is it true that low-carb diets, such as the Atkins diet, reduce insulin resistance?** Many people who have insulin resistance syndrome do lose weight and reduce resistance when they avoid "white" carbohydrates, such as white bread, white rice, white potatoes, etc. These are low in fiber and cause surges of glucose that require the pancreas to produce excess insulin.

•**What other dietary changes can reduce my risk?** *I recommend the following…*

•Eat fish at least twice a week. The omega-3 fatty acids in fish raise HDL and may reduce arterial inflammation.

•Limit alcohol to one drink a day for women and two for men—or avoid it if you have high triglycerides. Alcohol slightly raises HDL but also raises triglycerides.

•Avoid animal fats, including dairy, and the trans fats in margarine and other processed foods.

•Limit sodium intake to about 1,500 mg daily. More may raise blood pressure.

•**How important is exercise?** Very important. Even mild to moderate exercise—walking, swimming, biking, etc.—raises HDL, lowers blood pressure and promotes weight loss. Along with a healthful diet, regular exercise can reduce or even eliminate insulin resistance and the need for medication. Aim for at least 20 minutes of exercise a day most days of the week.

•**Do medications help?** There isn't one drug that manages the whole syndrome. The current approach is to control the syndrome's individual risk factors. *Thus, a patient may need to take several different drugs, including...*

•Insulin sensitizers, such as *metformin* (Glucophage), which lower insulin resistance. Some may also reduce triglycerides. Metformin is taken for life unless patients lose weight and have a significant decrease in insulin resistance.

New finding: Patients on *metformin* who discontinue it after about a year continue to have improved insulin sensitivity. It's possible that the drug can be used cyclically—one year on and one year off, for example.

•Weight-loss drugs, such as *orlistat* (Xenical) or *sibutramine* (Meridia), are FDA-approved for weight loss as part of a weight-management program under a doctor's supervision. The amount of weight lost through use of these drugs is usually sufficient to improve insulin sensitivity. And these drugs have been proven safe when appropriately supervised by a physician.

•Antihypertensive drugs, such as ACE inhibitors, calcium channel blockers, thiazide diuretics, beta-blockers, etc.

•Drugs to elevate HDL levels. *Fenofibrate* (Tricor) and *gemfibrozil* (Lopid) raise HDL and lower triglycerides. *Rosuvastatin* (Crestor), a newer drug, also raises HDL and lowers triglycerides.

Thyroid Disease Could Be the Cause of Your Symptoms

Richard L. Shames, MD, thyroid specialist in private practice, Mill Valley, CA, *www.thyroidpower.com.* He is coauthor of *Thyroid Power: 10 Steps to Total Health* (HarperResource).

America is in the grip of an energy crisis. Millions of men and women drag themselves around from day to day, feeling fatigued, unable to work productively or enjoy life. Many suffer additional ills, such as depression, anxiety, digestive misery, headaches and muscle pains.

What is their problem? It could be that they have low levels of thyroid hormone.

Trouble with the butterfly-shaped gland located at the base of the throat is surprisingly common—and since the symptoms of hypothyroidism are vague and nonspecific, thyroid disorders often go undetected.

THE MASTER GLAND

The thyroid functions much like a gas pedal for the entire body. Its hormones penetrate every cell to regulate the body's energy-producing "machinery." Too little thyroid hormone, and your organs can slow down—with consequences that range from irritating to devastating.

According to estimates, 5% of adult Americans have hypothyroidism. But recent surveys show that actually double that number—one in 10 Americans—have the problem. Among women who are in menopause, *one in five* has hypothyroidism.

Why the epidemic? No one knows for sure. But some endocrinologists theorize that the thyroid is affected by air pollution, pesticides and other chemical pollutants...increased radiation exposure from power plants, microwaves and cell phones...and chronic psychological stress.

Regardless of the reason, hypothyroidism can cause symptoms as diverse as the body systems the gland regulates.

In addition to the fatigue, low energy and mild depression that occur so frequently, many people with the condition have difficulty controlling their weight because their metabolism is sluggish. They may also feel cold when others are comfortable.

Additional problems that may point to thyroid disorder include allergies…dry skin, eczema or adult acne…poor concentration or forgetfulness…difficulty swallowing…or recurrent infections.

GETTING DIAGNOSED

Because the symptoms can have a number of causes, doctors* often mistake thyroid problems for another condition, such as menopause, irritable bowel syndrome or rheumatoid arthritis.

To avoid misdiagnosis, blood tests to assess thyroid function should be a routine part of any physical checkup—especially for people over age 35.

Make even more sure to have your thyroid checked if anyone in your family (even an aunt or a cousin) has had thyroid problems or a condition, such as diabetes or prematurely gray hair, which often suggests thyroid malfunction.

Caution: The most common test, which measures the levels of *thyroid-stimulating hormone* (TSH), sometimes gives a "false negative" (a normal reading even when there is thyroid trouble).

It's wise to follow up an all-too-frequent negative result with tests that can detect levels of the thyroid hormone *thyroxine* (T-4), which the body converts into *thyronine* (T-3).

Ask for: Free T-3 and free T-4 tests.

TREATMENT—THE HORMONE GAME

Standard treatment for low thyroid levels is a daily dose of T-4. But getting good results sometimes requires a little fine-tuning.

There are four brands of synthetic T-4, or *levothyroxine*—Synthroid, the largest seller and one of the most prescribed drugs in America …Levothroid…Levoxyl…and Unithroid. These formulations are *not* always equivalent. Some people fare much better on one than another. Unfortunately, it's impossible to tell in advance which will be best for you.

If symptoms persist for six months despite T-4 treatment, ask your doctor about switching

*To locate a thyroid specialist in your area, contact the Thyroid Foundation of America at 800-832-8321 or *www. allthyroid.org.*

brands. Generic T-4 is available. But its quality control may be less reliable than that of brand-name products, and potencies may vary.

It may be that no brand of T-4 hormone will do the job because your body can't convert it into T-3 properly. It this is the case, doctors often recommend adding a synthetic form of T-3, called *liothyronine* (Cytomel). This more active hormone works on its own and boosts the effectiveness of T-4 to help your body restore normal function. But in many instances, a better approach is a natural thyroid extract that contains both T-3 and T-4.

Bonus: Brands of natural thyroid hormone, such as Armour Thyroid and Westhroid, cost less than synthetic preparations.

WATCH YOUR DIET

Even the best medical regimen needs nutritional help. To keep your thyroid healthy, minimize exposure to chemicals found in processed foods. Eat natural foods—without preservatives, additives or artificial sweeteners. *Also take daily supplements that contain…*

- **Vitamin A**—10,000 international units (IU).
- **Vitamin C**—500 milligrams (mg).
- **Vitamin E**—400 IU. Check amount with your doctor.
- **Vitamin B complex**—At least 50 mg each of B-1, B-3, B-5 and B-6.
- **Folic acid**—800 micrograms (mcg).
- **Zinc**—25 mg.
- **Selenium**—200 mcg.
- **Manganese**—20 mg.

The thyroid needs iodine to function, but deficiencies of this mineral are largely a thing of the past due to Americans' high consumption of iodized salt. Especially if you live near a coast, you may be getting too much iodine, which is harmful to the thyroid.

To reduce iodine intake: Buy noniodized salt and minimize sodium intake by avoiding salty snacks and other high-sodium foods.

Fluoride is highly toxic to the thyroid. Don't use fluoridated toothpaste. If your water supply is fluoridated, drink bottled water.

Screening for Osteoporosis

Routine osteoporosis screening should be part of normal medical care for women over age 65.

Women age 60 to 64 with higher-than-average risk factors for bone thinning—such as thin women or women not taking estrogen—should also be screened routinely.

Best procedure: The *dual-energy X-ray absorptiometry* (DEXA), a painless scan.

Janet D. Allan, PhD, RN, dean of nursing, University of Maryland School of Nursing, Baltimore, and past vice chair of the US Preventive Services Task Force.

Bone Loss Warning

Irregular menstrual cycles may signal a hormonal shortage that could lead to osteoporosis. *Amenorrhea*—the absence of a menstrual period for three months or more—may mean a deficiency of estrogen and other reproductive hormones. These hormones help maintain bone density.

Most women don't consider the condition serious enough to warrant medical attention, leading to a delay in treatment that can result in further bone loss.

Lawrence M. Nelson, MD, reproductive endocrinologist, National Institutes of Health, Bethesda, MD, and investigator of a study of 48 women published in *Obstetrics & Gynecology*.

How to Build Strong Bones the Natural Way

Annemarie Colbin, PhD, CCP, CHES, food therapist and founder, the Natural Gourmet Institute for Food and Health, New York City. She is author of *Food and Our Bones—The Natural Way to Prevent Osteoporosis* (Plume Books).

If you're worried about preventing bone loss from osteoporosis, as most people are, you're probably trying to consume several servings of dairy products each day.

Problem: Concentrating just on dairy products is not the best way to build strong bones. Statistics show, for example, that the countries that consume the most dairy products (including the US) have the *highest* rates of osteoporosis. *Reasons...*

● **Calcium is not the only nutrient needed** for strong bones.

● **Magnesium and phosphorus are also important**—and these are found mostly in vegetable sources of calcium, such as green leafy plants. People who consume a lot of dairy products tend to eat fewer of these vegetables.

● **Heavy milk drinkers tend to eat more animal protein,** and more refined flour and sugar—all foods that make the bloodstream slightly acidic temporarily, causing the bones to release calcium to restore the normal pH balance of the blood.

● **Vegetables,** on the other hand, make the blood alkaline, encouraging calcium to be stored in the bones.

Bottom line: A diet that is high in animal proteins along with refined flour and sugar will actually encourage bone loss.

Better way: Get your calcium from the same places that cows and horses get theirs—plants.

A DIET FOR STRONG BONES

● **Eat vegetables, vegetables, vegetables.** For maximum calcium retention, you should eat at least two servings of vegetables (either raw or cooked) with every meal.

While virtually all vegetables and beans contain calcium, I recommend trying to eat high-calcium plants whenever possible—including kale, collards, mustard greens, arugula, bok choy, parsley, watercress, broccoli, cabbage, carrots and acorn or butternut squash.

Avoid spinach and swiss chard, though—they're high in oxalates, chemicals that interfere with the body's absorption of calcium.

Recommended: Organically grown vegetables, which tend to be higher in mineral content.

•**Moderate your protein intake.** Some dietary protein is essential for strong bones—collagen, a tough web of protein, makes up about one-third of your bone mass and is essential for keeping your bones flexible and resistant to fracture.

But too much concentrated animal protein will temporarily upset the pH balance of your blood, increasing the risk of bone loss.

I recommend limiting your intake to two or three servings a day of any of the following protein foods—fish, organically raised fowl or meat, organic eggs, beans (including lentils, split peas, kidney beans, navy beans and black beans), nuts (almonds, cashews, walnuts), sesame seeds (which are also high in calcium) and sunflower or pumpkin seeds.

•**Eat soy products occasionally.** Eating soy foods—such as tofu, unpasteurized miso and tempeh—two or three times a week will provide another source of protein. Soy products also contain phytoestrogens, which may help prevent bone loss.

I don't recommend regular consumption of highly processed soy products, such as textured vegetable protein, however.

•**Eat whole grains.** For a good source of fiber, B vitamins and complex carbohydrates, eat two or three servings a day of brown rice, barley, buckwheat or kasha, millet, quinoa, oats, cornmeal or whole wheat.

•**Eat sardines**—bones and all. The soft fish bones in sardines are an excellent source of calcium and other nutrients.

•**Make soups using vegetable, chicken or beef stock.** Boiling soup bones or vegetables for an extended period of time is another superb way to extract key nutrients.

•**Avoid calcium-draining foods and other substances.** Refined flour and sugar products top this list, since they acidify your blood the same way too much protein does.

This includes all pasta and any nonwhole-grain breads, muffins and rolls, as well as sugared drinks, candy, pastries, ice cream and any other sweet dessert.

Excessive caffeine will also deplete your calcium stores. Drinking two cups of coffee a day over a lifetime has been linked to reduced bone density later in life, unless the coffee drinkers also drink a daily glass of milk (which appears to blunt the calcium-draining effect).

Here are a few easy, bone-building recipes you can try…

SARDINE SPREAD

1 can (about 4⅜ oz.) sardines with skin and bones, packed in oil or water
1 Tbs. fresh lemon juice
1 Tbs. onion, grated
¼ tsp. sea salt
1 Tbs. tahini (optional)
1½ Tbs. fresh parsley, chopped
Freshly ground pepper

Open the can of sardines partway and drain out the oil or water. Then place the sardines, lemon juice, onion, salt, tahini and parsley in a bowl and mix with a fork until well blended. For extra flavor, top with freshly ground pepper. Makes about two-thirds of a cup.

This spread can be eaten as part of a light lunch or an appetizer. Spread the mixture on whole-rye crackers or whole-grain bread.

BASIC GARLIC GREENS

½ lb. kale, collards or mustard greens
1 tsp. extra virgin olive oil
2 garlic cloves, peeled and chopped
1 to 1½ cups vegetable or chicken stock (or water)
1 pinch of sea salt
1 pinch of grated nutmeg

Cut off the stems of the greens, then wash the remaining leaves and cut them into bite-sized pieces. Next, heat the oil gently in a saucepan, and add the garlic. Stir for a minute, then add the greens and the stock, using a wooden spoon to push the greens under the surface of the liquid. Simmer uncovered for 15 to 20 minutes. Then add the salt and nutmeg, and stir for another two minutes. Drain. (Drink the cooking liquid if there is any left or save it for soup.) Serves four.

CRISPY BAKED SMALL FISH

1 lb. fresh small whole fish, such as smelts, anchovies or whitebait

½ cup cornmeal

½ tsp. sea salt

½ tsp. pepper

½ cup olive oil

4 to 6 lime or lemon wedges

Have the fish cleaned, but leave the heads and tails on. Wash the fish in several changes of water, then pat dry with paper towels. Place the cornmeal, salt and pepper in a plastic or paper bag and shake until mixed. Add the fish to the bag and shake well until the fish is covered with the mixture.

Next, put the olive oil in a soup plate and dip the fish in it briefly. Then put the fish into a metal baking pan lined with parchment paper and bake at 400°F for 30 to 40 minutes (depending on the size of the fish) until the fish is crisp but not overbrowned. Fish 4" or longer should be turned over once halfway through cooking. Serve with lime or lemon wedges. Serves three to four.

BEEF STOCK

2 lbs. beef marrow bones

4 quarts water

1 large carrot, cut up

1 medium onion, cut into quarters

2 celery stalks, cut up

3 garlic cloves, peeled and chopped

2 Tbs. olive oil

½ cup parsley stems

1 cup red or white wine, or 2 Tbs. wine vinegar

Place the bones and water in a 6- to 8-quart stockpot. Bring to a boil, then simmer for 10 minutes. Skim the top of the liquid, then add the vegetables, garlic, oil, parsley and wine to the pot. Simmer on very low heat for two or three hours with the cover ajar, skimming occasionally.

When done, strain the liquid, then chill it. Remove all congealed fat. Makes two quarts.

Eating Prunes May Help Prevent Bone Loss

In a study, 58 postmenopausal women who consumed about 12 prunes per day for three months showed higher blood levels of enzymes and growth factors indicative of bone formation than women who did not eat prunes.

Theory: The polyphenolic compounds and other nutrients in prunes act as antioxidants to curb bone loss.

Although only women were studied, researchers believe that men can gain the same beneficial effects from eating prunes.

Bonus: Those studied suffered no significant gastrointestinal side effects.

Bahram H. Arjmandi, PhD, RD, professor and chair, College of Human Sciences, Florida State University.

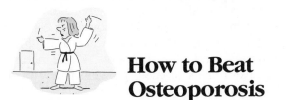

How to Beat Osteoporosis

George J. Kessler, DO, attending physician, NewYork-Presbyterian Hospital, clinical instructor of medicine, Albert Einstein College of Medicine, and clinical assistant professor, New York College of Osteopathic Medicine, all in New York City. He is author of *The Bone Density Program: 6 Weeks to Healthy Bones and a Healthy Body* (Ballantine).

Who should be concerned about osteoporosis? The short answer is *everyone.* Your body builds all the bone density it will ever have by the time you reach your late 20s. Bone density starts to decline after age 30, and this process accelerates as the body's synthesis of sex hormones slows.

Osteoporosis is especially prevalent among women, although approximately 20% of its victims are men.

Until recently, it was thought that osteoporosis affected mostly Caucasian women, but new evidence suggests that these women are simply more likely to *report* breaks due to osteoporosis. All races are at risk.

NUTRITION AND EXERCISE

Bones *seem* stable as rock. In fact, they're made up of living cells. These are constantly being broken down and replaced by new ones.

Osteoporosis develops when breakdown accelerates and/or rebuilding slows. *But lifestyle strategies can keep the process in balance...*

●**Minerals.** Most of us are well aware that calcium is necessary for bone health. Both premenopausal women and men under age 65 need to get 1,000 milligrams (mg) per day. For postmenopausal women and men over age 65, 1,500 mg is better.

Dairy foods are the classic source of calcium. One cup of milk contains 300 mg, one cup of plain yogurt 450 mg. But you can also get calcium from beans (100 to 200 mg per cup)...kale (90 mg per cup)...and collard greens (350 mg per cup).

Calcium-fortified orange juice contains 300 mg per cup, and fortified grapefruit juice has 280 mg per cup. Fortified breakfast cereals typically contain 250 mg per serving.

Soy milk, tofu and other soy products may contain supplemental calcium and also *phytoestrogens* and other nutrients. These natural plant estrogens promote growth of new bone tissue and slow bone loss.

Bones need other minerals, too—notably magnesium and phosphorus—as well as vitamin D. Fortunately, plant sources of calcium also contain the other minerals. You can get all the vitamin D you need from 32 ounces of fortified milk...or from just 20 minutes of sunlight a day. (Skin makes vitamin D upon exposure to sunlight.)

●**Exercise.** The physical stresses to which bones are subjected during exercise stimulate new bone growth. It's important to get at least 30 minutes of walking, weight lifting or another weight-bearing exercise, three times a week.

BONE ROBBERS

To slow the excretion of calcium from your body, it's essential to cut back on certain foods and activities. *Keep an eye on...*

●**Protein.** Each ounce of animal protein you eat causes elimination of roughly 25 mg of calcium. Most Americans get far more protein than they need.

●**Alcohol.** Have no more than three drinks per week.

●**Cigarettes.** Smoking doubles your risk for osteoporosis-related hip fracture.

●**Salt.** An eight-ounce serving of canned soup contains up to 3,000 mg of sodium chloride. Every 500 mg of sodium leaches 10 mg of calcium from your bones.

●**Caffeine.** Each cup of coffee pulls out 40 mg of calcium.

●**Soft drinks.** Phosphorus in sodas promotes calcium excretion.

DO YOUR BONES NEED HELP?

Bone densitometry is a 15-minute outpatient procedure that gauges bone strength. Most women should have the test at menopause—men, at ages 55 to 60. If it indicates a problem, doctors use one of the cross-linked collagen tests—*N-Telopeptide* (NTx) or *deoxypyridino-line* (Dpd)—to measure the rate of bone loss. Your doctor will use information from both tests to determine whether you need treatment for osteoporosis.

Depending on the degree of bone thinning, the rate of bone breakdown, your age, gender and other issues, your treatment may include hormones, bone-building drugs and/or medication for an underlying condition (such as an overactive thyroid).

HOW ABOUT HORMONES?

A woman who has significant bone thinning may be a candidate for *hormone replacement therapy* (HRT). It's the most effective way to slow bone loss. Even if bone loss was minimal up to menopause, HRT may be a good idea. Bone loss accelerates in the first three to five years after onset of menopause.

Whether or not to go on HRT is a personal decision. A woman with a family history of osteoporosis may want to remain on HRT. But women should take HRT only if the benefits outweigh the risks.

For women who do not want to use HRT because of the associated risks of breast cancer, heart disease and stroke, *selective estrogen receptor modulators* (SERMs) are similar to estrogen. They seem to provide all the bone-building benefits of HRT without the risks.

Several SERMs have been approved by the US Food and Drug Administration—*raloxifene* (Evista), *tamoxifen* (Nolvadex) and *toremifene* (Fareston). *Droloxifene* and other drugs are currently being studied.

HORMONE ALTERNATIVES

For people who want to avoid hormones, four drugs are worth asking a doctor about...

●*Alendronate* **(Fosamax).** Available by prescription, alendronate is the drug of choice for men and for bone loss linked to steroid drugs. It slows bone loss.

●*Risedronate* **(Actonel).** This prescription drug is similar to alendronate but is less likely to cause digestive problems.

●*Calcitonin* **(Miacalcin).** This prescription drug is often the best choice for people who cannot tolerate alendronate or who prefer a natural rather than a synthetic product. It slows bone loss and decreases bone pain.

●*Ipriflavone.* This over-the-counter derivative of soy protein resembles estrogen. It can be used by women and men and is the only drug that slows bone loss *and* builds new bone.

Osteoporosis Drug Warning

Osteoporosis drugs can cause potentially serious vision problems.

Recent study: In rare cases, people taking the *bisphosphonate* osteoporosis drugs, such as *alendronate* (Fosamax) or *risedronate* (Actonel), developed inflammation of the eye.

If this eye condition progresses unchecked, it could lead to blindness. Tell your doctor immediately if you experience eye redness or pain, blurred or lost vision, headache or sensitivity to light while taking an osteoporosis drug.

Alternative treatments for fragile bones include a diet that's rich in calcium and vitamin D, and weight-bearing exercises.

Frederick W. Fraunfelder, MD, professor of ophthalmology, Casey Eye Institute, Oregon Health and Science University, Portland.

How to Keep Your Hips Healthy

Marshall K. Steele III, MD, orthopedic surgeon, founder and medical director, the Center for Joint Replacement, Anne Arundel Medical Center, and president, the Maryland Knee & Hip Center, and the Orthopedic and Sports Medicine Center, all in Annapolis, MD. He is author of Sideline Help—A Guide for Immediate Evaluation and Care of Sports Injuries *(Human Kinetics).*

Each year, more than 150,000 Americans undergo hip-replacement procedures. But many of these surgeries could be postponed or avoided altogether if patients practiced better hip care.

Genetics may play a significant role in the primary causes of hip pain, such as osteoarthritis and osteoporosis. But anyone who suspects hip trouble should see a doctor for a proper diagnosis, because it may be caused by a variety of problems.

Important: Osteoporosis does not cause pain in its early stages but is a leading cause of hip fractures. Insist that your doctor order a *dual-energy X-ray absorptiometry* (DEXA) test if you have risk factors. These include being postmenopausal, fair-skinned or having a history of steroid use. The scan detects early signs of osteoporosis. Early treatment with a combination of drugs, hormones and calcium can stop or even reverse bone loss.

Regardless of the cause, hip discomfort may be prevented or minimized with exercise, diet and other lifestyle measures...

●**Maintain a healthful body weight.** Extra weight puts tremendous strain on the hips and increases damage caused by osteoarthritis.

Reason: The hips bear three times your body weight with each step. Each pound you lose reduces three pounds across your hip joint.

●**Avoid high-impact exercise.** Sports that subject the hips to impact, such as running, frequently increase pain and joint damage in people with a history of hip trouble. This does not appear to be a problem if your hips are normal.

Helpful: Perform low-impact exercise for at least 30 minutes, most days of the week. Walking is very effective. It strengthens the *abductors,*

73

muscles in the outer thigh that hold the body straight. Moving the hips also helps nourish the remaining good cartilage.

Walking also helps prevent osteoporosis. I recommend this weight-bearing exercise because it creates stress on the bones, improving calcium absorption. Hip patients who start exercising often report a decrease in symptoms within two weeks.

●**Try water workouts.** They're the safest form of hip exercise. You get the benefits of moving the joints through their full range of motion while reducing the pressure caused by gravity. Standing in waist-high water reduces pressure on the hip joints by 50%. In chest-high water, pressure is reduced by 70%.

Spend up to 30 minutes in a swimming pool, walking forward and backward in waist-high water. If your hips start to hurt, move into deeper water to reduce pressure.

●**Nourish bones and joints.** Nutrients found in foods and supplements repair injured muscles and tendons...strengthen cartilage... and make hip bones stronger.

Be sure to get these nutrients daily...

●1,200 milligrams (mg) of calcium and 200 international units (IU) of vitamin D. Taking more than 200 IU daily may be dangerous, check with your doctor. Calcium strengthens bones, and vitamin D aids in its absorption. *Good calcium sources:* Broccoli, kale, spinach and calcium-fortified cereals. *Good vitamin D sources:* Egg yolks and cod liver oil.

●60 mg of vitamin C. Vitamin C is a powerful antioxidant that aids in muscle and tendon repair. You'll get that much of the vitamin by eating one medium orange.

●1,500 mg of glucosamine and 1,200 mg of chondroitin. Glucosamine helps the body replenish damaged cartilage in the hip and other joints. Chondroitin appears to keep cartilage healthy by helping it absorb water.

●**Watch your posture.** The average adult loses 1% to 2% of muscle strength every year between the ages of 65 and 85. A loss of strength combined with age-related joint stiffness causes many people to sway or stoop when they walk. Poor posture puts additional pressure on the hips, and weakness increases risk for falls and fractures.

Helpful: Observe your gait while walking toward a full-length mirror. If you sway slightly from side to side, chances are the abductor muscles in the outer thigh are weak. Water workouts, leg lifts while you are lying on your side and abductor-strengthening exercises performed on machines in fitness clubs can strengthen the muscles, improve posture and reduce or prevent hip pain.

●**Don't ignore hip pain.** During flare-ups, wrap ice cubes in a washcloth or towel and apply them to the sore area for approximately 10 minutes several times per day.

If ice doesn't relieve the pain, try an over-the-counter (OTC) analgesic, such as *ibuprofen* (Motrin) or *naproxen* (Aleve). These drugs block inflammatory chemicals called *prostaglandins*. If you're at risk for stomach irritation, Cox-2 selective anti-inflammatories may be safer to use. Discuss treatment with your doctor.

Reducing inflammation minimizes pain and also helps injured hip joints heal more quickly. If you experience persistent hip pain, it usually means that you need to return to your physician for further evaluation and advice.

●**Safeguard your home.** Hip fractures most frequently occur when people fall in their own home or yard.

Identify—and remove—any potential tripping hazards, such as throw rugs, books, children's toys, etc.

Also: Replace 40- or 60-watt bulbs with 100-watt bulbs, so you can see household hazards more easily. (You may need to replace light fixtures that don't allow higher-watt bulbs.)

More from Marshall K. Steele...

Are You at Risk for Hip Problems?

If you answer "yes" to any of the following questions, your hips may be taking an unnecessary beating—and you should ask your doctor for advice.

●**Are you overweight?**

●**Do you have pain** in the groin?

●**Do you have trouble raising your leg** to cut your toenails?

●**Does your foot turn out** when you walk?

- **Are you stiff when arising** from a chair?
- **Do you walk all day** on concrete?
- **Have you had an injury** to your hip?
- **Do you have a family history** of arthritis?
- **Do you have osteoporosis?**

What You Must Know About Inflammation

William Joel Meggs, MD, PhD, professor and chief of toxicology, and vice chair for clinical affairs, department of emergency medicine, Brody School of Medicine, East Carolina University, Greenville, NC. He is coauthor of *The Inflammation Cure: How to Combat the Hidden Factor Behind Heart Disease, Arthritis, Asthma, Diabetes, Alzheimer's Disease, Osteoporosis and Other Diseases of Aging* (McGraw-Hill).

Every time you fight off a cold, sprain your ankle or cut your finger, your body reacts to protect or heal itself through a complex process called *inflammation.*

Marked by redness, swelling, heat and pain, inflammation involves the release of a cascade of chemical messengers in the body called *cytokines.* Depending on the type and severity of inflammation, the cytokines can trigger the immune system to attack and destroy foreign invaders, such as viruses or bacteria, or to heal a wound.

But too much inflammation, due to an infection, irritation, allergies or other reasons, can cause serious damage.

Examples: Inflammation of the joints contributes to arthritis, inflammation of the skin leads to dermatitis…inflammation of the gums leads to periodontitis.* In fact, most of life's most serious diseases—including heart disease, Alzheimer's disease and even some cancers—are fueled by inflammation.

INFLAMMATION CONNECTION

Scientists have known for generations that inflammation causes disease. Now, researchers

*In medical terminology, the suffix *–itis* indicates inflammation.

are finding that many inflammation-related diseases are connected. This discovery could lead to more effective prevention and treatment of these types of diseases.

Imagine placing one drop of blue dye in a glass of water. The dye starts out concentrated in one spot, but eventually all the water turns blue. Similarly, when there is inflammation in one part of the body, repercussions develop in other—often distant and otherwise unrelated—parts of the body.

Example: Cytokines released in response to inflammation associated with atherosclerosis (hardening of the arteries) circulate throughout the body and seem to be associated with gum disease, type 2 diabetes and other inflammatory conditions.

Inflammation-related diseases include…

- **Atherosclerosis and cardiovascular disease.** High blood pressure or other irritation causes damage to artery walls. This will trigger inflammation that attempts to "repair" the damage with plaque—the same way that we use spackle to patch holes in walls. Exposure to cigarette smoke and air pollution, high cholesterol and other factors can cause this process to go awry. Then, instead of a nice, smooth patch of plaque, thick layers accumulate until the arteries become blocked.

But heart attacks can also occur in people who have only small quantities of plaque in their arteries. In these cases, inflammation can make even tiny amounts of plaque fragile. If there is additional irritation, these plaques can burst, causing blood clots that block the arteries and result in heart attacks or stroke.

What you can do: Have your *C-reactive protein* (CRP) levels tested. This protein, which can be measured with a $20 blood test, is a powerful predictor of future heart disease. Even mildly elevated CRP *doubles* the risk for a future heart attack. In addition, elevated CRP can increase risk for stroke.

- **Diabetes.** Recent studies have suggested that chronic and low-grade inflammation may increase the risk of developing type 2 diabetes, a condition in which the body's cells become resistant to insulin, a hormone that controls the amount of sugar in the blood.

It's well known that people with diabetes are at greater risk for developing heart disease...and some scientists believe that the chronic inflammation associated with early atherosclerosis may actually contribute to the onset of diabetes.

What you can do: Decrease your overall inflammation load by losing weight. Body fat alone raises the levels of some pro-inflammatory body chemicals. Also, visit your dentist. Studies have shown that treating gum disease helps people with diabetes control their blood sugar better.

•**Fatigue.** If you have unexplained fatigue, that is an indication that there is inflammation somewhere in your body. The cytokines released during inflammation affect the brain to cause fatigue.

The reason we feel so exhausted whenever we have the flu is because of the inflammatory processes that gear up in the infected tissues to fight the virus.

What you can do: If you experience debilitating fatigue that interferes with your work and daily activities for more than two weeks, see your doctor for a checkup to make sure you aren't suffering from an underlying disease, such as a virus, allergy or cancer.

MORE WAYS TO
FIGHT OFF INFLAMMATION

Reducing inflammation in the body is the best way to curb your risk for developing inflammation-related diseases. It also helps to fend off age-related debilities, such as muscle weakness, an unsteady or slow gait and unintentional weight loss.

Because tobacco smoke is the single largest contributor to inflammation, anyone who still smokes must stop now. Avoiding secondhand smoke and other forms of air pollution, including furnace fumes and vehicle exhaust, is also important.

Other strategies to fight inflammation...

•**Start exercising.** Exercise—of any kind—is one of the most effective inflammation reducers. Studies have shown that walking 30 minutes every day cuts CRP levels in half—and reduces the risk for heart attack by 20%.

Recommended: Take music with you. Studies have shown that people who have difficulty exercising are able to walk farther when they listen to music they like.

•**Change cleaning habits.** Chemicals found in many cleaning products are irritants that can bring on inflammation of the mucous membranes of the eyes, nose, throat and lungs when inhaled. People with chronic asthma and sinus problems are most susceptible. Symptoms, such as headache, fatigue and wheezing, can result from irritant exposure.

Avoid breathing bleach and ammonia fumes, which are irritants that can lead to inflammation.

Never combine cleaning products. Combining bleach and ammonia can release highly toxic chloramine gas. When combined with other cleaning chemicals, toilet bowl cleaners containing hydrochloric acid can release chlorine gas, which was utilized as a chemical warfare agent during World War I.

Best approach: Use nontoxic cleaning products, such as those by Citra-Solv or Seventh Generation. They can be found at most health food stores and some supermarkets.

•**Use unscented products whenever possible.** Many of the chemicals often used in air fresheners, fragrances, perfumes, fabric softeners, detergents and scented household products can cause inflammation of the mucous membranes and skin.

To limit your exposure to potentially harmful artificial ingredients, personal hygiene products, such as deodorants, soaps, shampoo and anything else you use on your body, should also be unscented whenever possible.

•**Limit meat consumption to two to three servings a week.** Animal products (with the exception of fish) are among the top inflammation triggers. Studies show that populations that eat more red meat have a higher risk for heart disease and some forms of cancer.

Dairy products rich in saturated fat, such as butter, should be used in moderation.

•**Eat fish three times a week.** Salmon, tuna, bluefish, sturgeon, herring and sardines are among the richest sources of omega-3 fatty acids, which have an anti-inflammatory effect in the body. Avoid fish with a high mercury content. This includes shark, swordfish, tilefish and king mackerel.

As an alternative, take a 1,000-milligram (mg) fish oil supplement or one tablespoon of flaxseed oil daily.

Caution: If you take blood-thinning medications, such as *warfarin* (Coumadin), check with your doctor before using these supplements.

• **Limit alcohol consumption to one to two drinks each day.** Moderate alcohol use increases life expectancy and reduces risk for coronary artery disease. Wine and grape juice contain chemicals, such as *tyrosol* and *caffeic acid,* which have additional benefits in modulating pro-inflammatory compounds.

Caution: Heavy alcohol consumption may lead to addiction, liver damage and even some types of cancer.

Taking a Break May Save Your Life

Desk jobs put you at risk for life-threatening *deep vein thrombosis* (DVT), which is a blood clot that forms in the leg and can travel up to the lungs. The condition has long been known to occur during long-distance air travel, but research also links DVT to sitting at a desk for extended periods.

Self-defense: Be sure to take a short break every 30 to 60 minutes or so by getting up and walking around.

Richard Beasley, MD, director, Medical Research Institute of New Zealand, Wellington.

Love Your Liver—How to Care for Your Second-Largest Organ

James L. Boyer, MD, ensign professor of medicine and director, Liver Center, Yale University School of Medicine, New Haven, CT.

The liver is the second-largest internal organ by weight (the brain is the largest) in the human body. It removes toxic substances ingested, inhaled or absorbed through the skin...fights off invading bacteria and viruses...produces clotting factors, blood proteins, bile for digestion and more than 1,000 enzymes...stores iron and glucose needed for energy...and metabolizes cholesterol.

LIVER FITNESS PROGRAM

• **Go easy on alcohol.** Limit beer, liquor or wine to two drinks a day. More than two, especially for women, may harm the liver. Do not drink at all when taking certain medications, such as *acetaminophen* (Tylenol). Alcohol diminishes the liver's ability to metabolize many drugs—even over-the-counter products.

• **Use medication cautiously.** Don't take antibiotics for the sniffles—they fight bacterial infection, not viruses. Check with your physician about any herbal supplements—they may be toxic and/or contaminated due to poor manufacturing conditions.

Always ask about drug side effects. And don't combine medications without your doctor's approval.

• **Limit chemical exposure.** Use aerosol cleaners, chemicals such as carbon tetrachloride and paint sprays only in well-ventilated areas...and be sure to wear a mask, available in hardware stores.

• **Eat wisely.** A balanced diet helps maintain the health of your liver and your gallbladder, which stores bile.

• **Avoid fatty foods.** High fat consumption raises the risk of gallstones.

• **Minimize salt intake.**

• **Maintain your ideal weight.** Obesity is directly linked to gallbladder disorders, and it may cause fat buildup in the liver. Protein malnutrition can also produce fat buildup.

- **Exercise daily.**

DISEASE SELF-DEFENSE

There are numerous types of liver disease, including the following…

- **Hepatitis A (HAV).** Sources are contaminated water, food (particularly shellfish) and eating utensils. HAV does not cause chronic liver problems. Symptoms may include nausea, vomiting, fatigue and jaundice.

- **Hepatitis B (HBV).** Transmitted sexually and through exposure to infected blood and other bodily fluids, HBV may lead to other liver complications, such as chronic hepatitis, cirrhosis and even liver cancer.

Both HAV and HBV normally last only a few weeks. And they can be completely prevented with vaccines, which are advised for those in health-related or day-care fields and anyone traveling to developing countries. A vaccine for HBV is now recommended for all children.

- **Hepatitis C (HCV).** Transmitted through exposure to blood, intravenous drug users are at highest risk. HCV can lead to chronic—and potentially fatal—liver infections in 10% to 20% of infected individuals. Older males with HCV who also abuse alcohol have the greatest chance of developing cirrhosis.

- **Cirrhosis.** When scar tissue replaces damaged cells, limiting blood flow and handicapping liver function, the liver becomes cirrhotic. The most common causes of cirrhosis in the US are infection with HCV and heavy drinking. Cirrhosis has also been traced to congenital disease (occurring since birth), environmental toxins, autoimmune reactions and parasitic infection.

DETECT TROUBLE

While we do know what causes many liver disorders, few people can pinpoint the origin or onset of their ailment.

The liver can continue to perform despite some damage—so there may be no warning until effective treatment is impossible. *Symptoms of possible problems include…*

- **Chronic fatigue.**
- **Nausea or loss of appetite.**

- **Jaundice,** a yellow discoloration of the skin or eyes.

- **Abdominal swelling** or severe abdominal pain and discomfort.

- **Chronic itching.**

- **Very dark urine or pale stools.**

Precautions: Have your physician check your liver as part of your annual check-up. Blood tests measure liver function and indicate the presence of disease. You may also want to ask your doctor about getting ultrasound and CAT scans or a needle biopsy.

The Deadly Disease Most People Don't Know They Have

Raymond T. Chung, MD, associate professor of medicine, Harvard Medical School, and director, hepatology service and liver transplant program, Massachusetts General Hospital, both in Boston.

More than 5 million Americans have viral hepatitis—and most don't even know it. The most dangerous type, hepatitis C, typically causes no symptoms for up to 30 years. But it kills about 10,000 people annually—and this number is expected to triple as the baby-boom generation ages.

Hepatitis symptoms may not appear for decades. *When they do, they are similar for the various types of hepatitis…*

- **Fatigue**
- **Lack of appetite**
- **Nausea and vomiting**
- **Jaundice (yellowing of the skin)**
- **Fever of 100° or less**
- **Joint pain**

Hepatitis C is one of six currently identified hepatitis viruses—the others are A, B, D, E and G. All cause inflammation of the liver, which interferes with its ability to function.

Here's what else you need to know about the three main types—C, B and A—presented in order of severity.

Good news: Early detection and treatment can save lives—and all three types of hepatitis can be prevented.

HEPATITIS C

Nearly 4 million Americans have hepatitis C. It usually is detected only after serious and permanent liver damage has already occurred. Some people learn they have it when they try to donate blood—blood banks now routinely screen for the virus.

Causes: The virus is spread through infected blood. If you received a blood transfusion prior to 1992—the year that blood-screening tests for this infection became available—you could be at risk. Intravenous drug use with shared needles causes about 60% of infections. Hepatitis C can also be transmitted by sexual activity, but the risk from this exposure is small.

Prevention: Don't share toothbrushes, razors or other personal items that may come in contact with someone else's blood. If you go for electrolysis, ear piercing or a shave at the barber, make sure the equipment is sterilized. If you get a manicure or pedicure, bring your own equipment or have a set reserved exclusively for your use.

Treatment: About 20% of patients with hepatitis C fight off the virus on their own without liver damage. Unfortunately, there's no way doctors can predict who will be able to do this. Most doctors recommend early drug treatment.

Interferon alfa can eliminate the hepatitis C virus in more than half of patients. It is a synthetic version of the interferon that is produced by the body to fight viral infections. The drug can cause severe side effects, including extreme fatigue, depression, flu-like symptoms, anemia and a temporary drop in white blood cell count. Injections are given once a week for up to 48 weeks and may be combined with *ribavarin,* a drug that enhances interferon alfa's effectiveness.

A liver transplant is usually the only option for people who have advanced liver disease.

HEPATITIS B

One in 20 Americans gets hepatitis B at some time in their lives. As many as 5,000 die each year from it. About one-third of adults and most children who have the virus never develop symptoms.

Causes: Hepatitis B is transmitted in blood and body fluids. Risk factors include unprotected sex with an infected partner...sharing contaminated needles...or receiving a blood transfusion prior to 1970, the year when blood testing started for hepatitis B. The virus can be transmitted among children in day care and to babies during childbirth.

Prevention: Vaccination—three shots given over a six-month period—is more than 90% effective at preventing infection. The vaccine is administered to most children in the US. At-risk adults also should receive it. The US Food and Drug Administration recently approved a vaccine, Twinrix, that protects against both hepatitis A and B and has no known side effects.

Insist on sterile equipment during any procedure that breaks the skin...and never share a razor or a toothbrush.

Treatment: An injection of *gamma globulin* within 24 hours of exposure can prevent hepatitis B from developing.

Most people who are infected with hepatitis B develop an acute infection that lasts six months or less. They make a full recovery without treatment. About 5% go on to develop *chronic hepatitis.* The virus stays in the body, causing permanent liver damage and sometimes cancer.

If you have a chronic infection, your doctor may recommend an injection of interferon alfa, the drug used to treat hepatitis C, daily for four months. The virus usually isn't eliminated but is kept at safe levels even after the drug is stopped.

The drug *lamivudine* (Epivir), taken orally once a day, causes significantly fewer side effects than interferon alfa but usually must be taken for prolonged periods, generally several years.

Liver transplantation is the only option if the liver is severely damaged by chronic hepatitis B.

HEPATITIS A

About 23,000 Americans get the virus annually. Hepatitis A may or may not cause symptoms. When it does, it frequently is confused with the flu.

Causes: Hepatitis A is transmitted by the *fecal–oral route*. For example, a restaurant worker with the virus can transmit it by handling food without washing his/her hands after using the bathroom. Eating raw shellfish from contaminated water can cause it. So can close contact, including sexual contact, with someone who is infected.

Prevention: The best approach is to get vaccinated. Two shots given over a six-month period are more than 90% effective at preventing hepatitis A infection. It takes at least four weeks for the vaccine to work. Or you can get the Twinrix vaccine, which protects against both hepatitis A and B.

If you're traveling to a country with poor sanitation or if a member of your family already has hepatitis A, your doctor might recommend a shot of gamma globulin for immediate protection.

Other precautions…

●**Drink bottled water when traveling to high-risk areas.** Wash all fruits and vegetables with purified water and make sure your drinks don't have ice cubes in them. It is even advisable to brush your teeth with bottled water.

●**Avoid undercooked meats—and especially raw shellfish,** such as oysters or clams, etc., unless they're from uncontaminated water. Cooking kills the virus.

●**Wash your hands after using the bathroom,** changing a diaper, etc.

Treatment: There is no treatment for hepatitis A. The infection usually clears up within two months, and in nearly all cases, the liver recovers normally.

Eat bland meals to help prevent nausea…avoid alcohol…and ask your doctor if it's safe to continue taking prescription or over-the-counter drugs.

Protect Your Pancreas

Steven D. Freedman, MD, PhD, director, Pancreas Center, Beth Israel Deaconess Medical Center, and associate professor of medicine, Harvard Medical School, both in Boston.

The pancreas is a five- to six-inch organ that is nestled between the stomach and small intestine. It secretes insulin (the key hormone for sugar metabolism and storage) and enzymes that help digest fats, carbohydrates and proteins. When the pancreas malfunctions, it can lead to a variety of life-threatening conditions.

Cases of pancreatic cancer have become increasingly common in the US, although researchers are unsure why. It is currently the fifth leading cause of cancer death.

Here's what you must know about this deadly type of cancer and other diseases of the pancreas…

ACUTE PANCREATITIS

This condition causes inflammation of the entire pancreas. Each year, it strikes up to 80,000 Americans.

Causes: The most common are alcohol abuse and gallstones. Acute pancreatitis also has been linked to extremely elevated levels of triglycerides (over 1,000 milligrams per deciliter [mg/dl]). The condition also can be a side effect—fortunately, quite rare—of a number of drugs. *These include…*

●**Blood pressure medication,** such as the thiazide diuretic *hydrochlorothiazide* (Esidrix).

●**Sulfa drugs,** such as *sulfasalazine* (Azulfidine).

●**Seizure drugs,** such as *valproic acid* (Depakote).

Symptoms: Acute pancreatitis usually comes on suddenly, with severe pain that escalates within the upper abdomen, often spreading to the back. Nausea, vomiting and fever are common. Eating makes the pain worse.

Treatment: The condition cannot be reversed, so treatment aims to keep the body functioning until the crisis passes, usually within three to four days. Most patients must go to the hospital for pain control and intravenous (IV) fluids. In the majority of cases, acute pancreatitis causes no lasting damage.

But it can be life-threatening—about 5% of those affected die as a result of severe inflammation and shock that shuts down the kidneys, lungs and other organs.

Prevention: Eat a low-fat diet. If you drink alcohol, limit your intake to one drink per day for women and two drinks a day for men. If you have gallstone disease, get prompt treatment. If a drug causes an attack of acute pancreatitis, work with your doctor to find an alternative. If your triglycerides are sky-high, take medication, such as *gemfibrozil* (Lopid), to control your levels.

CHRONIC PANCREATITIS

Persistent inflammation and scarring of the pancreas affects about 288,000 Americans. Because chronic pancreatitis is less dramatic than the acute condition, it may go undiagnosed for years.

Causes: Alcoholism is responsible for up to 70% of chronic pancreatitis cases. The cause is unknown for the other cases. But recent research has focused on mutations in several genes, including one of those that causes cystic fibrosis.

Symptoms: Pain is often aching and bothersome, rather than severe. Some patients experience episodes of searing upper abdominal pain, accompanied by nausea and vomiting— sometimes several times weekly. These flare-ups are usually triggered by eating—especially high-fat foods, such as pepperoni pizza, steak, french fries, etc.

Diagnosis often is difficult because pancreatic enzymes are not elevated in chronic pancreatitis, as they are in the acute form of the disease. The organ also may look normal on *magnetic resonance imaging* (MRI) and *computed tomography* (CT) scans.

The most accurate test is *endoscopic retrograde cholangiopancreatography* (ERCP), in which an instrument is threaded through the small intestine to inject dye that makes the pancreatic ducts visible on an X-ray. This procedure requires IV sedation and must be performed in a hospital. Up to 6% of the time, ERCP triggers a bout of acute pancreatitis.

Treatment: There is no cure for chronic pancreatitis. Abstinence from alcohol and dietary prudence—avoiding fatty foods, in particular— may minimize flare-ups. Many patients require regular painkillers, sometimes including opiates, to control pain. Celiac nerve block (surgery to interrupt pain transmission from the abdomen) can be helpful in severe cases.

Prevention: Do not abuse alcohol.

PANCREATIC CANCER

Each year, about 25,000 Americans are diagnosed with pancreatic cancer, and 98% will die of the disease within six months. The malignancy is more common in men than women. Up to 85% of the time, it's detected too late for surgery.

Causes: Ninety-five percent of the cases have no known cause. The remaining 5% seem to be due to hereditary factors.

Symptoms: A gnawing pain often begins in the upper abdomen and spreads to the back as the malignancy moves along nerves. The patient often loses his/her appetite, and weight loss is common.

By the time the tumor is visible on an MRI or CT scan, it already has begun to spread. Blood tests, such as one that measures levels of CA 19-9, a protein produced by the tumor, can be helpful, but aren't very accurate.

Jaundice—yellowing of the skin and eyes— occurs when the tumor blocks the bile duct, but this typically occurs when the disease is fairly advanced.

Treatment: When caught early, it is possible to remove the cancerous part of the pancreas. It is an extremely complex, demanding operation that should be performed by an experienced surgeon who is affiliated with a medical center that specializes in pancreatic cancer.* If surgery is not an option, radiation

*To find such a medical center in your area, contact the National Pancreas Foundation at 866-726-2737, *www.pan creasfoundation.org.*

and chemotherapy aim to reduce pain and improve the quality of life.

Prevention: Giving up cigarettes is the best self-defense. Smoking doubles or triples the risk for pancreatic cancer. Chronic pancreatitis is another risk factor. Because alcoholism is a major cause of chronic pancreatitis, moderation or abstinence also is a prevention strategy.

In addition, take steps to reduce your overall cancer risk. Don't allow yourself to become overweight. Try to eat a low-fat diet and include antioxidant-containing red and yellow vegetables, such as tomatoes and peppers, in your diet. An antioxidant supplement—400 international units (IU) daily of vitamin E—also is recommended. But talk to your doctor—taking high amounts of vitamin E may be dangerous for some people.

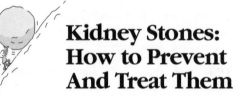

Kidney Stones: How to Prevent And Treat Them

David S. Goldfarb, MD, professor of medicine, New York University School of Medicine, clinical chief of nephrology, New York VA Medical Center, and director of the kidney stone prevention program, New York Harbor VA Medical Center, all in New York City.

If you ever have passed a kidney stone, you know that the pain can be excruciating. Each year, more than 1 million Americans experience this intense pain—and the number of reported cases is steadily increasing.

About 10% of Americans have kidney stones at some time in their lives. *Here's what you need to know to prevent and treat them…*

DIFFERENT SIZES

Kidney stones form when there is a high concentration of minerals—especially calcium, oxalate or uric acid—in urine. The pain is caused by contractions of a *ureter*—either of two tubes that carry urine from the kidneys to the bladder—as the stone passes through. Kidney stones that are very small (one to two millimeters [mm]) may cause little or no discomfort and pass on their own in a day or two. Bigger stones (5 mm or larger) are more likely to obstruct or abrade the ureter.

The pain can be felt in the side, back or groin and can range from mild to severe. The attacks typically last for five to 15 minutes. Pain keeps coming back over a period of hours, days or even months, until the stone passes out of the bladder in the urine.

Large kidney stones that obstruct the flow of urine can lead to serious infections or kidney damage—but they're not as dangerous as they used to be because of recent technology that can shatter or remove them before this happens.

If you have had kidney stones in the past, you are more likely to get another one than someone who never has had them. If you've had kidney stones twice, your risk of subsequent attacks is even greater.

Risk factors: Family history…missing a kidney…kidney disease. Men are more likely to get them than women, and people between ages 20 and 40 are most likely to be victims.

TYPES OF STONES

Prevention and treatment of kidney stones depends in part on the stones' mineral composition. *Four main types…*

• **Calcium.** Consisting mainly of calcium and oxalate, a type of salt, these account for 85% of kidney stones.

Main causes: Drinking too little water, high-sodium diet or, paradoxically, not getting enough calcium.

• **Uric acid.** Uric acid is a by-product of protein metabolism. A high-meat diet can increase the risk of kidney stones because meat breaks down to make uric acid.

• **Struvite.** These stones occur mainly in women who suffer chronic urinary tract infections. Infection-causing bacteria secrete enzymes that increase urinary ammonia, which causes the crystals in struvite stones. These stones are among the most serious because they are associated with kidney damage.

• **Cystine.** These rare stones form only in people with *cystinuria,* a genetic disorder that causes the kidneys to excrete excessive amounts of amino acids, which are the building blocks of protein.

If your doctor suspects that you have a kidney stone, he/she probably will order blood tests and 24-hour urine collection to measure the concentrations of different minerals.

PREVENTION

Most stones can be prevented...

●**Drink at least three quarts (12 cups) of water daily**—and even more if you live in a hot climate.

●**Eat calcium-rich foods.** Surprisingly, you need more calcium to prevent calcium kidney stones. Calcium in foods binds to oxalates in the digestive tract and prevents these stone-causing minerals from concentrating in the urine. Some studies have also found that high-calcium foods can help prevent calcium stones.

Good food sources of calcium: Low-fat milk, cheese and yogurt...sardines...fortified juice and cereal.

Caution: Unlike the calcium in foods, calcium supplements may increase the likelihood of kidney stones because they're less likely to bind with oxalates.

If you must take supplements, those made with *calcium citrate* are less likely to promote kidney stones than those made with *calcium carbonate.* Supplements should be taken with meals to bind oxalate.

●**Limit sodium to 2,000 milligrams** (just under one teaspoon) daily by restricting your intake of table salt, fast foods and packaged foods (unless labeled "low sodium" or "sodium-free"). Too much sodium in the diet leaches calcium from the bones and concentrates it in the urine.

●**Limit oxalate-rich foods**—such as organ meats (liver, heart, etc.), soy, herring, anchovies, tea, coffee, strawberries, spinach, cola, nuts, beets, wheat bran and chocolate—if you have recurrent kidney stones.

●**Limit protein to about 80 grams (g) daily** if you get uric acid stones. A four-ounce serving of chicken has about 34 g of protein.

●**Change urine chemistry with medications or supplements.** People who get frequent kidney stones may be advised to take thiazide diuretics, such as *hydrochlorothiazide.* Taken daily for life, diuretics reduce calcium concentrations in the urine. Potential side effects include headache, dizziness, constipation or diarrhea, low potassium in blood and low blood pressure.

Other options...

●*Allopurinol* (Aloprim, Zyloprim), a prescription drug, lowers uric acid levels and may prevent calcium and uric acid stones. A skin rash, which can be severe in some cases, is the main side effect but is quite rare.

●Urocit-K, a prescription potassium citrate supplement, inhibits the formation of calcium, uric acid and cystine stones. It is taken two to three times daily. *Home remedy:* Mix one-half cup of lemon juice in two quarts of water, add sweetener if desired, and drink during the day. It's high in citrate but doesn't work quite as well as prescription supplements.

●Antibiotics. Women who get struvite stones may need to take antibiotics to suppress urinary tract infections.

TREATMENTS

Usually your doctor will recommend that you take a prescription or over-the-counter painkiller, and then advise you to wait for the stone to pass. *Large stones may require one of these approaches...*

●**Extracorporeal shock wave lithotripsy.** Sound waves break large stones into smaller crystals that are easily passed in the urine. This outpatient procedure takes about 30 minutes.

Drawbacks: Lithotripsy isn't effective at shattering stones in the lower part of the kidney...it leaves fragments that may increase risk of recurrence...repeated treatments may cause kidney damage.

●**Ureteroscopic stone removal.** In this outpatient procedure, a surgeon threads a flexible wire into the urethra and up into the bladder and kidneys, snares the stone and removes it. Another form of this treatment includes destruction of the stone by a laser.

Gout Treatments That Really Work

H. Ralph Schumacher, Jr., MD, professor of medicine, University of Pennsylvania School of Medicine, and chief of rheumatology, Veterans Administration Hospital, both in Philadelphia.

Gout has been around for at least 2,000 years and is one of the oldest diseases known to man. It used to be called "the disease of kings" because it usually plagued wealthy men who overindulged in rich food and drink.

Today, more than 2 million Americans have gout. About 90% of them are men over age 40, although women become increasingly susceptible after menopause.

WHAT IS GOUT?

Gout is a form of arthritis triggered by high levels of uric acid, a waste product formed during the breakdown of purines. Purines are found naturally in the human body. Also, certain foods, including organ meats, are rich in purines. Smaller amounts are found in all meat, fish and poultry.

Gout causes sudden, severe attacks of pain, redness and tenderness around the joints. Even the pressure of a bedsheet can cause excruciating pain. You might not be able to move the joint normally for days. Pain is most intense for the first 24 to 36 hours, but it can linger for a week or more.

Most people with gout have a genetic inability to eliminate excess levels of uric acid from the body. Other causes include heavy alcohol consumption...the use of some diuretics...and diseases, such as diabetes and hypertension (high blood pressure).

More than half of those who have one gout attack will have a second within two years—and some people suffer attacks more frequently.

WHAT CAUSES THE PAIN?

Uric acid usually dissolves in blood and passes through the kidneys into the urine. In most people with gout, uric acid isn't excreted efficiently from the kidneys. When it reaches high concentrations, it may form needlelike crystals that accumulate in the tissues near joints—often the joint in the big toe.

The crystals don't cause any symptoms as long as they remain in solid tissue. For reasons that are unclear, they occasionally enter the joint. Then they stab into white blood cells, triggering an inflammatory response.

DIAGNOSING THE DISEASE

A simple blood test can measure uric acid levels. Levels between 4 and 8 milligrams per deciliter (mg/dl) of blood are considered normal. A reading higher than 8 mg/dl is indicative of gout.

But crystals can form when uric acid levels are as low as 6.2 mg/dl. The only way to be certain that you have gout is to have fluid drawn from the affected joint during an attack. Your doctor will look for the presence of uric acid crystals in white blood cells.

On rare occasions, it also may be important to check for tumors and rare genetic defects, which can cause the body to produce more uric acid—in excess of one gram in 24 hours—than the kidneys can process.

STOPPING ATTACKS

Drugs are the mainstay for treating gout. *But there are several other approaches to try for relief...*

• **Take an anti-inflammatory** at the first sign of symptoms. The longer you wait, the less effective the medication will be at halting the attack.

The prescription anti-inflammatory *indomethacin* (Indocin) usually is the first choice for treating gout attacks. Over-the-counter analgesics, such as aspirin, *ibuprofen* (Motrin, Advil) and *naproxen* (Naprosyn, Aleve), also may be effective for minor attacks. Your doctor probably will recommend high doses—for example, about 200 milligrams (mg) indomethacin or 1,500 mg naproxen daily—to reverse inflammation caused by gout. Take the drugs with food to prevent stomach upset.

• **Apply a cold pack or a few ice cubes wrapped in a towel to the affected joint.** Cold restricts circulation to the area and decreases the number of inflammatory white cells.

It also numbs the area and acts as a topical anesthetic. Apply cold for about 20 minutes, wait 20 minutes, then apply again. Repeat as often as necessary to get relief.

●**Steroids injected into a joint usually relieve pain within several hours or less,** and they are generally free of side effects. This may be all that is needed for gout that is limited to one joint. People who can't take anti-inflammatories because of ulcers or kidney disease often are treated with steroids.

Oral steroids are used only in rare cases—usually when gout is affecting multiple joints and other medications aren't effective. They can cause side effects, including appetite or mood changes, sweating and difficulty sleeping.

●**Colchicine,** an oral anti-inflammatory medication, can reduce the pain if taken early in an attack—but about 80% of people who take it can't tolerate the nausea, vomiting, diarrhea and other side effects. Low doses also may be prescribed between attacks to decrease the frequency of attacks.

PREVENTION

Medications to lower serum uric acid can prevent subsequent gout attacks. These medications are prescribed for patients who suffer two or more attacks per year or when crystal deposits are visible under the skin.

Important: Don't initiate long-term preventive therapy during a gout attack. The therapy causes swings in uric acid levels that can make symptoms worse. The time to begin preventive therapy is after an attack subsides.

Preventive drugs…

●**Probenecid (Benemid, Probalan) is a** prescription drug that increases the kidneys' ability to excrete uric acid. It will begin to show results within two weeks of starting treatment. The drug is taken daily, usually for life.

Probenecid rarely causes side effects, but it can't be used by those with kidney disease. Drink at least eight glasses of water daily to dilute uric acid in the kidneys and help prevent kidney stones.

●**Allopurinol (Aloprim, Lopurin, Zyloprim),** taken daily for life, also lowers uric acid levels by blocking its production. Unlike probenecid, it can be used by those who have kidney disease. Doses may need to be adjusted. A small number of people have a life-threatening hypersensitivity to allopurinol. Call your doctor immediately if you develop a rash to avoid a more serious reaction.

Other preventive measures…

●**Switch drugs if you're taking a thiazide diuretic and are having frequent gout attacks.** Often used to control hypertension, thiazide diuretics such as *bendroflumethiazide* and *hydrochlorothiazide* can trigger an attack of gout. Your doctor might be able to switch you to an ACE inhibitor or other blood pressure–lowering drug that doesn't have this side effect.

●**Drink only moderately.** Drinking more than small amounts of alcohol—up to one drink daily for women and two for men—causes uric acid levels to rise, increasing the risk of gout attacks.

●**Avoid excessive amounts of purines.** Organ meats—such as liver, brains, kidney and sweetbreads—are especially high in purines. So are anchovies, herring and mackerel.

●**Lose weight slowly.** This means a pound or two a week when you're dieting. And be careful—diets that severely restrict calories result in *lactic acidosis,* an increased acidity in the blood that impairs the ability of the kidneys to excrete uric acid.

Simple Cures For Gout

Jamison Starbuck, ND, naturopathic physician in family practice and lecturer at the University of Montana, both in Missoula. She is past president of the American Association of Naturopathic Physicians and a contributing editor to *The Alternative Advisor: The Complete Guide to Natural Therapies and Alternative Treatments* (Time-Life).

Many people associate gout with corpulent, older men who partake in rich food, strong alcohol, regular cigars and irregular exercise. Although I certainly know better, even I was a bit surprised that

Sam—a slim, 30-year-old sitting in my consultation room, with his right foot beet red and hugely swollen—was suffering from gout.

Classic gout is an acute arthritis of the lower extremities, most commonly in the big toe. Six out of every 1,000 men and one per 1,000 women have gout. But once women reach age 60, their risk of developing gout is almost equal to that of men.

Gout occurs when *monosodium urate* (MSU) crystals are produced in the fluid surrounding a joint. The big toe is a common spot because circulation to the feet is often less efficient than it is to other parts of the body.

Hyperuricemia—a high concentration of uric acid in the blood—will lead to the development of MSU crystals in susceptible people. A number of situations are associated with hyperuricemia. These include kidney disease... excessive alcohol consumption...use of some medications, such as aspirin and diuretics...a genetic predisposition to retain uric acid in the body...and a diet high in purine-containing foods, primarily proteins, such as liver, beef, chicken and pork, and legumes, such as navy and kidney beans. Purines—natural substances found in the body's cells and in concentrated amounts in some foods—form uric acid when broken down.

In Sam's case, it was genetics and a high-protein diet that caused his gout. His father had suffered from gout. What's more, Sam had been a vegetarian for most of his adult life. But recently an acupuncturist he had consulted for chronic fatigue had recommended that he eat meat again. When he came to my office, he had been consuming some form of animal protein—chicken, lamb, beef or pork—at two meals a day for the previous month.

To prevent gout: I suggest that all people over age 60 and men of any age with a family history of gout eat no more than one medium-sized portion of meat or fish daily. Keep your uric acid levels low by drinking lots of water— ½ ounce per pound of body weight daily. Twice a week, eat one eight-ounce portion of fresh or frozen cherries or dark berries, such as blackberries, blueberries or raspberries. They decrease uric acid.

For patients who have gout: Eliminate all protein, including less obvious sources, such as tofu, tempeh, lentils, dried peas, beans and cheese. Avoid vegetables with moderate purine levels, such as asparagus, spinach and mushrooms. Eat eight ounces of cherries daily. They are the most potent uric acid–reducing fruit. Drink ¾ ounces of water per pound of body weight daily. I recommend this regimen until the symptoms abate.

Two natural medicines can also help reduce inflammation and decrease uric acid levels—the bioflavonoid quercetin and the herb *Eupatorium-purpureum* (gravel root). The typical quercetin dosage is 1 gram, three times a day. Make a tea with two teaspoons of gravel root steeped in eight ounces of water, and drink three cups daily. Both are available in health food stores.

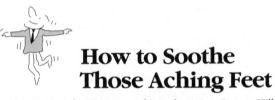

How to Soothe Those Aching Feet

Stuart Mogul, DPM, attending physician, Lenox Hill Hospital, and podiatric surgeon in private practice, both in New York City. He is author of *Perfect Feet* (Stewart, Tabori & Chang).

Some foot problems can be prevented by wearing comfortable shoes and maintaining a healthful weight. But that's not the case for all foot disorders.

Example: Many foot ailments are caused by natural foot flaws, such as high arches or flat feet. This can affect how the foot bears weight and recovers from injuries.

New treatments for common foot complaints due to natural foot flaws or other causes...

PLANTAR FASCIITIS

The band of soft tissue at the bottom of the foot (*plantar fascia*) tightens and relaxes every time you take a step. Walking or running can lead to tiny tears in the tissues, causing stabbing or burning pain at the bottom of the heel. Sudden weight gain or a new exercise program can trigger plantar fasciitis.

New approach: Stretching the plantar fascia.

What to do: Rest the affected foot on the thigh of your other leg...grip the base of the toes...and pull the toes toward the shin until you feel a stretch. Repeat twice daily. This technique works to relieve tension and tautness of the plantar fascia.

Also helpful...

●**Take an over-the-counter (OTC) analgesic.** *Ibuprofen* (Advil), *naproxen* (Aleve) and other nonsteroidal anti-inflammatory drugs (NSAIDs) reduce inflammation.

●**Use orthotics.** These custom-made plastic shoe inserts support the arch of your foot.

●**Tape the foot.** Have your podiatrist apply a series of one-inch, overlapping strips of medical tape to the bottom of the foot to reduce flexing. This takes pressure off the plantar fascia and allows the tissues to heal.

●**Wear the right shoes during a flare-up.** The heels of the shoe must be *at least* one-half-inch high—but no more than two inches. Elevating the heel puts more weight on the ball of the foot, which reduces pressure on the plantar fascia.

These approaches improve symptoms in nine out of 10 people with plantar fasciitis. Those who don't get better may need cortisone injections to eliminate inflammation. In severe cases, surgically cutting the plantar fascia will eliminate symptoms, usually without interfering with normal foot function.

NAIL INFECTION

Toenail infection (*onychomycosis*) usually is triggered by a fungus that causes the nails to discolor, thicken and develop crumbling edges. It's difficult to treat because topical drugs don't penetrate the nailbed. Prescription oral antifungal drugs, such as *itraconazole* (Sporanox) and *terbinafine* (Lamisil), often eliminate infection—but it may take three to six months.

New approach: Pulse therapy.

What to do: Under your doctor's supervision, take the antifungal drugs daily for one week...discontinue them for three weeks... then repeat the cycle. This technique can eliminate infection while reducing the risk for liver damage or other side effects from the drugs.

Also helpful: Dry the nails and in between the toes after showering or swimming...and change your socks at least once daily. Reducing moisture makes it harder for the fungus to thrive.

ATHLETE'S FOOT

This usually is caused by the same fungus that's responsible for toenail infections—but it's easier to treat because topical drugs kill fungal spores on the foot surface.

Apply an OTC antifungal ointment, lotion, powder or spray that contains *clotrimazole* (Lotrimin) or *terbinafine* twice daily. Most infections clear up in about 10 days.

New approach: Antifungal shoe treatment.

What to do: Spray your shoes with an OTC antifungal product, such as Desenex or Micotin. These products kill fungal spores that live inside shoes and often reinfect the feet even after successful drug treatment.

Also helpful: Keep your feet dry...wear open-toed sandals or flip-flops whenever possible (especially when using public showers or pools)...and wash your feet thoroughly with soap and water. Soap kills the fungus before it multiplies.

BUNIONS

Shoes with high heels or narrow toes can irritate—but not cause—these bony bumps on the sides of the big toe. Most bunions are due to inherited foot deformities—especially flat arches that put excessive pressure where the big toe meets the foot.

New approach: Orthotics. They support the arch, fight irritation and prevent bunions from getting worse. You can also apply a moleskin pad to the bump to prevent rubbing.

If bunions persist, take aspirin or ibuprofen to reduce inflammation...apply ice for 15 minutes two to three times daily...and wear sandals or round-toed shoes to prevent rubbing.

Also helpful: Your doctor can inject cortisone during painful flare-ups. If that's not enough, and the bunions continue to interfere with your normal lifestyle, outpatient surgery may be necessary to remove the bump and realign the joint. This eliminates pain in most cases.

HAMMERTOES

They're usually due to a tendon imbalance, which occurs when the *extensor tendon* (on top of the toe) overpowers the *flexor tendon* (on the bottom), or vice versa. This causes the toe to curl and press against the shoe.

Hammertoes also can be caused by nerve and muscle damage, resulting from diabetes or rheumatoid arthritis. Therefore, a podiatrist should always examine hammertoes to rule out these underlying problems.

New approach: Arthroplasty. This outpatient surgical procedure involves removing a small portion of bone from one of the joints in the toe to correct the tendon imbalance. The procedure slightly stiffens the toe joint and prevents it from bending and rubbing against shoes.

Also helpful: Stretch the Achilles tendon.

What to do: Lean your outstretched arms against a wall...put the affected foot behind the other foot, keeping the back leg straight...and then bend your front knee while leaning forward and keeping the affected foot flat on the floor. Hold the stretch for one minute. Repeat on the other side. Perform twice a day. This Achilles tendon stretch strengthens the flexor muscle and may stop the toe from curling.

More from Stuart Mogul...

Self-Test for Foot Problems

The type of foot you have tells a great deal about your risk for foot problems.

What to do: Moisten your feet in the tub, stand on a square of cardboard and look at the footprints. *If the impression shows...*

• **The entire foot.** This means your feet are *pronated,* or flat. You're predisposed to get plantar fasciitis, bunions, arch pain or leg pain after walking.

• **The heel and ball only.** Your feet are *cavus*—meaning you have a high arch. You're vulnerable to shin splints (inflammation of the shin muscles) and hip or back pain.

• **The heel and ball,** with a *faint* outline along the sides of the feet. You have an ideal foot shape and are less likely to have foot disorders or problems.

See a podiatrist if your prints show either of the first two trouble signs or if you're experiencing leg or foot pain on a regular basis.

To find a podiatrist in your area, consult the American College of Foot and Ankle Surgeons at 800-421-2237 or *www.acfas.org.*

4

Take Control of Your Health

The Ultimate Medical Checkup

The managed-care revolution has drastically reduced the amount of time doctors are willing to spend with their patients. During the typical office visit, your doctor barely has enough time to investigate troublesome symptoms and check your weight...pulse...heartbeat...blood pressure, etc. That is just not enough.

A thorough exam should also address your overall physical and emotional well-being... diet...lifestyle...and any "silent" symptoms that could potentially increase your risk for developing health problems.

Most doctors take a medical history, listing current health problems...prescribed medications...allergies...etc. This information is critical.

Helpful: When writing down your concerns, give your doctor additional information that he/she may fail to include in the medical history. *For example...*

●**How's your diet?**
●**Are you taking any herbal or dietary supplements?**
●**Do you get enough sleep?**
●**Are you physically active?**
●**Are you experiencing sexual problems?**

Also mention if you smoke, how much alcohol you drink and whether you're having difficulty in your personal relationships. Try to keep the list to one page.

THE PHYSICAL

To save time, doctors often take shortcuts during the physical. This can affect not only your current diagnosis and treatment—but also your future health. *Here are the steps most commonly omitted...*

●**Blood pressure.** This vital sign is typically checked in one arm while the patient is sitting. For a more accurate reading, blood pressure

---

Leo Galland, MD, director, Foundation for Integrated Medicine, New York City. His latest book is *The Fat Resistance Diet* (Broadway). *www.fatresistancediet.com.* Dr. Galland is a recipient of the Linus Pauling award.

89

should be tested in both arms, preferably while you're lying down.

If blood pressure differs by 15% or more between arms, there may be blockages in the large blood vessels.

Important: If you're taking blood pressure medication—or if you get dizzy when you change positions—your doctor should check your blood pressure immediately after you stand up. If blood pressure drops by more than 10%, a change in dosage of blood pressure medication may be needed.

●**Eyes.** Most people visit an ophthalmologist or optometrist. But if you don't see an eye specialist regularly and you're age 40 or older, your internist or family practitioner should measure the pressure on your eyeballs to test for glaucoma and look for lack of lens clarity—an early sign of cataracts.

Bonus: A careful eye exam can also reveal blood vessel narrowing or small hemorrhages on the retina—indicators of vascular conditions that increase your heart disease risk.

●**Hamstrings.** Few doctors test these muscles at the back of the thighs to identify potential back problems. To do so, the doctor should ask you to lie on your back and lift each leg to a 90° angle.

If you can't perform the lift, you may need a stretching program to relax the hamstrings.

●**Lymph nodes.** The lymph nodes in your neck are typically checked, but doctors should also check those in the groin and under arms. Swollen lymph nodes may signal infection. Lumps could indicate cancer.

●**Pulse points.** Your doctor probably checks your pulse in your neck and/or groin—but may skip your feet. If pulse strength differs in these three areas, it can be a sign of peripheral arterial disease.

●**Skin.** Many doctors ignore the skin altogether, assuming that it should be examined by a dermatologist. Not true. The skin should also be checked during a general medical checkup.

To thoroughly examine your skin, your doctor should ask you to disrobe so he can look for moles on every part of your body, even your scalp and the bottoms of your feet.

If you have moles larger than one-half inch—or if your moles have gotten larger, darkened or changed their shape—you should get a referral to a dermatologist for a melanoma screening.

●**Thyroid.** This butterfly-shaped gland at the base of the neck is often missed during the lymph node exam. By palpating the thyroid, your doctor can screen for thyroid cancer.

FOR WOMEN ONLY

●**Breast and reproductive organs.** Most doctors check the breasts for suspicious lumps, but few doctors show women how to perform monthly exams at home.

Helpful: When performing a self-exam, move all eight fingers, minus the thumbs, up and down instead of in a circle. That way, you will be covering the entire breast.

If you don't see your gynecologist regularly, your primary physician should also perform rectal and vaginal exams. These exams should be performed simultaneously—it makes it easier to identify suspicious masses.

FOR MEN ONLY

●**Testicles and rectum.** When examining men age 40 or older, most doctors perform a *digital rectal exam* (DRE) to screen for prostate cancer. However, they often fail to perform an exam to check for testicular cancer. Your doctor should also teach you how to perform a testicular self-exam.

Beginning at age 50—even earlier if there's a family history of prostate cancer—every man should undergo a *prostate-specific antigen* (PSA) blood test performed every three years...or more often if abnormalities are found.

LABORATORY TESTS

Routine blood tests include cholesterol levels ...liver and kidney function...blood glucose levels...and a white blood cell count. But we now know that other blood tests can be important if a patient shows signs of certain conditions. *These tests include...*

●**C-reactive protein.** An elevated level of this inflammation marker can indicate heart disease risk.

●**Homocysteine.** Elevated levels of this amino acid are associated with heart disease and stroke risk.

Helpful: The B vitamin folate, when taken at 200 to 400 micrograms (mcg) daily, reduces homocysteine levels.

•**Iron.** Elevated levels of this mineral contribute to iron overload (*hemochromatosis*).

•**Lipoprotein (a).** Elevated levels of this blood protein increase the risk for blood clots.

•**Magnesium.** Low levels of this mineral can bring about fatigue, generalized pain and/or muscle spasms.

•**Zinc.** If you're deficient in this immune-strengthening mineral, you may be prone to frequent infection.

More from Leo Galland...

Important Medical Tests Doctors Don't Tell You About

The special screening tests—for discovering heart disease, aneurysms, lung cancer and ovarian cancer—could save your life. But there's a good chance that your physician won't order them because insurance companies rarely pay for them.

Reason: Insurance companies typically pay for tests only when you have been diagnosed with a particular condition or when there is a high likelihood that you might have it. With some exceptions, such as mammograms, insurance rarely pays for screening tests aimed at early detection.

Ask your doctor if you should have any of the following tests, even if you have to pay for them yourself. They are available at most diagnostic and medical centers around the country. Ask your doctor for a referral.

These tests aren't appropriate for everyone, but early research suggests that they could be lifesavers for those with key risk factors...

CHOLESTEROL TEST

Traditional cholesterol tests only measure HDL ("good") cholesterol and triglycerides. The formula used to calculate levels of harmful LDL cholesterol isn't always accurate. This partly explains why half of people who have heart attacks have cholesterol levels that appear normal.

Better: Expanded cholesterol tests measure LDL specifically, giving more accurate readings.

About 40 million American adults have hidden heart disease. Expanded cholesterol tests could identify 95% of these patients before a heart attack occurs.

The tests also look at individual HDL and LDL particles and determine how helpful—or harmful—they are likely to be.

Example: HDL protects against heart disease, so high levels are desirable. But some people who appear to have high levels actually have a subtype of HDL that isn't very beneficial. Also, although all LDL particles are bad, the smaller ones are more dangerous than the bigger ones. These kinds of differences just aren't detectable with the conventional tests—but they can be detected with the expanded tests.

Who should consider them: Patients with mildly elevated cholesterol levels—200 to 230 milligrams per deciliter (mg/dl)—who smoke or who have cardiovascular risk factors, such as heart problems, high blood pressure or a family history of heart disease.

Cost: $75 to $175.

ANEURYSM TEST

Aneurysms are bulges in artery walls. If they rupture, they are fatal in 80% to 90% of the cases, killing approximately 30,000 Americans annually.

Better: An aneurysm scan uses an ultrasound wand to detect aneurysms in the abdominal aortic arteries. It's the only noninvasive test that allows doctors to identify aneurysms before they rupture. Surgery to repair aneurysms can increase survival rates to 99%.

Who should consider it: Anyone over age 60 who has cardiovascular risk factors, such as high blood pressure, or who smokes...as well as anyone over age 50 who has a family history of heart disease.

Cost: $60 to $200, depending on the extent of the scan.

HEART DISEASE TEST

Current methods for detecting heart disease risk, such as checking blood pressure, miss up to 75% of patients who later on develop heart problems.

Better: The *electron beam tomography* (EBT) heart scan is the first direct, noninvasive way of identifying atherosclerosis, the primary risk factor for heart disease. The patient lies in a doughnut-shaped machine while the electron beams map out calcium deposits in the arteries. The buildup of calcium indicates the presence of plaque—fatty deposits that hamper blood flow to the heart and increase risk of blood clots. The patients who are found to have early signs of heart disease can take the appropriate steps—such as lowering cholesterol, controlling blood pressure, stopping smoking, etc.—to prevent problems from progressing.

Drawback: Calcium deposits don't always indicate an elevated risk of heart attack. Some deposits may be harmless. On the other hand, a person who has a clear scan could actually have dangerous levels of plaque.

Patients with high calcium levels also may have to take a follow-up stress test. If this test is positive, the patient may have to undergo an angiogram—an invasive procedure. If the angiogram shows no heart disease, the patient has undergone these extra tests unnecessarily. Still the EBT is considered useful because traditional tests don't catch most heart problems.

Who should consider it: All men over age 45 and women over age 55. If you have heart disease risk factors—smoking, a family history of heart disease, etc.—consider having an EBT 10 years sooner.

Cost: About $400.

LUNG CANCER TEST

Lung cancer rarely causes symptoms until it reaches an advanced stage. The five-year survival rate is about 15%. Conventional X rays may fail to detect early-stage tumors.

Better: The spiral CT scan can detect cancerous tumors as small as one grain of rice. Eighty percent of lung cancers spotted in scanning studies were caught at a potentially treatable stage.

Drawbacks: The test can sometimes result in false-positives—findings that indicate cancer when none is present. This could lead to unnecessary and risky lung biopsies. The false-positive rate improves when patients have follow-up scans.

Who should consider it: Smokers as well as former smokers age 50 and over who have smoked at least one pack daily for 10 years or two packs daily for five years.

Cost: $200 to $450.

OVARIAN CANCER

More than 14,000 American women die from ovarian cancer every year. It is now the deadliest of female cancers. Like lung cancer, it often has no symptoms until it reaches an advanced stage of development.

Better: An ultrasound device inserted into the vagina allows doctors to inspect the ovaries for any malignant changes. University of Kentucky researchers used this test on 23,000 women. Twenty-nine showed cancerous ovarian tumors, 76% of which were detected at an early, more treatable stage. Typically, only 25% of ovarian cancers are caught early.

Drawback: The test isn't able to differentiate between malignant and benign growths—so positive test results could result in unnecessary medical procedures.

Who should consider it: Women age 45 and older with risk factors, such as a family history of ovarian, breast or colon cancer...or a history of fertility or hormone-replacement treatment...or who have never been pregnant.

Cost: About $250.

Also from Leo Galland...

Beware of "Normal" Test Results

Are you relieved when your doctor's office calls to say that your lab test results are "normal"?

Counts that look okay do not necessarily mean you are okay. Nor do high or low counts always mean health problems.

Key: Patients should ask their doctors for copies of test results and to compare current and past results to see if anything has changed significantly. Your doctor should be doing this—but don't rely on it.

Among the counts that patients should be sure to ask about...

●**Hemoglobin/hematocrit.** High levels may signal dehydration...low levels, anemia.

● **Mean corpuscular volume (MCV).** Low levels usually mean an iron deficiency. High values often disappear with retesting. If not, they may indicate liver disease or a vitamin B-12 deficiency, etc.

● **White blood cells and platelets.** Investigate high or low levels of either. Causes could range from an infection to bleeding disorders to leukemia.

● **Albumin.** Values under 4.0 may suggest liver problems or chronic inflammation.

● **Blood glucose.** A fasting level over 110 suggests a prediabetic condition…over 126, probably diabetes.

● **Calcium.** High counts usually disappear on repeat tests. If not, parathyroid glands may be malfunctioning.

● **Cholesterol.** High LDL ("bad") cholesterol counts are the most important. Total cholesterol is less significant.

There is no "one-size-fits-all" interpretation of results. Take a few minutes to discuss them with your doctor in conjunction with symptoms and personal or family history of disease. Those minutes could add years to your life.

How to Survive a Medical Emergency Without a Doctor

William W. Forgey, MD, past president, Wilderness Medical Society, Colorado Springs, *www.wms.org*. He is author of *Wilderness Medicine: Beyond First Aid* (Globe Pequot) and *Basic Essentials Wilderness First Aid* (Falcon). Dr. Forgey is in private practice in Merrillville, IN. For more information on medical treatment in the outdoors, visit *www.docforgey.com*.

When a medical emergency strikes, our first response is to call 911. But if you're camped on an isolated mountainside or exploring a remote island, you won't have that option. So what should you do?

Here's how to treat common medical emergencies when they occur in a remote area…

SEVERE CUT

Applying direct pressure with the heel of your hand should stop the bleeding. To avoid contact with the victim's blood, use a plastic bag as a barrier.

To clean the wound, fashion your own irrigation device. Do this by filling a plastic resealable bag with clean water from your canteen. Zip the top shut, punch a tiny hole (the size of a pencil tip) in one corner, and squeeze the bag to force the water out of the hole.

If you don't have a bandage, plastic food wrappers make an effective wound covering. Affix with tape. If tape is not available, rip clothes into strips and tie around the area to hold the covering in place.

If the wound becomes red, swollen or pus-filled, apply granulated sugar. It helps to kill off bacteria.

SPRAIN

Wrap the limb to provide support. T-shirts are a good source of stretchy cloth. If you need a cane, fashion one from a tree branch.

BROKEN BONE

To determine if a bone is broken, use three fingers to press along the length of the bone. If this pressure hurts at any spot, the bone could be broken. Stabilize the limb with splints made from the stays of a backpack frame or strips of a foam sleeping pad. Affix the splint with tape or torn cloth.

A crooked (angulated) fracture can compress arteries, stopping blood flow. To straighten it before applying a splint, grasp both sides of the fracture and gently pull in opposite directions.

POISON IVY

Soothe the rash by applying a cloth soaked in a concentrated salt/water solution.

HYPOTHERMIA

Even during the summer months, a person can experience acute hypothermia if he/she is immersed in water that is less than 50°F for more than 20 minutes.

If this occurs, the victim should be kept still. Physical activity increases blood flow to the skin. Since the skin is already very cold, moving the victim further reduces core body temperature. Place the victim inside a warm area, such as a tent. If no shelter is available, build a roaring fire to warm the victim.

HEATSTROKE

A person whose skin is hot, flushed and dry and who feels fatigued and/or disoriented should be immersed in cool water.

If no lake or stream is nearby, move the victim into shade. Cool him with ice, if available, or spray with water or any cold fluid while vigorously fanning the person.

Also, massage his limbs. That helps to move blood from the extremities to the core circulation more readily.

HEART ATTACK

If a person experiences chest heaviness or pain with exertion…pain in the neck or arms …sweating, clammy appearance…and/or extreme shortness of breath, have him lie down to lessen oxygen demand.

Position him so that his head is elevated at a 45° angle. If you have aspirin, give him one regular-strength tablet or two baby aspirin. If he is carrying any prescription heart medication, such as nitroglycerin, give him a dose.

EMERGENCY PREPAREDNESS

The best way to protect yourself in remote areas is to be prepared…

•**Dress to survive.** If you're going for a jog, walk or hike in the woods, carry emergency supplies. In addition to bottled water, a hat, sunglasses and insect repellent, your pack should include a few crucial items. *They are…*

•A rain poncho or large garbage bag to make into a poncho. It can also be used as a makeshift shelter.

•An extra set of dry clothing in case you need to spend the night outside.

•A signal mirror.

•**Bring a medical kit.** Carry a medical kit that contains sterile gauze…scissors…adhesive and elastic bandages…waterproof tape…splint …antibiotic ointment…eye drops…latex examination gloves…irrigation syringe…over-the-counter pain reliever, antihistamine, diarrhea and heartburn medications.

Such kits can be purchased at outdoor and sporting-goods stores for about $30 and up.

•**Make sure you use outdoor equipment safely.** Most serious burns in the wilderness happen when boiling water is spilled from a pot that's perched on a rock or when a cooking stove is used incorrectly.

How Doctors Stay Well With Sickness All Around All Day Long

Michael Janson, MD, general practitioner in private practice, in Arlington, MA, and New Smyrna, FL, and advisor, American College for Advancement in Medicine, a professional nonprofit medical educational organization. He is author of *The Vitamin Revolution in Health Care* (Arcadia Press).

Doctors provide the best of their science-based knowledge about health and disease to their patients. But many of them hold off recommending alternative treatments that they themselves use.

Here's what many doctors I know believe for themselves…and how they take care of themselves to limit the likelihood of illness. Consult your doctor to be sure this advice is right for you.

•**Vitamin supplements are essential to replenish cells with nutrients.** More than 60% of doctors say that they take supplements regularly even though they don't necessarily recommend them to their patients.

There's no question that a balanced diet is key to keeping your body functioning at its optimum level.

However, a variety of factors influence the value of the nutrients in our daily diets. Some factors include genetic makeup…pollution… overprocessed foods…and stress. Stress robs the body of important immune-boosting nutrients.

Vitamin supplements enhance a healthy diet and offer protection against the many factors that negatively influence our food supply and our health.

What I recommend: In addition to a multi-vitamin/mineral, I tell my patients to take 50 to 100 milligrams (mg) of vitamin B-6...400 to 800 micrograms (mcg) of folic acid...2,000 mg of vitamin C...and 6 to 15 mg of natural beta-carotene, daily.

●**Vitamin E.** Some studies show that vitamin E protects against heart disease. According to a recent survey, 80% of doctors said they took vitamin E.

Numerous studies have shown that vitamin E reduces heart disease risk by protecting the circulatory system from the consequence of cholesterol deposits. Those deposits can lead to clogged arteries—and to atherosclerosis.

Therapeutic doses range from 400 to 1,200 international units (IUs) per day of natural E (d-alpha-tocopherol). Check with your doctor for the proper amount. Doses higher than 200 IU may be dangerous for some people.

Caution: If you are taking anticlotting medications (for example, Coumadin or aspirin), you should consult your doctor before starting to take vitamin E. Its natural anticlotting properties may cause too much of that effect in your blood.

●**Niacin and glucosamine sulfate** can reduce joint pain and cartilage degeneration associated with osteoarthritis—without the side effects of anti-inflammatory drugs.

Osteoarthritis—which is a degenerative joint condition that affects about 80% of people older than age 70—is effectively treated with anti-inflammatory medicines.

But these medications can cause troublesome and sometimes serious side effects for many of the patients who take them.

That's why niacin (vitamin B-3) and glucosamine sulfate turn out to be an effective alternative for most of my patients.

Niacin has many uses in the body, including helping to maintain normal mental functions, energy in the cells, digestion and healthy skin.

Glucosamine sulfate is a natural compound found in connective tissue and cartilage that contributes to joint strength. Supplements help to repair joint cartilage and relieve pain within four to eight weeks.

Doses: I recommend two 500-mg glucosamine sulfate tablets taken twice daily and/or two 500-mg niacinamide tablets twice daily.

●**Headaches can be effectively managed through massage and diet.** Many of my colleagues ask their spouses or partners to massage their temples or necks after the working day, or they get professional massages.

Reason: Massage can help to relieve headaches that may be caused by muscle tension in various parts of the body. In fact, many pain clinics use massage as part of an overall program to treat tension headaches.

Your diet can play a large role in the onset or exacerbation of headaches—particularly processed, sugary foods, which cause blood sugar levels to fluctuate.

What you can do: Before you reach for an over-the-counter pain reliever, examine the foods you've been eating. Get rid of heavily processed foods, which often contain nitrates, white flour and sugar. Satisfy your cravings for sweets by eating fruit.

Standardized extracts of the herbal medicines feverfew (25 to 50 mg two to three times daily) or ginkgo biloba (60 mg twice a day) can also reduce the frequency and intensity of headaches without the rebound effect of medicines. (As with all herbs, pregnant or nursing women may need to take special precautions.)

●**Stress management can help lower and maintain blood pressure.** Many doctors are hesitant to discuss breathing and visualization exercises because they are still considered unconventional in most medical practices. But many others believe that they are key to lowering blood pressure and keeping it down, with or without medications.

Example: Sit in a comfortable position, and place one hand on your abdomen. While envisioning a warm, comfortable place, breathe in and out slowly, pushing your hand out each time you inhale. Do this for at least five minutes, three to four times daily.

It's also important to go to bed in a calm state. Read a relaxing book or listen to relaxing music just before bed.

●**Exercise has positive effects on more than two dozen chronic health problems,** ranging from rheumatism to diabetes. It's usual for doctors to recommend physical activity.

But has your doctor told you the reasons behind those recommendations? And how much exercise you should be doing?

Studies have demonstrated that regular exercise can improve cardiovascular health, including lipid levels, heart rate and blood pressure, and reduce breast cancer risk in women younger than age 40 by more than one-third.

Researchers have also demonstrated increases in strength and bone and muscle mass, by as much as 170% among individuals who are over age 80.

Best routine: Walk briskly at least four to five times every week.

Aim: Three miles in 45 minutes.

Go as fast as you can without getting out of breath—but work up a sweat. Strength-training three times weekly is a valuable addition.

How to Stay Healthy: Recommendations from Six Prominent Doctors

Robert Abel, Jr., MD, ophthalmologist in private practice, Wilmington, DE. He is author of *The Eye Care Revolution* (Kensington Health).

Samuel Meyers, MD, clinical professor of medicine, Mount Sinai School of Medicine, New York City.

Gail Saltz, MD, associate professor of psychiatry, New York-Presbyterian Hospital/Weill Medical College of Cornell University, and psychoanalyst in private practice, both in New York City.

Kenneth Offit, MD, MPH, chief of the clinical genetics service, Memorial Sloan-Kettering Cancer Center, New York City.

Sheldon G. Sheps, MD, emeritus professor of medicine, Mayo Medical School, Rochester, MN.

Lisa Meserole, ND, RD, former head of nutrition, Bastyr University, Seattle.

What's the best way to create a comprehensive strategy for staying healthy? Leading specialists—experts in heart disease, cancer prevention, eye health and more—give their recommendations.

OPHTHALMOLOGIST
Robert Abel, Jr., MD

• **Wear sunglasses outdoors**—even in the winter. This is the best way to minimize eye damage from ultraviolet (UV) light. Consistently wearing sunglasses that block UV rays will halve your risk for cataracts and macular degeneration—the leading causes of vision loss in adults.

If you're taking diuretics or antibiotics: Sunglasses are especially important because these drugs increase photosensitivity, which makes the eye lens much more vulnerable to UV damage.

• **Drink more water.** The body's blood supply does not feed the lens of the eye, so drinking lots of water to flush toxins can reduce the risk for cataracts.

• **Eat cold-water fish three times weekly.** Salmon, tuna, mackerel and sardines are the best dietary sources of *docosahexaenoic acid* (DHA), a long-chain fatty acid that rebuilds damaged cell membranes in the retina and may improve night vision.

If you don't eat fish: Take a fish oil supplement containing 500 milligrams (mg) of supplemental DHA daily...or consume 500 mg of supplemental algae, which is also rich in DHA.

GASTROENTEROLOGIST
Samuel Meyers, MD

• **Eat 30 grams (g) of fiber daily,** and limit your fat intake to 30% of total calories. These two changes alone could substantially reduce your risk for colon cancer and precancerous colon polyps.

Helpful: Start the day with All-Bran, 100% Bran, Raisin Bran or some other whole-grain cereal. Each of these cereals contains at least 8 g of fiber per serving. Other high-fiber foods include strawberries (3 g per cup) and sweet potatoes (4 g per potato).

• **Cook meats and fish thoroughly.** More than 90% of supermarket chicken is contaminated with disease-causing bacteria. Safe food preparation will prevent most cases of infection caused by *Salmonella, Shigella* and *Campylobacter*—and eliminate millions of doctor visits annually. Use a food thermometer to ensure that meats are cooked to 160°F and poultry to 180°F. Never let raw meat juices drip on foods.

●**Get a colonoscopy.** After a baseline test at age 50, repeat the screening at least once every five years. About 150,000 new cases of colon cancer are diagnosed each year. And most could be prevented—or treated early—with proper screening.

If you have a family history of colon cancer: Get your first colonoscopy 10 years before the earliest age at which a family member got the disease. Repeat the test every one to three years, following your doctor's advice.

PSYCHIATRIST
Gail Saltz, MD

●**Ask for help if you're suffering from depression**—even if you've had it for only a few weeks. One in 10 Americans suffers from depression. However, most of those people never seek help because they're embarrassed...or they wait so long that the depression becomes resistant to treatment.

If you feel symptoms, such as difficulty sleeping, loss of appetite, difficulty concentrating or hopelessness, for more than two weeks, see a mental-health professional. If you have thoughts of harming yourself, seek help immediately.

●**Look for negative patterns in your life.** Don't spend another year making the same bad decisions...sabotaging work success...or failing at relationships.

Break the cycle by reviewing all aspects of your life—family, friends, work, leisure, etc. If things are going poorly, ask yourself why. Look for behaviors that may be setting you back. It is the first step to finding healthier ways to live your life.

●**Acknowledge that you're not perfect.** We all experience anger, frustration and anxiety from time to time. You'll suffer more if you believe that these and other "negative" emotions are somehow abnormal.

When things don't go smoothly, regroup and move forward...and remember to appreciate the good things in your life, such as your health or loving relationships. It's impossible to be happy when your expectations are too high.

GENETIC ONCOLOGIST
Kenneth Offit, MD, MPH

●**Ask family members about their cancer histories.** Find out as much information as you can about your relatives' medical histories. Family history is one of the most important risk factors for breast, colon, prostate and other common types of cancer.

Example: If you have a strong family history of breast cancer, your risk of developing it could be 20 times higher than that of someone without the family history.

Knowing that cancer runs in the family will alert you to take the necessary steps to protect yourself. This includes getting regular screening tests and eating a more healthful diet.

Important: Family history goes beyond parents, siblings or other first-degree relatives. You also need to know the cancer histories of your grandparents, aunts and uncles.

●**Do not give up on mammograms.** In re-evaluating the previous studies, researchers questioned if women who received regular mammograms were less likely to die from breast cancer than women who did not get them. The preponderance of evidence, however, still supports the use of mammograms as a screening technique.

About 47 million American women ages 40 or older should be receiving mammograms. Deaths resulting from breast cancer could be reduced by up to 30% with regular screening. It's important to get tested annually.

CARDIOLOGIST
Sheldon G. Sheps, MD

●**Eat to lower blood pressure.** The DASH (Dietary Approaches to Stop Hypertension) diet is now the gold standard for preventing or reducing high blood pressure. It includes seven to eight daily grain servings...four to five servings each of fruits and vegetables...two to three servings of low-fat dairy...two servings of meat, poultry or fish...and four to five servings per week of legumes, nuts or seeds. People who follow the diet are less likely to suffer from heart disease, stroke, osteoporosis or kidney stones.

Important: The DASH diet limits sodium intake to 1,500 mg per day. In sodium-sensitive individuals, reducing sodium can prevent blood pressure in the high end of the prehypertension range (120–139/80–89) from progressing to true hypertension (140/90 or above)…and may reduce your need for medication if you already have hypertension.

●**Set modest weight-loss goals.** If you're overweight, losing as little as 10 pounds may be enough to lower blood pressure by five points. Losing up to 10% of your body weight is often enough to lower blood pressure to a healthful range.

Helpful: Physical activity promotes weight loss and lowers blood pressure—and you don't have to set aside "extra" time to do it. Incorporate more activity into your daily life by walking the halls at work…parking farther away from the entrance…and taking stairs instead of elevators. You'll get substantial health benefits as long as all forms of physical activity add up to at least 30 minutes daily.

●**Practice slow, deep breathing for 15 minutes most days.** It has the same benefits as other meditative techniques—lowering blood pressure…slowing the heart rate…reducing stress hormones, etc.

●**Don't forget the dangers of second-hand smoke.** Everyone knows that smoking contributes to heart disease, cancer and other serious illnesses. Secondhand smoke will also increase the risk for these ailments, but few people take the necessary steps to avoid prolonged exposure.

NATUROPATHIC PHYSICIAN
Lisa Meserole, ND, RD

●**Eat organic, locally produced foods.** Even so-called "safe" levels of pesticides, herbicides, hormones and other chemicals that are found in commercially grown produce and meats may increase the risk for cancer and other serious diseases.

In recent years, studies have shown a 50% drop in the sperm counts of American men…probably due to environmental toxins. Eating organic foods won't eliminate your exposure to toxins, but it will help minimize the amount you ingest.

●**Personalize your health decisions.** In addition to adopting new habits to improve your overall health, it's important to address specific medical conditions.

Suppose you get frequent sinus infections. Resolve to eat more vitamin C–rich foods to help your mucous membranes function effectively…keep the air moisturized with a humidifier…and exercise daily to improve immunity.

●**Balance work with play.** Don't try to do everything. Psychological stress is at epidemic levels in this country. Stress damages blood vessels, raises blood pressure and makes it hard to think clearly and make intelligent, life-affirming decisions. Relaxing isn't a luxury—you need it for your health. Make time each day for humor and love.

How to Stay in Touch with Your Doctor

Daniel Z. Sands, MD, MPH, assistant professor of medicine, Harvard Medical School, Boston, and coauthor of national guidelines on doctor–patient electronic communications.

After a doctor's appointment, patients almost always have some follow-up questions—about the lab results, symptoms, referrals, etc. But busy physicians receive up to 75 phone messages per day. The doctors just don't have time to answer them all.

Daniel Z. Sands, MD, explained how to stay in touch between office visits…

●**Rely on the doctor's assistant.** Nurses, physician's assistants and nurse practitioners can handle almost all questions. If you call the assistant, he/she is more likely than the doctor to call back the same day.

●**Call in the morning.** Afternoons are the busiest times in doctors' offices.

●**Write down what you want to say.** Limit it to *one* issue per message or conversation.

You might also try e-mail. If your doctor is willing to field questions via e-mail, put your name and patient identification number in the subject line. That way, your doctor knows the message is from a patient. Keep the message short—and use e-mail only for medical issues.

Because regular e-mail is about as secure as sending out a postcard, it may not be the best choice for discussing confidential issues, such as psychiatric disorders, or for addressing health issues that must be resolved right away.

Female Doctors Have Better Bedside Manners than Male Doctors

Women MDs spend an average of 23 minutes with patients, compared with 21 minutes for male doctors.

Female physicians who talk more about lifestyle and social issues, such as the advantages of exercising with a friend or the challenges of raising teenagers, are more likely to engage in positive health-related discussions, including the patient's feelings about diet restrictions. Other studies have linked this communication style to patient satisfaction, compliance with medical recommendations and improvements in health.

Debra Roter, DrPH, professor of health policy and management, Johns Hopkins University, Baltimore.

How to See a Specialist Faster

To get an appointment with a specialist sooner, tell the receptionist at the specialist's office that you are feeling anxious about your condition. If this does not work, emphasize that your primary-care physician wants you to be seen by the specialist quickly.

If this still does not work, ask your primary-care doctor to make the appointment for you. If your own doctor cannot get you a prompt appointment, call the specialist and ask for a referral to someone who is more readily available. This will often work, since doctors do not want to lose patients.

Susan A. Albrecht, PhD, RN, associate professor, University of Pittsburgh School of Nursing.

How to Guard Against Medical Misinformation

Dean Edell, MD, host of a nationally syndicated radio talk program "The Dr. Dean Edell Show." He is author of *Eat, Drink & Be Merry* (Harper).

Americans are setting records for good health and longevity—and are more worried about health than ever before. But much of this concern is misplaced. *A great deal of medical misinformation is afoot, and it's scaring us needlessly...*

***Myth:* All germs are harmful.** Despite worry about the AIDS and *Ebola* viruses and flesh-eating bacteria, the vast majority of viruses and bacteria coexist peacefully with humans.

Some germs are beneficial. Human skin, for example, is covered with bacteria that help prevent illness by "crowding out" other disease-causing bacteria.

The germs most likely to harm us are those that we worry about least. Food poisoning caused by *Salmonella* and *E. coli* is common. So is influenza. It kills 20,000 to 30,000 Americans each year.

Focus on germs that are likely to cause illness. Wash your hands frequently to reduce your risk of catching colds or flu. Regular soap is fine—no need for antibacterial varieties.

Food poisoning can usually be prevented by cooking meats thoroughly and taking care that raw meat juices don't come in contact with other foods.

***Myth:* Cold weather causes colds.** No matter what conventional wisdom says, colds are caused by viruses. These viruses are with us during warm weather and cold.

Colds are more prevalent in winter because we spend more time indoors then—in close proximity to other people. The viruses that cause colds are spread mainly by droplets from sneezes and coughs of infected individuals.

***Myth:* Herbal remedies are inherently safer than conventional drugs.** More than half of all conventional medications contain ingredients that are similar or identical to those found in herbs.

Getting these compounds in natural rather than synthetic form doesn't make them safer. In fact, just the opposite may be true.

When you take a conventional drug, you're getting a single active ingredient. Herbal remedies often contain *thousands* of active ingredients. We don't always know which of these compounds are truly beneficial.

Herbal remedies are reasonable alternatives to conventional medical treatment only as long as they've been proven to work.

Example: Reliable studies have shown that ginger prevents motion sickness and that feverfew is good for migraines.

Echinacea, on the other hand, does not seem to deserve its reputation as a cold-fighter.

***Myth:* Salt causes high blood pressure.** The recommended upper limit for salt intake is 2,400 milligrams (mg) per day. But most Americans consume three to four times that amount —and very few of us have high blood pressure problems.

Salt *does* elevate blood pressure in an estimated 30% of Americans who are "salt sensitive." Unfortunately, there's no way to predict who is sensitive.

The only prudent course of action is to have your blood pressure checked...and ask your doctor whether sodium restriction makes sense for you.

The biggest sources of sodium are not potato chips and other salty-tasting foods. Most sodium comes in the form of white bread, chocolate pudding and other foods that don't taste salty.

***Myth:* Caffeine is harmful.** Caffeinated coffee—and to a lesser extent caffeinated tea and soft drinks—can cause stomach upset. Too much caffeine can also be a problem for women who are pregnant or nursing and those prone to anxiety and insomnia. Otherwise, there's nothing wrong with it.

Caffeine is actually beneficial for people with asthma. It's chemically similar to the bronchodilating drug *theophylline* (Uniphyl).

To avoid insomnia and anxiety, limit your caffeine intake to about 250 mg a day. That's the equivalent of two cups of caffeinated coffee, six cups of black tea, eight cups of green tea or six 12-ounce cans of cola.

Otherwise, caffeine is one of life's little pleasures. Enjoy it.

***Myth:* Infections should always be treated with antibiotics.** In fact, viral infections, like colds and flu, should *never* be treated with antibiotics. Antibiotics have no effect on viruses—only on bacteria.

Since some infections are serious and require treatment, it's always smart to consult a doctor. But do *not* assume that antibiotics are called for.

If you think you have a cold and your doctor prescribes an antibiotic, ask why. Some doctors prescribe antibiotics because they think their patients expect them to.

***Myth:* Sugar makes children hyperactive.** Controlled studies have shown that behavior problems are no more common among kids who are fed sugar than among kids fed an inert sugar substitute.

The "sugar myth" got started when parents noticed that kids tend to act up at birthday parties—where large amounts of sugar are consumed. But it's the excitement of the party that causes the misbehavior—not the cake and ice cream.

***Myth:* Chocolate causes acne.** With the possible exception of seafood, no food has ever been shown to cause acne. Outbreaks occur when testosterone—found in females as well as males—stimulates glands in the skin to secrete oil (*sebum*). Excess sebum blocks pores, causing pimples.

Adolescents are prone to acne because of their changing hormone levels. In adults, psychological stress is often the culprit. It triggers a transient rise in testosterone levels.

If you're bothered by acne, do your best to avoid stress. Don't wash your face too often. Soap dries the skin, increasing flaking. That can block the pores.

Do Your Own Medical Research

Carol Svec, Raleigh, NC–based researcher, medical writer and patient advocate. She is author of *After Any Diagnosis: How to Take Action Against Your Illness Using the Best and Most Current Medical Information Available* (Three Rivers Press).

If you have always trusted your doctors to stay up-to-date on medical treatments, you are taking a big chance.

Every year, more than 3,000 biomedical journals are published. And every year, the US Food and Drug Administration (FDA) approves more than 500 new or updated drugs and more than 3,000 new medical devices. No doctor can keep up with all these innovations.

Patients must fill in the gaps by becoming experts on any medical condition from which they suffer. Studies show that informed patients spend fewer days in the hospital, lose fewer days of work, feel less depressed and report lower levels of pain.

EASIER SEARCHES

The Internet has made gathering medical information easier than ever before. There are nearly 10,000 Web sites on specific diseases and conditions.

To find reliable information, start with Web sites sponsored by government agencies (with URL addresses that end in *.gov*), educational institutions (with addresses ending in *.edu*) or nonprofit organizations (which end in *.org*).

Find one or two good Web sites and consult them periodically. For common disorders, such as diabetes, multiple sclerosis or asthma, checking back once a month is sufficient. For rare diseases, once every six months is plenty, because breakthroughs occur so infrequently.

Exception: For life-threatening diseases, check *every week* for updates and any new clinical trials.

However, try not to let the search become an obsession. Gathering information may help you feel "in control," but when the paper chase starts controlling you, it's time to scale back the search.

USING INFORMATION WISELY

Some physicians don't reveal all medical options to their patients—because they think patients will be confused by the choices or because the physicians specialize in a particular treatment.

For example, a surgical oncologist may be more inclined to recommend treating cancer with surgery, rather than with radiation or chemotherapy.

If you are well-informed, you'll be able to discuss all treatment options, make sound medical decisions and avoid health scams.

Work in partnership with your physician. Doctors know the medical facts, but patients know how they're feeling. *Some good ways to stay involved...*

●**Talk openly with your doctor about wanting to participate in your own care.** Most encourage their patients to become active information seekers. If your doctor objects, find a new one.

●**Keep your physician in the loop.** Don't try any new medication, supplement, herb or device without discussing it with your physician. Make sure it won't interfere with your current treatment.

●**Stay in touch *between* your appointments.** Questions often arise between office visits. Ask your doctor how he/she prefers to respond to these inquiries.

Good choices: Sending e-mail (if you're not worried about privacy), talking on the phone after office hours or consulting with a nurse or physician's assistant. If these strategies do not work, it may be necessary to book a separate appointment.

●**Don't deluge your doctor with written material.** Bring no more than three articles to your physician per visit. That's all a physician will be able to evaluate during the standard appointment.

●**Track your progress.** Request copies of all your medical reports (blood tests, X-rays, etc.) and keep them in a file. Log all monitoring information, such as blood pressure or glucose levels. Note any changes since your last office visit, including new pain or other symptoms and steps you've taken to control them.

Take your file to each doctor's appointment. This information lets the doctor know what's happening between office visits, and it provides a quick reference in case you change doctors or require emergency care.

STOP SCARING YOURSELF

Health statistics can be confusing and frightening. When assessing these numbers, remember that they are based on the average outcome of research involving thousands of patients.

Example: If a disease is said to have a 50% death rate, the statistic is based on reports from a broad sample of people who have had the disease. This includes those people who have had extensive treatment as well as others who opted for no treatment.

Statistics are used for understanding the seriousness of a disease, but they should never be used to predict an individual's outcome. Do not let numbers alone make you lose hope. *Before you worry over a study reported in the news, find out...*

●**Did the study involve humans?** Animal studies are a valuable first step, but the same results are not always found in people.

●**How many people participated in the study?** The more subjects, the better. If a study uses fewer than 100 subjects, don't take it too seriously.

●**Were the participants similar to you?** Did they have the same disease? Were they of the same sex and of a similar age? Unless the subjects were people just like you, the study may not be relevant.

How Much Do You Know About Your Doctor?

John J. Connolly, EdD, former president, New York Medical College, Valhalla, NY. He copublishes *America's Top Doctors* (Castle Connolly Medical Ltd.), an annual guide that lists the top specialists in a variety of fields, based on each doctor's credentials, experience and assessments by his/her peers.

When choosing a doctor, most people will rely on a recommendation given to them by a friend, family member, coworker or another doctor.

Few of us seek enough information from the prospective physicians themselves to predict the quality of care we will receive.

If you don't feel comfortable speaking directly to a doctor about his qualifications, ask to speak to the office manager when you call to make an appointment. This person should be knowledgeable about the doctor's background.

The American Medical Association (*www. ama-assn.org* or 800-621-8335 or 312-464-5000) also provides biographical information about physicians—but the AMA does not judge quality.

To ensure that you have enough information about a doctor, ask him these questions...

●**Are you board-certified?** Whether you're choosing a primary-care doctor or a specialist, board certification is the best indicator of competence and training.

Every medical specialty, including family practice and internal medicine, has a governing board that sets and enforces professional standards. Board certification means the doctor has completed an approved residency program and passed the board's stiff examination.

The American Board of Medical Specialties (*www.abms.org* or 866-275-2267) can tell you if a doctor is board-certified.

●**Where did you complete your residency?** Look for a physician who has at least three years of postgraduate specialty training in a residency program at a major hospital. This ensures that the doctor has gained experience in treating patients under the supervision of leading specialists.

It is fine to inquire where a doctor attended medical school, however, do not place too much emphasis on it. All accredited medical schools meet high standards, requiring graduates to pass standardized tests and compete for prestigious residencies.

A graduate from a foreign medical school must pass the same exam as a US medical school graduate—and complete the same residency requirements—to receive board certification from the appropriate governing board in the US.

●**How long have you been in practice?** If you put a premium on a doctor's clinical experience, you are more likely to prefer an older doctor who has been in practice for a number of years.

However, many people prefer doctors who completed their residency within the past five years, assuming they will be more familiar with the latest treatments.

Regardless of whether the doctor is old or young, he should have a lot of experience with your particular condition.

●**With which hospital are you affiliated?** Most doctors have admitting privileges at one or more hospitals. This allows them to admit patients to the hospital and care for them there.

Choose a doctor who has privileges at a major medical center with a good reputation. The very best doctors typically practice at the best hospitals.

Helpful: *U.S. News and World Report* ranks the best US hospitals each year. You can find details at *www.usnews.com.*

CHOOSING A SPECIALIST

For serious medical problems, including those that require surgery, your primary-care physician will often refer you to a specialist. Request more than one recommendation so that you'll have a choice.

Ask these questions to confirm a specialist's qualifications…

●**Are you board-certified in the appropriate subspecialty?** A doctor who is board-certified in a subspecialty has completed additional fellowship training in that area.

Example: A hand surgeon may be an orthopedist or a plastic surgeon who completed fellowship training in hand surgery.

●**How often have you performed this procedure?** Look for a doctor who has performed a procedure, such as laparoscopic surgery or open-heart surgery, as often as every day or every week for several years.

For rare procedures, such as the removal of certain types of brain tumors or liver malignancies, the frequency would be less. The more experience a doctor has performing a procedure, the greater the odds of success.

Caution: Every year, hundreds of physicians are disciplined or put on probation by their state medical authorities for improper behavior, substance abuse, fraud and other problems.

To avoid these doctors, call your state's medical licensing authority (check the state government listings in your phone book) or go to the Web site of the Federation of State Medical Boards at *www.fsmb.org.*

In addition to asking the questions above, patients can receive recommendations from area support groups and branches of national organizations, such as the American Diabetes Association, *www.diabetes.org.*

Use the triangulation method: If three people whose opinion you respect recommend the same doctor, he is likely to be a good choice.

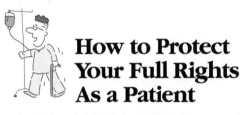

How to Protect Your Full Rights As a Patient

Charles B. Inlander, a consumer advocate and health care consultant based in Fogelsville, PA. He was founding president of People's Medical Society, a consumer health advocacy group. He is coauthor of more than 20 books on consumer health issues, including *Take This Book to the Hospital with You: A Consumer Guide to Surviving Your Hospital Stay* (St. Martin's).

Being ill or injured is a stressful experience—some injuries/illnesses, of course, are more stressful than others. The general feeling is one of being out of control—at the mercy of the "system."

You want answers…information…state-of-the-art treatment. You want to be treated with respect. And you want your medical information kept confidential.

Knowing your rights as a patient can protect you from abuse by the system.

GETTING COMPLETE INFORMATION FROM YOUR DOCTOR

In the past, many doctors viewed patients as unable to understand diagnoses, and so shared little about patient conditions and treatment alternatives (beyond what was required to obtain "informed consent").

Today, patients are savvier and demand more from their doctors. *How to proceed…*

•**Demand the time that is needed** to tell your doctor about all your symptoms. And—demand the time to hear his/her explanation of possible diagnoses and courses of treatment.

Helpful: Write down your symptoms so that you don't overlook them during the conversation with your doctor.

If you don't think your doctor is listening to you or giving you the time you need—*then speak up!*

•**Get a second opinion** before surgery or other invasive treatment. Most insurers are willing to pay for this—since a second opinion may indicate a less drastic and less costly course of action.

•**Do your own research.** While you aren't licensed to practice medicine (even on yourself), there's plenty of easy-to-understand medical information available on the Internet (try *www.ivillage.com* and *www.seekwellness.com*). Also check InteliHealth at *www.intelihealth.com*. Of course, don't rely solely on any information you find. Discuss it with your doctor.

PATIENT BILL OF RIGHTS

Most hospitals nationwide have adopted some or all of the 12 rights enumerated in the *Patient Bill of Rights,* which was approved by the American Hospital Association in 1992. *These rights include…*

•**Right to receive considerate and respectful care.**

•**Right to obtain relevant,** current and understandable information about diagnosis, treatment and prognosis from doctors and other caregivers. This includes disclosure of the financial implications of the alternatives presented.

•**Right to make decisions about the plan of care.** This includes the right to refuse a recommended treatment.

•**Right to have an advance medical directive**—a living will or a durable medical power of attorney. These documents permit you to express the kind of care you want and don't want.

•**Right to every consideration of privacy.** This extends not only to a patient's body during examination and treatment, but also to case discussions.

•**Right to expect confidentiality** for all communications and records pertaining to treatment.

•**Right to review records** pertaining to personal medical care. This includes the right to have such information explained.

•**Right to expect a reasonable response** from a hospital to a request for appropriate and medically indicated care. That may require transfer to another medical facility.

•**Right to be informed about business relationships among the hospital,** doctors and others that may influence a patient's treatment and care.

Example: The urologist owns an interest in the lithotripsy center, where kidney stones are sonically blasted. The urologist will be inclined to send you there even though there may be alternative treatments.

•**Right to consent or decline to participate in clinical studies** of an ailment that you suffer from.

•**Right to expect reasonable continuity of care.** You don't want a different doctor every other day.

•**Right to be informed of hospital policies and practices**—such as how to resolve billing disputes.

WINDOW DRESSING?

These rights sound great, but they're only "window dressing." Hospitals that say they support these rights might not. *Instead…*

•**Doctors may not adequately inform patients** of a prescribed drug's side effects.

•**Hospitals may not prepare itemized bills** when patients are discharged.

•**Hospitals may not even have a doctor** in the emergency room 24 hours a day.

Reality: No one else will be looking out for your rights.

If you're a patient and you believe that your rights have been or are being violated, you can take action.

Ask to speak with the hospital's patient advocate, a person employed by the hospital to be a go-between for patients and the hospital's administration.

You will find the name and number of the patient advocate (sometimes called a patient representative) on your hospital admission papers or posted in your hospital room.

Vocal objections to treatment you've received —or failed to receive—may be necessary. Don't hesitate to speak up.

REVIEW YOUR MEDICAL RECORDS

Review your medical records to ensure that there are no mistakes that could produce problems for you down the line.

The best course of action: Ask your doctor for a copy of your records. About half the states have statutes that give you the right to review your records. However, even in states without such statutes, you still have this right. Hospitals that have adopted the *Patient Bill of Rights* are supposed to provide your records upon request.

Note: Federal law ensures that nursing home residents in Medicare and Medicaid facilities can gain access to their records. Similar protection is provided to patients in federal facilities such as Veterans' Administration hospitals.

More from Charles B. Inlander...

How to Keep Your Medical Information Private

The medical privacy form is the long-awaited result of the *Health Insurance Portability and Accountability Act of 1996* (HIPAA), intended to protect privacy, not take it away (*www.hhs.gov/ocr/hipaa*).

Here are some examples of medical privacy problems....

•**Drug companies** obtaining patients' names for marketing purposes.

•**Insurers** telling employers about employees' health problems.

•**Embarrassing messages** concerning diagnoses or other confidential matters left on patients' answering machines.

•**Medical information** given to the media without the patient's consent.

•**Names of organ donors** released to the organ recipients without their consent.

The rules went into effect on April 14, 2003. Now, most health-care providers, health insurers and others who have access to your records are required to send you an explanation of how they use and disclose your medical information. Small health plans (those with annual receipts of no more than $5 million) had an extra year to comply.

Released information is limited to the minimum amount needed for the purpose of the disclosure. For example, physicians may send an insurer information about injuries from an accident—not the patient's entire medical file.

John Featherman, security consultant, suggests that you never sign blanket waivers. And, review privacy notices before receiving services. You can change them to limit information released to the specific date, doctor and condition. Patients have the right to ask for even more privacy restrictions. *Some examples...*

•**Requesting that all mail from the doctor** be sent to your address of choice.

•**If hospitalized,** requesting that your name, general condition, etc. not be included in the patient directory.

•**Seeing a copy of your file** before it is sent to a third party. Make sure it contains only relevant information.

A health-care provider does not have to agree to your add-on requests—but it must abide by any agreement that it makes with you.

Other newly mandated rights...

•**You may inspect and copy your medical records**—and request corrections to errors that you find. You can't demand them.

•**You may request a listing of what medical information has been sent out about you**—and to whom.

Lest you feel too safe, Mr. Featherman explains that many entities are exempt from the rules—law enforcement agencies, life insurance companies, auto insurers whose plans include health benefits, workers' compensation providers, agencies that deliver Social Security and welfare benefits, Internet self-help sites, cholesterol screeners at shopping centers or in other public places.

Also from Charles B. Inlander...

Don't Become a Victim of Medical Error

While doctors are facing a crisis surrounding the soaring cost of medical malpractice insurance, we medical consumers are facing a crisis of our own. The number of medical errors is on the rise, and despite a great deal of talk among medical experts, little progress has been made in reversing that trend.

Although most people think of medical errors as occurring in hospitals, they're just as common *outside* this setting. About four out of every 250 prescriptions filled at local pharmacies contain a mistake. That comes to 52 million erroneously filled prescriptions per year! Nonhospital-affiliated surgical centers are also a hotbed of errors and are rarely inspected by state governments or accrediting organizations.

I've always advised of the importance of getting second opinions and carefully checking out your doctor and hospital. *Additional advice to help you...*

•**Check your medications.** About 20% of all hospitalizations are related to pharmacy errors or reactions to medication. When your doctor prescribes a pill, ask him/her to give you a sample or show you a picture from a book, such as the *Physicians' Desk Reference.* Check out markings, size and color. If you get a sample, take it with you to the pharmacy and compare it with the drug that is dispensed to you. Anytime you fill or refill a prescription, ask the pharmacist (not the pharmacy tech) to review the product and usage with you. Ask him to check the medication again and to explain the best way to use it and any warnings. He is required by law to do so if you ask.

•**Make sure your doctor communicates.** Studies show the number-one reason malpractice suits are filed is that the physician fails to communicate the risks and options associated with a treatment and his experience performing it. Several years ago, I assisted a woman whose surgeon had recommended a specific treatment for cancer. When she started to ask questions, he said, "I'm an expert at this. I'm telling you

what you need." She acquiesced and did not question him further. The procedure was not only unsuccessful, but also caused her serious internal injury. She later found out the doctor had never performed the surgery before but had not told her. Afterward, she sued him and won. If your doctor dodges your questions or seems in a hurry to get out of the examining room, beat him to the door.

•**Use hospital-affiliated outpatient surgical centers.** While there is still a chance for error, the physicians at such surgical centers must have privileges at the hospital with which the center is affiliated, and personnel are usually hospital employees. Hospitals typically enforce stricter standards for their staffs than nonaffiliated centers. These centers are also accredited by the same agency that accredits hospitals.

By doing your homework and asking the right questions, you can greatly reduce your chances of being affected by a medical error.

How to Avoid Becoming a Medical-Error Statistic

Timothy McCall, MD, internist, medical editor of *Yoga Journal* and author of *Examining Your Doctor* (Citadel Press) and *Yoga as Medicine* (Bantam). *www.drmccall.com.*

Medical errors are frequently in the news. According to the Institute of Medicine (IOM), mistakes by doctors and other health-care workers kill up to 98,000 Americans each year. That's more than twice as many deaths as are caused by breast cancer.

The IOM report focuses on what doctors and health-care institutions can do to reduce the error rate, but there's a lot patients can do, too.

•**Surgical errors.** These account for about half of all medical mistakes. I'm talking about everything from accidentally nicking a vital organ or failing to monitor anesthesia properly to amputating the wrong leg. Fearing that the doctor will do the right procedure on the wrong side of the body, some surgical patients are using markers to indicate the correct surgical site right on their bodies. Even some surgeons have started to do it.

What's far more important is to focus on the surgeon's credentials. Studies show that patients are safer in the hands of a surgeon who does the particular operation frequently. There's no magic number, but I'd certainly prefer a surgeon who had done a procedure hundreds of times over one who had done it 10 times. And be sure to get a second opinion for any elective operation—to make sure you truly need it.

It's also smart to consider the hospital where the surgery will be done. You want an institution that employs a lot of registered nurses (RNs)—as opposed to nurse's aides, who may lack adequate training. It's impossible to give an exact number of nurses to look for, but the hospital you pick should assign no more than a few postsurgical patients to each RN. Given rising cost-cutting pressures, it's now commonplace for hospitals to assign a dozen or more patients to each RN. Having family members stay with you in the hospital can also help ensure that you get the care you need.

•**Drug errors.** This category encompasses everything from giving the wrong medication or dose to forgetting to check for allergies. Because one doctor may not realize what another is prescribing, I recommend bringing a list of all your medications—or a bag containing the bottles—to each visit. Be sure to include vitamins and other over-the-counter pills. These can interact dangerously with some foods, prescribed drugs—and with each other.

Use common sense. If a pill looks different than usual, alert your doctor, nurse or the pharmacist. If you develop new symptoms after starting to take a medication, call promptly to ask whether they might be caused by the medication. Never leave the doctor's office until you know *exactly* what you're being given and why, how to take it and what side effects to watch out for.

•**Missed or delayed diagnoses of cancer or another life-threatening condition.** If you don't respond to treatment or have worrisome symptoms your doctor can't explain, consider getting a second opinion. You might have another pathologist review a biopsy specimen or another radiologist read a questionable mammogram, for example.

•**Sloppy practice.** In the rushed world of modern medicine, doctors sometimes forget to wash their hands or follow up on an abnormal X-ray. A doctor who's too busy to keep up with the medical literature may be unaware of a new life-saving treatment for your condition.

When it comes to countering doctors' sloppiness, there's no substitute for paying attention and being politely assertive. Scrutinize the quality of your physician's care. Switch if you're not satisfied. Good doctors shouldn't feel threatened by patients who take an active role in their care. They should welcome it, because two heads really are better than one.

More from Timothy McCall...

Your Responsibilities for Your Health

I frequently write about what doctors should —and shouldn't—be doing. But to ensure first-rate medical care, patients need to do their part, too. *Here's what I suggest...*

•**Know your medical history.** One patient I was seeing for the first time, a high-powered civil engineer, was able to identify the blood pressure medication he'd been taking for several years only as "a little pink pill." That made my job tougher.

I suggest that you keep a record of all major diagnoses. Be sure to include medical terminology *and* what it means in plain English. The record should also include the dates and descriptions of all operations you've had, results of diagnostic tests, any allergies and all medications you take.

•**Prepare for your visits.** Before your appointment, prepare a list of questions you have about your condition—and problems you'd like the doctor to address. The doctor's time is limited, so try to focus on the matters of greatest concern.

•**Don't let embarrassment get in the way.** If you are drinking 12 cups of coffee a day, having sex problems or bowel trouble or seeing an alternative healer, tell your doctor. Don't let embarrassment stop you.

If you'd like certain information to be kept out of your medical record, ask if the doctor will agree not to write it down.

●**Be honest.** If you haven't been taking a medication the doctor has prescribed, tell him/her. Maybe the doctor didn't realize your concern about the cost of the drug or its side effects. Similarly, tell the doctor if you have no intention of filling a prescription, giving up cigarettes or showing up for a scheduled test. If your doctor knows precisely what you are—and are not—willing to do, you may be able to reach a mutually satisfactory solution.

●**Get to the point.** Try not to have a hidden agenda for your visit. It's best to reveal your major concerns as early as possible during the visit. Many patients waste precious minutes on trivial matters, only to spring their real concern at the last minute. This makes it virtually impossible for the doctor to address the problem fully.

●**Describe your symptoms.** Doctors are more interested in hearing a description of your symptoms than your theory about what might be causing them. If you've been having abdominal pain, for example, you might say to the doctor, "I've been having gnawing abdominal pain." Do not say, "My ulcer's been acting up." After all, not all abdominal pain is caused by ulcers.

The more detailed your description of your condition, the easier it will be for your doctor to sort things out.

●**Put yourself in your doctor's shoes.** If you're unable to make it to a scheduled appointment, call your doctor to cancel as soon as possible.

Don't call your doctor in the middle of the night for a problem you've had for weeks, unless it has suddenly become much worse. If a doctor's fee is reasonable, pay it. If you can't afford to pay right away, ask the doctor if you can make arrangements to pay in installments. Always try to be polite and respectful—even if you need to assert yourself.

Especially in this age of managed care, it's important to keep your doctor on your side. And you'll be a lot more likely to get your needs met if you consider your doctor's needs, too.

Also from Timothy McCall...

How to Get the Most Out of Your Annual Physical

In recent years, experts have begun to question the value of the routine annual checkup. Since most health plans allow a free or low-cost physical each year, you may wonder if it's worthwhile to get one. I believe it is—although perhaps not for the reasons you might suspect.

Many elements of the typical exam—blood counts, EKGs and other routine tests—provide little useful information in people who are in apparent good health. The same applies to listening to the heart, checking the reflexes and most other parts of the traditional exam.

What is of value is a detailed discussion of diet, exercise and other aspects of preventive medicine. Ideally, doctors would discuss these matters with their patients during routine office visits. Yet with the speedup in medical visits, many doctors now find that they lack the time. So an annual exam may afford you and your doctor the only opportunity to review the overall state of your health. *Here's how to get the most out of it...*

●**Discuss each of your major medical problems.** Ask your doctor whether there have been any significant advances in treatment during the past year. Is there anything more you could be doing to boost your health? Any new specialists you could be seeing? New drugs you should be taking?

●**Review your medications.** Bring all your medications to the doctor's office, along with a typewritten list of these drugs. Include over-the-counter drugs and dietary supplements as well as prescription medications. That way, you can be sure that your doctor knows exactly what you're taking.

Since every drug carries risks, it's a good idea to ask if you really need to be taking each one. Are there safer alternatives to any of the drugs? Are there potentially dangerous interactions between any of the pills?

●**Get the few screening tests proven to work.** Like most doctors, I urge my patients to have their blood pressure checked at least once every other year. I also recommend checking total cholesterol and HDL cholesterol levels every few years.

Tests for colon cancer should include yearly checks for hidden blood in the stool and flexible sigmoidoscopy every three to five years after age 50. Colonoscopy, a more thorough examination, can be done less frequently.

I also side with the experts who say that women should have a Pap smear every one to three years, as well as an annual breast exam and, starting at age 50, mammograms.

Mammograms *before* age 50 are of uncertain value. So is the PSA test for prostate cancer. Some experts believe in these tests. Others suspect that they do more harm than good—for instance, by leading to unnecessary surgery. Carefully review the pros and cons of each test with your doctor.

•**Review your immunizations.** Parents tend to be good about remembering to have their kids vaccinated—but forget about themselves. Doctors, too, often neglect this vital issue. Studies show that most people at risk for hepatitis B, influenza and pneumonia have not had the protective vaccines. The result? More than 60,000 American adults die of vaccine-preventable diseases each year—compared with fewer than 1,000 children.

Your doctor needs to devote enough time to the exam to do it right. How long is long enough? That depends on your age and overall health. Expect 20 to 30 minutes if you're young and healthy—twice that if you're not.

The longer time usually allotted for annual exams should allow you and your doctor to get to know each other a bit better. And that could be the most valuable part of all.

Timothy McCall on Second Opinions…

What to Do When Your Doctors Disagree

Medical experts say it's always prudent to get a second opinion before elective surgery. I agree. But I also recommend getting a second opinion if your doctor seems unable to diagnose your problem, if you fail to get better, as anticipated, or if you've just been diagnosed with cancer or another life-threatening ailment.

What do you do when the doctors' opinions differ? Just because doctors disagree does not necessarily mean one of them is wrong. There are reasonable differences of opinion, and often more than one approach will work. Sometimes we simply don't have enough scientific data to say which treatment is best.

Here's what I suggest to help you resolve conflicting advice…

•**Do your own research.** Learn as much as you can about your diagnosis and the recommended treatments. The more you know, the smarter your questions to the doctors will be—and the better your ability to evaluate what each doctor says.

•**Think things through.** Don't feel pressured to make your decision right away. Except in true emergency situations, a couple of weeks' delay in making a decision is unlikely to cause any problems. Some people go along with treatments or tests they really don't want because they sense that their physician favors it.

I think it's good to get out of the doctor's office, read about your problem, talk over the options with your loved ones—and then make your decision.

•**Ask for explanations.** Find out each doctor's reasons for recommending a particular test or treatment. If you can understand the rationale for each doctor's recommendation—and not just the recommendation itself—you'll be in a better position to evaluate it.

Are there scientific data behind the advice? Is the advice based on personal experience? What would happen if you declined to do what is recommended? Would a delay be harmful?

•**Ask each doctor to evaluate the other's advice.** One doctor may spot weaknesses in another doctor's reasoning that might not have occurred to you—or to the other doctor. If possible, get each doctor's advice in writing and show it to the other.

•**Follow the money.** In sorting out a doctor's recommendations, it pays to know where the financial incentives lie. It stands to reason—and studies confirm—that doctors are more likely to recommend treatments or tests when

109

they stand to profit by doing so. That's the case with most traditional fee-for-service health insurance. Under managed care, doctors are less likely to recommend costly interventions—even if they might benefit you.

•**Get another opinion.** If you think it's necessary, don't hesitate to get a third or even a fourth opinion. It's usually a good idea to consult doctors who are unaffiliated with either of the other doctors.

Given the financial incentives in HMOs against providing expensive services, it's often a good idea to get an opinion from a doctor who is outside of the plan—even if you have to pay a bit extra.

•**Go with your gut.** Ultimately, many medical questions have no right answers. Since you're the one who will have to deal with the consequences of any medical decision, it ought to be your values—and not those of your doctors—that determine which path you'll follow.

How to Make Sure Your Mammogram Is Read Accurately

Alexander J. Swistel, MD, director, Weill Cornell Breast Center, and chief of surgery, New York-Presbyterian Hospital/Weill Medical College of Cornell University, both in New York City. Dr. Swistel is widely recognized as a pioneer in the improvement of breast cancer care. He is also past president of the Metropolitan Breast Cancer Group, the oldest and largest group of breast cancer specialists in the US.

Mammograms are one of the best diagnostic tools to detect breast tumors. So it's important to make sure they are done effectively. There are several questions you need to ask to find the right facility for your mammogram. *They are...*

•**Has the office been accredited by the American College of Radiology?** If the facility is accredited, then the doctors must maintain accurate files on you, especially if cancer is suspected. The staff also is more likely to be well trained.

•**How many mammograms are performed there yearly?** Volume makes a difference. A facility that performs 50 mammograms a year is not going to be as competent as one that does 500.

•**Is the mammogram read at the facility?** Some places will send mammograms out to be read. The outside reader may not have pertinent clinical information or old films for comparison. If that's the case, the facility probably is not the best choice.

•**Is the mammogram read more than once?** A recent practice has developed called double-reading. One physician reads the mammogram, and then a second doctor reads it as well to guard against human error.

•**How old is the equipment?** Newer machines produce better images.

•**Can the facility perform biopsies and sonograms on-site?** This is an indication of a top facility. If there is any question regarding a reading, get a second opinion. Areas that might look cancerous can be benign—and vice versa. A second screening at a different facility may give the answer.

Biopsy Alert

Susan L. Blum, former editor, *Bottom Line/Health,* 281 Tresser Blvd., Stamford, CT 06901.

When pathologists at Johns Hopkins University School of Medicine took a second look at more than 6,000 biopsy samples previously analyzed at other institutions, the results were shocking. Almost two out of every 100 analyses were erroneous. Nearly 25% of the misdiagnoses mistook a benign growth for a cancer.

Scary: Six percent gave patients an "all clear" when in fact they had cancer.

As a result of these errors, some healthy patients underwent grueling cancer treatment —unnecessarily. And some cancer patients failed to receive needed treatment.

Why so many potentially life-threatening errors? Jonathan L. Epstein, MD, professor of pathology at Johns Hopkins and lead author of the study, said that the trend is the ironic result of medical progress.

New, less invasive techniques such as needle biopsies are easier on patients, since they remove less tissue. But that gives pathologists smaller samples to examine—which means signs of disease may be missed.

Also, earlier biopsies are now the norm, thanks to cancer screening procedures like blood tests and mammograms. But early biopsies are more likely to be ambiguous...and the potential for "false positives" greater.

To protect yourself, Epstein advises patients to have biopsy samples double-checked by a pathologist specializing in the tissue type under scrutiny.

If you've had a prostate biopsy, for instance, find a prostate cancer expert. Ask your doctor for help in locating the right specialist. The sample can be sent anywhere in the country. A second opinion will take about a week and approximate cost ranges between $125 to $175. But the answer may be priceless.

What You Need to Know About All the Scary Errors in Medical Tests

Richard N. Podell, MD, MPH, medical director, the Podell and King Medical Practice, Somerset and Springfield, NJ, *www.drpodell.org*. Dr. Podell is one of several doctors nationwide who are conducting studies on Ampligen, an experimental drug for chronic fatigue syndrome. He is author of several books, including *Doctor, Why Am I So Tired?* (Fawcett).

No medical test is perfect. Even when it is performed by a skilled technician and analyzed at a reliable laboratory, what you do *before* the test can significantly alter the test results.

No news: At least 2% of test paperwork gets lost and never reaches the doctor's attention.

So—don't assume all is well if your doctor doesn't contact you. Always call for results a week or two after having a test.

Here are practical guidelines for the most common tests to ensure your results are as accurate as possible...

BIOPSY

Biopsy is vital for people with suspicious results on preliminary cancer tests. It is also used to diagnose skin ailments.

Procedure: Suspect tissue is removed with a "punch" biopsy device or with a scalpel...then analyzed under a microscope. Depending on the location of the suspicious tissue, you may require sedation and/or stitches.

Accuracy: Results can be ambiguous. A pathologist's judgment and experience are critical for an accurate assessment.

Results: One to two weeks.

BONE DENSITY

Women should have this painless test for osteoporosis within one year of menopause... and every 12 to 24 months thereafter. Appropriate frequency varies by individual. Have the test earlier if there is a family history of the disease or if you've ever had a bone fracture...especially an "easy break" that occurs in low-trauma situations—for example, falling on grass and breaking your wrist.

Men should have the test if they've ever suffered a severe fracture or have a family history of osteoporosis.

Patients taking corticosteroids, such as those for asthma, lupus or rheumatoid arthritis, should be tested at the start of therapy and every one to two years thereafter (frequency varies by individual). These drugs make bones brittle.

Procedure: You lie fully clothed on a special table or stick your heel, wrist or finger into an ultrasound or *dual-energy X-ray absorptiometry* (DEXA) machine.

Preparation: None is necessary.

Accuracy: Varies depending on the site measured and the test used. DEXA is the most accurate test, especially when performed at the spine or hip.

Results: One week.

CHOLESTEROL TEST

Every five years, men and women over age 20 should have a blood test to measure their total HDL ("good") and LDL ("bad") cholesterol levels. This test is especially important for women after menopause, when LDL tends to rise and HDL tends to fall. If the level of LDL cholesterol is elevated, the test should be performed more often.

Procedure: Blood is taken from your arm.

Preparation: None is necessary prior to total and HDL tests. Before LDL and triglyceride testing, fast for 12 hours and don't drink alcohol for three days.

Accuracy: Very precise if the guidelines are followed.

Results: Within two days.

COLON CANCER TESTS

Both men and women should have an annual test for hidden (occult) blood in the stool starting at age 50—earlier if there is a family history of colon cancer. Also see your doctor for a rectal exam every year beginning at age 40.

Accuracy: There are many benign causes of blood in the stool, such as hemorrhoids and ingestion of certain foods or medications. False-positive results can occur.

Better: Have a sigmoidoscopy every three years or a colonoscopy every five years. These tests are far more accurate than a stool test.

Procedure: For the stool test, your doctor will likely give you a kit to obtain a stool sample. You'll collect the sample at home and then bring it to the office or lab for evaluation.

Colonoscopy is performed at a hospital or an outpatient medical facility. Sigmoidoscopy is usually done in the doctor's office.

For either procedure, you'll lie on your side on a table and the doctor will insert a scope into your anus.

Sedation—either general or local—is needed for colonoscopy, which examines the entire length of the colon.

There is usually mild to moderate discomfort—fairly brief—during sigmoidoscopy, which only examines the lower third of the colon. Anesthesia is usually not given.

Preparation: Four days prior to having a stool test, don't take aspirin, ibuprofen or vitamin C supplements. Don't eat red meat for three days before the test.

Stay on a liquid diet for 24 to 36 hours before a colonoscopy or sigmoidoscopy. You will also have to take medications or perform enemas the night before the test to clean out the bowel.

Results: Three days for the stool test... immediately for the other tests.

MAGNETIC RESONANCE IMAGING (MRI)

MRIs are important for those who may have disorders of the brain, spinal cord, other organs or blood vessels.

Procedure: You lie inside a narrow tube for 30 minutes or more. During this time, you'll hear the the MRI scanner make loud clicking noises.

Preparation: If you are claustrophobic, request a sedative prior to the procedure...or ask your doctor about having an open MRI, which has a less-confining tube but is not quite as sensitive.

Accuracy: The clarity of the image varies depending on the body site scanned. MRIs require the radiologist's interpretation and judgment.

Results: Within one week.

MAMMOGRAM

All women age 40 and over should undergo annual mammography and clinical breast exams. Schedule the mammogram during the two weeks after your menstrual period.

Reasons: Just prior to and during menstruation, breasts may be tender, making the test more painful. Breast tissue is also more dense at this time, making it harder to spot abnormalities.

Procedure: A technician positions your breast on a plate, compresses it and takes X-ray images.

Preparation: Don't wear any aluminum-containing antiperspirant on the day of the test. It can produce specks on the X-ray that look like abnormalities. Be sure to shower if you wore antiperspirant the day before.

Accuracy: Approximately 10% to 15% of breast cancers are missed by mammograms—

but most of these may be detected on physical exam by a doctor or during self-examination. Almost any mass that is found will require further evaluation, often a biopsy.

Results: Federal guidelines require that negative results be mailed to patients within two weeks of the test. Suspicious or positive results must be conveyed even more quickly.

PAP SMEAR

All women age 18 and over should have an annual Pap smear to screen for cervical cancer. The risk of this cancer is greatly increased for women with multiple partners or who became sexually active at a young age. Tests can be performed anytime except during a menstrual period.

Procedure: You sit on an examining table and place your feet in stirrups at the end of the table. The doctor inserts a speculum into the vagina to prop it open. He/she inserts either a long cotton swab or a brush into the vagina to scrape off a few cells from your cervix. These cells are smeared on a slide for analysis. The test may be mildly uncomfortable.

Preparation: Don't douche, have sex or use vaginal medication for 24 hours before the test.

Accuracy: After a normal test, the chance of developing cervical cancer within the next three years is less than one in 20,000.

Important: A Pap smear detects only cervical cancer—not uterine or ovarian cancer. Endometrial biopsies to screen for uterine cancer are offered to women who have irregular vaginal bleeding or postmenopausal women on estrogen therapy. A pelvic ultrasound can be used to screen for ovarian cancer, as can a CA-125 blood test, but they are not routinely given.

Results: One to two weeks.

PROSTATE CANCER TESTS

All men over age 40 should have an annual rectal exam, in which the doctor feels for lumps or enlargement of the prostate.

All men over age 50 should have a *prostate-specific antigen* (PSA) blood test. Men with a family history of prostate cancer should begin testing at least five years before the age at which the relative developed cancer.

Procedure: Blood is drawn from your arm.

Preparation: Avoid sexual activity and rectal exams for 24 hours prior to the test. Either may falsely raise the PSA level.

Accuracy: At very high levels, it strongly suggests prostate cancer. Lesser elevations can be caused by either prostate enlargement or prostate cancer.

Results: Within two days.

STRESS TEST

This test is important for men and women with suspected or known heart disease, such as those with chest pain. It is also important for those with risk factors for heart disease, such as a family history of heart attack at a young age.

Procedure: Blood pressure and electrical heart activity are measured while you walk or run on a treadmill or pedal a stationary bike. The test detects whether blood flow to the heart is compromised.

Preparation: Wear gym shoes and comfortable clothing. Don't eat anything for six hours prior to the test.

Accuracy: Relatively high false-positive rate in people with a low risk of heart disease. It is much less useful to screen for heart disease in people who do not have symptoms or risk factors.

In those with symptoms, a stress test can provide an estimate of the risk of dying in the next five years. If you develop any discomfort during the test, tell your doctor promptly.

Results: Available immediately.

Do You Really Need That Diagnostic Test?

Lynne McTaggart, editor of the newsletter *What Doctors Don't Tell You,* 2 Salisbury Rd., London SW19 4E2. She is author of *What Doctors Don't Tell You* (Avon).

In the "good old days," medical diagnoses were made with little more than a stethoscope and good judgment. Now doctors have an array of high-tech tools that can scan and probe every inch of a patient's interior.

Used properly, this equipment saves lives. Too often, however, diagnostic tests are performed needlessly. That wastes patients' time and money...and can subject them to needless concern and even danger.

Examples: An X-ray involves exposure to cancer-causing radiation...and a misread angiogram can lead to unnecessary heart surgery.

Next time a doctor recommends diagnostic testing for you, ask these questions...

•**Do I really need this test?** Most doctors will automatically answer "yes." Follow up by asking whether there's a less risky alternative that can yield the same information.

Example: *Magnetic resonance imaging* (MRI) and *computed tomography* (CT) yield similar information. A CT scan involves radiation. An MRI scan does not.

Helpful: Ask what doctors did before the diagnostic test was developed. In many cases, older doctors know how to provide excellent care without being overly reliant on the latest technology and gadgetry.

•**What will you advise me to do if the test result is abnormal?** Consider the likely chain of events as far as possible. Try to find a way to cut the number of procedures you'll have to undergo.

Example 1: If an abnormal reading on one test means that another test will be needed, is it possible to have that second test performed right away?

Example 2: If an abnormal test result suggests a treatment that you find unacceptable, why have the test in the first place?

Many pregnant women undergo testing for *alpha-fetoprotein* (AFP), which can indicate Down syndrome or spina bifida. If you're unwilling to consider an abortion, getting tested may be pointless.

•**How reliable is this test?** Diagnostic tests sometimes indicate that you have a disease when you really don't (false positive)...or that you don't have a disease when you really do (false negative).

A test with a false-positive/false-negative rate in excess of 25% is so unreliable as to be of questionable value.

Example: The test for *prostate-specific antigen* (PSA)—an indicator of prostate cancer—has a false-negative rate of 40% and a false-positive rate of up to 75%.

Three out of every four men who have an abnormal PSA reading are subsequently shown via biopsy *not* to have prostate cancer.

•**What risks are involved with this test?** Ask how often people who undergo the test experience side effects and what kind. Decide whether the risks associated with being tested outweigh the risks of not being tested.

Example: One of every 1,000 cardiac angiography procedures—used to diagnose heart disease—results in stroke or heart attack. Ask your doctor what risks you face if you decline to get tested.

•**Is the equipment operator fully qualified?** If your doctor doesn't know, ask the manager of the testing facility—or the test operator.

Look for certificates detailing the operator's training. You want someone who has administered the test at least 50 times.

Especially important: The operator's track record for accuracy. His/her record should match the equipment's standard for accuracy (the rate of false positives/false negatives).

If the operator acknowledges having more or fewer inaccuracies than the standard, try to find out why.

A high number of inaccuracies may mean he isn't fully qualified. A low number suggests that his skill level is unusually high...or that he is being dishonest.

Helpful: When scheduling a test, ask to be one of the first three appointments on the operator's shift. This will help eliminate errors associated with end-of-shift exhaustion.

•**When was the equipment last calibrated?** There are different standards for each machine, but most equipment should be checked for safety and accuracy at least once a year.

If the most recent calibration occurred more than 12 months ago, discuss the calibration guidelines with the operator.

If you must have an X-ray: Make sure you will be getting the smallest possible dose of radiation.

Find out the typical radiation dose for your particular X-ray, then compare it with the dose you'll receive from the equipment to be used to test you.

Doses in excess of the standard mean that the machine is needlessly inefficient. Find another X-ray facility.

Important: Use lead shielding on body parts that aren't being X-rayed.

•Is it possible to make use of previous test results? Whenever possible, have your doctor rely on results from a previous test. That saves you time and money…and keeps you from being exposed to additional risk.

•If a family member of yours were in my shoes, would you urge him to have this test? This question forces the doctor to think on a different level. You shift from being just another workload case to being compared with a family member.

Watch for signs of ambivalence. If the doctor pauses or frowns when you pose this question, follow up with questions about what the concerns might be.

Don't be needlessly confrontational when probing for information. Calmly let your doctor know that you want to be fully informed about your options before making your decision regarding the diagnostic test.

Full-Body CT Scan Hype

E. Stephen Amis, MD, chairman of radiology, Albert Einstein College of Medicine and Montefiore Medical Center, Bronx, NY.

Full-body *computed tomography* (CT) scans, in which a symptom-free person gets scanned in an effort to detect early-stage cancer, heart disease or some other illness, have become increasingly popular.

Are full-body CT scans a good idea? The American College of Radiology, the American Cancer Society and the American Heart Association do not recommend them. *Here's what consumers should know…*

•There's no scientific evidence to support the use of full-body CT scans as a screening technique for people without symptoms. However, the targeted CT scans, such as chest scans to detect lung cancer in smokers and former smokers, are effective.

•Early-stage cancer can be missed. Although full-body CT scans examine the entire torso, from neck to pelvis, they are unlikely to detect small malignancies of the colon, breast or prostate.

Better: Colonoscopy, mammography or a *prostate-specific antigen* (PSA) test.

•Radiation doses are high. A full-body CT scan delivers up to 300 times the amount of radiation of a chest X-ray. Because radiation risks are cumulative, people who get full-body CT scans regularly increase their risk for radiation-induced cancer.

To learn more, visit the American College of Radiology's Web site at *www.acr.org.*

Best Home Medical Tests

Steven I. Gutman, MD, director, US Food and Drug Administration's Office of In Vitro Diagnostic Device Evaluation and Safety, Rockville, MD, *www.fda.gov.*

Home medical testing kits and devices sold at pharmacies and on the Internet allow anyone to conveniently test for illnesses and other medical conditions in the privacy of his/her own home.

Home-test manufacturers must prove to the US Food and Drug Administration (FDA) that their products are as accurate as the laboratory tests used by medical offices.

None of the tests requires a doctor's prescription, but they aren't substitutes for doctor visits. These tests are not covered by insurance.

Important: Carefully read the instructions that come with any test. Doing a test improperly—taking urine at the wrong time of day, for example—can invalidate the results.

Editor's note: Home medical tests are available at retail and on-line pharmacies and from such Web companies as *www.home-health testing.com* and *www.homeaccess.com*.

Some of the best home tests...

CHOLESTEROL

High cholesterol is a leading risk factor for stroke, heart disease and other cardiovascular conditions.

How the test works: Place some blood from a finger prick on a chemically treated strip. Cholesterol readings will appear on a thermometer-like scale in about 10 minutes. Some tests provide separate breakdowns for LDL ("bad") and HDL ("good") cholesterol levels. For this, you must send the blood sample to the manufacturer and then wait several weeks for the results.

Average cost: $20 to $25 for a package of two tests.

COLON CANCER

Fecal occult blood tests (FOBTs) can detect small, often invisible amounts of blood in the stool—an early sign of colon cancer.

How the test works: Traditional FOBTs require you to take stool samples at home, then bring them to a lab for analysis. A newer FOBT doesn't require stool samples. You drop a chemically treated tissue into the toilet after you've had a bowel movement. A color change indicates that blood is present. If so, you need additional tests, such as a colonoscopy, to check for cancerous or precancerous growths.

To ensure accuracy: You must repeat the test for three consecutive bowel movements. Do not take aspirin, *ibuprofen* or other nonsteroidal anti-inflammatory drugs for one week prior to testing. They may cause bleeding that can skew the results.

For three days prior to the test, avoid eating red meat and don't take vitamin C supplements in excess of 250 milligrams (mg) daily. Don't use this test if you have bleeding hemorrhoids or anal fissures.

Average cost: $24.95 per test kit.

DRUG USE

Parents who suspect their children of drug use may want to do a home test. Some tests check for a specific drug, such as marijuana. Broader tests detect multiple drugs—including cocaine and amphetamines.

How the test works: Some urine is dropped in a test cassette. Markings or color changes show if drugs are present. Marijuana generally can be detected within two to 30 days after use.

Important: About 5% of all urine drug tests result in false positives—the tests indicate that drugs are present when they're not. A positive home test should be confirmed with a laboratory drug test, such as a gas chromatography.

Average cost: $10 for one test.

Drugs can also be detected in hair clippings, which are sent to a laboratory for analysis.

Cost: About $65.

HIV

Privacy concerns prevent many people from getting tested for HIV, the virus that causes AIDS. Home-test manufacturers that analyze results follow strict confidentiality guidelines.

How the test works: Prick your finger, and apply the blood to special paper. Call a toll-free number to activate your personal code. Mail the blood sample and an anonymous personal identification number to a laboratory. To get the test results, you call a toll-free number and give your personal code.

Average cost: About $60 for one test.

MENOPAUSE

Women in their 40s and 50s commonly experience hot flashes, mood swings or other menopause-like symptoms. They can confirm that they are entering menopause with a simple home test.

How the test works: Place a few drops of urine on a test strip. The test measures levels of follicle-stimulating hormone and indicates whether a woman has entered menopause.

Home-test manufacturers advise women to repeat the test every six to 12 months when the symptoms of menopause occur.

Average cost: $30 for two tests.

OVULATION

The home-test kits have taken much of the guesswork out of when women may be able to get pregnant.

How the test works: Wet a test strip with urine to measure luteinizing hormone. Levels peak 24 to 36 hours prior to ovulation, which is the optimal time to try to conceive.

Average cost: $10 for five tests.

URINARY TRACT INFECTIONS (UTIs)

With a home test, you can confirm that you have an infection. Then your doctor may prescribe antibiotics for you over the phone.

How the test works: Wet a plastic strip with urine. Part of the strip will change color if a UTI is present.

These tests are recommended only for people who get recurrent UTIs and are familiar with the symptoms, including frequent and/or painful urination.

If you have not experienced a UTI before, you should see your doctor to rule out any other possible conditions, such as chlamydia or kidney stones.

Important: The test fails to detect infections about 30% of the time. See your doctor if the test is negative but you have symptoms.

Average cost: $25 for four tests.

What You Need to Know Before You Get a Blood Test

Hospital blood technicians routinely draw up to 10 times more blood than is needed to perform diagnostic tests. Blood draws can significantly reduce a patient's blood volume, causing anemia or other health problems.

A generation ago, diagnostic equipment required large volumes of blood for testing. But today's equipment is so sophisticated that only tiny samples are needed. Patients should request minimal blood draws.

Jocelyn M. Hicks, PhD, past chair, department of laboratory medicine, Children's National Medical Center, Washington, DC.

These Genetic Tests Could Save Your Life

Aubrey Milunsky, MD, founding director, Center for Human Genetics, Boston University School of Medicine. He is author of *Your Genetic Destiny: Know Your Genes, Secure Your Health, Save Your Life* (Perseus).

Genes influence much more than appearance and personality. More than 8,600 disorders and traits have been traced to specific genes, and many more are known to involve *several* genes.

But heredity doesn't have to be your destiny. Understanding your genetic makeup will give you a weapon to protect your health. It may even save your life.

Here's what you should know about common hereditary illnesses…

HEMOCHROMATOSIS

One person in 200 has two copies of the defective gene that causes *hemochromatosis*— a condition in which the body stores excessive iron, resulting in potentially fatal damage to the heart, liver and pancreas.

Consider DNA testing if: You experience persistent malaise and joint aches…and a close family member (parent, sibling, aunt, uncle, first cousin, grandparent) suffers from or died of heart failure, diabetes or unexplained cirrhosis of the liver. In advanced stages of hemochromatosis, distinct skin pigmentation appears —you look as if you have a tan even though you haven't been out in the sun.

If the test is positive: Your physician will arrange for you to "donate" a pint of blood once a week for three months…then once every three months. This keeps blood iron levels in check.

PULMONARY EMBOLISM

About 3% to 5% of Caucasians carry defective genes for the blood component factor V Leiden. About 2% carry a prothrombin gene mutation. These put individuals at risk for sudden death from pulmonary embolism (a blood clot in the lung).

Consider DNA testing if: You or a member of your family has suffered either *deep vein* *thrombosis* (a blood clot in the thigh or calf) or a *pulmonary embolism* (a clot in the lung) before age 50.

If the test is positive: Women should avoid oral contraceptives. These increase clotting risk. Anyone, male or female, should alert his/her doctor if he/she will be immobile for a long period of time, such as after surgery—or even on a long plane or car trip.

BREAST CANCER/OVARIAN CANCER

Five to 10 percent of breast cancers are inherited—most through mutations in two specific genes, *BRCA1* and *BRCA2*. A woman who has inherited one of these two genes has an 85% risk of developing breast cancer in her lifetime—and a 40% to 65% risk of developing ovarian cancer.

Consider DNA testing if: Two or more close relatives had breast or ovarian cancer ...or one relative had cancer in both breasts.

If the test is positive: Surgical removal of both breasts is an option. This does not eliminate cancer risk—some susceptible tissue is left behind—but reduces it to less than 10%. Removal of both ovaries is also an option.

If you opt against surgery: Discuss with your doctor how to watch for early signs of breast and ovarian cancers. He may recommend that you have regular mammograms, ultrasounds, blood tests, etc.

Important: Sons of women with breast cancer who inherit a breast cancer gene mutation are also vulnerable. The half who inherit the mutant gene have a greater risk for prostate, intestinal, pancreatic or even breast cancer. Ask your doctor about how to maintain close surveillance of these organs to catch cancer early.

COLON CANCER

One to three percent of colon cancers are caused by *familial polyposis.* In this condition, hundreds—possibly thousands—of growths develop along the intestinal lining. Some of these turn malignant. There are other hereditary forms of colon cancer, too.

Consider DNA testing if: Two members of your family have had colon cancer...or one family member had familial polyposis.

If the test is positive: Removal of the colon is an option. Otherwise, keep close watch by having an annual colonoscopy.

POLYCYSTIC KIDNEY DISEASE

One person in 1,000 has this illness, which causes multiple cysts in the kidneys and leads to hypertension and kidney failure. It also raises the risk of *cerebral aneurysm*—a brain artery dilation (bubble) that is prone to rupture.

Consider DNA testing if: A close relative has the condition.

If the test is positive: Consult your doctor about kidney transplants—you may need one eventually—and about CAT or MRI scans of the brain.

FAMILIAL MEDITERRANEAN FEVER

This disease is characterized by progressive deposits of *amyloid,* a waxy substance, in the kidneys, leading to kidney failure and, if left untreated, death.

Consider DNA testing if: You are of Armenian, Turkish, Arab or Sephardic Jewish descent...and you suffer from intermittent fever, abdominal and chest pain, arthritis or other symptoms that doctors cannot explain.

If the test is positive: Treatment with *colchicine,* an alkaloid medication in tablet form, will prevent serious kidney damage.

EMPHYSEMA

People who do not possess the *alpha-1-antitrypsin* enzyme are prone to emphysema.

Consider DNA testing if: A close family member developed chronic lung disease, particularly if he also had cirrhosis of the liver.

If the test is positive: Avoid smoking as well as prolonged contact with any dust or industrial pollutants.

WHAT ELSE YOU SHOULD KNOW

If you think you have a familial disorder, ask your doctor if he recommends DNA testing. Think carefully about the decision and the treatment options. Be aware that most—but not all—states have legislation prohibiting the use of genetic information when being considered for life or health insurance or employment.

To find a clinical geneticist, call the department of genetics at a university medical center. Or contact the American College of Medical Genetics at 301-634-7127 or *www.acmg.net.*

Why You Must Know Your Family's Medical History

Christopher Friedrich, MD, PhD, associate professor of medical genetics, University of Mississippi Medical Center, Jackson. He is also a member of the working group on family history at the US Centers for Disease Control and Prevention Office of Genomics in Atlanta.

An accurate, up-to-date family medical history is one of the most important tools you have for safeguarding your health. It offers a road map to your own genetic strengths and weaknesses, pinpointing the ailments for which you need frequent screening tests and an aggressive prevention plan.

Christopher Friedrich, MD, PhD, talks about what you need to know about your family medical history, and what you should do with this information...

●**If I have a healthful lifestyle, do I still need to learn my family medical history?** Absolutely. Most diseases have an environmental *and* genetic component. For example, a high-fat diet and smoking may lead to coronary artery disease. But genetic factors help determine your vulnerability.

Likewise, your risk of developing lung cancer or emphysema depends on your smoking habits *and* on your genetic susceptibility to the effects of smoking.

Knowing your family medical history will allow you and your doctor to monitor your health for symptoms and alter your lifestyle so that you can drastically reduce your chances of developing these diseases.

Thousands of rare diseases, such as cystic fibrosis and hemophilia, are entirely hereditary. If one of these diseases runs in your family, you may want to consider genetic testing.

●**Isn't it my doctor's responsibility to ask about my family medical history?** Your doctor should ask about your family medical history during your first visit. However, completing this history is a cooperative effort, requiring your active input.

Your physician needs to know about any medical condition affecting your first-degree relatives—parents and siblings.

Tell your doctor if any first- or second-degree relative (grandparent, aunt or uncle) suffered from inherited diseases, such as sickle cell anemia...cystic fibrosis...hemophilia...Parkinson's disease...Marfan syndrome (a connective tissue disorder)...or muscular dystrophy.

Also tell your doctor if any of the following diseases are in your family: Alzheimer's, asthma/allergies, blood disorders, cancer, diabetes, epilepsy, eye conditions, heart disease, high blood pressure, kidney disease, mental illness, osteoporosis and stroke.

And indicate if there has been any substance abuse or smoking in your family.

●**What other things do I need to know about the medical conditions that have affected my relatives?** The age when a disease first strikes can be *extremely* important, because this may indicate your family's level of genetic vulnerability.

A heart attack, stroke, bypass surgery or angioplasty in a first-degree male relative under age 45 or in a female relative under age 55 may indicate strong genetic susceptibility.

The age when high blood pressure, diabetes or cancer strikes is also significant. The earlier these conditions show up, the more likely a genetic risk factor is involved.

●**Will my family medical history tell me anything other than possible lifestyle changes I should make?** Your family history can also indicate when screening is warranted to detect diseases in their early stages when they're most treatable. *For example...*

•If you have a first-degree relative with hypertension, you should get annual blood pressure checks starting at age 18.

•If you have a first-degree relative with heart disease or high cholesterol, you should start cholesterol testing in your mid-teens and continue on a regular schedule recommended by your doctor.

•If cancer of the breast, ovaries or colon has occurred in three or more relatives (or two relatives, including one under age 40), you should get mammograms (for breast cancer), CA-125 blood tests (for ovarian cancer) and colonoscopies (for colon cancer) beginning at age 40, or at the earliest age of diagnosis in the family, if under the age of 40.

•If you're male and your father, uncle or brother had prostate cancer, you should consider annual examinations and *prostate-specific antigen* (PSA) testing starting at age 45.

•If my family history suggests a specific genetic vulnerability, should I undergo genetic testing? Most genetic vulnerabilities have not yet been traced to specific gene mutations, so they can't be tested for. Even with diseases such as polycystic kidney disease and Marfan syndrome, which are linked to specific mutations, the case for testing isn't always clear.

In families with a history of breast cancer, which has been linked to two specific gene mutations (BRCA1 and BRCA2), testing is probably a good idea. If you turn out to have one or both mutations, then you can be extra vigilant with self-exams and mammograms.

One of the major advantages of genetic testing for cancer susceptibility is that it identifies those who may benefit from earlier and more frequent monitoring than is recommended for the general public. Testing will also identify those who did not inherit their family's mutation and do not need to undergo more intensive monitoring.

With inherited diseases, such as sickle cell anemia, it makes sense to test the extended family (aunts, uncles, cousins, nieces and nephews) as well as the immediate family to identify the carriers for the gene mutation (meaning they could pass the mutation to their own children).

Better Emergency Medical Care

Emergency medical care goes more smoothly when patients provide doctors with their medical histories.

What to do: In your wallet or purse, keep a brief, up-to-date account that includes your doctor's name and phone number...all medications you take...diagnoses and treatments...results of major diagnostic tests...list of drug allergies you have...and—if you have heart trouble—a copy of a recent electrocardiogram.

This information helps doctors pinpoint your problem rapidly. Parents should carry this information for their children—but children can carry their own, too.

Frank Rasler, MD, MPH, emergency room physician, Dekalb Medical Center, Atlanta.

Self-Defense Against Prescription Mistakes

To avoid prescription mistakes, take time at your doctor's office to write down the generic and brand names of the medicine and its purpose and proper dosage.

Also, remind your doctor and pharmacist of any drug allergies you have and other medicines you are taking—including any over-the-counter or herbal medicines and vitamins.

Check refills to be sure pills are the same color and size as before. Call in refills a day or two ahead so the pharmacist doesn't rush to fill them.

Finally, avoid ordering prescriptions on Monday—which tends to be pharmacists' busiest day.

Rosemary Soave, MD, associate professor of medicine, Weill Medical College of Cornell University, New York City.

Has Your Medication Been Switched?

Health insurers often switch patients to a different prescription drug based on the *drug formulary* (a listing of prescription drugs covered by an insurance company).

But, according to research, 22% of those patients who were switched to another prescription drug reported side effects from the new medication.

In addition, switching drugs can cost patients an average of $58.50 more in out-of-pocket expenses, including extra trips to their health care providers, additional medications and/or hospital visits.

Self-defense: If your health insurer changes your prescription based on a drug formulary, check with your doctor.

David Chess, MD, chairman and president, Project Patient Care, a nonprofit organization dedicated to improving patient care. *www.projectpatientcare.org*.

How to Shrink Your Medical Bills by 25% Or More

Sue Goldstein, host of *The Diva of Discounts,* a radio program on KAAM-AM 770, Dallas/Fort Worth. She maintains the Web site *www.biggerbetterbargains.com*.

The cost of medical care continues to climb. And even if you do have health insurance, it rarely covers everything. *But you can cut costs...*

NEGOTIATE A BETTER DEAL

More patients are negotiating with their doctors for reduced fees. If you would like to try, phone your physician *before* scheduling an appointment. Ask what you can do to lower your bill. Would there be a discount if you paid with cash...or scheduled your appointment for an off-peak time? What if you agreed to come in on short notice when the doctor had a cancellation? You could get 25% off your bill—possibly more.

You might even be able to barter for medical care if you have a skill or service that the medical professional needs. Are you a Web designer, landscaper, architect or accountant? Ask the physician if he/she is interested in trading services.

If a procedure is medically necessary but you have no insurance and money is tight, tell your doctor. Most physicians are willing to bend on price under these circumstances.

COSMETIC SURGERY SAVINGS

Cosmetic surgery is rarely covered by health insurance, so cosmetic surgeons are often open to negotiation. Some board-certified surgeons may offer significant discounts to patients who are flexible about scheduling.

About 13% of all scheduled cosmetic surgeries are postponed. This can leave doctors with open operating-room time. If you're ready to jump in when one of these gaps occurs, the doctor might discount his regular rate by as much as 15%.

Important: Ask the surgeon to show you his portfolio of patients' before-and-after pictures. Get at least three references. Also call your state's medical society—listed in the *Yellow Pages* under "Medical Associations"—to learn about disciplinary actions, license suspensions or other complaints.

GO TO A TEACHING HOSPITAL

Local teaching hospitals, dental schools and chiropractic schools often offer inexpensive medical care. Students lack the experience of older doctors, but they typically are well supervised. If they can't handle something, more experienced doctors are on hand to help. Contact local teaching hospitals or schools for more information.

Resource: The Association of American Medical Colleges (202-828-0400 or *www.aamc.org*).

DISCOUNT HEALTH CARE CLUBS

Discount health care clubs offer big savings on prescription drugs...doctor visits...even eyewear and hearing aids.

121

The best club I have found is Meds of America (800-388-8284 or *www.medsofamerica.com*). For about $10* a month, uninsured or under-insured people can purchase prescription medications at discounts of up to 85% off regular rates. Check the Web site to see if the drugs you need are among the more than 3,500 offered.

For approximately $30 a month, members have access to the discount pharmacy and also receive price breaks from medical providers. There are more than 275,000 physicians participating nationwide, offering savings of 30% to 50% on average...and over 15,000 dentists offering savings of up to 80%. Discounts do vary, so members should ask about prices before making their appointments.

There is also an average savings of up to 30% at a variety of neighborhood pharmacies for those who need prescriptions immediately or who would like to deal with a pharmacist face-to-face.

These discounts are available because the participating doctors, dentists and pharmacies want to build their businesses and don't want insurance company hassles.

FREE MEDICATIONS

Major pharmaceutical companies may provide drugs to certain people at no cost or at steep discounts. There are more than 1,100 drugs available through 78 pharmaceutical company programs.

To be eligible for these discounts, your insurance must not cover the prescription. You also must make enough money that you don't qualify for government health care programs—but not so much that the pharmaceutical company thinks you can afford to pay.

Income requirements vary from company to company, but people making less than $25,000 a year are generally eligible for most programs. Anyone with big prescription drug bills—$300 per month or more—who is making less than $50,000 annually may also qualify.

These programs are based on income, not assets. Even if you own a nice home, you still could qualify if you are retired or temporarily unemployed.

*All prices subject to change.

To find out if you are eligible and if the drug you need is covered, call the drug manufacturer.

You can also download a pamphlet, *Free and Low Cost Prescription Drugs, www.institute dc.org,* listing the drugs covered from the Cost Containment Research Institute, a public interest group.

FREE COUPONS

Many pharmaceutical companies run free, week- to month-long trial-offer programs for certain drugs. All that consumers need to do is clip a coupon from a magazine or download one from a Web site and have a doctor write a prescription. Rules vary, but in many cases, you can use the coupon even if it is not your first prescription for the medication.

Don't assume that these coupons are always good deals. The drugmaker might be offering the free trial because a competing drug—perhaps even a cheaper generic version of the drug—is coming to market. The drug company is banking that you won't want to go through the bother of switching medications. Always ask your doctor if there are cheaper or more effective alternatives.

To find out if a coupon is available for a particular drug, check the company's Web site.

DISCOUNTS ON ADJUSTABLE BEDS AND NONALLERGENIC MATTRESSES

For people with certain heart conditions or back problems, adjustable beds are medical necessities. For allergy sufferers, nonallergenic mattresses can be a must.

City Mattress Factory (800-834-2473) sells all types of mattresses and adjustable bed frames, typically for half the retail price of brand-name mattresses even after factoring in shipping.

Example: An adjustable double bed at City Mattress costs about $1,100, rather than the $2,000 you would pay for one that's advertised on television.

IF MONEY IS EXTREMELY TIGHT

If you have no insurance and require medical treatment, one option is to participate in a clinical trial. You receive free complete medical exams, free treatment and may even get paid for your trouble.

Downside: The treatment that you receive might not yet be proven effective—it could even be dangerous, although this is rare. Also, if you participate in a "blind" study, you might be given a placebo instead of the experimental drug.

If you are interested in participating in a clinical trial, contact Research Across America (972-241-1222 or *www.researchacrossamerica.com*)...or Radiant Research (425-468-6200 or *www.radiantresearch.com*).

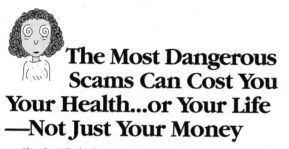

The Most Dangerous Scams Can Cost You Your Health...or Your Life —Not Just Your Money

Chuck Whitlock, noted scambuster, consumer advocate and speaker on television and radio. He is author of *Chuck Whitlock's Scam School* (Hungry Minds).

Medical fraud is the most dangerous fraud facing older Americans—and it is becoming more prevalent and more dangerous every day.

Experts say health-care fraud costs $100 billion to $250 billion every year. And it is aimed directly at seniors, who use more health-care services than any other group.

Caution: Financial fraud and consumer fraud can cost you only money. Medical fraud can cost you your health...even your life.

SELF-DEFENSE

To protect yourself from medical fraud, it's important first to recognize...

•**The risk is growing.** More medical scam artists are operating today than ever before—in response to the growing population of seniors who are exhibiting maladies of advancing age as well as being squeezed by rising medical costs incurred on fixed budgets.

•**Everyone is vulnerable.** Medical fraud is even more seductive to potential victims than financial fraud.

Financial fraud offers only easy money. Medical fraud offers longer life, better looks, more

potency, less weight, greater strength, the return of lost functions and—for the desperate—even life itself. And it often offers an easy way out, such as a pill to "absorb" body fat while eliminating the need for diet or exercise.

Everybody wants these things, so everybody is potentially vulnerable to the false promises of medical fraud.

BIGGEST DANGERS

There are specific areas you should be wary of. *Here's how to protect yourself...*

•**Over-the-counter (OTC) drugs and supplements.** The first problem here is that most consumers have no way of verifying the contents of what they buy. Sellers know this and can take advantage of it by selling something other than what is promised. *Examples...*

•Food supplements sold as "97% protein" have been found under chemical analysis to be as little as 4% protein.

•Items that are expensive to produce, such as vitamin E, occasionally are "shorted," so less is in the product than is promised on the label.

Self-defense: Buy only OTC items that carry the brand of major firms that have had the quality of their products confirmed by testing conducted by independent consumer groups.

Recommended: Drugs and supplements from major firms, such as Twinlab, Rexall and Nature Made.

A second problem is that clerks in stores that sell OTC products often act like doctors. Don't ask them to recommend a product— they don't have the medical training to do so.

Much better: Ask your doctor what to buy, then tell the sales clerk exactly what you want.

•**Prescription drugs.** The same problem exists here as with OTC drugs—the consumer has no way of verifying what's in the product.

Scam: Store pharmacists sometimes cut costs by reselling drugs acquired not from drug companies, but from wholesalers with aging stocks, or from scam artists who sell drugs they've bought cheaply using mass-produced phony prescriptions. As a result, the drugs you buy may be expired or adulterated.

Self-defense: Buy prescription drugs from reputable drugstore chains, such as Rite Aid and

Walgreens. These have centralized purchasing departments that assure product quality and eliminate opportunity for store-level fraud.

●**Bogus doctors.** The fact that a person claims to be a doctor doesn't mean he/she is one. A diploma mill in the Bahamas that was recently shut down was selling 1,100 medical diplomas *per month*.

In addition, it's very easy for a fake doctor to adopt the identity of a real physician, referring to the real doctor's education and certifications as his own.

When considering a new doctor, be sure to check with...

●Your state's Board of Medical Examiners to confirm that he is registered in your state. (A fake doctor won't be registered.)

●Your County Medical Association to see if any complaints or lawsuits have been filed against the doctor.

Smart idea: When looking for a new doctor, call your local hospital's head nurse in the area of specialization you are interested in, such as cardiology. Ask whom he/she would go to if he had a medical problem. Head nurses can be a fount of valuable information.

●**Bogus treatments.** If a doctor (or anybody else) offers a medical treatment that is too good to be true—or a price that is too good to be true—it probably is.

Self-defense: Get a second opinion. Go to another doctor and ask for an opinion about your case. Don't reveal to him/her what the first doctor said.

If, after getting the second opinion, you still feel uncertain, get a third opinion. If insurance won't pay for it, pay for it yourself. It's your health and life that are at stake.

●**Bogus medical equipment.** Scam artists make fortunes selling bogus medical equipment that is supposed to alleviate the maladies of advancing age. *Examples...*

●The ACCU-STOP 2000 was an earpiece worn at night to intercept hunger signals going to the brain and help the wearer lose weight. Medically worthless, it cost only 14 cents to produce but was sold for $39.95—and 3.5 million

were sold before the scam artist behind it fled the country.

●The medical alert device that had the unforgettable "I've fallen and I can't get up" TV advertisement was sold with a $7,200 two-year service contract, when the same device was available for $50 with free service from the phone company. The maker's salespeople made sales calls lasting up to five hours each to intimidate seniors into buying it, until the government shut them down.

Danger: At best, bogus medical devices are expensive and useless. At worst, relying on them could jeopardize your health and life.

Self-defense: Ask your doctor if the claims for a device are legitimate. If he says, "No," believe him. (If your doctor says, "Yes," but you have nagging doubts, get a second opinion.)

MORE DEFENSES

Purveyors of medical fraud often use very persuasive advertising. They can, because they are not constrained by the truth. *Self-defense...*

●**Never believe testimonials.** The vast majority are made by accomplices. But even "honest" ones can be bogus. *How...*

●It may be the placebo effect or power of suggestion that gave someone relief with a worthless treatment.

●Even those suffering the most serious diseases experience a small percentage of remissions due to unknown reasons. These may be touted as "miracle cures," and the patients may believe it, even though the remissions had nothing to do with the treatment.

Example: Those practitioners in Mexico who treat cancer with apricot seeds point to their patients who survive—and ignore the vastly larger number who die.

●**Don't talk to telemarketers.** When a telemarketer calls selling a medical product, just hang up. Seniors, especially, have been raised to be polite on the phone, and telemarketers use this to exploit them.

Exception: If you think an offer may be legitimate, get the name and address of the firm that is calling. Check it out and then call back if you wish.

More from Chuck Whitlock...

Internet Fraud Warning

Use the Internet—but beware of it, too. The Internet gives consumers access to great quantities of medical information.

Many top medical groups, such as the American Cancer Society, the American Diabetes Association and the National Kidney Foundation, have legitimate Web sites that can be extremely useful to consumers, as do most hospitals, medical schools and government organizations.

Caution: The Internet is unregulated and crawling with scam artists. So be sure you use it to obtain information only from recognized organizations with unquestionable integrity.

Beware of These Health Scams

Hal Morris, veteran Las Vegas–based consumer affairs journalist who writes about scams, schemes and rip-offs.

Don't let yourself become a prime target for slick characters with sticky fingers. *Here are a few of the latest and recycled rip-offs making the rounds...*

•**Dangerous drugs.** The US Food and Drug Administration (FDA) warns about the risks associated with drugs you might be tempted to buy from foreign countries. In some cases, drugs exported from Canada are actually manufactured in Mexico, Costa Rica, Taiwan, Pakistan, India or Thailand, among other nations.

Many drugs do not bear adequate labeling—sometimes it's in dual languages or there are no labels or instructions for safe use. In some cases, drugs are loose in plastic bags or simply wrapped in tissue paper. In addition, some foreign-source drugs have been found to be contaminated or lacking medicine entirely.

Self-defense: Scrutinize all prescription labels. Verify potential foreign sources for drugs with your pharmacist.

•**Wheeler dealers.** Have you been offered a free power wheelchair or other mobility product lately? Beware! The Centers for Medicare & Medicaid Services, which administers Medicare, has encountered scammers that exploit the Medicare power wheelchair benefit by offering free equipment to those who don't need it or never received it.

Their tempting offer: "We'll give you a free power wheelchair or other mobility product if you promise to use our doctors and agree to waive all of your coinsurance or Medicare Part B deductibles."

Scammers get money by inflating billings to Medicare, charging for equipment and supplies not delivered and falsifying documents to qualify beneficiaries for wheelchairs and other equipment that they often do not need. Very few actually receive power wheelchairs.

Self-defense: Review any supplier's recommendations with your personal doctor, who can best determine your needs. With questions, call the Medicare hotline at 800-633-4227 or visit *www.medicare.gov.*

•**Battling the bulge.** As the average size of the nation's midriff swells, so do weight-loss schemes. Most of them offer pills or capsules that lead to losing weight without exercising or improving your diet. Key rip-off buzzwords that are linked to eliminating fat from the system include "secret," "breakthrough," "guaranteed" and "miraculous."

Self-defense: Giving in to these claims only lightens your wallet. Any legitimate weight-loss program requires slicing calories and increasing exercise.

Consult your doctor before starting a weight-loss program.

5

Medications, Drugs, Vitamins & Supplements

Protect Yourself and Your Family from Medication Mishaps

Prescription medications are supposed to make us well. But each year, according to a study conducted by researchers at the University of Toronto, approximately 100,000 Americans die from adverse reactions to drugs prescribed by their doctors. Another 2 million are injured as a result of the drug reaction.

And these are unfortunate patients who got the correct drug at the correct dosage. Thousands more deaths and injuries occur each year from medication errors, in which the wrong dose was administered...or the patient was given the wrong drug altogether.

The key to avoiding these problems is information. Patient, doctor and pharmacist should all be fully informed about dosages as well as side effects, allergy risks, etc.

All should be fully aware of the patient's medical history, too, including any other medications being taken.

AT THE DOCTOR'S OFFICE

When your doctor prescribes a drug, ask him/her exactly why it's being prescribed. Find out the exact dose being prescribed and when and how the drug should be taken.

Ask about side effects, too. Although you should already have filled out a form listing other drugs you take, it's best to double-check this list with your doctor at the time he writes the prescription.

Ask the doctor for a list of pertinent medical facts that your pharmacist should know—including the results of any kidney function tests you've had. Adverse drug reactions are often associated with kidney problems.

THE PRESCRIPTION FORM

The written prescription should include your height and weight...the drug's generic and

---

Michael Cohen, RPh, president, Institute for Safe Medication Practices, 1800 Byberry Rd., Suite 810, Huntington Valley, PA 19006. *www.ismp.org.*

brand names…the dosage being prescribed…and the reason for taking the drug (unless confidentiality is an issue).

For children and cancer patients, the prescription should also include the dose relative to body weight (milligrams per kilogram), which is used to calculate the total dose.

Handwriting trap: Half of all medication errors occur when pharmacists misread doctors' scribbled prescriptions. If you have trouble reading what your doctor has written, ask him to rewrite it neatly.

The doctor should write out the word "unit" at all times, instead of using a capital "U"—which can be misread as a zero.

If the dose being prescribed is less than one unit, the doctor should place a zero before the decimal point.

Example: For a dose of three-tenths of one milligram, the doctor should write "0.3 mg" instead of ".3 mg."

Doctors often use a set of abbreviations that can be misinterpreted by pharmacists…

- **pc…**after meals.
- **po…**take orally.
- **qd…**every day.
- **qid…**four times a day.
- **tid…**three times a day.
- **tiw…**three times a week.

To avoid confusion, ask your doctor to eschew these abbreviations and use plain English instead. If you or your pharmacist have any questions about any aspect of your prescription, contact your doctor immediately.

AT THE DRUGSTORE

Have all your prescriptions filled at one drugstore—ideally one with a computerized screening system.

These systems automatically warn of interactions with other drugs…as well as the risk of allergies and side effects.

If your doctor offers you free samples of the drug he is prescribing, take these to the drugstore to have the pharmacist check them using his/her system.

Do not rely on your doctor to remember all pertinent information about the drug. With thousands of prescription drugs now on the market, it's impossible for even the smartest person to know all drug–drug and food–drug interactions, side effects, etc.

Double-check the name of the drug, and what the pills look like. Some spellings are easily confused when handwritten.

Example: The antihypertensive *amlodipine* (Norvasc) is often confused with the antipsychotic *thiothixene* (Navane).

Review the dosage and means of administration with the pharmacist. Be sure he knows about any other drugs you take, as well as whether you're pregnant or nursing…have high blood pressure or diabetes…or suffer from kidney disease or impaired liver function.

Ask the pharmacist for a plain-language information sheet on the drug. These sheets—developed by the US Pharmacopeia—are easier to understand than package inserts provided by drug manufacturers.

For more detailed information, consult a consumer drug reference. A good example is *Consumer Reports Consumer Drug Reference 2007,* Consumer Reports Books/$44.95. 800-500-9760.

AT THE HOSPITAL

Each time a nurse arrives to administer medication, ask him/her to double-check the name of the drug and the exact dosage.

If the doctor has ordered a change in your medication, ask that the hospital pharmacist screen the drug for interactions.

The day before your discharge, ask a friend or relative to bring in all the drugs you'll be using at home. Go over each with the doctor who prescribed it.

AFTER TAKING THE MEDICATION

If you experience any unexplained symptoms after taking a drug, contact your doctor immediately.

Do not stop taking any prescription drug without your doctor's knowledge. Discontinuing certain medications abruptly can be dangerous and may cause a serious reaction.

How Dangerous Medication Mistakes Can Be Avoided

Netra Thakur, MD, clinical assistant professor of family medicine, Jefferson Medical College, Philadelphia. She is a member of the American Academy of Family Physicians.

Medication mistakes—such as forgetting to take drugs at the proper time or taking more or less than the prescribed amounts—account for about 10% of all hospital admissions.

Here are the most common mistakes—and how to prevent them…

Mistake #1: **Ignoring directions on the label.** Check the label carefully for the right dosage. Taking the wrong dose of a medication can be very dangerous.

Example: Taking too much of a blood thinner can cause internal bleeding.

Labels also state other directions. For example, you may need to take painkillers with food to prevent stomach upset.

What to do: Every time you get a new drug or a refill, review the label and the pharmacy drug summary.

Mistake #2: **Missing doses.** It's easy to forget to take your medications at the appropriate times every day.

What to do: Keep medications where you will see them, such as on your desk or next to your toothbrush. If you take multiple medicines, use a pillbox that has a compartment for each day.

Important: If you forget to take a dose, read the package insert for directions, or ask your doctor or pharmacist. For some drugs, such as antibiotics, you can usually take a double dose at the next scheduled time. For others, such as blood pressure drugs, it is safer to skip the missed dose and then take your usual amount at the next scheduled time.

Mistake #3: **Not knowing which drugs you take.** If you don't know the names of all the drugs you're taking—and you aren't sure why you're taking them—there is no way to know if your doctor or pharmacist accidentally gives you the wrong ones.

Different drugs will sometimes have similar names. For example, the cough medicine Benylin can be very easily confused with the antihistamine Benadryl.

If you don't know what drugs you're taking, you also won't be able to alert doctors in an emergency. You could be given the wrong treatment in a hospital emergency room.

Example: Beta-blockers, which are often used to control high blood pressure, can cause severe asthma-like symptoms.

What to do: Before leaving your doctor's office with a prescription, ask him/her to write down the medication's name and why you need to take it. Review this information with the pharmacist.

Mistake #4: **Failing to recognize side effects of the drug.** Patients do not always make the connection between a drug and symptoms that are actually side effects.

Example: Blood pressure drugs called ACE inhibitors can cause a dry cough that may be dismissed as a sign of a cold or allergy.

What to do: Tell your physician about any symptom that begins after starting a new drug, even if it seems unrelated. Most side effects can be reduced or eliminated by switching drugs or adjusting the dose, with medical supervision.

Mistake #5: **Insisting on new drugs.** Both patients and doctors can be influenced by magazine and TV advertisements for "new and improved" drugs. The vast majority of new drugs have few or no advantages over older ones. They also may be riskier because they haven't been on the market long enough for doctors to know much about their side effects or complications, some of which might not emerge until years later.

What to do: Ask your doctor if the new drug he is prescribing is clearly superior to older available medication.

Mistake #6: **Combining prescription drugs with supplements.** The risk of side effects rises sharply when you combine prescription drugs with herbs, dietary supplements or over-the-counter (OTC) medicines.

Examples: Garlic supplements increase the risk of internal bleeding when combined with the blood-thinner *warfarin* (Coumadin)...vitamin C may increase iron absorption, which can be dangerous for some people...and the herb ephedra may interact with many cardiac drugs.

What to do: Tell your doctor about all supplements and OTC drugs you take.

***Mistake #7:* Stockpiling drugs.** No one wants to throw away expensive medication that might be useful in the future. Keeping drugs that you are not using, however, increases the chance that you might take the wrong one by mistake.

What to do: Throw out any medication that you are no longer using or is well beyond its expiration date.

***Mistake #8:* Poor communication.** People with multiple health problems usually receive drugs from different specialists—rheumatologists, cardiologists, internists, etc. It is unlikely that any one of the physicians knows exactly what medications the others are prescribing. Patients can sometimes even get prescriptions for the same drug from two different doctors. The same drug may be sold under different names...or different drugs may be prescribed for the same purpose.

What to do: Ask your primary doctor to review all your prescriptions. Put the drugs in a bag, and take them to the doctor. Or e-mail, fax or mail a list to your physician. A "brown-bag review" ensures that you aren't taking drugs unnecessarily...you aren't getting incorrect dosages...and the drugs aren't interacting in harmful ways.

Buy all prescription drugs at the same pharmacy. Most pharmacies use computers to track prescriptions and can alert you to duplications or potential interactions.

Pill Dosage Danger

Tablet splitting may result in inaccurate dosing. Talk to your physician or pharmacist before splitting any drug.

In one study, when older patients used one of two commercially available tablet splitters, doses varied from 9% to 37% of the intended 50/50 split. Patients split tablets more accurately depending on the splitter used, the shape of the tablet and whether they received instructions beforehand.

Brian T. Peek, PharmD, clinical assistant professor, Campbell University school of pharmacy, Buies Creek, NC.

The Very Simple Secret Of Stopping Side Effects From Medications

Jay S. Cohen, MD, adjunct associate professor of family and preventive medicine and of psychiatry, University of California, San Diego. He is author of *What You Must Know About Statin Drugs & Their Natural Alternatives* (Square One). Dr. Cohen has published several journal articles on medication safety. He maintains a Web site at *www.medicationsense.com*.

Each year, medication side effects account for an estimated 115 million doctor visits and 8.5 million hospitalizations.

And each year, 100,000 Americans die as a direct result of the drugs they take. That's more than are killed in automobile accidents and all other accidents combined.

Less dramatic, but often just as serious, many people are so bothered by side effects that they stop taking the medicines that are needed to fight their illnesses.

TOO MUCH MEDICATION

More than 80% of all side effects are dose-related. The higher the dosage, the greater the risk for side effects.

Research has shown that low dosages often work just as well. But few doctors—perhaps one in 10—make a serious effort to find dosages that maximize the benefits to patients while minimizing side effects.

Most physicians do just what they learned in medical school, prescribing the dosages listed in the *Physicians' Desk Reference (PDR)*. The dosages listed in this giant reference book are supplied by drug manufacturers.

How do drug manufacturers calculate the dosages listed in the PDR? In most cases, they test just a few dosages, then settle on one that is effective for about 75% of patients.

Trap: People differ in how they react to drug amounts. One person might do well on 10 milligrams (mg). Another might need several times as much.

In general, older people are more sensitive to the effects of a drug than younger people are. And women often do much better on a lower dosage than men.

SMALLER BUT STILL EFFECTIVE

The dosages listed in the *PDR* are only part of the story. Once a new drug begins to be widely prescribed, it often becomes clear that many patients fare well on smaller dosages—with a smaller risk for side effects. *Here are a few examples...*

●**Antidepressants.** The recommended initial dosage of *fluoxetine* (Prozac) is 20 mg per day. But a study published in *The New England Journal of Medicine* demonstrated that 5 mg per day is often effective—and less likely to cause headaches, anxiety and other side effects. Other studies show that 2.5 mg is often enough.

Similar success has been reported with lower-than-usual dosages of other antidepressant drugs.

●**Ulcer drugs.** Acid-blocking drugs like *omeprazole* (Prilosec) and *lansoprazole* (Prevacid) can cause headaches, joint pain, nausea and constipation or diarrhea.

The usual dosage of omeprazole is 20 mg per day. But studies have shown that 10 mg works well for many people. Some elderly people do fine on 5 mg.

●**Cholesterol-lowering drugs.** Preliminary testing of *simvastatin* (Zocor) and other "statins" suggested that these drugs had few side effects. Now it's clear that statins can cause severe muscle pain and gastrointestinal problems.

The starting dosage usually prescribed for simvastatin is 10 mg per day. But many people achieve significant cholesterol reduction with 5 mg or even 2.5 mg.

●**Blood pressure drugs.** ACE inhibitors like *enalapril* (Vasotec) are less likely than other blood pressure drugs to cause side effects. But these drugs can cause a constant cough or lightheadedness.

The manufacturer recommends a starting dosage of 5 mg per day for enalapril. But a report issued by the Joint National Committee on Prevention, Detection, Evaluation and Treatment of High Blood Pressure suggests starting at 2.5 mg per day. Unfortunately, few doctors have read this report.

●**Pain medications.** *Ibuprofen* (Motrin) and other *nonsteroidal anti-inflammatory drugs* (NSAIDs) are highly effective at controlling pain and inflammation caused by conditions like arthritis or tendinitis.

But these drugs can cause severe stomach irritation, ulcers and bleeding.

USING DRUGS PROPERLY

Doctors have no desire to prescribe more of a drug than is needed. It's just that they're unaware that lower, safer doses are often found to be effective after a medication has been approved. *That's where the patient comes in...*

●**Alert the doctor to side effects you've experienced in the past.** If a drug you once took caused fatigue, odds are you'll be sensitive to a new drug for which fatigue is also a common side effect. The doctor may be able to suggest an alternative.

●**Encourage the "start low, go slow" approach.** Unless your ailment is severe, it's often prudent to begin at the lowest possible dosage and—if that doesn't work—boost the dosage gradually.

This strategy lets the doctor find the smallest effective dosage. It also gives your body a better chance to adjust to a new medication.

●**Try intermediate dosages.** Most drugs come in just a few strengths. But often the lowest effective dosage falls between two different strengths.

Finding a way to get this intermediate dosage can require a little creativity—taking a fraction of a pill, for instance, or dissolving the contents of a capsule in juice and then dividing the dose.

Example: The drug fluoxetine is available in both 10-mg and 20-mg pills. It's usually prescribed at 20 mg per day—then, if necessary, 40, 60 or 80 mg. But a patient might not respond to 40 mg...and 60 mg might cause serious side effects.

For this patient, taking 50 mg (two 20-mg pills and one 10-mg pill) might work perfectly.

●**Bring the dosage down.** Especially for blood pressure drugs and other medications that must be taken on an indefinite basis, it's important to find the lowest effective dosage. No one wants to endure troublesome side effects for a lifetime.

Good news: While a high dosage may be needed at first to bring a condition under control, it's often possible to notch down to a "maintenance dose" later on.

●**Divide the dose.** Most people find it most convenient to take medication once a day. But a single large dose can cause a high concentration of the drug in the bloodstream.

Ask your doctor about dividing one large dose into two or three smaller doses.

Caution: Never start or stop taking any prescription medication—or alter the dosage—without first checking with your doctor.

More from Jay S. Cohen...

Don't Take Antidepressants With Aspirin

Taking painkillers and antidepressants can cause dangerous stomach bleeding. Long-term use of aspirin, *ibuprofen* or other types of *nonsteroidal anti-inflammatory drugs* (NSAIDs) increases the risk of gastrointestinal bleeding. Prozac, Zoloft and other *selective serotonin reuptake inhibitor* (SSRI) antidepressants also can cause bleeding. Taking both types of drugs further increases risk.

Self-defense: People using SSRI antidepressants should ask their physicians about taking painkillers that don't cause bleeding—such as *acetaminophen* (Tylenol).

Important: To minimize side effects, talk to your doctor about taking the lowest effective dose of any drug.

Antidepressant Alert

Doctors often misprescribe tranquilizers and antidepressants. Especially among older adults, some of these medications' potentially harmful effects—like urine retention, sedation and confusion—may outweigh their potential benefits. It's estimated that 20% of people age 65 and older take a drug that could be especially dangerous for them.

Self-defense: At least once a year, review with your doctor all over-the-counter and prescription medications you take. Discuss side effects you are experiencing and whether you can reduce the dosage or stop taking the drug.

Important: Never discontinue a medication without consulting your doctor.

Arlene S. Bierman, MD, chair, Women's Health Council, University of Toronto, and senior scientist, Inner City Health Research Unit faculty, St. Michael's Hospital, Toronto.

Medications that Cause Weight Gain

Some medications can trigger weight gain by increasing appetite, slowing down metabolism or causing fluid retention.

Common culprits: Newer antipsychotics, such as Risperdal, Seroquel and Zyprexa... mood stabilizers, such as *lithium* and the anticonvulsants Depakote and Tegretol...steroids... tricyclic antidepressants, such as Aventyl, Elavil and Remeron...drugs to treat diabetes, such as Actos and Avandia.

Weight gain may be experienced fairly early in the course of therapy. If you gain weight after starting any medicine, consult your doctor. Prescription diuretics can help take off water weight. Increased exercise may be needed if a drug slows your metabolism.

Stephanie DeGraw, PharmD candidate and researcher, Institute for Safe Medication Practices, Huntingdon Valley, PA. The Institute publishes the consumer newsletter *Safe Medicine*. Its Web site is *www.ismp.org*.

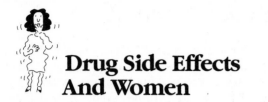

Drug Side Effects And Women

Women experience drug side effects more often and differently than men. Women's systems may absorb drugs at different rates or are just more sensitive to them.

Examples: The antibiotic *erythromycin* is more likely to cause dangerous heart arrhythmias in women…asthma and epilepsy medications may not work as well during menstruation.

Women need to tell their doctors if they take more than one of these drugs, use alcohol or take any dietary supplements.

Raymond I. Woosley, MD, professor of medicine and vice president for health sciences, University of Arizona, Tucson.

Drug Patches: Healing With Fewer Side Effects

Richard D. Hurt, MD, professor of medicine, Mayo Medical School, and director Mayo Clinic Nicotine Dependence Center, Rochester, MN. He is a leading researcher in the use of patches for smoking cessation.

Many drugs are available in patch form, and more are awaiting approval from the US Food and Drug Administration (FDA). Drug patches—or transdermal drug-delivery systems—offer important advantages and, in some cases, cause fewer side effects.

HOW PATCHES WORK

The medication's active ingredient is integrated into the adhesive gel on the "active" side of the patch. When you peel off the plastic cover and apply the patch to your skin, drug molecules pass through the skin into the bloodstream.

Several kinds of drugs are available in patch form, including…

●**Testosterone** for men with low levels of this hormone.

●**Estrogen and progesterone** for women as birth control or hormone replacement therapy.

●**Narcotic analgesics** (painkillers).

●**Antinausea drugs** for motion sickness and chemotherapy-related nausea.

●**Nitroglycerine** for angina.

●**Nicotine** to help people quit smoking.

Patches stay in place even when you swim or shower and can be removed with little or no discomfort. Some testosterone patches need to be placed on scrotal tissue, but most drug patches can go anywhere. Follow the manufacturer's instructions.

Do not put patches on elbows, hands or the bottoms of feet. The tough skin in these areas inhibits absorption.

You can generally wear more than one patch at a time—for example, a nicotine patch along with a patch for pain relief. Drug interactions can occur with patches just as they can with pills. If you're using one or more patches and/or taking oral medication and experience side effects, tell your doctor right away.

ADVANTAGES

Oral drugs need to be given in relatively high doses. That's because up to 90% of some active ingredients may be inactivated when they pass through the digestive tract and the liver. Patches bypass the liver and the intestines and deliver drugs directly into the bloodstream. This allows the use of lower doses and reduces the risk of dangerous side effects, including liver damage. *Other advantages…*

●**Patches deliver steady doses of medication over hours or days,** without the surges that occur with oral drugs.

●**Applying a patch just once a day**—or once a week or every few weeks—is more convenient and easier to remember than taking oral drugs several times a day. With oral drugs, noncompliance—forgetting to take the drugs or skipping doses—is a huge problem, especially for people with chronic conditions.

●**Patients who have difficulty swallowing pills can use the patch form.**

DRAWBACKS

Some people get hives where the patch is applied. This generally can be prevented just by applying patches to different areas of the skin on different days. Other patients may experience a generalized allergic reaction, such as an allover rash—but this is rare.

Be sure to remove old patches before applying new ones. Accidentally wearing multiple patches of the same medication could cause an overdose.

WHAT'S AHEAD?

Researchers are developing patches that deliver drugs for asthma, depression, diabetes, Parkinson's disease and other conditions. These may be available within the next several years.

They're also working on patches that incorporate tiny electronic circuits and use ultrasound, heat or electric current to facilitate the passage of drugs—especially those with large molecules, such as insulin—through the skin. These high-tech patches also may be used to deliver painkillers more rapidly than conventional patches.

Emergency Warning: Know Your Medications

Charles B. Inlander, a consumer advocate and health care consultant based in Fogelsville, PA. He was founding president of People's Medical Society, a consumer health advocacy group. He is author of more than 20 books on consumer health issues, including *Take This Book to the Hospital with You* (St. Martin's).

If you take medication regularly, make sure emergency medical personnel have fast access to this information.

Reason: Emergency procedures can harm people using certain drugs.

Examples: Nitrate drugs used during anesthesia can be dangerous to people who take Viagra…drugs used to dissolve blood clots can harm people who take blood-thinning *warfarin* (Coumadin) or aspirin daily.

Lifesaver: Carry a card listing medications in your wallet, next to your driver's license. It should also list dietary supplements…chronic conditions…allergies…contact lenses.

Alternative: Use an emergency medical information service. MedicAlert (888-633-4298) sells bracelets and necklaces engraved with health information and a number to call for your medication information.

More from Charles B. Inlander…

How to Get Drugs Not Yet FDA Approved

Medicines that have not yet been approved by the US Food and Drug Administration (FDA) may be available for patients who demonstrate real need. The patient's doctor has to recommend the patient, and the drug has to be in the human-testing stage or beyond.

Find out about *compassionate use* programs, for conditions ranging from lung cancer to obesity, at drug manufacturers' Web sites or search at *www.clinicaltrials.gov.*

Also from Charles B. Inlander…

Older Drugs May Be Better than Newer Versions

Updated—and more expensive—versions of old drugs may not be much better for you. Some drug companies will make small changes to existing medications and apply for new patents. The new products typically are only 3% to 5% more effective than the older ones. But they can cost 40% to 50% more.

Example: Clarinex is a slightly stronger form of Claritin, an allergy medication that is now available over-the-counter.

Self-defense: Ask your doctor about drug options. Don't switch blindly.

New-Drug Dangers

One-fifth of the 548 drugs approved by the US Food and Drug Administration (FDA) over the past 25 years turned out to have serious side effects that were not known when they were approved. Seven of the drugs, which were later withdrawn from the market, had side effects so severe that they may have contributed to more than 1,000 deaths.

Self-defense: Avoid drugs that have been on the market for fewer than five years. If your doctor prescribes a new drug, ask whether there are older, time-tested alternatives.

Karen Lasser, MD, MPH assistant professor of medicine, Harvard Medical School, Boston, and leader of a study published in the *Journal of the American Medical Association*.

Do Drug Companies Call the Shots?

Timothy McCall, MD, an internist, medical editor of *Yoga Journal* and author of *Examining Your Doctor* (Citadel Press) and *Yoga as Medicine* (Bantam). *www.drmccall.com.*

Drug companies spend an enormous amount of time and money trying to influence the prescribing habits of physicians. And they do it for one reason—it works. Millions of dollars spent in swaying physicians can result in billions of dollars of revenue from exorbitantly priced "blockbuster" drugs.

Unfortunately, this practice is usually not in the best interest of the patient. This point was driven home by a major study that showed that old-fashioned diuretics—"water pills" costing pennies a pill—were more effective for high blood pressure than heavily promoted drugs costing a buck or more a pill.

As a patient, you simply want the best medical care you can get. You'd like your doctors' recommendations to be based on science and common sense—not on the marketing efforts of the drug companies.

How can you tell if your doctor is overly influenced by the drug companies? There are a few warning signs. (Keep in mind, however, that it's a pattern—not an individual transgression—that most suggests a problem.) *A few to look out for...*

●**The doctor prescribes drugs promoted with freebies.** Be careful if the name on your prescription matches the name on the pens, notepads, posters or other drug company freebies littering your doctor's office. Personally, I don't think doctors should accept any such promotional materials. It can subtly influence their prescribing behavior, and the expense contributes to the high cost of drugs.

●**The doctor never prescribes generics.** For most drugs, generics are every bit as effective as the name brand. Doctors who prefer a name brand ought to have a good reason why and be able to articulate it if you ask. Similarly, if there is *never* a generic version of the drugs your doctor recommends, it means that he/she is favoring the newer, more expensive drugs. (Generics become available only after the patent expires on brand-name drugs.)

●**The doctor gives "a pill for every ill."** Handing a patient a prescription is one way some busy doctors signal that your appointment time is up. But often, what's best is to explore nondrug options, such as exercise, dietary changes and stress-reduction strategies, before resorting to drugs. It takes longer to explain nondrug options, however, so this route is increasingly a thing of the past for too many doctors.

●**The doctor is always willing to prescribe drugs you request.** In recent years, drug companies have realized that another way to manipulate doctors is to advertise directly to patients, who then ask their doctors for specific medications. But often, direct-to-patient ads are for drugs that you don't need or that may not be the best choice for your condition. Good doctors refuse to go along—at least some of the time—with these patient requests. They may suggest a better alternative or explain why no drug is needed. Some patients may be disappointed, and it can be bad for business. But the best doctors know when to just say "no."

More from Timothy McCall...

Are Cholesterol-Lowering Medications Safe?

When the popular cholesterol-lowering medication *cerivastatin* (Baycol) was recalled after being linked to several deaths, millions of Americans who take the statin drug were left wondering whether their health was at risk. The Baycol users who died had suffered muscle inflammation (myositis)—a side effect that can progress to kidney failure and death.

Six statins remain on the market—*lovastatin* (Mevacor), *simvastatin* (Zocor), *pravastatin* (Pravachol), *atorvastatin* (Lipitor), *fluvastatin* (Lescol), and *rosuvastatin* (Crestor). Each of these can cause myositis. Overall, however, the drugs appear to be fairly safe. *Here's what I suggest to lower your risk of problems...*

● **Try nondrug options before committing to medication.** Renowned cardiologist Dean Ornish, MD, has found that a comprehensive program of lifestyle change—including yoga, group psychotherapy, walking regularly and a low-fat vegetarian diet—can reverse the buildup of fatty deposits in coronary arteries. Interestingly, the control group in his experiments, some of whom took various cholesterol-lowering drugs, had more symptoms and heart attacks than those who followed his program. Dr. Ornish's program isn't for everyone. But those people who are willing to change their lifestyles may have a more powerful—and safer—alternative than drug therapy.

Other nondrug options that may help lower cholesterol include fiber supplements (such as Metamucil) and oat bran. Alcohol in moderation, low-dose aspirin therapy, black or green tea and antioxidants, such as vitamin E, may independently lower heart attack risk. Discuss dosages with your doctor.

● **Get monitored for side effects.** Most people who take statins don't observe any side effects, which has given some patients—and some doctors—a false sense of confidence. Blood tests for liver function are advised six weeks after starting statin therapy and every four to six months thereafter. Unfortunately, few doctors insist on these tests.

If you develop unexplained muscle soreness, weakness or fever, stop taking the drug and consult your doctor. If your urine turns brown, seek care immediately. This can be a sign of kidney failure.

● **Watch out for drug combinations.** One-third of the Baycol users who died were also taking *gemfibrozil* (Lopid), another cholesterol-lowering drug. Tragically, doctors were warned not to prescribe these drugs together.

In general, the more medications you take—especially if they're newer ones—the greater your risk for drug interactions.

My advice: Avoid new drugs for the first several years unless they offer significant advantages over older, time-tested drugs.

The Baycol recall reminds us that you cannot always count on physicians to do what they are supposed to do. Some don't bother to look up a medication to check for side effects, drug interactions and warnings before prescribing it. Some are too busy and simply make mistakes. Whatever the cause, you can help avoid this kind of problem by reading the package insert for every drug you're prescribed. Request it from your pharmacist.

Although we often seem to forget it, all drugs have side effects. What matters most is whether the potential benefits outweigh the risks. If a person is at high risk for heart disease—but hasn't had much success with diet, exercise and other nondrug approaches—a statin is clearly appropriate. In fact, the side effects of not taking the drug could be much worse.

Avoid Expensive Combo Drugs

Many brand-name combination drugs are simply expensive repackagings.

Examples: Caduet combines an existing blood pressure pill and cholesterol pill...Symbax combines an antidepressant and antipsychotic drugs.

Patients should use combo products only if there are no generics or similar drugs and the combo costs about the same as the two separate medicines. Insured patients may pay only one co-pay for a combo drug—but that is a false saving if there are cheaper alternatives.

Jerry Avorn, MD, professor of medicine, Harvard Medical School, and chief, division of pharmacoepidemiology and pharmacoeconomics, Brigham and Women's Hospital, both in Boston.

Are You Taking Medications Properly?

The term *with food* means during a meal, not with a glass of milk or juice. *Before meals* means at least one hour before eating. *After meals* means at least two hours afterward. *On an empty stomach* means one hour before or two hours after eating. The type of food you eat also matters.

Examples: Grapefruit juice will intensify some drugs, and calcium-fortified juice can prevent proper absorption.

Ask your doctor and pharmacist for the best way to take each medicine.

Joe Graedon, pharmacologist in Durham, NC, and coauthor, with Teresa Graedon, PhD, of *The People's Pharmacy* (St. Martin's). Their Web site, *www.peoples pharmacy.org*, provides information about the uses and side effects of herbs and drugs.

Is Your Medication Depleting Your Body Of Nutrients?

Some popular prescription drugs can remove nutrients from the body.

Examples: Drugs used to treat high blood pressure, such as *propanolol* (Inderal), appear to

lower levels of coenzyme Q10 in the body—yet this nutrient is critical to heart health...nonsteroidal anti-inflammatories, such as aspirin and *ibuprofen,* and birth-control pills are among the drugs that can lower levels of folic acid.

Self-defense: Ask your doctor if you need supplements to counter the effects of any medicines you take regularly.

Ross Pelton, PhD, RPh, pharmacist, Ashland, OR, and coauthor of *The Nutritional Cost of Drugs: A Guide to Maintaining Good Nutrition While Using Prescription and Over-The-Counter Drugs* (Morton).

Don't Mix Culinary Herbs And These Drugs

Several culinary spices and herbs can affect the body's ability to metabolize medications. Garlic, ginger, cloves, sage, turmeric and oregano may cause drug interactions when taken with anticoagulants, heart drugs and chemotherapy drugs. The risk of an interaction may increase with the number of medications taken and the amount of highly flavored foods eaten.

Self-defense: Talk with your physician and pharmacist about the risk for such interactions with the medications you are taking.

Brian C. Foster, PhD, senior science adviser, Health Canada, Ottawa.

 # Timing Your Medications for Maximum Benefit

Michael Smolensky, PhD, professor of environmental and occupational health, and cofounder and former director, Hermann Hospital Clinical Chronobiology Center, both at the University of Texas, Houston. He is editor of the medical journal *Chronobiology International* and coauthor of *Body Clock Guide to Better Health* (Owl Books).

Most medical students are taught that the body is *homeostatic*—that is, having a "steady state" of biological functions. However, scientists now know that the body functions rhythmically.

The symptoms of chronic medical conditions, such as high blood pressure, arthritis and hay fever, vary greatly according to so-called *circadian* (24-hour) *rhythms*. By timing medications to your body's biological rhythms—a treatment approach known as *chronotherapy*—you can recover faster from a health problem or live better with a chronic illness. *Here are the latest findings in chronotherapy…*

HIGH BLOOD PRESSURE

One in every four American adults has high blood pressure. Most physicians agree that ideal blood pressure should be 115/75. (The top number is *systolic* pressure, when the heart beats…the bottom number is *diastolic,* when the heart relaxes between beats.)

Using a technique called *ambulatory blood pressure monitoring,* which measures pressure automatically 24 hours a day, doctors now know blood pressure exhibits a circadian rhythm.

In most people, blood pressure is highest after awakening, rising by at least 25 systolic points. Blood pressure remains elevated during the day and declines in the evening, reaching its lowest level during nighttime sleep. It is important that prescription blood pressure medications control daytime highs without overcorrecting nighttime lows.

Medical advances: In the US, there are four medications specifically designed to keep drug levels in the body in sync with the circadian rhythms of blood pressure. These medications, called chronotherapies, are the calcium channel blockers *verapamil* (Verelan PM and Covera-HS) and graded-release *diltiazem* (Cardizem LA)…and the beta-blocker *propranolol* (Inno-Pran XL).

Intended to be taken at bedtime, their drug-delivery technology ensures that no medication is released until four hours after ingestion. Medication is then released so that peak levels of the drug are circulated during the day when blood pressure rises and the lowest levels of the drug are circulated at night when blood pressure is lowest.

Clinical studies indicate that these medications optimize the control of the morning blood pressure rise, which has been linked to stroke in at-risk patients. These drugs may also minimize risk for morning heart attack.

Caution: If you are taking a nonchronotherapy drug, do not change your dosing schedule. Studies show that taking certain medications at the wrong times can cause extreme lowering of blood pressure during nighttime sleep and may not control hypertension throughout the day.

Important finding: Low-dose aspirin, when taken at the correct time of day, may have a blood pressure–lowering effect. A study published in the journal *Hypertension* found that taking low-dose aspirin before going to bed reduced systolic blood pressure by an average of five points but had no effect when taken first thing in the morning.

More research is needed, but this finding suggests the importance of the body's circadian rhythm, even when taking a nonprescription medication, such as aspirin.

ARTHRITIS

Osteoarthritis (OA) is an age-related disease of painful, stiff and swollen joints. *Rheumatoid arthritis* (RA) is an autoimmune disease that causes joint inflammation. These two conditions are typically treated with the *nonsteroidal anti-inflammatory drugs* (NSAIDs), like *ibuprofen* (Advil), *ketoprofen* (Orudis) and *indomethacin* (Indocin).

Important finding: Large clinical studies show that NSAIDs are more effective against symptoms of RA when taken at bedtime.

Moreover, NSAIDS produce fewer gastrointestinal (GI) complications, such as indigestion and stomach discomfort, when taken at bedtime than when taken in the morning.

Additional studies have found that patients with OA who experience their most severe symptoms in the afternoon and evening get the most relief from NSAIDs when they are taken at breakfast (even though there may be an increase in the risk for GI side effects at this time) or at midday with lunch.

If NSAIDs do not relieve arthritis symptoms, your doctor may prescribe anti-inflammatory corticosteroid medications, such as *prednisone* (Deltasone). These medications can cause side effects, such as insomnia, mood changes and appetite enhancement, especially when taken in high doses. Studies show that these medications are the most effective, and the least likely to cause side effects, when taken once a day, either in the morning or early afternoon.

HAY FEVER

Allergens, such as pollens, mold spores, dust mites or animal dander, cause this respiratory problem, also known as *allergic rhinitis.* Symptoms will include sneezing, an itchy, stuffed or runny nose and swollen, puffy eyes.

One in 10 sufferers experience symptoms seasonally, while the remainder suffer year-round. As all hay fever sufferers know, symptoms typically are worst in the early morning, after waking up, although many sufferers complain that sleep is disrupted at night due to severe nasal congestion.

The circadian rhythm of hay fever symptoms is thought to be due to fluctuations in adrenaline and cortisol. That's because these hormones, which counter allergen-caused inflammation and swelling, are at their lowest during the night.

To better control morning symptoms, such as sneezing and/or a stuffy, runny nose, take an antihistamine in the evening or at bedtime.

Best Time to Take Heart Pills

The best time to take heart medication is in the morning. Cardiac medicines (such as beta-blockers or ACE inhibitors) taken in the morning take effect when you are up and about, and therefore putting greater demands on your cardiovascular system.

Exception: Take statins at bedtime—they work in conjunction with cholesterol synthesis, and the liver makes more cholesterol at night.

Thomas H. Lee, MD, editor in chief, *Harvard Health Letter,* 10 Shattuck St., Boston 02115.

Blood Pressure Trap

If you take medication for high blood pressure, make sure your drug regimen controls your hypertension 24 hours a day.

Recent study: People who had high blood pressure underwent psychological testing to measure hostility.

Those with high scores were found to have elevated blood pressure even while asleep. Ordinarily, blood pressure dips during sleep.

Those with low scores experienced a blood pressure dip at night but had sharp rises in blood pressure upon waking. These surges have been linked to early morning heart attack.

Implication: Hypertensives who tend to be hostile should generally take their antihypertensive medication at bedtime.

Those who are less hostile should generally take a slow-release pill in the morning.

In addition, hostile hypertensives should consider psychotherapy and/or relaxation techniques to help them curb their hostility.

Jagoda Pasic, MD, PhD, attending physician, department of psychiatry, University of Washington Medical Center, Seattle.

Over-the-Counter Drugs: Some Are Much Safer And More Effective Than Others

Michael B. Brodin, MD, a dermatologist in private practice in Scarsdale, NY. He is author of *The Encyclopedia of Medical Tests* and *The Over-the-Counter Drug Book* (both from Pocket Books).

There are approximately 300,000 over-the-counter (OTC) medications on the market. How does one make a smart selection?

Select products with only a *single active ingredient*—one that's been shown to be safe and effective for your primary symptom.

Reason: Each active ingredient in a medication carries its own side effects. Don't subject yourself to these side effects unless you really need the medication.

Doctors and pharmacists tend to talk about brand-name products, but it makes sense to opt for the generic equivalent whenever one is available. Generics are just as safe and effective. They're also less costly.

Here are the best OTC products for several common ailments…

ACHES AND PAIN

The *acetaminophen* in Tylenol is your best bet. While it doesn't combat inflammation, it's less likely than aspirin or nonsteroidal anti-inflammatory drugs like *ibuprofen* (Advil) to cause stomach upset or ulcers.

Acetaminophen is safe for children, too. Aspirin can cause a potentially fatal disorder known as Reye's syndrome when given to children under age 16.

Acetaminophen is also the best OTC drug for lowering fever.

CONSTIPATION

Many people continue to take *senna* (Ex-Lax) or another stimulant laxative. But there's now ample evidence that "bulk-forming" laxatives are effective—and less likely to result in dependency.

Bulk-forming laxatives absorb liquid and swell in the gut. The resulting increase in stool size stimulates the muscles of contraction and evacuation.

Different bulk laxatives contain different active ingredients—*psyllium* in Metamucil, *methylcellulose* in Citrucel, *malt soup extract* in Maltsupex and *calcium polycarbophil* in FiberCon. They're all approximately equivalent in performance.

COUGH

The best OTC medication for a cough depends upon the kind of cough you have.

•**Productive cough**—one that produces phlegm. Your best bet is the expectorant *guaifenesin,* which is found in Robitussin. By helping to liquefy mucus, guaifenesin seems to shorten the duration of a productive cough… and make the cough less painful.

•**Dry, hacking cough.** Use *dextromethorphan,* which is found in Benylin Adult Formula Cough and similar products. A morphine derivative, dextromethorphan is more effective at suppressing coughs than *diphenhydramine* (Benadryl), an OTC antihistamine that's often used as a cough suppressant.

Dextromethorphan does not cause drowsiness…but diphenhydramine can.

CUTS AND SCRAPES

Choose an antibiotic ointment that contains only *bacitracin* or a combination of bacitracin and polymycin.

The *neomycin* found in Neosporin and similar products can cause an allergic reaction.

DIARRHEA

Loperamide, found in Imodium and similar products, is safe and easy to take. It works by curbing the muscular contractions that lead to defecation.

Loperamide is more effective than adsorbent compounds—*attapulgite* (Kaopectate) and *kaolin/pectin* (Kao-Paverin). It's also more effective than *bismuth subsalicylate* (Pepto-Bismol).

NASAL CONGESTION

Pseudoephedrine, which is found in Sudafed and other similar products, is the best option for regular daytime use. It reduces congestion by narrowing blood vessels, helping to shrink swollen tissues.

Since pseudoephedrine has a mild stimulating effect, it should be avoided for at least four hours before bedtime. If you have hypertension, do not take this drug without talking to your doctor first.

For controlling congestion at night, diphenhydramine is often a better choice. Besides drying mucous membranes, it also has a mild cough-suppressant effect.

Caution: Consult a doctor before taking diphenhydramine or any other antihistamine if you have glaucoma, heart disease, thyroid disease, diabetes, high blood pressure or an enlarged prostate.

SORE THROAT

The best way to soothe throat pain is with a saltwater gargle…or with the natural painkiller *menthol.* One good source is Halls Mentho-Lyptus Ice Blue Cough Suppressant drops.

Each drop contains 12 milligrams of menthol—more than most other cough drops.

YEAST INFECTION

The four leading antifungal medications are *clotrimazole* (Gyne-Lotrimin, Mycelex-7), *miconazole* (Monistat 7), *butoconazole* (Femstat 3) and *tioconazole* (Vagistat-1).

These products are so similar as to be virtually interchangeable. Buy the one that you find most convenient to use.

Aspirin Isn't Just For Headaches

Peter Elwood, MD, professor of epidemiology, University of Wales College of Medicine, Cardiff.

Over the past 25 years, more than 140 studies have shown that taking aspirin can help to prevent heart attack and stroke. Recent research suggests that it may cut the risk for other diseases as well.

Peter Elwood, MD, lead author of a landmark 1974 study that was the first to link aspirin with reduced heart disease risk, discussed the latest research on this remarkable medication—and who should and who should not be taking it.

●**Just how effective is aspirin at preventing heart attack and stroke?** In studies involving men who had already sustained a heart attack or stroke, low-dose aspirin therapy—typically one tablet or less a day—cut the risk for heart attack and stroke by 30% to 40%.

The vast US Physicians' Health Study indicates that aspirin reduces heart attack risk in healthy men as well as in male heart patients. However, since healthy, nonsmoking men (and presumably women) have an extremely low risk for heart attack, the actual benefit to these individuals is probably too small to make daily aspirin therapy worthwhile.

But for people at high risk for heart attack —older people, smokers, those with high blood pressure or elevated cholesterol and/or a family history of heart disease—aspirin therapy is often worthwhile.

Aspirin prevents heart disease by reducing the "stickiness" of platelets. Those are the cellular fragments that clump together to start a blood clot.

●**Doesn't aspirin also play a role in heart attack treatment?** Absolutely. Taking an aspirin tablet as soon as symptoms become apparent may substantially boost the chance of survival, studies have shown.

The more promptly aspirin is taken, the better the odds for survival.

Since heart attack can kill within minutes, anyone at risk for heart disease should always carry a pillbox containing aspirin...and take a tablet at the first sign of chest pain.

To get aspirin into the bloodstream as quickly as possible, it's important to *chew* the tablet before you swallow it.

●**Which other conditions can aspirin help prevent?** Preliminary evidence suggests that aspirin can help prevent Alzheimer's disease.

Evidence is much stronger that aspirin helps prevent *vascular dementia*, a form of cognitive impairment associated with *transient ischemic attacks* (TIAs) and strokes.

Researchers believe that TIAs and strokes caused by blood clotting contribute to about half of all cases of dementia. Unless there's a good reason not to take aspirin (such as a history of ulcers), anyone who shows signs of mental deterioration suggestive of vascular dementia should probably be taking aspirin.

There is also good evidence that aspirin can help prevent certain forms of cancer. Three large-scale studies and many smaller ones have found that patients who take aspirin on a daily basis face a reduced risk for colon cancer.

Cancers of the rectum, stomach and esophagus also may be prevented by regular aspirin use, according to some studies.

Taking aspirin also seems to reduce the risk for developing cataracts...and to prevent the potentially blinding diabetes-related condition known as *diabetic retinopathy*.

●**Can't aspirin cause stomach trouble and other side effects?** About 8% of people on a low-dose aspirin regimen report nausea and/or stomach pain. Taking aspirin *after* a meal helps alleviate these symptoms.

Some people notice that they bruise more easily after going on aspirin therapy. This is nothing to worry about. Rarely, aspirin causes acute bleeding—vomiting blood or blood in the stool. This is a medical emergency.

To be safe, consult a doctor before taking aspirin—especially if you have a peptic ulcer… if you're taking an anticoagulant, such as *warfarin* (Coumadin)…or if you're allergic to aspirin.

● **What dosage of aspirin is appropriate?** When it comes to preventing illness, low dosages work fine. The World Health Organization recommends taking 100 milligrams (mg) per day to prevent heart attack. This dosage is probably appropriate for preventing other illnesses as well.

A standard aspirin tablet contains 325 mg. Some manufacturers have begun making 100-mg aspirin tablets. But it's okay to take half of a 325-mg tablet…or one 81-mg children's aspirin.

● **Does the type of aspirin make a difference?** Plain aspirin is fine for use in daily aspirin therapy…as well as for treating a suspected heart attack.

Enteric-coated aspirin bypasses the stomach and dissolves in the small intestine. It was developed to minimize gastrointestinal effects in chronic pain patients and other individuals who take large doses of aspirin. Since aspirin therapy involves low dosages, there's no reason to prefer enteric-coated over plain aspirin.

Aspirin Therapy Alert

Baby aspirin may not be enough to protect against stroke and heart disease. A daily baby aspirin—81 milligrams (mg)—is supposed to thin blood enough to lower disease risk. But in one study, 56% of people taking baby aspirin had no blood-thinning effects.

Also: Coated aspirin—which has a hard yellow coating or shell to ease digestion of the tablet—may not be effective. Sixty-five percent of the people studied didn't benefit from it.

Self-defense: Talk to your doctor about taking an uncoated adult-strength aspirin (325 mg) daily instead.

Mark J. Alberts, MD, director, Stroke Program, Northwestern Memorial Hospital, Chicago.

Protect Your Stomach If You Take Aspirin Daily

Commonly taken as a blood thinner or pain reliever, aspirin can irritate or damage the stomach lining.

Important finding: Taking vitamin C along with aspirin can help mitigate this damage. Vitamin C appears to decrease levels of free radicals, unstable molecules that damage the stomach lining.

If you take daily aspirin therapy: Ask your doctor about taking 250 milligrams (mg) of vitamin C along with the aspirin.

Thorsten Pohle, MD, internal medicine specialist, Medicinal Clinic and Polyclinic B, University of Muenster, Germany.

When to Take Your Daily Aspirin

Nighttime is the best time to take a daily aspirin to protect your heart. In one study, people with mild hypertension who waited until bedtime to take an aspirin tablet lowered their systolic blood pressure by an average of seven points after three months. Those who did not take aspirin or who took aspirin in the morning showed no change in blood pressure. Check with your doctor.

Ramon C. Hermida, PhD, director, bioengineering and chronobiology labs, University of Vigo, Spain.

Beware of Accidental Acetaminophen Overdose

Peter Draganov, MD, associate professor of medicine, division of gastroenterology, hepatology and nutrition, University of Florida College of Medicine, Gainesville.

Many over-the-counter medications contain *acetaminophen,* including some varieties of Alka-Seltzer, Benadryl, Contac, Dimetapp, Drixoral, Excedrin, Midol,

Robitussin, Tavist, Theraflu and Vicks. If you take one of these products *and* the recommended dose of acetaminophen, as found in Tylenol, you risk liver damage. Risk for liver damage is also greater if you take acetaminophen and drink more than a moderate amount of alcohol.

Self-defense: Read labels carefully or ask your doctor or pharmacist. The maximum daily acetaminophen dosage from all sources is 4,000 milligrams.

More from Peter Draganov...

Acetaminophen/Alcohol Alert

Alcohol and *acetaminophen* do not mix. Acetaminophen—in Darvocet, Tylenol, Vicodin and other products—causes 70 to 100 deaths per year from acute liver failure, usually due to overdoses or use in combination with alcohol.

Self-defense: Never take more than eight 500-milligram acetaminophen tablets in one day. Don't take it within 48 hours of drinking alcohol. And, never use acetaminophen to treat a hangover.

Are You Taking The Wrong Pain Pill?

George E. Ehrlich, MD, pain specialist and adjunct professor of medicine, University of Pennsylvania School of Medicine, Philadelphia, and the New York University School of Medicine, New York City. He is coauthor of *Conquering Chronic Pain After Injury* (Avery).

Far too many people fail to get adequate pain relief. This frequently occurs because pain sufferers are overly concerned about potential side effects of pain relievers. Or pain sufferers prefer to "tough" it out without using any medication.

This is unfortunate because pain is a leading cause of depression and stress. Pain can also escalate when it's not treated early.

Example: Suppose you hurt your knee while working in the backyard. A pain-causing chemical, *substance P,* released at the time of the injury irritates nearby tissues. To compensate for the pain, you'll put more weight on the other leg. Over time, this can cause chronic *secondary* pain in the back, leg or hip.

Pain that persists longer than 10 days should be evaluated by a doctor. He/she should examine you and perhaps order tests to rule out any underlying problem that will worsen without treatment. It's also important to ensure that you're taking the right analgesic.*

NONPRESCRIPTION ANALGESICS

In most cases, over-the-counter (OTC) analgesics work well. They often contain the same active ingredients as prescription drugs, though in lower doses.

The best choices...

•**Aspirin.** Also known as *acetylsalicylic acid,* aspirin reduces inflammation, blocks the transmission of pain signals through nerves and may lower levels of pain-causing chemicals called *prostaglandins.* The usual dosage is two 325-milligram (mg) tablets, four times every day—although your doctor may recommend larger doses for serious pain.

Use it: For arthritis, sports injuries, etc. The least expensive analgesic, it has been used for pain relief for more than 100 years. However, since it can cause heartburn and other side effects, especially when taken for long periods, many people choose newer painkillers that are better tolerated. Although most people can tolerate extended use of low-dose aspirin to prevent clogged arteries, painkilling doses should typically not be taken for more than 12 days without a physician's approval.

Avoid it: If you experience stomach pain, nausea, rectal bleeding or other gastrointestinal side effects. Aspirin inhibits the action of certain chemicals that are protective to the lining of the digestive tract.

Important: Do *not* use aspirin if you're taking an anticoagulant, such as *warfarin* (Coumadin), or any herbal products, such as ginkgo

*Women who are pregnant or nursing should consult their doctor before taking any painkiller.

biloba, which also has blood-thinning effects. Never give aspirin to children, except in rare instances when it may be recommended by a physician. The salicylates in aspirin may trigger Reye's syndrome, a potentially fatal disorder that causes severe brain inflammation. Aspirin can also aggravate asthma.

●**Acetaminophen.** *Acetaminophen* is as effective as aspirin for short-term and chronic pain. It is also less likely to cause stomach upset or the other side effects associated with aspirin use. Children can take acetaminophen because it doesn't trigger Reye's syndrome.

Use it: For pain that isn't accompanied by swelling or inflammation, such as aches due to overexertion or headaches. Unlike aspirin, acetaminophen works only as a painkiller—it has no effect on inflammation. The recommended adult dosage is two 325-mg tablets, taken three to four times daily.

Avoid it: If you drink heavily. When combined with heavy alcohol consumption, acetaminophen can cause liver damage. In elderly people, liver damage can occur even without excessive alcohol consumption.

Caution: Extra-strength acetaminophen is generally no more effective for pain than regular acetaminophen, and the higher dosage is more likely to cause liver damage.

●**Nonsteroidal anti-inflammatory drugs (NSAIDs).** Aspirin is an NSAID, but the term usually refers to other drugs that are less likely than aspirin to cause side effects.

Examples: Ibuprofen (Advil, Nuprin, Motrin)…and *naproxen* (Aleve).

Many people will choose an NSAID when aspirin or acetaminophen doesn't give them adequate relief or causes side effects.

Use it: For all types of pain, especially pain accompanied by inflammation, such as arthritis, sprains and other injuries.

The recommended dosage varies for each NSAID. Check the label for instructions. The drugs are similar, but not interchangeable. You might get relief from one NSAID but not another. Count on trying several before finding the one that works best for you.

Avoid it: If you experience the same side effects as aspirin—stomach upset, bleeding, ulcers, etc.

NSAIDs may also inhibit kidney function and shouldn't be taken by people with kidney disease without a doctor's supervision.

PRESCRIPTION ANALGESICS

Most patients will self-medicate with an OTC product, then consult a physician and progress to prescription-strength drugs if they don't get adequate relief. *I often prescribe…*

●**Cox-2 inhibitors.** Drugs in this class help to reduce pain and inflammation. They are less likely than aspirin to cause ulcers and other gastric side effects because they suppress only inflammation-causing Cox-2 enzymes—*not* the Cox-1 enzymes that protect the stomach lining.

Use it: For long-term pain that is accompanied by inflammation—injuries, arthritis, etc. Cox-2 inhibitors are expensive and may not be covered by insurance so they are generally prescribed when the older NSAIDs don't work or cause too many side effects.

Be aware that some studies show that Cox-2 inhibitors may increase the risk of heart attack or stroke after 18 months of use. Talk to your doctor to see if these drugs are safe for you.

Avoid it: When you need fast-acting relief. Cox-2 inhibitors may take at least five days to be effective.

●**Narcotics.** These are the most effective of the analgesics. Codeine, acetaminophen with codeine, *oxycodone* (OxyContin) and others are taken orally, by injection or in slow-release patch forms.

Use it: For relief from acute pain.

Example: After surgery or to ease any type of severe pain. Narcotics are usually prescribed only for one to two days because of risk for abuse or addiction. They do not control inflammation.

Avoid it: When side effects—mainly drowsiness, mental confusion or constipation—are severe, or if you have a history of drug or alcohol abuse.

Six Dangerous Myths About Antibiotics

Stuart B. Levy, MD, president, Alliance for the Prudent Use of Antibiotics, *www.apua.org,* and director, Center for Adaptation Genetics and Drug Resistance, Tufts University School of Medicine, both in Boston. He is author of *The Antibiotic Paradox: How the Misuse of Antibiotics Destroys Their Curative Powers* (HarperCollins).

After the terrorist attacks of 2001, the antibiotic *ciprofloxacin* (Cipro) was taken by thousands of Americans who may have been exposed to deadly spores of the anthrax bacterium.

Unfortunately, practically one out of five of these people suffered side effects, including itching, breathing problems and swelling of the face, neck or throat, according to the US Centers for Disease Control and Prevention.

Even though people tend to think that antibiotics are relatively harmless, they can endanger your health—and the health of your family.

Here are the six most common misconceptions about antibiotics…

Misconception: Antibiotics kill viruses.

Antibiotics attack only bacteria—they do not kill off viruses. Antibiotics are not effective for upper-respiratory viral ailments such as colds, flu and coughs.

Misconception: It's a good idea to stockpile antibiotics in case you get sick.

By stockpiling antibiotics in your home, you may be tempted to take them without a physician's advice.

Self-medication could cause unexpected side effects and propagate resistant bacteria, which can pass to other family members and the rest of your community. Also, taking antibiotics or any drugs that are not stored properly and/or are used after the expiration date can cause liver and kidney damage.

Misconception: There's really no harm in taking antibiotics even if you do not need them.

Any time you take an antibiotic unnecessarily, you risk side effects.

Also, some of the bacteria in your body survive and develop resistance to the drug. These bacteria inevitably pass to other people, creating a pool of antibiotic-resistant bacteria. When someone else develops an infection with antibiotic-resistant bacteria, the drugs may be rendered ineffective and will not work.

The only way to prevent this problem is for each of us to use antibiotics *only when necessary.* This means relying on a physician to properly diagnose your condition and prescribe antibiotics accordingly.

Misconception: It is okay to stop taking antibiotics when your symptoms begin to subside.

You may start feeling better shortly after starting an antibiotic, but you must continue to take the drug for the full course of the prescription.

If you don't, surviving bacteria can reactivate the infection. Taking only a partial course of antibiotics is also more likely to create antibiotic-resistant bacteria.

Misconception: Antibiotic resistance is only a theoretical problem.

In fact, bacteria have developed resistance to multiple antibiotics. Some bacteria now exist that are resistant to every antibiotic on the market today.

In 1992, less than 10% of US patients infected with *Streptococcus pneumoniae* (which causes pneumococcus pneumonia, ear infections and meningitis) experienced penicillin resistance.

A recent report in *The New England Journal of Medicine* showed that the frequency increased to 21% in 1995 and 25% in 1998. During that time, the bacteria's frequency of resistance to three or more types of antibiotics increased from 9% to 14%.

In hospitals, once-powerful antibiotics, such as methicillin, can no longer be relied upon to kill the common *Staphylococcus aureus* bacterium, which causes life-threatening blood poisoning. In fact, this bacterium is often resistant to whole classes of antibiotics, including *penicillins, cephalosporins, aminoglycosides* and *quinolones.*

Misconception: **It's easy for researchers to develop new, stronger antibiotics.**

This was true when penicillin was first being widely used back in the 1940s. At that point, scientists knew that pathogenic bacteria died when put in the soil and theorized that the earth might be a rich source of additional antibacterial chemicals.

They were right. They discovered new antibiotics in soil all over the world.

Now, most of those antibiotics are no longer effective because so many bacteria are resistant to them. As a result, scientists are creating synthetic versions—a process that is much more expensive and time-consuming than finding an antibiotic in nature.

What's more, scientists are finding it difficult to produce synthetic antibiotics to treat drug-resistant strains of bacteria. The days of rapid discovery of new, ever-stronger antibiotic miracle drugs are over.

Antibiotics and Calcium Don't Mix

Taking *fluoroquinolone* antibiotics, such as Cipro, Levaquin or Tequin, with calcium-rich or -fortified foods, such as milk, orange juice and breakfast cereals, can reduce antibiotic absorption. This makes treatment less effective and may produce antibiotic-resistant bacteria.

Self-defense: Whenever possible, take these antibiotics with water—and either two hours before or after meals.

Ask your doctor how to take other antibiotics, which also may need to be taken separately from meals.

Guy Amsden, PharmD, Bassett Healthcare, Cooperstown, NY, and leader of a study of antibiotic absorption, reported in Journal of Clinical Pharmacology.

Many Herbal Supplements And Drugs Shouldn't Be Combined

Mark Blumenthal, founder and executive director, American Botanical Council (ABC), *www.herbalgram. org*, an Austin, TX–based nonprofit organization that disseminates information on herbs and medicinal plants. He is also senior editor of *The ABC Clinical Guide to Herbs* (American Botanical Council).

One in six Americans takes prescription drugs *and* herbal supplements. Most herbal remedies are safe, but some herbs can pose potential risks when mixed with prescription or over-the-counter (OTC) drugs.* That's because herbal formulas can have a physiological effect on the body, such as raising or lowering blood pressure, blood sugar levels or heart rate.

RISKY COMBINATIONS

Drugs that should not be combined with some herbs…

•**Antacids.** Medications that ease the discomforts of persistent heartburn, indigestion or peptic ulcer are among the most popular OTC and prescription drugs in the US. These drugs include substances that either neutralize gastric acid (antacids) or inhibit its secretion (proton pump inhibitors).

People who take antacids, such as Alka-Seltzer or Mylanta, or proton pump inhibitors, such as *omeprazole* (Prilosec) or *esomeprazole* (Nexium), should avoid herbal formulas that *enhance* stomach acid secretion. This includes cayenne fruit (red pepper), which is typically used to treat peptic ulcer.

•**Anticoagulants.** Millions of Americans use aspirin or prescription blood thinners, such as *warfarin* (Coumadin), to protect against heart attack and stroke.

What many people fail to realize is that some herbs can also have a blood-thinning effect. *These include…*

•Feverfew, used for migraines.

•Garlic, used for cardiovascular health.

*Tell your doctor and pharmacist about all herbal supplements you are taking. Women who are pregnant or nursing should avoid most herbs.

• Ginger, used to aid digestion.

• Ginkgo, used to improve cognitive impairment in adults.

• Ginseng, used to boost physical endurance.

People who combine any of these herbs with an anticoagulant may experience excessive bleeding if they suffer a cut or a wound...as well as increased risk for internal bleeding if they sustain an injury.

•**Antidepressants.** If you take a prescription antidepressant, you should avoid the herbal remedy St. John's wort.

Although St. John's wort can be an effective treatment for mild to moderate depression, it can act in concert with the class of antidepressant drugs known as *selective serotonin reuptake inhibitors* (SSRIs) to produce "serotonin syndrome."

The condition causes drowsiness, rapid eye movement, restlessness and confusion. Commonly used SSRIs include *fluoxetine* (Prozac), *paroxetine* (Paxil), *sertraline* (Zoloft) and *citalopram* (Celexa).

•**Anti-anxiety drugs.** Kava, an herbal supplement used to relieve anxiety and stress, should not be taken with prescription medication for anxiety, such as *chlordiazepoxide* (Librium), *diazepam* (Valium), *alprazolam* (Xanax) and *lorazepam* (Ativan). Combining kava with one of these drugs can result in a loss of motor skills.

Caution: The US Food and Drug Administration (FDA) has warned consumers that kava has been linked to severe liver damage. Regulatory agencies in some European countries have also issued warnings or banned the herb from the marketplace.

If you have a history of liver disease...drink moderate or large amounts of alcohol...or take *acetaminophen* (Tylenol) or other drugs with possible toxic effects on the liver, you should avoid kava unless your treatment is supervised by a physician.

•**Antihypertensives.** If your doctor has prescribed drugs, such as thiazide diuretics, to help lower your blood pressure, don't eat licorice candy or use licorice supplements that contain true licorice extract. Licorice can counteract the medication's ability to lower blood pressure. Check the ingredients listed on the licorice label.

Licorice candy flavored with anise—rather than true licorice extract—is considered safe if you're taking diuretics.

Licorice supplements that contain *deglycyrrhizinated licorice* (DGL), often used for gastric ulcers, can also be used safely.

•**Oral contraceptives.** Women who take oral contraceptives should avoid chastetree. Commonly used to ease *premenstrual syndrome* (PMS), this herb affects the regulation of hormones and may interfere with the effectiveness of oral contraceptives.

Oral contraceptive users should also consult a physician before taking St. John's wort. Recent reports from Scandinavia have found that St. John's wort lowers the effectiveness of birth control pills, which could result in an unwanted pregnancy.

BUY WISELY

To help ensure the purity and integrity of an herbal product, check the label for a seal from one of the following...

•**ConsumerLab.com,** an independent testing organization that publishes on the Internet results for products that pass its tests.

•**NSF International,** a nonprofit organization that assesses factory procedures and product quality.

•**United States Pharmacopeia (USP),** a government-commissioned organization that establishes standards for drugs and dietary supplements.

Any of these seals ensures that the product contains the ingredients and amounts that are listed on the label.

The nonprofit American Botanical Council also provides information about drug interactions and other safety guidelines on some product labels.

For professional advice about using herbal supplements, consult a naturopathic physician, a healthcare practitioner who is qualified to prescribe a variety of alternative therapies, including herbal remedies.

To find a naturopath in your area, contact the American Association of Naturopathic Physicians at 866-538-2267 or *www.naturopathic.org*.

Drugs and Sun Don't Always Mix

Certain medications can make your skin unusually reactive to ultraviolet (UV) light. This condition, called *chemical photosensitivity,* can result in sunburn or a rash after even brief exposure to sunlight.

Photosensitivity can be a side effect in people taking an antihistamine, diuretic, nonsteroidal anti-inflammatory drug (NSAID) or antibiotic, including tetracycline or "sulfa" drugs.

Sunscreens offer only limited protection for people taking these drugs. Talk with your doctor about a sun-avoidance strategy.

Barney J. Kenet, MD, dermatologic surgeon specializing in skin cancer, New York-Presbyterian Hospital/Weill Medical College of Cornell University, New York City, and coauthor (with Patricia Lawler) of Saving Your Skin—Prevention, Early Detection, and Treatment of Melanoma and Other Skin Cancers (Four Walls Eight Windows).

Peanut Alert

If you are allergic to peanuts, be sure to remind your physician of your allergy whenever he/she prescribes a new medication.

Reason: Common drugs can trigger potentially fatal allergic reactions in people who are sensitive to peanuts, soybeans or soya lecithin.

Examples: *Ipratropium* (Atrovent) for asthma and *ipratropium with albuterol* (Combivent) for chronic obstructive pulmonary disease. Some forms of these drugs contain some of the same proteins as the foods.

Important: Food allergies do not always appear in patients' medical charts.

Amy M. Karch, RN, associate professor of clinical nursing, University of Rochester, Rochester, NY.

Secrets to Living Longer: Miraculous Supplements

Ronald Klatz, MD, president, American Academy of Anti-Aging Medicine, Chicago, www.worldhealth.net, and cofounder, National Academy of Sports Medicine, Calabasas, CA. He is author of many books, including The New Anti-Aging Revolution (Basic Health).

Aging damages the cells in our bodies—in our eyes, ears, brain, heart, lungs, skin, etc. The cells are assaulted by *free radicals* (by-products of the cells' normal metabolism) as well as by sunlight and pollutants. The accumulation of toxins hinders cell growth and repair. If we can prevent or reverse this cell damage, we can slow aging and live longer.

An important way to combat cell damage is with antiaging supplements. Below are seven of the most effective. You can choose to take one, several or all of them.*

Important: Don't take supplements without the approval of a qualified physician. To find one in your area, contact the American Academy of Anti-Aging Medicine at 773-528-4333 or go to the organization's Web site, *www.world health.net,* and click on "Physician Directories."

ALPHA-GPC

This nutrient, derived from soy, provides high levels of *choline,* which protects brain cells. It also increases levels of the neurotransmitter *acetylcholine,* which triggers an increased release of *human growth hormone* (hGH)—a hormone that is naturally present in the human body when we are young, but that decreases steadily as we age.

Studies show that increased hGH can reduce body fat, boost energy levels and restore youthful immune function.

In animal studies, alpha-GPC corrected age-related brain decline. And, in human studies, it

*Women who are pregnant or nursing should check with their doctor before taking any supplements.

helped stroke victims retain cognitive functioning and improved the mental functioning and mood of people with dementia.

Dose: 600 to 1,200 milligrams (mg) per day.*

ASHWAGANDHA ROOT

This herb is used extensively in Ayurveda, the traditional medicine of India. It stimulates immunity and, as an antioxidant, reduces cell-damaging free radicals, particularly within the brain cells. The herb's anti-inflammatory properties have been shown to be helpful for such inflammatory conditions as arthritis.

In one study, it increased oxygen-carrying hemoglobin, which rejuvenates cells. In addition, 70% of the men in the study said that their sexual performance improved—some men even reported fewer gray hairs.

Dose: 3 to 6 grams (g) of the dried root in capsule form per day.

BETA-GLUCAN

This nutrient is derived from baker's yeast, young rye plants and medicinal mushrooms. It activates *macrophages,* key immune cells that fight bacteria, viruses and other organisms that cause disease. Beta-glucan enhances the effectiveness of conventional antibiotic therapy. It acts as a free radical scavenger, removing cells damaged by exposure to radiation, chemotherapy and environmental pollutants. It also decreases total and LDL ("bad") cholesterol while increasing HDL ("good") cholesterol. In addition, it reduces risk of infection by stimulating white blood cell activity.

Dose: 300 to 1,000 mg per day.

LEMON BALM

Lemon balm is an important antioxidant. It contains a high concentration of *phenols,* chemicals that fight cell-damaging toxins. This herb can improve sleep…decrease pain caused by inflammatory conditions including arthritis…boost mental functioning…and combat viruses and bacteria.

Dose: 1,000 to 1,500 mg per day.

Caution: Avoid taking lemon balm if you have been diagnosed with glaucoma. Some animal studies have shown that it may raise

*Dosages vary by body weight. Consult your doctor for the appropriate amount for you.

pressure in the eye, which can worsen the symptoms of glaucoma.

OMEGA-3 FATTY ACIDS

Also known as *essential fatty acids* (EFAs), omega-3 fatty acids aren't manufactured by the human body and must be supplied by diet or supplements. They are found primarily in fish but also are present in smaller amounts in green, leafy vegetables…soybeans…nuts…and flaxseed and canola oils.

Omega-3s work to decrease blood levels of triglycerides (bad fats) and homocysteine (an artery-damaging amino acid) and decrease blood pressure. They help thin the blood, preventing blood clots. These effects lower the risk of heart disease and stroke, the number-one and number-three killers of Americans (cancer is number two).

Omega-3s also act like anti-inflammatories, helpful in the treatment of such autoimmune diseases as rheumatoid arthritis, chronic inflammatory bowel disease and psoriasis. They are a building block of the outer layer of brain cells and may help treat depression.

Dose: 3 to 10 g daily of fish oil capsules. Follow instructions on label.

Caution: If you have heart disease or diabetes, consult your doctor before taking these high doses, which may raise cholesterol and blood sugar levels.

To get omega-3 fatty acids from your diet, eat oily fish three to four times a week. These include mackerel, salmon, sea bass, trout, herring, sardines, sablefish (black cod), anchovies and tuna. Use omega-3–rich canola oil in cooking and salad dressings.

EVENING PRIMROSE OIL

Evening primrose oil is derived from the seeds of the evening primrose plant. The active ingredient is *gamma linolenic acid* (GLA), an omega-6 fatty acid.

As the body ages, it loses its ability to convert dietary fats into GLA. Supplementing with evening primrose oil is important in combating the general effects of aging. It also may help in treating rheumatoid arthritis, diabetes, nerve damage (neuropathy), multiple sclerosis and Alzheimer's-related memory problems.

Dose: 3,000 to 6,000 mg daily, which contains about 270 to 540 mg of GLA.

Caution: Evening primrose oil may worsen temporal-lobe epilepsy. It should be avoided by epileptics and schizophrenics who are prescribed phenothiazine epileptogenic drugs.

RESVERATROL

This is a naturally occurring antioxidant that's found in many plants—including the skins of grapes. Red wine is the main dietary source. Resveratrol decreases the "stickiness" of blood platelets, reducing the risk of blood clots. It also may help prevent the development and progression of various cancers.

Dose: 200 to 650 micrograms (mcg) daily. One eight-ounce glass of red wine contains roughly 640 mcg.

Supplements Adults Should Take Daily

Adults should take a multivitamin that provides 100% of the daily value (DV) of most vitamins and minerals and lists an expiration date on the label.

All adults over age 50, especially women, should also take a 600-milligram (mg) calcium supplement, since multivitamins typically provide only about 10% of the DV for calcium.

Also consider taking a vitamin E supplement. Even though evidence is inconclusive, some studies suggest that vitamin E supplements may reduce risk for heart disease, cancer and Alzheimer's disease. Try 200 international units (IU) of the natural *d-alpha-tocopherol* or 400 IU of the synthetic *dl-* form.

Supplements of fish oil, containing DHA and/ or EPA omega-3 fatty acids, also may reduce heart disease risk.

Important: Check with your doctor before taking any new supplement.

Jeffrey Blumberg, PhD, professor of nutrition, Friedman School of Nutrition Science and Policy, Tufts University, Boston.

Use Melatonin Wisely

Use melatonin only on the advice of your doctor. Marketing campaigns urge older people to take melatonin supplements to make up for its decline as they age. Melatonin is touted for resetting the biological clock and fighting jet lag and insomnia.

Reality: The level of melatonin, which is produced by the pineal gland, does not automatically drop as people age. It is lower in many older people because of illness, not aging.

Trap: Melatonin's sale is unregulated, and its long-term effects are unknown.

Martin Scharf, PhD, director, Tri-State Sleep Disorders Center, Cincinnati.

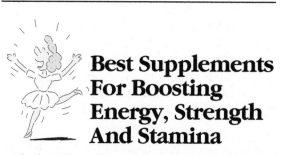

Best Supplements For Boosting Energy, Strength And Stamina

The late Edmund R. Burke, PhD, former professor of exercise science and director, exercise science program, University of Colorado, Colorado Springs, and coauthor of *Avery's Sports Nutrition Almanac.*

If you've ventured into a health food store or a drugstore recently, you've probably seen shelves lined with creatine, DHEA and other "performance enhancing" products.

Which of these over-the-counter products really enhance athletic performance? Which ones are safe and reliable? *Here's a product-by-product rundown...*

CREATINE

Of all the products that purportedly have a strength-building effect, creatine is the top contender. There's ample scientific evidence to support creatine's effectiveness.

This protein-like substance—made up of three amino acids found naturally in meat and fish—is not a substitute for exercise. It does not build muscle or boost strength on its own. But it can help boost the muscle-building effect of your weight-lifting workouts. It can also put more power in your tennis serve...and make you a faster runner. It's safe, too.

Creatine may also be effective at preventing and even reversing the muscle loss that typically accompanies aging. This condition is known as sarcopenia.

Typical dosage: 2 to 3 grams (g) per day, preferably with a meal or carbohydrate-rich beverage, such as Gatorade.

GLUCOSAMINE

If your joints and muscles often feel sore after exercise, consider taking *glucosamine.* This amino acid supplement promotes repair of cartilage and ligaments.

Typical dosage: 500 to 750 milligrams (mg) in the morning and again at night.

VITAMIN SUPPLEMENT

A multivitamin/mineral tablet is perhaps the most important overall performance enhancer you can buy. It's also the safest and cheapest.

Every morning with your breakfast, take a supplement that contains a minimum of 100% of the RDA for most vitamins and minerals.

ANDROSTENEDIONE

Andro is said to stimulate muscle growth by boosting testosterone levels. It's been touted as a natural alternative to anabolic steroids, the dangerous drugs used by many bodybuilders.

There is no scientific evidence that andro builds muscle mass or strength. Research has shown that it increases testosterone for less than one hour, even when taken in large doses. Increased testosterone could raise the risk for prostate cancer in men and of acne or excessive body hair in women.

If you still choose to take andro, take it only under medical supervision. If you're male, make sure your *prostate-specific antigen* (PSA) level—a marker for prostate cancer—is monitored.

DHEA

Dehydroepiandrosterone is a substance that is naturally produced by the adrenal glands and ovaries.

DHEA is supposed to build muscle mass and increase strength. But as with andro, there's no evidence that it does either. It may also carry the same serious risks and side effects as andro.

DHEA is beneficial only for men whose blood tests have shown chronically low levels of testosterone.

It should be taken under a doctor's supervision so that testosterone levels and PSA levels can be monitored.

GINSENG

The herb ginseng is purported to boost energy and endurance...and to help reverse fatigue. Russian athletes have used it for years. Yet there's little scientific evidence to back up these claims.

If you want to try ginseng anyway, the usual dosage is 100 mg, two to four times daily.

Caution: Ginseng can raise blood pressure. Do not take it if you have that condition.

Glucomannan: A Wonder Supplement

Andrew L. Rubman, ND, director, Southbury Clinic for Traditional Medicines, Southbury, CT, *www.naturopath.org.*

Most people would benefit from taking the powdered root of the Japanese *konjac* plant (*glucomannan*) every day. By improving the liver's ability to excrete fat-soluble waste, it will lower cholesterol...promote weight loss ...alleviate menopausal symptoms...and relieve headaches and premenstrual syndrome.

Take one capsule before your largest meal. And be sure to consult your doctor before starting any supplement.

Cost: About $12 for 60 capsules, available in health food stores.

More from Andrew L. Rubman...

Get the Most from Vitamin and Mineral Supplements

Take your vitamins and minerals at the right times and in the right combinations to maximize effectiveness.

Examples: Take vitamin C by itself—it interferes with the absorption of some vitamins

—and not with meals. Taking vitamins A and E and zinc together makes them work better. Take calcium and magnesium by themselves for maximum absorption—but with food. Take selenium by itself, between meals.

Information: National Institutes of Health Office of Dietary Supplements, 301-435-2920 or *http://dietary-supplements.info.nih.gov.*

Look for the USP On the Label

If a vitamin supplement does not disintegrate in the digestive tract, it will provide little benefit.

The best guarantee that pills will disintegrate properly is to look for the letters "USP" on the label. That means they meet the disintegration standards of US Pharmacopeia, an independent, nonprofit pharmaceutical-testing organization. Generic vitamins approved by USP meet the same test standards as more expensive name brands.

Robert Russell, MD, director, USDA Human Nutrition Research Center on Aging, Tufts University, Boston.

The Omega-3 Solution: Fatty Acids Fight Heart Disease, Arthritis and Obesity

Andrew L. Stoll, MD, director, psychopharmacology research laboratory, McLean Hospital, and associate professor of psychiatry, Harvard Medical School, both in Boston. He is author of *The Omega-3 Connection* (Free Press).

In Japan and other nations where fish is a dietary staple, many disease rates are significantly lower than in Western countries.

Omega-3 fatty acids—lipid compounds that are a major constituent of fish oil—receive much of the credit for this difference.

Many people now take omega-3 supplements to reduce their risk for heart disease, rheumatoid arthritis, obesity and other health problems. But do omega-3s really deliver all these salutary effects?

Distinguished researcher Andrew L. Stoll, MD, provided the facts…

●**Why are omega-3 fatty acids important?** Essential fatty acids are dietary constituents that promote good health.

In addition to omega-3, there's another essential fatty acid known as omega-6. For optimum health, we need to consume roughly the same amount of omega-3s and omega-6s.

But Americans eat small quantities of fish and even less omega-3-containing plants, such as flax and the salad green purslane. Instead, our diets are loaded with omega-6-rich oils— corn, sunflower and most oils in processed foods. We eat 10 to 20 times more omega-6s than omega-3s.

●**Why is this unhealthful?** Omega-3s contain *eicosapentaenoic acid* (EPA). When we consume this beneficial fat, much of it gets converted into *eicosanoids,* hormone-like substances that direct the inflammatory response and other functions within the immune system, heart and brain.

Omega-6s contain the fatty acid *arachidonic acid.* This substance also turns into eicosanoids —but with a critical difference.

Omega-6 eicosanoids are strongly inflammatory. On the other hand, omega-3 eicosanoids are only slightly inflammatory or, in some instances, anti-inflammatory.

That's why balance is so important. Without it, uncontrolled inflammatory responses can damage virtually any organ system in the body.

●**How do omega-3s protect the heart?** By offsetting omega-6s, omega-3s reduce *atherosclerosis* (hardening of the arteries). Without omega-3s, omega-6s can inflame and damage coronary arteries, allowing plaque buildup.

Omega-3s also raise levels of beneficial high-density lipoprotein (HDL), which transports plaque-causing cholesterol out of the body.

EPA prevents blood platelets from sticking together, reducing the risk for clotting.

Omega-3s also help to inhibit *arrhythmia* (erratic heartbeat), the leading factor in fatal heart attacks. Research shows that at least 1 gram (g) daily of omega-3s reduces the heart patient's risk for sudden death by 30%.

●**How do omega-3s help prevent obesity and diabetes?** Obesity is a diabetes risk factor. Omega-3s are the only fats that may actually promote weight loss, since they cause the body to burn calories. Plus, people who eat omega-3-rich foods or take supplements often report fewer cravings for other more fattening foods, such as ice cream, butter and cookies.

Omega-3s fight diabetes by making the body's insulin receptors more responsive. In adult-onset (type 2) diabetes, the body's insulin receptors fail. This can lead to a dangerously high level of blood sugar.

●**What about diseases of the immune system?** The highly inflammatory eicosanoids produced by omega-6s are great infection fighters. But when left unchecked by omega-3s, they can damage healthy tissue.

In the digestive disorder known as Crohn's disease, the gut becomes inflamed…in rheumatoid arthritis, it's the joints…in asthma, the airways are inflamed.

A remarkable Italian study published in *The New England Journal of Medicine,* showed that 60% of Crohn's patients who took 2.7 g of fish oil supplements daily went into remission for more than one year. No medication has proven to be more effective in treating Crohn's disease.

Studies have also indicated that omega-3s reduce the inflammation of rheumatoid arthritis and asthma.

●**Do omega-3s help fight other diseases?** Research conducted at Brigham and Women's Hospital in Boston indicated that omega-3s block abnormal brain cell signaling in patients who have bipolar disorder (manic depression). Therefore, omega-3s can be a powerful adjunct in treating this illness.

Many bipolar patients who take the antidepressant *lithium* (Lithonate) and other mood stabilizers, such as *divalproex* (Depakote) and *lamotrigine* (Lamictal), improve initially but then later relapse. Omega-3s can enhance the drug's effectiveness and may allow some people to reduce their dosage.

Caution: If you're taking a mood stabilizer, do not alter the dose without your doctor's approval. Stopping these medicines abruptly can make the illness worse.

●**How much omega-3 does a healthy person need?** To maintain health, 1 to 2 g daily. But it's difficult to get that much in food alone. You would have to consume, say, a large salmon steak daily.

You should certainly try to eat more omega-3–rich foods, such as salmon, tuna, mackerel, sardines…wild game meats, including buffalo and venison…flax…purslane…and walnuts. Add one to two servings a day of these foods to your diet. Still, you may not get enough omega-3s in dietary sources. To ensure adequate intake, take a daily 1 to 2 g supplement.

●**How do I choose the right supplement?** Look for distilled fish oil capsules that have an omega-3 concentration of 50% or more.

Quality supplements cost more, but they do enable you to take fewer and smaller pills, without the fishy aftertaste you often get with other brands.

●**What do you recommend for vegetarians?** Flaxseed oil is a good option for strict vegetarians or those allergic to fish. Consume one-half tablespoon of this plant-based source of omega-3 every day.

Some people will take flaxseed oil straight. Others can't tolerate the strong taste. However, it's virtually imperceptible when used in waffle batter and other recipes.

●**Do omega-3 supplements have any side effects?** Omega-3s may inhibit blood clotting. If you're taking a blood thinner, such as *warfarin* (Coumadin), or high-dose aspirin, check with your doctor before starting a regimen of omega-3 supplements.

Some people experience stomach upset, but this usually goes away within seven days. You'll be less likely to have this problem if you use a quality supplement…take it with food… and divide your daily intake among two or three equal doses.

By the way, it's a good idea to take vitamins C and E with omega-3s. These antioxidant vitamins scavenge disease-causing molecules known as "free radicals." Once free radicals are eliminated, omega-3s can do their job.

I typically recommend 800 international units (IU) of vitamin E (but check with your doctor first—large amounts can be dangerous for some people) and 1,000 mg of vitamin C daily. In addition to other benefits, your colds won't last as long.

Unexpected Benefits of Vitamin D

Michael F. Holick, MD, PhD, professor of medicine and dermatology, Boston University Medical Center. He is editor of *Vitamin D: Physiology, Molecular Biology and Clinical Applications* (Humana Press).

Everyone knows that vitamin D strengthens your bones, but recent scientific evidence suggests that vitamin D protects against a wide range of diseases from high blood pressure to diabetes to cancer—in addition to helping the body absorb calcium.

WHAT IS VITAMIN D?

Vitamin D is supplied by food and supplements. It is also produced by your own skin tissue when it is exposed to adequate sunlight.

In the body, vitamin D travels to the liver and kidneys, where it is chemically modified into a biologically active form.

Vitamin D is widely recognized for its ability to triple the amount of calcium your digestive system can absorb from food and/or supplements. This function helps protect your bones, from which the body might otherwise rob calcium to compensate for a deficiency of the mineral.

LATEST FINDINGS

Compelling evidence shows that adequate vitamin D can reduce the risk for developing breast, prostate, ovarian and colon cancers.

For example, researchers have shown that the risk for some cancers is cut in half among people with high blood levels of vitamin D. A study conducted in Finland found fewer cases of prostate cancer among men who had been exposed to the most sunlight.

Vitamin D also appears to reduce the risk for autoimmune diseases, in which immune cells attack the body's own tissues. High doses of the vitamin have been shown to prevent type 1 diabetes in children. Evidence also suggests that adequate sun exposure may help prevent multiple sclerosis.

Vitamin D may shield the heart as well, possibly by inhibiting the production of *renin,* an enzyme that raises blood pressure.

Although vitamin D deficiency is a common cause of osteoporosis (brittle-bone disease), it can also trigger *osteomalacia,* a lesser-known problem in which bones become soft. Osteomalacia occurs when the body does not properly deposit calcium into the bone. The condition is associated with bone and muscle pain, muscle weakness and an increased risk for fracture. Osteomalacia, which chiefly afflicts older adults but can occur at any age, is an often overlooked source of chronic pain.

ARE YOU DEFICIENT?

A surprising number of people of all ages lack adequate vitamin D. More than one-third of 69 Boston University Medical Center students and residents ages 18 to 29 were deficient at the end of winter. Even a summer's worth of sunshine left 4% below par.

Anyone over age 60 is at greater risk, in part because older bodies are less efficient at manufacturing vitamin D from sunlight. At Johns Hopkins in Baltimore, researchers found severe vitamin deficiencies in more than half of adults over age 65.

Are you at risk? The test that measures blood levels of *25 hydroxy-vitamin D,* the partially activated form of vitamin D, costs about $100 and may be covered by health insurance. Talk to your doctor, and consider making it part of your regular physical.

HERE COMES THE SUN

Diet rarely gives you all the vitamin D you need. To get enough vitamin D, you would have to consume a substantial amount of cod liver oil or oily fish, such as salmon, eel or mackerel, several times a week.

Milk is enriched with vitamin D, but it takes two to six eight-ounce glasses daily to provide the recommended daily intake—up to age 50, 200 international units (IU)...ages 51 to 70, 400 IU...and age 71 or older, 600 IU.

What's more, strong evidence suggests that the recommended intake is too low. To maintain adequate blood levels of vitamin D, some people may actually need to get as much as 1,000 IU daily.

For most people, sun exposure is the primary source of vitamin D. Every time you go out in the sun in the spring, summer and fall, your body immediately starts manufacturing the nutrient.

Because vitamin D is stored in fatty tissues, sensible sun exposure during the warm months can typically supply all you'll need of the vitamin for the entire year. What's sensible depends on the season, time of day and your individual skin type.

Here's a simple formula: Find out how much sun it takes to turn your skin just slightly pink—the very beginnings of sunburn. Expose your unprotected hands, face and arms (or arms and legs) to direct sunlight for *one-quarter* this time, then apply an SPF-15 sunscreen to prevent skin damage. Do this twice a week. The more of your body you expose, the more vitamin D you manufacture.

Example: If you turn pink in one hour, expose yourself to 15 minutes of sun. This should result in the body manufacturing 600 to 1,000 IU of vitamin D—without increasing your skin cancer risk.

To ensure that you're getting enough vitamin D daily, take a 400 IU supplement (it's usually part of a multivitamin formula). If you're over age 50, ask your doctor about taking up to 1,000 IU daily.

Vitamin D Boosts Calcium Absorption

Many people take calcium supplements and/or increase the amount of calcium in their diets to help avoid losing bone mass with aging. But the body doesn't absorb all of the calcium that is consumed.

Remedy: Studies show that taking vitamin D supplements can increase the body's absorption of calcium by up to 65%.

Recommended daily allowances of vitamin D are 200 international units (IU) up to age 50, 400 IU from ages 51 to 70 and 600 IU for persons over 70. Vitamin D also is found in fish, liver, egg yolks and vitamin D–fortified milk.

Medical Update, Box 2166, Indianapolis 46206.

Tired? Forgetful? You May Need More B Vitamins

Michael Hirt, MD, assistant clinical professor of medicine, University of California, Los Angeles School of Medicine, and medical director, Center for Integrative Medicine, Encino-Tarzana Regional Medical Center, Encino, CA.

It's fairly common knowledge that *folate* (also called *folic acid*) helps to prevent birth defects when taken by pregnant women.

But there's strong evidence that folate and other B vitamins provide many additional benefits. In fact, B vitamins do a better job of protecting the average adult's *overall* health than any other vitamin.

A study of more than 9,000 Americans showed that people with the highest dietary intake of folate—400 micrograms (mcg) a day—have an 86% lower risk for heart attack and a 79% lower risk for stroke than those with the lowest intake (100 mcg).

Evidence also suggests that a high intake of folate may decrease the risk of developing colon and breast cancers. In addition, B vitamins may help prevent Alzheimer's disease as well as other memory problems older adults experience.

How can one nutrient provide so many health benefits? Michael Hirt, MD, one of only a handful of US physicians who is board-certified in nutrition, answered this question and more. *Here are the details...*

●**What is the function of B vitamins?** There are seven different B vitamins. In addition to folate, there are B-1 (thiamine), B-2 (riboflavin), B-3 (niacin), B-5 (pantothenic acid), B-6 (pyridoxine) and B-12 (cobalamin).

Each of these vitamins is critical for optimum health. Collectively, they play an important role in how our bodies metabolize sugar, fat and protein and in the production of energy.

B vitamins also aid the functioning of the nerves and brain chemistry and boost immunity.

●**Why is folate so important in protecting the heart?** Folate helps lower blood levels of the amino acid homocysteine. A high level of homocysteine (above 10) is a risk factor for heart disease and stroke.

Low-fat diets, regular exercise and other heart-healthy actions don't affect the body's homocysteine levels. Getting enough folate is the only way to lower homocysteine.

●**Is that why flour-containing foods are fortified with folate?** No. This practice was mandated in 1998 to prevent birth defects. Along with vitamin B-12, folate is essential for synthesis of DNA—the genetic molecule that "instructs" cells how to form and act.

If a pregnant woman doesn't get enough folate, fetal DNA can't multiply properly. That can result in spina bifida, a neural tube defect in which the spinal bones and spinal cord don't fuse correctly as the body forms.

Fortifying flour with folate helps to ensure that all women receive enough folate in their diets to prevent spina bifida. Every woman of childbearing age should consume 400 mcg to 800 mcg of folate daily.

●**What about the other B vitamins?** Vitamin B-12 is probably second to folate in therapeutic power. In large doses prescribed by a physician, vitamin B-12 can help to ease symptoms of low-grade depression, chronic fatigue, chronic pain, dust, pollen and other allergies and the mood swings of *premenstrual syndrome* (PMS).

Vitamin B-12 can also help control the side effects of psychoactive medications, such as those used to treat Parkinson's disease and schizophrenia.

●**Which foods contain high levels of B vitamins?** Some of the best sources of B vitamins are whole grains, beans, peas and vegetables. Since most Americans don't eat a lot of these foods, they usually consume less than the government's recommended dietary intake of B vitamins.

Helpful: Everyone should be sure to get a blood test every two years to check for any B vitamin deficiencies.

●**Is low dietary intake the sole cause of a deficiency?** No. Stress depletes the body of B vitamins, so anxiety or a hectic lifestyle can cause a deficiency.

Also, cooking vegetables—one of the best sources of these nutrients—reduces B vitamin content. To avoid this problem, steam your vegetables—which destroys fewer vitamins—or even better, eat them raw.

Older adults—particularly those over age 65—are at risk for a deficiency of vitamin B-12 no matter how much they get in their diets.

As the stomach lining ages, its ability to absorb B-12 decreases. This condition causes a deficiency that can usually be corrected with a B-12 injection or a tablet that dissolves under the tongue. Discuss these options with your doctor.

●**Should all adults take a B vitamin supplement?** Yes. Because these vitamins help lower levels of homocysteine in the blood, we would see a dramatic decrease in the incidence of heart disease in this country.

Each year, more than 500,000 Americans die from heart disease—many of those lives would be saved if everyone included a B vitamin in their supplement regimen.

●**What do you look for in a B vitamin supplement?** I recommend taking a B-complex supplement that contains 100% of the recommended daily intake, or daily value (DV), of each of the seven B vitamins. Be sure to check the label.

Important: Under certain conditions, you should take more than the DV of vitamin B-12. For example, I recommend supplementing your B-complex intake for a total of 100 mcg to 200 mcg of vitamin B-12 if blood tests determine that you have difficulty absorbing the nutrient...if you're over age 65...or if you have frequent indigestion, which can indicate an inflammation of the stomach that decreases absorption of B-12.

•**Is it possible to consume too much in B vitamins?** Yes. More than 200 milligrams (mg) daily of vitamin B-3 (niacin), which may be prescribed to lower cholesterol levels, can cause skin flushing and dangerously high levels of liver enzymes.

With vitamin B-6, which can be taken to alleviate symptoms of PMS, you should never take more than 25 mg a day without a doctor's supervision. Taken on a daily basis, high levels of vitamin B-6 can cause permanent nerve damage.

Too Much of a Good Thing?

Restrict your intake of vitamin-fortified foods if you take a daily multivitamin. The argument that taking too much of a vitamin or mineral is harmless applies only to water-soluble vitamins, which the body excretes—such as vitamin C and the B vitamins. The body stores fat-soluble vitamins—A, D, E and K.

Example: Too much vitamin A increases risk of osteoporosis for women and men.

Safest: Take multivitamins that provide 100% of the recommended daily intake, not more. Try to limit foods fortified with vitamins whose daily intake you already meet.

Richard Wood, PhD, associate professor of nutrition, Friedman School of Nutrition Science and Policy, Tufts University, Boston.

Get More Vitamin C from Orange Juice

Ready-to-drink orange juice loses half of its vitamin C one week after opening. In fact,

vitamin C levels begin to drop immediately after opening—regardless of the expiration date.

Reason: Once open, the juice is exposed to oxygen, which destroys vitamin C. Oxygen can also pass through wax and plastic containers.

Better: Drink orange juice that's made from canned concentrate. Because juice from concentrate contains higher vitamin C levels, it can be used for up to 14 days after preparation.

Carol S. Johnston, PhD, RD, professor of nutrition, Arizona State University East, Mesa.

Vitamin C and Stress

Supplementing with vitamin C may help to prevent illness in people who are experiencing severe psychological stress.

A dose of vitamin C equal to several grams a day in humans reduced levels of *corticosterone* in rats stressed by being immobilized. High levels of corticosterone and other stress hormones have been linked to heart disease, ulcers and other illnesses. It is likely that vitamin C has the same effect in people.

When under stress: Consume more orange juice, citrus fruits and other vitamin C–rich foods...or take a daily 500-milligram vitamin C supplement.

P. Samuel Campbell, PhD, emeritus professor, department of biological sciences, University of Alabama, Huntsville. His study was presented at a meeting of the American Chemical Society.

Antioxidant Therapy

Jeffrey Blumberg, PhD, professor of nutrition and chief, Antioxidants Research Laboratory, Tufts University, Boston.

Most people know about *free radicals* and the harm they do to the human body. Free radicals are thought to contribute to cancer, cataracts, heart disease, Alzheimer's disease and other chronic ailments.

And antioxidants—which are found in food and nutritional supplements—help minimize free radical damage.

But many people are still confused. *Leading antioxidant researcher Jeffrey Blumberg, PhD, cleared up the confusion...*

WHAT ARE FREE RADICALS?

Free radicals are molecular fragments that are created when the body burns oxygen...or when it's exposed to "insults" like tobacco smoke or sunlight.

Free radicals react eagerly with other molecules in a process known as *oxidation*. Antioxidants neutralize free radicals by scavenging and destroying them before they reach the other molecules.

There's growing evidence that an antioxidant-rich diet helps stop free radical damage. How can you be sure you're getting enough antioxidants? The best strategy is to eat a variety of fruits and vegetables—five to nine servings per day. Taking antioxidant supplements may also be a good idea.

Caution: Although antioxidant supplements do seem to enhance a well-rounded diet, they are not a substitute for such a diet.

KEY ANTIOXIDANTS

Scientists have just begun to identify the thousands of antioxidants found in foods. *So far, five seem especially important...*

•**Vitamin C** helps prevent heart disease by blocking oxidation of cholesterol and other fatty substances in the blood. It also blocks the effects of *nitrites,* carcinogens found in bacon and other preserved meats.

Sources of vitamin C include citrus fruits, cantaloupe, strawberries, peppers, tomatoes and broccoli. A one-cup serving of cantaloupe or broccoli contains about 100 milligrams (mg) of vitamin C.

Daily supplement: 250 to 1,000 mg of vitamin C. Studies have shown that the incidence of heart disease—as well as of cataracts and cancer—is significantly lower among people whose vitamin C intake falls within this range.

Caution: Excess vitamin C can cause diarrhea. To avoid trouble, start at 250 mg per day, and increase the dosage gradually over several weeks. Do not take more than 1,000 mg per day without a doctor's supervision.

The beneficial effects of vitamin C have been demonstrated in numerous scientific studies. In 1998, however, scientists at the University of Leicester in England published a study that suggested that vitamin C supplements could raise the risk for cancer.

The English researchers found evidence of DNA damage—a harbinger of cancer—among individuals who took 500 mg of vitamin C each day for six weeks.

This study cannot be taken seriously. It contained insufficient detail for other researchers to evaluate the methodology.

In addition, the authors never subjected the study to peer review, the process in which weaknesses in methodology are often detected.

Most telling: Other researchers who attempted to replicate these findings didn't achieve the same results.

•**Vitamin E** fights heart disease by preventing oxidation of LDL ("bad") cholesterol... blocks sunlight-induced oxidation of skin cells ...and helps prevent cataracts.

One study suggested that vitamin E may slow the progression of Alzheimer's disease. Other studies suggest that it enhances the clot-preventing power of aspirin, suggesting that the aspirin–vitamin E combination might be a good idea for many heart patients.

Good sources of vitamin E include vegetable oil...almonds and other nuts...and especially wheat germ.

Because food sources of vitamin E tend to be high in fat, it's hard to get enough E from food without getting too much fat. Vitamin E supplementation is a better idea.

Daily supplement: 100 to 400 international units (IU) of vitamin E. However, more than 200 IU may be dangerous, so check with your doctor for the proper amount to take.

Most studies showing the protective effects of vitamin E supplements have used *dl-alpha-tocopherol*, the synthetic form of the vitamin. The natural form—*d-alpha-tocopherol*—costs more but is somewhat more potent.

•**Beta-carotene and other carotenoids** help prevent heart disease, stroke, cataracts and cancer of the breast, cervix and stomach.

Carotenoids also block development of lung cancer—at least when taken by nonsmokers.

In the mid-1990s, Finnish and American researchers discovered that smokers who took high-dose beta-carotene supplements seemed to be at increased risk for lung cancer.

In light of these studies, heavy smokers should avoid beta-carotene supplements. Studies involving nonsmokers have not found beta-carotene or any other carotenoid to be toxic.

Good sources of beta-carotene and other carotenoids include cantaloupes, apricots, carrots and squash and other red and yellow fruits and vegetables...broccoli...and green, leafy vegetables.

Daily supplement: 15,000 IU of beta-carotene—for nonsmokers only.

Preliminary research suggests that other carotenoids may be even more protective than beta-carotene...

•*Lycopene* seems to reduce the risk for prostate cancer.

•*Lutein* and *zeaxanthin* seem to guard against age-related macular degeneration, a potentially blinding retinal ailment.

•**Selenium** boosts the disease-fighting power of other antioxidants. In several recent studies, people who took a selenium supplement had a substantially reduced risk for lung and prostate cancer.

Good sources of selenium include Brazil nuts and seafood (especially mackerel, oysters, tuna and shrimp).

Daily supplement: 200 micrograms (mcg) of selenium. Higher doses can cause loss of hair and fingernails and possibly nerve damage.

•**Flavonoids** have been linked to reduced risk for heart disease and stroke—and possibly some types of cancer.

Sources of flavonoids include onions, apples and grapes...green and black tea...and red wine.

Several flavonoid supplements are on the market, including pine bark extract and grape seed extract. But until the effectiveness of these supplements has been demonstrated in clinical trials, it's probably a good idea to depend upon food sources of flavonoids.

Antioxidant Supplement Warning

Get your antioxidants from fruits and vegetables instead of supplements. An analysis of 15 large-scale studies showed that taking supplemental beta-carotene actually *increases* risk of dying from all causes by a small but significant amount and from heart disease in particular. It also showed that there are no significant cardiovascular benefits from vitamin E supplements.

New recommendation: Stay away from dietary supplements that contain beta-carotene or its close cousin, vitamin A. The jury is still out on whether they protect against cancer.

Marc S. Penn, MD, PhD, staff cardiologist, the Cleveland Clinic Foundation, Cleveland. His analysis was published in *The Lancet*.

Vitamins and Colon Polyps

Multivitamins and calcium supplements fight precancerous polyps. Use of vitamins and calcium also makes it less likely that colorectal polyps will return in patients who have already had them removed. Nearly all cases of colon and rectal cancer start as benign polyps.

Richard Whelan, MD, associate professor of surgery and director, colon and rectal surgery, Columbia University College of Physicians and Surgeons, New York City.

Vitamin Danger

Bradley Bongiovanni, ND, naturopathic physician in private practice, Atlanta.

It's fair to say that most people would benefit from taking nutritional supplements. But certain vitamin and mineral supplements can have serious consequences for some people. *Such as...*

•**Smokers.** Synthetic beta-carotene may raise lung cancer risk, according to one study.

Better: Get your daily dose from carrots, spinach and other food sources...or take a natural *mixed* carotenoid supplement.

•**People with kidney disease or hyperparathyroidism.** Avoid getting too much calcium, as these ailments can disrupt calcium metabolism. Limit supplemental intake of calcium to 300 milligrams (mg) a day.

•**Adult men and menopausal women.** Too much iron can lead to heart disease and other illnesses.

Better: Plenty of foods are fortified with iron, so iron supplements make sense only for premenopausal women, children under age 13 and anyone who is iron deficient.

•**People with the metabolic disorder hemochromatosis,** or a history of kidney stones. Limit supplemental intake of vitamin C to 250 mg a day.

•**People on blood-thinning medication** and/or daily aspirin therapy. Vitamin E, ginger, ginkgo biloba, St. John's wort and garlic can all intensify the blood-thinning effect.

Better: Ask your doctor about adjusting your medication and your supplement intake.

To avoid drug interactions: Tell your doctor and pharmacist about all herbs and over-the-counter medicines you are using.

Ron H.J. Mathijssen, MD, PhD, scientist, department of medical oncology, Erasmus Medical Center–Daniel den Hoed Cancer Center, Rotterdam, the Netherlands.

Vitamin A Danger

Too much vitamin A can weaken bones, increasing fracture risk. No one should get more than 1.5 milligrams (mg) per day. Women really need only 0.7 mg of vitamin A per day... men, 0.9 mg. A healthful diet that includes liver, milk, fish and fish oil will supply that much.

Check fish oil labels for vitamin A content, and don't eat liver more than once a week. Choose a multivitamin that contains no more than 5,000 international units (IU)—or 1.5 mg of vitamin A. There is no reason to take vitamin A supplements in addition to a multivitamin.

Donald Louria, MD, chairman emeritus of preventive medicine, University of Medicine and Dentistry of New Jersey, Newark.

Does St. John's Wort Interfere with Cancer Drugs?

In a study, St. John's wort, which is used by many people who suffer from mild depression, reduced the effectiveness of *irinotecan* (Camptosar), a drug commonly prescribed to treat colorectal cancer.

Patients taking the herb and the drug were found to have 40% less medicine in their bloodstream than patients not using St. John's wort.

Men Need Calcium, Too

After age 50, men should consume 1,200 milligrams (mg) of calcium per day. In one study, men took calcium supplements to boost their daily intake from 700 mg to 1,200 mg.

Result: They experienced significantly reduced rates of bone loss.

Some men may need a supplement to meet the 1,200 mg level, but food sources of calcium are preferred. Sources include low-fat milk and yogurt and green, leafy vegetables.

Bess Dawson-Hughes, MD, chief, Calcium and Bone Metabolism Lab, Jean Mayer US Department of Agriculture Human Nutrition Research Center on Aging, Tufts University, Boston.

Potassium Warning

Unless you exercise enough to have heavy loss of fluids and minerals from sweating, potassium supplements—in the form of sports drinks, pills or powder—are unnecessary and may actually cause harm.

Potassium can irritate the esophagus, stomach lining and small intestine, and it may cause an irregular heart rate. You can get all the potassium you need—and you can't possibly get too much—from foods.

Some good sources: Fruits, particularly figs, oranges, bananas and cantaloupe...vegetables, including potatoes, beets and radishes...any meat or seafood.

Michael Mogadam, MD, clinical associate professor of medicine, George Washington University, Washington, DC, and physician in private practice, Alexandria, VA.

Zinc Alert

Prostate cancer risk has been linked to high zinc intake. Zinc, popularly used as a cold preventive, is also found in many vitamin/mineral combinations.

New study: Men who took more than 100 milligrams (mg) of zinc daily over 10 or more years were more than twice as likely to develop advanced prostate cancer as men who took no supplementary zinc.

Self-defense: Avoid any supplements that contain many times the recommended dietary allowance—which is 11 mg a day for men.

Michael Leitzmann, MD, DrPH, nutritional epidemiologist, National Cancer Institute, Rockville, MD. His study of 46,974 men was published in the *Journal of the National Cancer Institute.*

Hidden Ephedra

Stephen Bent, MD, ephedra expert and assistant professor of medicine, University of California, San Francisco.

We've all heard plenty of frightening news about the popular herb ephedra, also known as *Ma huang.*

The active ingredient in many weight-loss and body-building supplements, ephedra contains *ephedrine,* a potentially dangerous chemical compound that constricts blood vessels and increases the heart rate.

Poison control centers have received reports of adverse reactions—such as headache, anxiety and insomnia—and several *deaths* due to ephedra. There's also evidence that it may increase stroke risk.

The American Heart Association has urged a ban on the sale of over-the-counter (OTC) ephedra supplements, and the US Food and Drug Administration has proposed warning labels on products that contain the herb.

Unfortunately, it's not always easy to determine whether a product contains the herb or one of its derivatives. *To protect yourself...*

●**Check labels carefully for ephedra or ephedra derivatives,** such as *Ephedra sinica,* horsetail or Chinese ephedra.

●**Be cautious when considering products labeled "ephedra-free."** Many contain *Citrus aurantium,* a plant compound containing *synephrine*—a chemical cousin of ephedrine that may have similar side effects.

●**Avoid OTC asthma remedies that contain ephedrine.** They may be just as risky as ephedra supplements. Safer alternatives are available from your doctor.

Does Cookware Boost Your Intake of Iron?

Stainless steel cookware boosts the iron content of some foods an average of 14%.

Recent study: Iron leached into scrambled eggs, hamburgers, stir-fried chicken breast and pancakes...but not into rice, green beans or medium-thick white sauce.

Approximately 6% of Americans are believed to have too little iron in their bodies, while 1% are believed to have too much. Either condition can be dangerous.

If you're unsure of your status, ask your doctor about getting your iron level tested.

Helen C. Brittin, PhD, professor of food and nutrition, Texas Tech University, Lubbock.

Fish Oil Supplements Are Harmful for Some

Fish oil supplements can be dangerous for some people. They can increase the risk of hemorrhagic stroke in people who have bleeding disorders or uncontrolled hypertension and those taking anticoagulants. Large doses—more than 3 grams every day—can suppress the immune system, increase glucose levels in people with diabetes and cause nausea, diarrhea and other side effects.

Bottom line: Consult your physician before taking any supplement, and be sure to take only the recommended dose.

University of California, Berkeley Wellness Letter, Box 412, Prince Street Station, New York City 10012, *www. wellnessletter.com.*

Beware of Chromium Picolinate

An over-the-counter nutritional supplement, chromium picolinate is supposed to build muscles and reduce body fat. But one study suggests that it triggers chemical reactions that may lead to cancer.

John B. Vincent, PhD, professor of chemistry, University of Alabama, Tuscaloosa.

6

Diet & Nutrition Solutions

Prevent Asthma, Cataracts, Gallstones, Heart Failure and IBS by Eating the Right Foods

Almost every major medical condition is either caused or affected by what you eat. Yet very few medical doctors are knowledgeable about nutrition. As a result, they rarely give nutritional advice—even when specific foods can help curb symptoms or correct underlying problems as well as or *better than* prescription medications.

Here are the best food treatments for five common diseases…

ASTHMA

This respiratory ailment affects up to 20 million Americans and is becoming increasingly common, presumably because of worsening levels of air pollution.

Best foods: Chili peppers…fish…and coffee.

People who regularly consume hot sauces or chili peppers may have less frequent—and less severe—asthma attacks. *Capsaicin,* the chemical that makes peppers hot, may stimulate nerve endings to help keep airways open.

The fatty acids in cold-water fish, such as salmon, tuna and sardines, lower levels of *prostaglandins* and *leukotrienes,* chemicals that increase airway swelling.

Helpful: Three or more two- to three-ounce servings of fish each week can reduce the frequency of asthma attacks.

Doctors traditionally have advised people to drink one cup of strong coffee at the onset of asthma attacks if none of their usual medications are available. One of coffee's active ingredients, *methylxanthine,* relaxes airway muscles.

Isadore Rosenfeld, MD, Rossi Distinguished Professor of Clinical Medicine, Weill Medical College of Cornell University, New York City. He is author of many books, including *Doctor What Should I Eat?*, *Power to the Patient* (both published by Warner) and *Dr. Isadore Rosenfeld's Breakthrough Health* (Rodale).

162

Adult asthmatics who drink several cups of caffeinated coffee daily have 30% fewer asthma attacks than noncoffee drinkers. I recommend three to four cups a day, provided you don't have active ulcers or cardiac arrhythmias.

CATARACTS

A cataract is a clouding (opacity) of the lens of the eye, which results in impaired vision. Much of the damage is caused by free radicals, harmful oxygen molecules that are produced as a by-product of metabolism.

Best foods: Brightly colored fruits and vegetables—especially squash, spinach, broccoli, oranges, carrots and sweet potatoes. They're rich in vitamins C and A as well as beta-carotene, all of which reduce eye damage.

Helpful: Eat five or more servings daily.

CONGESTIVE HEART FAILURE

It occurs when an underlying condition—such as a viral infection, hypertension, a narrowed heart valve, etc.—inhibits the heart's ability to pump blood.

Best foods: Brown rice, spinach, oatmeal, legumes (such as beans and peas), potatoes and bananas. They're rich in magnesium and potassium, both of which help to improve cardiac function.

Warning: These minerals often are depleted by the use of diuretics—standard drugs for the treatment of heart failure.

Helpful: Eat two daily servings of magnesium- and potassium-rich foods.

Also: Eat four to six small daily meals instead of three big ones. Blood flow to the stomach following big meals increases energy demands on the heart.

Limit total daily sodium intake to less than 2,000 milligrams (mg) daily—a little less than one teaspoon. Excessive salt increases fluid retention and reduces the heart's pumping ability.

GALLSTONES

About half of the 20 million American adults who have gallstones don't have symptoms. In the remaining sufferers, these collections of solid crystals in the gallbladder or bile ducts may cause severe pain under the breastbone or in the upper right side of the abdomen, especially after meals.

The presence of such crystals can irritate the gallbladder and promote infection. Even a single, large stone developing in the gallbladder predisposes that organ to cancer.

Best foods: Fruits…legumes…and vegetables—anything that's low in fat. Fatty foods tend to stimulate gallbladder contractions that can precipitate attacks.

Bonus: The fiber found in plant-based foods interacts with bile in the gallbladder and reduces stone formation. A high-fiber diet may dissolve existing gallstones and also helps with weight reduction.

Warning: People who are just 10% overweight are twice as likely to get gallstones as those who maintain a healthful weight.

Helpful: Get 35 to 45 grams (g) of fiber daily. Eat at least five daily servings of fruits and vegetables, along with whole-grain pasta and breads, legumes and other high-fiber foods.

Good choices: One cup of baked beans (13 g of fiber)…one medium baked potato (4 g) …one large apple (5 g)…or one-half cup of All-Bran (10 g).

IRRITABLE BOWEL SYNDROME (IBS)

This condition is associated with excessively strong and frequent contractions of intestinal muscles. Symptoms include gas, bloating, diarrhea and abdominal cramps.

Best foods: Legumes, whole-grain breads and cereals. They're high in soluble fiber, which reduces diarrhea without adding too much "bulk" to the intestine.

Coarse miller's bran, available in health food stores, is very high in soluble fiber.

Helpful: Slowly increase your consumption to two tablespoons of miller's bran, twice daily. To reduce constipation when eating high-fiber foods, it helps to drink several extra glasses of water a day.

Avoid milk and other dairy foods for a few weeks to see if your symptoms subside. Many people with IBS are unable to digest the lactose in dairy foods. If you are among them, take a supplement, such as Lactaid, with meals.

How Nutritionists Shop For Groceries

Ramona Josephson, registered dietitian and nutritionist (RDN) in private practice, Vancouver. She is author of *The HeartSmart Shopper: Nutrition on the Run* (Douglas & McIntyre).

Grocery shoppers are overwhelmed by choice. The average supermarket now stocks 25,000 items, and these products are packaged, promoted and displayed so as to encourage consumers to buy them whether they are healthful or not.

Here's the smart way to shop for food...

●**Ignore the front of the box.** This is where manufacturers trumpet information that exploits our desires. We gravitate to items labeled "NO CHOLESTEROL," "LOW-FAT" or "LIGHT" because we think these are good for our health.

Those words are often misleading. Plant-based foods *never* contain cholesterol, since cholesterol is found only in animal products. And potato chips, margarine and other foods that are labeled "cholesterol-free" may be very rich in fat—and fat promotes synthesis of cholesterol in the body.

Similarly, many items labeled "low-fat" may be high in calories. So eating these foods may do little to help you control your weight.

Self-defense: Read the ingredients list and "Nutrition Facts" box printed on the label before putting any item into your shopping cart.

●**Examine the *order* of ingredients.** Ingredients are listed in descending order of weight. To judge how healthful a particular food is, consider the first four ingredients.

Example I: If you want to buy whole wheat bread, the first ingredient should be whole wheat flour, not enriched white flour.

Example II: If you pick up a bottle of "juice" that has water and sugar among the first ingredients, it's not really juice.

●**Watch for ingredient "aliases."** Fat, salt and sugar have many different names. If you need to watch your intake of these nutrients, you must be able to identify them in all their forms. *For example...*

●Fat can be listed as lard, shortening, hydrogenated vegetable oil, coconut oil, palm oil, tropical oil, tallow, monoglycerides or diglycerides.

●Salt can be listed as monosodium glutamate (MSG), baking soda, baking powder, brine, kelp, soy sauce or a variety of names containing the word "sodium."

●Sugar can be listed as honey, molasses, dextrose, sucrose, fructose, maltose, lactose, dextrin, maltodextrin, maple syrup, corn syrup or malt syrup.

●**Avoid trans fats.** When it became clear that butter and saturated fat were harmful to the heart, food manufacturers started using vegetable oil instead.

But vegetable oil is often chemically altered—via a process known as *hydrogenation*—to render it more solid. Hydrogenation causes formation of trans fatty acids, which are now thought to be even more dangerous to heart health than saturated fat.

Hydrogenated or partially hydrogenated oils are used to make french fries, donuts, margarine and many baked goods, including crackers and cookies.

Self-defense: If you see that hydrogenated or partially hydrogenated oil is among the first four items in a food's ingredient list, try to choose another product.

●**Pay attention to serving size.** The "Nutrition Facts" label explains, among other things, just how much of the particular food constitutes a single serving. This is the quantity on which all the other nutrition information is based.

Serving sizes are often confusing. A serving of yogurt may be one-half cup, for example, yet the container may hold three-quarters of a cup. In some cases, similar cereals made by the same manufacturer have different serving sizes.

Example: One serving of Post Great Grains cereal is two-thirds of a cup, while a single serving of Post Cranberry Almond Crunch is one cup.

Self-defense: When comparing products for fat grams, calories and nutrients, don't forget to take serving size into account.

●**Beware fantasy thinking.** Food ads would have us believe that we can be transformed by eating certain foods. Not true.

The term "granola" might sound as if eating it would turn us into vigorous outdoors enthusiasts, but granola bars are often very high in fat and sugar.

And while athletes use sports drinks, you won't become more athletic if you drink them. In fact, sports drinks can be high in calories. Nonathletes who use them often gain unwanted weight.

Self-defense: Base your food purchases on ingredients, not on seductive advertising.

•**Pay attention to product placement.** Food manufacturers pay a premium to have their products shelved at eye level. These are often heavily promoted products—and are not necessarily the most healthful.

Cast your eyes higher and lower on the shelves to discover other healthful options.

•**Scrutinize impulse items.** Items at the ends of aisles and at checkout counters are placed there because these positions are conspicuous. The idea is for you to buy something you hadn't planned on buying.

Think twice before adding these items to your basket.

•**Avoid the snack food aisle.** Don't think you're being health-conscious by buying baked chips instead of regular potato chips. While they're less fatty, baked chips aren't much more healthful than fried ones.

Snack foods should be healthful mini-meals, not chips and other nutritionally empty foods.

Good snack choices: Fruit, raw vegetables, yogurt or mini-pizzas made with low-fat mozzarella and tomato sauce.

Don't Be Fooled by Food Labels

Franca B. Alphin, MPH, RD, assistant clinical professor, student health dietitian, Duke University, Durham, NC.

The US Food and Drug Administration (FDA) ruled that food manufacturers must disclose the amount of trans fatty acids contained in food products on their "Nutrition Facts" panels. These chemically altered oils, which extend the shelf life of packaged foods, increase heart disease risk. The ruling went into effect in 2006. But until then, manufacturers are free to use this harmful ingredient without clearly labeling it as "trans fat" or listing the amount that has been added to the product. Most chips, crackers and baked goods are loaded with trans fat.

Without the new labeling, it's impossible for consumers to know the exact content of food products. To protect yourself, limit intake of food products that list "hydrogenated" or "partially hydrogenated" ingredients on the label. These are code words for trans fat.

Whenever it is possible, choose foods with labels that clearly state no trans fat is present. Health food stores typically stock such products. Frito-Lay, which sells snacks and chips in major grocery stores, also has removed trans fat from its products.

Beware: If you do buy foods that contain trans fat, make sure it does not appear among the top five ingredients. These ingredients add the most content (by weight) to the product. You owe it to yourself to find a more healthful alternative.

 # Smart Food Choices Boost Brainpower

Arthur Winter, MD, neurosurgeon and director, New Jersey Neurological Institute, Livingston. He is coauthor, with his wife, science writer Ruth Winter, of *Smart Food: Diet and Nutrition for Maximum Brain Power* (ASJA Press).

Everyone knows that diet has a profound effect on weight, as well as risk for heart disease, cancer and many other serious illnesses. But very few people recognize the impact that food has on brain function.

Brain chemicals known as *neurotransmitters* carry messages that alter both mood and the ability to think. One such neurotransmitter, *serotonin,* is the body's natural antidepressant. Another, *cholecystokinin,* aids memory.

Research now shows that you can influence neurotransmitter activity through your food choices. By eating the right foods, you can improve memory, maintain alertness throughout the day and soothe anxiety.

Situation: Mental fatigue causes you to lose your focus during an intensely competitive round of bridge.

What to eat: There's nothing like caffeine to reverse a sinking mental performance or snap you out of fatigue. But you must consume a considerable amount for the best effect—150 to 600 milligrams (mg) for a 150-pound person. Six ounces of coffee contains about 100 mg of caffeine.

Natural forms of sugar also act as mental boosters because they increase blood sugar levels. Glucose, found in grapes, oranges and corn, is a fast-acting form of natural sugar. It takes only two minutes to raise blood sugar.

Fructose, found in many fruits and vegetables, is slow acting—it takes about 25 minutes to increase blood sugar—but its energy effect is longer lasting. Munch on fresh fruits and crudités throughout your game to stave off mental fatigue.

Situation: You face a day-long seminar. You need both mental alertness and endurance.

What to eat: Protein is key. It provides the building blocks to create *norepinephrine* and *dopamine*—neurotransmitters that help you maintain your mental edge.

Best protein sources: Eggs, fish, beans, meat, yogurt, cheese and milk.

Everyone experiences a decline in alertness about two hours after lunch. The bigger the lunch, the bigger the drop-off. If you must stay in high gear, consider skipping lunch.

If midday fasting doesn't work for you, opt for easy-to-digest protein choices, such as tuna or egg salad.

Carbohydrates elevate levels of the amino acid *tryptophan,* which helps to produce the calming neurotransmitter serotonin. Loading up on protein and limiting carbohydrates, such as pasta and french fries, will help to minimize post-lunch drowsiness.

Situation: You are giving a presentation at work. You need quick recall.

What to eat: Cholecystokinin is a neurotransmitter that improves memory by releasing tryptophan and another amino acid called *phenylalanine*. However, timing is everything if you want to achieve cholecystokinin's optimal effect.

Review your presentation *before* you eat. Immediately after you finish memorizing the material, have a snack or meal that contains cholecystokinin-releasing foods to help you memorize what you have just learned.

Foods that release cholecystokinin include milk, nuts and rice.

Situation: You feel cranky and out of sorts.

What to eat: Foods rich in the omega-3 fatty acids—salmon, trout, walnuts, canola oil and soybeans—help to curb depression.

Chocolate, which boosts levels of serotonin, also eases a depressed mood.

For a calming effect, choose to eat foods that contain tryptophan, such as turkey, bananas and peanuts.

Three Foods that Are No Longer Taboo

Three good-for-you foods that were once considered unhealthful...

Nuts: About 170 calories and 14 grams of fat per ounce. But people who eat them a few times a week actually consume fewer total calories than people who eat no nuts. And some nuts, such as almonds, pecans and walnuts, can help cut cholesterol.

Shellfish: Contain cholesterol—but saturated fat, not cholesterol, is the main culprit in raising cholesterol levels in humans. And shellfish are low in saturated fat.

Eggs: Also high in cholesterol, but low in saturated fat. It is all right to eat up to one a day, unless your doctor has advised otherwise.

Gene A. Spiller, PhD, DSc, director, Health Research and Studies Center and Sphera Foundation, both in Los Altos, CA.

Beware! Six Healthy Foods That Can Be Very Dangerous…*to You*

Julie Avery, RD, nutrition projects manager, Preventive Cardiology Program, Cleveland Clinic Heart Center, Ohio.

Foods that are universally recognized as "good for you" can actually cause problems in some people. *It is important to be aware of the potential risks…*

GRAPEFRUIT JUICE

Medical researchers discovered that the digestion of grapefruit juice utilizes the same liver "pathway" as some drugs. So if you drink grapefruit juice and take certain medications at the same time, the effects of the drugs may be increased or decreased.

Drugs that may be affected by grapefruit juice: Blood pressure medications…antihistamines…cholesterol-lowering drugs…some antidepressants.

Bottom line: Ask your pharmacist if any of the drugs you're taking may be affected. If the answer is yes, avoid grapefruit and grapefruit juice for at least four hours before and after taking medication.

Otherwise, enjoy it. It is rich in both vitamin C and fiber. Pink and red grapefruits also contain *lycopene,* an antioxidant that protects against heart disease and cancer.

AVOCADOS

Avocados are loaded with nutrients and fiber but are also high in fat. One medium avocado has 30 grams of fat—more fat than six teaspoons of oil. Ounce for ounce, avocados are loaded with calories, too—more than five times the calories of most other fruits.

Bottom line: Avocados are healthful when consumed in moderation. A safe limit would be to have one thin slice a day. If you use avocado to make guacamole (add diced tomato, chopped onion and garlic), try to have no more than three tablespoons.

GREEN LEAFY VEGETABLES

Broccoli, spinach, Swiss chard and other leafy greens are rich in vitamin K, which is involved in blood clotting. If you're taking a blood-thinning medication, such as Coumadin (*warfarin*), eat consistent amounts of these foods.

Eating a lot more—or a lot less—leafy greens than usual can alter the effects of these drugs, resulting in abnormal clotting.

Bottom line: Leafy greens are loaded with vitamin C, folate and other essential nutrients. Everyone should have at least two servings daily. If you're taking a blood thinner, be sure to eat the same amount all the time.

WINE

Red wine contains *flavonoids,* which appear to keep cholesterol from accumulating in the arteries. Moderate amounts of red wine reduce the risk of heart disease and stroke.

Downside: Drinking too much alcohol can interfere with certain medications. It also increases the risk of liver disease, depression and other health problems.

Bottom line: Women should limit wine consumption to five ounces daily…men, 10 ounces daily. Or, for other alcoholic beverages, the upper limit is one drink daily for women and two for men. These amounts provide the benefits without as much risk.

RAW FISH

Raw fish is sometimes contaminated with parasites. This is true of the raw fish served in sushi bars as well as raw oysters and clams. Raw shellfish also may transmit hepatitis.

For a healthy person, the parasites aren't a problem—they're destroyed in the intestine. For those with weak immune systems, however, parasites may cause digestive discomfort—and even illness.

Bottom line: Anyone with weakened immunity—such as the elderly…very young children…those undergoing chemotherapy, etc. —should avoid raw fish and shellfish.

Eating cooked fish is fine—heat destroys the harmful parasites.

TOMATOES

Tomatoes, a great source of vitamin C and lycopene, occasionally cause food allergies.

Tomatoes can also cause hives and/or difficulty breathing in those who are allergic to aspirin, since they contain *salicylates,* compounds similar to aspirin.

Bottom line: Eating tomatoes is unlikely to cause problems for most people. But food allergies are potentially serious, so talk to your doctor about any food to which you suspect you may be sensitive.

Time Bombs—Hidden Salt, Sugar And Fat in Everyday Foods

John A. McDougall, MD, founder and medical director, McDougall Program, Santa Rosa, CA, *www.drmcdougall. com.* He is author of numerous books, including *The McDougall Program for Women: What Every Woman Needs to Know to Be Healthy for Life* (Plume).

Even "good" eaters will compromise their health with poor dietary habits—and they often don't even realize it.

Most dangerous culprits: Salt, sugar and fat. Make the appropriate changes to avoid these "hidden" ingredients to reduce your risk of disease.

HIDDEN SALT

Table salt and high-sodium ingredients flavor and preserve everything—from pudding and cake mix...to salad dressing and frozen entrées...to canned food and condiments.

About 20% of the US population is sodium-sensitive, suffering from increased blood pressure or fluid retention due to excess sodium. Excess sodium also causes bones to release calcium and therefore contributes to the development of osteoporosis.

The average American consumes 3,000 to 5,000 milligrams (mg) of sodium per day. Aim for no more than 2,000 mg per day. People with congestive heart failure, gout, hypertension and kidney problems should avoid foods with added salt.

Sodium is added in various forms, including monosodium glutamate (MSG)...sodium bicarbonate...sodium chloride (table salt)...and sodium nitrate.

One cup of soup can easily contain 800 mg to 1,000 mg of sodium, and a few handfuls of chips can contain up to 400 mg. Read labels to compare the sodium content of similar products. *Other strategies...*

• **Buy foods in their natural states.** Avoid processed foods. They are likely to have lots of added sodium.

• **Do not add salt while cooking.** If you must add salt, use it sparingly on the surface when you're ready to eat—don't mix it in. Your tongue will detect the salt and you will be satisfied without a lot of it laced throughout the dish.

• **Use lemon juice,** lime juice, vinegar and extra herbs and spices to flavor foods. All add punch without extra sodium. Add a few squirts or pinches to cooked greens, low-sodium tomato juice and low-sodium soup.

HIDDEN SUGAR

Refined and even natural sugars are added to everything—from baby food and breakfast cereal...to pasta sauce and processed foods. On food labels, sugar is listed in many ways—as sucrose, fructose, high-fructose corn syrup, fruit juice concentrate, honey, molasses, maple syrup and others. An ingredient ending in -ose is usually a form of sugar.

If you are overweight, eating excess sugar can slow weight loss or even cause weight gain. Dried fruit, fruit juice and foods flavored with added sugar are concentrated in calories. All sugar—whether refined or natural—can contribute to elevated blood triglyceride levels, a risk factor for heart disease.

Sugar-avoidance strategies...

• **Eat fresh fruit.** Limit processed fruit products, such as fruit juices and canned and dried fruits. I advise my patients to eat no more than three servings of fruit per day...or one serving per day for maximum weight loss.

• **Think of fruit as dessert.** Fruit is a wonderful source of vitamins, minerals and health-supporting phytochemicals as well as fiber. Make fresh fruit the sweet ending to a meal.

Skip fattening desserts, which are devoid of nutritional benefits.

●**Add sugar—but just to the surface.** As with salt, a little bit of sugar sprinkled on the surface of food adds flavor without many extra calories. A bowl of cooked oatmeal topped with a teaspoon of brown sugar is satisfying and contains less sugar than many presweetened packaged varieties.

Likewise, you can buy unsweetened cold breakfast cereals and drizzle a bit of honey on top. You will get much less sugar than in presweetened cereal.

HIDDEN FAT

Fat is added to processed foods to enhance the flavor and texture and blend ingredients. Everyone needs to monitor fat intake. In addition to obesity, consuming excess dietary fat promotes cancer, coronary artery disease and diabetes. Both animal and plant fats are a concern.

I advise consuming *no* added fat. Those who need to lose weight should also avoid high-fat plant foods, such as avocados, nuts, olives, seeds and soy products.

Food manufacturers list fat on labels in different ways…

●**Mono- and diglycerides.** These are the fats that are added to bread and other baked goods to soften them.

●**Hydrogenated fat (trans fatty acids).** Commonly used in margarine and processed foods, it raises blood cholesterol levels even more than butter and cream.

●**"Fat-free."** Foods that contain less than one-half gram of fat per serving can be labeled "fat-free." The trouble is that many standard "servings" are small by consumers' standards. If you eat several servings of a so-called fat-free food, you may be consuming a fair amount of total fat.

●**Choice of fats.** Foods are often labeled with *possible* fat sources. A product label might say, "May contain soybean and/or cottonseed oil." Manufacturers can then use whichever fat is most cost-effective for them.

Fat self-defense strategies…

●**Eat fresh foods.** Baked potatoes, steamed vegetables and cooked rice do not have any extra fat unless you put it there.

●**Choose wisely.** Eat less meat and fewer dairy products and more whole grains and fresh fruits and vegetables.

●**Cook and bake from scratch**—to control the amount of fat used.

Examples: Use only nonstick cookware …experiment with decreasing the amount of fat in recipes…substitute mashed bananas, unsweetened applesauce or prune paste for fat.

The Truth About Fats and Oils

Jamison Starbuck, ND, naturopathic physician in family practice and lecturer, University of Montana, both in Missoula. She is past president of the American Association of Naturopathic Physicians and a contributing editor to *The Alternative Advisor: The Complete Guide to Natural Therapies and Alternative Treatments* (Time-Life).

Most health-conscious consumers are aware that some types of dietary fats are necessary and healthful, but not many people know *why*.

Fat is a necessary component for energy, hormone production, brain and nerve activity, healthy skin, good digestion and the absorption of nutrients from the gastrointestinal tract. If you suffer from depression, fatigue, eczema, memory problems, premenstrual syndrome (PMS), gallbladder disease or an autoimmune disease, such as rheumatoid arthritis or lupus, you may feel better if you add healthful fats and oils to your diet and supplement list.

As a general rule, 20% of your daily calories should come from fat. To keep track of your intake, read food labels and keep a food diary. Choose healthful sources, such as fish (excluding shellfish), eggs, soybeans, nuts, seeds and avocados. Use olive and canola oils for cooking. Limit your intake of saturated fats, such as red meat (no more than twice a week) and high-fat cheese (two ounces a day).

Remember, too, that oils are easily damaged by light, air and heat. This produces free radicals, substances that can lead to inflammation and cancer. To protect your cooking oils, store them in tightly sealed glass jars, placed in a cool, dark cabinet. (Oily foods, such as nuts and seeds, must be similarly stored.) Do a rancidity "sniff test" before you consume any food that is high in fat or oil. If it's rancid, you'll notice a peculiar sour odor.

If you have one of the health conditions listed here—or if you exercise more than two hours a day—simply adding healthful fats and oils to your diet may not be adequate. You may need to supplement with medicinal oil, such as flaxseed and fish. The indications for each are slightly different.

I prefer flaxseed oil in treating fatigue, eczema, gallbladder disease and autoimmune disease. I recommend organically grown flaxseed oil. The typical daily dose is 3,000 milligrams (mg), taken with food. Be forewarned that some people are allergic to flax. The most common symptom is a skin rash, which disappears after discontinuing the flaxseed oil.

I recommend fish oil for patients with depression, memory problems, PMS and menstrual irregularity. Fish oil works within 10 days—more quickly than plant oil—in solving brain and hormonal problems. Fish oil is available in liquid or capsules. In liquid form, fish oil is best taken with food—mixed in cottage cheese or orange juice, for example—to mask the taste. I take a spoonful of fish oil every morning with breakfast. The typical dose is 2,000 mg daily. Look for fish oil with 300 mg of *eicosapentaenoic acid* (EPA) and 200 mg of *docosahexaenoic acid* (DHA).

Caution: If you are taking *warfarin* (Coumadin) or another blood thinner, check with your doctor before taking fish oil, which can also have a blood-thinning effect.

Breaking the Sugar Habit

Nancy Appleton, PhD, researcher and nutritional consultant, Santa Monica, CA. She is author of *Lick the Sugar Habit* and *Lick the Sugar Habit Counter* (both from Avery).

The average American consumes more than 20 teaspoons of refined sugar each day. That's 20% more than the amount we consumed a decade ago.

If you think tooth decay and weight gain are the only health consequences, think again.

By replacing fruits and vegetables and other nutrient-dense, disease-fighting foods, sugary foods and beverages can cause increased blood sugar (glucose) levels and obesity. These conditions may then lead, in turn, to chronic health problems, such as heart disease, high blood pressure and diabetes.

Cakes, cookies, candy and ice cream aren't the only sources of refined sugar. It can also be found in the seemingly wholesome foods and beverages, such as muffins, flavored instant oatmeal, canned sweet potatoes and even old-fashioned lemonade.

For some people, sugar—like alcohol or tobacco—can be addictive.

Example: Sugar addicts time their meals and snacks so they have some form of sugar in their body at all times. They crave sugar and experience withdrawal symptoms, such as fatigue, headache, depression or shaking, if they stop eating sugar "cold turkey."

That's why it's important for sugar addicts to *slowly* reduce the sugar in their diets.

Whether you're a "sugarholic" or just an average American who consumes too much sugar—often unknowingly—your long-term health will benefit if you gradually reduce your intake. *Here's how...*

●**Read the "Nutrition Facts" panel on food labels.** A healthy person can metabolize 8 grams (g)—two teaspoons—of sugar at one time. Stay away from foods that contain more than 8 g of sugar per serving.

This means foregoing soft drinks and many fruit juices, which average about 40 g (10 teaspoons) of sugar per 12-ounce serving.

●**Avoid foods and drinks containing artificial sweeteners.** Even though artificially sweetened foods don't contain sugar, they can stimulate your sweet tooth. Instead of diet soda, for example, opt for tap or mineral water with a spritz of lemon.

●**Use *half* as much sugar.** Start by cutting back on what you normally add to your coffee, tea, cereal, etc.

Also, halve the amount of sugar you use in recipes. But—because sugar adds tenderness to dough and golden-brown surfaces to baked goods, some recipes may not survive without it.

What to do: Switch to recipes that can be made without sugar. Its absence won't affect the texture of many foods.

Example: Fruit pies that are made with fully ripened fruit taste plenty sweet without the half cup—or more—of sugar frequently called for in the recipe.

Gradually reduce sugar intake until your taste buds adjust. If you are a sugar addict, try eliminating sugar altogether.

●**Satisfy sugar cravings.** Fruit is your best choice. Besides nutrients and disease-fighting plant chemicals known as *phytochemicals,* fruit provides fiber. This slows the absorption of sugar into your bloodstream.

Fruit won't give you the same energy rush that you get from refined sugar. That's partly what makes sugar so addictive for some people.

Once you are accustomed to eating fruit instead of, say, cookies or candy, add vegetables to your snacking repertoire.

Steam some white potatoes, sweet potatoes, squash and other vegetables containing complex carbohydrates.

Complex carbohydrates are converted into sugar in your digestive tract. This provides a steady flow of sugar into the bloodstream.

Keep these foods in your refrigerator along with fresh green and red pepper strips, jicama, carrots and celery.

Helpful: Brush your teeth when you crave sugar. Most toothpastes contain artificial sweetener. It often satisfies a craving.

●**Don't keep sugar-laden foods in your home.** That way, if you need a sugar fix, you'll be forced to go to the store to feed your habit.

This delaying tactic will give you time to change your mind and temper—if not lessen—the urge.

Sugar cravings often subside within 15 minutes. If you still must have sugar after you've traveled to the store, buy the smallest size of whatever it is you crave—and enjoy it. Then throw out what you don't eat...or give it away.

●**Be aware of psychological stress.** Is there something that's making you anxious? Are you putting that sweet morsel in your mouth to calm emotional upset?

Rather than opening the refrigerator, try exercising, writing in a journal, deep breathing, yoga, listening to music, praying or meditating —anything that helps alleviate stress.

Once you've successfully eliminated—or at least cut back on—your sugar consumption, you'll begin to appreciate the natural sweetness of many healthful foods. A carrot or a piece of fruit will taste as good as candy once did.

Sweet Treat Lengthens Life

Honey may help prevent heart disease and cancer. It is as rich in antioxidants as some fruits and vegetables. The darker the color, the higher the antioxidant level. Buckwheat honey has the highest levels. Clover honey—the most commonly available type—has two to three times less but still is a good antioxidant source. Use honey instead of sugar in cereal, tea, etc.

Nicki J. Engeseth, PhD, associate professor of food chemistry, University of Illinois, Urbana, and leader of a study of honey's effect on human blood, published in the *Journal of Agricultural and Food Chemistry.*

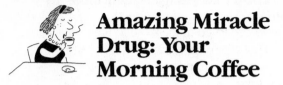

Amazing Miracle Drug: Your Morning Coffee

Bennett Alan Weinberg and Bonnie K. Bealer, coauthors of *The Caffeine Advantage* (Free Press) and *The World of Caffeine* (Routledge). They have been researching caffeine for several years, working with leading scientific and medical experts. Based in Philadelphia, they develop continuing education programs that train physicians in the use of pharmaceuticals.

We all know that caffeine makes us feel more alert. But did you know that it can be a powerful drug with remarkable healing powers?

For decades, asthma sufferers have gotten relief from caffeine. Some findings have shown that it also helps prevent Alzheimer's disease and Parkinson's disease…limits stroke damage …and reduces the incidence of skin, colon and breast cancers. Mopping up damaging free radicals, it is a stronger antioxidant than vitamin C.

In addition to preventing illness, caffeine can help us in our day-to-day lives by doing everything from boosting mood to maximizing weight loss.

Is there a downside? Scientific studies looking at tens of thousands of people have shown that caffeine is not the villain it has been made out to be. For example, despite what many people think, it does not cause or exacerbate hypertension or heart problems.

Some people experience insomnia or "jitters" after having a lot of caffeine. These and other side effects usually disappear when it is consumed regularly or in smaller amounts. Pregnant women should limit their intake of caffeine. More than 300 milligrams (mg) a day raises the risk of miscarriage. Check with your doctor.

HOW IT WORKS

Many of the day-to-day benefits we receive from caffeine stem from its effects on *neurotransmitters,* the chemicals that regulate communication between nerve cells. Caffeine boosts the effects of the neurotransmitters *dopamine* and *serotonin,* which improve mood. It also boosts levels of *acetylcholine,* a neurotransmitter that improves short-term memory.

Scientists at the National Addiction Centre in London studied more than 9,000 people and found that those who ingested caffeine scored higher on tests of reaction times, reasoning and memory. Other studies have shown that caffeine improves IQ test scores.

As little as 100 mg of caffeine—the amount in four ounces of drip-brewed coffee—boosts mood and memory. Larger amounts—200 mg or more—are needed for optimal mental or physical performance.

You won't develop a tolerance to the beneficial effects of caffeine. If 300 mg helps you run faster the first time you take it, the same dose will deliver the same benefit even after taking caffeine for years.

It takes about 15 minutes for caffeine to kick in. The effects usually last three to four hours, but this varies from person to person. Women who take oral contraceptives metabolize caffeine more slowly and may feel the effects in their systems for twice as long. But smokers metabolize caffeine more quickly and experience a shorter "buzz."

The amount of caffeine that is "right" for you also varies by individual. A small number of people can barely tolerate a 50-mg dose of caffeine, while many others can have 500 mg or more every day with no problems. Start with about 100 mg in the morning, and gradually increase your dose until you experience the benefits without side effects.

Also, determine your personal "caffeine cutoff point," the point in time after which consuming caffeine interferes with your sleep. This is different for each person. Some people find they can't have caffeine after noon, while others can consume it right before bed and sleep soundly. The cutoff point for many people is five to six hours before bed.

Helpful: Caffeine pills, such as NoDoz, give a better boost than coffee or tea. One of the chemicals in coffee and tea, *chlorogenic acid,* partially dampens the effects of caffeine. Caffeine pills don't work any faster, but the effects are more dramatic and predictable.

Here are five ways in which caffeine can enhance your life…

RELIEVE HEADACHES

Caffeine is an active ingredient in some over-the-counter painkillers, such as Anacin and Excedrin, and prescription painkillers, such as Darvon Compound-65.

It is particularly helpful for tension and migraine headaches because it stimulates the body's natural painkilling mechanisms. Studies at Chicago's Diamond Headache Clinic showed that caffeine eliminated headaches in nearly two-thirds of participants—and took effect 30 minutes faster than *ibuprofen.*

Caffeine Rx: Take 200 mg of caffeine at the first sign of a tension headache or migraine… and continue to take 100 mg every two to three hours, as needed. For additional relief, take caffeine with 200 to 400 mg of ibuprofen. This combination increases the analgesic effects, without risk.

LOSE WEIGHT

Caffeine stimulates the release of *cholecystokinin* (CCK), a hormone that suppresses appetite, delays the onset of hunger and promotes a feeling of fullness. In addition, caffeine promotes efficient fat-burning (*lipolysis*) and increases metabolism.

Caffeine Rx: A daily 200-mg dose helps burn 50 to 100 extra calories. That means a loss of five to 10 pounds a year. You will eat less if you consume caffeine 15 minutes before a particularly tempting meal.

MAXIMIZE WORKOUTS

Caffeine enhances nearly every aspect of physical activity, including endurance, speed and lung capacity. It also helps damaged muscle cells recover.

Caffeine Rx: A 200-mg dose will improve endurance by as much as 20% when riding an exercise bike, running on a treadmill or doing other moderately strenuous workouts. Prior to more strenuous exercise—like running a marathon—take 300 to 400 mg of caffeine.

DRIVE SAFELY

Driver fatigue is the leading cause of highway fatalities. A study by the US Department of Health, Education and Welfare showed that drivers who consumed 200 mg of caffeine had significant improvements in alertness and reaction times as compared with people who were not given caffeine.

Caffeine Rx: If you feel sleepy while driving, pull off the road…drink coffee or take a caffeine pill…and then take a nap for 15 minutes. The caffeine will enter your bloodstream while you rest, making you more alert when you're back on the road.

Warning: Most people rest, *then* drink coffee when they resume driving. That's dangerous—you are groggy from the nap, and the caffeine hasn't had time to take effect.

FIGHT JET LAG

About 94% of long-distance travelers suffer fatigue, irritability, headaches and/or gastrointestinal discomfort due to jet lag. Your body needs one day to adjust for every time zone you cross, especially traveling west to east.

Caffeine Rx: Before your trip, avoid caffeine to increase its effects later. But don't stop using caffeine suddenly. This can result in withdrawal symptoms, such as headaches and anxiety. Instead, taper off, reducing your intake by about 150 mg a day—for example, by eliminating one cup of coffee. By the time you leave for your trip, you should have stopped having caffeine entirely for a day or two.

Take one 200-mg caffeine pill or drink about one-and-a-half cups of coffee immediately after arriving at your destination. You can repeat the dose every three hours until you reach your personal caffeine cutoff point. The boost in energy will help you stay awake and shift your body clock to the new time zone.

Cinnamon for Diabetes

One-half teaspoon of cinnamon a day can reduce blood sugar levels in diabetics by 20%. Sprinkle ground cinnamon on toast or cereal, and stir it into juice or coffee.

Richard Anderson, PhD, research chemist, US Department of Agriculture's Human Nutrition Research Center, Beltsville, MD, and leader of a study of type 2 diabetics, published in *Diabetes Care.*

Drink Your Cocoa

Hot cocoa fights disease better than wine or tea. One cup of hot cocoa contains about 611 milligrams (mg) of *phenols* and 564 mg of *flavonoids,* two powerful antioxidants that protect against cancer and heart disease.

In comparison, a glass of red wine has 340 mg and 163 mg, respectively, of these compounds, while green tea has 165 mg and 47 mg …and black tea has only 124 mg and 34 mg.

Bonus: Although chocolate also is very rich in antioxidants, it is high in saturated fat. The equivalent amount of cocoa contains less than 1 gram (g) of saturated fat.

Chang Y. Lee, PhD, professor and chairman, food science and technology, Cornell University, Geneva, NY.

Cranberries Protect Against Disease

Cranberries top the list of disease-fighting foods. Ounce for ounce, they contain more beneficial compounds than other nutritional powerhouses, like broccoli and blueberries.

Fresh and dried cranberries provide the greatest antioxidant protection against heart disease and cancer, followed by cranberry sauce and cranberry juice.

Good idea: Eat one-half cup of fresh or dried cranberries daily.

Joe A. Vinson, PhD, professor of chemistry, University of Scranton.

Apples Really Do Keep The Doctor Away

In a recent finding, incidence of lung cancer was reduced by 60%…asthma by 20%…and death from heart disease by 20% in people who ate one apple a day.

Theory: Apples are rich in the bioflavonoid *quercetin,* which helps block the accumulation of free radicals in the body. The cell damage caused by free radicals contributes to the development of these diseases.

Self-defense: Eat one small apple every day to achieve this benefit.

Other quercetin-rich foods: Onions, cabbage, blackberries and cranberries.

Paul Knekt, PhD, epidemiologist, National Public Health Institute, Helsinki, Finland. His study was published in the *American Journal of Clinical Nutrition.*

Let Oregano Help Keep You Healthy

Ounce for ounce, oregano has 42 times more antioxidant activity than apples… 30 times more than potatoes…and 12 times more than oranges. One tablespoon of fresh oregano (or one-half teaspoon of dried oregano) contains the same amount of antioxidants as one medium-sized apple.

Other antioxidant-packed herbs are chives, coriander, dill, parsley, sage and thyme.

Helpful: Try adding herbs to hot water for a potent tea…or sprinkle them on lean meats and vegetables.

Shiow Y. Wang, PhD, plant physiologist and biochemist, US Department of Agriculture, Beltsville, MD. Her study was published in the *Journal of Agriculture and Food Chemistry.*

Cooked Carrots Are More Nutritious than Raw Ones

Antioxidant levels increased more than 34% after carrots were cooked—and continued to increase while the vegetables were kept at 104°F for one week.

Heating softens carrot tissue, allowing the release of antioxidants attached to cell walls.

This phenomenon may also occur in other vegetables as well.

Luke Howard, PhD, professor of food science, University of Arkansas, Fayetteville.

Choose Rye Bread Over Wheat

Rye breads are more healthful than wheat breads. Starches in rye bread break down more slowly than those in wheat bread, and so do not produce high insulin spikes. Researchers believe that repeated high post-meal insulin spikes, caused by high intake of carbohydrates, may increase risk of developing insulin resistance and type 2 diabetes.

Self-defense: Replace wheat bread with rye in your daily meals.

Hannu Mykkanen, PhD, professor of nutrition, University of Kuopio, Finland.

Cook Your Pasta al Dente

Pasta that's slightly firm has a lower *glycemic index* (GI) than pasta cooked until soft. Foods with low GIs are absorbed into the bloodstream more slowly than high-GI foods and do not cause your blood sugar to rise as quickly. Slower absorption may protect against weight gain, heart disease and diabetes.

Natural Health, 70 Lincoln St., Boston 02111.

Grape Juice and Aspirin

Purple grape juice boosts the heart-protective effects of daily aspirin therapy. Aspirin helps guard at-risk individuals against heart attack by preventing blood clots. But the adrenaline produced by exercise or during periods of psychological stress can counteract this clot-inhibiting effect.

Result: Reduced protection from heart attack.

Good news: *Flavonoids* in grape juice—as well as in dark beer and red wine—block the effects of adrenaline.

Best: 10 to 12 ounces of grape juice per day.

John Folts, PhD, professor of medicine and director, coronary thrombosis research and prevention laboratory, University of Wisconsin Medical School, Madison.

Soy Milk and Calcium

Robert P. Heaney, MD, professor of medicine, Creighton University School of Medicine, Omaha. His comparison of calcium in cow's milk and soy beverages was published in the *American Journal of Clinical Nutrition.*

Soy milk doesn't provide as much calcium as dairy (cow's) milk.

Reason: Soy milk calcium is less easily absorbed by the body.

If you drink soy milk: Try to get more calcium through nonfat or low-fat dairy products. Or look for soy milk that contains 500 milligrams (mg) of calcium per cup—your body will absorb 300 mg, the equivalent of one cup of cow's milk.

More from Robert P. Heaney...

Nondairy Ways to Get Calcium

There are a variety of ways to get more calcium in your diet besides drinking milk. Try one cup of raw chopped broccoli (42 milligrams [mg])...one-half cup dried unblanched almonds (126 mg)...one can of bone-in sardines (351 mg)...one eight-ounce glass of calcium-fortified orange juice (300 mg)...and other calcium-fortified foods. The typical American diet provides about 600 mg of calcium. The recommendation is 1,000 mg per day. You may need supplements.

Important: Avoid supplements made from natural sources, such as oyster shells and bonemeal—they are more likely to contain impurities.

Caution: Taking calcium with tetracycline or iron can reduce their absorption.

Tea Drinking Builds Strong Bones

In a recent finding, the lumbar spine and hip-bones in people who drank an average of two cups of tea a day for six years were approximately 2% denser than those of people who did not drink tea. After 10 years, the bone density among tea drinkers was 6% greater.

Theory: Fluoride and chemical compounds in tea called *flavonoids* enhance bone density. Different types of tea—black, green and oolong—all offer the same benefit.

Chang Chin Jen, MD, director, diabetes and obesity research center, National Cheng Kung University Hospital, Taiwan.

Black Tea Boosts Immunity

People who consumed five cups of black tea a day for one week had five times more germ-fighting proteins in their blood than they did before they started to drink tea.

Theory: The immune-boosting capacity of black tea is derived from *L-theanine,* an amino acid that is found in black tea as well as other nonherbal teas.

Good news: Regularly drinking just two cups a day may confer many of the same benefits.

Because tea can reduce absorption of iron, people with iron-deficiency anemia should be sure to limit their intake of tea.

Jack Bukowski, MD, PhD, assistant clinical professor of medicine, Harvard Medical School and Brigham and Women's Hospital, both in Boston.

The Simple Drink that Fights Cancer, Heart Disease, Colds and Cavities

Lester A. Mitscher, PhD, distinguished professor of medicinal chemistry, University of Kansas, Lawrence. Dr. Mitscher received the American Chemical Society's lifetime achievement award for his work with teas and antibiotic resistance. He is coauthor of *The Green Tea Book: China's Fountain of Youth* (Avery).

You know that green tea is good for you. But did you know that both green *and* black teas help ward off many types of cancer, fight heart disease and colds—and even help prevent cavities?

A Chinese emperor first touted the health benefits of green tea more than 4,000 years ago. *Here's what the latest scientific research shows…*

WHY TEA HELPS

Green and black teas are made from the leaves of the *Camellia sinensis* plant. The leaves contain *catechins,* antioxidants that block the action of free radicals (harmful molecules).

The most powerful catechin is *epigallocatechin gallate* (EGCG). A study conducted at the University of Shizuoka in Japan showed that the antioxidant power of EGCG in green tea was 200 times stronger than that of vitamin E, another antioxidant.

Green tea is made from fresh, young leaves, which are steamed right away to preserve catechins and then dried. Black tea contains about half the catechins as green tea because it undergoes more processing before leaves are dried.

SPECIFIC BENEFITS

The health benefits of the catechins that are found in tea include…

• **Reducing risk of certain types of cancer,** including cancers of the lung, breast and digestive tract. In a University of Minnesota study of more than 35,000 women over eight years, those who drank two or more cups of green or black tea daily had a 10% lower risk of developing any cancer than those who seldom drank tea.

• **Reducing heart disease** by blocking the formation of plaque in the coronary arteries. A four-year study conducted at Harvard Medical School indicated that participants who drank 14 cups or more of green or black tea weekly had a 44% lower death rate after a heart attack than people who didn't drink tea.

●**Fewer colds and other illnesses.** Tea prevents free radicals from undermining the immune system. In one scientific article, researchers at Toyama Medical and Pharmaceutical University in Japan confirmed reports that catechins in green tea extract inhibit the growth of the influenza virus. Scientists at the Health Science Center of the State University of New York in Syracuse reviewed this literature and concluded that green tea enhances immunity.

●**Building bone density.** One study of more than 1,000 participants indicated that drinking two or more cups of tea a day for at least six years strengthened bone density.

●**Preventing cavities** by blocking growth of *Streptococcus mutans,* bacterium associated with dental plaque.

●**Aiding digestion** by fostering the growth of beneficial bacteria in the intestines.

HOW MUCH TEA?

Aim to drink four cups of green tea or six cups of black tea daily. Expensive teas may taste better, but they don't necessarily provide more health benefits.

Brew tea for three minutes or less to ensure the release of antioxidants. Longer steeping only produces more tannins, which taste bitter.

Iced tea yields the same benefits, but antioxidants degrade with time, so drink the tea soon after brewing.

Tea contains less caffeine than coffee—up to 30 milligrams (mg) per cup of green tea...up to 90 mg for black, versus 160 mg for brewed coffee. People who are sensitive to caffeine may prefer decaffeinated tea. The process that removes caffeine from tea does not interfere with its health benefits.

Alternative: Try caffeine-free green tea capsules, available at health food stores. Look for a brand that is organic, free of preservatives and has an expiration date to ensure freshness. The usual dose is two 250-mg capsules daily.

Nuts vs. Cholesterol

Eating moderate amounts of pecans (three-quarters of a cup daily for eight weeks) can lower LDL ("bad") cholesterol levels by 10%, a study has shown.

The monounsaturated and polyunsaturated fats in the nuts are responsible for this effect, especially when nuts take the place of saturated fats in the diet.

Studies conducted with almonds and walnuts have shown similar results. Nuts are also high in heart-healthy fiber, vitamin E, copper and magnesium.

Wanda Morgan, PhD, RD, associate professor of human nutrition and food science, New Mexico State University, Las Cruces.

Organic Food Trap

Advertisers may claim that organic produce is grown without pesticides. But a study has found that 23% of these fruits and vegetables contain trace amounts of pest-fighting chemicals. That's because long-lived pesticides, such as DDT, which has been banned in the US, can remain in the soil for years.

Seventy-three percent of nonorganic produce contains pesticide residue, according to recent research. To be safe, wash *all* fruits and vegetables thoroughly.

Edward Groth III, PhD, environmental health and risk communication adviser, Groth Consulting Services, Pelham, NY.

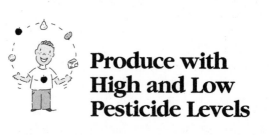

Produce with High and Low Pesticide Levels

Apples, cherries, grapes, celery, lettuce and winter squash retain high levels of pesticide residue. Bananas, blueberries, mangoes, watermelon, broccoli, cauliflower and eggplant are likely to have little residue.

Self-defense: Buy organic produce, which has less residue…wash all produce thoroughly before you serve it.

Caroline Smith DeWaal, JD, food safety director, Center for Science in the Public Interest, Washington, DC, and coauthor of *Is Our Food Safe?* (Three Rivers).

Separate Your Produce

Some fruits and vegetables give off *ethylene,* a gas that causes other produce to get overripe. Keep ethylene-sensitive produce separate from fruits and vegetables that emit the gas.

Ethylene producers include apricots, bananas, cantaloupe, honeydew, kiwis, peaches, pears, plums and tomatoes.

Keep them away from ethylene-sensitive fruits and vegetables, such as apples, broccoli, carrots, cucumbers, eggplant, green beans, lettuce, potatoes and watermelon.

Real Simple, Time-Life Building, 1271 Avenue of the Americas, New York City 10020.

Does Washing Produce With Water Remove All Bacteria?

Washing fruits and vegetables with water doesn't completely clean away bacteria, such as *E. coli* and *Listeria,* which can cause food poisoning.

Better: Fill one spray bottle with white or apple cider vinegar, another with 3% hydrogen peroxide, the same strength commonly available in drugstores. Spray all produce with the vinegar first. Its acidity kills the majority of organisms. Then spray with peroxide, which is a strong oxidizer that helps eliminate Listeria. Rinse well with water.

These precautions are recommended for all produce, including organic products.

Susan Sumner, PhD, professor and head, department of food science and technology, Virginia Polytechnic Institute and State University, Blacksburg, VA.

Keep Mercury Levels Down

To minimize mercury exposure from canned tuna, eat only the chunk light tuna instead of albacore or solid white tuna. Chunk light tuna is darker than albacore and comes from smaller types of tuna, which tend to contain less mercury.

University of California, Berkeley Wellness Letter, *www.wellnessletter.com.*

 ## Make Sure Your Water Is Safe to Drink

Timothy McCall, MD, internist, medical editor of *Yoga Journal* and author of *Examining Your Doctor* (Citadel Press) and *Yoga as Medicine* (Bantam). *www.drmccall.com.*

Tap water can be contaminated with hundreds of potentially harmful substances. Experts—including doctors—disagree on the risk. It's naive, though, to dismiss the potential for harm.

Most Americans get their drinking water from a municipal water system. If you do, ask your local water utility for a copy of the *municipal drinking water contaminant analysis.* Utilities are required by law to test their water on a regular basis—and to make test results available to the public.

But there's a problem with relying solely on these analyses. Lead can leach into water from the pipes and faucets in your home—after the water leaves the utility. To find out if your water contains lead, you can arrange to have it tested. The cost is usually around $40.

There are two other potential problems with the contaminant analyses provided by local water utilities. First, they give only a "snapshot" of toxins. A transient contamination might not be evident at the time the water was tested. Second, hundreds of harmful chemicals aren't looked for at all.

If your water comes from a private well—or if you're worried about your community's water system—consider having it tested...not only for lead, but also for other heavy metals, pesticides, nitrates and bacteria. A battery of tests generally costs less than $200, but shop around. Even among certified labs, the price varies quite a bit. One lab, National Testing Laboratories (800-458-3330), offers an extensive battery of tests for about $170.

If you need help locating a certified water-testing lab, contact your state's water-quality department—or the Environmental Protection Agency's Safe Drinking Water Hotline (800-426-4791). Watch out for outfits offering free water testing. They're usually trying to sell a filtration system that you might not need.

You could invest thousands of dollars testing your water for every conceivable contaminant. I don't think that's practical—or affordable—for most people. I recommend that you test only for the most likely contaminants. Call your local health department and ask what sorts of contaminants are common in your area. If tests reveal—or if you suspect—particular pollutants, choose a water-purification system to deal specifically with those problems. *The best systems to consider are...*

● **Carbon filters remove bad taste,** chlorine and some hazardous organic compounds. They're ineffective against viruses and bacteria.

● **Reverse osmosis filters remove a large array of potentially toxic minerals,** heavy metals and infectious microorganisms. But they're expensive and waste a lot of water.

● **Distillation filters remove lead,** microbes and most man-made contaminants. They're ineffective against *volatile organic compounds* like benzene and chloroform, which have been linked to cancer.

For more information about water-filtration systems, contact the National Sanitation Foundation at 800-673-6275 or *www.nsf.org.*

Bottled water is one potential solution, of course, but be wary. Some is less healthful than good municipal tap water. Given the high cost of premium brands, a home purification system may be a better deal in the long run.

Be careful, though. Virtually all bottled water lacks fluoride and many home filtration units remove fluoride. Children may need another source of this tooth-protecting element.

Foods that Relax You

Annemarie Colbin, PhD, certified health education specialist and founder, Natural Gourmet Institute for Health and Culinary Arts, New York City. Ms. Colbin is author of the chapter "Food for Relaxation" in *The Big Book of Relaxation* (The Relaxation Company). She is also author of *Food and Our Bones: The Natural Way to Prevent Osteoporosis* (Plume).

You probably know that foods that are rich in carbohydrates and fiber—and free of hydrogenated fat (the fat in fried foods, margarine, shortening)—help you stay healthy. But—did you know the same foods also help your mind and body relax?

Steamed vegetables, fruits, whole wheat bread, brown rice, polenta or oatmeal help you relax by providing your body with a source of energy that is steadily metabolized and continuously absorbed—and by stimulating the relaxing brain chemical serotonin.

When these foods are consumed with some protein—fish or chicken—they leave you feeling calm and focused.

FOOD MYTHS

Refined sugar and alcohol seem to have a relaxing effect on the body. In fact, they often make you sleepy. But don't be fooled.

After the initial ease of tension, the effects of alcohol wear off, leaving many people tense and angry.

The same is true for sugar. After an initial sugar "rush"—the surge that leaves you feeling temporarily alert and clear-headed—many people feel exhausted.

They typically crave more sugar to get them going again, and a cycle of highs and lows becomes a way of life.

RELAXING FOODS

To help keep your energy in balance and feel tension-free, eat a variety of the following healthful foods…

•**Breakfast.** Start your day with a small piece of fish with dark rye bread…or with an organic egg on whole-grain toast…or oatmeal cooked with raisins and cinnamon and topped with toasted sunflower and pumpkin seeds.

The protein/carbohydrate combination will leave you feeling relaxed and focused—unlike a high-fat, high-sugar breakfast (a donut or muffin), which may create a need for caffeine and more sugar as the morning wears on.

In general, I don't recommend eating dairy products. Among other things, they tend to make some people feel heavy and congested.

•**Lunch out.** Have a sandwich made with whole wheat bread or a pita, an English muffin or rye toast.

Great fillers: Thinly sliced natural meats like turkey, chicken breast or roast beef…a dab of mustard or a bit of mayonnaise…and vegetables like lettuce, tomato, onion, grated carrots or sprouts.

Another good lunch option is soup—anything with dried beans or peas—such as split pea, lentil, Yankee bean or black bean. Also good are hearty vegetable soups and chicken soup, served with bread and salad.

If your goal is to be alert and energetic, have more protein and fewer carbohydrates.

Good choice: Broiled fish or grilled chicken and a side salad. Avoid dessert.

Poor choice: Pasta and green salad—it's likely to leave you feeling relaxed and ready for a siesta, not raring to go.

•**Lunch at home.** Mash avocado with a little salsa and eat it on whole wheat pita bread. Mash canned salmon or sardines with some lemon juice, chopped onion and celery and spread on rye crackers.

One potato: A great low-fat, relaxing side dish or snack is a baked yam or sweet potato.

To keep yams on hand, bake six at a time in a 400°F oven for one hour—but don't wrap or puncture the skin. Store them in the refrigerator and serve cold, sliced and steamed, grilled or pan-fried.

•**Dinner out.** For a good night's sleep, choose pastas (skip the heavy Alfredo sauce), polenta, rice dishes, cooked vegetables, salads, curries, baked or broiled fresh fish…and other dishes that are low in protein and high in complex carbohydrates.

Dessert: Strive to eat something fruit-based, like sorbet. Avoid chocolate, which contains caffeine and sugar.

•**Dinner at home.** A high-fiber vegetarian dinner cooked at home will relax you and give you the nutrients you need.

Good choices: Brown rice, barley, polenta, kasha, bean soups and green vegetables like broccoli, baked yams or squash, salad.

Dessert: Something sweetened with fruit juice, barley malt or maple syrup (which has the added benefit of being high in calcium).

FOODS TO AVOID

Some foods and drinks stimulate the nervous system and cause tension and insomnia—whether they're consumed in the morning or at night. *To stay relaxed, avoid…*

•**Caffeine.** Caffeine-containing foods and beverages include sodas, chocolate, teas—even green tea—and some over-the-counter and prescription medications.

•**Alcohol.** It's OK to occasionally have a cocktail or a glass of wine with dinner, but drinking alcohol every day can interfere with sleep and cause mood swings.

•**Sugar.** When you crave something sweet, try a dessert sweetened with fruit juice, grain malt or maple syrup. Chamomile tea with honey is relaxing. *Here's one of my favorite sweet treats…*

BANANAS VERMONT

4 bananas, ripe but firm
1 Tbs. unsalted butter
1 Tbs. maple syrup
2 Tbs. water

Peel bananas, cut once in half across, then cut each piece in half again lengthwise. Melt the butter and pour into a 9" x 13" baking pan. Arrange the bananas in it, turning once to get a little butter on the other side. Mix water and maple syrup and drizzle over the bananas. Broil five minutes, or until bananas soften. Four pieces per person. Serves four.

If you're allergic, these foods and herbs also may trigger hives, watery eyes, a metallic taste or itchy palate (roof of the mouth).

Leonard J. Bielory, MD, director, division of allergy/immunology and rheumatology, University of Medicine and Dentistry of New Jersey, New Jersey Medical School, Newark.

Yogurt Eases Allergies

It may sound like an old wives' tale, but in a study, adults who ate 16 ounces of plain yogurt a day had fewer allergy symptoms, such as sneezing, runny nose and nasal congestion, than those who drank an equal amount of skim milk.

The yogurt contained two types of "beneficial" bacteria, *Lactobacillus acidophilus* and *Bifidobacterium bifidum,* which help create a healthy balance of microflora in the gastrointestinal tract. This makes you better able to fight allergens in your body.

If you suffer from allergies: Consume yogurts, such as Stonyfield Farms, Cascade Fresh and Horizon, which list these two bacteria on the label.

Carlo Aldinucci, researcher, department of physiology, University of Siena, Italy.

Foods that Trigger Hay Fever

Some foods and herbs contain proteins similar to those found in ragweed pollen and can cause allergy symptoms ranging from mild (itching, sneezing) to severe (asthma, sudden blood pressure drop).

Foods and herbs to avoid: Bananas, cantaloupes, cucumbers, honeydew, watermelon, zucchini, chamomile and echinacea.

Helpful: Avoid these items if they make your mouth tingle or itch when you eat them.

Beans—the Perfect Food

George L. Hosfield, PhD, research geneticist, US Department of Agriculture, and director of bean research, Sugarbeet and Bean Research Unit, Michigan State University, East Lansing.

Beans are a well-known source of protein and fiber. But few people realize just how versatile and nutritious they really are. *For example...*

A standard serving size of beans (one-half cup, cooked) contains 8 grams (g) of protein. If you eat beans with a serving of a whole grain food—such as a slice of whole wheat bread or one-half cup of rice—you'll get a "complete protein," containing all the amino acids essential for keeping the body healthy.

A serving of beans has one-third the calories of beef and contains less than 1% fat. Meanwhile, beef contains no fiber, while a serving of beans has approximately 7 g of fiber—about 25% of the daily recommendation.

Because beans are digested slowly and do not quickly increase blood sugar levels, they are said to have a low glycemic index.* This means that beans keep insulin levels relatively stable.

Foods with a high glycemic index, such as white rice, bagels and white potatoes, cause fluctuations in blood sugar and insulin, which may contribute to the development of diabetes in some people.

VITAMINS AND MINERALS

One-half cup of most types of beans provides about one-third of your daily requirement of folic acid—a vitamin that helps manufacture

*The glycemic index ranges from 0 (no sugar) to 100 (pure sugar). Most beans have a glycemic index of about 30.

vital proteins and DNA in the body. Folic acid may also decrease the risk for heart attack.

That same serving of beans also provides about 15% of your daily recommended dose of potassium (important for nerve and muscle function) and more than 10% of the recommended amount of iron (critical for immune functioning).

Beans are a good dietary source of bone-building calcium, with one-half cup providing about 3% of the daily recommended amount. That may not sound like much, but it's more calcium than we get from many other foods, with the exception of dairy products.

ANTIOXIDANTS

Scientists have discovered that the bean's seed coat—the exterior covering—is rich in cancer-protecting antioxidants called *flavonoids*. The bean's color dictates its flavonoid content —the darker the bean, the more antioxidants it contains.

For that reason, black beans are the richest source of antioxidants. They contain *anthocyanins,* the same antioxidants that are found in dark-colored berries and grapes. In fact, one cup of black beans contains the same antioxidant levels as a six-ounce glass of red wine.

Red beans (kidney or chili beans) are the next best source of antioxidants, followed by brown beans (pinto beans or lentils) and yellow beans (chickpeas). White beans (Great Northern or navy beans) provide the least antioxidants of all bean varieties. However, white beans are still nutritious, due to their fiber, protein, vitamin and mineral content.

Soybeans are rich sources of antioxidants known as *isoflavones,* which may reduce the risk for osteoporosis and prevent certain cancers, including prostate malignancies.

Because the isoflavones in soybeans have an estrogen-like activity in the body, they seem to help prevent breast cancer in some women—but may actually promote tumor growth in others.

Until we know more, most physicians believe that soybeans are beneficial for most people, but women with breast cancer (or risk factors, such as family history) should talk with their physicians before adding soybeans to their diet.

DISEASE PREVENTION

Numerous studies have shown that eating beans can prevent the development of both heart disease and colon cancer.

Beans' salutary effect on the cardiovascular system is due primarily to their high soluble fiber content. Soluble fiber has been shown to lower levels of "bad" low-density lipoprotein (LDL) cholesterol, which is responsible for the buildup of plaque in arteries. Soluble fiber also raises levels of "good" high-density lipoprotein (HDL) cholesterol, which helps remove arterial plaque.

In addition, people who eat beans more than twice a week are 47% less likely to develop colon cancer than people who eat beans less often, according to some studies.

Several theories have been offered to explain why people who eat beans regularly are less likely to develop colon cancer. Beans keep insulin levels low, which may fight colon cancer. High insulin levels have been shown to promote colon cancer.

Beans also help eliminate free radicals, the tissue-damaging by-products of metabolism that may be partly responsible for colon cancer. Fiber flushes waste material out of the intestines so that fewer free radicals are formed.

CANNED OR DRIED?

Canned beans are convenient and can be prepared in minutes. However, they typically contain more than 300 milligrams (mg) of sodium per serving. (Daily sodium intake should not exceed 2,000 mg.) To reduce sodium levels, rinse canned beans with water. Dried beans typically contain less than 10 mg of sodium per serving but require up to 12 hours of soaking and need to be cooked for one to two hours.

To maximize their nutritional benefits, eat at least one-half cup of beans four days a week. (That's about the amount found in a single 19-ounce can.) Of course, you'll get additional benefits if you eat more.

To get the full spectrum of flavonoids, vary the type of bean you eat. For example, eat black beans one day, kidney beans or white beans the next day, etc.

NO MORE FLATULENCE

Beans cause intestinal gas because humans lack an enzyme called *alpha-galactosidase,* which is needed to digest the complex sugars found in beans.

We can reduce the effect of complex sugars by draining or rinsing canned beans before serving. (Soaking dried beans overnight and replacing the soaking water with fresh water fights gas but may reduce mineral content.)

You can also add the missing enzyme to your digestive system by taking a product called Beano (available in drug stores and supermarkets) before eating beans.

Better Bean Digestion

To stop beans from causing flatulence, cook them thoroughly and discard the cooking water. Uncooked starch from beans is one major source of intestinal gas. Rinse canned beans well after removing them from the can, and throw away the water, which contains indigestible sugars. Build up your consumption of beans gradually over a few weeks, so your body has time to adjust.

If you still have gas: Try Beano, an over-the-counter product that aids in the digestion of gas-causing sugars.

Reminder: Beans are very nutritious, containing fiber, protein, potassium, magnesium and other nutrients.

Franca Alphin, MPH, RD, nutrition director, Duke University Student Health Services, Durham, NC.

Secrets of Avoiding Digestive Problems

Raphael Kellman, MD, Kellman Center for Progressive Medicine, New York City. He is author of *Gut Reactions* (Broadway).

Ulcers…heartburn…gastric reflux…bowel disease. More than half of all American adults have been diagnosed with these or other problems of the digestive tract.

Gastrointestinal (GI) problems prompt more doctors' visits than any other medical condition except the common cold. But few sufferers are getting effective treatment.

Now there's evidence that GI problems contribute to heart disease, arthritis and some neurological problems, such as dementia.

Sound hard to believe? Researchers have determined that the gut (30 feet of tube that runs from your mouth to your anus) contains two-thirds of your body's disease-fighting immune cells. It acts as the "gatekeeper" to your overall health.

In one study, published in the British medical journal *Lancet,* patients with congestive heart failure were found to have high blood levels of *endotoxins,* proteins derived from bacteria that are normally confined to the gut. Irritation or inflammation of the intestinal wall causes bacteria and their toxins to pass into the bloodstream and spread throughout the body. This triggers inflammatory reactions that can lead to heart disease, arthritis and autoimmune disease.

ARE YOU HURTING YOUR GUT?

Digestive problems often result from some of the very treatments and dietary practices that people follow to help ensure their gastrointestinal and overall health.

Example: Americans spend more than $1 billion every year on over-the-counter (OTC) antacids in an attempt to curb heartburn and stomach upset.

Problem: Prolonged use of antacids reduces stomach acid levels, causing an imbalance in the microbes in the digestive tract. This not only allows stomach viruses and infections to flourish, but also blocks the absorption of calcium, zinc and magnesium.

Better than OTC antacids: Deglycyrrhizinated licorice (DGL) root. Licorice root makes the intestinal lining more resistant to food-borne illnesses and inhibits growth of the *Helicobacter pylori* bacterium, a leading cause of ulcer formation. Ask your physician about taking one 500-milligram (mg) tablet of DGL root 30 minutes before each meal.

NATURAL HEALING

Herbal and dietary regimens can prevent and heal most common gastrointestinal disorders.

Unlike most prescription and OTC drugs, the natural approach treats the cause of the problem rather than the symptoms. Natural treatments are also usually safer than medication.*

•**Gastroesophageal reflux disease (GERD).** This happens whenever stomach acid backs up into the esophagus, causing a burning sensation in the chest.

What to do: Take just one 1,000-microgram (mcg) tablet of vitamin B-12 and one 800-mcg tablet of folic acid daily. Avoid eating pasta and bread, as well as chocolate and coffee.

•**Ulcers.** Lesions in the stomach's mucous membrane bring on gnawing, cramping and severe pain.

What to do: Take 800 mcg of folic acid twice daily and 500 mg of DGL root 30 minutes before each meal. Take 2 grams (g) of the herb goldenseal twice daily for 14 days.

Helpful: Cabbage juice promotes healing of ulcers by building the stomach's mucosal lining. Drink two glasses daily.

To mix up your own: In a juice machine, blend two cups of chopped cabbage with four celery sticks and two carrots.

•**Heartburn and indigestion.** This causes gas, bloating, belching and stomach malaise.

What to do: Take 4 g of the amino acid *L-glutamine* three times a day and 500 mg of DGL root 30 minutes before each meal. Take 1,000 mg of mastic (an oil derived from tree sap) twice daily. Drink ginger tea after meals. Avoid the OTC *nonsteroidal anti-inflammatory drugs* (NSAIDs), which can worsen symptoms.

Note: My clinical experience shows that patients who suffer from GERD, ulcers and/or heartburn often benefit from short-term use of high-dose vitamin A. Consult your doctor for advice on dosage. Too much vitamin A can cause liver toxicity and birth defects.

•**Irritable bowel syndrome.** This condition causes diarrhea and/or constipation, excessive gas and GI pain.

*Caution: Do not stop taking your current medication or begin the regimens described here without your doctor's approval. Also, some supplements can be dangerous for women who are pregnant or nursing.

What to do: Drink peppermint, lemon balm or ginger tea to reduce gas. Avoid wheat products. Instead, gradually increase your consumption of oat and rice products. Apples, legumes, raisins and grapes can exacerbate gas problems.

•**Crohn's disease.** This causes severe abdominal pain, bloody bowel movements, fever and rectal bleeding.

What to do: Take one 800-mcg tablet of folic acid a day, along with a dietary fiber supplement. Take a 500-mg tablet of DGL root 30 minutes before each meal. Take 2 g of fish oil or flaxseed oil three times daily and 2 g of the bioflavonoid *quercetin* and 4 g of L-glutamine twice daily with meals. In addition, take 2 g of goldenseal twice daily with meals for 14 days. Avoid any foods containing hydrogenated fat, such as margarine, cookies, cakes and most processed snack products.

EXERCISING YOUR GUT

Just as regular aerobic exercise strengthens your heart, your gut also needs a daily workout to ensure proper functioning. This is true even if you do not have gastrointestinal problems.

Proper physical activity stimulates blood flow and keeps the neurotransmitters lining the intestinal wall healthy and active.

I also recommend practicing deep breathing or yoga or doing sit-ups or stomach crunches for about 10 minutes a day.

Helpful: While lying on your back, massage your stomach area twice a day for approximately 10 minutes.

Avoid Heartburn When Eating Out

To prevent heartburn when eating out, choose meals carefully. Salads are usually safe—but ask for the dressing served on the side so you use less.

Reason: Most salad dressings contain fat, which makes heartburn more likely in people who are prone to it.

More options: Pasta in a simple sauce, such as pesto or lemon sauce, but avoid spicy Italian food, especially in tomato-based sauces. Meat should be very lean. Mexican food usually is OK if you avoid the extra cheese and use mild salsa—but black beans sometimes cause heart-burn. Avoid fried or sautéed foods—instead, order grilled or broiled.

David Peura, MD, professor of medicine, University of Virginia, Charlottesville and president of the American Gastroenterological Association.

How Long to Keep Foods

Unsure about whether it's time to toss the lunch meat or milk? *The US Food and Drug Administration has guidelines on how long it's safe to keep various foods...*

●**Ground beef.** Up to two days refrigerated ...four months frozen.

●**Lean fish**—such as cod or flounder. Up to two days refrigerated...six months frozen.

●**Fatty fish**—such as bluefish or salmon. Up to two days refrigerated...no more than two to three months frozen.

●**Whole chicken.** Up to two days refrigerated...12 months frozen.

●**Luncheon meat.** Up to five days refrigerated...one to two months frozen.

●**Milk.** Five days refrigerated...only one month frozen.

FDA Consumer, US Government Printing Office, Box 37195, Pittsburgh 15250.

Is Microwaving In Plastic Safe?

Clair Hicks, PhD, professor of food science, University of Kentucky, Lexington.

You can microwave plastics with recycling codes that indicate they are safe for your microwave. Plastic containers labeled number 1 (*polyethylene terphthalate*) and number 5 (*polypropylene*) can be used. Number 6 (*polystyrene*) may be microwaved only if it is covered with a barrier film, such as a microwave-safe plastic wrap.

Most baby bottles and their disposable liners are safe to microwave. Anything that is labeled *nylon, dual ovenable* or *microwave safe* also can be put in the microwave.

But don't microwave plastic containers labeled number 2 (*high-density polyethylene*)...3 (*polyvinyl chloride*)...4 (*low-density polyethylene*) ...or 7 (which is made of other resins).

Also: Don't microwave plastic wrap or plastic bags—except for those specifically labeled *microwave safe.* Wax paper and paper towels are fine to use in the microwave.

Better: Glass or ceramic bowls that are made for the microwave—they will usually have a plastic top with a steam vent specifically designed for the microwave.

7

Exercise & Weight Loss

Secrets of the Diet Masters

People who lose weight and keep the pounds off for longer than three years are true diet experts. To learn their eating and exercise secrets, I surveyed 208 women and men whose average weight loss was 64 pounds.

Here's what they said works...

•Drink a glass of water before eating. There really is no metabolic reason why drinking water should make you shed pounds.

But to my surprise, two out of every three people I questioned told me that they make a serious effort to drink more water, specifically to control their weight.

While downing a glass of water (eight to 10 ounces) won't necessarily stem the craving for a candy bar, the water will fill you up. Having a glass of water before or between meals leaves less room in your stomach and is likely to help you eat smaller portions.

If water is not appealing, drink sparkling water with lemon or lime...or flavored sparkling water...or even diet soda.

When you feel hungry or have a food craving between meals, try drinking a glass of water and then waiting 20 minutes to see if the desire to eat passes. If not, have a small amount of the item you desire—along with a big glass of water.

•Kick the red meat habit. For years, health experts have been telling us to get less of our protein from meat—particularly steaks and burgers, which tend to be high in total fat and the saturated fat that is associated with heart disease.

The people I interviewed cut back dramatically on red meat consumption. Most told me they eat little or no red meat, with more than half indicating that at most they eat meat once

Anne M. Fletcher, MS, RD, registered dietitian and former executive editor of Tufts University Health & Nutrition Letter. She is author of *Eating Thin for Life: Food Secrets & Recipes from People Who Have Lost Weight & Kept It Off* and *Thin for Life* (both from Houghton Mifflin).

or twice a week. Instead of meat, they favored poultry, seafood and legumes—all of which are lower in fat and calories.

From a nutritional standpoint, there is no reason to shun lean meats. But red meat seems to be associated with past unhealthy ways of eating that maintainers want to avoid.

Helpful: Think of meat as a condiment rather than as the main course. When you eat red meat, your portion should be no bigger than a deck of cards.

Substitute a three-ounce portion of skinless poultry, fish or shellfish for meat at dinner. On other nights, have a meatless pasta dish...or a vegetarian meal consisting of a hearty bean soup or rice and beans.

Example: A filling, tasty combination is rice, seasoned canned beans and salsa. Mix and warm, then top with some reduced-fat cheese or fat-free sour cream.

• **Eat low-fat and fat-free foods carefully.** There is evidence suggesting that when some people see the words "low-fat" or "fat-free" on food labels, they eat much more.

The diet masters consume reduced-fat foods carefully, watching their portion sizes. Given a choice between two similar foods with similar calorie values, they tend to choose the one with less fat, but they consume it in a portion equal to the regular one.

Helpful: The next time you reach for a bag of low-fat chips or cookies, read the label and parcel out only the amount listed as a "serving size." Then put the bag away. Also, compare labels of reduced-fat and regular versions of the same foods to see if there really is that much of a difference.

My rule of thumb: If there is no more than a two- to three-gram fat difference and no more than a 25-calorie difference per serving, the reduced-fat item probably doesn't have much of an edge.

To stick to reasonable portions of all snack foods, have a piece of fruit along with each snack or sweet.

• **Keep track of what you eat.** Most diet masters do not obsessively weigh and measure the foods they eat. But they do track their consumption occasionally.

Some count calories or keep track of food groups, while others keep food diaries, writing down the foods they eat as the day progresses.

Keeping a food diary pinpoints where your extra calories are coming from if you get stuck at a plateau while losing weight. It also makes you stop and think before grabbing a handful of snacks.

Helpful: Buy yourself a lined notebook or a weight-loss journal. For one week, write down what you eat, the amount and the total calories in the portion. There is no need to count sugar-free beverages or gum.

Women trying to lose weight should stick with 1,200 to 1,500 calories a day...for men, the daily caloric intake should be 1,500 to 2,000 calories.

• **Don't let exercise become boring.** Exercise is the cornerstone of successful weight control. Most diet masters told me that they exercise at least three times a week, with 25% of them working out five or six times weekly. Most important, many of them had more than one way to keep physically fit.

Example: Six out of 10 people engage in at least two different forms of exercise, such as walking and light weight training. Some change their exercise with the season—outdoor cycling in the summer and aerobics in the winter.

Others vary their exercise within a workout session. Spending 45 minutes on a treadmill is boring, but spending 15 minutes on each of three different pieces of equipment is more bearable.

Helpful: Since exercise goals that are too rigorous are usually short-lived, you should start small, start easy and do a form of exercise that you enjoy.

Begin by walking for 15 to 20 minutes every day—this is the top form of exercise among diet masters. After a few weeks, increase each walk to 30 minutes, and on alternate days, ride your bike or lift weights.

Important: Give yourself a break—schedule some days off from exercise each week, and don't feel you have to keep increasing your exercise to benefit. That's a good way to get hurt or discouraged.

Outsmart Your Fat Triggers to Lose Weight and Keep It Off

Stephanie Dalvit-McPhillips, PhD, registered dietitian with a doctorate in nutritional biochemistry. Ms. Dalvit-McPhillips has a private counseling practice in Willoughby, OH, where she treats people with weight problems and eating disorders. She is author of *The Right Bite: Outsmart 43 Scientifically Proven Fat Triggers and Beat the Dieter's Curse* (Fair Winds).

If you've tried every fad diet but failed to reach your ideal weight, stop blaming yourself. No single diet can address all the complex factors that contribute to weight gain.

In two decades of nutrition research and clinical practice, I've identified dozens of hidden triggers that can cause weight gain—in some cases, even *when you don't overeat.*

Some triggers alter your metabolism, causing you to burn fat and calories inefficiently. Others spark irresistible cravings that give way to out-of-control bingeing.

The key is to identify and avoid your personal triggers. *Here are eight of them that may surprise you...*

SENSORY CUES

Have you ever claimed to put on weight just by looking at food? Well, you may be right.

In a Yale University study, insulin levels skyrocketed in hungry individuals who were exposed to the sight, smell and even the mere mention of charcoal-broiled steaks. Participants' bodies started converting glucose to fat even before they had taken their first bite.

What to do: Don't linger near buffet tables or dessert trays—especially if you are hungry.

LACK OF FIBER

Low-fiber diets typically provide a lot of fat and calories but few nutrients. Such diets also lack bulk, which means you need to eat more to feel full.

High-fiber foods are filling, nutritionally dense and relatively low in fat and refined sugar. High-fiber foods also help stabilize blood glucose and insulin levels.

What to do: Get at least 25 grams (g) of fiber in your daily diet. Good sources include whole grains, fruits, vegetables and legumes.

INSUFFICIENT CALORIES

When you limit calories to 1,000 or fewer daily, your body starts to pilfer protein from lean body tissue, destroying the muscle mass necessary to burn fat and calories. You also begin to manufacture an overabundance of *lipoprotein lipase,* an enzyme that stores fat in your cells.

You may drop pounds on an extremely low-calorie diet. But once you resume eating normally, your body will convert what it now perceives as excess calories into fat.

What to do: Don't eat fewer than 1,400 calories daily. Total calories should be divided among several meals and snacks.

DIET FOODS

You may assume that you can eat more if foods are labeled "low-fat" or "lite." Wrong. Despite the catchy labeling, these foods can be packed with sugar *and* calories. "Sugar-free" products may contain aspartame or saccharin—sweeter-than-sugar substitutes that can provoke a sweet tooth.

What to do: Read ingredient and nutrition labels. Avoid foods that derive more than 20% of calories from fat.

SALT AND FLAVOR ENHANCERS

Scientists are not sure why salt triggers compulsive eating. It may trigger hormonal changes that amplify hunger, or we may eat more of the foods we find flavorful.

In addition to salt, food manufacturers can choose from more than 2,000 flavor enhancers to make packaged snacks and meals irresistible. But many of these ingredients, such as monosodium glutamate (MSG) and ammonium carbonate, may cause you to not only eat more, but also to store more of what you do eat as fat.

What to do: Avoid salt and foods with artificial flavor-boosters. Use lemon, herbs, balsamic vinegar and no-salt substitutes.

THIRST

People frequently confuse thirst for hunger. What's more, we neglect to count the calories we drink. For example, most 12-ounce sodas contain 150 calories.

What to do: Before surrendering to your cravings, drink a glass of water—then reassess your hunger. When choosing beverages, stick to water or herbal tea.

CAFFEINE AND NICOTINE

Often trumpeted as appetite suppressants, caffeine and nicotine actually increase hunger and cravings in certain individuals.

Both substances trigger the fight-or-flight response. This causes glucose to flood into the bloodstream, providing quick energy and temporarily suppressing appetite. But as blood glucose levels rise, so do insulin levels.

Result: Within one hour of consuming caffeine (even as little as one cup of coffee) or nicotine, glucose levels take a nose-dive. This leaves you feeling ravenous.

Worrisome: Secondhand smoke. People exposed to smoke experience the same fluctuations in blood sugar, but—unlike a smoker—won't light up when they feel hunger.

What to do: Avoid caffeine for three months. Are you able to forgo that midmorning donut? Have you shed pounds? If so, caffeine is a trigger to be avoided. Nicotine should be eliminated—weight-gain trigger or not. Talk to your doctor about quitting smoking…and avoid secondhand smoke.

NOT ENOUGH SLEEP

Sleep-deprived people may increase their daily calorie consumption by as much as 15%, according to research conducted at Emory University School of Medicine in Atlanta.

What to do: Strive to get at least eight hours of sleep every night.

Almonds for Weight Loss

In one finding, people who ate a moderate amount of almonds, three ounces a day, lost more weight than those on high-carbohydrate diets who ate the same number of calories.

Theory: The fat in almonds may not be completely absorbed by the body.

Try a handful of almonds between meals to satisfy hunger and stop unhealthy snacking.

Michelle Wien, DrPH, RD, CDE, program dietitian and researcher, City of Hope National Medical Center, Duarte, CA, and leader of a study of 65 overweight and obese adults, published in the *International Journal of Obesity.*

Weight-Loss Secrets That Really Work

Lawrence J. Cheskin, MD, director, Johns Hopkins Weight Management Center, and associate professor of medicine and human nutrition, Johns Hopkins University Bloomberg School of Public Health, both in Baltimore. He is author of *New Hope for People with Weight Problems* (Prima).

Consume fewer calories. Exercise daily. Reduce fat intake. Everyone knows the standard advice for losing weight. Unfortunately, up to 90% of those who initially lose weight gain it back within one year.

HIDDEN CAUSES OF WEIGHT GAIN

Only 2% of people who cannot lose weight have physical reasons for gaining the weight, including a slow metabolism or inefficient fat-storing mechanisms. The adrenal gland disorder Cushing's syndrome and an underactive thyroid (*hypothyroidism*) can also lead to weight gain.

More often, people put on weight because they eat too much and/or do not get enough exercise. Sadly, our sedentary lifestyle makes it difficult for us to maintain a healthful weight. Many people also eat to relieve stress or boredom. They fail to lose weight because they don't recognize the cues that cause them to eat inappropriately.

Helpful: Wear your watch upside down for a few weeks. Most people look at their watches when they're thinking about eating. When you see it's upside down, ask yourself *why* you want to eat. If you're truly hungry, eat—but resist the urge if you're merely doing it out of habit. Instead, go for a walk…read the newspaper…or call a friend.

When buying food, it's not enough to check the labels for fat and calories. You must also check serving sizes. Many packaged foods that appear to contain one serving actually contain two or more. This means you might be consuming more fat and calories than you think.

Example: Bottled cranberry juice has approximately 120 calories per eight-ounce serving. But a 20-ounce bottle contains two-and-a-half servings. If you drink the whole bottle, you're really getting 300 calories.

Surprisingly, gyms can also be a problem for dieters. They are often inconvenient, and people sometimes feel too self-conscious to go. Instead, I favor home and neighborhood workouts—riding an exercise bike or walking around the block.

Many people fail to realize that medication can cause unintended weight gain, too. These drugs include hormones…steroids…and antidepressants, such as *amitriptyline* (Elavil) and *imipramine* (Norfranil). If you've gained more than a few pounds within one month of starting a drug, ask your doctor or pharmacist to review your medications. There may be effective alternatives.

For people who *still* can't lose weight, the best approaches…*

WEIGHT-LOSS PROGRAMS

If you are too busy or self-conscious to participate in a group weight-loss program, such as Weight Watchers (800-651-6000 or *www.weightwatchers.com*)…or Take Off Pounds Sensibly (414-482-4620 or *www.tops.org*), the interactive, Internet-based weight-loss programs can be an effective alternative.

A recent study in the *Journal of the American Medical Association* found that people who participated in an Internet-based program lost an average of 10 pounds in six months.

Good weight-loss information on the Web: *www.ediets.com.*

Cost: $65** for a 13-week program.

WEIGHT-LOSS DRUGS

People who combine drugs with diet and exercise may lose an additional 5% of their weight over six months. But all drugs have side effects, so I recommend them only for

*Use of weight-loss drugs and the diets described here require a doctor's supervision.

**Price subject to change.

people who are at least 40 pounds over their recommended ideal weight.

Leading weight-loss drugs…

• **Fat-blockers.** *Orlistat* (Xenical) attaches to enzymes that digest fats. Fats pass out of the body in the stool instead of entering the bloodstream.

• **Appetite suppressants.** *Phentermine* (Fastin), *sibutramine* (Meridia) and the other appetite suppressants alter brain chemistry to make you feel satisfied with eating smaller amounts of food.

Warning: Do *not* take over-the-counter weight-loss drugs. They often contain such ingredients as caffeine and ephedrine, which may cause heart irregularities.

KETOGENIC DIETS

Seriously obese patients can benefit from so-called ketogenic diets.

How they work: A high-protein diet, in which 60% to 80% of calories come from protein, curbs appetite and helps maintain muscle mass during weight loss. Restricting carbohydrate intake results in *ketogenesis*—a process in which the production and breakdown of fat by-products curbs appetite and increases the burning of fat tissue.

However, this approach may cause heart and kidney damage. To prevent this, I recommend a *modified* ketogenic diet that consists of 20% to 30% carbohydrates…10% to 20% fat …and the rest protein.

VERY LOW-CALORIE DIET

People who are 100 pounds or more over their ideal weight often get good results from a very low-calorie diet—defined as less than 800 calories daily. This approach can cause weight loss of up to three pounds per week. But this type of diet *must* be supervised by a physician.

SURGERY

People with a body-mass index (BMI) of 40 or higher* are candidates for a surgical procedure that uses a *laparoscopically adjustable gastric band,* which was approved by the US Food and Drug Administration in June 2001.

*To calculate your BMI, go to the National Heart, Lung and Blood Institute Web site at *www.nhlbisupport.com/bmi.*

How it works: A plastic band is tightened around the stomach to reduce the amount of food it can hold. To perform this procedure, a bariatric surgeon inserts flexible instruments through keyhole incisions in the abdomen.

To locate a bariatric surgeon in your area: Contact the American Society for Metabolic & Bariatric Surgery at 352-331-4900 or *www.asbs.org.*

Feel-Full Snacks That Are Only About 150 Calories Each

Barbara J. Rolls, PhD, professor and Guthrie chair of nutrition, Pennsylvania State University, University Park, and coauthor of *The Volumetrics Weight-Control Plan* (HarperCollins).

Snacking in the evening is one of the chief culprits in weight gain. Here are healthful snacks that are roughly 150 calories each…

ANGEL FOOD CAKE

Top one slice of angel food cake with one cup of whole fresh strawberries and two tablespoons of light, nondairy whipped topping.

BAKED APPLE

Peel an apple one-quarter down from the top. Core it, and place two teaspoons of brown sugar in the center. Sprinkle with cinnamon. Microwave on high in a small, covered bowl for two to three minutes.

CARROTS, CELERY AND DIP

Place 15 prewashed baby carrots and a sliced stalk of celery on a plate. Dip them into three tablespoons of nonfat ranch dressing.

POPCORN AND FRUIT

Two and one-quarter cups of fresh air-popped popcorn—plain or lightly salted. Enjoy with one-half an apple and one cup of grapes on the side.

FRUIT SMOOTHIE

Use a blender to mix four ounces of light yogurt…one-quarter cup of nonfat milk…three-quarter cup of frozen or fresh sliced strawberries…one-third of a ripe banana…and one cup of ice. The banana will help to give any smoothie a rich, filling texture.

MILK AND COOKIES

Have three-quarter cup of nonfat milk along with eight *bite-sized,* reduced-fat chocolate chip cookies.

OAT CEREAL WITH MILK

Mix three-quarter cup of toasted oat cereal with three-quarter cup of nonfat milk.

TOMATO SOUP

One and one-quarter cups of tomato soup made with water. Have three saltine crackers along with the soup.

More from Barbara Rolls…

Asian Weight-Loss Secret

Stop eating when you are 80% full. Elders on the Japanese island of Okinawa call this *hara hachi bu*—and it helps them eat 10% to 40% fewer calories than Americans consume.

Rationale: It takes the stomach 20 minutes to signal the brain that it is full. Stopping when you are almost full—and waiting 20 minutes—helps your body feel satisfied without eating additional food.

Helpful: At the first faint sign of fullness, put down your utensils, and leave the table.

Lose Belly Fat and Save Your Life

Arthur Agatston, MD, cardiologist and associate professor of medicine, University of Miami School of Medicine, and consultant, National Institutes of Health Clinical Trials Committee, Bethesda, MD. He is author of *The South Beach Diet* (Rodale), *www.southbeachdiet.com.*

The size of your waist is a better indicator of health dangers than your weight. Men who have waists that measure more than 40 inches and women whose waists measure more than 35 inches generally have excess visceral fat. Large amounts of visceral fat—which wraps around the internal organs, such as the heart—greatly increase your risk of diabetes, heart disease, stroke and cancer.

CARBOHYDRATE CONNECTION

Diet is fundamental to reducing visceral fat—specifically, a diet that contains little or no refined carbohydrates.

The carbohydrates that dominate the typical American diet—white bread, pasta, cereals, snack foods, cakes, cookies, candies, etc.—are stripped of fiber during processing. All these foods are quickly digested and absorbed as glucose, the form that sugar takes in the bloodstream.

The body needs to produce ever-increasing amounts of insulin to remove excess glucose and fat from the blood. Elevated levels of insulin promote fat storage in the abdomen.

Higher insulin levels will end up removing too much glucose from the blood. The resulting low blood sugar, called *reactive hypoglycemia,* triggers food cravings. The more you give in to the cravings, the more weight you gain.

I have developed a three-phase strategy that reduces insulin resistance and food cravings without the dramatic calorie reductions. People typically lose eight to 13 pounds during the first two weeks and then one to two pounds per week thereafter.

PHASE 1

For 14 days, eat all the lean meat, chicken, turkey and seafood that you want. Eliminate the refined carbohydrates—bread, pasta, rice, baked goods, candy and alcohol. All of these foods exhibit high glycemic indexes. The glycemic index measures the amount by which a specific food raises blood glucose levels.

Eliminating these foods for 14 days reduces cravings for carbohydrates and helps normalize glucose levels. Eventually, you will be able to add some high-glycemic foods back into your daily diet.

Fruits and certain root vegetables, such as carrots and potatoes, also have high glycemic indexes and should be avoided in this phase. You can have as much as you want of other vegetables. To find the glycemic index of various foods, go to *www.glycemicindex.com.*

You also can have mono- and polyunsaturated fats, such as olive and canola oils. These satisfy appetite, reduce food cravings and help lower levels of harmful triglycerides and LDL cholesterol—main risk factors in people with large stores of visceral fat.

Nuts also are allowed. They are filling and contain mainly monounsaturated fats. Nuts are high in calories, so limit yourself to about 15 almonds or cashews, 30 pistachios or 12 peanuts (technically a legume) daily.

Don't worry about eating too much. Eat until you're satisfied—you'll still lose weight. Most of the weight loss that occurs during this phase will come from your midsection.

PHASE 2

During the third week, you can reintroduce some refined carbohydrates into your diet. Your body will respond more normally to insulin's effects. You can allow yourself a small serving of bread, pasta, potatoes or rice twice a day. Cookies, cakes, candy, alcohol and snack foods, such as potato chips, still should be avoided.

Continue to focus on foods that have low glycemic indexes. Foods that are rich in fiber, such as brown rice, whole-grain breads, etc., have the lowest glycemic numbers because they are digested slowly and release glucose into the bloodstream gradually.

Helpful: Prepare foods whole, or chop them as coarsely as possible. The more work your stomach has to do to digest the food, the more slowly glucose enters the bloodstream. Finely chopped foods—shredded potatoes in hash browns, for example—allow glucose to enter the bloodstream more quickly. Whole fruit is better than juice for the same reason.

Other Phase 2 strategies…

●**Eat fish at least twice a week.** The omega-3 fatty acids in fish have been shown to reduce heart attack and stroke risk. Salmon, mackerel and herring are particularly rich in omega-3s.

●**Eat a high-protein breakfast.** Morning protein suppresses food cravings and promotes weight loss. People who skip breakfast experience morning drops in blood glucose that trigger cravings. They also tend to eat more calories during the day. A study of teenagers found that those who ate sugary breakfast cereals consumed 80% more calories over the following five hours than those who ate omelettes.

Try an omelette with cheese or vegetables, such as asparagus or broccoli, or have Canadian bacon, turkey bacon, farmer cheese or low-fat cottage cheese.

●**Snack when you're hungry.** Always try to keep some food in your stomach. It's the best way to prevent sudden food cravings.

Rather than grabbing fast foods that are high in the glucose-raising carbohydrates, try cheese sticks or a serving of sugar-free yogurt. These foods are ideal because they provide appetite-suppressing protein with very little sugar.

PHASE 3

This is the maintenance phase of the diet. Once you have reached your desired weight, continue to limit refined carbohydrates to keep food cravings under control, minimize insulin resistance and maintain low levels of visceral fat.

Six Ways to Lose That Too-Big Potbelly

Garry Egger, PhD, MPH, director, Centre for Health Promotion and Research, Sydney, Australia, and adjunct professor of health sciences, Deakin University, Melbourne, Australia. He is coauthor of *GutBuster: Waist Loss Guide* (Allen & Unwin).

Whether it's called a potbelly or a spare tire, fat deposits concentrated around the middle of a man's body have long been the butt of jokes.

But mid-body fat is no laughing matter. It raises the risk for heart disease, diabetes, high blood pressure, back pain, knee problems, snoring and even impotence.

Almost every man develops at least a bit of a paunch as he grows older. How can you tell if yours is reason for concern?

Do not rely on your bathroom scale—either to check yourself now or to monitor your weight loss later. A scale can tell you if you weigh more than most other men your height.

But muscular men are sometimes overweight without being fat.

Your waist measurement is a more reliable indicator of potential health problems. Any man whose waist spans 39 inches or more should take immediate steps to lose his belly.

To find your waist size: Place a tape measure around your waist at the level of the navel. Do not suck in your gut. That will only give you an artificially small number—reassuring, perhaps, but dangerously misleading.

SIX WAYS TO SHRINK A BELLY

The good news for men is that it's not especially difficult to lose a potbelly. Abdominal fat tends to be more "mobile" than weight deposited at the hips and thighs—as women's fat often is.

Follow these guidelines, and you should lose an inch of fat in your waist measurement every two to three weeks…

1. Cut fat consumption *dramatically.* Most health experts continue to recommend getting about 30% of total calories in the form of fat. But it's not really the percentage of dietary fat that counts. It's the total amount of fat that you eat that controls how fat your body is.

Important: Eat no more than 40 grams (g) of fat per day. Pick up a fat-count book, such as Karen J. Bellerson's *The Complete & Up-to-Date Fat Book* (Avery).

Recent research suggests that dietary fat is actually addictive—the more you eat, the more you crave. Stop eating fatty foods for just two weeks, and you should lose most, if not all, of your craving.

Helpful: Pay attention to your eating. Do you tend to snack while watching television? Do you eat in your car? At your desk? Many men are surprised to discover that they can break these bad habits—and cut down on unconscious eating—simply by paying attention to their eating habits.

2. Eat small, frequent meals. Doing so boosts your metabolic rate, speeding the rate at which the body burns calories and helping you avoid the hunger that sometimes leads to uncontrolled eating.

Never go more than four hours without eating. Do *not* skip breakfast. If you have no appetite upon rising, start the day with toast and juice.

3. Focus simply on moving more—not necessarily getting more exercise. Vigorous exercise is unnecessary. Your goal should be simply to boost the amount of time you spend in motion—going up stairs, walking the dog, mowing the lawn, etc.

Helpful: Use a pedometer to count how many steps you take each day. At least 7,500 steps are necessary to lose weight, but 10,000 to 12,000 steps per day are better.

Stomach exercises do firm the abdominal muscles. But they have no special magic against belly fat. Walking is actually more effective, since it's a more efficient way of burning calories.

4. Cultivate a caffeine habit. Too much coffee or any other caffeinated beverage can cause health problems, including anxiety. But it's now clear that a little caffeine each day constitutes a safe way to speed your metabolism and lose weight.

Because the body quickly develops a tolerance to caffeine, drinking coffee, cola, etc., is most effective after a period of abstinence.

If you're a habitual coffee, tea or cola drinker, go "cold turkey." After two weeks, gradually reintroduce caffeine into your diet. Limit consumption to two cups of coffee—or four cups of tea or cola—per day.

If you're not much of a caffeinated beverage drinker right now, start slowly. Have one-half cup of coffee in the morning and one-half cup in the afternoon.

5. Season your food with hot peppers. *Capsaicin,* the compound that makes hot peppers hot, fights body fat in two ways. It boosts your metabolism…and helps reduce the amount of food eaten at each meal. It does the latter by curbing your appetite.

Sources of capsaicin: Red and green chili peppers, cayenne pepper, Tabasco sauce and jalapeños.

6. Observe your drinking habits. Contrary to popular belief, alcohol is not a significant contributor to a potbelly. It's the chips, cheese, etc., that you eat while drinking alcohol that add on the pounds.

What if you're a teetotaler? At least as far as your belly is concerned, there is no reason to start drinking.

A Harvard MD Weighs In on the Eating Debate

George L. Blackburn, MD, PhD, associate professor of surgery and nutrition, and associate director, division of nutrition, Harvard Medical School, Boston. He is also chief, the Nutritional/Metabolism Laboratory and director, the Center for the Study of Nutrition Medicine, both at Beth Israel Deaconess Medical Center, Boston.

For years, we've been told that a low-fat, high-carbohydrate diet is the best way to lose weight and reduce the risk of heart disease. It is the basis of the federal government's Food Pyramid for healthful eating.*

However, some reputable researchers have suggested that a high-protein, high-fat, low-carb diet is actually more healthful and effective. The premise behind this diet—often called "the Atkins diet" because it was first popularized by the late Robert Atkins, MD, over 30 years ago—is that it is carbohydrates, not fat, that make us gain weight. If we consume fewer carbohydrates, we will lose weight—and live much longer.**

A distinguished expert in the field of nutrition and obesity, Harvard's George L. Blackburn, MD, PhD, helped to sort fact from fiction…

●**When trying to lose weight, is what you eat more important than the number of calories?** Probably not. The bottom line is always total calories taken in minus total calories expended. If you burn more calories than you consume, regardless of the source, you will lose weight. If you consume more calories than you burn, you will gain weight.

*For more information on the USDA Food Pyramid, go to *www.mypyramid.gov.*

**For more information on the Atkins diet, go to *http://atkins.com.*

• **But people lose weight on the Atkins diet, which can be high in calories. Why?** Like almost all fad diets, a high-protein, high-fat diet cuts down on variety, which reduces interest in food and thus limits intake. Also, protein—especially animal protein—seems to induce the feeling of being satisfied.

Some proponents claim that the Atkins diet burns fat by controlling insulin production. Another theory is that *ketones*—chemicals produced when carbohydrate intake is very low—play a role. But these are just hypotheses.

Whatever the mechanism, obese people will generally lose 20 to 30 pounds over a three- to six-month period.

• **What happens long term?** There are no scientific control studies that prove weight loss continues past that point, or that the weight lost will stay off.

• **Is the Atkins diet better than other diets for losing weight?** The jury is still out on that one. There have been no head-to-head trials in which a control group was following a different weight-loss regimen. It's an area that deserves serious study.

• **The Atkins diet encourages fat consumption. Is that healthful?** High LDL ("bad") cholesterol remains the number-one risk factor for coronary heart disease, and saturated fat is known to increase it. But it appears that you can take in substantial amounts of fat without increasing cholesterol—*while your weight is decreasing*. As long as you burn all the fat you consume, it doesn't end up in your arteries.

But once you stop losing weight, it's another story. We don't know if someone can exceed the recommended levels of dietary fat and still stay healthy.

There are other health problems as well. Low-carbohydrate, high-protein diets, such as Atkins, raise blood acid levels, which can increase the risk of osteoporosis and promote the formation of kidney stones in vulnerable individuals. You shouldn't start the Atkins diet or change your eating habits in any radical way without talking to your doctor.

• **How about the high-carbohydrate, low-fat diet promoted in the Food Pyramid?** Some people say it causes obesity. But there is no evidence of this. It is true that the rate of obesity in this country has gone up markedly over the last 20 years. But that's probably because people are dining out more—and eating larger portions than they would at home. Also, people are exercising less.

As for carbohydrates themselves, it is important to distinguish among different kinds. The Food Pyramid calls for fiber-rich whole-grain foods, vegetables and fruits. No one is advocating unlimited refined carbohydrates, such as white bread, white rice and sugar.

Some people do need to be cautious about consuming too many carbohydrates. They have *Syndrome X*—a condition marked by high triglyceride levels, low HDL ("good") cholesterol and an increased risk of heart disease and diabetes—which could be aggravated by any simple sugars and refined starches. This is another reason to discuss diet plans with your doctor.

• **Overall, what is a sensible plan for losing weight?** It doesn't matter what you do for a few days, weeks or even months. You need a diet *for the rest of your life*. The idea is to find one that is flexible and satisfying.

One thing people tend to overlook even though it makes a real difference in weight control is water. Volume makes you feel satisfied, and water, especially when it's in food, has a lot to do with that. Eat lots of fruits and vegetables—they have a high water content and are rich in dietary fiber, which also fills you up. Soup is also a good diet food.

It takes some time and practice to change the way you eat. Most people eat 21 meals a week. In at least 10 of them, try to include whole grains, vegetables and fruits, moderate amounts of protein and limited fats. This may mean brown-bagging some lunches.

For the other meals, concentrate on controlling your portions and eating slowly. Take at least 20 minutes between the first and last bites of the meal.

Guidance from a dietitian or other health professional can be worthwhile. It is also helpful to have family members and others with whom you eat regularly eating healthfully, too. Healthful eating should be a communal effort.

High-Protein Diet Danger

High-protein diets may encourage the formation of kidney stones. Studies show that a high-protein diet will result in acidic, calcium-rich urine. These conditions encourage the formation of kidney stones.

Instead: Dieters should find a balanced diet that allows them to lose weight…it's important to drink plenty of water, too.

Shalini Reddy, MD, associate professor of clinical medicine, Pritzker School of Medicine, University of Chicago.

The Calcium Diet: Lose Weight Faster with This Vital Mineral

Michael B. Zemel, PhD, professor of nutrition and medicine and director, Nutrition Institute, University of Tennessee, Knoxville. He is coauthor of *The Calcium Key: The Revolutionary Diet Discovery That Will Help You Lose Weight Faster* (John Wiley & Sons).

Why are two out of every three Americans so overweight? Certainly we are eating more and exercising less. But there is another cause—a lack of the mineral calcium in our diets.

If you are among the Americans who are getting the lowest average level of calcium—which is 255 milligrams (mg) per day—you are 84% more likely to be overweight than if you are among those people getting the highest average level of calcium—1,346 mg per day—according to an examination of statistics from the federal government's Health and Nutrition Examination Survey.

Simply by getting adequate calcium in our diets, as many as four out of five of us could lose the extra weight.

CALCIUM AND YOUR FAT CELLS

Calcium does far more than just keep your skeleton strong. Without enough calcium

circulating in your bloodstream, your heart wouldn't beat, your blood wouldn't clot, your hormones wouldn't regulate your metabolism and your nerves wouldn't transmit signals.

If calcium levels fall—if you eat a diet low in calcium, for example—the body releases more of the hormone *calcitriol*. Calcitriol increases absorption of calcium in the intestines, so you get the most calcium possible from food.

In addition, it increases reabsorption through the kidneys, so that you lose as little calcium as possible through excretion.

Calcitriol also controls how fat cells work. When you get too little calcium and more calcitriol is released, your fat cells make and store more fat, causing weight gain.

MORE PROOF

In a study we conducted at the University of Tennessee, overweight people were put on one of three eating plans for six months.

●**Group 1** ate a diet that was 500 calories below maintenance level—the level at which you neither gain nor lose weight—and had no more than one serving of dairy a day for a total of 400 to 500 mg of dietary calcium.

●**Group 2** ate the same calorie-restricted diet but took an 800-mg calcium supplement for a total intake of 1,200 to 1,300 mg of calcium.

●**Group 3** also ate the calorie-restricted diet but included three servings of low-fat dairy a day, bringing their total calcium intake to 1,200 to 1,300 mg.

Results: Group 1 lost 6% of total weight…Group 2 lost 7.5%…and Group 3—the low-fat dairy group—lost 11%. Group 3 also lost more body fat than the other groups, particularly around the waist area.

This is an important finding because a slimmer waist is associated with a lower risk of heart disease, stroke, diabetes and cancer.

This means that adding three servings of low-fat dairy to your daily diet can…

●**Increase the amount of weight you lose by 70%.**

●**Increase the amount of body fat you lose by 64%.**

• **Help you lose 47% more fat** from around your belly.

Other studies have replicated these findings as well. In a 10-year study of 3,000 people ages 18 to 30, researchers at Harvard University discovered that people who ate three servings of dairy a day had a 60% lower risk of being overweight than those who consumed less calcium.

FOOD VERSUS SUPPLEMENTS

Studies show that calcium from dairy foods is more effective for weight loss than supplements. Why? Food is a complex mixture of known and unknown components. There is a cooperation among the components that can't be reproduced in a nutritional supplement.

Dairy contains calcium and a host of other biologically active components, including the amino acid *leucine*. Recent research reveals that leucine may increase the ability of muscle to use fat.

WHAT TO DO

To lose an average of one pound per week, you need to reduce calorie intake and increase calorie burning by about 500 calories per day, or 3,500 calories per week.

To boost the loss to 1.5 to two pounds, you need three or four servings of dairy a day, for a total of 1,200 to 1,600 mg of calcium.

The easiest way to get that is with three servings of no-fat (skim) or low-fat milk (eight ounces per serving), yogurt (eight ounces) or cheese (1.5 ounces or two ounces processed).

Strategy: Have milk before a meal. Studies show that getting a liquid form of dairy before eating helps you feel full sooner at that meal and eat less at the next meal.

If you are lactose intolerant, try eating yogurt that contains live cultures or cheese (it has very little lactose), or take a lactose supplement when consuming dairy.

To cut 3,500 calories a week: One brisk, hour-long walk will burn about 250 calories. If you do that four times a week, you still need to cut 2,500 calories per week, or about 350 calories a day. Look for one or even two high-calorie items that you can eliminate from your daily diet.

Examples: A 12-ounce cola has 150 calories...two tablespoons of full-fat salad dressing, 150...a glazed doughnut, 250...one four-ounce bagel, 300.

Just eliminating these items from your diet will help you to lose weight, but boosting calcium intake will help you lose more.

When It's OK to Use Diet Drugs

Prescription diet drugs are safe and effective when taken under a doctor's supervision. Many people are unaware that they are available and so have turned to potentially dangerous alternatives.

Effective diet medications: *Phentermine* is an appetite suppressant. *Xenical* blocks fat absorption. *Wellbutrin* is an antidepressant that has some weight-loss effects.

All these drugs can have side effects and require medical supervision. Your doctor will determine how long you can take them.

Louis J. Aronne, MD, director, weight-control program, New York–Presbyterian Hospital, New York City.

How to Recognize a Dangerous Diet

Beware of diets that claim weight losses of more than one to two pounds per week... promote "miracle" foods or supplements...restrict or recommend large quantities of specific foods to the detriment of a balanced diet... imply you can lose weight—and keep it off—without making any lifestyle changes or exercising...rely heavily on case histories, testimonials and anecdotes—but offer no scientific research to back up those claims...typically promise a "money-back guarantee."

Consult your doctor before starting any weight-loss program.

Stephen P. Gullo, PhD, president, Center for Healthful Living, Institute for Health and Weight Sciences, New York City and author of *The Thin Commandments Diet* (Rodale).

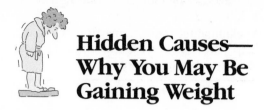

Hidden Causes— Why You May Be Gaining Weight

David E. Cummings, MD, endocrinologist and associate professor of medicine, University of Washington and Seattle Veterans Administration Medical Center, both in Seattle.

Most people put on pounds as they get older. However, if there's been a sudden change in your weight, you could have a hidden health problem. *Certain medical conditions can lead to obesity...*

HYPOTHYROIDISM

The thyroid gland helps regulate your body's metabolism. *Hypothyroidism* means that this gland is underactive, producing low levels of thyroid hormone. This causes the body to slow down and to burn fewer calories, leading to weight gain.

Other symptoms: Fatigue...a slow heart rate ...dry skin...brittle hair...constipation...depression...reduced blood flow to arms and legs, which can make you feel cold all the time.

About 7 million Americans suffer from hypothyroidism. Most gain a total of 10 to 20 pounds with this condition.

Hypothyroidism is typically diagnosed with two blood tests. One of the tests measures a person's levels of *thyroid-stimulating hormone* (TSH), which is produced by the pituitary gland. The other measures levels of the thyroid hormone *thyroxine.*

Treatment: The standard drug prescribed is the synthetic hormone *levothyroxine* (Levothroid, Synthroid). Taken every day for life, it will restore the body's normal metabolism with virtually no side effects.

CUSHING'S SYNDROME

This rare syndrome is caused by excess levels of *cortisol,* a stress hormone produced by the adrenal glands. People with this condition slowly gain a total of 10 to 25 pounds, usually in the upper body, face and neck.

Other symptoms: Elevated blood pressure ...high blood sugar...purplish stretchmark-like patterns (called *stria*), on the abdomen.

The most common cause of Cushing's syndrome is the long-term use of corticosteroids. These drugs are used to treat the inflammatory diseases such as rheumatoid arthritis, asthma, lupus and inflammatory bowel disease, and to prevent the rejection of a transplanted organ.

This condition also could be due to other causes, such as a benign tumor on the pituitary gland. In this case, it is called Cushing's disease, instead of syndrome.

Treatments: If the cause is corticosteroid use, your physician may be able to treat the syndrome by decreasing the drug dosage or by discontinuing the drug. If the cause is a tumor, surgery usually is recommended.

POLYCYSTIC OVARY SYNDROME

Women who have *polycystic ovary syndrome* (PCOS) can gain 50 pounds in two years. It is caused by excess production of *androgens*— the male hormones that promote weight gain. PCOS also has been linked to insulin resistance, a decline in insulin's ability to transport glucose into cells.

Other symptoms: Irregular or absent periods...infertility...acne...facial hair.

Up to 10% of women suffer from PCOS. It usually begins in puberty but often goes undetected for decades because the symptoms are subtle. PCOS is easily diagnosed with blood tests that measure hormone levels.

Treatment: Your doctor may prescribe one or more medications to manage the symptoms and risks of PCOS. He/she may prescribe *metformin* (Glucophage), which improves sensitivity to insulin. Taken daily for life, it reduces androgen levels, regulates the menstrual cycle and lowers risk of diabetes and heart disease.

For excessive hair growth, your doctor may add a drug such as *spironolactone* (Aldactone), which blocks the effects of androgens and lowers their production.

PRESCRIPTION DRUGS

Dozens of medications cause weight gain as a side effect, including steroids, antipsychotics and antidepressants, such as *tricyclic antidepressants* (TCAs) and *monoamine oxidase inhibitors*

(MAOIs). Ask your physician or pharmacist to review all of your prescriptions. If one or more has weight gain as a side effect, ask if other drugs can provide the same benefits without adding pounds.

Stop Food Cravings And Lose Weight

Elizabeth Somer, MA, RD, nutritionist in Salem, OR. She appears regularly on NBC's *Today* show and is a contributing editor to *Shape* magazine. She is author of *Food & Mood* and *The Origin Diet* (both from Henry Holt).

If you're berating yourself because you simply can't seem to cut back on potato chips, ice cream or some other tempting food—*stop*. Your problem may *not* come from a lack of willpower.

Food cravings are linked to low levels of critical nutrients and/or an imbalance of brain chemicals that affect appetite as well as mood.

Example: Low levels of *serotonin,* a "feel good" neurotransmitter, trigger cravings for carbohydrate-rich foods, including cookies, pasta and candy. Such foods elevate levels of *tryptophan,* an amino acid that is converted into serotonin in the brain.

Cravings can often be reduced by eating a healthful breakfast and a nutritional meal or snack every four hours throughout the day… and getting at least 30 minutes of exercise five days a week.

Some other helpful solutions for common problem foods…

FAT

The craving for fat is driven, in part, by a brain chemical called *galanin.* Galanin levels are lowest in the morning, rise during the day and peak in the afternoon. Eating fatty food keeps galanin circulating in the body, which stimulates a strong craving for more fat later in the day.

This physiological response makes sense in evolutionary terms. At one time, fat was scarce, so people had to eat as much as possible whenever it was available in order to survive.

Today, with rich food all around, fat cravings can lead to obesity, diabetes and heart disease. *Much better for you…*

● **Eat half a small avocado or one ounce of nuts daily.** These foods usually satisfy fat cravings because they contain monounsaturated and polyunsaturated fats, which are more healthful than the saturated fat found in meat and rich desserts.

● **Satisfy cravings with fat-free creamy foods,** such as fruit-and-yogurt smoothies or puréed squash soup. Their creamy textures help reduce cravings.

CARBOHYDRATES

Simple carbohydrates, such as candy, pie, doughnuts and cake, provide a temporary serotonin boost. But the cravings return as soon as serotonin levels wane. *Better approach…*

● **Eat complex carbohydrates.** Whole wheat toast…a whole wheat bagel…a bowl of air-popped popcorn are all low in fat and calories, but raise serotonin levels.

● **Stock up on healthful snacks** so you will be prepared if you tend to crave carbohydrates in the afternoon.

Good choices: Low-fat bran muffin, English muffin, baked tortilla chips and salsa, or lemon sorbet with fruit.

● **Use artificial sweeteners,** such as *aspartame* (NutraSweet), *sucralose* (Splenda) or *acesulfame K* (Sunett). Consumed in moderation, these products satisfy your sweet tooth but spare you the calories found in sugary snacks.

SALT

The human body needs only about 500 milligrams (mg) of sodium daily, or about one-quarter teaspoon. Most Americans consume *10 times* that amount. Salty foods increase blood pressure in people who are sensitive to salt. These foods also contribute to weight gain because they are typically high in fat.

Salt cravings usually result from eating habits that are surprisingly easy to unlearn. *Here's how…*

● **Snack on crunchy foods,** such as baby carrots or celery. Foods with a crunchy texture help satisfy the craving for salty snacks, such as potato chips.

●**Use seasonings.** Lemon juice, fresh ginger, cilantro, red pepper flakes and other spices enhance the flavor of unsalted foods.

CHOCOLATE

Chocolate boosts levels of serotonin and the morphine-like neurotransmitters called *endorphins*. It also contains caffeine and *theobromine*, a caffeine-like compound that provides a mental lift...*phenylethylamine*, the so-called "love" chemical that increases heart rate and blood pressure...and *anandamide*, a brain chemical that mimics the mood-lifting effects of marijuana.

It's no wonder chocolate is the most commonly craved food. Those who crave it find it is almost impossible to give up. *Instead...*

●**Eat very *small* amounts.** Just two small pieces of chocolate, one cup of sugar-free hot chocolate or one small cookie will often correct your brain chemistry without providing too many calories or fat.

●**Eat chocolate only *after* meals.** You will enjoy the taste treat and the boost in brain chemicals, but you'll be less likely to overindulge than if you eat chocolate between meals when you are hungry.

●**Substitute fat-free chocolate syrup for regular chocolate.** It provides the same pleasurable effects with only a fraction of the calories. I often advise clients to use one-quarter cup of chocolate syrup as a dip for fresh fruit.

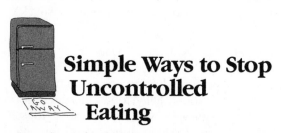

Simple Ways to Stop Uncontrolled Eating

Joyce D. Nash, PhD, clinical psychologist in private practice, Menlo Park, CA. She is author of *Binge No More* (New Harbinger). For more on binge eating disorder, contact the National Eating Disorders Association (800-931-2237; *www.myneda.org*), or go to Dr. Nash's Web site, *www.joycenashphd.com*.

A re you unable to control your eating? If so, you have plenty of company. One American in 10 suffers from *binge*

eating disorder* (BED), which involves frequent bouts of overeating.

BED strikes both men and women, especially obese individuals. It often goes hand-in-hand with chronic stress.

The binges can be triggered by hunger...or, more commonly, by restrictive dieting, anxiety, anger or simply boredom.

BED interferes with work and personal relationships. In addition to poor self-esteem, it can lead to persistent depression.

In severe cases, psychotherapy—either alone or with prescription antidepressants—may be necessary. But there is much sufferers can do for themselves.

RECORD YOUR BINGES

Binges often seem to run on some sort of "automatic pilot." *Self-monitoring can reveal just how and why you binge...*

●**Mark the time,** place and content of every meal, snack or drink. How hungry were you before you began eating? Underline any episode you deem a binge...and record what might have provoked it.

●**Look for patterns after two weeks—** when, where and on what you binged... whether you were hungry...what decisions, thoughts or emotions preceded the binge... and how you felt about yourself afterward.

NORMALIZE YOUR EATING

Binge eaters often fall into a destructive cycle in which restrictive dieting—denying all foods or certain "forbidden" foods—is followed by a binge.

Some binge eaters skip breakfast or lunch and gorge on dinner. Others "graze" all day.

Better: Establish a regular eating schedule. That means three balanced meals each day plus two or three snacks. Plan to have one meal or snack every three to four hours.

Important: Limit meals to 30 minutes apiece...and snacks to 15 minutes each. Focus on *when* you eat, not on *what* you eat.

*A binge is any loss of control over eating—whether it's two hours of fast food or two days of carrot sticks. Unlike the better-known eating disorders, bulimia and anorexia nervosa, BED does not involve regular vomiting or self-starvation.

Avoid diets that prohibit certain foods. For example, saying that you will never again eat ice cream or french fries virtually guarantees that you will crave those foods.

LEARN TO CONTROL CRAVINGS

It's almost inevitable to feel some cravings. Don't panic or give in. *Instead, whenever you feel a craving coming on, invoke the "five Ds"…*

• **Delay** eating for at least 10 minutes—to let the craving pass.

• **Distract** yourself. Go for a walk, call a friend, fold laundry, etc.

• **Distance** yourself from temptation. Leave the kitchen, avoid the cafeteria, throw out tempting foods.

• **Determine** how important it is to satisfy the craving.

• **Decide,** if the craving persists, how much food you can prudently consume. Then *enjoy* what you have chosen to eat.

ACCENTUATE THE POSITIVE

More so than most people, binge eaters base their self-worth on their physical appearance.

Relentlessly bombarded with images of perfection—airbrushed models and actors in magazines and movies and on TV—they silently berate themselves for failing to measure up.

The result? Low self-esteem. The antidote? Set more realistic standards.

Helpful: Write down at least five positive attributes of yours that are *unrelated* to weight or body shape. Don't overlook traits you have that might be considered mundane (being able to sew, for instance) or offbeat (being able to read upside down).

Review the inventory whenever you need a boost of confidence.

BANISH NEGATIVE THOUGHTS

· Binge eating is fueled by negative thinking. To encourage a more constructive inner voice, write out a series of positive thoughts, one each on 3"x5" index cards.

On each "reminder" card, jot down a single positive thought that rebuts a negative.

Example: If you often find yourself thinking, *No one will ever love me,* write down, *My mother, sister and best friend love me.*

The positive messages must be brief and believable. Platitudes such as *I have much to be thankful for* ring false.

Carry the cards with you to reflect on whenever you have time—first thing in the morning, when waiting on line, etc.

BEFRIEND YOUR BODY

Binge eaters frequently see their bodies as "the enemy." To make friends with your body instead, it's critical that you hold periodic "peace talks."

What to do: Stand naked in front of a mirror. Tell your body what you like about it… and what you'd like to change. Thank it for all it does for you. Apologize for mistreating or criticizing it. Ask what it needs from you now. Imagine and write down its response.

IMPROVE YOUR COPING SKILLS

Binge eaters often use food to cope with stressful situations.

Better: Practice problem-solving skills. Identify and describe every problem in detail… brainstorm possible solutions…implement the most reasonable one…assess its effectiveness.

Muscle relaxation exercises and deep breathing can help ward off cravings.

Muscle relaxation: Lie down and get comfortable. Alternately tense and relax the large muscle groups, beginning with the fists and arms, then the legs, torso, neck and head.

Deep breathing: Take a deep breath that fills your abdomen like a balloon. Exhale, letting yourself relax. Repeat until stress melts away.

SEEK OUT PLEASURE

Binge eaters often put obligations to others ahead of their own needs, leaving no time for themselves. Too many "shoulds" and not enough "wants" can cause feelings of deprivation…and the inevitable binge.

To restore balance: List all daily activities. Mark each with an "H" (*have to*), "W" (*want to*) or "M" (*mixture of the two*). Next, rank how much satisfaction each activity provides—high, medium or low.

If the Hs far outnumber the Ws or Ms—or if your satisfaction ratings are mostly medium or low—reassess your priorities. Eliminate some obligations to include enjoyable things.

Most People Don't Realize When They're Full

People who wore blindfolds while eating a meal consumed 22% less food than those who could see their plates.

Reason: Most of us rely on external cues—an empty plate or the bottom of a bag—to tell us when we're full. Blindfolded subjects rely instead on signals from their stomachs.

If you are trying to lose weight: Try using a blindfold once or twice to become more aware of your satiety cues.

Yvonne Linne, MD, PhD, researcher, obesity unit, Huddinge University Hospital, Stockholm.

Reduced-Fat Foods Could Cause Weight Gain

Low- or reduced-fat foods actually may cause weight gain. That's because many people eat more of these foods in the mistaken belief that they are also low in calories. No scientific evidence exists to support the use of low- or reduced-fat foods as a weight-loss tool.

Better: Eat at least five servings of fruits and vegetables daily. They are naturally low in fat and calories and are filling.

Judith Wylie-Rosett, EdD, RD, professor and head of the department of epidemiology and population health, Albert Einstein College of Medicine, Bronx, NY.

Healthier Peanut Butter

Regular peanut butter is healthier for you than reduced-fat peanut butter. Reduced-fat versions contain less monounsaturated fat, the kind that is good for the heart. To replace fat, manufacturers add sugar—so you end up with as many calories in reduced-fat peanut butter as in the regular type.

Holly McCord, RD, author of *Prevention's The Peanut Butter Diet* (St. Martin's) and nutrition editor, *Prevention,* Emmaus, PA 18098.

Eating Out with America's Top Food Cop

Michael F. Jacobson, PhD, executive director, Center for Science in the Public Interest, a nonprofit group that has led a nationwide campaign to improve America's nutrition and health, Washington, DC, *www.cspinet.org.* Dr. Jacobson is coauthor of *Restaurant Confidential* (Workman).

The average American eats at a restaurant more than four times a week. This practice may be very convenient—but it's not always healthful. Restaurant food has more fat, salt and cholesterol than home-cooked meals.

LUNCHTIME TRAPS

Is a veggie sandwich the ideal lunch? Not necessarily. The two ounces of cheese typically added to these popular lunchtime meals contain three-quarters of a day's allowance for saturated fat. Tuna salad, thanks to the mayonnaise usually used as a base, is packed with 720 calories. Chicken salad has 550 calories.

Best choices: Opt for a turkey, roast beef, chicken breast or veggie sandwich *without* cheese. Ask for extra veggies, light mayo, mustard, ketchup or light salad dressing.

Don't assume that a salad is diet food, either. A taco salad is served in a fried taco shell filled with ground beef, cheese, sour cream and guacamole. It contains 1,100 calories and a day's quota of saturated fat.

Greek salads are usually weighted down with feta cheese, which is high in saturated fat.

An Oriental chicken salad contains 750 calories, due to the dressing, nuts and fried noodles.

Helpful: If you're ordering salad, ask for light dressing on the side. Use no more than a few teaspoons. Also order cheese, nuts and noodles on the side—and use them sparingly.

For the best lower-calorie fast-food lunch, consider the following…

• **Burger King's BK Veggie Burger**—with reduced-fat mayonnaise—contains 340 calories and 2 grams (g) of saturated fat. It's better than just about any burger at any other chain.

• **McDonald's Fruit 'n Yogurt Parfait**—low-fat vanilla yogurt layered with berries and topped with granola—is a nutrient-rich bargain at only 380 calories.

• **Subway's "7 subs with 6 g of fat or less."** These include ham, roast beef, chicken and turkey—ranging from 200 to 300 calories for a six-inch sub.

• **Wendy's Mandarin Chicken Salad.** This creative salad of mixed greens, chicken and mandarin orange sections, roasted almonds and half a packet of Oriental sesame dressing is hard to beat at 470 calories.

Here's how to make the most healthful dinner choices when you're eating the following cuisines…

AMERICAN

The worst thing you can eat at a steak house isn't the steak—it's the appetizers. A fried onion served with dipping sauce has more than 2,000 calories. An order of cheese fries with dressing contains about 3,000 calories. Have a salad and bread instead.

The wrong choice of entrée can also send your calorie intake soaring. One trimmed, 16-ounce prime rib has about 1,000 calories and two days' worth of saturated fat. One trimmed, 20-ounce porterhouse steak isn't much better with a day-and-a-half's limit of saturated fat. A trimmed, 16-ounce T-bone steak has 700 calories and a day's quota of saturated fat.

As for side dishes, french fries or a loaded baked potato (sour cream, butter, cheese and bacon) add 600 calories.

Best choices: Sirloin steak or filet mignon are by far the leanest choices, containing about 400 calories each and less than half a day's saturated fat per serving. A baked potato with sour cream or a cooked vegetable is the best side dish.

CHINESE

Many people assume that all Chinese food is low in fat and calories. Not so. A breaded and fried chicken main dish, such as General Tso's Chicken, contains 1,600 calories. And, one order of orange (crispy) beef or sweet-and-sour pork also contains 1,600 calories each.

Best choices: You can cut calories by ordering steamed rice instead of fried…braised or stir-fried foods instead of deep-fried ones… vegetable-rich dishes, such as Szechuan shrimp, chicken chow mein, shrimp with garlic sauce or beef with broccoli.

Helpful: Use chopsticks or a fork to lift the food out of the fat-laden sauce in the serving plate and transfer it into your rice bowl.

ITALIAN

Most people know that a cream-and-cheese-based dish, such as fettuccine Alfredo, is an "artery-clogger." But they may not realize that a single order has 1,500 calories.

There are other less obvious danger zones when eating Italian food. Most spaghetti (with meatballs or sausage) and parmigiana dishes (eggplant, chicken or veal) contain more than 1,000 calories each. And the typical order of lasagna, one of the most popular Italian dishes, packs as much saturated fat as two McDonald's Big Macs, not to mention about 1,000 calories.

Best choices: Pasta topped with marinara or meat (Bolognese) sauce (skip the meatballs) …red or white clam sauce…or chicken Marsala.

A serving (a quarter of a large pie) of Pizza Hut's Stuffed Crust Pepperoni Lover's Pizza is about the same as eating two McDonald's Quarter Pounders. A typical serving of Pizza Hut's Hand-Tossed Veggie Lover's Pizza, on the other hand, has half the calories (550) and one-fourth the saturated fat (6 g).

Best choices: When ordering pizza, ask for half the usual amount of cheese. Vegetable toppings are lowest in calories. Chicken and ham are second best. Sausage and beef are the worst choices.

MEXICAN

At Mexican restaurants, the trouble starts with the appetizers. A complimentary basket of tortilla chips runs 650 calories. An order of cheese nachos or cheese quesadillas hits 900 calories. If you opt for the beef and cheese nachos, calories climb to 1,400.

Most platters at Mexican restaurants weigh in at more than 1,500 calories and a day's limit of saturated fat. This is due to the hefty side dishes (refried beans and rice) and rich condiments (sour cream and guacamole) that typically accompany the meat- and cheese-filled entrées (chimichanga, enchilada, burrito)—all of which contain high saturated fat levels.

Best choices: Stick with shrimp, chicken or vegetable fajitas…nonfried ("charro") beans instead of refried beans…soft tortillas with salsa instead of chips…or a couple of chicken tacos. Substitute salsa for sour cream and cheese.

Easy Way to Increase Fat Burning

Drink caffeine before a workout to accelerate fat burning. This works best when it's taken on an empty stomach.

For maximum absorption, drink one cup of coffee or tea without sugar and with a little milk.

If you are sensitive to coffee or dislike black tea, try *guarana tea*, a natural caffeine source that is often sold in health food stores.

Ori Hofmekler, New York City–based fitness expert and author of *The Warrior Diet* (Blue Snake Books), *www.warriordiet.com.*

Six Ways to Trigger Your Natural Fat Burners

Robert K. Cooper, PhD, Ann Arbor, MI–based researcher, speaker and writer. He is author of several books, including *Low-Fat Living: Turn Off the Fat-Makers, Turn On the Fat-Burners for Longevity, Energy, Weight Loss, Freedom from Disease* (Rodale). *www.robertkcooper.com.*

We have trouble shedding excess fat because our bodies and brains have an innate drive to create and store body fat. Combine this tendency with the typical American high-fat diet, and you've got a prescription for weight problems.

Good news: By switching on your natural fat-burning mechanisms, you can counteract the body's fat-storing tendencies…and boost energy levels at the same time.

Fat Burner 1: **Turn up the light.** To jump-start your metabolism each morning, expose yourself to sunlight by opening the curtains or blinds and standing there for several minutes.

If your bedroom doesn't get direct sun, turn on all the lights.

Alternative: Install full-spectrum lightbulbs—available at hardware and lighting stores.

Fat Burner 2: **Eat three low-fat meals a day, along with several low-fat snacks in between, and eat breakfast.** The more food you consume early, the higher your metabolic rate will be later in the day. Skipping breakfast also encourages bingeing at the end of the day, when your body's tendency to store fat is at its peak.

Follow the "Three plus Four" eating plan—this includes three low-fat meals a day, plus four low-fat snacks.

Recommended snack times…

• **10 am**—making it less likely that you'll stuff yourself at lunch.

• **3 pm**—to head off the desire for a salty snack later in the day.

• **5:30 pm**—a predinner appetizer, so you won't binge at dinner.

• **9 pm**—a small snack of fruit or grains, if you desire.

Appropriate snacks include…

•**Whole-grain bread,** crackers, bagel or English muffin topped with low-fat cottage cheese, fresh fruit or all-fruit preserves.

•**Low-fat granola bar.**

•**One cup of nonfat plain yogurt** with fresh fruit added.

•**A cup of nonfat or low-fat soup.**

•**A whole-grain–bread sandwich with Dijon mustard,** nonfat mayonnaise and two slices of turkey or chicken breast (not a good choice for a nighttime snack, however).

•**A piece of fresh fruit.**

Fat Burner 3: **Drink eight glasses of water daily.** Most people don't drink enough water to replace fluids lost throughout the day. Dehydration inhibits your body's ability to metabolize fat for energy.

To maximize fat-burning, drink eight eight-ounce glasses of water or an equivalent low-calorie noncaffeinated beverage every day. (Caffeinated drinks act as diuretics, contributing to fluid loss.)

Fat Burner 4: **Fit in 30 minutes of daily aerobic activity.** Thirty minutes of daily aerobic exercise burns *hundreds* of extra calories each week, while training your body to burn fat more efficiently. Exercising a few minutes at a time is just as beneficial to your health as doing it all at once.

Follow the "Four Fives and a Ten" plan—a five-minute walk just before or after breakfast, another five-minute walk before and after lunch, five minutes of walking or other light activity when you get home and a brisk 10-minute walk or cycle after dinner.

To accelerate fat-burning…

•**Add walks of 20 to 30 consecutive minutes,** three or four times a week.

•**Add in regular strength-training sessions** every other day. This will help increase your muscle mass.

Fat Burner 5: **Practice on-the-spot stress reduction.** When you feel frustrated, anxious or upset, your body produces stress-related hormones that promote the storage of body fat. Stress also leads people to overeat and eat foods rich in fat and sugar.

To keep your fat-burning mechanism in full gear, use diaphragmatic breathing whenever a stressful situation arises…

•**Sit or stand with your shoulders relaxed,** your spine straight.

•**Place your hands on your stomach just below your rib cage.** Slowly inhale through your nose, feeling your abdomen expand slightly downward and forward. As you complete the inhalation, feel your chest expand comfortably.

•**Exhale slowly through your mouth,** feeling a wave of relaxation flood your abdomen, chest, throat and face.

Other ways to reduce stress…

•**Shift your attention to focus on what you can control,** rather than what you can't.

•**Trigger calming regions of your brain** by imagining a "relaxation wave" running through your body—beginning in your face, then passing through your neck and shoulders and down your arms and legs, ending in your fingertips and toes.

•**Close your eyes and visualize the special people,** possessions or memories that you value and love.

•**Write to or call someone you love.**

Fat Burner 6: **Get deeper sleep to boost your metabolism.** No matter how much shut-eye you get, improving the *quality* of your sleep will help to increase the amount of fat you burn at night…and speed the building of new muscle tissue.

For deeper, more restful sleep…

•**Switch to a lighter blanket or just a sheet,** to allow your normal body thermostat to kick in. (Cooler temperatures increase metabolism.)

•**Do light exercise or take a hot bath or shower** three hours before bed. This will trigger a drop in body temperature as you're falling asleep, which helps deepen your rest.

•**Make your bed a time-free environment.** Set an alarm if you must, but turn the clock so you cannot see the face if you wake up during the night.

How to Exercise to Burn More Fat

Do the toughest exercise first. Then ease into more moderate effort. You'll burn up to 3% more fat.

Bonus: Exercising this way feels less difficult than starting moderately and building up.

Caution: Give yourself extra warm-up time to get muscles ready for high-intensity activity.

Jie Kang, PhD, assistant professor, department of health and exercise science, The College of New Jersey, Ewing.

How Hollywood Stars Shape Up—Fast!

Greg Isaacs, celebrity trainer and former director, corporate fitness, Warner Bros. Movie Studios, Burbank, CA. He is author of *The Ultimate Lean Routine* (Tapestry).

As a trainer who works with professional actors and actresses—who are some of the most body-conscious people in the world—I have found that they aren't very different from you and me.

Like average people, many actors eat out of emotion...have sedentary jobs...often dislike exercising...have erratic work schedules...and are frequently exposed to tempting, high-calorie foods.

What makes them different is that their jobs depend on being fit and trim. That gives them a very special incentive to get in shape and stay that way.

You don't have to be a celebrity to have a body like one. You just have to be willing to work out like one. I recommend the following exercises to all of my clients.

Important: For each exercise, do three sets of eight to 12 repetitions. Perform each of the exercises slowly. You'll strengthen your muscles faster and with fewer repetitions this way. Increase the weight of your dumbbells as soon as an exercise becomes easy for you to perform.

SCULPTED ARMS AND SHOULDERS

Do push-ups. Position yourself on all fours on the floor. Keep your upper body and your elbows straight and place your hands beneath your shoulders.

Either bend your legs at the knees and cross your ankles—the easiest way to do push-ups—or keep your legs straight and balance on your toes for the greatest benefit.

Lower your chest to the floor using only your arms. Then raise your chest off the floor using only your arms until your elbows are straight again—but not locked. Repeat.

BULGING BICEPS

Do a biceps curl using an eight- to 10-pound weight. Stand or sit. Stick your chin up and your chest out. Keep your elbows in—close to your sides—palms forward. Don't cheat by letting your elbow swing back and forth as you lift the weight or by leaning forward to begin a lift. Curl up one weight with a "one-two" count. Pause briefly. Lower and repeat with the other arm.

WELL-DEFINED CHEST

Do the dumbbell fly. Lie on your back on a flat bench with your feet on the floor and an eight- to 10-pound dumbbell in each hand.

Slightly bend your arms, and place them directly out to your sides. Keep your palms up and the dumbbells in line with your chest. Let the dumbbells pull your arms down so you feel a slight stretch.

In an arcing motion, bring both the dumbbells together over your upper chest with your palms facing together. Slowly lower the dumbbells, and then repeat.

RIPPLING BACK

Do a one-arm dumbbell row with the weights described for the biceps curl.

Lean over a flat bench, and place your left knee on the bench and your left hand at the top with your fingers curling over the side of the bench. Position yourself so your back is flat. Place your right foot securely on the floor. Hold a dumbbell in your right hand.

Fully extend your arm down with your palm facing your foot. Pull the dumbbell up to your hip, rotating your palm inward as you do so. Bring your elbow as far upward as you can.

Slowly return to the starting position. Repeat on each side.

WASHBOARD STOMACH

Do leg lifts. Lie on the floor on your back, and place your hands behind your head to elevate it. Lift your legs up to a 75° to 90° angle. Using your abdominal muscles, roll your buttocks off the floor, keeping your legs up.

Pull your elbows in toward your knees. Do not jerk your neck. Then slowly ease your buttocks back to the ground.

Simpler: If you can't lift your buttocks with your legs held up, do the exercise with your knees at a 45° angle.

FIRM BUTTOCKS

Squats are the answer. Stand against a wall. Elevate your heels on a book (or books) two inches thick. Bend your knees and slide down until you reach a sitting position. Keep your back straight. Hold for a few seconds. Slowly come back up.

Squeeze your buttocks muscles as you return to the starting position. Don't lock your knees. Repeat.

STRONG THIGHS

Do pliés—the ballet exercise. They'll also tone your abdominal muscles. Stand with your legs shoulder-width apart, toes pointed outward—what's known in ballet as second position.

Keeping your back, buttocks and hips aligned, bend your knees and go down as far as you can without lifting your heels off the floor. As soon as you reach the bottom of your plié, slowly return to the starting position. Squeeze your inner thighs as you raise your body.

SHAPELY LEGS

Do walking lunges down a hallway or outside. Stand erect. Take a large step forward. Bend your knees and lower your body. Keep the knee of your forward leg above the ankle, and let the rear knee almost touch the floor.

Return to an upright position, and drag the trailing leg forward. Press the heel of your front leg down as you come up, and squeeze your buttocks together as your bring your legs back to the starting position.

Repeat on each leg.

DROP POUNDS FAST

The basic fundamentals of weight loss never change. You must expend more calories than you consume. This becomes harder as you age because your metabolic rate slows.

Best: Jump-start your day with at least 45 minutes of cardiovascular exercise (running, swimming, biking). You'll not only burn calories, you'll also work off some of your stored energy so it won't be converted to fat.

And…do strength-training exercises twice a week. As you build muscle, you'll raise your metabolic rate and burn more fat—even when you're resting—since muscle cells burn more calories than fat cells do.

Important: Don't be lured by fad diets, such as the popular high-protein plans. The best way to lose pounds fast, safely and for good is to follow a diet high in fruits, vegetables and whole grains…and low in fat.

Be Your Own Personal Trainer

Miriam E. Nelson, PhD, director, Center for Physical Fitness, School of Nutrition Science and Policy, Tufts University, Boston. She is coauthor of the Strong Women series of exercise books and founder of *www.strong women.com.*

If you exercise on a regular basis, then you probably already know the value of a good personal trainer.

A trainer can help you establish and maintain a regular exercise schedule…suggest appropriate workouts…push you harder for better results …and teach you proper form and technique.

But trainers typically charge $45 or more for each one-hour session.

Good news: It's possible to achieve all of these benefits on your own—without a trainer. *Here's how…*

A REGULAR SCHEDULE

•**Work out with a friend.** Commit to specific times and days each week. You're less likely to miss a workout if another person is counting on you.

●**Make a realistic time commitment.** How much time can you devote to exercise each week? Thirty minutes a day? Thirty minutes three times a week? If you set unrealistic goals, you're likely to quit.

Choose the days you'll exercise, then write them in your calendar. Check them off once you've completed each workout.

Helpful: Think of each session as an "appointment" with yourself.

Having difficulty fitting your workout routine into a busy schedule? Try exercising before work or during your lunch hour…getting up early two mornings a week…dropping a low-priority item from your schedule…or performing three 10-minute workouts, rather than one 30-minute session.

●**Choose a suitable location.** Look for a convenient site that offers the services and equipment you need.

If winters are severe where you live, try to exercise indoors. Buy a stationary bicycle or treadmill, or use an exercise video.

When traveling, stay at a hotel with a fitness center. Ask the concierge for a walking or running route. Or pack a jump rope.

●**Keep a detailed exercise log.** Charting your ongoing progress will motivate you to maintain your program.

Include the date you exercised…how long you worked out…and what kind of exercise routine you performed.

Note at the bottom of the log the intensity of each routine—*too easy, just right, too hard.* This helps you recognize when a routine is no longer challenging.

Example: February 15…40 minutes…running and weights…intensity—just right.

For a weight-training routine, list the type of exercise…pounds or level of the workout… and number of repetitions.

THE BEST ROUTINES

There are three basic types of workouts…

●**Aerobic exercise.** Brisk walking, jogging or bicycling increases the heart rate.

●**Strength training.** Lifting weights preserves muscle strength and function.

●**Flexibility training.** Stretching expands your joints' range of motion.

Find a routine that satisfies your requirements for exercise, such as preventing back pain or tightening your abdomen.

Participate in aerobic exercise at least three times a week…strength or flexibility training at least twice a week. Begin each session with five minutes of easy exercise, warming up to full intensity. End with a five-minute cool-down that includes stretching.

THE RIGHT INTENSITY

Exercise won't do you much good unless you work out at an appropriate level of intensity.

To "push yourself" as a personal trainer would, ask yourself after your workout… *Could I have exercised longer? Could I have done more difficult exercises?* If so, try to increase your intensity next time.

Or you might be exercising too hard. Ask yourself after the routine…*Am I exhausted? Do my limbs feel heavy and sore?* If so, decrease your intensity.

Exercise physiologists have devised these exercise intensity guidelines…

●**Aerobic activity.** At least three times a week for a minimum of 20 minutes, exercise at a level that requires strenuous movement, elevating your heart rate to 60% of its maximum.* Breathing is rapid. Sweating starts within 15 minutes.

Incorporate into your daily life easy, sustainable movement that increases your heart and breathing rates slightly.

Sample activities: Strolling…gardening… playing golf.

Avoid overexertion. You've overdone it if your heart is pounding to the point of discomfort or nausea or if breathing becomes too rapid for you to speak easily.

●**Strength training.** For the first four weeks —while you are learning the exercises—work out at a moderate exertion level. This causes fatigue only if prolonged, like carrying a full briefcase that gets heavier as the day goes on.

To measure heart rate: Find your pulse on your neck or wrist. Count the number of beats for 15 seconds and multiply by four. *To calculate maximum heart rate:* Subtract your age from 220. If you're age 50, for example, your maximum heart rate is 170.

Stabilize at a level that begins at moderate intensity and gets harder after six or seven repetitions. You should be able to maintain good form while performing the movement eight times, but you will need to rest afterward.

Avoid any movements that require all your strength. These can cause injuries to bones and muscles.

● **Flexibility training.** Hold the pose and push it to the maximum stretch—but not to the point of pain. And *never* bounce.

Exercise Opportunities: Use Anything... Anywhere

Porter Shimer, author of several books on health and fitness, including *Too Busy to Exercise* (Storey Books).

Many people find it difficult to take extra time to exercise, due to their work, family and social commitments. *But there are many ways that you can make your own exercise opportunities...*

● **Anything that has weight can be lifted** —phone books...portable TVs...table lamps.

● **Exercise your muscles against each other isometrically...**when forced to sit for long periods.

Example: Brace yourself by putting your palms on your thighs just above your knees and try to lean forward with slightly bent arms, held rigid.

● **Do horizontal exercises...**when you have a chance to lie down.

Examples: Lie on one side, with one hand propping up your head and the other in front, slowly raise your top leg as far as you comfortably can, hold for five seconds, lower slowly and repeat nine times. Then switch sides and repeat the set.

● **Don't just stand there waiting for the bus or train**—walk.

● **Never ignore a flight of stairs at home or elsewhere.** Stair climbing is such good exercise that people pay good money for machines that duplicate this motion.

● **Carry your own luggage.**

● **Burn off calories with courtesy.** Small active acts of politeness—like holding elevator doors...opening car doors...approaching people so you can speak quietly rather than holler to them—add up, little by little, to a gain in physical fitness...and may even help you make new friends.

● **Don't be embarrassed if you look a little odd exercising.**

Example: When people see you in the act of lifting yourself up by pressing with your palms on the armrests of your bus seat, explain it is an exercise to develop your triceps.

Painless Ways to Build Exercise Into Your Daily Routine

Steven N. Blair, physical education doctor (PED), president, The Cooper Institute, Dallas, *www.cooperinst.org*. Formerly senior scientific editor of the *Surgeon General's Report on Physical Activity and Health,* he is coauthor of *Active Living Every Day: 20 Weeks to Lifelong Vitality* (Human Kinetics).

Improving your physical fitness need not require an arduous exercise regimen. And you certainly do not have to go to a gym, wear special clothes and sweat a lot.

But if you want to improve your health and fitness, you must increase your physical activity. This can be done gradually, at home or at work or with the help of a professional program. Your goal should be to change your behavior, not wear yourself out.

Burning 200 to 300 more calories per day through moderate-intensity exercise lowers the risk of heart disease, stroke, diabetes, some cancers and other conditions related to stress or being overweight. You'll also increase fitness, which will give you more energy and lead to greater enjoyment of life.

ACTIVITIES FOR HEALTH

Some of the most effective ways to boost physical activity are often overlooked…

•Increase the number of steps you take each day. That by itself will go a long way toward burning calories and exercising muscles.

Helpful: Wear a pedometer to record the total number of steps you take every day. My favorite is the DIGI-WALKER, which accurately documents how many steps you take. It is sold at sporting-goods stores and is also available directly from New Lifestyles (816-373-9969 or *www.new-lifestyles.com*).

Cost: Starting at $16.95* plus shipping and handling.

Most people over the age of 50 who work in sedentary jobs and do not exercise regularly take about 2,000 to 4,000 steps a day. It's easy to increase this.

When you go to the mall, for instance, don't drive around until you find a parking place next to the door. Park in the first available space and walk to the entrance. You'll increase the number of steps you take and often save time in the long run.

Before taking the car out for a short errand, think about walking. You'll often be delighted at how much you see in the neighborhood. If you take public transportation, getting off one stop early can be similarly enjoyable and will add exercise to your trip as well.

•Stand instead of sit. Standing burns more calories than sitting, which is what many people do for 12 hours a day.

When you talk on the phone, get in the habit of standing. And at least sit up when you watch television instead of stretching out on a sofa. Sitting burns more calories than lying down.

•Move around. Even slow walking burns twice as many calories per minute as sitting. If you have a mobile phone or a phone with a long cord, don't merely sit or stand in place each time you have a conversation. Instead, walk around as you talk.

•Do household chores. Catch up on your gardening. Or repaint a wall, repair the kitchen cabinet, hang some new pictures or rearrange the furniture.

*Price subject to change.

•Take up a sport or physical activity. Try one that always interested you or one you once enjoyed but had to give up as your responsibilities grew.

Examples: Bicycling, tennis, swimming, bowling, golf, running.

Call local clubs in your area. You may be surprised to find out how many people are resuming a sport after many years or taking it up for the first time.

KEEP ON TRACK

Increasing your physical activity, even gradually, isn't always easy. The big problem is reversing the long-established behavior of avoiding unnecessary exertion. *Helpful…*

•Set goals. Aim low at first. When you reach your first objective, set the next goal slightly higher. The satisfaction of reaching a goal will inspire you to go on to the next.

On the other hand, nothing is more discouraging than setting a high goal and then failing to meet it. *Examples of reasonable goals…*

•If a pedometer shows that you take about 3,000 steps a day, set a goal for increasing the number by 500 a week until your daily rate is in the 8,000 to 10,000 range.

•If your goal is to lose 30 pounds, set a goal of five pounds a month.

•Monitor your progress. Recording your physical activities in a diary can help develop momentum for reaching your goals. Keep the entries short so the diary itself doesn't become a chore. Simply record each day's physical activity, and make a note of whether you met your goals.

If you use a pedometer, record the number of steps you take each day. It also helps to estimate how many hours a day you sit and how many you spend moving around. Over a period of several weeks, the log should show a decrease in the amount of time spent sitting and an increase in moving around.

•Join a group. Although you can easily increase your physical activity without joining a health or fitness club, being a member of a group offers two major advantages—you'll have access to a professional trainer and the support of fellow members.

210

Look for a group that helps its members to achieve a modest, but steady, increase in their physical activity.

Human Kinetics, a publisher with which I'm affiliated, is currently in the process of establishing Active Living fitness centers at health clubs, hospitals, work locations and Ys throughout the country. These centers teach changes in lifestyle, encourage goal-setting and establish support systems to help people stay physically active. Those are the qualities to look for in any activity group.

Information: 800-747-4457 or *www.active living.info.*

•**Gather support.** Research on physical activity shows that people with support from friends or family members are far more likely to succeed than those who try to do it on their own. Support can be especially critical during the early stages of a physical fitness program. *Recommended...*

•When you decide to increase your level of activity, tell two or three friends about your goals, and ask them to help you. Choose these people on the basis of how supportive they've been in the past—those who will phone you periodically to check on your progress or to encourage you to reach difficult goals...or better still, those who will go for a walk with you at lunchtime.

•If someone you hoped would support you doesn't follow through, immediately enlist the support of someone else.

•When you evaluate fitness programs, ask what type of support they offer. The best programs encourage participants to support one another after class and to find support among other friends.

Safety: All the moderate-intensity lifestyle activities discussed here are safe. You are just doing more of what you normally do. If you have a history of heart problems, osteoporosis or other conditions that could interfere with physical activity, check with your doctor. If you experience worrisome symptoms during exercise, such as pressure in your chest or extreme breathlessness with mild exertion, stop the activity and check with your doctor.

Information: Visit *www.americanheart.org.*

More from Steven N. Blair...

Can Fat Be Fit?

A growing number of experts are challenging the standard belief that being overweight indicates that a person is unfit and subject to serious health risks.

They say that being unfit and sedentary may contribute to weight gain—but it is the lack of fitness that creates health risks associated with high body weight, not the weight itself.

In fact, people who are "fat but fit" face fewer health risks than those who are thin and unfit.

Example: Long-term studies done at the Cooper Institute in Dallas have found that death rates for both women and men who are thin but unfit are at least twice as high as for their counterparts who are obese but fit.

Being fit in these studies means merely engaging in a cumulative 30 minutes of moderate intensity activity, such as walking, daily.

Key: The greatest health benefits come from taking the first steps toward fitness—study data show about 50% lower mortality in the moderately fit as compared with the low fit...while highly fit individuals lower their mortality risk by only another 10% to 15%.

Recommended: Be physically active. This will greatly reduce health risks regardless of your weight.

How to Exercise Anytime, Anywhere

Joan Price, fitness speaker, writer and instructor, Sebastopol and Santa Rosa, CA, who specializes in helping beginning exercisers. She is author of *The Anytime, Anywhere Exercise Book—300+ Quick and Easy Exercises You Can Do Whenever You Want!* (Adams Media). *www.joanprice.com.*

We all know we should exercise on a regular basis—but only about one in every five Americans actually gets a 30- to 60-minute workout most days of the week. Even these committed exercisers often run into trouble when their schedule is disrupted by work, travel or family responsibilities.

The solution? Stop thinking of fitness as a separate undertaking and instead, start taking advantage of all the exercise opportunities that crop up during the course of your day-to-day activities.

In addition to keeping up with your regular schedule of cardiovascular exercise, here are eight strengthening and stretching exercises you can perform without missing a beat in your daily routine...

ABDOMINAL ALERT

This simple movement will give you an abdominal workout *and* improve your posture.

What to do: From a sitting position, sit up tall and pull your abdominal muscles in, lifting your chest and rib cage as you exhale. Hold for four to six seconds, then release slowly as you inhale. Repeat eight to 12 times.

Perform this: While driving, watching television or sitting at your desk.

Helpful: If you perform this exercise while driving, adjust your rearview mirror so you can see out of it only when you're in the "sitting tall" position. This will remind you to maintain this posture.

BACK STRETCH

If you spend long hours sitting in a chair, a back stretch provides welcome relief.

What to do: Stand about arm's length behind a chair, with your hands resting on the top of the backrest. Keeping your head upright, bend forward from the hips, lowering your upper body and pushing your buttocks away from the chair until you feel a stretch in your mid and upper back. Hold for 10 to 60 seconds. If your chair has rollers, increase the stretch by pushing it forward slightly as you lower yourself.

Perform this: While standing at your desk or watching television.

CALF STRENGTHENER

Here's a good way to strengthen your lower legs, back and abdomen.

What to do: Stand on a telephone book (the bigger, the better) with your toes facing the book's spine and your heels hanging over the edge opposite the spine. For better stability, this exercise can also be done standing on a step while holding a railing or on a curb while holding a signpost for balance.

Keeping your back straight, push up onto the balls of your feet while counting for two seconds, hold for another two seconds, then count for four seconds as you lower yourself back down. To help stay balanced, tighten up your abdominals and buttocks.

Keep doing for two minutes or until your calves tire, whichever comes first.

Perform this: While waiting for a bus or watching television.

OUTER THIGH LIFT

This exercise strengthens and tones up your outer thighs while standing.

What to do: While standing on a step or on a curb, bend your left leg just slightly at the knee and slowly lift your right leg out to the side, keeping your knee facing forward and your foot flexed. Do this eight to 12 times, then switch legs and repeat.

BUN SQUEEZE

Here is an efficient way to tone up the muscles in your buttocks whenever you're standing.

What to do: Squeeze the buttock muscles in both cheeks as tightly as you can, then hold the contraction for two seconds. Release for two seconds. Repeat eight to 12 times.

Perform this: While in line at the store.

NECK ROLL

A good neck stretch helps relieve neck and shoulder tension.

What to do: Let your head fall gently to the left side, until your ear is close to your left shoulder. Return to the upright position. Repeat the same movement on the right side. Continue alternating left and right four to six times.

Next, slowly roll your head from one shoulder down toward your chest, then back up to the opposite shoulder. Repeat in the opposite direction. Perform the full movement four times.

Do *not* tilt your head back. This can compress the neck and spine and may cause dizziness by impinging blood flow.

Perform this: While sitting at a desk, talking on the phone or taking a shower. In the shower, stand with your back facing the showerhead so the water hits your neck and shoulders.

JUNK-MAIL CRUMPLE

Believe it or not, crumpling up junk mail is a great way to strengthen your forearms and relieve wrist tension from typing or writing.

What to do: Open an envelope, pull out the letter and hold it in one hand. Starting at one corner, crumple the letter into your palm, bit by bit, until it forms a tight ball. Squeeze the ball a few times, then throw it away.

Perform this: While opening your mail.

Exercise illustrations by Shawn Banner.

Best Time to Exercise

Although some people enjoy waking themselves up with an early morning jog, a recent study suggests that morning exercise can suppress the immune system.

Reason: Levels of *Immunoglobulin A,* a class of antibodies that protect the body against infection, are markedly lower early in the day. Exercising when the immune system is most vulnerable can increase risk of infection.

However: Recreational athletes should exercise whenever they can, whatever the time of day. The benefits of exercise will most likely outweigh the risks.

Craig Sharp, DSc, professor of sports science, Brunel University, Middlesex, England.

How to Avoid Injury When Working Out

Jolie Bookspan, PhD, sports medicine specialist and physiologist in private practice, Philadelphia. She is author of several books, including *Health & Fitness in Plain English* (Healthy Learning). *www.drbookspan.com.*

Fitness enthusiasts often assume that they won't get injured as long as they work out frequently. Unfortunately, that's not true. Even people who exercise several days a week are at risk for injury if they spend most of their time sitting, slouching and/or bending or walking incorrectly.

THE WARM-UP

For years, we've been told to stretch before working out. But warming up is key to avoiding exercise injury. In fact, stretching itself can cause injury if it's attempted before warming up.

To warm up, you must perform enough physical activity to raise your body temperature.

Helpful: For 10 minutes—or until you break a sweat—move around. For example, walk, jog slowly or bike.

After warming up, slowly ease into your stretch and hold each position. Don't bounce while you're stretching—it can cause muscle and joint pulls and tears. And *never* stretch to the point of pain.

AVOIDING INJURIES

Here are some surprisingly simple ways to avoid five common exercise injuries…

•**Strain of the Achilles tendon.** A sedentary lifestyle, walking with your toes pointing out (that is, duck-footed) and/or wearing shoes with heels can shorten the Achilles tendons. Short, tight tendons are subject to strain during almost any activity. When this occurs, pain is felt anywhere from the heel to the calf.

Self-defense: Stretch your Achilles tendons with a simple exercise. Stand facing a wall. Place the ball of your right foot against the wall with your heel resting on the floor. Lean forward, pressing your right hip toward the wall. Stretch the whole foot for a few seconds. Repeat with left foot. Perform this exercise a few times each day.

If you have Achilles tendon pain: Have your cholesterol checked. High cholesterol levels can stiffen blood vessels in the tendon and predispose it to injury.

•**Ankle sprain.** People who have loose ligaments and stretched muscles on the sides of their ankles, weak leg muscles, prior ankle sprains that were incompletely rehabilitated and bad balance are especially prone to ankle sprain. This is because their ankles tend to roll outward, either overstretching or tearing the ligaments.

Self-defense: Forget high-top shoes and elastic bandages. Prevent ankle sprain with strengthening and balancing exercises.

To strengthen your *evertor* muscles (those that lift the outside edge of your foot), loop a bungee cord (without the hook), any stretchy tubing or band or a pair of pantyhose around both feet while sitting or standing. Roll the outside edges of your feet upward. Hold for a few seconds. Repeat. Gradually increase to 10 repetitions. Do this exercise at least once daily.

Helpful: Balance exercises are crucial to preventing recurrence of ankle sprain. While talking on the phone or waiting in line, stand on one foot for as long as you can. Repeat with other leg.

•**Anterior cruciate ligament (ACL) tear.** When you stop short while lunging for a ball during tennis or hit a mogul too hard while skiing—but do not have the muscular strength to compensate—you can overstress or tear the ACL inside your knee. This causes pain and swelling.

Self-defense: Strengthen your leg muscles, including the quadriceps (the muscles in your front thighs) and hamstrings (the muscles in your back thighs).

Running, biking and stair climbing are the most effective ways to build these muscles. For best results, combine with squats and lunges.

Helpful: When lifting things, hold your torso upright, use your leg muscles and bend with your knees.

•**Rotator cuff strain.** Also known as swimmer's, tennis or pitcher's shoulder, rotator cuff strain often comes from bad head and arm posture during activities that require you to lift the arm. This can even include movements that do not lift the arm completely overhead.

If you hold your head forward in a "craned" posture, it can impinge on any of the four muscles and tendons that make up the rotator cuff. This can lead to pain anywhere from the shoulder to the middle of the arm. People who do not use the muscles of the torso when moving their arms also experience stress on the shoulder.

Self-defense: Begin by always practicing good posture.

To strengthen your rotator cuff, tie a strip of rubber tubing (found in most medical-supply and sporting-goods stores) around a vertical pipe, pole or anything that will hold it securely, at shoulder height.

While gripping the rubber tubing with your right hand, turn sideways and bend your right elbow. Pull the tubing across your torso, keeping your posture straight by using your leg, back and abdominal muscles.

Return the tubing to the starting position while continuing to use your muscles. Don't let the band pull your elbow back. Repeat with your left arm. Work up to 10 repetitions daily with each arm.

•**Shin splints.** Weak shin muscles, poor shock absorption when you land during walking, running or jumping, and running on your toes can all contribute to shin splints.

Self-defense: While sitting or standing, place your feet flat on the floor, with your toes under anything that provides resistance, such as the bottom of your desk. Lift your toes, and hold for two seconds.

You can do this exercise either one foot at a time or with both feet at once. If there's no object nearby to create resistance, you can even use the toes of one foot to hold down those of the other foot.

Repeat 10 times on each foot, working up to at least a few sets of 10 each day.

Helpful: Walk and run lightly, coming down heel first, then with the rest of the foot.

When you jump, land toes first, then allow your heels to come down, bending your knees and using your leg muscles to ensure a soft landing on your feet.

Injuries: When To Use Heat... Or Cold

First aid rules for injuries can often be a bit confusing. *Here is the lowdown...*

•**Cold reduces inflammation.** Apply cold to acute injuries, such as a newly sprained ankle or a pulled muscle.

•**Heat improves circulation.** It's best for chronic pain, such as from tight muscles or a sore back.

•**Alternate heat and cold** if you have soft-tissue damage and/or stretched ligaments, such as an ankle sprain. Heat aids in restoring range of motion.

Apply cold for 20 minutes per hour as desired for the first 24 hours. The next day, use warmth for 20 minutes per hour as desired.

Caution: Don't apply cold for more than 24 hours or warmth for more than 72 hours after the injury. If the inflammation continues beyond 72 hours, see a doctor.

Richard O'Brien, MD, spokesperson, American College of Emergency Physicians, and emergency physician, Moses Taylor Hospital, Scranton, PA.

Raisins Before a Workout

Although exercise offers many health benefits, a strenuous workout can trigger the formation of free radicals. The damage caused by these harmful molecules can contribute to cancer or heart disease.

Helpful: Eating a handful of raisins (approximately one ounce) 15 minutes before a workout can significantly lower levels of free radicals—and the damage they cause.

Raisins are rich in *antioxidants,* powerful compounds that protect the body.

Gene A. Spiller, PhD, DSc, director, Health Research and Studies Center and Sphera Foundation, both in Los Altos, CA.

A Stronger Body in Only 30 Minutes a Week

Fredrick Hahn, president and cofounder, National Council for Exercise Standards, an organization of exercise, medical and scientific professionals. He is owner of Serious Strength Inc., a Slow Burn strength-training studio in New York City, and coauthor of *The Slow Burn Fitness Revolution* (Broadway). His Web site is *www.seriousstrength.com.*

We know the benefits of strength training. It will restore muscle...increase bone density...improve balance, decreasing the likelihood of falls...and promote weight loss and cardiovascular fitness. But conventional strength training requires several hours a week and frequently causes injury.

Better way: Slow Burn, in which the weights are lifted and lowered with incredible slowness—about 10 seconds up and 10 seconds down. *The benefits...*

•**It's safer.** Slow lifting reduces stress on the ligaments, tendons and joints, which can cause injury. This means that even the elderly can do it safely.

•**It's more effective.** Without the aid of momentum, more muscle fibers are exercised.

•**It's more efficient.** A person can get a complete workout in about 30 minutes each week—compared with at least three hours for conventional lifting.

HOW TO DO IT

In a Slow Burn workout, you complete a set of three to six repetitions of each exercise in 60 to 90 seconds. If you perform 10 exercises, you can complete your workout in approximately 10 to 15 minutes. Two workouts a week are all you need for total fitness.

To obtain the best results, raise and lower weights at the rate of about one inch per second. Allow a total of about 100 seconds for all repetitions of each exercise—push-ups, leg curls, etc. Breathe normally.

Helpful: Use a metronome to maintain the one-inch-per-second rhythm.

Repeat each exercise until the muscles are fatigued and you can't do another repetition in perfect form. If you pass the 90-second point and feel as though you could keep going, the weights are too light. If you cannot complete three repetitions in 90 seconds, the weights are too heavy. Experiment to find the right weight.

The following program stimulates all muscle groups. Do three to six repetitions of each exercise. For exercises that require switching arms or legs, do three to six repetitions with each arm or leg. You will need adjustable hand and ankle weights. Look for sets that adjust from one to 20 pounds.

•**Push-ups.** Kneel on a towel with both your hands flat on the floor in front of you, shoulder-width apart. Keep your back straight—don't let it sway or arch.

Take three seconds to lower yourself the first inch and at least seven seconds to lower yourself all the way, until your forehead almost touches the floor. Without resting at the bottom, reverse direction. Don't lock your elbows at the top. Just as soon as your arms are almost straight, reverse and go back down. If kneeling push-ups are too easy, do regular push-ups, with your toes on the floor.

•**Doorknob squats.** Open a door halfway so that you can grip both knobs. Place a stool or chair about two feet from the edge of the door. Stand arms' length away from the door. Then, lightly grasp the knobs for balance, and slowly bend your knees and lower your body as though you were sitting down.

Take three seconds to lower yourself the first inch and seven seconds to go all the way down, until your bottom just touches the stool. Then reverse and rise back up. Be careful not to pull yourself up with your arms—use the muscles of your buttocks and thighs.

•**Side-lying leg lifts.** Try this exercise without ankle weights at first. If it's too easy, start with five-pound weights. Lie on your left side with your head propped on your left hand. Bend your left leg slightly so that your right leg rests on top of the calf. Slowly raise your right leg up toward the ceiling, moving from the hip. Take three seconds to move it the first inch and then seven seconds to raise it all the way. Pause at the

top, tightly squeeze the hip and buttock muscles for a few seconds, then slowly lower the leg back down. Repeat with the other leg.

•**Single-leg curls.** Attach one five-pound weight to your right ankle. The weight may be too light, but it's a good place to start. Lean forward and put both hands on a stool or chair...keeping your right knee slightly bent and spine straight.

Curl your right leg so that the heel comes close to your bottom. Take three seconds to curl the leg the first inch and seven seconds to curl it the rest of the way. Pause at the top, squeeze the muscles in the back of your thigh, then slowly reverse direction. Repeat with the other leg.

•**Side shoulder raise and overhead press.** This movement combines two exercises. Start with five-pound dumbbells. With a dumbbell in each hand, sit on a chair with your back straight and your feet flat on the floor. Slowly raise the weights away from your sides, taking three seconds to move them the first inch and seven seconds to raise them until they're parallel to the floor. Pause at the top for a few seconds, then slowly lower the weights.

Without resting, move to the second phase of the exercise. Elbows bent, hold the weights at shoulder height, then slowly raise them over your head, taking three seconds to move them the first inch and seven seconds to extend all the way up. Pause for a second, then gradually lower the weights until they're back at shoulder height. Do not lock your elbows at the top. Let your muscles support the weights.

•**Single-arm back pull-ups.** You need a stool or chair and a six- to eight-pound dumbbell. Hold the dumbbell in your right hand... then face the stool with your left leg forward...and support yourself with your left hand on the stool. Let your right arm hang beside the stool.

Slowly pull the dumbbell back and upward, taking three seconds to move it the first inch and seven seconds to raise it all the way. Your right elbow will be facing up and behind you. Pause at the top, squeeze the arm and back muscles for a few seconds, then lower the weight back down. Don't let your arm hang down at the end of the movement. Keep tension on the muscles all the time. Repeat with the other arm.

•**Biceps curls.** Sit on a stool or straight-back chair with a five-pound dumbbell in each hand. Tuck your elbows into your sides, and focus on keeping them there throughout the exercise. The only thing that should move is your lower arm.

Curl the dumbbells toward your shoulders, taking just three seconds to move them the first inch and seven seconds to curl them all the way. Squeeze the muscles in the forearms and upper arms for a few seconds at the top of the movement, then slowly lower the weights back down.

•**Shoulder shrugs.** Sit on a stool or straight-back chair with a 10-pound dumbbell in each hand. Let your arms hang down away from your hips, with the elbows slightly bent.

Then, raise up the tops of your shoulders as though you're trying to touch them to your earlobes. Sit up straight. Don't slouch forward or backward. Take three seconds to move your shoulders the first inch and seven seconds to raise them as far as they'll go. Pause at the top to squeeze the muscles in your shoulders, then lower them back down.

•**Abdominal crunches.** Lie on your back with your feet flat on the floor and your knees bent at a 90° angle. Tuck a rolled towel under your lower back ...hold your arms straight in front of you... and keep your chin tucked into your chest. Curl your torso upward and forward, taking three seconds to move the first inch and seven seconds to move forward. Do not try to sit up all the way. Keep your lower back in contact with the towel throughout the movement. Pause and squeeze your abdominal muscles at the top of the movement, then slowly lower

your torso down. Don't rest your shoulders on the floor at the end. As soon as they brush the floor, repeat the exercise.

Exercise illustrations by Shawn Banner.

Revised Exercise Guidelines

Be physically active for 60 minutes a day to maintain health and normal body weight. The previous recommendations of 30 minutes of daily or almost-daily physical activity were not enough. Daily physical activities should be moderately intense, such as cycling, swimming or brisk walking.

Joanne Lupton, PhD, professor of nutrition, Texas A&M University, College Station, and chairperson of the Institute of Medicine panel that made the revised exercise recommendations.

Exercise as Medicine

Mitchell Krucoff, MD, and Carol Krucoff, coauthors of *Healing Moves: How to Cure, Relieve, and Prevent Common Ailments with Exercise* (Harmony). Dr. Krucoff is professor of cardiology, Duke University Medical Center, Chapel Hill, NC.

Study after study has shown that physical activity enhances a person's overall health while inactivity impairs it. Everyone—no matter what his/her level of ability—deserves and needs physical activity.

Our exercise prescriptions for people who have specific ailments are low-tech, low-risk, low-cost—and easy to do.

Take an incremental approach to our "healing moves." If all you can do today is walk to your mailbox, fine. Tomorrow, walk to your neighbor's mailbox. On day three, walk a little farther.

You will improve your health as long as you make a commitment to being active every day. Little strategies—a 10-minute walk first thing in the morning, 15 minutes of yard work, taking the stairs instead of the elevator, parking in the farthest space—add up and can make a dramatic difference in your health.

Important: For best results—and to ensure safety—speak with your doctor and consult a qualified exercise professional who can design a program for you.

Here are several exercise suggestions that will help you manage your illness...

ARTHRITIS

It may seem counterintuitive, but most forms of exercise can help to prevent the progression of arthritis. *For example...*

Stationary bicycling is good for people who should avoid putting stress on their hips, knees and feet. Swimming and water aerobics are also excellent because they put little stress on joints.

New studies indicate that resistance exercises with weights may be very helpful for rheumatoid arthritis sufferers.

CANCER

A major problem for some cancer patients is fatigue. Yoga, walking and other forms of moderate exercises can boost energy levels, mood and stamina. Walking is ideal for cancer patients because it improves lung function, stimulates bone and muscle growth and is easy on joints.

COLDS

One of the most potent immune enhancers —and cold preventers—is exercise. Moderate activity can help your immune system even if you're fighting a cold—as long as your symptoms are above the neck. If you have a fever, muscle aches or a hacking cough that produces phlegm, don't exercise.

Rule of thumb: Wait until the worst is over, then start activity slowly until you feel like yourself again.

DIABETES

Walking and other forms of aerobic exercise help prevent and manage diabetes because they help the body control blood glucose.

People with diabetes should work with their physicians to develop individualized programs. In general, moderate aerobic exercise, such as walking for 20 to 45 minutes at least three days every week, is recommended. Frequency is essential to moderate blood glucose. Exercising every day, or nearly every day, confers maximum benefit.

HIGH BLOOD PRESSURE

If you have mild to moderate hypertension (up to 159/99), talk with your doctor about trying moderate-intensity aerobic activity, such as brisk walking for 30 to 45 minutes a day most days of the week. This regimen may bring your blood pressure into an acceptable range without medication. Meditative practices, such as yoga and tai chi, can also be very effective.

Markedly elevated blood pressure should be controlled with medication before you embark on an exercise program, since vigorous exercise can temporarily raise blood pressure even more.

HIGH CHOLESTEROL

Amid all the hoopla over oat bran and fish oil, synthetic fats and prescription drugs, one of the most effective strategies for improving cholesterol—exercise—is frequently neglected.

Regular exercise raises the level of HDL ("good") cholesterol and lowers the level of LDL ("bad") cholesterol.

Do some form of moderate-to-hard aerobic exercise five days a week for at least 30 minutes per session. Try to burn at least 1,000 calories a week—the equivalent of walking or running eight to 10 miles—through movement. While moderate- to high-intensity activity is most beneficial for improving cholesterol levels, even low-intensity activities—such as gardening or strolling—can help if done daily.

OBESITY

For lasting weight loss, aim to create a 300- to 500-calorie deficit each day through a combination of eating less and exercising more.

The best calorie burner is aerobic exercise— activity that demands large quantities of oxygen for long periods of time. This includes walking, running, bicycling and in-line skating.

In general, taking a three-mile walk five days a week, plus practicing good eating habits, results in significant weight loss.

Creating a calorie deficit solely through diet can be dangerous. About half the weight lost on extremely low-calorie diets is from muscle and bone. And metabolism slows down with excessive caloric restriction.

OSTEOPOROSIS

No matter how much calcium you consume, you won't build bone unless you exercise. *It's important to perform exercises that put force on the skeleton...*

•**Weight-bearing exercise,** such as walking and dancing, in which your legs bear the weight of your body.

•**Resistance exercise,** such as working out with free weights or weight machines. The force of maximally challenged muscle pulling against bone stimulates bone building.

The higher the impact, the greater the bone strengthening. Stair climbing, running and racquet sports, for instance, are high-impact. Swimming and biking are not weight-bearing.

Perform weight-bearing activity for 30 minutes a day, most days of the week. Lift weights two to three times a week for 20 to 40 minutes.

REPETITIVE STRESS INJURIES

While a mouse click isn't strenuous, performing thousands of clicks for hours on end can be extremely troublesome.

Result: Microscopic tears in tendons, nerves, muscles and other soft tissues.

People who do hand-intensive work should do a few minutes of warm-up stretches for the hands, wrists, neck, shoulders and arms. Stretch throughout the day and cool down at the end of the day. *Best stretches...*

•**Shoulder shrugs.** Lift shoulders toward ears...hold five seconds...lower.

•**Wrist curls.** With open hands, rotate wrists in circles.

•**Neck circles.** Draw imaginary circles in front of you with your nose.

•**Fist flings.** Form a loose fist, then fan out fingers as far as comfortable.

For people who use a keyboard: Grasp the fingers of one hand with the other hand and gently pull back until you feel an easy stretch in the wrist.

If you hunch over a desk: Once every half-hour, raise your arms and stretch back over your chair, looking up at the ceiling. Take a brief walk once an hour to boost circulation and give overused muscles a break.

Finally, perform exercises that strengthen the back and abdominal muscles, such as abdominal crunches and back extensions.

RESPIRATORY DISORDERS

Asthmatics are often afraid to exert themselves because some forms of physical activity can trigger an attack.

People with emphysema or chronic bronchitis are often short of breath just getting through the activities of daily living. They assume they haven't enough "wind" for even gentle exercise. In reality, inactivity promotes a vicious cycle in which muscles weaken...heart and lungs lose tone...and self-esteem deflates.

Asthmatics: Ask your doctor about appropriate medication, especially if exercise brings on symptoms. Work up to at least 30 minutes of aerobic activity, such as walking or swimming, most days of the week. Stay well hydrated to thin secretions, so they lubricate airways rather than clog them.

Emphysema sufferers: Consult your doctor, who may recommend drugs, monitors or supplemental oxygen during exercise. Walking is often the easiest exercise, although stationary cycling and water aerobics are also fine. Start slowly and progress gradually, adding a few minutes each week.

Exercise Fights Ulcers

Men who are physically active on a regular basis are 30% to 50% less likely to develop ulcers than sedentary men.

Theory: Exercise reduces acid secretion in the stomach, improves immune function or simply relieves anxiety. The more a man works out, the less likely he is to develop an ulcer.

Caroline Macera, PhD, researcher in a study of 11,000 people, US Centers for Disease Control and Prevention, Atlanta, published in the *British Journal of Sports Medicine.*

Heartburn and Weight Lifting

Exercise-induced heartburn affects weight lifters three times as often as it hits other athletes. The process of lifting apparently causes excess stomach acid to enter the esophagus, creating the problem.

Self-defense: Do not eat for one to two hours before a workout. During a session, always exhale while pushing or pulling a weight.

Philip Schoenfeld, MD, spokesperson, American College of Gastroenterology, Bethesda, MD.

Muscle Loss Prevention

Muscle mass in the average adult declines by more than six pounds per decade. The rate of muscle loss accelerates after age 45.

Good news: Age-related muscle loss can be prevented and even reversed by exercising 30 to 50 minutes a day four or five days a week.

Best: A fitness routine that encompasses stretching, weight lifting and aerobic activity.

William J. Evans, PhD, professor of geriatrics, physiology and nutrition, University of Arkansas for Medical Sciences, Little Rock.

Yoga Is for Everyone

Miriam Austin, Otis, MA–based yoga instructor and author of *Yoga for Wimps: Poses for the Flexibly Impaired* (Sterling).

Many people think you must be super-flexible to perform yoga. But that's simply not the case.

When I first started taking yoga 20 years ago, the poses proved too difficult since I had so many athletic injuries. Luckily, I found a teacher who helped me modify the poses so that they were easy enough for any beginner.

These yoga poses reduce stress, relieve lower back pain, enhance athletic ability and boost your sense of well-being.

The following seven poses do not require a lengthy workout session. They can be performed between your daily activities. You can use them for a light workout—or as a stepping stone to more advanced poses or a formal yoga class.*

If you've never tried yoga, here are a few things to know before you get started…

• **Perform all of the poses in bare or stocking feet.**

• **Keep two towels handy** for poses that require extra support.

• **Begin and end each pose slowly.**

• **Relax and breathe normally** while holding each pose.

• **Never do any movement that causes you pain.**

CHAIR STRETCH

This is a great pose to relax your back and shoulders. When you're feeling tense, use it to stretch out your back—or as a break during shopping or sightseeing.

Sit in a chair with your feet placed slightly wider than your hips. Bend forward at the waist, relaxing your entire body. When you're leaning all the way forward, grasp each elbow with the opposing hand and drop your head in the space between your knees.

Relax your neck completely. Hold the pose for one minute.

KITCHEN COUNTER POSE

This pose relieves back pain by stretching out the lower and upper back. You can do it while waiting for your coffee or tea to brew in the morning.

Place a folded towel on your kitchen countertop. Stand with your hips pressed against the side of the counter. The countertop edge should be even with the bend in your hip crease. (If you're too low, stand on your toes or on a phone book…too high, bend your knees.)

*To find a teacher in your area, visit the *Yoga Journal* Web site at *www.yogajournal.com.*

Lean over the counter. Place your head and crossed arms on the towel, with your head turned to one side. Rest comfortably in this position for five minutes.

If your neck feels tight, do this facedown instead, resting your forehead on your arms or a rolled towel.

RECLINING HAMSTRING STRETCH

This pose limbers up your walking muscles by stretching the backs of your thighs. I recommend doing it before you get out of bed each morning.

Lie on your back with your legs extended. Place the midpoint of a man's necktie under the ball of your right foot and grasp the ends in either hand. Holding the tie, lift your right leg toward the ceiling, keeping your leg straight and your toes flexed in toward you. Hold for 30 seconds. Switch legs and repeat. Then place both feet in the tie and stretch for 60 seconds.

ROCK THE BABY

This chair exercise is a terrific way to loosen a stiff hip or to stretch out your hips before more strenuous exercise, such as walking, jogging or bicycling. It also helps relieve lower back pain.

Sit in the middle of the chair seat, holding your back straight. Bring your right leg up to your chest, grasping your knee in your right hand and your foot in your left hand.

Bring your calf as close as possible to your chest, keeping it parallel to the floor. Move your right leg from side to side as though you were rocking a baby. Do this for 30 seconds. Switch legs and repeat.

DOWNWARD FACING DOG

This is one of the most famous yoga poses. It stretches and strengthens your legs, torso, arms and shoulders. When you're feeling tired or stressed, perform this exercise anywhere—in the kitchen or at your desk.

Place the back of a chair against the wall. Kneel two feet in front of the chair and place your hands securely on the sides of the seat.

Keeping your arms straight, slowly raise up on your toes by straightening your knees. Your torso should angle downward. Hold the pose for 20 seconds, lengthening your back as much as possible.

STAFF POSE

This is a great way to stretch your legs and hips before and after physical activity, such as skiing, running or racquet sports.

Lie on your back with your buttocks as close to the wall as possible. Extend your legs straight up the wall. As you're doing this, straighten your knees and flex your feet toward you. Hold the pose for another 20 seconds.

To stretch your hips *and* inner thighs, slowly open your legs as far as you comfortably can and flex your feet toward you.

Remember, gravity is your friend. Allow it to ease your legs wider as the muscles relax. Hold for 30 seconds. To take pressure off your inner thighs, do this pose with a rolled-up towel placed between the outside of each upper thigh and the floor.

PASSIVE BACK BEND

This pose is perfect for unwinding at the end of the day. It stretches and strengthens the back and allows more oxygen into the lungs.

Roll up a large towel. Lie on your back. Place the roll under your upper back, behind your breastbone. Extend arms and legs straight outward. Relax and breathe naturally.

Rest as long as you want. I like to stay in this pose for at least 20 minutes. To enhance the relaxation effect, cover your eyes with a small towel and insert earplugs.

Exercise illustrations by Shawn Banner.

The Stretch Cure

Michelle LeMay, Marina del Rey, CA–based fitness and dance instructor. She is author of *Essential Stretch—Gentle Movements for Stress Relief, Flexibility and Overall Well-Being* (Perigee).

Everyone knows just how great a stretch feels upon awakening. But very few people realize that stretching can actually help alleviate stress-related ailments, such as headaches, anxiety, insomnia and overeating. Many people even report feeling more focused and energetic after several weeks of stretching.

Stretching will also increase your range of motion by lengthening tight muscles and increasing the movement of synovial fluid into joint cartilage, which lubricates and cushions your joints. Once your mobility begins to return with daily stretching, you'll find all physical activity—including sex—much easier and more enjoyable.

You can perform the following six stretches at least three times weekly. The entire workout takes less than 10 minutes to perform.

During all these exercises, visualize yourself breathing into the area that you are stretching. Exhale fully—then push a little more air out. This will automatically induce a deep, relaxing inhalation. Stretching is easiest to perform in a quiet, carpeted space.

OVERHEAD REACH

Stand up straight, with your feet placed shoulder-width apart. Inhale deeply as you open your arms and reach toward the sky. Then interlace your fingers as you extend your torso. Release fingers and return your arms slowly to your sides. Repeat the overhead reach four more times. Doing this exercise will stretch muscles in the torso and increase your range of motion.

CALF STRETCH

Get down on your hands and knees, with your shoulders aligned directly over your wrists and the hips directly over your knees.

Extend your right leg straight behind you, with the ball of your right foot touching the ground. Press your right heel down toward the ground, feeling the stretch in the upper part of your calf.

While continuing to press your heel down, bend your right knee slightly, until you feel a stretch in your lower calf. Repeat four more times with each calf.

This exercise will extend the muscles of the upper and lower calves and feet.

BUTTERFLY CONTRACTION

Sitting on the floor, with your head up, knees apart and the soles of your feet pressed together, grasp your ankles with your hands.

Exhale and round your upper back as you bring your chin to your chest. You'll feel the stretch in your neck and back. Inhale and return to the starting position. Repeat these steps eight times. The butterfly will loosen the muscles in your neck, back, hips and inner thighs.

CLAM

Lie on your back and pull your knees into your chest. Then wrap your hands around your lower legs and allow your back to sink into the ground. Hold for 30 to 60 seconds. This exercise helps to relax and loosen your lower back and buttocks.

SEATED FORWARD BEND

Sit on the floor with your legs straight out in front of you. Gently lean forward, while dropping your head toward your knees.

Place your hands on the floor to the side of each leg, and gently rock side to side for 20 seconds. Do not move so much that you experience discomfort. Roll up slowly and return to the seated position. This exercise relaxes and loosens the neck, back, buttocks and hamstrings.

CHILD'S POSE

Rest on both your knees, with your shins flat against the floor. Relax and bend forward until your chest is resting on your thighs and your forehead touches the ground. If you like, place a pillow or towel under your forehead.

Breathe deeply and slowly, and allow your lower back to expand with each breath. Hold the pose for two minutes.

This exercise expands lower back muscles and provides deep relaxation.

For quick tension relief, I recommend performing the following stretches at least twice daily. Ideal times are midmorning and at the end of the day, before you go to sleep. The tension-relief workout takes about three minutes to perform.

SPINAL ROLL

Stand up straight, with feet shoulder-width apart. Relax your neck and gently drop your chin onto your chest. Allow your shoulders to slowly collapse forward, feeling the stretch in your upper back. This is a half-spinal roll.

To do the full spinal roll, continue to roll down until both of your hands touch the floor, allowing your knees to bend gradually. Keep your arms, neck and back relaxed, feeling the stretch along the length of your spine.

When you've rolled down as far as you can, slowly roll back up to the starting position. Repeat four times.

The spinal roll helps to relax muscles in the neck and upper, middle and lower back.

SEATED FORWARD BEND AND CLAM

Both of these exercises are also helpful in tension relief.

Exercise illustrations by Shawn Banner.

Walk and Live Longer

To lengthen your life—*walk*. Men who walked more than two miles a day were almost half as likely to have died during a 12-year period as men who walked less than one mile a day. The earlier you establish a walking habit, the more you reduce your risk of cancer and heart disease in later life.

Robert Abbott, PhD, professor of biostatistics, University of Virginia School of Medicine, Charlottesville, and author of a study published in *The New England Journal of Medicine*.

Walking Boosts Brainpower

In one study, sedentary adults who were 60 to 75 years of age started walking briskly three times a week, gradually increasing the length of their walks from 15 to 45 minutes. After six months, their mental function had improved by 15%. Similar adults who did stretching and toning exercises for one hour, three days a week, showed no improvement.

Theory: By increasing oxygen flow to the brain, walking averts the earliest mental changes that occur with aging.

Arthur Kramer, PhD, professor of psychology, University of Illinois, Urbana-Champaign.

Fitness Walking to Cure Disease

Therese Iknoian, exercise physiologist and walking instructor, Grass Valley, CA. She is author of *Walking Fast—Techniques and Workouts for High-Level Fitness and Performance* (Human Kinetics). For more tips, visit *www.totalfitnessnetwork.com*.

A casual, 30-minute walk every day can reduce your risk of developing cardiovascular disease and diabetes—and it may also increase your life span.

Fast "fitness" walking brings even greater benefits. You'll slim your waistline, improve muscle tone and increase your endurance. Plus, fast walking is fun! *But first...*

ASSESS YOUR HEALTH

Fast walking puts extra strain on your cardiovascular system. Be sure to get the OK from your doctor before starting a fitness walking program. *Undergo a complete physical exam especially if you...*

- **Are mostly sedentary.**
- **Smoke cigarettes.**

•**Have a medical history of heart disease or chest pain.**

•**Have a family member who was diagnosed with heart disease** before age 50.

•**Have diabetes or high blood sugar,** or blood pressure of 140/90 or above.

•**Have joint pain** that generally worsens with exercise.

•**Are taking medication** that may interfere with your ability to exercise—such as for diabetes or high blood pressure.

MIND AND FEET

Walking faster requires concentrating on your walking form. Start by evaluating your normal walking style.

Find a stretch of open sidewalk where you can watch yourself in shop windows. Or have a friend videotape you walking. Make sure that he/she films your entire body, including your feet. Pay special attention to the swing of your arms and the movement of your hips—how you walk normally.

Fitness walking should *not* be done in tennis shoes, aerobics shoes or cross-trainers—they aren't built for straight-ahead movement and walking-specific foot impact.

Instead: Spend at least $50 on a pair of shoes designed strictly for walking...or a pair of lightweight running shoes with a low heel. The shoe should bend easily across the ball of the foot when you flex it in your hand.

HONE YOUR TECHNIQUE

Pick a smooth walking route—a clear sidewalk, a bike path, a running track or an open field. *Do several 30-second bursts of fast walking, keeping these points in mind...*

•**Keep your arms bent at the elbows at a 90-degree angle.** Swing your arms from the shoulder at a faster-than-normal tempo. When you swing your arms faster, your legs automatically move faster, too.

•**Hold your elbows close to your body.** Concentrate on a strong backswing, pulling your fist all the way back to the hipbone. Don't overdo the forward motion of your arms—reaching out in front of you robs your walking stride of power.

•**Keep your chin pulled in.** Make sure your ears are positioned directly in line with your shoulders.

•**Resist the urge to lean forward.** Keep yourself tall with tight abdominals.

•**Land on your heel,** and roll forward onto the ball of your foot. Keep your toes pointed straight ahead.

•**Keep the area from just below your rib cage to your hipbones as relaxed as possible.** As you stride, imagine that your legs start at your waist.

•**Don't take big steps.** Try to glide along—as if you are rolling on wheels—taking shorter, quicker steps.

SUPPLEMENTAL EXERCISES

To avoid sticking out your elbows: Practice walking close to a hedge or wall. Keep your elbows tucked in on that side to avoid hitting the barrier.

For a quicker stride: Mark off a 10- to 30-yard section of sidewalk, street or track. Walk this stretch as fast as you can, counting your steps. Repeat several times. Try to increase the number of steps with each repetition.

Practice pushing yourself: Walk up a short hill several times, being careful not to lean forward from the waist.

To limber up your walking muscles: Try out the following...

•**Hip stretch.** Sit on the floor with the right leg straight in front of you and the left knee bent with the foot on the floor to the outside of the right leg. Sit up straight.

Use the right arm to pull the bent left knee to your body. Gently rotate the right shoulder to the left knee. Hold for 15 to 30 seconds, then switch legs and repeat.

•**Lower-back stretch.** Lie on your back. Grasp behind your right knee with both hands. Use a towel if you have trouble reaching with your hands.

Pull your knee to your chest so you feel a slight stretch in your lower back and upper hips. Hold for 15 to 30 seconds. Switch legs and repeat.

DEVELOP A WALKING PROGRAM

Once you've mastered the technique, start incorporating fast fitness walking into your regular daily walks.

After warming up for five to 10 minutes, pick a stationary object a short distance away —such as a mailbox or a telephone pole—and walk as fast as you can until you reach it. Then return to your normal walking pace. Repeat this several times.

Over the next few weeks, gradually increase the length of these "speed bursts" until you're able to keep going at a fast pace for a minute or two at a time.

Next, do a three-minute session of fast walking in the middle of your workout. Every other day, add a little time to it, until you can walk fast for five minutes with good form and without stopping.

When you've accomplished this, begin adding a second fast walk right after the first, with a minute or two of slow walking in between to recover. Do this every other day until you can manage to perform two or more five-minute stretches back to back. As a final step, try to eliminate the "rest period," and walk fast for 10 or more minutes straight.

Continue fitting in 10 minutes of fast walking into your regular walks every other day. This can be done all in one stretch...or you can break up the 10 minutes into smaller pieces for variety.

On one or two days per week, add three to six "speed bursts" of one minute, alternated with one to two minutes of easier walking. Don't overdo it—you should always have one easy workout after every hard workout. Once a week, walk for 45 to 60 minutes at a steady, brisk pace—this will help increase endurance.

Enlist a training partner for some workouts: Walking fast is even more fun when you share the experience with a friend or your spouse—and you'll both come away from your fitness walks feeling trimmer, stronger and more energetic.

More from Therese Iknoian...

Better Fitness Walking

Take more steps—not longer ones. Long strides can cause knee, shin and foot pain. A smooth, rolling stride—at a faster pace—is more effective than a long stride to speed up a walk and better for the body.

8

Headaches, Arthritis & Chronic Pain

Little-Known Headache Triggers

 The International Headache Society (*www.i-h-s.org*) has identified more than 150 different types of headaches. Most headaches are generally nothing to worry about, but some could be dangerous and even life-threatening.

Important: See your doctor if you experience headaches daily...have severe head pain that comes on suddenly or isn't relieved with over-the-counter painkillers, such as aspirin or *ibuprofen*...or have pain accompanied by other symptoms, such as fever, stiff neck, seizures, strange smells, changes in vision, numbness in an arm or leg, etc.

Various causes of headaches...

CARBON MONOXIDE

Poor ventilation or a faulty heating system can cause a buildup of *carbon monoxide,* an odorless gas that displaces oxygen in the blood and brain. It can cause persistent symptoms—such as headache, fatigue and general weakness—for months, even years.

If you only get headaches at home and the pain disappears when you're away, suspect carbon monoxide poisoning, especially if other family members also get frequent headaches.

Hire a heating specialist to check your furnace. Leave the garage door open when working on a car with the engine running—and don't warm up the car while it's in the garage.

SEX

A throbbing or stabbing headache may build up during intercourse or occur only during orgasm. Known as *coital* or *orgasmic* headaches, these usually are benign—but not always.

A small number of sex headaches are caused by an *aneurysm* (a damaged blood vessel) in the brain or by a brain tumor. See your doctor.

Seymour Diamond, MD, founder and director, Diamond Headache Clinic, and director, Diamond In-Patient Headache Unit, St. Joseph Hospital, both in Chicago. He is author of *Conquering Your Migraine* and *Headache and Your Child* (both from Fireside).

He/she probably will recommend a *magnetic resonance imaging* (MRI) scan as well as a *magnetic resonance arteriogram* (MRA) to examine blood vessels in the brain.

When healthy people get sex headaches, the pain usually is due to increased pressure in the brain and cerebral spinal fluid. The prescription drug *indomethacin* (Indocin), taken one hour before intercourse, often prevents this type of headache.

STRAINING

Straining may cause the same kind of pain as a sex headache, probably for similar reasons. Coughing—as well as sneezing, laughing, moving your bowels and exercise—increases pressure in the brain.

See your doctor if the pain is severe or occurs every time you cough or sneeze. That could indicate a more serious problem that might need medical attention.

Most straining headaches are mild and go away in a few minutes.

ALCOHOL

Alcohol dilates blood vessels and increases blood flow to the brain. The increase in pressure can trigger headaches.

Dark-colored liquors—whiskey, rum, scotch, red wine, etc.—are more likely than clear liquors (such as vodka) to cause headaches. Dark liquors contain acetone and other impurities.

During or right after drinking alcohol, have one tablespoon of honey or a glass of orange juice. These contain *fructose,* a sugar that burns off alcohol. A cup of coffee also helps because caffeine constricts blood vessels—the opposite effect of alcohol. Caffeine is as effective as ibuprofen but, unlike ibuprofen, the positive effects wear off after 90 minutes.

SODIUM NITRITE

This chemical preservative, which is found in hot dogs, bacon and other cured meats, dilates blood vessels. As little as one milligram can trigger headaches in people who are sensitive to the chemical.

These headaches usually start within one hour of ingesting sodium nitrite. They're bothersome but benign. The pain almost always goes away within an hour.

MONOSODIUM GLUTAMATE (MSG)

The food additive MSG often is used in Asian foods, which is why MSG-induced headaches are sometimes called "Chinese restaurant syndrome." This name is misleading because MSG is added to thousands of packaged foods.

MSG causes the blood vessels to dilate in individuals sensitive to this additive. Headaches usually start within 30 minutes after eating MSG and end within an hour. Other symptoms include pressure in the chest, facial flushing and abdominal discomfort. In some people, symptoms may be delayed by up to 24 hours.

People who are sensitive to MSG should check all food labels. When dining out, ask that dishes be prepared without MSG. Most restaurants are familiar with the problem and happy to oblige.

ICE CREAM

Consuming ice cream or iced drinks too quickly can trigger a short but intensely painful headache. About one-third of Americans experience this, and it's nearly universal among migraine patients.

Cold stimulates the sphenopalatine nerve complex within the sinuses. The resulting headache is harmless and usually lasts a few seconds to no more than two minutes.

Eat ice cream and other cold foods slowly. Sip cold drinks rather than gulping them.

DROPS IN BLOOD PRESSURE

When you rise from a sitting or prone position, blood pressure drops. People whose blood pressure is already low—a common side effect of anti-hypertensive drugs as well as some antidepressants and heart medications—may experience pounding headaches when they stand or move too quickly. This type of headache, called an *orthostatic* headache, is harmless. The blood vessels naturally dilate and constrict when you move, and the pain rarely lasts more than a few seconds.

Get up in stages. When you're lying down, slowly rise to a seated position, wait a few seconds, then slowly stand up all the way.

If you take drugs for blood pressure or other conditions, tell your doctor if you experience orthostatic headaches. Changing the drug and/or dose may eliminate the headaches.

More from Seymour Diamond...

Caffeine and Ibuprofen

Caffeine boosts the headache-fighting power of ibuprofen. When volunteers took the pain reliever along with the caffeine equivalent of two cups of coffee, 71% experienced total pain relief. Only 58% of those who took ibuprofen alone experienced total relief. The combination should also relieve other types of pain, including backache and muscle soreness.

If you suffer from pain: Ask your doctor about taking 400 milligrams (mg) of ibuprofen along with two eight-ounce cups of coffee.

Anti-Headache Diet Keeps You Pain-Free

David Marks, MD, former medical reporter, WNBC-TV and WCBS-TV, and practicing internist, Norwalk, CT. He is former medical director, New England Center for Headache, Stamford, CT, and is coauthor (with Dr. Laura Marks) of *The Headache Prevention Cookbook—Eating Right to Prevent Migraines and Other Headaches* (Houghton Mifflin).

Red wine and other alcoholic beverages are notorious headache triggers. But several other less-obvious foods and beverages can also cause problems.

Eliminating these foods from your diet can often provide relief and allow you to reduce or stop your use of headache medications.*

Important: Tell your doctor about your diet plans, so he/she can help monitor your progress and be able to adjust your headache treatment accordingly.

Here's how to get started...

IDENTIFY YOUR FOOD TRIGGERS

Dozens of foods can cause migraines and other headaches, but most people are bothered by only a few. To identify the foods that affect

*Contact a doctor immediately if your headache is worse or "different" than usual...comes on rapidly and severely...first occurs after age 50...and/or is accompanied by neurological symptoms, such as paralysis, slurred speech or loss of consciousness. These symptoms may indicate an aneurysm, brain tumor, stroke or some other serious problem.

you, avoid *all* potential triggers (see the following list) for two weeks. If your headaches are food-related, you'll notice an improvement.

REINTRODUCE PROHIBITED FOODS

After the two-week period, resume eating *one* food from the prohibited list each week. If you experience no change, the food is not a headache trigger for you. If your headaches return or worsen, the reintroduced food is probably a trigger and should be permanently eliminated from your diet.

FOODS TO AVOID

• **All alcoholic beverages,** including cooking sherry.

• **All cheeses,** except for American, ricotta, cottage, Velveeta and cream cheese.

• **Any food containing monosodium glutamate (MSG) or preservatives,** including those found in canned soups.

• **All seeds and nuts.**

• **All chocolate,** carob and licorice.

• **Bacon,** hot dogs, pepperoni, sausage, salami, bologna, ham and all canned, cured or processed meat products.

• **Pickles,** chili peppers and olives.

• **Nonorganic dried fruits,** such as raisins, dates and apricots.

• **Soy sauce,** olive oil and vinegar, except for white and cider.

• **All artificial sweeteners,** including those found in diet sodas.

• **Non-dry varieties of mustard,** ketchup and mayonnaise.

• **All beans,** including lima, string, garbanzos and lentils.

• **Whole milk,** sour cream, buttermilk, whipped cream and ice cream.

FOODS TO LIMIT

• **Tomatoes and onions** (½ cup each daily).

• **Oranges,** grapefruits, tangerines, lemons and limes (½ cup each per day).

• **Bananas** (½ banana per day).

• **Skim-milk yogurt** (½ cup per day).

• **Caffeinated drinks** (16 ounces per day).

Get to the Root of The Headache

Suffering from "mystery headaches"? Foods likely to trigger headaches include corn (a very common trigger)...any overripe fruit...anything pickled, fermented or marinated...and baked goods containing yeast, especially when hot from the oven.

Also watch out for: Preserved or processed meats—bologna, hot dogs, hard sausage, etc. ...ripened cheese...eggs...chocolate...beverages containing caffeine or alcohol...anything containing preservatives.

Robert Milne, MD, founding member, American Academy of Medical Acupuncture; member, California State Homeopathic Society; and coauthor of *An Alternative Medicine Definitive Guide to Headaches* (Future Medicine Publishing).

Faster Pain Relief

For quicker pain relief, use a liquid pain reliever, such as Alka-Seltzer (which is liquid aspirin), liquid Tylenol (*acetaminophen*) or liquid Advil (*ibuprofen*) for the first dose.

Liquid pain relievers are absorbed by the body much faster than tablets and capsules. Switch to an anti-inflammatory medicine such as Advil or Aleve several hours later.

Warren Scott, MD, sports medicine specialist, Santa Cruz, CA.

Quick Headache Relief

When a headache comes on, start moving. Exercise produces painkilling endorphins and relieves stress.

Also: Drink a caffeinated beverage to speed absorption of aspirin...massage your head and neck. *Guided imagery*—close your eyes...imagine water moving over you on a sunny beach, the waves easing tension. When you relax, picture your headache as an object. Turn it into liquid—and let it pour through your fingers.

Roger Cady, MD, medical director, Headache Care Center, Springfield, MO.

Foot Massage Helps Headaches

Reflexology—massaging specific pressure points on the feet and other extremities— helped 81% of migraine and tension headache sufferers in one recent study. Many people were able to stop taking headache medicine after using reflexology for six months.

To find a reflexology practitioner in your area, visit *www.reflexology-usa.org.*

Laila Launso, PhD, associate professor, department of social pharmacy, The Royal Danish School of Pharmacy, Copenhagen, Denmark.

Natural Remedies for Headache Pain

Alexander Mauskop, MD, associate professor of clinical neurology, State University of New York, Brooklyn, and director, New York Headache Clinic, New York City. He is coauthor of *The Headache Alternative: A Neurologist's Guide to Drug-Free Relief* (Dell).

Which medication works best for headache pain? The answer depends on the type of headache you have. *There are several different kinds...*

●**Migraines** are usually treated with *sumatriptan* (Imitrex), *zolmitriptan* (Zomig) or another "triptan" drug.

●**Tension headaches** are usually treated with anti-inflammatory drugs like *ibuprofen* (Motrin) or *naproxen* (Aleve).

●**Cluster headaches** are usually treated with sumatriptan or inhaled oxygen.

These treatments are reliable and safe for occasional use. But when patients start to use

229

headache medication more than twice a week, stomach upset and other side effects become a serious concern.*

For this reason, headache sufferers should be sure to ask their doctors about trying non-drug approaches as well.

DIETARY MODIFICATION

Chronic headaches often have their origins in food sensitivities. To identify the food or foods underlying your pain, try an elimination diet. *Here's what to do...*

•**For one week,** keep a list of all foods and beverages you consume. Be sure to include seasonings and condiments.

•**For the next 30 days,** avoid all foods and beverages you consumed during the 24 hours preceding each headache you had during the week.

•**After 30 days,** reintroduce suspect foods one per meal. Before eating the food, take your resting pulse. Twenty minutes after eating, take your pulse again.

If your pulse after eating is 10 beats or more per minute faster than your pulse before eating, you may be sensitive to the food you've just reintroduced. Try to avoid this food for another 30 days.

If you remain sensitive to this food for several months, eliminate it permanently.

NUTRITIONAL SUPPLEMENTS

Headaches occur less frequently in individuals whose intake of certain key nutrients is adequate. *Ask your doctor about taking...*

•**Magnesium** (400 milligrams [mg] a day). This mineral has no effect on tension headaches but is moderately effective against migraines and cluster headaches.

Most effective: Slow-release or chelated magnesium tablets. They're better absorbed than conventional tablets.

•**Fish oil or flaxseed oil** (15 grams per day). These oils are rich in omega-3 fatty acids, which have been associated with reduced migraine frequency and severity.

*Contact a doctor at once if your headache is accompanied by confusion, convulsions or loss of consciousness...pain in the eye or ear...slurred speech, numbness, blurred vision or trouble walking...fever or nausea.

•**Lecithin** (200 mg a day). This protein—sold as a powder that can be mixed into beverages—reduces symptoms of cluster headaches.

•**Vitamin B-2** (riboflavin). Megadoses of this B vitamin—400 mg a day for two to three months—have been shown to reduce the frequency and severity of migraines.

Megadoses should be taken only under a doctor's supervision.

ACUPUNCTURE

Acupuncture works to combat tension and migraine headaches. Typically, the patient undergoes weekly or twice-weekly treatment sessions for 10 weeks, followed by monthly "maintenance" sessions.

For the name of an acupuncturist in your area, contact the American Academy of Medical Acupuncture at 323-937-5514 or *www. medicalacupuncture.org.*

Caution: Make sure the acupuncturist uses disposable needles.

In many cases, headaches can be prevented via acupressure, which is the self-help variant of acupuncture. *Try these techniques at the first sign of pain...*

•**Press your thumbs against the hollows between the muscles in the neck**—just below the base of the skull and in line with your ears. Hold for two minutes. Breathe deeply throughout.

•**Use your thumbs to press the upper inside corners of the eye sockets.** Hold for one minute while breathing deeply.

•**Use your right thumb to press on the top of the fleshy mound between your left thumb and index finger.** Hold for one minute while breathing deeply. Switch hands and repeat.

ENVIRONMENTAL FACTORS

To avoid the eyestrain that triggers some headaches, be sure to have adequate lighting for the task at hand.

Fluorescent bulbs often produce a barely perceptible flicker that can cause headaches. If there's a chance fluorescent flicker is behind your headaches, switch to incandescent bulbs.

Important: Have a professional eye exam once a year. Straining to compensate for poor vision can cause headaches.

Mold, dust mites and fungi can trigger headaches. To eliminate these airborne irritants, install exhaust fans in your bathroom and kitchen...and a dehumidifier in your basement or any other damp area. Indoor humidity should stay between 35% and 40%.

Use scent-free hypoallergenic soap and non-aerosol sprays.

Some headaches are triggered by chronic low-level exposure to *carbon monoxide* (CO). Never leave a car idling in an attached garage. Consider installing a CO detector in your home.

HERBAL REMEDIES

Feverfew can reduce the frequency and severity of migraines. If you'd like to try this herb, chew two fresh or freeze-dried leaves a day...or take 125 mg of dried feverfew that contains at least 0.2% parthenolide.

There's no evidence that herbal remedies are effective for tension or cluster headaches.

MASSAGE THERAPY

Massage has been found to reduce pain caused by tension and migraine headaches—but not cluster headaches.

For referral to a massage therapist in your area, contact the American Massage Therapy Association at 877-905-2700 or *www.amtamas sage.org.*

BIOFEEDBACK

By using devices that measure muscle tension and blood flow, biofeedback teaches you to relax tense muscles...and boost blood flow to your scalp. Each technique can ease headache pain.

For adults, 10 or more 30- to 60-minute sessions may be necessary. Children typically need only five or six.

To find a biofeedback therapist in your area, contact the Biofeedback Certification Institute of America at 303-420-2902 or *www.bcia.org.*

EXERCISE

Aerobic activity is beneficial for people with chronic headaches. Adding a *mantra*—a word repeated over and over to focus the mind—enhances the effect.

Caution: Exercising when you have some headaches can intensify the pain.

FOR PERSISTENT HEADACHES

If nondrug therapies fail to work within three months, consult a headache specialist.

For a list of specialists in your area, contact the National Headache Foundation (NHF) at 888-643-5552 or *www.headaches.org.*

More from Alexander Mauskop...

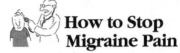 ## How to Stop Migraine Pain

Painkilling medications have brought welcome relief to millions of migraine sufferers. But medications aren't the only effective weapons against migraine.

Many alternative therapies, from acupuncture to nutritional supplements, can enhance the effectiveness of migraine drugs. In some cases, they eliminate the need for drugs altogether.

STRESS MANAGEMENT

Psychological stress can trigger migraines. Some migraineurs get headaches during periods of intense stress. Others get "letdown" headaches after stress has subsided.

By retraining your nervous system, biofeedback can be extremely effective at countering psychological stress.

It doesn't have to be conventional biofeedback, in which the patient—hooked up to electrodes—monitors his/her anxiety level via visual or audible signals. Almost any relaxation technique can work—including meditation, yoga, self-hypnosis, progressive relaxation or gentle martial arts like tai chi.

ELIMINATING CAFFEINE

In small amounts, caffeine eases migraine pain. Not surprisingly, many aspirin-based painkillers contain caffeine...and migraineurs often gulp coffee at the first sign of pain.

But among those who consume more than the equivalent of two cups of coffee a day, skipping a cup can cause caffeine withdrawal. That can trigger migraine.

Lesson: Migraineurs who drink lots of caffeinated coffee, tea or cola—or who eat lots of chocolate, which also contains caffeine—can benefit by giving up their habit.

DIETARY TRIGGERS

Headache frequency and severity can be reduced by avoiding certain food triggers…

•**Aged cheese,** red wine, pickled food, figs, bananas and other foods containing the amino acid tyramine.

•**Yogurt,** beer, freshly baked bread and other fermented foods.

•**Dried fruit.** Most contain sulfites, preservatives that can trigger headaches. Raisins contain a red pigment that can trigger migraine.

•**Foods containing nitrites and/or monosodium glutamate (MSG).**

•**Bread and pasta made from wheat.** Although a true wheat sensitivity is rare, some migraineurs find that avoiding wheat helps curb their headaches.

SLEEP HABITS

Migraines can be triggered by getting too little sleep—or too much. Aim for eight hours of sleep a night. Do not try to "catch up" by sleeping late on weekends. Take short naps during the day instead.

VITAMINS AND MINERALS

Magnesium plays a key role in brain function. Among other things, it influences blood vessel dilation and serotonin levels—each of which is a factor in migraine pain.

Up to 50% of migraineurs have a magnesium deficiency, according to recent research.

Spinach and other dark green, leafy vegetables are rich in magnesium. But other good magnesium sources—including nuts and beans—contain compounds that can trigger migraines. For this reason, it's hard to correct a magnesium deficiency through diet alone.

Better: Ask your doctor about taking a supplement containing 300 to 600 milligrams (mg) of magnesium per day.

Also helpful: Vitamin B-2 (riboflavin) supplements. A double-blind study published in the journal *Neurology* found that taking 400 mg of B-2 daily helped to significantly reduce migraine frequency.

You may have to take B-2 supplements for up to four months before you notice any effect.

FEVERFEW

Feverfew, an herb related to chamomile, has been used against migraine for centuries. Recent studies have found that daily use of feverfew reduces migraine frequency by up to 25%.

Feverfew is sold at health food stores. The usual dosage is 100 mg a day.

ACUPUNCTURE AND MASSAGE

Acupuncture can be quite effective at relieving migraine pain. You might try one 20- to 30-minute session per week for 10 weeks as a preventive measure…plus periodic "touch-ups" if headaches recur.

To find an acupuncturist in your area, contact the American Academy of Medical Acupuncture at 323-937-5514 or visit its Web site at *www.medicalacupuncture.org.*

Massage fights migraine indirectly, by relieving stress. But certain forms of massage seem to do more to relieve migraine than simply relieve stress.

Several migraine-fighting massage techniques—described by Toru Namikoshi in his classic book *Shiatsu and Stretching*—have proven to be particularly effective. *Try these…*

•**Place your thumbs on each side of the spine,** in the hollows between the neck muscles just below the base of the skull. Tilt your head back. Press firmly for two to three minutes, breathing deeply as you do.

•**Press the web between your thumb and forefinger with the thumb and index finger of your opposite hand.** Press hard for one minute, breathing deeply. Repeat with the other hand.

WHEN MEDICATION IS NEEDED

The 1993 introduction of *sumatriptan* (Imitrex) was hailed as a breakthrough for migraine sufferers—and no wonder.

Taken at the first sign of migraine, this prescription medication constricts dilated blood vessels, relieving not only pain but also the nausea and sensitivity to light and noise that often accompany migraine headaches.

Sumatriptan can be taken orally or—for faster relief—sprayed into the nose or injected.

Unfortunately, sumatriptan can cause unpleasant side effects, including chest pressure and a transient rise in blood pressure.

Sumatriptan and the newer "triptans"—including *zolmitriptan* (Zomig), *rizatriptan* (Maxalt) and *naratriptan* (Amerge)—are off limits for most heart patients and individuals who are at risk for heart disease.

Other drugs proven effective in preventing migraine include...

• **Anticonvulsants,** such as *valproic acid* (Depakote) and *gabapentin* (Neurontin).

• **Antidepressants.** Tricyclics, such as *nortriptyline* (Pamelor), *imipramine* (Tofranil) and *desipramine* (Norpramin), are most effective.

• **Beta-blockers,** such as *propranolol* (Inderal) and *atenolol* (Tenormin).

Breakthroughs for Headache Relief

Robert B. Daroff, MD, professor of neurology and interim vice dean, CASE School of Medicine, Cleveland. He was also chief of staff and senior vice president for academic affairs, University Hospitals of Cleveland, and president, American Headache Society, www.american headachesociety.org.

When patients complain of headaches, most doctors simply pull out their prescription pads.

Fortunately, researchers have discovered many new approaches to preventing and treating this all-too-common condition. *The latest developments...*

BETTER MIGRAINE DETECTION

Fewer than half of the estimated 30 million Americans who suffer from migraines receive an accurate diagnosis. Patients—and their doctors—often mistake it for a tension or sinus headache. Because the treatments that may be effective for these conditions are not effective for migraines, a missed diagnosis often leads to unnecessary discomfort and frustration.

Headache experts have no trouble recognizing migraines. That's primarily because they typically will take an hour to evaluate each new patient. Primary care physicians don't have the time—or, in some cases, the expertise—to properly identify migraine symptoms.

New study: Researchers at Albert Einstein College of Medicine in New York City gave a simple survey to 443 patients who had a history of headaches. More than 90% of those who answered "yes" to two of three key questions were found to have migraines. *The questions...*

• **Has a headache limited your activities** for one or more days in the last three months?

• **Are you nauseated** when you have a headache?

• **Does light bother you** when you have a headache?

Implication: This three-question test provides a quick and accurate guideline that can help physicians make a proper diagnosis.

This test is not a perfect diagnostic tool. For example, some patients who answer "yes" to two of the questions may turn out to have an underlying disease, such as cancer.

Caution: Patients as well as physicians frequently confuse migraine with chronic sinusitis. *Don't believe it.* Migraine symptoms—intense pain along with nausea and/or visual disturbances, such as auras, in the absence of fever—are almost never caused by sinus infections.

HERBS AND HEADACHES

Nearly half of all Americans use herbal remedies on occasion. This includes ginkgo biloba for memory...ginseng for energy...echinacea for colds...St. John's wort for depression...garlic supplements for heart health, etc. What most people don't realize is that some of these common herbs can actually trigger headaches or interact with conventional headache treatments.

New study: University of Utah researchers identified the herbal products that are most commonly utilized in the US. The researchers then scoured the scientific literature and identified possible side effects and/or potential drug interactions.

Ginkgo biloba, ginseng, echinacea, St. John's wort and garlic supplements interfere with liver enzymes that break down the migraine drug *sumatriptan* (Imitrex) and the tricyclic antidepressants *amitriptyline* (Elavil) and *nortriptyline* (Aventyl), which are also commonly used for migraine prevention and treatment.

Possible result: Dangerous drug levels can accumulate in the bloodstream.

Combining herbs with drugs may also make treatments less effective, causing your doctor to prescribe unnecessarily high doses.

Ginkgo biloba may even cause headaches in some people.

Implication: Patients undergoing treatment for migraines or cluster headaches should *not* use ginkgo biloba, ginseng, echinacea, St. John's wort or even garlic supplements without being supervised by a physician.

BOTOX AND HEADACHES

Because over-the-counter (OTC) analgesics taken at the onset of a headache do not always relieve symptoms, some patients take these drugs daily. But the long-term daily use of such medication increases the risk for side effects, such as gastric irritation or bleeding.

In addition, daily use of OTC or prescription drugs can also cause severe *rebound* headaches —chronic daily headaches that happen when a medication wears off.

New study: Researchers at Kaiser Permanente in San Diego gave injections of *botulinum toxin* (Botox), the popular antiwrinkle treatment, to 271 headache patients who failed to get relief from standard treatments. Patients in the study were given injections every three months, for a period of six to 15 months.

At the conclusion of the study, 80% of participants said their headaches were less frequent, less intense or both. About 95% reported no side effects. This study confirms the results of previous studies.

Most patients receive 30 small injections per treatment, usually in areas of the scalp where pain is present.

Implication: Botox reduces the frequency of headaches and is a good choice for sufferers who don't get relief from other methods. The use of Botox for headaches is still experimental, so insurance will not pay for it.

BENEFITS OF COUNSELING

The debilitating pain of migraines can affect emotional as well as physical health. It's common for people who get frequent migraines to feel misunderstood or frustrated by friends and colleagues who fail to appreciate the degree of their discomfort. Although doctors routinely treat physical symptoms, they often don't give

sufficient attention to the emotional components of chronic headache pain.

New study: Researchers at Ohio University gave more than 100 migraine patients a battery of psychological and neurological tests. Nearly one-third of them were found to have mood or anxiety disorders, with depression being the most common diagnosis, followed by generalized anxiety disorder.

People who suffer frequent migraines understandably get depressed and anxious, but migraines are not the cause. It is possible that there's a third, underlying factor—perhaps an imbalance in serotonin or other neurotransmitters—that triggers migraine headaches as well as mood disorders.

Implication: Migraines, in addition to other kinds of chronic pain, are frequently accompanied by depression and/or anxiety. People who are depressed tend to experience even more pain. They're also less likely to pursue positive coping strategies, such as exercise or healthful dietary changes.

All migraine patients should consider seeing a therapist for psychotherapy treatment and/or medication, which might help them cope with the psychological stress associated with having migraine headaches.

Treatment Options for Migraine Relief

Fred Sheftell, MD, director and founder, The New England Center for Headache, Stamford, CT, and national president, American Council for Headache Education. He is coauthor of *Conquering Headache* (Decker).

An estimated 28 million Americans suffer from migraine headaches. But fewer than half of those people receive treatment for their pain. Because migraine symptoms tend to be so varied, many doctors fail to give a proper diagnosis, much less prescribe the appropriate treatment.

As a result, migraine sufferers often rely on over-the-counter painkillers, such as *acetaminophen* (Tylenol) or *ibuprofen* (Advil).

These may relieve mild pain, but not moderate to severe pain. Taken too frequently or at a high dosage, these pain relievers can aggravate—rather than relieve—headache pain.

Good news: If you suffer from migraines, you can lessen the frequency and severity of your attacks by avoiding certain foods and getting enough exercise. If you often get severe migraines, prescription drugs can halt or even prevent the pain.

IS IT REALLY A MIGRAINE?

Migraines affect 6% of men and 18% of women. The migraine predisposition is inherited.

Fluctuations in the brain chemical *serotonin* trigger a migraine. These changes affect blood vessel activity, resulting in swollen, inflamed blood vessels.

Migraines last from four to 72 hours and are accompanied by nausea...vomiting...and/or sensitivity to light or sound. Migraines also cause at least two of the following symptoms —they occur on one side of the head...cause throbbing or pulsating pain...interfere with or restrict activity...worsen with physical activity.

Before diagnosing a migraine, your doctor must rule out any other possible causes of your headache—particularly high blood pressure or allergies. These conditions require separate treatment.

THE ROLE OF DIET

Certain foods that contain the amino acid *tyramine* can trigger migraine attacks by dilating blood vessels.

Sources of tyramine include red wine, beer and dark-colored alcohol, such as scotch and bourbon...chocolate...nuts...bananas...onions ...pizza...avocados...processed meats...pork... sour cream...pickled and fermented foods... and aged cheese.

The food additives *monosodium glutamate* (MSG), *hydrolyzed fat* and *hydrolyzed protein* can also result in migraines by causing fluid retention and blood vessel dilation. These are found in potato chips and canned foods.

Magnesium helps reduce the frequency of migraine attacks by stabilizing nerves that, when excited, can act as triggers. Migraine sufferers should be sure to eat plenty of foods that contain this mineral. Spinach and other green, leafy vegetables are good choices.

To ensure that you get enough magnesium: Ask your doctor about taking a daily 400-milligram (mg) magnesium supplement. You may need to take magnesium for four months before seeing results.

Foods that are rich in vitamin B-2 (riboflavin)—such as broccoli, fish and dairy products—also help fight migraines. Riboflavin is thought to help by increasing the efficiency of *mitochondria,* the microscopic "power plants" inside the body's cells.

Consider taking a supplement containing 400 mg of vitamin B-2 each day. This dosage has been shown to decrease the frequency of migraines by more than 50%.

A doctor should supervise vitamin treatment taken at this high dosage. It takes three to four months to see results.

EXERCISE IS HELPFUL

Aerobic exercise improves blood flow to the brain and triggers the release of painkilling compounds called *endorphins.* Following four months of regular exercise, migraine sufferers have fewer attacks.

Walk, bike, swim or do some form of aerobic exercise for 30 to 40 minutes, three or four days a week. Build up to this amount gradually.

IS IT TIME FOR DRUG THERAPY?

Moderate to severe migraines often require drug therapy. The *right* medication—used at the first sign of a migraine attack—can relieve pain quickly.

"Triptans" are the most effective medications to stop migraines that do not respond to lifestyle changes, such as diet and exercise.

•***Zolmitriptan* (Zomig)** tablets typically relieve pain in about 60 minutes. They also help prevent recurrences.

•***Sumatriptan* (Imitrex)** is available in the form of self-injection, nasal spray or tablet. The injection stops pain in an hour. The nasal spray and tablets take longer to work but are ideal for patients who dislike injections.

•***Naratriptan* (Amerge)** tablets alleviate pain more slowly than either zolmitriptan or sumatriptan tablets but are more effective at preventing recurrence.

●*Rizatriptan* **(Maxalt)** is a tablet or wafer that dissolves on the tongue. Migraineurs who also suffer nausea often prefer the wafer. Rizatriptan may also work faster than other triptans.

Side effects: Fatigue, mild chest discomfort and tightness of the neck and shoulders can occur with any triptan. Injections tend to be faster-acting but may be more troublesome than tablets or wafers.

Newer triptans, such as *eletriptan* (Relpax), *almotriptan* (Axert) and *frovatriptan,* may stop recurring migraines better than existing triptans.

Warning: Triptans are off-limits to people with coronary artery disease, uncontrolled high blood pressure (above 140/90) and individuals who have suffered a stroke. Those who smoke or have another risk factor for heart disease—obesity or total cholesterol above 220 mg/dl—must be monitored closely while taking these medications.

PREVENTIVE DRUGS

If triptans don't ease migraines within four hours, or if attacks are frequent, the next step is preventive medicine.

Everyone responds differently to these drugs, so work with your doctor to find the right medication for you. *They include…*

●**Beta-blockers.** *Atenolol* (Tenormin), *nadolol* (Corgard), *propranolol* (Inderal) and *timolol* (Blocadren).

●**Calcium-channel blockers.** *Verapamil* (Calan).

●**Antidepressants.** *Amitriptyline* (Elavil) and *nortriptyline* (Pamelor). *Fluoxetine* (Prozac), *paroxetine* (Paxil) and *sertraline* (Zoloft) are excellent for depression but less effective for headache.

●**Anticonvulsants.** *Divalproex* (Depakote).

●**Seratonin-2 antagonists.** *Cyproheptadine* (Periactin).

●**Alpha-2-adrenoceptor agonists.** *Clonidine* (Catapres).

●**Pain relievers/sedatives.** Aspirin or acetaminophen, caffeine and a mild sedative (Fiorinal or Fioricet).

TRACKING MIGRAINE SYMPTOMS

Migraine symptoms and your response to treatment can vary. To help you—and your doctor—identify patterns, it's helpful to keep a headache diary.

Record the duration of each migraine…any medication you take…severity of the pain on a scale of 1 (least) to 10 (greatest)…and the degree of relief.

Migraines can often be triggered by specific events, such as emotional upset…skipping a meal…weather changes…certain foods…flickering or bright lights…sleep changes.

Record any triggers and try to avoid them.

Acid Reflux May Cause Migraines

R eflux—also called acid indigestion—can cause pain to radiate from the upper teeth and gums into cheeks and eyes, a common location of migraine headaches.

Self-defense: If you have acid reflux and frequent migraines, see your doctor. An increased dose of acid reflux medicine may help prevent headaches.

Egilius L.H. Spierings, MD, headache expert, department of neurology, Brigham and Women's Hospital, Harvard Medical School, Boston.

Arthritis Relief

John D. Clough, MD, a retired rheumatologist in the department of rheumatic and immunologic disease at the Cleveland Clinic, is the author of *Arthritis: A Cleveland Clinic Guide* (The Cleveland Clinic).

M ore than 21 million Americans suffer from osteoarthritis, a degenerative joint disease. That's the bad news.

The good news—we know more about the disease now than ever before, including how to slow its progression.

CAUSES

There are many different forms of arthritis. Osteoarthritis is the most common form. When you have osteoarthritis, the cartilage that cushions the ends of the bones in your joints deteriorates. Over time, the cartilage may wear down completely, leaving bone rubbing on bone.

Osteoarthritis commonly affects the fingers, neck, lower back, hips and knees. *The exact cause of the disease isn't known, but the following are key risk factors...*

• **Advancing age.** People 45 years and older are at greater risk for the disease. In older people, the joint cartilage contains less fluid and may become brittle, which leads to deterioration.

• **Family history.** Heredity plays a role, especially in osteoarthritis of the hands. This particular type of osteoarthritis, which ultimately gives the fingers a gnarled appearance, is more common in women whose mothers also suffered from the condition.

• **Previous injury.** Not every joint injury causes a problem, but if you have had torn cartilage or a disruption of the ligaments in a major joint, then you are more likely to develop a problem in that area.

• **Obesity.** Being overweight puts unnecessary stress on weight-bearing joints—particularly hips and knees.

EARLY WARNINGS

Osteoarthritis often progresses slowly, but there can be early signs...

• **Joint pain** during or after use, after a period of inactivity or during a change in the weather.

• **Swelling and stiffness** in a joint, particularly after using it.

• **Joint instability,** especially noticeable in the knees, which can even take on a knock-kneed or bowlegged appearance as the cartilage deteriorates.

• **Bony lumps.** With osteoarthritis of the hands, these lumps (called Heberden's nodes and Bouchard's nodes) can appear on the middle or end joints of the fingers or at the base of your thumb.

PROTECT YOURSELF

There is no known cure for osteoarthritis, but lifestyle measures can help. *To prevent or slow progression of the disease...*

• **Lose weight.** While it's obvious that running and jumping can be hard on the joints, if you're overweight, even everyday tasks such as walking and climbing stairs can be problematic. Shed pounds, and you can ease the pressure on your weight-bearing joints.

• **Exercise.** Choose low-impact activities, such as walking, cycling and swimming, so that you don't put too much pressure on your joints.

If you've had a knee injury, it also pays to do quadriceps-strengthening and hamstring-stretching exercises so that those muscles can better stabilize and operate the knee.

New finding: A study recently published in *Arthritis & Rheumatism* shows that people with knee osteoarthritis who exercised regularly for as long as 18 months had less disability and were able to walk much greater distances than people who dropped out of the program.

Check with your doctor before beginning a regular exercise program. He may recommend working with a physical therapist to design an exercise program to meet your specific needs.

MEDICATIONS

Osteoarthritis sufferers have a range of treatment options...

• **Oral medications.** The most commonly used drugs for osteoarthritis are pain relievers, such as *acetaminophen* (Tylenol) and nonsteroidal anti-inflammatory drugs (NSAIDs), which fall into two categories...

• Nonselective NSAIDs. Drugs such as aspirin, *ibuprofen* (Advil), *diclofenac* (Voltaren) and *naproxen* (Aleve) are commonly used to treat the symptoms caused by inflammation (pain, swelling, redness, etc.), and they work very well for some people. However, long-term use of NSAIDs can cause problems ranging from stomach upset to gastrointestinal bleeding.

• Selective Cox-2 inhibitors. These drugs were originally touted as being less likely to cause gastrointestinal problems than traditional NSAIDs, but most have been pulled from the shelves because of potentially devastating side effects. *Rofecoxib* (Vioxx), for example, was pulled in September 2004 after a study showed that the drug predisposed people to heart attacks. Currently, there's only one Cox-2 inhibitor, *celecoxib* (Celebrex), still in use although its safety is being scrutinized. Celebrex does not seem to cause the same heart risks as Vioxx. Check with your doctor.

Recent finding: In a paper published in *The Journal of the American Medical Association,* three researchers at Harvard University examined 114 clinical trials of Vioxx, Celebrex and other drugs. The researchers found that Celebrex was associated with lower blood pressure readings (unlike Vioxx, which was associated with higher blood pressure readings).

•**Injections.** In cases where a particular joint is acutely inflamed, a physician might opt to inject a corticosteroid preparation into the joint. This can provide rapid relief for up to several months, but long-term use of corticosteroids can be harmful to tissue and bones.

SUPPLEMENTS

Glucosamine and *chondroitin sulfate* play a role in the structure of cartilage and other connective tissue—and you can get them over-the-counter in supplement form. A massive study, known as the "Glucosamine/Chondroitin Arthritis Intervention Trial (GAIT)," coordinated by the University of Utah School of Medicine, found that in patients with moderate to severe pain, glucosamine and chondroitin provided statistically significant pain relief. However, the combination did not work any better than a placebo for the overall group of patients.

Also, a study done on glucosamine suggests that it could potentially slow the progression of osteoarthritis of the knees, although not all studies of this supplement confirm this finding. More research is needed, but the supplements seem safe to use if you choose to try them.

Exception: People who are allergic to shellfish should steer clear of glucosamine, which is made from shellfish.

JOINT REPLACEMENT

In joint-replacement therapy (arthroplasty), the damaged joint is removed and replaced with a plastic or metal prosthesis. Joint replacement can be very effective, particularly for the major weight-bearing joints, such as the hips and knees, allowing you an active, pain-free life. Shoulder replacement also is effective, and the technology for smaller, more complex joints, such as the wrist and ankle, is improving.

Relieve Arthritis Pain... Naturally

James M. Rippe, MD, associate professor of medicine, Tufts University School of Medicine, Boston. Dr. Rippe is founder and director, Rippe Lifestyle Institute, Shrewsbury, MA, and author of many books, including *The Joint Health Prescription* (Rodale).

More than half of Americans over age 40 are dealing with some type of joint problem, from stiffness to arthritis pain. In people over age 60, joint problems account for more than 50% of all cases of disability.

In the past, doctors typically relied on painkilling drugs to treat joint ailments. But these medications do not solve the underlying problems. *Here's how to get lasting relief…*

EXERCISE

A decade ago, doctors told their patients with joint pain to avoid exercise. We now know from dozens of studies that regular exercise is one of the best things you can do for your joints.

The perfect exercise program for healthy joints will include aerobics and stretching as well as strengthening…

•**Aerobics.** The safest workouts are low-impact activities such as walking, swimming and bicycling.

Avoid running, step aerobics and jumping rope. They could cause joint injury.

•**Stretching.** Do head rolls, shoulder rolls and hamstring stretches.

•**Strengthening.** Use dumbbells or weight machines. Stretching and strengthening exercises help cushion and stabilize the joints.

To start an exercise program: Begin by performing 10 minutes of aerobic exercise each day. Every week, increase that time by five minutes until you are getting 30 minutes of moderate aerobic activity every day. Do stretching exercises every morning and night. Strengthening exercises should be done every other day.

You do not have to do all your daily exercise at one time—as long as you accumulate 30 minutes of activity throughout the day. Gardening, housework and taking the stairs all count.

Caution: If you already have arthritis or another serious joint condition, such as a prior injury, have your doctor and/or physical therapist recommend appropriate exercises for you. Anyone who has been sedentary should consult a doctor before beginning an exercise program.

WEIGHT LOSS AND NUTRITION

If you are overweight, losing even 10 pounds will reduce wear and tear on your joints. Even if you are not overweight, proper nutrition can help keep your joints healthy.

Be skeptical of any "arthritis diet" that claims to cure joint pain by promoting a single type of food or eliminating whole categories of foods. *Instead, just follow basic principles of good nutrition...*

●**Avoid unhealthy fats.** A high-fat diet triggers inflammation—a key component of joint problems. This is especially true of saturated fat (found in many animal products, such as red meat) and omega-6 fatty acids (found in many processed foods and vegetable oils).

Helpful: Substitute monounsaturated fats, such as olive oil and canola oil. Eat foods rich in "good" omega-3 fatty acids, such as nuts, flaxseed and cold-water fish, including salmon and mackerel. These foods help fight inflammation.

●**Eat more vitamin-rich foods.** Fruits and vegetables are good sources of antioxidant vitamins. Antioxidants will neutralize the free radicals, which damage cells and contribute to joint inflammation.

Also, certain vitamins may act directly on joints. Vitamin C is involved in the production of collagen, a component of cartilage and connective tissue. Beta-carotene and vitamins D and K help in the development of strong bones.

For more information on healthy eating and nutrition, contact the American Dietetic Association at 800-877-1600 or *www.eatright.org.*

SUPPLEMENTS

Research suggests that certain supplements can help relieve joint problems. *Ask your doctor whether any of the following supplements are right for you...**

●**Vitamins.** Even though food is the best way to get your vitamins, it's a good idea to

*Supplements can interact with other drugs, so tell all your doctors what you are taking.

take a multivitamin supplement to make sure you are getting *all* the vitamins you need. These include beta-carotene and vitamins C, D and E. Vitamin E is especially hard to get in sufficient quantities from food alone. But high amounts of vitamin E may be dangerous, so ask your doctor for the proper amount.

●**Gelatin.** It contains *glycine* and *proline,* two amino acids that are important for rebuilding cartilage. These amino acids are found in products made with hydrolyzed collagen protein (such as Knox NutraJoint). Such products dissolve in juice without congealing—unlike cooking gelatin.

Typical daily dosage: 10 grams.

●**Glucosamine.** This sugar is one of the building blocks of cartilage. Increasing evidence suggests that supplementing with glucosamine helps relieve arthritis pain and stiffness—without major side effects.

Typical daily dosage: 1,500 milligrams (mg).

●**Chondroitin.** Naturally present in cartilage, chondroitin is believed to guard against destructive enzymes. A number of supplements combine glucosamine and chondroitin.

Typical daily dosage: 1,200 mg.

Water Helps to Fight Osteoarthritis

Osteoarthritis pain may be a symptom of dehydration in the joint. Increasing water intake often improves the condition after about four weeks—the time needed to rehydrate the body. Drink half your body weight in ounces.

Example: If you weigh 160 pounds, drink 80 ounces—10 eight-ounce glasses. Drink more during the summer, when humidity is high, or when exercising.

Ronald Lawrence, MD, PhD, founding member, International Association for the Study of Pain, Seattle, and coauthor of *Preventing Arthritis* (Putnam).

Use Ginger to Ease Arthritic Knee Pain

Among arthritis patients who were taking 225 milligrams of a ginger extract twice a day, 63% reported less pain while standing and after walking 50 feet.

Theory: Ginger contains *salicylates,* the same anti-inflammatory compounds that are found in aspirin.

When taken in high doses, aspirin, unlike ginger, can cause stomach irritation. Ginger extract is available in most drugstores and health food stores.

Roy D. Altman, MD, professor of medicine and chief, division of rheumatology and immunology, University of Miami School of Medicine.

Knee Surgery May Not Help Arthritis

Arthroscopic surgery for an arthritic knee may not be effective. This surgery involves removing injured cartilage. In one study, some patients underwent real arthroscopic surgery and others a placebo surgery (small incisions were made, but cartilage was not removed).

During the following two years, patients who had the placebo surgery consistently reported the same improvement as patients who underwent the real thing.

Nelda Wray, MD, chief of general medicine, Houston VA Medical Center, and professor of medicine and medical ethics, Baylor College of Medicine, Houston. Her study of 180 patients was published in The New England Journal of Medicine.

Stop Knee Pain— Without Surgery

Brian C. Halpern, MD, sports medicine specialist and assistant attending physician, Hospital for Special Surgery, and clinical assistant professor in medicine, Weill Medical College of Cornell University, both in New York City. He is author of The Knee Crisis Handbook (Rodale).

The knee is the largest hinged joint in the human body and is subjected to the most physical stress.

Example: A 150-pound adult exerts 300 to 400 pounds of knee pressure when running or jumping.

As we age, we become increasingly susceptible to osteoarthritis. This wear-and-tear arthritis affects the knee more than any other joint.

The knee is also vulnerable to injuries, most of which are caused by overuse—pushing the muscles and tendons beyond their capacity.

In sedentary people, underuse is the main problem. People who don't exercise regularly lack the necessary muscle strength to give the knee full support when performing daily activities, such as working in the yard or running to catch a bus.

Main types of knee injury…

• **Ligament damage.** The knee has four major *ligaments,* tightly woven cables that limit the joint's range of motion. Pushing the knee past its normal range of motion during activities, such as skiing or soccer, can result in a sprain or tear. Many ligament injuries can heal on their own, although torn ligaments may require surgical repair.

• **Meniscal injuries.** The two *menisci* in the knee act like rubber washers. They cushion the thighbone and absorb shocks. Injuries can occur while twisting, bending or squatting and typically involve tears in the cartilage, usually due to sudden movements. The menisci also harden and degenerate over time. Small tears in the cartilage usually heal naturally. More serious tears may require surgery.

• **Tendinitis.** This irritation or inflammation of a *tendon*—the thick end of a muscle that attaches to bone—can result from running or jumping. It typically improves with home care, such as using ice packs, doing stretching and strengthening exercises and taking anti-inflammatories. A completely torn tendon, on the other hand, almost always requires surgery.

•**Bursitis.** This is often called "housemaid's knee" because inflammation of the *bursa*—small, fluid-filled sacs located where tendons connect to bone—is often caused by the type of pressure that occurs when a person kneels, as one might do when scrubbing floors. Bursitis can be intensely painful, but symptoms abate when fluid in the sac is reabsorbed into the body, usually within a few weeks.

KEYS TO PREVENTION

There are certain factors that predispose a person to knee injury—such as problems with leg alignment, differences in leg length or loose-jointedness—which can't be changed. *But the majority of knee problems can be prevented with proper care...*

•**Drink fluid throughout the day.** Fluid intake nourishes muscles and structures around the knee by increasing circulation, bringing in nutrients and eliminating lactic acid and other toxins that can promote pain and injury. Aim for about six eight-ounce glasses of any fluid each day.

•**Train "in phase."** If your workouts are casual—occasional weight lifting, brisk walks, etc.—exercise at *different* times of the day.

Reason: The muscles will adjust to a wider range of body conditions, such as changing levels of the stress hormone cortisol. This helps provide more overall fitness and knee strength.

•**Take glucosamine/chondroitin.** Combination supplements that contain both substances help cartilage regenerate and reduce joint inflammation.

Typical dose: 1,500 milligrams (mg) glucosamine and 1,200 mg chondroitin daily.

•**Replace exercise shoes every 300 to 400 miles.** This is especially important if you engage in high-impact sports, such as tennis, jogging, basketball, etc. Stress on the knee is greater when shoes age and lose resilience.

•**Avoid the "knee killers."** Exercises, such as deep squats, jumping or bending at the knees, are among the main causes of knee injuries. Exercises that use bouncing or springy movements to lengthen muscles often can trigger the muscle to contract rather than stretch. Do more controlled exercises, such as biking, swimming or walking, if you have a history of knee pain or injury.

•**Get enough calcium.** Most adults need 1,200 to 1,500 mg daily to maintain adequate bone strength. The loss of bone density that often occurs with age weakens the bones, increasing strains on muscles, tendons and ligaments that support the knee.

TREATMENT SECRETS

It's common for knee injuries to take weeks or months to completely heal. *Here are the best treatment options...*

•**Ice it.** Applying cold—such as an ice pack or ice cubes wrapped in a towel—to the knee for about 20 minutes as soon as possible after an injury shrinks blood vessels and reduces swelling. Repeat the treatment every few hours, and keep doing it for two days.

Helpful: A product called Knee Cryo Cuff, available from some pharmacies, compresses and ices the knee at the same time. Compression reduces pain as well as swelling.

Typical cost: $120.

•**Get moderate rest.** You don't want to overwork the knee while it's healing, but you do want to keep moving it through its normal range of motion—*short of pain.* Movement stimulates all of the cells as well as that of lubricating synovial fluid, which also supplies nutrients to surrounding cartilage. Patients who stay moderately active recover sooner than those who get total rest.

•**Take analgesics.** Medications such as aspirin, *ibuprofen* (Advil), *naproxen* (Aleve) and other nonsteroidal anti-inflammatory drugs (NSAIDs) reduce levels of prostaglandins, pain-causing chemicals that increase swelling and tissue damage.

•**Apply analgesic cream.** Topical OTC ointments, such as Zostrix, contain *capsaicin,* the substance that makes chili peppers hot. These analgesic creams deplete nerve cells of pain-causing *substance P.* The ointments won't do much for severe pain but do seem to help ease minor knee discomfort. Expect to use an analgesic cream one to two times a day for at least a week before getting relief.

BETTER SURGICAL OPTIONS

If you and your doctor determine that you need knee surgery, don't worry—it isn't the ordeal it used to be. Orthopedic surgeons routinely perform arthroscopy for everything other than total knee replacement.

During arthroscopy, thin viewing scopes and instruments are inserted into very small punctures in the knee, allowing a well-lit and magnified picture of the knee joint to be shown on a TV monitor. The surgeon can more accurately diagnose the injury and repair it if necessary.

Arthroscopy can be performed on an outpatient basis. Typically, recovery is within four to six weeks.

More from Brian C. Halpern...

Is It Serious?

Some knee injuries can be treated at home, but others need immediate attention. *See your doctor if...*

●**You can't put any weight on the knee.** This can be a sign of a cartilage tear or other serious injury.

●**It isn't getting better after a few days.**

●**The knee is infected.**

Main signs: Heat, redness or swelling.

●**The knee locks or gives out** when you're trying to walk.

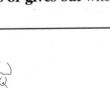

Amazing Advances in Joint-Replacement Surgery

Andrew A. Shinar, MD, assistant professor of orthopedic surgery and director, Joint Replacement Center, Vanderbilt University Medical Center, Nashville.

Physicians used to discourage all adults younger than age 65 from having joint-replacement surgery. It was thought that artificial joints would last only about 10 years and you would require subsequent surgery if you had decades of life ahead of you.

That's no longer true. The materials used now in artificial joints are very durable and can last 20 years or more.

Although most people have few or no complications, joint-replacement surgery isn't free of risks. Patients must take an active role to ensure that the new joints stay trouble-free.

Andrew Shinar, MD, who performs about 300 joint-replacement surgeries per year at Vanderbilt University's Joint Replacement Center, answered some questions...

●**Who should consider joint-replacement surgery?** Each year, as many as 400,000 Americans undergo joint-replacement surgery to relieve pain, stiffness and immobility. Most suffer from osteoarthritis, the gradual breakdown of cartilage and bone. Joint replacement also is an option for those who have been injured or who have severe rheumatoid arthritis or other conditions affecting the joints.

Joint replacement is most successful in large joints like hips, knees and shoulders. It is less effective in the small hand joints, although this procedure is improving.

There's never a rush to undergo surgery. It's often possible to control discomfort with over-the-counter analgesics, exercise and other lifestyle approaches. Artificial joints may wear out, so it's better to delay the procedure if possible.

Patients usually opt for surgery if they have persistent, severe joint pain or have trouble with daily activities, such as walking, climbing stairs, getting out of a chair, etc. The patient—not the surgeon—decides when "enough is enough."

•**What are prosthetic joints made of?** Usually metal (titanium or cobalt chrome), plastic or a combination. The "ball" of an artificial hip joint, for example, typically is made of metal, while the "socket" is made of hard plastic.

One type of plastic—cross-linked polyethylene—is incredibly durable. It shows virtually no wear after 10 years.

A new approach—ceramic-on-ceramic joints —seems to have very impressive wear characteristics, but we don't yet have long-term data.

•**What causes replacement joints to wear out?** Abrasion. The parts move against each other, which causes them to wear over a long period of time. These newer, harder materials should eliminate such problems.

•**What does the surgery involve?** The patient is given a general, spinal or epidural anesthetic. I usually recommend an epidural— it offers better pain control after surgery.

The surgeon then makes an incision. Minimal incision hip replacement requires only a three- to five-inch incision, versus the standard 10- to 12-inch incision in standard hip replacement.

In all joint-replacement procedures, the surgeon removes the damaged bone and tissue, keeping healthy bone and tissue intact, and then implants the new joint.

Younger patients will often receive custom-made, "pressed-fit" implants—precise parts that are essentially banged into place. Surrounding bone gradually grows into the implant and gives additional support.

Older patients, who have more fragile bones, cannot always withstand the force that is necessary for pressed-fit implants. An alternative is to cement the joint to the bone. Some surgeons use this approach with all of their patients because cementing will give the implant immediate strength and speeds recovery. However, it can complicate subsequent procedures should the artificial joint need to be replaced.

Most people leave the hospital after two or three days, regardless of the technique or the type of joint being replaced.

•**What happens after surgery?** You want to get the joint moving as soon as possible. Your surgeon probably will arrange for you to meet with a physical therapist, who will design an appropriate exercise plan.

•**What else can I do to improve my recovery?** If you smoke, quit right away. Smoking delays the growth of new blood vessels in the bone surrounding the new joint. It can prevent the bone from growing into the artificial joint. Smoking also causes surgical incisions to heal more slowly.

•**What are some of the biggest risks of joint-replacement surgery?** Infection is one. Bacteria readily colonize on foreign material in the body, including artificial joints. The resulting infection can loosen the joint.

After replacement surgery, inform your dentist or doctor that you have an artificial joint. You may need to take antibiotics prior to any dental work or other invasive procedures for two years after the joint replacement.

Also, if you develop any kind of infection (urinary, skin, etc.), be sure to get medical treatment immediately.

Dislocation is another risk. The moving parts in prosthetic joints can separate or dislocate. This is common in hip replacements.

Increasing muscle strength helps prevent dislocations. It's also important to avoid combination movements that cause the hip to move in two directions at once. Examples are crossing your legs at the knee or leaning to the side to pick up something.

Blood clots can form, but this is rare and usually not life-threatening. Your physician will give you blood-thinning medicine before, during and after the surgery to prevent this.

It is also important to flex your feet and calves several times a day. Keep doing this exercise diligently for at least three months after the operation. It pumps blood through the veins and helps prevent clotting. Also avoid taking long car or plane trips.

•**How successful are the results?** Some results are remarkable. With the new minimally invasive hip-replacement procedure, motivated patients can return to office work in as little as two weeks. I have had similar results with unicondular knee replacement, which is one-half of a total knee.

With other procedures, you can resume normal activities six to eight weeks after surgery, though certain activities may be restricted. For example, if you have hip- or knee-replacement surgery, high-impact activities, such as running or basketball, may never obtain your doctor's approval. You probably can swim, play golf, walk or ride a bike comfortably. With shoulder replacement, you may be able to lift light loads but should avoid playing tennis.

●**Will the artificial joint set off airport alarms?** Yes. Security devices are more sensitive than they used to be. Ask your surgeon to give you a card that explains you have an artificial joint. It will help you get through checkpoints more quickly.

If You Think Osteoarthritis Is Inevitable, You're Wrong!

Brenda D. Adderly, MHA, author of *The Arthritis Cure Fitness Solution* (Lifeline Press).

Some experts believe that *osteoarthritis* (OA) of the hands, hips, knees and other joints is actually brought on by a chemical change in the cartilage of the affected joint, caused in part by important nutrients being flushed out of the cartilage.

This makes the cartilage less spongy and more vulnerable to inflammation.

One way to reverse this chemical change is to take two specific food supplements—*glucosamine* and *chondroitin sulfate*—on a daily basis. These over-the-counter nutritional supplements (available in pharmacies and nutrition stores everywhere) help promote the growth of healthy cartilage tissue, reversing arthritic symptoms.

In addition to a daily dose of these two supplements, the main thing you can do to ward off the symptoms of OA is to exercise…

●**Exercise helps you maintain a healthful weight,** which puts less stress on your joints as you stand and walk.

●**Exercise encourages the flow of nutrient-rich lubricating fluids** into the cartilage tissue of the joints—helping to repair arthritis-related damage caused by the loss of nutrients.

●**Exercise also strengthens the muscles around your joints,** providing added support and cushioning for the joints themselves.

My Arthritis Cure Fitness Plan includes three parts in its program—stretching, strength building and cardiovascular workouts.

STRETCHING

Most people with osteoarthritis experience limited flexibility and range of motion in their affected joints. This makes it easy to strain adjoining muscles and tendons, and puts more stress on other parts of the body that compensate for the inflexible areas.

That's why stretching exercises, done five days a week, should be the first step in your fitness program.

Try starting with just one of the stretches listed below. Do it for a couple of days, then add a stretch or two…then more.

You'll find that these exercises improve your flexibility and reduce the discomfort of muscle exertion.

Chest stretch: In a standing position, clasp your hands together behind your back. Next, pull back your shoulders while lifting your hands a few inches higher, as though you wanted to flaunt your favorite necklace or necktie. Your chest will automatically expand. Hold for 10 to 30 seconds.

Back and torso stretch: Lie flat on your back, with your lower back pressed to the floor. Bend both knees, and then lower them both slowly to your left side, so your right knee and ankle rest on top of your left knee and ankle.

Spread both arms out to either side, pushing your shoulders as flat as possible, and gently turn your head in the opposite direction from your knees.

Relax and hold this position for 30 seconds, feeling the stretch in your back and legs. Then switch sides and repeat.

Upper arm and back stretch: Cross your right arm over your chest and rest the upper part of it on your left palm, so that your left hand completely supports your right arm.

Hold the "lazy arm" and gently pull it across your body until you feel a stretch in your upper right shoulder. Hold for 10 to 30 seconds, then switch sides and repeat.

Hamstring stretch: Sit on the edge of a sturdy chair with your hands on your hips. Straighten your right leg in front of you, keeping your left leg bent.

Lean forward from the hips, pushing your chest toward your knee until you feel a good stretch in the back of your right thigh, knee and calf. Hold for 10 to 30 seconds, then switch sides and repeat.

Buttocks stretch: Lying flat on the floor, grasp your right leg behind the knee with both hands, keeping your left leg straight.

Gently and slowly pull the right knee as close to your chest as possible, feeling the stretch in your lower back and buttocks. Hold 10 to 30 seconds, then switch legs and repeat.

Calf stretch: Step forward with your left leg as if you're about to start a running race. Keeping your right leg straight and your right heel flat on the floor, bend your left knee slightly and shift your weight onto your left leg. You should feel a stretch in your right calf as you lean forward. Hold 10 to 30 seconds, then switch legs and repeat.

STRENGTH BUILDING

Developing better muscle strength is the most important part of the Arthritis Cure Fitness Plan. Strong muscles can take weight off arthritic joints and also act as shock absorbers, reducing pain when you move about. Muscle strengthening has the added benefit of building bone mass.

The following exercises can be done with or without weights. You'll know you're at the right resistance level when you feel a slight burning sensation in the muscle you're working after about 10 repetitions.

For best results, these exercises should be done at least three times a week.

Shoulder and biceps: Holding dumbbells or full cans of food in each hand (or with your hands empty, if cans are too heavy), bend your elbows so your fists are even with your shoulders. Slowly raise both arms straight over your head. Do eight to 10 repetitions of this movement.

Shoulders and triceps (back of upper arms): Sitting in a sturdy armchair, grasp both arms of the chair and push yourself up until you're half-standing, using only your arms—no leg power.

Repeat this "chair pushup" eight to 10 times.

This exercise should be avoided by people with arthritic hands or wrists.

Quadriceps I (front of the thighs and lower back): Lie on your back with both knees bent. Pushing from your feet, raise your buttocks three or four inches off the floor. Hold this position for 10 seconds, then slowly release and lie flat for five seconds. Repeat eight to 12 times.

Quadriceps II (front of the thighs): Sit in a chair and place the handles of a plastic grocery bag containing one or two full cans of food over your right ankle.

Lift your right leg straight out in front of you, lifting the bag off the ground, and hold for a count of five. Then slowly lower your leg back down to the ground, and repeat up to 10 times, if possible. Switch legs and repeat.

CARDIOVASCULAR WORKOUTS

Cardiovascular (aerobic) workouts do not merely strengthen your heart and circulatory system—they also bring sinovial fluid into the joints and build muscular strength and endurance. They also give additional support to your joints. They're the best way to keep your weight at a healthful level.

Begin by doing whatever you can, even just a block or two of walking at a comfortable pace (slow is fine). Add a small increment of distance each time you work out, until you're up to a half hour or more.

Cardiovascular workouts should be done two or three times a week, alternating day to day with strength-building workouts. *Other good aerobic activities…*

●**Walking.** Especially good for those with arthritis in the hips, knees and ankles.

●**Swimming.** Good for improving joint flexibility and decreasing arthritis-related pain—swimming is also recommended for people with OA who are overweight.

●**Water aerobics.** This can be as simple as walking in the shallow end of the pool. Many people with arthritis find it beneficial to alternate a few minutes of water aerobics with a few minutes of easy swimming.

●**Bicycling.** This activity is especially good for people with arthritis in the knees.

●**Aerobics classes.** Low-impact activity is good for arthritis in all parts of the body.

●**Ballroom dancing.** Good for arthritis in all parts of the body.

Breakthrough Treatments For Arthritis

Harris H. McIlwain, MD, specialist in pain-related diseases, Tampa Medical Group, Tampa, FL. He is board-certified in rheumatology and geriatric medicine, and is coauthor of *Pain-Free Arthritis: A 7-Step Program for Feeling Better Again* (Henry Holt).

If you have arthritis, chances are you have a well-worn heating pad and a medicine cabinet full of painkillers. Unfortunately, these approaches provide only temporary relief for both *osteoarthritis* (an age-related disease that causes joint pain and stiffness) and *rheumatoid arthritis* (an autoimmune disease that triggers joint inflammation).

Even though there is no cure now for arthritis, several underutilized treatments can dramatically curb your symptoms...

EXERCISE

Arthritis patients often avoid exercise, fearing it will exacerbate muscle and joint pain. Yet research consistently shows that exercise alleviates arthritis symptoms and improves strength and flexibility. Exercise also helps to prevent weight gain, which has been shown to worsen arthritis pain.

Scientific evidence: Researchers at Wake Forest University School of Medicine discovered that aerobic or resistance exercise reduces the incidence of disability for key daily activities (eating, dressing, bathing, etc.) in arthritis patients by about 50%.

What to do: Stretch for at least 10 minutes daily. Perform an aerobic activity (such as biking or walking) very slowly, working up to 30 minutes five days per week. Do strengthening exercises—either resistance machines or weight lifting—gradually working up to 15 minutes, three times a week.*

To minimize pain and prevent injury, apply warm, moist heat to arthritic joints or sore muscles for 15 minutes before and after exercise.

BOOST YOUR C AND D

Vitamin C seems to slow down the cartilage loss that comes from osteoarthritis, while a diet low in vitamin D may speed up the progression of osteoarthritis.

Scientific evidence: In research conducted as part of the ongoing Framingham Heart Study, doctors discovered that patients who ate a diet that was high in vitamin D, or who took D supplements, decreased their risk for worsening arthritis by 75%. And, a study of 25,000 people by the Arthritis Research Campaign in England found that a low intake of vitamin C may increase the risk of developing arthritis.

What to do: Take daily supplements that provide 500 to 1,000 milligrams (mg) of vitamin C and 400 international units (IU) of vitamin D.

DRINK TEA

Tea may help reduce arthritis inflammation and bone deterioration.

Scientific evidence: Researchers recently discovered that green tea contains a *polyphenol,* or chemical compound, that suppresses the expression of a key gene associated with arthritis inflammation. Black tea is made of the same leaves and may be as beneficial, even though it is processed differently.

What to do: Drink one to two cups of hot or cold tea daily.

*A physician or physical therapist can help you to devise a safe movement program that combines stretching, aerobic and strengthening exercises.

EAT GRAPES

Grape skins contain *resveratrol,* the only natural compound known to perform like Cox-2 inhibitors. Like pharmaceutical Cox-2 inhibitors, resveratrol both suppresses the Cox-2 gene and deactivates the Cox-2 enzyme, which produces inflammation at the site of injury or pain.

Scientific evidence: A study published in the *Journal of Biological Chemistry* confirmed that resveratrol acts as an antioxidant and a Cox-2 inhibitor.

What to do: Eat one cup of white or red grapes daily.

Good news: Imbibing your grapes may be as healthful as munching them. All wines have some resveratrol, with red wine packing the biggest punch. But, for the best overall health benefits, limit your wine consumption to no more than one or two glasses a day.

TRY SUPPLEMENTS

Dietary supplements can be a valuable adjunct to traditional drug treatments, allowing patients to reduce or, in some cases, eliminate expensive medications altogether.* *The most effective are...*

•**Glucosamine.** Derived from the shells of shellfish, this supplement appears to aid in the lubrication of joints and reduce arthritis pain and stiffness.

Scientific evidence: In a report published in the *British Medical Journal,* taking 1,500 mg of glucosamine daily was found to slow cartilage deterioration in patients with osteoarthritis.

What to do: Ask your doctor if taking 1,500 mg of glucosamine daily would be helpful. Glucosamine is often packaged with chondroitin, but there is less evidence to support the effectiveness of chondroitin.

Warning: People who have shellfish allergies should *not* take glucosamine.

•**SAMe.** Doctors in Europe commonly prescribe this natural supplement for depression and arthritis.

Scientific evidence: Studies indicate that it relieves pain and inflammation about as well as

*Always consult your doctor before taking supplements. Some may interfere with the action or efficacy of certain drugs.

naproxen (Aleve), but without the stomach upset and other side effects. It has the added benefit of boosting mood, possibly by increasing production of the brain chemical *dopamine.*

What to do: If your arthritis does not get better with glucosamine, ask your physician about taking 400 to 1,200 mg of SAMe every day.

GET A MASSAGE

Manual manipulation by physical or massage therapists is among the most effective of treatments for relieving neck and back pain.

Scientific evidence: In a study recounted in the *Archives of Internal Medicine,* back pain patients who underwent 10 weeks of therapeutic massage took fewer medications the following year than did back pain patients who were not massaged.

What to do: Consider getting regular massages, as needed, for pain management.

Whenever possible, choose a state-licensed massage therapist. To locate one, contact the American Massage Therapy Association at 877-905-2700 or *www.amtamassage.org.*

CONSIDER THERAPEUTIC TAPING

Therapeutic taping—wrapping rigid tape around a joint to realign, support and take pressure from it—may have significant pain relief benefits for some osteoarthritis patients.

Scientific evidence: In one Australian study, 73% of patients with osteoarthritis of the knee experienced substantially reduced symptoms after three weeks of therapeutic taping. The benefits were comparable to those achieved with standard drug treatments and lasted three weeks after taping was stopped. Though the study looked only at knees, taping may work as well for elbows, wrists and ankles.

What to do: Ask your doctor if therapeutic taping is right for you.

Important: Taping must be done properly to be effective. If you try taping, you should first have your sore joint wrapped by a physician or physical therapist who is familiar with the procedure. He/she can show you or a family member the proper technique.

If taping proves too difficult or cumbersome, a fitted neoprene sleeve (an elastic sleeve used by athletes) may provide similar benefits. It is available at most drugstores.

More from Harris H. McIlwain…

Arthritis Pain Relief Strategies

To minimize arthritis pain and protect your joints, follow this helpful advice…

•**When grocery shopping, request plastic bags that can be looped over your arms,** between the wrist and elbow. This shifts the weight to your shoulders and upper body, instead of the more delicate wrist and hand joints.

•**Put foam "grips" around pens and pencils** (you can find the grips in office-supply stores). You can use these same covers around crochet hooks and knitting needles, too.

•**Use pump toothpastes** rather than the squeeze tubes.

•**Choose clothing with Velcro closures** instead of zippers and buttons.

•**Women should wear bras that open in the front.**

Arthritis Food Cures

Isadore Rosenfeld, MD, Rossi Distinguished Professor of Clinical Medicine, Weill Medical College of Cornell University, New York City. He is also author of several books, including *Doctor, What Should I Eat?* (Warner) and *Dr. Isadore Rosenfeld's Breakthrough Health* (Rodale).

Both osteoarthritis and rheumatoid arthritis cause painful inflammation that usually becomes worse with age. But the proper food choices can help reduce this pain—without the side effects caused by some painkillers.

Best food: Fatty fish (salmon, mackerel, sardines, etc.). The omega-3 fatty acids in fish counter the effects of *prostaglandins,* chemicals that promote inflammation. Eat three or more fish meals weekly. If you are pregnant, ask your doctor whether you should eat fish.

Also helpful: Brazil nuts. They contain *selenium,* a trace mineral that may reduce arthritis symptoms. One Brazil nut supplies the recommended daily intake of 70 micrograms (mcg).

Approximately 20% of all osteoarthritis and rheumatoid arthritis cases are linked to food allergies. Common offenders include soy, coffee, eggs, milk, corn, wheat, potatoes, beef, pork and shellfish (especially shrimp).

I advise patients with severe arthritis to stop eating these problem foods, one at a time, to see if their symptoms diminish.

Amazing New Ways to Control Rheumatoid Arthritis

James F. Fries, MD, professor of medicine and rheumatology, Stanford University School of Medicine, Palo Alto, CA. He is coauthor of *The Arthritis Helpbook* (Perseus Books).

If you're among the 2 million Americans who have *rheumatoid arthritis* (RA), there's good news. New treatment strategies are proving to be much more effective than the strategies that were considered state-of-the-art just a few years ago.

Implication: If you have RA but haven't seen a doctor recently, your current treatment regimen may not be optimal.

An autoimmune disease, RA occurs when the immune system attacks the body's own cells as if they were invaders.

This attack causes the joints to become swollen and warm to the touch. Enzymes produced in the joints as a result of this inflammation slowly digest adjacent tissue, causing permanent damage to bone and cartilage.

Joint damage begins earlier in the disease process than many RA patients—and even some doctors—realize. For this reason, it's crucial that treatment be initiated without delay.

Important: Consult a rheumatologist. Especially given all the recent advances, few primary care physicians are up-to-date on rheumatoid arthritis treatments.

DRUG SEQUENCING

The most important recent advance in the treatment of RA is in the way medications are "sequenced." Traditionally, doctors prescribed potent *disease-modifying antirheumatic drugs* (DMARDs) only after *nonsteroidal anti-inflammatory drugs* (NSAIDs) proved ineffective.

New thinking: It's more effective to prescribe DMARDs first. Doing so ensures that the disease is brought under control as quickly as possible.

Ironically, *naproxen* (Naprosyn), *ibuprofen* (Advil) and other NSAIDs don't quite live up to their reputation for mildness.

Some research indicates that NSAID-induced gastrointestinal problems and other serious side effects cause more than 16,000 deaths and 100,000 hospitalizations each year.

Methotrexate (Rheumatrex), *hydroxychloroquine* (Plaquenil) and other DMARDs now appear to be no riskier than NSAIDs, and are more effective.

Bottom line: Virtually every rheumatoid arthritis patient should be taking a DMARD. With early and consistent use of DMARDs, lifetime disability can be cut by up to two-thirds.

COMPLETE PAIN RELIEF

The old approach to treating RA was simply to keep pain levels tolerable. But since pain stems from tissue damage, even mild discomfort means the disease process is continuing.

Better: Treat the disease until pain and stiffness disappear. Speak up if you still feel pain. Don't put up with it…and don't assume that it is normal.

Becoming pain-free may take time—some drugs take as long as six weeks to work. And if one DMARD doesn't work, your doctor may try another…or may try a combination of drugs.

NEW MEDICATIONS

If older, established DMARDs don't work—or if they cause severe side effects—you may be a candidate for one of the new medications.

The US Food and Drug Administration has approved several medications for the treatment of rheumatoid arthritis. *Two that show promise are…*

●*Leflunomide* (**Arava**) slows the rate of cell division, inhibiting the reproduction of joint-damaging inflammatory cells. It's often a good option for people who cannot tolerate methotrexate, which can cause mouth ulcers, liver problems and other side effects.

●*Etanercept* (**Enbrel**) and *infliximab* (**Remicade**) work by blocking *tumor necrosis factor* (TNF), a naturally occurring compound that activates the inflammatory response.

THE ROLE OF EXERCISE

Exercise cannot cure RA, but it can be highly effective at reducing joint pain and improving flexibility. Nearly everyone benefits from a walking program.

Also, to prevent morning stiffness, do gentle stretching before going to bed at night…and before getting out of bed in the morning. Spend extra time stretching any joint that has become "frozen."

Include hand and wrist exercises, since those joints are often affected by RA. One particularly effective hand exercise is the thumb walk.

What to do: Keeping your wrist straight, touch your index finger to your thumb, forming an "O." Straighten and spread your thumb and fingers. Then touch your middle finger to your thumb. Repeat for all fingers.

Choose exercises on the basis of which joints are affected and how well the disease is controlled. Discuss the matter with your rheumatologist.

Don't do any exercise that puts excessive force on an inflamed joint.

Rheumatoid Arthritis/ Heart Attack Link

According to scientific research, women with rheumatoid arthritis have up to three times the normal risk for heart attack.

Theory: Inflammation of the lining of the joints—a characteristic of rheumatoid arthritis—is associated with an increased risk for heart attack. While the reasons are not completely understood, it's likely that the same inflammatory process that leads to rheumatoid arthritis also plays a role in *atherosclerosis* (fatty plaque buildup in the arteries) and heart attack. Although only women were studied, researchers suspect the same association applies to men.

Self-defense: People who have rheumatoid arthritis should be carefully monitored and treated for cardiovascular risk factors, such as high blood pressure, high cholesterol, diabetes and smoking.

Daniel H. Solomon, MD, MPH, associate professor of medicine, Harvard Medical School, Boston. His 20-year study of 114,342 women was published in Circulation.

Ten-Step Program for Chronic Pain Works Very, Very Well

Dharma Singh Khalsa, MD, founding director, Acupuncture Stress Medicine and Chronic Pain Program, University of Arizona College of Medicine, Phoenix. He is also founding president and medical director, Alzheimer's Prevention Foundation, Tucson, and coauthor of The Pain Cure *(Warner Books).*

Approximately 25 million Americans are bedeviled by some form of chronic pain —sciatica, migraine, arthritis, muscle pain, etc. There are effective ways to curb chronic pain, but these *aren't* the ways typically recommended by mainstream physicians.

In addition to surgery and narcotics, mainstream doctors often recommend nonsteroidal anti-inflammatory drugs (NSAIDs) like *ibuprofen* (Motrin) to their patients with chronic pain.

These drugs can be highly effective against acute pain, such as sprains or toothaches. But they're less effective against chronic pain. And—NSAIDs can cause bleeding ulcers and other side effects.

Following are 10 pain-relieving strategies that really work…

●**Eat more fish and poultry.** Doctors often prescribe *fluoxetine* (Prozac) for chronic pain. This prescription antidepressant helps curb pain by boosting levels of the neurotransmitter *serotonin* in the brain. Serotonin blocks synthesis of *substance P,* one of the main chemical messengers involved in chronic pain.

But many people can keep serotonin levels high simply by eating foods that are rich in *tryptophan,* an amino acid that the body converts into serotonin.

Two excellent sources of tryptophan are poultry and fish. If you suffer from chronic pain, try eating three ounces of chicken, turkey, salmon, etc., five days a week.

In addition to blocking substance P, serotonin helps make people less aware of pain by improving mood and regulating disturbed sleep cycles.

●**Eat a banana every day.** Most chronic pain stems from arthritis, muscle pain or another inflammatory condition, which invariably goes hand in hand with muscle spasms. These spasms contribute to chronic pain.

Eat one banana a day—along with a bit of the lining of the peel that you've scraped off with a spoon. Doing so will supply you with lots of magnesium and potassium. Both minerals help control spasms.

●**Get regular exercise.** Exercise triggers the synthesis of the natural painkillers that are known as *endorphins.*

If you're experiencing severe pain, of course, you probably don't feel like doing vigorous exercise. That's fine. Endorphin synthesis can be triggered by any form of activity that pushes the body a bit harder than it's accustomed to.

If you've been sedentary for a long time, something as simple as rotating your arms for a few seconds can work. So can sitting in a chair and raising your legs a few times.

●**Take steps to control psychological stress.** Stress plays a central role in chronic pain. Meditation and other relaxation techniques reduce muscle spasms, limit the release of pain-causing stress hormones and improve breathing. Each of these helps reduce pain intensity.

One study found that pain sufferers who meditated for 10 to 20 minutes a day visited a pain clinic 36% less often than did their non-meditating peers.

What to do: Carve out at least 15 minutes of quiet time each day. If you aren't comfortable meditating, use the time to pray…visualize a tranquil scene…or sit quietly.

●**Avoid harmful fats.** Red meat and cooking oil stimulate production of *arachidonic acid,* a compound that the body converts into hormone-like substances that trigger inflammation. These substances are known as *prostaglandins.*

Chronic pain sufferers should avoid red meat entirely...and use cooking oil sparingly.

●**Take omega-3 fatty acid supplements.** Taking 1,000 to 3,000 milligrams (mg) of fish oil or flaxseed oil each day helps block synthesis of prostaglandins.

In addition to blocking prostaglandin synthesis, a type of omega-3 fatty acid known as *eicosapentaenoic acid* (EPA) improves circulation by making the platelets—cell-like structures that are responsible for blood clotting—less "sticky." This helps keep blood from pooling and causing inflammation and irritation.

Fatty acid supplements are unnecessary for individuals who eat cold-water, dark-flesh fish several times a week. Salmon, tuna, mackerel and sardines all fit the bill.

●**Take a vitamin B-complex supplement.** Chronic pain is often accompanied by fatigue. When you feel more energetic, your pain is more manageable.

To increase your energy, ask your doctor about taking a daily supplement that contains at least 50 mg of B-complex vitamins. Vitamin B helps increase energy levels by facilitating the production of ATP, the high-energy compound found in *mitochondria,* the "power plants" inside cells.

●**Season food with turmeric.** Its primary constituent, *curcumin,* has been shown to be as effective at relieving pain as cortisone or ibuprofen—without any risk of side effects. A pinch or two a day is all you need.

●**Try acupuncture.** There's now solid evidence that acupuncture can be more effective than drug therapy for relieving many types of chronic pain.

Acupuncture that is done by a physician seems to be especially effective. So-called medical acupuncture often involves the application of electrical current to needles inserted into the skin. This variant of traditional acupuncture is called *electroacupuncture.*

For referral to an acupuncturist in your area, contact the American Academy of Medical Acupuncture at 323-937-5514 or *www.medical acupuncture.org.*

●**See a chiropractor or osteopath.** Most physicians rely upon drug therapy and surgery for controlling pain. Chiropractors and osteopaths incorporate physical manipulation into their treatments. For some types of pain, especially back pain, manipulation often works better than drugs or surgery.

Stop Pain Fast with Self-Hypnosis

Bruce N. Eimer, PhD, clinical psychologist and hypnotherapist in private practice, Philadelphia. He is author of *Hypnotize Yourself Out of Pain Now! A Powerful, User-Friendly Program for Anyone Searching for Immediate Pain Relief* (New Harbinger).

As a clinical psychologist, I have specialized for many years in treating people who are suffering from chronic pain.

However, only after a car accident left me in severe, unrelenting pain did I start to fully appreciate the power of hypnosis to pick up where prescription drugs, physical therapy and surgery leave off.

WHY HYPNOSIS?

Hypnosis is an altered state of consciousness. It magnifies your ability to focus and temporarily sharpens your concentration.

All hypnosis is *self*-hypnosis. Even if the altered state is achieved with the help of an expert, you can become hypnotized only if you allow yourself to be.*

The nature of hypnosis makes it helpful for treating chronic pain. It is a state of concentrated attention, which in itself can reduce pain and emotional anguish associated with physical suffering. It also eases tension and curbs insomnia.

*To locate a qualified clinical hypnosis practitioner in your area, contact the American Society of Clinical Hypnosis at 630-980-4740 or *www.asch.net.*

ENTERING THE HYPNOTIC STATE

The first step in hypnosis is called *induction*. In this process, you employ techniques that focus your attention (on the ticking of a metronome or the sound of a voice, for example) and provide suggestions to deepen your relaxation.

Try this two-minute induction method, which many people find effective...

Raise one hand. Concentrate on a single finger, with your eyes open (staring at the finger) or closed (imagining it). Then, let the other fingers fade away from your awareness.

As you continue to concentrate, feel your hand and arm start to grow heavier. Lower your arm slowly, and allow yourself to enter into a comfortable state of relaxation.

By the time your hand comes all the way down and is resting in your lap or on the armrest of your chair, your eyes should be closed and you should feel relaxed. Focus on your breathing. Feel your belly expand with each inhalation and contract as you exhale.

To relax more deeply, close your eyes and imagine you are walking down a set of 20 stairs. Feel the thick, plush carpeting beneath your feet as well as the smooth, polished wood of the handrail.

With each step, allow yourself to fall into a deeper state of relaxation. At the bottom of the stairs, find a door. Open it, and "enter" the place where you feel the most happy, content and pleased (a balmy beach, a peaceful mountain meadow or a sidewalk café in Paris). Imagine this "favorite place" in rich detail, and stay there as long as you want.

To emerge from the hypnotic state, walk back up the stairs, feeling more awake with each step. When you reach the top, you'll feel alert and refreshed.

The more often you repeat the induction, the better you will get at it. Practice at least twice a day, for 10 minutes each time.

USING THE HYPNOTIC STATE

After you have practiced induction daily for three weeks, you should be able to elicit deep relaxation at will and go to your "favorite place" whenever you need a stress break or a respite from pain.

Once you have mastered the induction process, the following techniques can be added. Practice the technique of your choice for 10 minutes daily.

●**Distraction.** Most people naturally cope with pain by focusing their attention elsewhere. For a simple distraction technique, rub the fingers of one hand together. Concentrate on the sensations in your fingers, the texture of the skin and the temperature.

Do this *before* inducing the hypnotic state. This will give your subconscious the suggestion that you can distract yourself the same way whenever you feel discomfort. After the first month, you'll find that even when you are in your normal waking state, you'll be able to divert your attention away from pain more effectively.

●**Dissociation.** This is perhaps the most powerful way to cope with severe pain. Your pain is not gone, but your subconscious mind takes over the task of feeling the pain while your conscious mind is relaxed.

Practice this technique by visualizing your shadow. It moves with you and is attached to your body, but it is not inside your body. While in a hypnotic state, imagine your shadow... then visualize yourself merging with it.

Put the pain in your shadow. Then imagine yourself floating away from the shadow and the pain. The pain is in your shadow, but not in your body.

●**Self-suggestion.** This technique helps to develop attitudes and beliefs that strengthen your ability to cope with pain.

Choose messages that have particular meaning for you, and write them in a journal or on index cards. Repeat one to yourself three times before inducing the hypnotic state.

Some helpful self-suggestions...

●I am in charge.

●I can manage the pain. I can stand this.

●Whenever I feel stressed, I accept the feelings and stay calm.

●I take satisfaction every day in handling my problems better and better.

Unraveling The Mysteries of Fibromyalgia

Timothy McCall, MD, an internist, medical editor of *Yoga Journal,* and author of *Examining Your Doctor: A Patient's Guide to Avoiding Harmful Medical Care* (Citadel Press) and *Yoga as Medicine* (Bantam). *www.drmccall.com.*

Fibromyalgia is a frustrating disease for both doctors and patients alike. Because there is no definitive lab test to diagnose the condition, some physicians aren't sure it even exists. Many patients bounce from doctor to doctor, enduring a series of unrevealing lab tests and unhelpful drugs, until finally someone hits on the diagnosis.

The typical symptoms of fibromyalgia include widespread pain, fatigue and poor sleep. Sufferers often have other conditions, such as irritable bowel syndrome, depression and *sleep apnea,* a condition that temporarily interrupts breathing during sleep. Fibromyalgia is diagnosed by identifying characteristic symptoms as well as "tender points" that typically occur on the hips, shoulders and on either side of the spine. The condition affects seven times more women than men.

Although the cause of fibromyalgia is unknown, studies show that the condition is not "all in your head." Researchers have found, for example, significantly elevated levels of a pain mediator, called *substance P,* in the spinal fluid of fibromyalgia patients, which suggests abnormalities in the way pain sensations are processed within the spinal cord and brain.

Because fibromyalgia is a chronic disease, it responds best to a holistic program of both conventional interventions (including drug therapy), alternative measures (such as acupuncture and massage) and lifestyle changes. *Here are some useful strategies…*

●**Get gentle exercise.** Exercise can help fibromyalgia, but be careful. Too much too soon can exacerbate symptoms. Gentle yoga is a good choice, because it is safe, easy and can be performed at home. Start slowly and gradually build up to 30 minutes daily.

●**Consider trigger point injections.** Doctors can treat pain by injecting a local anesthetic directly into tender points, then stretching the underlying muscles to relieve tension in them. The treatments usually need to be repeated a few times for optimal effect. Since the skill of the doctor doing the injections is key, if you don't feel any relief after a few treatments, try another doctor before giving up on this approach entirely.

●**Try drug therapy.** While over-the-counter pain relievers should be tried first, doctors have found that a weak opiate called *tramadol* (Ultram) brings significant relief to the majority of fibromyalgia patients. Other options include tricyclic antidepressants and muscle relaxants.

●**Deal with psychological stress.** While stress and depression may not cause fibromyalgia, they can fan the flames. In addition to stress-reduction measures (such as yoga, meditation and walking), you may need antidepressants and/or cognitive-behavioral therapy, which identifies and changes negative thought patterns that lead to psychological suffering.

●**Connect with others.** Consider joining a local or online support group. To learn more, contact the Fibromyalgia Network at *www.fm netnews.com* or 800-853-2929. The group publishes a useful newsletter and a list of doctors who have experience in treating this misunderstood condition.

Getting Relief from Mysterious Muscle Pain

Jamison Starbuck, ND, naturopathic physician in family practice and lecturer, University of Montana, both in Missoula. She is past president, American Association of Naturopathic Physicians, and contributing editor of *The Alternative Advisor: The Complete Guide to Natural Therapies and Alternative Treatments* (Time-Life).

Do you have chronic muscle pain, especially in the neck and shoulders and around joints? Are you bothered by poor sleep, daytime fatigue and listlessness? If so, you may be suffering from *fibromyalgia.*

Approximately 3 to 5 million Americans have this mysterious ailment. And 80% are women between 35 and 60 years of age.

Fibromyalgia wasn't recognized as a disease until 1990. The cause of the disorder is still unknown, and many doctors remain unaware of the "diagnostic criteria" used to identify it. These consist of muscle pain on both sides of the body for a minimum of three consecutive months…along with pain in at least 11 of 18 "tender points," including at the knees and elbows, the base of the neck and skull and other areas as well.

Fibromyalgia can be very tricky to diagnose. No blood test is available to confirm the diagnosis. And since it affects muscle (soft tissue) rather than bone, X-rays are not useful. Not surprisingly, many cases go undiagnosed.

If you think you might be suffering from fibromyalgia, it's important to consult a health-care practitioner who is well acquainted with the condition. Look for someone who can recite the diagnostic criteria and who has successfully treated at least a handful of cases. If you need help finding a qualified practitioner, contact the Fibromyalgia Network at 800-853-2929 or *www.fmnetnews.com* for a referral.

Since no single drug alleviates all symptoms of fibromyalgia, medical doctors often use several. If you work with a medical doctor, you may be given prescriptions for a muscle relaxant, a sedative or an antidepressant. These drugs can cause nasty side effects, including nausea, bowel changes, dry mouth and headaches. To control these problems, doctors often prescribe additional medications—which can cause side effects of their own. As you might imagine, this approach to treatment isn't always successful.

Many cases of fibromyalgia can be controlled simply by eliminating meat, dairy products, refined sugar, hydrogenated fats and alcohol. These foods aggravate symptoms by robbing the body of inflammation-fighting essential fatty acids.

If you have fibromyalgia, consider switching to a diet rich in fish, seeds, soy and grains. If one month of this semi-vegetarian diet causes symptoms to abate, you might want to make the dietary change permanent.

In my practice, I've noticed a strong correlation between fibromyalgia and the health of the patient's adrenal glands. In simple cases, fibromyalgia pain and lethargy can be eliminated by boosting adrenal function with Siberian ginseng (*Eleutherococcus senticosus*). Take one teaspoon twice daily of a 1:1 alcohol extract of dried herb—available in health food stores. This dosage is safe for most people, but check with your doctor first.

Another remedy that often helps alleviate trigger point tenderness is a combination of magnesium and malic acid (malate). This one-pill combo—available at health food stores and some drugstores—improves the health of muscle tissue. It's safe for most people—but, again, check with your doctor.

Although fibromyalgia is a physical ailment, many sufferers make matters worse by "over-doing" things. I give patients this advice—learn to leave some projects unfinished, and use the time you free up to do something nice for yourself. You can always finish the project later.

More from Jamison Starbuck…

Get Pain Relief from Natural Remedies

For many people, reaching for pain relievers is as instinctual as eating. Hungry? Go to the refrigerator and grab a bite. In pain? Swallow a pill. But pain pills have their costs.

Acetaminophen (Tylenol, Panadol, etc.) can cause liver damage. Nonsteroidal anti-inflammatory drugs (NSAIDs), such as *naproxen* (Aleve) and *ibuprofen* (Advil, Motrin, etc.), can cause gastrointestinal bleeding and impaired kidney function. They can also inhibit cartilage repair in the knees, hips and other joints.

In addition to being addictive, Lortab, Percocet and other narcotic painkillers can cause drowsiness and clouded thinking. The muscle relaxant *cyclobenzaprine* (Flexeril) has been linked with dizziness, rash, arrhythmia and even convulsions.

In certain cases, the risks posed by these adverse reactions are offset by clear benefits. When pain is especially severe, nothing can replace the merciful relief of medication. But for run-of-the-mill discomfort—tension headache, ankle sprain, joint stiffness, back pain and postsurgical pain—it's often better to skip drugs and opt instead for natural treatments.

Ice may seem old-fashioned, but it remains one of the best natural painkillers available. It's great for back pain, aching, swollen joints and headache. It reduces congestion, improves blood flow and promotes healing. A bag of frozen peas works as well as an ice pack, and it can be refrozen and reused many times. Usually a 10-minute application, two or three times each hour, is effective.

If headaches are your problem, drinking lots of water is often all that's needed. In particular, tension headaches and "toxic" headaches from drinking too much alcohol or consuming too much caffeine respond well to "hydrotherapy." Have eight ounces of water every 10 minutes for one hour. Make sure a bathroom is nearby before starting this remedy!

For acute sprains, strains and scrapes, bruises and other minor trauma, nothing beats *arnica*. This homeopathic remedy—available in health food stores and many drugstores—reduces bruising and pain. Unless you are accident-prone, a single vial costing less than $10 should last several years. I recommend arnica in 30C potency—typically two homeopathic pellets, one to three times daily, for up to seven days.

For tendinitis and sciatica—and to speed recovery from surgery—I often recommend *bromelain*. This natural anti-inflammatory agent —an enzyme derived from pineapple—stimulates the breakdown of inflammatory compounds at the injury site. Bromelain is available in capsules at health food stores and pharmacies. The typical dosage is 250 milligrams (mg) one to four times daily. However, bromelain is off-limits for people with high blood pressure.

Boswellia serrata (frankincense) has a long tradition as an arthritis treatment in India and the Middle East. Though human studies on this herb are inadequate, the clinical experience of many practitioners—myself included—has been extremely promising. I routinely recommend Boswellia as a substitute for NSAIDs in cases involving back pain, arthritis, inflammatory joint pain and acute muscle and bone injuries. Even

with long-term use, Boswellia does not seem to cause the gastrointestinal bleeding and pain that can be a problem with NSAID use.

Boswellia can be found in health food stores. Look for Boswellia alone, or combined with ginger and turmeric, two additional herbal pain relievers that are easy on the stomach. The typical dose is 300 mg of Boswellia, three times a day, as needed for pain.

Seven Myths About Multiple Sclerosis

David H. Mattson, MD, PhD, professor of neurology and director, Neuroimmunology/Multiple Sclerosis Center, Indiana University School of Medicine, Indianapolis. Dr. Mattson has done extensive research on the use of beta-interferon and other medications for treating and controlling multiple sclerosis.

Many people equate *multiple sclerosis* (MS) with profound disability and early death. Not true.

Reality: Although MS can be debilitating in some cases, new treatment approaches allow most sufferers to live relatively normal lives.

MS is an autoimmune disease that affects about 400,000 Americans. In people with MS, antibodies and white blood cells damage the myelin sheath that surrounds nerves in the brain and spinal cord.

Result: Scarring (*sclerosis*) that damages multiple areas on nerves and slows or blocks normal nerve-signal transmission, causing varying degrees of physical disability.

Approximately three out of four MS sufferers never need a wheelchair. Most patients are able to continue working, exercising, enjoying outings with their families, etc. MS may slow them down, but it rarely curtails their ability to live full lives. Almost all have normal life spans.

Other misconceptions…

Misconception #1: **MS is easy to diagnose.**

Reality: MS can be difficult to diagnose because symptoms vary from person to person, depending on the exact location of the nerve damage. Symptoms also tend to wax and wane over a period of months—or even years—and patients can have normal neurological examinations in between early attacks.

Common early symptoms include blurred or double vision, weakness in a leg or hand as well as numbness, tingling—even burning or itching in the extremities, trunk or face. Fatigue, depression, tremor, constipation, dizziness and difficulty reaching orgasm also occur in some MS sufferers. That's why MS can easily be confused with other disorders, such as lupus, arthritis of the neck and Lyme disease, which produce similar symptoms.

If MS is suspected: After a comprehensive clinical exam, your doctor will most likely have you undergo a *magnetic resonance imaging* (MRI) scan…a spinal tap to check for antibody markers…and a series of electrical-impulse tests that measure how fast your nerves are conducting visual, auditory and sensory signals to your brain.

Misconception #2: MS is always caused by hereditary factors.

Reality: Viral or bacterial infections may trigger attacks of MS in someone who may have a genetic susceptibility. Symptom flare-ups have also been linked to flu and other infectious illnesses, such as bladder infections or nonspecific respiratory viruses. The reason? People with MS have overactive immune systems, which not only attack foreign bodies but can attack "good" brain tissue as well.

While it is true that heredity is probably a risk factor for MS (if you have a first-degree relative who has it, your chances of getting it are 20 to 40 times greater), scientists have not yet been able to determine the exact causes of the disease.

Misconception #3: All MS sufferers experience the same frequency and severity of symptoms.

Reality: The degree of disability varies widely from person to person. Patients with *benign* MS—about 10% of cases—have only mild symptoms that don't get worse and don't lead to long-term disability.

About 80% of MS sufferers have a form of the disease called *relapsing-remitting*. They have symptom flare-ups every one to three years, followed by variable periods of having no outward symptoms. After about 10 years, half of the patients in this group get progressively worse.

Only about 10% of MS patients—those with a type known as *primary progressive*—invariably experience a steady worsening of symptoms from the very beginning.

Misconception #4: MS cannot be diagnosed until it is at an advanced stage.

Reality: Doctors are now starting to diagnose and treat patients who have had just *one* attack of MS symptoms (for example, vision, strength or balance disturbances), which typically last more than one day and are followed by recovery in two to four weeks.

Patients who have a relapsing form of MS should start a drug regimen as soon as possible, when the medication is most likely to curb the disease's progression.

Misconception #5: There are no effective treatments for MS.

Reality: Drugs don't cure MS, but they do slow the progression of the disease and ease or eliminate symptoms. *Common treatments…*

• **Beta-interferons.** Given by injection once a week, three times a week or every other day, beta-interferons can slow the progression of MS by 35%. Side effects include flulike symptoms.

• ***Glatiramer*** **(Copaxone).** A synthetic peptide given by daily injections, glatiramer is as effective as beta-interferons but has none of the flulike side effects, although you might experience chest tightness or anxiety. The drug is believed to block immune-system attacks on nerve myelin.

• **Corticosteroids.** Taken orally or by injection, corticosteroids reduce brain inflammation during MS attacks and help shorten attacks. These drugs can cause side effects, such as fluid retention and increased appetite.

• **Muscle relaxants.** Taken several times a day, muscle relaxants, such as *tizanidine* (Zanaflex) and *baclofen* (Lioresal), are frequently used to control muscle spasms. Side effects include sedation and dizziness, but most people tolerate these drugs well.

Misconception #6: MS relapse cannot be predicted.

Reality: Unfortunately, there is no current way to accurately predict an MS relapse. But that may change in the future. According to a study published in *The New England Journal of Medicine,* two simple blood tests can detect antibodies that may help determine if MS sufferers are likely to suffer a relapse.

These tests may also help confirm a diagnosis and help predict the future severity of the disease. The results of such tests could enable doctors to determine which patients could forgo drug therapy—and the related side effects.

***Misconception #7:* People who have MS shouldn't exercise.**

Reality: Exercise helps to boost muscle strength and energy. Studies show that MS patients who engage in regular exercise experience less fatigue than those who are sedentary.

Determine how much exercise it takes before you start to experience fatigue, then cut back. If you normally get tired after jogging two miles, for example, limit your runs to a mile and a half.

Helpful: Swimming is ideal for people who have MS. Using different strokes works all the major muscle groups, and submersion in water helps prevent overheating, which can cause extreme fatigue and muscle weakness in some MS sufferers.

Surprising Secret to Stopping Back Pain

Arthur H. White, MD, former president, North American Spine Society, and retired orthopedic spine surgeon, Walnut Creek, CA. He is coauthor of *The Posture Prescription* (Three Rivers).

The word "posture" has negative connotations for many people who were bullied into standing up straight as children. But good posture can help you to avoid, reduce—or even eliminate—most types of back pain. An exercise program that focuses on posture can help you forgo powerful painkilling drugs or surgery—the standard treatments recommended by most doctors.

Fortunately, the type of posture I recommend is *not* the straight-as-an-arrow position most of our parents nagged us about.

MECHANICS OF THE SPINE

When we stand, sit and move properly, the bones and disks maintain their optimum alignment and healthy function. If we add physical stress, such as repeated bending, lifting and sitting, to any part of the back, then the disks can tear, bulge and press on a nerve—or even rupture. When disks are damaged, large muscles of the back go into spasm to protect the spine, and body tissue may become inflamed and painful.

PROPER SPINE ALIGNMENT

Three separate exercises will help you attain proper posture. Repeat these exercises 10 times each, twice a day.

Important: Be patient. Although proper posture will feel awkward at first, these positions will seem comfortable and natural after about three weeks of practice.

- **Dorsal glide.** Sit in a chair with your back supported. Thrust your head forward without moving your back or shoulders. Feel the strain in your neck. Pull your head back, centered between your shoulders. Then squeeze your shoulder blades to bring your shoulders upright.

Most people carry their heads forward, a position that contributes to neck pain and headaches. Your head should always be centered over the body with your chin parallel to the floor.

- **Shoulder squeeze.** Stand with your feet shoulder-width apart and your knees slightly bent. Clasp your hands together behind your back at about the level of your hips.

  Without moving your lower back, lift your hands and arms to straighten your shoulders and squeeze your shoulder blades together.

- **Straight stick.** Grasp a yardstick or a three-foot dowel, pole or broom handle with both hands and hold it behind you at the level of your waist. Straighten your back so that your head, upper back and lower back are all touching the stick.

To straighten your lower back, tilt your pelvis forward by "tucking in" your buttocks. Then hold that position for about 30 seconds.

Better: Walk around for a few minutes while holding the stick behind your back to feel what it is like to move with a straight back.

PUTTING IT TOGETHER

•**Standing straight.** Stand with your feet a few inches apart, toes forward. Bend your knees slightly. Balance your weight evenly on both feet, without too much weight on either the toes or the heels. Don't shift your weight from one leg to the other.

Make your lower back straight by tilting your pelvis forward. Relax your shoulders, then squeeze your shoulder blades together.

Finally, center your head over your body. Ideally, you should maintain this position whenever you are standing.

When you sit, the position of your lower back, upper back and head needs to be straight. Do not lean against the back of the chair. If you do, support your lower back with a cushion.

Smart idea: Watch yourself as you walk by mirrors, store windows or any other reflective surface to "catch" yourself if you start to slump. If you regularly sit for long periods, make sure the front of the chair seat is tilted upward so your knees are above your hips. As an alternative, rest your feet on a phone book or footstool. When standing for long periods, place one foot on a footstool.

MOVING PROPERLY

Your back compensates for weaknesses elsewhere. For example, if you lift a box that is too heavy for your arms, you are likely to lift with your back. Although back muscles are large and strong, using them improperly can cause strains, sprains and disk injury.

The following exercises will help you to develop the strength and flexibility you need to get through the day without injuring your back.

As these movements become more comfortable, integrate them into your daily life.

Example: Squat while pulling weeds in the garden or do the leg stretch while talking on the telephone.

•**The squat.** The best overall exercise is the squat because it allows a total stretch of your ankles, knees and hips, as well as your Achilles tendon and calf muscles. Just getting up from a squat will strengthen and firm up your thighs. This allows you to stand for extended periods without putting stress on your back.

With your feet apart, squat all the way down. Keep your feet flat on the floor, and bring your buttocks as close to your heels as you can. Keep your weight back on your heels.

Once you are in this position, straighten your back. Use the straight stick, if necessary.

If you cannot get all the way down, hold on to a flat, stationary surface, such as a desk or kitchen counter, and lower yourself as far as you can go. Hold this squat for at least 30 seconds, then raise yourself up using just your thigh muscles.

Perform the half-squat 20 to 30 times a day. When you can do 30, switch to full squats. Then do one to two full squats five to 10 times a day. You can incorporate these into your daily activities, such as getting something out of a low cabinet.

Caution: Do *not* perform the full squat if you have arthritis or total knee or hip replacement. Also, do not perform this exercise with dumbbells or barbells. The additional weight can damage the knees.

•**Leg stretch.** While in proper standing posture, position yourself in front of a table or other flat, stationary surface. Put one leg out straight and rest your left heel on the table. Hold on to the wall or other object for balance, if necessary. Hold for at least 30 seconds, then repeat with the other leg.

If this exercise is too difficult, start with a lower surface, such as a chair or a stair step. If

Exercise illustrations by Shawn Banner.

this exercise feels too easy, you can gain an extra stretch by leaning your upper body toward your raised leg, keeping your back straight.

Perform the leg stretch 10 to 20 times a day. You can do it while reading, watching TV or even talking on the phone.

You Can Beat Chronic Back Pain

Art Brownstein, MD, clinical instructor of medicine, University of Hawaii, Mano, and medical director, Princeville Medical Clinic, Princeville. He is author of Healing Back Pain Naturally *(Harbor Press).*

I suffered from debilitating back pain for more than 20 years, starting in the early 1970s. Surgery didn't help. The pain got so bad I became hooked on painkillers...and plunged into a deep depression.

Out of desperation, I spent five years studying with healers in the US and the Far East, exploring alternatives to conventional medical treatment for back pain. *What I learned...*

●**Surgery is rarely the answer.** It is appropriate in certain cases, such as when there's a cyst on the spine or a congenital spine abnormality. But for most back problems, surgery only weakens the spine.

●**Back pain originates in the muscles.** Both doctors and patients often think of back pain as a skeletal problem. In fact, the spine's curvature, alignment and movement are all governed by the surrounding back muscles.

Tight muscles and muscle spasms in the back squeeze the vertebrae. This compresses the disks between the vertebrae, and an X ray of the back shows an apparent disk problem. The real source of the trouble, however, is the muscles.

One major contributor to back pain is sitting. Sitting causes the back muscles to shorten, stiffen and grow weaker. That leaves them vulnerable to injury.

●**Psychological stress plays a key role.** My first serious episode of back pain occurred during medical school, which is a notoriously stressful environment.

In the four years leading up to my surgery, I had lost four family members...and my wife was dying of cancer.

At the time, I didn't connect any of these stressors with my back pain. But I learned that the brain is "hardwired" to the back muscles, and that psychological stress inevitably causes these muscles to contract.

This can throw the back out of alignment. It can also constrict blood vessels, choking off the blood supply to the back.

The holistic approach I learned during those five years worked wonders. I now surf, teach yoga and run a busy medical practice—all without pain.

Here are the strategies you can use to beat back pain...

STRETCHING

Daily stretching decompresses the spine, improving its flexibility and boosting blood flow to the back muscles.

Stretching also helps reverse muscle atrophy caused by a sedentary lifestyle. *Some simple, safe stretches to try...*

●**Gluteal squeezes.** Lie on your back with your knees bent and your feet flat on the bed or floor. Squeeze the muscles in your buttocks as tightly as you can, then slowly relax.

●**Knee raises.** Lie on your back with your legs either bent or straight. Then slowly raise your right knee to your chest. Place your hands on your right shin, and gently pull your leg closer to your chest.

Notice the expansion of your chest and abdomen and the stretching in your hip, knee and lower spine. Lower your right knee and repeat with your left knee.

●**Cat/horse stretch.** Get on your hands and knees, keeping your weight distributed equally from front to back and side to side. Slowly arch your spine like a cat. Lower your head, and relax the muscles in your neck and shoulders.

Hold this position for several breaths, feeling your back muscles stretch. Then slowly release the arch and let your back droop like an old horse's. Raise your head and look up, extending your buttocks upward and feeling the stretch in your neck, upper back and spine.

Caution: Don't force yourself into any position that is painful. Breathe smoothly and slowly throughout each stretch.

The best overall stretching program for the back is yoga. Unfortunately, yoga classes offered by health clubs are often too vigorous for people with back trouble.

Before signing up, make sure the instructor has experience working with back patients.

EXERCISE

Once you've been doing daily stretches for a month or two, add a program of walking, swimming or another gentle form of exercise to further strengthen your back muscles.

Important: Pay attention to how your back feels as you move.

Caution: If you ride a bicycle, avoid the bent-over position. It can exacerbate back pain.

STRESS REDUCTION

Meditation and other relaxation techniques —practiced for 20 minutes or so each day— are very effective at alleviating stress.

Easy relaxation technique: Sit comfortably with your eyes closed. Notice your back moving slightly with each breath. Also notice the gentle pulling on your spine that occurs with each breath.

As you relax, visualize your back as strong, healthy and flexible. See yourself bending and moving with grace and vigor.

Leisure activity—play—is perhaps the most effective way to alleviate the stress that can cause back pain. Spend time on your hobbies. Listen to music. Pursue your favorite sport— but be sure to protect your back.

Crucial: Avoid the win-at-all-costs mentality. Learn to play for the joy of the game.

UNDERSTANDING PAIN

Like me, many of my patients have found it helpful to have an "internal dialogue" with their back pain.

What to do: Close your eyes. Imagine that your pain has taken the form of an animal, cartoon character or anything else that occurs to you. *Ask your pain...*

- **Why are you here?**
- **Why do you hurt so much?**
- **How can I get rid of you?**

To conclude the dialogue, express your gratitude and slowly open your eyes. Repeat this process once or twice a day.

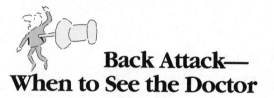

Back Attack— When to See the Doctor

Carol Hartigan, MD, rehabilitation expert, New England Baptist Hospital, Boston.

If you are suffering from a "back attack," you should see a physician if one or more of these conditions applies...

- **The back pain is a result of significant trauma,** such as from a bad fall.
- **Fever is present.**
- **Legs or feet are weak, numb or tingly.**
- **You have a personal history of cancer.**
- **You are over age 50.**
- **It doesn't improve after four weeks.**

If you don't meet any of these conditions, chances are that a doctor won't do much for you. Time often is the only effective treatment for back pain. Some people sing the praises of massage or other therapy—but they most likely would have gotten better on their own. Treated or not, a back problem usually resolves within six weeks.

I advise against bed rest, since being immobile can aggravate inflammation. Exercise acts as a natural anti-inflammatory. I recommend starting with mild aerobic exercise, such as walking or swimming, as soon as possible—but no tennis or other high-impact, variable activity.

If you are able to take *ibuprofen* (Advil or Motrin), it can reduce pain and inflammation.

Ice the area with a bag of frozen vegetables or a body-conforming ice pack. Do this for 15 minutes every few hours for the first 24 hours to reduce inflammation. After several days, applying heat before activity may help.

How to Manage Back Pain

Michael S. Sinel, MD, assistant clinical professor of medicine, University of California, Los Angeles Medical Center, and spine specialist in private practice, Beverly Hills. He is coauthor of *Win the Battle Against Back Pain: An Integrated Mind-Body Approach* (Dell).

Back pain is often blamed on a herniated disk or another anatomical problem. Yet about 85% of all cases stem from non-anatomical causes—psychological stress, depression, anxiety or anger...or simply being in poor physical condition.

Consequently, the remedy for back pain usually isn't bed rest or surgery. It's improving your emotional and physical conditioning. *Here's how to do it...*

•**Start a diary.** Just days after experiencing physical pain or emotions, it's hard to remember them accurately. Keeping a *pain–activity–mood–medication* (PAMM) diary helps.

Every waking hour, rate your pain from 0 (no pain) to 10 (worst pain imaginable). Also rate your moods from 0 (feeling great) to 10 (severe emotional distress). Simultaneously, record any medicine you take and any activity—whether it's "fighting with spouse" or "can't sleep." Also keep track of your exercise routine.

Periodically review this diary to help identify what situations and reactions lead to pain ...and act to avoid them.

•**Evaluate your personality.** Certain traits are linked to psychological stress—and to back pain. These personality traits often include extreme self-discipline...strong drive to succeed ...perfectionist and compulsive tendencies... and harsh self-criticism.

If you think that you have any of these traits, strive to temper them.

•**Recognize and reprogram negative thoughts.** People under psychological stress often give in to irrational negative thoughts. These produce depression, anxiety and fear— as well as back pain.

In stressful situations, identify negative thoughts like "I'll never get better at this job," and practice changing them to coping thoughts —"I'm doing better than a week ago."

The same goes for thoughts about back pain. Change "I'll never lose this pain" to "The pain isn't so bad anymore."

•**Talk back to your brain.** Tell it that you're not going to take the pain anymore. Put up "pain gates"—defenses that shut out pain.

Examples: Distract yourself with a hobby or call a friend.

•**Feel the anger.** Hit a pillow or yell in a room by yourself. By keeping difficult emotions like anger inside, you can cause muscle tension that leads to back pain.

•**Learn a relaxation technique.** Relaxation in any form can offer stress relief. But formal relaxation techniques are more effective for handling stressful situations. They decrease heart and breathing rates, blood pressure and muscle tension.

Learn deep breathing...progressive relaxation...meditation...or imagery (visualizing peaceful situations or enjoyable activities).

Buy a book or audiotape to master one of these techniques. Then use the technique in times of stress to fend off back pain.

•**Talk to a psychotherapist.** Counseling fosters positive attitudes and provides an outlet that helps prevent back pain.

•**Change your job.** Stress at work and job dissatisfaction can trigger back pain. Find a less stressful, more rewarding job...or improve the one you have. Alter your hours or duties.

•**Find purpose.** Don't let pain be the center of your life. The more purpose you have in life—the more things you care about—the less pain you'll have.

•**Set concrete goals.** Build short-term, achievable goals into every area of life. Daily success eases stress and builds good feelings that help prevent back pain.

Examples: Tell yourself you'll make 10 sales today...or do something nice for your spouse and kids.

•**Improve fitness.** Regular low-impact aerobic exercise is vital. Just 30 minutes every other day of brisk walking, swimming, water aerobics or recumbent stationary bicycling (easier on the back than upright bicycling) reduces levels of stress hormones and triggers the release of pain-relieving endorphins.

Combined with weight training, aerobic exercise also strengthens muscles that support the back. If you have severe back pain, keep away from high-impact sports, like football and basketball, as well as such sports as racquetball or golf that require sudden pivoting or twisting.

●**Do back exercises.** An orthopedist, physiatrist (physician who specializes in the diagnosis and nonsurgical treatment of musculoskeletal disorders) or physical therapist can suggest exercises to strengthen back and abdominal muscles—which help support the spine.

Also ask the doctor or physical therapist for slow stretching exercises to improve flexibility.

●**Maintain proper weight.** Being overweight increases stress on every body structure, including the back.

A protruding stomach, in particular, burdens the lower back, making it more susceptible to injury and pain.

●**Lift things properly.** We've all heard about the proper way to lift a heavy object. Bend at the knees, not at the waist...hold the object close and push straight up with your legs so that they support most of the weight ...keep your spine straight as you lift...and never twist while lifting. If you have to turn in another direction, turn your entire body.

●**Sit down and stand up correctly.** When you stand, do a "pelvic tilt." With palms on the small of your back, slightly push your lower back inward and tilt your pelvis forward as you gradually extend your back upward.

To sit, move your tailbone as far back as possible above the chair, with your upper body tilting forward. Bring your upper body upright as you sit down.

●**Change position frequently.** Don't stand or sit in one position for long periods. If you have to stand still, lean against something. If you can, rest one foot on a stool or rail. Wear shoes with cushioned soles and low heels.

Long periods of sitting tax the lower back. Driving can be especially troublesome because road vibrations are transmitted to the spine. On extended car trips, stop at least once an hour to stretch and walk around.

●**Use a good chair.** It should place your back in the proper position—maintaining the curve in your spine. If you can't get such a chair, roll up a towel and place it against the small of your back. Prop your feet on a footstool or large book.

●**Sleep on your side,** with hips and knees bent toward your body—as in the fetal position. Place a small pillow between your knees. If you must lie on your back, place pillows under your knees.

Should You See A Chiropractor?

Rand Swenson, MD, DC, PhD, associate professor of neurology and anatomy, Dartmouth Medical School, Hanover, NH. He maintains a clinical practice in neurology at Dartmouth-Hitchcock Medical Center, Lebanon and Monadnock Community Hospital, Peterborough, both in New Hampshire.

A scientific study shows that spinal manipulation is about as effective as pain pills or exercise in treating low back pain. So is chiropractic treatment really worthwhile?

Absolutely, according to Rand Swenson, MD, DC, PhD, a distinguished medical physician who is also trained in chiropractic.

For people who suffer side effects from painkillers, such as stomach irritation, or for those whose back pain does not improve from exercise alone, chiropractic treatment can offer long-lasting relief.

Here's what you should know...

WHAT IS CHIROPRACTIC?

With chiropractic treatment, the relationship between the structure of the spine and the function of the nervous system is key to maintaining or restoring health.

During each five- to 20-minute session, chiropractors manipulate the spine in specific directions with varying degrees of force. It's believed that these manipulations, also known as *spinal adjustment,* restore the normal range of motion in spinal joints...improve posture...

and relax back muscles. They may activate sensory fibers in spine tissues that promote short-term (days to weeks) pain suppression.

Long-term benefits haven't been clearly established, but studies suggest that a series of five or more chiropractic treatments can provide pain relief for a year or more.

Orthopedists, neurologists and neurosurgeons often refer patients to chiropractors for nonspecific back pain, which arises from the muscles, ligaments and joints of the spine and doesn't require medical intervention, such as surgery.

Most private insurance plans, Medicare and worker's compensation will pay to cover chiropractic care.

Solid evidence supports the use of chiropractic for several conditions, including…

LOW BACK PAIN

Dozens of scientific studies show that chiropractic treatment can relieve back pain that has lasted less than four weeks. It also appears to be helpful for chronic back pain, although this hasn't been as well studied.

A large study of more than 700 patients published in the *British Medical Journal* found that chiropractic was more effective for nonspecific low back pain than standard medical treatments—bed rest, anti-inflammatory medications and physical therapy. Patients in the study had strong initial improvements, but the benefits were even more pronounced a year later.

Important: Chiropractic for low back pain is most effective when combined with a vigorous rehabilitation program that includes stretching and strengthening exercises. Acupuncture and other pain-relieving procedures can also be used in conjunction with chiropractic.

NECK PAIN

A Dutch study of 183 patients with neck (cervical spine) pain lasting at least two weeks showed greater improvements from spinal manipulation than from physical therapy or painkillers. Patients treated with *both* manipulation and physical therapy had the most improvement.

Caution: Chiropractic neck manipulation may trigger stroke in people with undetected abnormalities in neck blood vessels. The risk is estimated at one in 1 million. Do *not* seek chiropractic treatment if you suffer any neurological symptoms, such as vision loss, double vision, loss of sensation or paralysis.

HEADACHE

Tension headaches caused by cervical spine abnormalities (*cervicogenic headaches*) respond particularly well to chiropractic treatment. These headaches typically cause pain in the upper neck at the base of the skull.

Migraines and other headaches can also be helped by chiropractic treatment, although usually to a lesser degree.

Researchers in Denmark recently reported that up to 70% of patients with cervicogenic headaches had significant improvement—in headache frequency as well as pain—after undergoing chiropractic manipulation.

Some studies even suggest that chiropractic works as well as *amitriptyline* (Elavil), an antidepressant drug used for tension headaches. The benefits from a single chiropractic treatment can last a month or more. In comparison, drugs stop helping as soon as the medication is discontinued.

WHAT TO EXPECT

Each year, up to 10% of Americans see chiropractors. Most get eight to 14 treatments (one to three times weekly), with occasional "tune-ups" as needed. Five visits should be enough for a recent flare-up of back or neck pain. Conditions that have lasted months or years might require up to 15 treatments.

Chiropractic has a good safety record. It can be normal to feel sore after treatments. The soreness usually disappears within a day or two.

A chiropractor should take a complete health history before the initial adjustment. He/she will perform reflex and range-of-motion tests to rule out potentially serious problems, such as *sciatica* (irritation of or damage to the spinal sciatic nerve). These are the same tests that you'd get from a neurologist or orthopedist. And X-rays may be recommended to check for spinal stability. Tell your chiropractor if you suffer from osteoporosis.

Important: Your chiropractor should estimate the number of treatments you're likely to need. Don't settle for a vague answer. Ask him what progress you can expect during the treatment period—less pain, fewer headaches, etc. See your physician if you don't achieve this goal or your problem gets worse.

WHEN TO AVOID CHIROPRACTIC

Anecdotal evidence suggests that chiropractic may be helpful for irritable bowel syndrome and some types of menstrual pain. However, the evidence for these uses is very weak.

Chiropractic is also reputed to help with asthma, but again, the research isn't very solid. Two well-designed studies failed to find any real benefits in lung function following chiropractic care.

Chiropractic is not appropriate as the main form of treatment for diabetes, cancer, Parkinson's disease or other systemic diseases.

Patients who suffer from back pain that is accompanied by weakness in the leg, pain radiating down the leg, fever and/or loss of bladder or bowel control should consult a medical doctor before considering chiropractic treatment. These symptoms may indicate a serious medical problem, such as a tumor, abscess or fracture of the vertebrae.

In addition, spinal manipulation should be avoided by anyone with...

•**Spinal cancer.** The manipulation can break or fracture bones that are already weakened by the cancer.

•**Spinal infection.** Bacterial infections can weaken the spine and increase the risk for fracture during chiropractic manipulation.

•**Severe rheumatoid arthritis.** Manipulation can increase pain and inflammation.

•**Severe sciatica.** Manipulation could worsen sciatica and other problems with spinal nerves.

•**Large disk herniation.** There is a small risk that patients will get worse after some types of manipulation.

9

Heart Disease & Stroke

Heart Attack Prevention Secrets: Low-Tech Strategies Are Effective

Even with all the modern advances in cardiology, natural strategies continue to be useful tools for preventing heart attack—and often they are the only ones needed. You may find that a few simple lifestyle changes make a real difference. *Some healthful suggestions...*

LOWERING CHOLESTEROL

Atorvastatin (Lipitor) and other cholesterol-lowering "statin" drugs can be highly effective at lowering elevated cholesterol levels.

But statins can cause nausea, muscle aches, insomnia and other side effects. For this reason, it's a good idea to explore dietary strategies for keeping cholesterol levels down.

Some of the cholesterol that is found in our bodies comes from eating eggs, whole milk, meat and other animal food sources. But most is produced by the body itself.

What determines how much cholesterol your body makes? Dietary fat is key. The more fat you consume—particularly saturated fat—the more cholesterol your body makes.

CUTTING OUT THE FAT

The average American gets 40% of his/her calories in the form of fat. The American Heart Association recommends cutting this back to 30%. But for most people, that's still too high to reduce cholesterol.

To have a significant impact on cholesterol levels, you must get no more than 20% of your total calories from fat. *To do this, take steps to eliminate fatty foods from your diet...*

- **Oil-based salad dressings.** Switch to a mixture of mustard and balsamic vinegar, rice vinegar or wine vinegar.

David Heber, MD, PhD, founding director, Center for Human Nutrition, University of California, Los Angeles, School of Medicine. He is author of *Natural Remedies for a Healthy Heart* (Avery).

265

●**Butter, margarine and mayonnaise.** Use broth or wine for sautéing. Use cooking spray to keep food from sticking to pans.

Whenever possible, eat bread while it's still warm. That way, it's moist even without a fatty spread. Spread jam or roasted garlic on your toast instead of butter.

●**Red meat.** Substitute white-meat chicken or turkey...or give up meat altogether. Recent studies show that replacing animal proteins with tofu, tempeh and other soy foods can reduce cholesterol levels by up to 8%. That translates into a 16% reduction in heart attack risk.

●**Farm-raised fatty fish,** including catfish and trout. Substitute low-fat fish, such as snapper, halibut, shellfish or tuna packed in water.

●**Whole or low-fat milk and cheese.** Choose skim milk. While reduced-fat cheeses are available, it's better to avoid even these varieties. They often contain up to 70% of the fat found in ordinary cheese.

●**Egg noodles.** Use rice or pasta instead.

●**Baked goods.** Commercially baked cookies, pies and crackers tend to be high in fat. Better to stick with homemade baked goods made with applesauce instead of oil. Applesauce can be substituted cup for cup for oil.

THE IMPORTANCE OF FIBER

The undigestible part of fruits and vegetables, fiber helps lower cholesterol levels by promoting excretion of cholesterol-rich bile acids. You should be getting 25 to 35 grams (g) of dietary fiber each day. That's 15 g to 25 g more than the average American gets.

To boost your fiber intake...

●**Have a bowl of oatmeal or another high-fiber cereal** as part of each breakfast. Look for cereals that contain at least 8 g of fiber per bowl.

●**Consume five to 11 servings of fruits and vegetables a day.** Good choices are brussels sprouts, broccoli, carrots, tomatoes, bananas, oranges and berries.

SUPPLEMENTS

Cholesterol forms artery-obstructing deposits in the coronary arteries only if it has been oxidized. Antioxidant nutrients such as vitamins C and E interrupt the oxidation process.

It's hard to get enough antioxidants from diet alone. For this reason, it's a good idea to take 400 international units (IU) of vitamin E each day, plus 500 milligrams (mg) of vitamin C. However, check with your doctor first—more than 200 IU of vitamin E may be dangerous.

Folic acid serves primarily to lower levels of *homocysteine,* an amino acid now thought to be a risk factor for heart disease. Consider taking 400 micrograms (mcg) of folic acid in supplement form each day.

Garlic seems to cut cholesterol and lower blood pressure, too. Consider taking two to four 500-mg garlic capsules each day.

If your total cholesterol remains above 240 after 12 weeks of starting this natural heart-health plan, you may need to take a statin. Ask your doctor for more information.

STRESS REDUCTION

Stress spurs the release of adrenaline-like chemicals that raise blood pressure and make the heart beat faster. This extra workload raises the risk for heart attack, even if your cholesterol level is low. That's why stress reduction is a crucial part of any heart-health program. *Here are some suggestions...*

●**Avoid stressful situations.** Keep a diary of the stressors in your life. Think about how you could change each situation—or your response—to ease the wear on your cardiovascular system.

Example: To avoid heavy traffic, you might try leaving for work earlier.

●**Find ways to refresh yourself between stressful episodes.** Gardening, reading, yoga or even something as simple as stopping briefly to breathe deeply when tension builds can be very effective.

In addition to stress relief, regular workouts bring marked reductions in cholesterol levels and blood pressure. They promote weight loss, too, helping to reduce the heart's workload even more.

Exercise needn't be strenuous. One brisk 30-minute walk per day is enough to reap most of the benefits. Check with your doctor before starting an exercise program.

#1 Heart Attack Trigger

Many heart attacks are triggered by a fatty meal. Researchers have found that heart attacks are most likely to occur in the six hours following the consumption of a meal *high in fat,* regardless of the source of the fat.

Studies conducted recently have shown that fatty foods increase the blood level of a substance that encourages the formation of blood clots and makes arteries stiffer, constricting blood flow.

Prevention: Men and women who have not had heart attacks should eat meals with less than 20 grams (g) of saturated fat. A "killer meal" would be, for instance, a prime beef hamburger (20 g), plus french fries fried in beef tallow (10 g) and one cup of premium ice cream (20 g).

William P. Castelli, MD, medical director of the Framingham Cardiovascular Institute and former director of the Framingham Heart Study, Framingham, MA.

If You're Having a Heart Attack...

Chew an aspirin tablet if you think you may be having a heart attack. Do not just swallow the aspirin—chewing the aspirin gets it to work nearly twice as fast, bringing a quicker beneficial effect on your blood's clotting.

Richard O'Brien, MD, spokesperson for the American College of Emergency Physicians and an emergency physician at Moses Taylor Hospital, Scranton, PA.

Chill Therapy for Cardiac Arrest Victims

The American Heart Association has endorsed *therapeutic hypothermia,* which involves cooling a comatose cardiac arrest victim's body after the heart has been restarted with a defibrillator. Body temperature is reduced by 5°F to 9°F by using cooling blankets and ice bags within six to eight hours of cardiac arrest.

Theory: Cooling the body slows brain-damaging inflammation that occurs when oxygenated blood is restored to the brain.

Therapeutic hypothermia is available at most major hospitals.

Terry L. Vanden Hoek, MD, professor of emergency medicine, University of Chicago.

How to Help Heal Yourself

Rachael Freed, MSW, founder of Minneapolis–based Heartmates, Inc., which provides resources for heart patients and their families.

After a loved one suffers a heart attack, life changes forever. We mourn our old innocent ways...and our lost certainties. And—we face changes in lifestyle, financial security, retirement and our spouses' physical capabilities.

Learning to live with uncertainty is one of the greatest challenges for the partner of a person with heart disease.

Over the years, you may have developed an idea of security. Now the rules have changed.

Important: Give yourself permission to break with family protocol and do whatever it takes to get all of you through. The task of a cardiac couple is to develop a "new normal" that incorporates heart disease.

The upside: A brush with mortality can reorder a couple's priorities for the better.

You don't have the power to eradicate your spouse's heart disease or to eliminate its effects on your life. Your goal is to be prepared to support his/her recovery—*and yours.*

Years after a cardiac event, people expect the heartmate to be a constant cheerleader.

My experience: During the crisis period, friends asked only about the patient. And when the emergency was over, they were too uncomfortable to rally around me. But I needed help—a lot of help.

GRIEF AND LOSS

After my husband's heart attack, I was coping, but I felt overwhelmed by strong feelings that took months to define. It was the grief that accompanies loss.

Since my husband was still alive, how could I be feeling grief and loss? Because our life together had changed forever.

During an early presentation I made to spouses of heart attack survivors, I said, "You are feeling grief." Their tears and thanks convinced me that I was on the right track.

YOU'RE A TOP PRIORITY, TOO

The most important person in a heart patient's recovery is not the doctor, but the spouse. To maintain your role as a positive caretaker, you must pay attention to your own recovery.

Example: Airplane travelers are instructed to put their own oxygen masks on before helping someone else.

Taking care of yourself helps you come to terms with a life-changing crisis. *Steps to take...*

•**Make a list.** It should contain actions that would nourish your body, feelings, mind and spirit. Write one action on your calendar every day—and do it.

Examples: Listen to music...sit in a chapel ...take a walk.

•**Gather information.** Learn how diet, exercise and stress affect heart patients.

•**Confide in someone.** To reduce your sense of isolation, share your concerns with a nonjudgmental sibling, close friend or neighbor.

Many people find great relief by communicating with others in similar situations.

Good resource: The Heartmates Web site at *www.heartmates.com.*

TAKE YOUR TIME

The nagging fear of another attack always churns below the surface. The fear never disappears entirely, but you'll begin to believe that your mate won't collapse every time he coughs.

Healing is a process, not an event. It takes at least a year, often two, to recover from a spouse's heart attack or cardiac event. No one but you can know the limits of your grieving period.

EMBRACE YOUR HEALING ROLE

Take these steps to reinforce family bonds and your vitality as a couple...

•**Involve the whole family.** The patient and family members may experience different realities. Learn what your family is feeling. At weekly problem-solving meetings, ask each person to describe his/her greatest concerns. Then discuss them.

Example: If your children are grown and living elsewhere, performing this exercise even once during a visit can break the tension and be extremely helpful.

•**Fight your guilt and fear of stressing the patient.** Use caution in all things, but be aware that the patient won't die if you accidentally sprinkle a little salt on his food...use a noisy vacuum cleaner...take some time for yourself...or cry.

•**Repair the heartmate connection.** Fear of communicating is common after the hospital stay has threatened the marriage bond.

The trauma pulls some cardiac couples apart, intensifying existing conflicts. For others, the crisis provides an opportunity for enriching the relationship.

Honest confrontation of the changes in your relationship is a step toward deepening the marriage connection. *Avoid these traps...*

•**Concealing your concerns and fears** from the patient.

•**Thinking you can reduce stress and tension by withholding your anger** and other negative feelings.

•**Assuming you must always agree with the patient.**

•**Disregarding your own legitimate emotional needs.**

•**Letting TV preempt precious time** to communicate with each other.

SEX: THE UNASKED QUESTION

At my group presentations, people almost never ask about sex. Privately, they are distraught by the silence, isolation and lack of information about impotence.

These misconceptions contribute to spouses' fear and apprehension...

Myth: **Sexual activity is hazardous for heart patients.**

Reality: For most, not so. The amount of energy expended during sex is roughly equivalent to climbing two flights of stairs. A patient who can do the latter can probably do the former safely.

Myth: **Heart disease decreases sex drive and impairs sexual functioning.**

Reality: Fatigue, depression and medications for angina, high blood pressure or palpitations can cause impotence. Fatigue and depression can be treated. If a particular medication is the problem, the doctor may be able to prescribe a different one.

Myth: **Heart disease signifies the end of normal sexual activity.**

Reality: After a few weeks of rest and recuperation, the overwhelming majority of cardiac couples can resume their sexual relationship...and mend their bond through affection and physical intimacy.

How to Recover from a Cardiac Crisis

Barry A. Franklin, PhD, director, Cardiac Rehabilitation and Exercise Laboratories, William Beaumont Hospital, Royal Oak, MI. He is coauthor of *Take a Load Off Your Heart—109 Things You Can Actually Do to Prevent, Halt and Reverse Heart Disease* (Workman).

Each year, 1 million Americans survive a heart attack. Another 1.2 million undergo balloon angioplasty or heart surgery. These people often think that life as they knew it is over. That's a mistake.

Two analyses of 21 clinical trials, which included more than 4,000 patients with heart disease, found that rehabilitation reduced the risk for dying in the three years following surgery by 20% to 25%.*

A cardiac rehab program offers...

*For a list of cardiac rehab programs, contact the American Association of Cardiovascular and Pulmonary Rehabilitation, 312-321-5146, *www.aacvpr.org*.

•**Psychological support.** Rehabilitation from a heart attack or heart surgery is mentally stressful. An experienced rehab staff reduces this burden by providing education and supervised activity in a supportive environment.

Important: A positive mind-set. Invariably, patients who thrive are those who *believe* they can achieve longevity and a high quality of life.

The support of family and friends also is essential. Cardiac rehab patients who live alone and have few family and friends do much worse than those who have a strong, supportive social network. If you live alone, it is especially important to cultivate friendships and be socially active.

•**Personalized advice.** After assessing your individual case, the rehab staff provides personalized advice on diet, exercise and other lifestyle issues.

•**Monitoring of symptoms.** The rehab staff monitors your progress and informs your doctor if you experience symptoms, such as shortness of breath, heart-rhythm irregularities or angina.

A typical program has four phases...

•Phase I occurs while you're still hospitalized and includes self-care activities, frequent sitting or standing and low-level walking (at a slow pace for brief periods).

•Phase II begins as soon as one week after leaving the hospital and may last for up to 12 weeks. A moderate intensity exercise program is initiated. Insurance typically covers rehab through phase II.

•Phase III lasts three to six months. The exercise level is gradually increased. The staff offers counseling on risk-factor reduction, stress management and diet.

•Phase IV consists of a lifetime exercise program, combined with permanent diet modification and other preventive health measures.

PREVENTION WORKS

In addition to rehab, cardiac patients should consider following my "ABCDE" program. *Each letter represents one or more proven or promising interventions...*

•**A—Aspirin.** A daily baby aspirin (81 milligrams [mg]) reduces heart attack survivors' risk for recurrent cardiac events by up to 30%.

●**A—ACE inhibitors.** These drugs relax blood vessels, reducing blood pressure and increasing oxygen flow to the heart. A study of more than 2,200 heart attack survivors found that treatment with ACE inhibitors reduced recurrent heart attacks by about 25%.

●**B—Blood pressure control.** Strive for blood pressure below 140/90, through diet and exercise and, if necessary, drug therapy.

●**B—Beta-blockers.** These are among the most effective medications (along with diuretics) for lowering blood pressure. They've been shown to reduce risk for future heart attacks by approximately 25%.

●**B—Behavior change.** The fight against heart disease is a marathon, not a sprint. You should adopt permanent, ongoing lifestyle changes.

●**B—B vitamins.** Elevated blood levels of the amino acid *homocysteine* have been linked to arterial damage. Homocysteine levels can be markedly reduced by taking daily supplements containing at least 400 micrograms (mcg) of folic acid...2 mg of vitamin B-6...and 6 mcg of vitamin B-12, and by eating foods that are rich in B vitamins, such as bananas or prunes.

●**C—Cholesterol control.** Your total cholesterol should not exceed 200 milligrams per deciliter (mg/dl). For those who have had a heart attack and/or undergone angioplasty or bypass surgery, LDL ("bad") cholesterol should be under 70 mg/dl. If you're at risk for heart disease, your LDL level should not exceed 100 mg/dl.

HDL ("good") cholesterol should be above 40 mg/dl, and triglycerides should be below 150 mg/dl. If these goals can't be reached through diet and exercise alone, treatment with statin drugs should be considered.

●**D—Diet modification.** No more than 20% of your total daily calories should come from fat. Limit your intake of saturated fat to 7% of your total calories.

To reduce fat intake in your daily diet, check food labels for fat content, eat more fruits and vegetables, fiber and fish, limit meat intake and avoid whole milk and cheese.

●**D—Depression.** Identifying and treating depression in cardiac patients is critical. New evidence suggests that depressed patients are less likely to seek medical care and/or stick to a rehab program. As a result, they are more likely to have a recurrent cardiac event.

●**E—Exercise.** Performing at least 30 minutes of moderate exercise most (or preferably all) days of the week will improve several coronary risk factors, such as blood pressure and cholesterol levels, and encourage weight loss.

For best results, slowly build up to the point where you are burning 1,500 to 2,000 calories per week. For a 160-pound person, that's the equivalent of walking 15 to 20 miles.

●**E—Vitamin E.** Daily supplements of 400 international units (IU) of vitamin E may have a protective effect on the heart. Although a major recent study found that vitamin E supplements did *not* affect cardiovascular outcomes in patients at high risk for cardiac events, I believe the existing evidence supports the use of this vitamin.

Heart Attack Self-Defense

Dennis Sprecher, MD, cardiologist, University of Pennsylvania Health System, and former director of preventive cardiology and rehabilitation, Cleveland Clinic Foundation. He is a contributing author of *The Cleveland Clinic Heart Book* (Hyperion).

You've cut back on dietary fat and cholesterol. You've started exercising and lost weight. If you ever smoked, you've now stopped. Perhaps you've even taken to drinking green tea. What else can you do to reduce your risk of heart disease?

Quite a lot, actually. The following advice comes from Dennis Sprecher, MD, a heart attack specialist at the world-renowned Cleveland Clinic. *He believes people should...*

●**Consume more apples,** onions and green beans...and more purple grape juice. These foods are rich in the heart-protective antioxidants called *flavonoids.*

Flavonoids benefit the heart by inhibiting oxidation of cholesterol—a chemical process that promotes artery blockages.

Flavonoids also help dilate the arteries that supply oxygen-rich blood to the heart.

Caution: Unsweetened grape juice—at 154 calories per eight ounces—is too calorie-dense to be consumed on a daily basis.

Like purple grape juice, red wine contains flavonoids. But given the risks associated with alcohol, men should have no more than two five-ounce glasses a day…women no more than one five-ounce glass a day.

•**Boost intake of omega-3 fatty acids.** Fish oil is a good source of omega-3 fatty acids, which are believed to account for the lower incidence of heart-related deaths among people who eat at least some fish.

Omega-3s increase levels of HDL ("good") cholesterol and reduce blood pressure by relaxing arteries…stabilizing heartbeats…and inhibiting the formation of artery-clogging blood clots. Try to eat fish high in omega-3s, such as salmon and trout, twice a week.

Caution: Fish oil is a highly concentrated source of fat calories. Consuming too much of it raises LDL (bad) cholesterol levels.

If you don't like fish, ground flaxseed—sold in health-food stores—is an alternative source of omega-3s. Add it to cereal.

Another little-known source of omega-3s is arugula lettuce.

•**Eat more beans and other low-fat foods** —and less meat. One cup of black beans provides as much protein as two ounces of lean ground beef. But the beans contain only one gram (g) of total fat, compared with 12 g for the meat.

Also, beans contain no saturated fat or cholesterol. The meat contains 4 g of saturated fat and 43 milligrams (mg) of cholesterol.

•**Eat more soy- and oat-based foods.** Both protect the heart by encouraging the excretion of cholesterol circulating in the bloodstream.

Use soymilk instead of cow's milk on high-fiber bran or oat cereal. Low-fat soy cheese and tofu—found in the dairy section of many supermarkets—are other good sources of soy. Or have oatmeal or oat bread for breakfast instead of sugary cereals.

•**Cut way back on salt.** It's well known that excess sodium—found in table salt and many processed foods—can damage the heart by raising blood pressure. Yet the average American still consumes 6,000 mg a day—far more than the recommended 2,400 mg.

To lower your salt intake, follow the diet that was developed as part of a landmark study known as Dietary Approaches to Stop Hypertension (DASH).

The DASH diet consists primarily of fruits, vegetables, whole grains and low-fat dairy products. People who followed the DASH diet experienced a 15% reduction of atherosclerosis (stiff, clogged arteries), a cause of heart attack.

The DASH diet also reduces blood pressure about as much as medications do.

More information: *www.nhlbi.nih.gov/ health/public/heart/hbp/dash/how_plan.html.*

•**Eat six small meals a day.** Small, frequent meals make it less likely that the body will turn the calories you consume into fat.

If you plan to go out and eat at a restaurant, have an apple or another low-fat snack beforehand. This takes the edge off your hunger so you are less likely to load up on calorie-laden breads or appetizers.

•**Work out more frequently.** In addition to burning excess calories, physical activity boosts levels of HDL cholesterol.

Although most experts recommend exercising for 30 minutes at least three times a week, new research confirms that *daily* activity yields the greatest benefits.

Jog, walk, run, dance or do some other moderately vigorous exercise for at least 30 minutes a day. If you cannot manage one continuous 30-minute workout, do three 10-minute sessions spread throughout the day.

•**Curb psychological stress.** In response to a stressful situation—be it a traffic jam or a difficult boss—your body produces two key hormones. *Epinephrine* increases heart rate. *Cortisol* raises blood pressure.

If your body constantly generates these hormones, you overwork your heart—and that increases your risk for heart attack.

When we are under stress, our breathing becomes rapid and shallow. That deprives the heart of oxygen.

To reverse this oxygen-robbing tendency, inhale deeply through your nose for a count of 10 when you feel stress. Then exhale for a count of 10. Repeat twice more.

Ask your doctor about heart-protecting medication. Taking a daily aspirin helps reduce the blood's tendency to clot. And that makes a heart attack less likely.

Caution: Do not take aspirin to protect your heart without talking to your doctor first. In some people, regular use of aspirin can cause internal bleeding.

If your total cholesterol is 200 or higher and/or you have a strong family history of heart disease, you should probably take *pravastatin* (Pravachol) or another prescription "statin" drug.

Triglycerides: Too-Often Overlooked Culprit In Heart Disease

Daniel Rader, MD, director, Preventive Cardiovascular Medicine and Lipid Clinic, department of medicine, University of Pennsylvania School of Medicine, Philadelphia.

If you get your cholesterol levels checked regularly, you no doubt know the difference between the "bad" form of cholesterol (low-density lipoprotein, or LDL) and the "good" form (high-density lipoprotein, or HDL). But there's another type of blood lipid that deserves equal attention—triglycerides.

Here's what you should know…

WHAT ARE TRIGLYCERIDES?

Triglycerides, which circulate in the bloodstream, are fats that have been digested and are ready to provide energy to muscle cells or be deposited in fatty tissues. Like cholesterol, triglycerides do not float freely in the blood but are attached to larger molecules known as lipoproteins.

In a recent analysis of 17 studies comprised of over 46,000 men and approximately 11,000 women, it was found that elevated triglycerides

significantly increased the risk for heart disease during the next decade—by 14% for men and 37% for women—even after other factors, such as smoking, obesity and high blood pressure, were taken into account.

According to the most recent guidelines published by the National Heart, Lung and Blood Institute (NHLBI), a normal triglyceride level is less than 150 milligrams per deciliter (mg/dl)…borderline-high is 150 to 199…high is 200 to 499 …and very high is 500 or above.

Important: If your triglyceride level is very high (especially if it's above 1,000 mg/dl), there is a more immediate risk for acute pancreatitis, a sudden inflammation that can be deadly.

ELEVATED TRIGLYCERIDES

Like high cholesterol, elevated triglyceride levels tend to run in families.

Certain medications can also increase triglyceride levels. They include estrogen (even the low-level hormones found in birth control pills)…steroids, such as *prednisone* (Deltasone) or *cortisone* (Cortone)…beta-blockers, such as *propranolol* (Inderal) or *atenolol* (Tenormin) …and diuretics. *Tretinoin* (Retin-A), which is often prescribed for skin conditions, can trigger particularly steep increases in triglycerides.

Triglyceride levels may also be elevated by diseases, such as type 2 (adult-onset) diabetes and kidney failure.

LIFESTYLE CHANGES

To lower your triglyceride level, follow these proven strategies…

●**Cut back on carbohydrates.** Although the amount and type of fat is critical for cholesterol, the key factor for triglycerides is carbohydrates. When digested carbohydrates pass through the liver, they are believed to stimulate the release of triglycerides.

The simple carbohydrates—sugar and refined starches—are broken down most quickly and have the strongest effect on triglyceride levels. Avoid pastries, candies, white bread and pasta. Beverages that contain sugar are particularly bad. Eliminate soft drinks, and substitute fruit for fruit juice. A single orange contains approximately half the sugar of an eight-ounce glass of orange juice.

Alcohol has the same effect as sugar. Scale back to no more than one drink a day.

•**Get enough exercise.** If you now have a sedentary lifestyle, any increase in activity may be helpful. Take a walk at lunchtime…use the stairs…garden instead of watching television.

More is better. You'll probably see a much bigger drop in triglycerides if you get at least 30 minutes of aerobic exercise (brisk walking, jogging, swimming or bike riding) at least three times a week.

•**Lose weight, if necessary.** Being obese is strongly linked to elevated triglycerides. To determine if you are overweight, calculate your *body mass index* (BMI).

Formula: Multiply your weight in pounds by 703, and divide this by your height (in inches) squared. If the result is 25 or above, you may need to lose weight. For a BMI calculator, visit the NHLBI Web site at *www.nhlbi support.com/bmi.*

DRUG TREATMENT

If lifestyle changes don't lower your triglyceride level to 150 or below within six months, you may need medication…

•**Fibrates.** *Gemfibrozil* (Lopid) and *fenofibrate* (Tricor) are the most effective medications. These drugs lower triglycerides by as much as 50%—and raise HDL cholesterol by up to 20%.

Side effects: Mild gastrointestinal problems (stomach upset, nausea, diarrhea).

•**Niacin.** It's almost as effective as fibrates. An over-the-counter B vitamin, niacin must be taken in large doses of 1,000 to 2,000 milligrams (mg) daily and should be used only under a doctor's supervision. Niacin also raises HDL.

Side effects: Hot flashes—a flushing which spreads upward from the chest to the face… stomach upset…and ulcer.

Note: An extended-release prescription form of niacin, *Niaspan,* has fewer side effects.

•**Statins.** They may be prescribed if LDL cholesterol also needs lowering. Statins reduce triglycerides, but not as much as fibrates or niacin. The more potent statins, such as *simvastatin* (Zocor) and *atorvastatin* (Lipitor), are most effective.

Side effects: Mild gastrointestinal difficulties (constipation, gas, cramps). In rare cases, muscle pain may occur.

•**Fish oil.** Fish oil supplements also lower triglycerides. However, this treatment requires a high dose (six to nine 1,000-mg capsules per day). Check with your doctor before taking this dose. Fish oil capsules are usually added only when drugs aren't effective.

Side effects: Fishy odor on the breath and stomach upset.

❓ Syndrome X…the Little-Known Cause Of Many Heart Attacks

Gerald M. Reaven, MD, professor of medicine emeritus, Stanford University School of Medicine, Stanford, CA. He is coauthor of *Syndrome X: Overcoming the Silent Killer That Can Give You a Heart Attack* (Simon & Schuster).

It's well known that a high cholesterol level —especially a high level of LDL ("bad") cholesterol—is a major risk factor for heart attack. Now, there's another risk factor which is finally getting the attention it deserves as a major contributor to heart disease. That factor is insulin resistance.

Insulin—produced by the pancreas—is the hormone that ushers blood sugar (glucose) into cells. Cells can become resistant to insulin's action. When they do, the pancreas pumps out more insulin in an attempt to "force" sugar into the cells.

Excess insulin directly damages coronary arteries. It also triggers an array of metabolic abnormalities that contribute to the development of artery-clogging fatty plaques and to blood clots.

The constellation of abnormalities, which affects 70 million Americans, is called "syndrome X." *It includes…*

•**Excess fibrinogen,** a substance that promotes blood clots.

273

●**Excess plasminogen activator inhibitor-1 (PAI-1),** a substance that slows the breakdown of clots.

●**High levels of triglycerides,** the body's main fat-storage particles.

●**Low levels of HDL ("good") cholesterol,** which sweeps fat out of arteries.

Many people with syndrome X also have high blood pressure. And they're likely to have glucose intolerance—a condition characterized by slightly elevated blood sugar levels.

Important: Glucose intolerance is not diabetes. But up to 5% of people who have syndrome X go on to develop type 2 diabetes. That's the form that occurs when, due to insulin resistance, blood sugar levels rise into the diabetic range.

DIAGNOSING SYNDROME X

The results of five simple tests point to a diagnosis of syndrome X. *Risk for heart attack rises with each out-of-bounds test score...*

●**Fasting triglyceride level** in excess of 200 milligrams per deciliter (mg/dl).

●**Fasting HDL cholesterol level** that is less than 35 mg/dl.

●**Blood pressure** higher than 145/90.

●**Being overweight** by 15 pounds or more.

●**Fasting blood sugar level** higher than 110 mg/dl...or a level higher than 140 two hours after drinking a glucose solution.

FIGHTING SYNDROME X

●**Eat the right diet.** Americans are besieged by a glut of high-concept diets, all of them purporting to be best for weight loss and health.

The American Heart Association diet counsels cutting down on fat and boosting consumption of carbohydrates. *The Zone* diet advises boosting protein intake and lowering fat.

These diets may work for people who don't have syndrome X. But protein and carbohydrates stimulate insulin production—which is a dangerous outcome for people with the syndrome.

The Atkins diet counsels consumption of low levels of carbohydrates and as much fat as desired. But that diet is too high in artery-clogging saturated fat.

The ideal diet to combat syndrome X supplies 45% of calories from carbohydrates... 15% from protein...and 40% from fat.

Key: Emphasize beneficial mono- and polyunsaturated fats. These should supply 30% to 35% of the diet. Only 5% to 10% should come from saturated fats.

Good sources of healthful fats include avocados...fatty fish (such as sea bass, trout, sole and salmon)...natural peanut butter...nuts and seeds...canola, corn, olive, safflower, peanut, soybean, sesame and sunflower oils.

●**Lose weight.** Shedding pounds improves insulin resistance.

Recent study: Insulin resistance fell an average of 40% in overweight individuals who lost 20 pounds.

●**Exercise.** People who exercise daily use insulin 25% more efficiently than those who do not exercise. Forty-five minutes of aerobic exercise a day is ideal.

●**Stop smoking.** Smoking promotes insulin resistance.

MEDICATION

If lifestyle changes alone don't overcome syndrome X, medication can help...

●**Triglyceride-lowering medication.** Three drugs can lower triglyceride levels. They also lower PAI-1 levels and raise HDL cholesterol.

One of them—niacin—has the added benefit of lowering LDL cholesterol. A common side effect of nicotinic acid is facial flushing.

Self-defense: To minimize flushing from nicotinic acid, increase the dose gradually.

Two other effective drugs are *gemfibrozil* (Lopid) and *fenofibrate* (Tricor). In rare cases, however, they can cause liver damage.

Self-defense: Talk to your doctor about testing liver function periodically.

●**Blood pressure medication.** Fifty percent of people diagnosed with high blood pressure also have syndrome X. But some blood pressure drugs can worsen the condition.

Talk to your doctor about the potential risks of high-dose diuretics and beta-blockers if you have syndrome X.

Because syndrome X is caused by insulin resistance, it's logical to ask whether *thiazolidinediones*—drugs that increase insulin sensitivity—might be helpful. Currently, such drugs are used to treat type 2 diabetes.

Ongoing research will determine if thiazolidinediones improve syndrome X. Until the studies are completed, these drugs should not be used to treat the condition.

What's Your Risk For Heart Disease?

For years, doctors have considered the body mass index (BMI) to be a strong indicator of heart disease risk. (BMI is calculated by dividing your weight in kilograms by the square of your height in meters. A BMI over 25 suggests that a person is overweight…over 30 indicates obesity.)

But research shows that a person's waist size is actually more accurate than BMI in assessing heart disease risk.

To determine your waist size: Measure just above the top of the hip bone at the end of a normal exhalation. Men are at risk for heart disease if their waist measurement is 35 inches or above. For women, it's 33 inches or above.

If your waist measurement puts you in one of the danger zones, make sure that you talk to your doctor about reducing your heart disease risk by losing weight, lowering high blood pressure and LDL "bad" cholesterol, and raising HDL "good" cholesterol.

Shankuan Zhu, MD, PhD, former research fellow, New York Obesity Research Center, and currently assistant professor, family and community medicine, Medical College of Wisconsin.

The Ultimate Cholesterol-Lowering Diet

John McDougall, MD, founder and medical director, McDougall Program, Santa Rosa, CA, *www.drmcdougall. com.* He is author of several books, including *The McDougall Program for a Healthy Heart: A Lifesaving Approach to Preventing and Treating Heart Disease* (Plume).

The importance of lowering cholesterol levels was underscored again when the National Institutes of Health (NIH) released new guidelines calling for aggressive treatment for total cholesterol levels of 240 milligrams per deciliter (mg/dl) or higher. The NIH recommended aiming for a level of 200 mg/dl or below.

With my patients, I go even further—I work with them to achieve and maintain a total cholesterol level *no higher than 150 mg/dl.* This is the point where heart disease stops progressing and begins to reverse itself. This is also a level of cholesterol where the risk of dying from heart disease is almost zero. If you settle for a total cholesterol of 200 mg/dl instead, you still subject your arteries to toxins and plaque buildup—and risk a heart attack.

Here is how I helped my high-cholesterol patients get their levels under control…

CUT OUT ANIMAL PRODUCTS

The single most effective way to lower your blood cholesterol is to stop eating foods that contain cholesterol. In other words, *avoid all animal products*—red meat, poultry, shellfish, fish, eggs, dairy products and foods made with them.

As far as the health of your arteries is concerned, there is no "safe" amount in regard to the consumption of animal products.

Forbidden foods (many of which have long been perceived as permissible) include…

•**Fish and fowl.** Studies show that these foods will raise cholesterol just as surely as beef or pork.

•**Low-fat or skim milk, cheese or other dairy products.** Even when the fat is taken out, the animal proteins in these foods can raise cholesterol levels and damage the artery walls.

●**"Free" fats such as margarine, corn oil, olive oil and canola oil.** These fats are easily oxidized in the bloodstream, making plaque likely to build up on artery walls.

If you follow a strict vegetarian diet for several months, you should be able to lower your cholesterol levels by 25% or more. At the same time, blood levels of triglycerides, homocysteine, uric acid and other heart disease risk factors will also decline.

VEGETARIAN DELIGHTS

Giving up animal products does not mean you must eat poorly. The foods in my program are varied and delicious. They provide all needed nutrients in optimal amounts.

You can eat *all you want* of the following…

●**Whole grains,** including barley, brown rice, buckwheat, bulgur, corn, oatmeal and wheat, as well as noodles that are made from these sources.

●**Potatoes, sweet potatoes and yams.**

●**Root vegetables,** including beets, carrots and turnips.

●**Squashes,** such as acorn, buttercup and zucchini squash.

●**Beans and peas,** including chickpeas, green peas, kidney beans, lentils as well as string beans.

●**Other vegetables,** such as broccoli, brussels sprouts, cabbage, celery, the darker lettuces, spinach, cucumbers, okra, onions, peppers and mushrooms.

●**Mild spices and cooking herbs.**

Eat only limited amounts of fruit and fruit juice (no more than three servings a day), sugar and other sweeteners, salt and fatty plant foods, such as peanut butter, seed spreads, avocados, olives and soybean products—including tofu. Simple sugars, even fruit and juice, raise cholesterol and triglycerides.

HEART-HEALTHY MENU PLAN

There are many excellent vegetarian cookbooks to choose from, but you don't have to be a gourmet to prepare heart-healthful meals. Start with potatoes, rice, beans or spaghetti, then add some low-fat, plant-based sauces and soups. Throw in a salad and bread, and you've got a meal. *Other tips…*

●**For breakfast,** toast, bagels, oatmeal, cereals, hash browns and pancakes (all made from the right ingredients) are all fine. Use rice milk or soy milk on cold cereal.

●**Sauté food in soy sauce,** wine or sherry, vinegar (rice or balsamic), vegetarian Worcestershire sauce, salsa or lemon or lime juice.

●**Eat until you're satisfied…**and eat as often as you need to.

●**To boost feelings of fullness,** include beans and peas in your meals.

A typical day's menu might include…

Breakfast: Pancakes, oatmeal, French toast or a breakfast tortilla.

Lunch: Vegetable soup, along with a vegetarian sandwich or a veggie burger.

Dinner: Bean burritos, mu-shu vegetables over rice, chili and rice, or spaghetti with marinara sauce, along with some fresh bread and a chickpea salad.

After a week or two on this diet, most people find themselves craving healthful foods—and not missing all that poisonous dietary fat.

CHOLESTEROL-LOWERING DRUGS

With a high-risk patient—someone who's had a heart attack or appears headed for a heart attack, coronary bypass or angioplasty—I would not wait several months to "see what happens." If his/her total cholesterol hasn't fallen to 150 mg/dl after 10 days of healthful eating, I then suggest supplementing the diet with drugs.

Between a vegetarian diet and cholesterol-lowering medication, virtually anyone's cholesterol can be brought down to 150 mg/dl.

First, try out some of the natural cholesterol-lowering "medications"…

●**Garlic**—up to 800 milligrams (mg), or one clove every day.

●**Oat bran**—two ounces a day or oatmeal (three ounces, dry weight), a day.

●**Vitamin C**—2,000 mg a day.

●**Vitamin E**—dry form, 400 international units [IU] a day. But check with your doctor first—more than 200 IU may be dangerous.

●**Beta-carotene**—25,000 IU a day.

●**Gugulipid.** Recently, I have been recommending this Indian herb—500 to 1,500 mg, three times a day.

●**Immediate-release niacin** is yet another potentially useful medication. But it has been known to damage the liver, so it should be taken only under a doctor's supervision.

If the patient doesn't respond, I typically prescribe *simvastatin* (Zocor), *pravastatin* (Pravachol), *lovastatin* (Mevacor) or *fluvastatin* (Lescol). Since my patient may have to take this medication for years, it's important to match him/her with the drug that's most effective, but with the fewest side effects.

EXERCISE AND GOOD HABITS

While exercise isn't as crucial as diet, a brisk walk of at least 20 minutes each day benefits your heart and arteries in many ways.

Regular exercise helps to train the heart to beat more efficiently...increases levels of HDL ("good") cholesterol...lowers levels of triglycerides...increases oxygen flow to your heart, brain, muscles and other tissues...and boosts the immune system.

As if you didn't know: Don't smoke. Limit coffee consumption (both regular and decaffeinated raise cholesterol levels about 10%). Drink alcohol moderately if at all. Your arteries will thank you.

OJ for Your Cholesterol

Drinking orange juice can increase the amount of HDL ("good") cholesterol in your body. When researchers gave people with high blood cholesterol levels orange juice daily for three months, increasing the amount until they were drinking three glasses a day in the third month, they found that the amount of HDL cholesterol in their blood increased by more than 21%. Five weeks later, when the subjects were back on their original diets, their HDL was still at the elevated level.

Elzbieta M. Kurowska, vice president, research and development, Research Park Corp., University of Western Ontario, London.

Cranberry Juice Fights Heart Disease

Cranberry juice has long been used to help prevent urinary-tract infections in people who are susceptible to this condition.

Recent finding: Drinking three eight-ounce glasses of cranberry juice daily for one month raises HDL ("good") cholesterol levels by 10%. This theoretically would reduce heart disease risk by about 40%.

Theory: The juice's antioxidant activity confers the heart-protecting benefit.

Helpful: Only drink unsweetened varieties, which contain half the calories of regular cranberry juice.

Joe Vinson, PhD, professor of chemistry, University of Scranton, PA.

Trans Fatty Acids Are Worse than Butter

Trans fatty acids are even worse for your health than the saturated fats in sour cream, butter and lard.

According to the National Academy of Sciences, trans fatty acids increase your risk of heart attack by raising LDL ("bad") cholesterol and lowering levels of protective HDL cholesterol as much as or more than saturated fats. There is no safe level of intake.

In addition to being present in high-fat dairy products, trans fats are in foods containing hydrogenated or partially hydrogenated vegetable oils, such as cakes, pies and cookies...and fast-food french fries, chicken and other deep-fried foods.

Suzanne Havala Hobbs, DrPH, RD, registered dietitian and adjunct assistant professor, School of Public Health, University of North Carolina, Chapel Hill. She is author of several books, including *Being Vegetarian for Dummies* (For Dummies).

Easier Cholesterol Control

Twice-yearly injections of an experimental vaccine raised HDL ("good") cholesterol levels by 40% in animal studies. If it's successful in humans, this could be a convenient, less-expensive alternative to statin drugs, which are typically taken twice daily for life.

Arteriosclerosis, Thrombosis, and Vascular Biology, an American Heart Association journal, 7272 Greenville Ave., Dallas 75231.

The Miracle Heart Drugs Millions of Americans Take

Steven E. Nissen, MD, chairman, cardiology, the Cleveland Clinic Foundation, and professor of medicine, Ohio State University, Cleveland.

Everyone knows that too much cholesterol is bad. High levels of this fat-like substance in the blood raise the risk of heart attack and sudden death.

But how much is too much? And what's the best way to reduce cholesterol levels? The answers have changed recently, largely because of cholesterol-lowering drugs called *statins*. Already, millions of Americans take them…and each study seems to enlarge the circle of people who may benefit from statin therapy. How about you?

LATEST GUIDELINES

The National Cholesterol Education Program issued guidelines designed to help people decide if they need to lower their cholesterol levels.

Healthy people should keep LDL ("bad") cholesterol—the kind linked to heart disease—below 130 milligrams per deciliter (mg/dl). Those who have had a heart attack or stroke or who have diabetes or cardiovascular disease should aim for an LDL level of 70 mg/dl. The same is true if you smoke cigarettes or have a family history of heart disease.

If a low-fat, high-fiber diet doesn't reduce cholesterol enough within three months, you may need drug therapy to bring down levels.

SURPRISING FINDINGS

Some data suggest that these guidelines do not go far enough. The British Heart Protection Study observed over 20,000 people with cardiovascular disease or diabetes who were randomly selected to take either *simvastatin* (Zocor) or a placebo for five years.

The results were striking. People who were given simvastatin had 33% less heart attacks and strokes than those who were given the placebo. They also required significantly fewer heart surgeries, angioplasties and amputations.

Most important: The benefit was not limited to people who have high cholesterol. Simvastatin appeared to prevent heart attacks and strokes even in those whose LDL levels were below the recommended level.

WHAT DOES IT MEAN FOR YOU?

If you have had a heart attack or stroke or have been diagnosed with cardiovascular disease or diabetes, you would probably benefit from statin therapy. This is true even if your cholesterol levels are in the healthy range.

If you don't fit into these categories but have several risk *factors* for heart disease—you are male, middle-aged, smoke cigarettes, have high blood pressure or a family history of heart attacks—you are in a gray zone. But I generally recommend statins for such individuals.

Statin medication does not mean you can become complacent. Lifestyle still counts. You should take steps to lower your heart attack risk—exercise, improve your diet and maintain a healthy weight.

CHOOSING THE BEST STATIN

Statins are usually taken to lower cholesterol. *Atorvastatin* (Lipitor) and *simvastatin* (Zocor) seem to be the most effective.

But while statins are usually the best medications for lowering LDL cholesterol, other drugs are sometimes more suitable for people with certain cholesterol problems…

●**Your HDL cholesterol level is too low.** If levels of this "good" cholesterol (which removes fatty deposits from the arteries) are too low, your doctor may prescribe niacin. Niaspan, a prescription-only, sustained-release formulation, has minimal side effects.

● **Your level of triglycerides—another blood fat—is high.** Your doctor may advise you to take a fibric acid derivative, such as *gemfibrozil* (Lopid) or *fenofibrate* (Tricor). These also raise HDL cholesterol levels.

Both niacin and fibric acid drugs may be taken along with a statin for double-barreled action against heart disease.

HOW SAFE ARE STATINS?

Several years ago, *cerivastatin* (Baycol) was pulled off the market. The drug was linked to more than 100 deaths from *rhabdomyolysis,* a serious condition marked by severe muscle pain and weakness. The risk with other statins is exceedingly low—an estimated one person in 3 million has a fatal reaction.

A minority of people taking statins experience muscle aches. They usually feel better when they switch to a lower dose or a different type of statin.

Some people may worry that their cholesterol levels will drop too low. The body does need some cholesterol for such biological functions as the formation of cell membranes. But the amount needed is very small.

TWO MORE POSSIBLE BENEFITS

According to a study presented at a meeting of the American Academy of Neurology, more than 2,500 people who took statins were far less likely to develop Alzheimer's disease, the leading cause of dementia.

More research needs to be done on this front, but brain protection could turn out to be another compelling reason to consider statins.

There is also preliminary evidence that statins may help reduce the risk of colon cancer, especially when they are taken in combination with the nonsteroidal anti-inflammatory drugs (NSAIDs), such as aspirin. But, again, more research needs to be conducted.

Lower Your Cholesterol Without Drugs

Robert E. Kowalski, medical journalist and author of *The New 8-Week Cholesterol Cure: The Ultimate Program for Preventing Heart Disease* (Harper Torch). He is editor of *Diet-Heart Newsletter,* Box 2039, Venice, CA 90294, *www.thehealthyheart.net.*

It is possible to lower your cholesterol without medication. Medical journalist Robert E. Kowalski discussed his recommendations for reducing cholesterol naturally…

● **How is your cholesterol level these days?** I'm a shining example of how successful "secondary prevention" can be. When I left the hospital after my first bypass operation in 1978, the doctors basically told me, "We've fixed the problem—now go out and enjoy your life."

Six years later, I was back in the hospital for another bypass. That's when I started to research cholesterol and came up with the idea of controlling my cholesterol through a diet low in fat and high in oat bran—plus daily doses of the vitamin niacin.

My total cholesterol dropped from 269 to 184 in only *eight weeks.* And, angiograms show that my coronary vessels are clear.

● **What is your current advice for people who are at risk for heart disease?** Start by taking a daily multivitamin supplement, along with an additional 1,000 micrograms (mcg) of folic acid…6 milligrams (mg) of vitamin B-6* and 500 mcg of vitamin B-12.

These B-vitamins work to "normalize" blood levels of *homocysteine*—an amino acid that is as much a predictor of heart attack risk as is high cholesterol.

Ask your doctor to check your cholesterol levels—including total cholesterol, LDL ("bad") cholesterol and HDL ("good") cholesterol. Make sure he/she checks your triglyceride levels also.

These numbers indicate your risk for coronary artery disease. Regardless of your age, try to get your total cholesterol below 200—ideally 160 to 180—with an LDL level that's no higher than 70.

*This is a very small amount, so look for B-6 in a vitamin mixture.

●**What if a person's total cholesterol exceeds 200?** You can lower your cholesterol level by about 10% simply by eating oat bran. When you eat one cup of oat bran (the equivalent of three bran muffins) or one-and-one-half cups of oatmeal each day, the bran binds with bile in your digestive tract. The bile is then excreted in bowel movements.

Since bile contains cholesterol, more blood cholesterol must then be used up to make additional bile. Other foods high in soluble fiber, such as dried beans, raisins, prunes and figs, also help eliminate bile.

●**What other dietary approaches do you suggest?** You can reduce your blood cholesterol by another 10% by taking a cholesterol-blocking substance called *phytosterol*. When you take phytosterol before eating a meal containing animal products, phytosterol molecules occupy the cholesterol receptors in your intestines. This prevents cholesterol from passing into your bloodstream.

A company called Endurance Products sells a 450-mg phytosterol pill.

Cost: $58* for 400 tablets. (To order, visit *www.endur.com.*)

I recommend taking one or two tablets, 30 minutes prior to each meal. If you're eating eggs, take one tablet per egg yolk.

●**What about soy foods?** Eating soy can yield another 10% drop in cholesterol, but you have got to consume a fair amount—25 grams of soy protein a day. That's the equivalent of three eight-ounce glasses of soy milk, plus soy nut snacks.

If you adopt all these approaches, you'll make a real dent in your cholesterol level. The other step is to cut back on dietary fat.

●**Does this mean cutting out all fat?** No. You can eat all the fish you want, especially fatty fish, since it contains the heart-protective omega-3 fatty acids. Also, use as much olive oil and canola oil as you want.

Just be sure to cut back on trans fat (referred to on food labels as "hydrogenated" or "partially hydrogenated" fat or vegetable oil). Saturated fat, too, should be limited.

*Price subject to change.

Trans fat not only raises levels of total and LDL cholesterol, but also lowers levels of protective HDL cholesterol.

Another huge source of trans fat is fast-food restaurants, which fry their products in hydrogenated fat. Have fast food no more than once a week. Never is best.

To reduce your intake of saturated fat, substitute avocados, nuts or peanut butter for meat whenever possible. Consume skim milk instead of low-fat milk products. Remove skin from chicken. And eat only lean cuts of meat.

If you plan on eating hamburgers or meat loaf, pick out a piece of lean London broil or top round at your supermarket and ask the butcher to trim the fat before grinding it. You'll have ground beef that's only 5% fat—the same fat content as skinless chicken breast. Regular ground beef is 15% to 30% fat.

●**Where does niacin come into the picture?** If your cholesterol is in the mid-200s or higher, bite the bullet and talk to your doctor about taking cholesterol-lowering medication.

I'm not a doctor, but I prefer niacin, a vitamin of the B-complex group, to statin drugs—for several reasons. First, statins are expensive, and not everyone has insurance that covers the cost. Second, we know next to nothing about the long-term side effects of statins. Finally, while statins lower LDL and total cholesterol, they don't affect HDLs, triglycerides or other cholesterol "subfractions."

Niacin lowers levels of total and LDL cholesterol *and* triglycerides. It also raises HDL and lowers levels of two other dangerous particles—*lipoprotein subfraction alpha,* or lp(a) cholesterol, and small, dense LDL cholesterol, both of which are especially prone to lodging in artery walls.

Niacin does have a downside. You have to take it three times a day (typically one 500-mg tablet with each meal) and have your liver enzymes checked *every six months,* since the high dosage required for cholesterol reduction can cause liver disturbances. Niacin can also cause flushing.

A new therapy that combines statins and niacin is also showing promise in clinical trials.

In one recent study of heart patients at the University of Washington, the results of this approach virtually halted the progression of heart disease. Statin drugs alone did not.

Beyond Cholesterol: Six Threats to Your Heart Doctors Often Overlook

Michael Mogadam, MD, clinical associate professor of medicine, Georgetown University, Washington, DC, and an internist and lipid specialist in private practice in Alexandria, VA. He is author of *Every Heart Attack Is Preventable* (Lifeline Press).

M ost doctors believe that high cholesterol is the primary cause of heart disease. But seven out of 10 heart attack victims have cholesterol levels in the "borderline" range of 180 to 240 milligrams per deciliter (mg/dl).

Clearly, cholesterol levels are important. High levels of LDL ("bad") cholesterol or triglycerides and/or low levels of HDL ("good") cholesterol are risk factors. So are smoking, obesity, hypertension, diabetes, etc. *But other risk factors are also important...*

CHLAMYDIA INFECTION

A common respiratory tract germ, *Chlamydia pneumoniae* can migrate to the arteries and spark an infection that can damage the linings. (*C. pneumoniae* is related to, but different from, the microorganism that causes the sexually transmitted disease commonly known as chlamydia.)

More than half of adults with atherosclerosis (hardening of the arteries) are believed to be infected with C. pneumoniae. Only 5% of people with healthy arteries are infected.

Self-defense: Anyone with chronic sinusitis or bronchitis who has two or more risk factors for heart disease should have a blood test for C. pneumoniae.

Treatment typically includes a 14-day course of the oral antibiotic *arithromycin* (Zithromax), followed by one pill a week for three months.

DEPRESSED MOOD

Ten percent of American adults have a syndrome known as HAD—hostility, anger and depression. HAD increases the risk for coronary artery disease as much as high cholesterol or hypertension.

Self-defense: People who get frustrated easily...lose their temper...and often feel angry should discuss this with a physician.

Stress-reduction techniques, such as meditation, deep breathing and yoga, are helpful. In fact, one study conducted at Duke University found that stress reduction can reduce the risk for coronary artery disease by 70%.

ELEVATED FIBRINOGEN

Fibrinogen is a blood protein involved in clotting. An elevated level (above 250 mg/dl) *triples* the risk for coronary artery disease.

Self-defense: A person who eats a high-fat diet and has one or more risk factors for heart disease should receive a blood test to measure his/her fibrinogen level.

Eliminate fried foods, margarine and other foods that contain trans-fatty acids from your diet. These fats stimulate the liver to produce elevated fibrinogen.

Also helpful: Consuming fatty fish, such as tuna, mackerel and salmon, three or four times per week. The omega-3 fatty acids in fish lower fibrinogen and reduce the risk for blood clots. Taking an 81-milligram (mg) aspirin tablet (one baby aspirin) along with 400 to 800 international units (IU) of vitamin E daily should also counteract elevated fibrinogen levels. However, check with your doctor first—more than 200 IU of vitamin E may be dangerous.

Important: If you have elevated fibrinogen and have suffered a heart attack or stroke or have peripheral-artery disease (poor blood circulation in the legs), your doctor may recommend the B vitamin niacin and/or a cholesterol-lowering drug, such as *pravastatin* (Pravachol).

HIGH HEMATOCRIT

Hematocrit is the percentage of your whole blood volume that is comprised of red blood cells. At the higher levels—48% to 51%—red blood cells make blood thicker and impair circulation. Elevated hematocrit can *triple* the risk for heart attack.

Self-defense: Anyone with a ruddy complexion…morning fatigue…or occasional dizziness or confusion should be tested. Your hematocrit level is routinely measured during blood tests—and when donating blood.

Your doctor will need to rule out conditions that increase levels of red blood cells, such as lung or bone marrow disorders.

If you're otherwise healthy: Donate one pint of blood every few weeks until your hematocrit level drops to 42% to 45%. Continue donating blood every 90 days to maintain a healthful level.

ELEVATED HOMOCYSTEINE

An abnormally high level of this blood protein can actually *double* the risk for heart attack and stroke.

An elevated homocysteine level damages artery linings and increases the risk for clots.

Self-defense: Anyone with a personal or family history of cardiovascular disease—or with one or more risk factors—should be tested for elevated homocysteine.

If your blood contains more than nine micromoles per liter, ask your doctor about taking B-vitamin supplements. I recommend 1,000 to 2,000 micrograms (mcg) each of folate and vitamin B-12, taken twice daily.

If your homocysteine level remains high after eight to 10 weeks, I recommend adding 50 to 100 mg of vitamin B-6 twice daily.

PLATELET ABNORMALITIES

In some people, blood platelets—cell-like structures that assist in clotting—function more than they should, increasing the risk for clots that can cause a heart attack. Excessive platelet levels—above 250,000 per milliliter of blood—are also a threat.

Self-defense: People with one or more heart disease risk factors should receive a blood test to measure platelet levels.

If platelet levels are elevated, take one 81-mg aspirin tablet daily and one 325-mg aspirin every two weeks to boost the effectiveness of your daily low-dose aspirin.

The prescription drug *clopidogrel* (Plavix) also has antiplatelet effects. It is useful for people who are allergic to aspirin.

All men over age 35 and women over 45 should ask their doctors about taking a low-dose aspirin daily—even if they have no coronary risk factors. Doing so may save their hearts—and their lives.

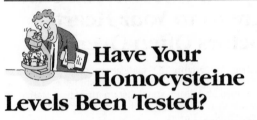

Have Your Homocysteine Levels Been Tested?

David W. Freeman, former editorial director, *Bottom Line/Health,* Boardroom Inc., 281 Tresser Blvd., Stamford, CT 06901.

There's solid evidence that too much *homocysteine*—an amino acid that forms in the body after consumption of meat and dairy foods—means a heightened risk for heart disease and stroke.

Yet few doctors are urging their patients to have their homocysteine levels checked.

Why is that? According to Kilmer McCully, MD—the Providence, Rhode Island, pathologist who originated the homocysteine theory of heart disease—many doctors are unaware of the studies showing how dangerous *hyperhomocysteinemia* can be.

Others fail to recommend the test because they think it's too costly…or because the necessary apparatus isn't available at the diagnostic lab they use.

NO MORE EXCUSES

Two new homocysteine tests have been introduced that use standard lab apparatus. Doctors don't have to track down a new lab, and the cost of testing should be in the range of only $25 to $30.

Testing makes sense for anyone age 65 or older…as well as anyone over age 50 who has a family history of heart trouble.

In some cases, a high homocysteine level is caused by an underlying illness—which needs treatment. More often, the problem is simply eating too much meat and dairy products and not enough fruits and veggies.

It's often possible to keep homocysteine low by eating right and taking three B-vitamins daily—folic acid (1 milligram [mg]), B-6 (10 mg) and B-12 (0.1 mg). Higher doses may be needed to lower an elevated level.

If you think you could benefit from homocysteine testing and your doctor has never mentioned the test to you, ask him/her about it. Don't let a doctor who's out-of-date place your life in jeopardy.

Reason: Often these patients come in with shortness of breath and wheezing, symptoms that mimic lung disease. As a result, ER doctors are less likely to order tests that screen for heart failure. And, the treatment for COPD may even worsen heart failure.

If you go to the ER with shortness of breath: Ask your doctor to measure your level of *B-type natriuretic peptide* (BNP). A BNP of less than 100 can rule out heart disease. If your BNP exceeds 100, and especially if it is over 500, you probably have heart failure.

Peter A. McCullough, MD, MPH, consultant cardiologist and director, division of nutrition and preventive medicine, William Beaumont Hospital, Royal Oak, MI.

Better Test to Predict Heart Attack Risk

The *C-reactive protein* (CRP) blood test is a better predictor of heart attack than cholesterol or homocysteine levels. This test measures a protein in the body, elevations of which have been correlated with both heart attack and stroke. The test generally costs between $50 and $100 and may not be covered by insurance.

Good news: Diet, exercise and statin drugs can reduce CRP significantly.

Richard Milani, MD, director, Cardiovascular Health Center, and vice chairman, department of cardiology, Ochsner Clinic Foundation, New Orleans.

Self-Defense Against ER Misdiagnosis

Hospital emergency rooms (ERs) misdiagnose about one in five patients with heart failure as having either asthma or *chronic obstructive pulmonary disease* (COPD).

Bypass Surgery Danger For Women

Women who are between the ages of 50 and 59 are three times more likely to die after having coronary-artery bypass surgery than men who are the same age.

Possible reasons: Since doctors are less inclined to suspect that younger women have heart disease, women are referred for surgery only when heart disease is advanced.

Also: Women have smaller arteries, making bypass surgery more difficult.

But women shouldn't avoid this potentially lifesaving surgery.

Self-defense: Undergo regular screening for heart disease risk factors, such as high blood pressure, high blood sugar and high cholesterol, beginning in young adulthood.

If any of these levels is elevated, seek prompt treatment to reduce your risk.

Viola Vaccarino, MD, PhD, professor of medicine, Emory University School of Medicine, Atlanta, and leader of a study of more than 57,000 bypass-surgery patients, reported in *Circulation*.

Heart-Bypass Surgery Side Effect

Heart-bypass surgery can be hard on the brain. In one study of 300 patients, 39% showed a decline in thinking skills six weeks after surgery. The greatest decline occurred in patients with the highest fevers in the 24 hours after surgery.

Self-defense: Ask your surgeon what steps will be taken to protect the brain.

Examples: Slow postoperative rewarming...temperature monitoring...arterial line filters, which remove harmful debris...cell-saving devices that recycle a patient's blood and decrease debris in the bypass circuit.

Hilary Grocott, MD, associate professor of anesthesiology and critical-care medicine, Duke University Medical Center, Durham, NC. His findings were published in *Stroke.*

Baldness Linked To Heart Trouble

Men who are losing the hair on the crowns of their heads have a 36% greater risk of heart problems than men who are not going bald...or who have mildly receding hairlines.

Going bald at the crown is an inherited characteristic that may be linked to elevated male hormone levels. Any man who is going bald in this way should carefully watch his blood pressure and cholesterol levels, and be especially careful to exercise regularly, not smoke and eat a heart-healthy diet.

JoAnn Manson, MD, DrPH, chief of preventive medicine, Brigham & Women's Hospital, Boston, and coauthor of a study of 22,000 male doctors, ages 40 to 84, reported in *Archives of Internal Medicine.*

Good News About Nutraceuticals

Stephen L. DeFelice, MD, chairman, Foundation for Innovation in Medicine (*www.fimdefelice.org*), Cranford, NJ, and former chief of clinical pharmacology, Walter Reed Army Institute of Research, Washington, DC. Dr. DeFelice coined the term "nutraceutical" and was among the first researchers to study carnitine's effects on the heart. He is author of *The Carnitine Defense* (Rodale).

There's now compelling evidence that certain foods contain special nutrients that guard against heart disease. The most important of these so-called "nutraceuticals" is *carnitine,* an amino acid found in red meat and in smaller amounts in chicken, fish, dairy products and certain fruits and vegetables.

Carnitine's primary function in the body is to ferry fatty acids from the foods we eat into the mitochondria. These microscopic "furnaces"—found inside every cell—convert fatty acids into the chemical energy that is put to use throughout the body.

CARNITINE SUPPLEMENTS

Biologists have been studying carnitine since the 1940s. Recent studies suggest that high levels of carnitine improve cardiac function in people suffering from coronary artery disease.

Other studies have shown that carnitine given immediately before or after a heart attack helps stabilize the heart rhythm. That improves the heart's pumping efficiency.

Carnitine has also been shown to minimize the damage caused to the heart in the aftermath of a heart attack.

No one can predict when a heart attack will strike. For this reason, it's often a good idea for people age 35 or older to take a daily carnitine supplement—to ensure that carnitine levels in the body are sufficient to protect the heart. Consult your doctor.

Carnitine supplementation is especially important for individuals with one or more risk factors for heart attack—obesity, family history of heart disease, elevated cholesterol level, high blood pressure and diabetes.

Carnitine supplements are sold over-the-counter in drugstores and health food stores. Check labels carefully. Animal studies suggest that carnitine *fumarate* is more cardioprotective than other forms of carnitine.

Typical daily dosage: 1,500 to 3,000 milligrams (mg). Taking carnitine twice daily—in divided doses 12 hours apart—helps keep blood levels consistent.

At this dosage, carnitine is extremely safe. Any excess is simply excreted in the urine.

BEYOND CARNITINE

Carnitine isn't the only heart-healthy nutraceutical. Vitamin E, magnesium, folic acid and other B vitamins, chromium and ethyl alcohol *in moderation* are all proven to reduce heart attack risk.

Since these compounds are present in food only in minute quantities, it can be hard to get enough of them from food alone. For this reason, supplementation is often a good idea.

VITAMIN E

Vitamin E helps neutralize free radicals, helping keep these highly reactive molecular fragments from triggering the buildup of fatty deposits in coronary arteries.

Typical daily dosage: 400 international units (IU). However, you should check with your doctor—taking more than 200 IU may be dangerous for some people. And, to get that much vitamin E from food alone, you'd have to eat 48 cups of wheat germ or 100 cups of spinach every day.

One recent study of patients at high risk for heart disease seemed to suggest that vitamin E supplementation did not protect the heart against a lack of oxygen. This study contradicts numerous other studies showing that the supplements are heart-protective.

It may turn out that vitamin E is more effective at preventing the development of high cholesterol and high blood pressure than at reducing heart attack risk in individuals who already have these risk factors.

Caution: Check with a doctor if you've had a stroke or are on daily aspirin therapy and/or are taking *warfarin* (Coumadin) or another prescription anticoagulant. In such cases, vitamin E supplementation can thin the blood to the point that hemorrhage is likely.

MAGNESIUM

Magnesium works to prevent platelets in the blood from clumping together and clogging coronary arteries. It also stabilizes heart rhythm, reducing the risk of damage to the heart muscle during a heart attack.

Typical daily dosage: 400 to 500 mg. Divide into two doses and take twice a day to keep blood levels up all day.

Dietary sources of magnesium include artichokes, beans, shellfish, nuts and whole grains.

B VITAMINS

The B vitamin folic acid cuts blood levels of *homocysteine,* a blood protein that's been linked to heart disease. Folic acid's homocysteine-busting effect is especially pronounced when it's taken in combination with vitamins B-6 and B-12.

Typical daily dosages: 400 micrograms (mcg) folic acid...400 mg vitamin B-6...500 to 1,000 mcg vitamin B-12.

ALCOHOL

Moderate alcohol consumption fights heart disease in three ways—it boosts levels of HDL ("good") cholesterol...helps rid the body of LDL ("bad") cholesterol...and helps prevent platelet clumping.

Typical daily "dosage": The equivalent of one drink for women...one or two drinks for men. One drink equals 12 ounces of beer, four ounces of wine or 1.5 ounces of distilled spirits.

If you have a family or personal history of alcohol abuse: Consult a doctor before using alcohol. Pregnant women should not drink alcohol.

CHROMIUM

Chromium has been shown to reduce insulin resistance, in which cells' increasing insensitivity to insulin causes glucose levels to rise. This is a significant problem for people with diabetes.

Typical daily dosage: 500 to 1,000 mcg.

Dietary sources of chromium include brewer's yeast, liver, egg yolks, wheat germ and whole-grain cereal.

If it's too hard to keep track of which supplements to take once a day and which twice a day, divide all the doses in half and take all your supplements twice a day.

Caution: Consult a doctor before taking any nutritional supplement. Like prescription medications, supplements can interact with other drugs you take.

Your doctor should carefully monitor the effects of the supplements...and, if necessary, adjust dosages.

Chocolate Is Good For The Heart

A *bit* of chocolate may be good for your heart. Chocolate contains flavonoids—antioxidant compounds also found in fruits and vegetables that protect against heart disease. Dark chocolate contains more flavonoids than milk chocolate.

Francene Steinberg, PhD, RD, associate professor of nutrition, University of California, Davis.

Eat Citrus to Reduce Heart Disease

G rapefruit and oranges protect the heart, reports Pamela Mink, PhD, MPH.

New finding: In a study of nearly 35,000 women ages 55 to 69, researchers found that women who consumed the most *flavanones,* a flavonoid antioxidant found primarily in citrus fruits (such as grapefruit and oranges), had a 22% lower risk for death from heart disease than those who consumed the least.

Theory: Flavonoids help prevent blood clots and promote blood vessel health. If you take medication, ask your doctor whether citrus affects the drug's effectiveness.

Pamela Mink, PhD, MPH, senior managing scientist, Health Sciences, Exponent Inc., Washington, DC.

Consume Split Peas for a Healthier Heart

B etter than soybeans for heart protection are kudzu and yellow split peas. These legumes are richer in *genistein* and *dadzein*—isoflavones thought to protect against heart disease—than soybeans. Kudzu seedlings contain at least 10 times more of these beneficial substances than soybeans...yellow split peas, almost twice as much as soybeans.

Important: To get the most protection from any of these legumes, wash and consume the seedling shoots as well as their roots, which contain the greatest concentration of genistein and dadzein.

Peter B. Kaufman, PhD, professor emeritus of plant physiology and plant biotechnology, University of Michigan, Ann Arbor.

Drinking Beer Combats Blood Clots

I n a recent finding, men who consumed 12 ounces of beer a day for one month had 10% less of the clot-promoting protein *fibrinogen* in their blood than those who drank only mineral water. Blood clots increase the risk for heart attack and stroke.

Theory: Compounds known as *polyphenols* found in beer—as well as in wine and fruit juice—act as antioxidants and may trigger this beneficial effect.

Self-defense: Ask your doctor whether moderate consumption of beer, wine or fruit juice is appropriate for you.

Shela Gorinstein, PhD, chief researcher and head of the international research group, department of medicinal chemistry and natural products, The Hebrew University of Jerusalem, Israel.

New Strategies For Controlling High Blood Pressure

Sheldon G. Sheps, MD, a cardiologist and emeritus professor of medicine, Mayo Medical School, Rochester, MN. He was editor-in-chief of *Mayo Clinic on High Blood Pressure* (Kensington).

Most people assume that high blood pressure (hypertension) is relatively easy to diagnose and treat. Not so. Even experienced doctors can fail to treat effectively all the complexities of the condition.

To avoid many of the serious health threats associated with hypertension—heart attack, stroke, kidney failure, etc.—here are the latest research findings...

●**Even mild hypertension needs treatment.** Optimal blood pressure is 115/75. Traditionally, doctors have treated blood pressure only when readings climb to 140/90 or higher.

But recent research shows that a systolic reading (the top number) of 130 to 139 and a diastolic reading (the bottom number) of 85 to 89 can cause artery damage.*

Any increase in blood pressure needs to be lowered, either with lifestyle changes (a healthful diet, regular exercise, etc.) or medication.

●**Systolic pressure is just as important as diastolic pressure.** Many doctors continue to focus on diastolic pressure because they were taught it was the main cause of organ damage.

Fact: Mildly elevated systolic pressure (140 to 150) needs to be lowered—even if diastolic pressure is normal.

●**"Pulse pressure" may predict heart disease more accurately** than systolic and diastolic readings. Pulse pressure is the numerical difference between systolic and diastolic pressure. Some researchers believe that pulse pressure is even more important than systolic pressure in determining long-term health risks.

A pulse pressure below 50 indicates that the arteries are elastic and healthy. But when arteries are stiff and inelastic, systolic pressure rises

*Systolic pressure is the force that's generated when the heart's main pumping chamber contracts. Diastolic pressure is that which occurs between these contractions.

and diastolic pressure falls. This increases pulse pressure to 60 or greater.

New medications: Vasopeptide inhibitors target pulse pressure by lowering systolic pressure while having relatively less effect on diastolic pressure. These drugs, which are currently in clinical trials, will eventually be available by prescription.

●**Blood pressure readings taken in a doctor's office are not always enough.** People who regularly check their blood pressure at home tend to control their hypertension more effectively than those who get only periodic readings in a doctor's office.

Bonus: Monitoring done in your home can detect two common types of faulty blood pressure readings...

● *White-coat hypertension* is a spike in blood pressure that occurs when people feel anxiety during a doctor's appointment.

● *White-coat normotension* is a drop in blood pressure that occurs in people who feel especially relaxed in their doctors' offices (compared with home or work).

Consider at-home monitoring if your blood pressure is mildly elevated during office visits ...or if you're being treated for high blood pressure. Your doctor can give you specific recommendations on the frequency. *For accurate home readings...*

●Use an electronic (digital) blood pressure-measuring device. Most models are easy to use. *Cost:* $35 to $400. *Important:* Ask your doctor to measure your arm to determine the proper cuff size. Cuffs that are too small give artificially high readings. Cuffs that are too big give low readings.

●On the days you measure your blood pressure, take two readings in the morning (a few hours after you wake up)...and two in the evening...then average the results. Always wait at least a half-hour after eating...smoking...or drinking caffeine or alcohol to take your blood pressure. *Important:* Go to the bathroom first. A full bladder elevates readings.

●Bring a log of the readings to your next doctor's appointment. If the readings seem to be unusually high—or are rising over time—call your doctor right away.

●**Salt really does matter.** Research shows that restricting salt intake to 1,500 milligrams (mg) daily—down from the current recommendation of 2,400 mg—can reduce systolic pressure by 11.5 points and diastolic pressure by an average of 5.5 points.

●**Drinking alcohol can raise blood pressure.** Excessive alcohol consumption is thought to contribute to hypertension in one out of 10 people who suffers from this condition.

Men should have fewer than two drinks per day...women, one.

●**Deep breathing helps.** People who practice deep breathing for 15 minutes daily—inhaling through the nose for about four seconds... holding it momentarily...then exhaling through the mouth for four seconds—may reduce their blood pressure.

Helpful: The FDA has approved a prescription device called RESPeRATE for lowering high blood pressure. The device measures breathing rate, then creates audio-guided exercises to slow breathing down.

More information: Contact the manufacturer, InterCure, at 877-988-9388 or on the Web at *www.resperate.com.*

●**Even minor weight loss makes a difference.** In a recent study, 40% of people with hypertension who lost eight to 10 pounds were able to stay off antihypertensive medication.

Key: Exercise regularly, eat less fat and cut your calories.

●**Exercise daily.** Most experts recommend exercising at least three days a week, but new research shows that exercising every day or most days can lower blood pressure by five to 10 points.

Best choices: Aerobic exercises, such as walking, biking or swimming.

Eat Your Way to Lower Blood Pressure

Michael F. Roizen, MD, former dean, School of Medicine, SUNY Upstate School of Medicine, Syracuse, NY. He is author of *Real Age: Are You as Young as You Can Be?* and *The RealAge Diet: Make Yourself Younger with What You Eat* (both from Harper Resource). *www.realage.com.*

High blood pressure is more than simply a leading cause of heart disease and stroke. It is also a major factor in memory loss, wrinkling of the skin, impotence and decreased sexual response in women. Most Americans have blood pressure well over the ideal of 115/75. In fact, less than 10% of those over age 50 have ideal pressure.

While many people require medication, a diet rich in fruits, vegetables, fiber, calcium and potassium can help to reduce blood pressure...

●**Eat two to four servings of fruits and three to five servings of vegetables each day.** A colorful variety is best.

●**Up to 25% of daily calories should come from healthful fat** (monounsaturated and polyunsaturated). These fats are found in olive, canola and flaxseed oils...avocados... unsalted nuts...and fish. When you cook, use oil sparingly. A mere half-teaspoon per meal contains all the necessary nutrients.

●**Eat one clove of garlic and as much onion as you can tolerate each day.** These contain flavonoids, which help the arteries to resist hardening.

●**Avoid saturated fat,** found in all animal products. Eat red meat no more than once a week. An hour before eating a fatty meal, take 400 milligrams (mg) of vitamin C and 400 international units (IU) of vitamin E (check with your doctor for the proper amount). These vitamins may contribute to healthier arteries.

●**Get 1,200 mg of calcium daily**—and 400 IU of vitamin D to help with absorption.

●**Make exercise part of your "daily diet."** I start hypertension patients with 30 minutes of walking a day. After three weeks, they add 10 minutes of weight lifting, three times a week. Any exercise is good exercise...and some is better than none.

Better Blood Pressure Reduction

Ask your doctor if you can try weight loss and sodium reduction instead of hypertension drugs to reduce your blood pressure.

A study of 975 people between 60 and 80 years old found that one-third of them could stop taking blood pressure medication after losing less than eight pounds and reducing their sodium intake by 25%. And among those people who only lost weight *or* reduced their sodium consumption, one-third were able to stop taking medication.

Paul Whelton, MD, senior vice president for health sciences, Health Sciences Center, School of Public Health and Tropical Medicine, Tulane University, New Orleans.

Falling Blood Pressure Alert

Falling blood pressure can be a sign of failing health.

Background: Blood pressure tends to very slowly increase with age. But a study shows that adults age 65 or older who had a decline in systolic blood pressure of 20 points or more or a decline in diastolic blood pressure of 10 points or more over a three-year period had a 60% greater chance of dying from heart disease during the succeeding three years than those people who had no change in their blood pressure.

Speak with your physician if your blood pressure declines by more than 20 points without any blood pressure–lowering medications.

Shiva Satish, MD, MPH, assistant professor of internal medicine, University of Texas, Galveston.

How to Avoid a Stroke...and Get the Right Life-Saving Help If It Strikes

Harold P. Adams, Jr., MD, professor and director, division of cerebrovascular diseases, University of Iowa College of Medicine, Iowa City, and chairman of the advisory committee of the American Stroke Association. www.strokeassociation.org.

Stroke is the leading cause of disability in this country—and the third leading cause of death, after heart attack and cancer.

Strokes are sometimes called "brain attacks." Like heart attacks, they result from interrupted blood flow to critical tissue. *There are two kinds of stroke...*

•**Ischemic stroke** is by far the more common type. It is caused by a blood clot that forms within the brain's arteries or is carried by the blood to the brain from elsewhere in the body.

Ischemic stroke can also occur when fatty deposits (plaques) rupture inside an artery in the brain or neck.

•**Hemorrhagic stroke** is more likely to result in death. It occurs when a blood vessel in the brain ruptures, allowing uncontrolled bleeding into the brain or surrounding spaces.

AN OUNCE OF PREVENTION

In addition to quitting smoking and keeping blood sugar in check, follow these guidelines...

•**Keep your blood pressure down.** Check pressure annually—more often if you have borderline numbers. Blood pressure should be 115/75 or below.

People who develop high blood pressure in midlife have higher stroke risk. Most require medication, but stroke risk can be reduced by changes in diet, weight and exercise.

One effective strategy was developed as part of an ongoing study known as Dietary Approaches to Stop Hypertension (DASH). The DASH diet, which emphasizes the consumption of fruits, vegetables and low-fat dairy products, appears to help reduce blood pressure.

For more information on the DASH diet, visit the Web site at *www.nhlbi.nih.gov/health/pub lic/heart/hbp/dash/how_plan.html.*

• **Control cholesterol.** Regular exercise and a healthful diet can help you maintain the proper ratio of LDL ("bad") cholesterol to HDL ("good") cholesterol—which reduces the formation of artery-narrowing plaques.

The same DASH diet that controls blood pressure helps keep cholesterol down. So does the Mediterranean Diet, which emphasizes grains, fruit, vegetables and olive oil.

If a healthful diet and regular exercise aren't sufficient, your doctor may prescribe cholesterol-lowering medication.

• **Relax.** Chronic psychological stress elevates stroke risk in two ways. It raises blood pressure and can lead to overeating, smoking or heavy drinking.

Helpful: Meditation. A recent study showed that transcendental meditation can reduce both stroke and heart attack risk.

• **Drink alcohol in moderation.** Moderate alcohol use seems to lower stroke risk. But don't exceed two glasses of wine daily. And since alcohol can cause other health problems, nondrinkers should not start drinking to reduce stroke risk.

• **Use aspirin—maybe.** Taking aspirin on a regular basis may prevent stroke and heart attack by keeping clot-forming platelets from clumping together. Most patients take one 81-milligram (mg) tablet daily or a 325-mg tablet every other day. But the data are stronger for prevention of a heart attack.

Discuss the matter with a doctor before starting aspirin therapy. Aspirin can cause bleeding in the stomach and other problems.

Aspirin is especially beneficial for people who have experienced a *transient ischemic attack* (TIA). A TIA is often a warning sign that a full-blown stroke is imminent.

Symptoms: TIA symptoms are similar to those of stroke—sudden weakness or numbness of the face, arm or leg, especially on one side of the body...sudden confusion...trouble speaking or understanding speech...vision loss...sudden severe headache...or sudden trouble walking, accompanied by dizziness and loss of balance or coordination.

Seek immediate treatment for these symptoms even if they resolve quickly.

Some patients can't tolerate aspirin or have TIA symptoms despite taking aspirin. In such cases, doctors often prescribe other antiplatelet agents, such as *ticlopidine* (Ticlid) or *clopidogrel* (Plavix).

THE GOLDEN WINDOW

Treatment within three hours of the stroke's onset offers the best chance of full recovery. Like a heart attack, stroke is a 911 emergency. Before emergency strikes, ask your doctor the location of the nearest "stroke center"—where stroke experts are always on hand.

Using a *computed tomography* (CT) brain scan or ultrafast *magnetic resonance imaging* (MRI), a stroke team determines if a stroke is ischemic or hemorrhagic. Clot-busting *tissue plasminogen activator* (tPA) cannot be given to patients with hemorrhagic stroke. If the stroke is ischemic, tPA given within three hours can be a lifesaver. Delivered by injection into a vein—or via a catheter directly into the brain—tPA breaks up blood clots, restoring normal circulation to the brain.

The treatment of hemorrhagic stroke is more difficult, but surgery is sometimes helpful.

Ambulance crews are starting to get sophisticated stroke-treatment tools that until recently were available only in emergency rooms. So, it's usually best to go to the hospital by ambulance.

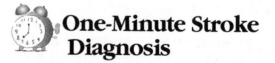

One-Minute Stroke Diagnosis

Stroke researchers have devised a simple three-step test to tell if someone has suffered a stroke. *Here's what to do...*

1. Ask the person to show his/her teeth. The "smile test" helps to determine one-sided facial weakness.

2. Have the person close his eyes and raise his arms straight out in front of his body. Stroke victims usually cannot raise both arms to the same height.

3. Ask the person to repeat a simple sentence, such as "Don't cry over spilled milk." Listen for slurring.

This three-step test should not be used as a substitute for appropriate medical evaluation and can miss some types of strokes. However, if you or someone you know shows *any* of the symptoms described above, call 911 immediately.

Spotting stroke symptoms early is critical. Potentially lifesaving clot-busting drugs must be given within the first three hours of the onset of stroke.

Jane H. Brice, MD, MPH, assistant professor of emergency medicine, University of North Carolina–Chapel Hill School of Medicine.

Better Stroke Detection

Fast *magnetic resonance imaging* (MRI) lets physicians diagnose stroke in as little as three minutes, enabling life-saving clot-buster drugs to be administered earlier. A fast MRI can be performed about as quickly as a *computed tomography* (CT) scan, the test currently used to diagnose stroke. However, the new technology provides a better image of the brain and blood vessel blockage than a CT scan.

Fast MRI is now offered at some major US medical centers and should become increasingly available within the next few years.

Jonathan H. Gillard, MD, lecturer and consultant neuroradiologist, Addenbrooke's Hospital, University of Cambridge, England.

Do You Know the Symptoms of a Ministroke?

Nearly four out of five primary care physicians surveyed could not identify the typical symptoms of a ministroke. *Transient ischemic*

attack (TIA) occurs when an artery to or in the brain becomes blocked. Symptoms include numbness or weakness in the face, arm or leg, especially on one side…visual difficulties in one or both eyes…confusion or trouble speaking …trouble walking…and dizziness.

Self-defense: Anyone who experiences these symptoms needs to get to a hospital immediately. Treating the TIA risk factors, such as high blood pressure and cholesterol, can prevent a full-blown stroke.

S. Claiborne Johnston, MD, PhD, director, Stroke Service, University of California, San Francisco.

Surprising Stroke Risks Even Doctors Overlook

Gregory W. Albers, MD, professor of neurology and neurological sciences, Stanford University Medical Center, and director, Stanford Stroke Center, both in Palo Alto, CA. He also is chairman of the American College of Chest Physicians' expert panel for both stroke and atrial fibrillation, cochairman of the National Stroke Association's Stroke Center Network and chairman of the American Heart Association's Stroke Council.

Stroke is a leading cause of brain damage and death. Most of us know that stroke risk can be reduced by controlling high blood pressure and cholesterol, eating a well-balanced diet and exercising on a regular basis. But it is what you may *not* know about this disabling disorder that could save your life.

Often overlooked stroke risks…

PREHYPERTENSION

Until just recently, blood pressure less than 140/90 was considered normal. However, studies now indicate that a reading higher than 115/75 raises the risk for stroke and should be treated with a combination of exercise, diet and medication, if needed.

What you may not know: Although diuretics, beta-blockers and ACE inhibitors have long been utilized to lower blood pressure, recent research reveals that a newer class of antihypertensive medication, called *angiotensin II receptor* *blockers* (ARBs), may provide unique protection against stroke.

Recent study: An ARB known as *losartan* (Cozaar) reduced stroke risk by an additional 25% over the beta-blocker *atenolol* (Tenormin). Several large trials are under way to further study ARBs. If the results are as promising as this preliminary one, ARBs could become the antihypertensive medication of choice for preventing stroke.

Bonus: ARBs cause fewer side effects than other blood pressure medications.

Self-defense: If you take blood pressure–lowering medication, ask your physician if an ARB would be appropriate for you.

ATRIAL FIBRILLATION

This heart rhythm disturbance affects two million Americans. With *atrial fibrillation* (AF), the upper chambers of the heart quiver rapidly or irregularly and fail to pump efficiently.

What you may not know: Each year, up to 70,000 strokes are caused by AF. During AF, some patients experience a racing heart, palpitations or a fluttering in their chest, dizziness and/or shortness of breath. For other patients, the first symptom of AF may be a stroke.

Self-defense: To determine if you may have AF, put your index finger on your wrist and check your pulse for an irregular or random rhythm. AF can be confirmed with a routine *electrocardiogram* (EKG).

If you are diagnosed with AF, your doctor may prescribe an antiarrhythmic medication, such as *digoxin* (Lanoxin) or *amiodarone* (Cordarone), or a type of electric shock, known as cardioversion, to correct the arrhythmia.

However, the recurrence rate for AF is high with these therapies. It is usually preferable to choose a treatment that prevents blood clots, rather than focusing on the heart rhythm disturbance. Lifetime use of anticoagulants can reduce stroke risk in AF patients by 68%.

The most frequently prescribed anticoagulant, *warfarin* (Coumadin), is extremely effective at preventing clots and reducing stroke risk in people with AF. Unfortunately, it has a narrow "therapeutic index"—slightly too much in your system can cause bleeding...slightly too little will permit stroke.

Warfarin also interacts with other drugs, supplements and even foods.

Example: Vitamin K, which is found in leafy greens and margarine, counteracts the effects of warfarin.

Because warfarin interferes with so many common substances, people taking it need to undergo monthly blood tests...and physicians must adjust the dosage frequently. As a result, less than half of AF patients who should take Coumadin actually do.

Good news: An anticoagulant called *ximelagatran* (Exanta) promises to revolutionize stroke and blood clot prevention. Early data suggest that it's as effective as warfarin for preventing stroke, causes less bleeding, has no known food, drug or alcohol interactions, and blood doesn't have to be tested regularly for coagulation. If the additional tests are positive, Exanta will go to the FDA for approval before being made available to patients.

LEG PAIN

Just as atherosclerosis can narrow blood vessels to the heart and brain, it also can block arteries in the extremities, causing *peripheral artery disease* (PAD). Leg pain—especially in the calves—is the chief symptom. Known as intermittent claudication, the pain typically begins with walking and ends when you stop. PAD affects up to 20% of Americans who are age 65 or older.

What you may not know: If you have PAD, you also may have atherosclerosis elsewhere in the body, such as the heart or the brain. This puts you at increased risk for stroke. What's more, you also can have "silent," or asymptomatic, PAD. Risk factors for PAD are the same as those for cardiovascular disease—high blood pressure, high cholesterol, diabetes and age.

Self-defense: PAD is easily and painlessly diagnosed with an ankle brachial index test, which measures the ratio of blood pressure in the arm and ankle. If you're diagnosed with PAD, your physician might prescribe an antiplatelet medication, such as aspirin or *clopidogrel* (Plavix). Moderate exercise to reduce leg pain and blood pressure or cholesterol-lowering medications also may be recommended.

SLEEP APNEA

This disorder occurs when breathing is temporarily interrupted during sleep. An estimated 24% of men and 9% of women suffer from significant sleep apnea.

What you may not know: People with sleep apnea are three to six times more likely to suffer a stroke. Their blood pressure increases dramatically during the night, which can raise the risk for atherosclerotic blockages of the carotid—or neck—arteries, a chief cause of stroke.

In one recent study involving men ages 45 to 77, more than 21% of patients with sleep apnea had calcified plaques, which block blood flow, in their carotid arteries. Only 2.5% of the healthy control patients had calcified plaques.

Self-defense: Obesity is the leading risk factor for sleep apnea...and loud snoring and excessive daytime sleepiness are telltale signs. If you suspect you may have sleep apnea, consult your physician about diagnosis and the best treatment options.

Caution: It's important for AF patients who have symptoms of sleep apnea to undergo sleep apnea screening. Mayo Clinic researchers have reported that AF is twice as likely to recur in patients with untreated sleep apnea.

The Migraine–Stroke Link

Migraines that are preceded by an aura increase ischemic stroke risk fivefold. Auras, which affect about 15% of all migraine sufferers, happen up to one hour before the headache strikes.

An aura will typically include bright or flashing dots or other sensory disturbances. The reason for the association between migraines and stroke is unknown.

If you have migraines with auras: See your doctor for treatment and to discuss a plan to reduce your risk for stroke.

Neil R. Poulter, MD, professor of preventive cardiovascular medicine, Imperial College, London. His study of 286 women was published in the *Journal of Neurology, Neurosurgery and Psychiatry.*

Stents May Help Prevent Stroke—Safely

Stroke patients may receive stents as an outpatient alternative to surgery for clogged carotid (neck) arteries.

Stents are small wire-mesh devices that hold clogged arteries open and can reduce risk for stroke. Most patients can go home four hours after the procedure is completed instead of staying overnight in the hospital.

A recent randomized study of high-risk surgery patients has shown that the procedure has half the risk of traditional surgery. An angiogram is used to determine if a patient is a candidate for carotid stents.

Gary S. Roubin, MD, PhD, chairman, department of interventional cardiology, Lenox Hill Heart and Vascular Institute of New York, New York City.

Potential Risk of Artery Surgery

Artery-clearing surgery makes sense only if arterial blockages are severe.

Trap: In people whose carotid (neck) arteries are only mildly blocked, *carotid endarterectomy* is more likely to cause a stroke than to prevent one.

The surgery can loosen a tiny piece of the fatty plaque that makes up the blockage...and send it to the brain, where it blocks circulation.

Bottom line: If your carotid arteries are blocked by 70% or more, endarterectomy can dramatically reduce your risk of stroke. But if your arteries are less severely blocked, it may be safer to live with the blockages.

Henry J. Barnett, MD, principal investigator, North American Symptomatic Carotid Endarterectomy Trial, Robarts Research Institute, London, Ontario. His 11-year study of 2,885 people who had had a stroke or a transient ischemic attack (TIA) was presented at a meeting of the American Heart Association.

10

Cancer Prevention & Treatment

Proven Ways to Reduce Your Risk of 12 Common Cancers

Statistics show that cancer kills one in four Americans. And each year, more than 1 million new cases are diagnosed. Some cancer risk factors—family history, age, ethnicity, etc.—can't be changed. *But you can lower your risk of developing cancer by making basic lifestyle changes...*

- **Don't smoke.**
- **Eat a healthy diet.**
- **Maintain a healthy weight.**
- **Get regular physical activity.**
- **Limit alcohol consumption.**
- **Protect yourself from the sun.**
- **Avoid sexually transmitted infections.**

As much as 50% of cancers in this country could be prevented. *Here are some specific*

steps you can take to decrease your risk of the most common ones...

PROSTATE CANCER

More than 198,000 new cases are diagnosed annually. *Risk reducers...*

●**Limit the amount of animal fat in your diet.** Men who eat fewer than five servings a day of meat, milk, cheese, etc. have a lower risk of prostate cancer. One serving of these foods, which is four ounces, is about the size of a deck of playing cards.

A great deal of research is being done to identify the factors in animal fat that increase prostate cancer risk. One explanation may be that animal fat can affect different hormone levels, increasing cancer risk.

●**Eat one or more servings daily of tomatoes or tomato-based foods,** such as tomato juice and spaghetti sauce. One serving equals

Cynthia Stein, MD, MPH, associate director, Center for Cancer Prevention, Harvard School of Public Health, Boston. The Center's Web site, *www.diseaseriskindex. harvard.edu,* helps individuals evaluate their risks for different types of cancer.

one-half cup of whole or chopped tomatoes or sauce, or three-quarters of a cup of tomato juice. Tomatoes are rich in the antioxidant *lycopene,* which may protect the prostate from cancerous cells. Other fruits and vegetables contain lycopene, but tomatoes are the best source.

●**Talk to your doctor about screening tests,** especially if you are at high risk—African-Americans and men with a close relative who had prostate cancer at a young age are at increased risk.

BREAST CANCER

More than 190,000 American women are diagnosed with breast cancer every year. Although the overwhelming majority of people with breast cancer are women, about 1,500 American men are also diagnosed with this disease each year. *Risk reducers...*

●**Eat at least three servings of vegetables daily.** A serving equals one cup of green, leafy vegetables or one-half cup of other vegetables, cooked beans or peas. There are numerous vitamins and nutrients in vegetables that may reduce the risk of different types of cancers. Specifically, low levels of vitamin A have been associated with breast cancer risk.

●**Limit your alcohol intake.** Alcohol may affect levels of estrogen and other hormones, increasing the risk of breast cancer. Women who have less than one drink per day have a lower risk of developing breast cancer. One drink is equal to a can of beer, a glass of wine or a shot of liquor.

●**Get regular screening.** All women should get clinical breast exams regularly and should start getting mammograms at age 50 (earlier if there is a strong family history or other risk factors).

LUNG CANCER

Lung cancer is the third most common cancer in the US, and the leading cause of cancer death. Nearly 170,000 cases are diagnosed annually. *Risk reducers...*

●**Do not smoke**—and avoid secondhand smoke. Tobacco smoke causes 90% of lung cancer cases. Quitting not only decreases the risk of lung cancer, it also reduces the risk of heart disease, stroke and cancers of the mouth, esophagus, pancreas, kidney, bladder, cervix and colon.

●**Eat a diet rich in fruits and vegetables.** They have many cancer-fighting ingredients, including vitamins A and C. People who eat three or more servings per day have a lower risk of lung cancer. One serving equals one cup of leafy greens...one medium-sized fruit ...one-half cup of cut fruit or vegetables...or one-third cup of juice.

Although fruits and vegetables can help protect against many kinds of cancer, nothing will decrease your risk of lung cancer nearly as much as avoiding tobacco smoke.

COLORECTAL CANCER

Cancer of the colon and rectum is currently the second-leading cause of cancer deaths in the US. More than 130,000 new cases are diagnosed every year. *Risk reducers...*

●**Maintain a healthy weight.** Researchers have found that people who maintain a healthy weight have a lower risk of developing colon cancer. This may be because weight affects different hormone levels in the body.

●**Limit the amount of red meat in your diet.** People who eat less than one serving per day of beef, pork, lamb or veal have a lower risk of colon cancer. One serving is about four ounces. Cooked meat contains chemicals that may increase cancerous cells.

●**Avoid alcohol.** As with breast cancer, it has been found that people who have less than one alcoholic drink per day have a lower risk of colon cancer. Alcohol decreases levels of folate, a B vitamin that may provide protection against cancer.

●**Take a daily multivitamin.** It should contain 400 international units (IU) of folate.

Also: Eat folate-rich foods, such as spinach, asparagus, beans, peas and fortified cereals.

●**Exercise at least 30 minutes each day.** There are many benefits to physical activity. One way it may help against colon cancer is by speeding up the movement of waste through the body.

●**Get screened.** Screening allows early discovery and removal of polyps—small growths that can become cancerous. People who are screened regularly have a lower risk of colon cancer. Ask your doctor about the appropriate screening frequency for you.

BLADDER CANCER

More than 54,000 new cases are diagnosed every year. It most commonly afflicts men. *Risk reducers...*

•**If you smoke, quit now.** Tobacco contains more than 40 carcinogens. Many of these can concentrate in the urine and damage cells lining the bladder walls. As little as one cigarette per day can increase your cancer risk. Quit, and the risk drops almost immediately.

•**Beware of workplace chemicals,** especially those used in the rubber, aluminum and dye industries. Chemicals including aromatic amines have been linked to an increase in bladder cancer. Adequate safety equipment—gloves, respirators, protective suits and eye protection—is essential.

MELANOMA

The deadliest form of skin cancer, melanoma strikes more than 50,000 Americans each year. Other forms of skin cancer like basal cell and squamous cell are more common (more than 1 million cases per year) but also more easily treated. *Risk reducers...*

•**Use sunblock.** Avoid prolonged sun exposure, especially between 10 am and 4 pm. Wear a hat, sunglasses and long sleeves as often as possible. Always use sunblock with a sun protection factor (SPF) of 15 or higher. Reapply often, especially if you have been in the water or perspiring.

•**Protect your children.** As much as 80% of lifetime sun exposure can occur before age 21. Sunburns early in life increase the risk of skin cancer in later years. Don't let your children go outside without sunblock, a hat and protective cover.

UTERINE CANCER

Also called endometrial cancer, this is the most common cancer of the female reproductive tract. About 36,000 cases are diagnosed annually. *Risk reducer...*

•**Maintain a healthy weight.** High levels of estrogen, especially after reaching menopause, can increase the risk of uterine cancer.

And excess fat increases the amount of estrogen in a woman's body.

KIDNEY CANCER

It strikes about 30,000 Americans annually. *Risk reducers...*

•**Don't smoke.** Many of the same carcinogens that damage the bladder also increase kidney cancer risk.

•**Maintain a healthy weight.** In addition to the other benefits of a healthy weight, people who are not overweight also have a lower risk of kidney cancer.

PANCREATIC CANCER

This type of cancer strikes about 29,000 Americans every year. It is often diagnosed at a late stage because there may be no early warning signs. Survival rates are terrible—20% at one year...4% at five years, according to the American Cancer Society. *Risk reducers...*

•**Eat at least three servings of vegetables every day.** Vegetables may offer protection against cancer in different ways. One way they do this against pancreatic cancer is by adding fiber to the diet.

•**Don't smoke.** People who smoke have a higher risk of pancreatic cancer than do non-smokers. The chemicals in tobacco smoke will cause cell damage throughout the body, increasing the risk of many types of cancer and other diseases, such as heart disease and stroke.

OVARIAN CANCER

Each year, it strikes 23,000 American women. Like pancreatic cancer, the disease is often difficult to detect and, in many cases, spreads prior to the diagnosis. *Risk reducers...*

•**Breast-feeding,** which can cause a woman to ovulate (produce an egg) less frequently, may help decrease ovarian cancer risk.

•**Taking birth control pills** for at least five years can also decrease the risk of ovarian cancer. They may be protective by preventing ovulation.

However, there are also risks involved in taking oral contraceptives, and a woman should discuss the risks and benefits with her doctor.

STOMACH CANCER

There are more than 20,000 new cases every year. *Risk reducers...*

●**Eat three or more daily servings of fruit.** One vitamin in fruit that may be particularly helpful is vitamin C. Low levels have been associated with stomach cancer.

●**Limit salt intake.** High salt content may affect the lining of the stomach, and thereby increase the risk of cancer. Large amounts of salt are often found in processed foods, soups and sauces.

CERVICAL CANCER

Cervical cancer tends to grow slowly, which is why it can often be prevented or treated successfully when detected early with a Pap test. About 13,000 American women are diagnosed with cervical cancer annually. *Risk reducers...*

●**Use safer-sex practices**—condoms, abstinence or monogamy. Women who are exposed to sexually transmitted infections, especially certain types of *human papillomavirus* (HPV) —and especially at young ages—have a higher risk. The infections may cause cell changes that lead to cervical cancer.

●**Do not smoke.** Again, the chemicals in tobacco smoke cause cell damage and increase the risk of cancer.

●**Have regular Pap tests.** Pap tests can identify changes in cells before they become cancerous. Women who have regular Pap tests have a lower risk of cervical cancer.

Beware of Hidden Carcinogens

Christopher J. Portier, PhD, director, environmental toxicology program, National Institutes of Environmental Health Sciences, Research Triangle Park, NC.

Every two years, the federal government publishes their *Report on Carcinogens* (ROC), a list of all environmental substances that are either known—or appear likely—to cause cancer. The ROC does not calculate the odds that an individual exposed to these substances will get cancer. Nor does it offer ways to offset cancer risks.

Common carcinogens to avoid...

ESTROGENS

Every woman is exposed to various forms of the hormone estrogen. This includes the natural form secreted by the ovaries and fat tissue, as well as, in some cases, the estrogens used in birth control pills, *hormone replacement therapy* (HRT), vaginal creams, etc.

Estrogens are carcinogenic. And, the greater a woman's exposure, the greater her risk for developing uterine and breast cancer. In rare cases, men must take estrogen to treat prostate cancer. They are also at increased risk for developing breast cancer.

Women cannot reduce their exposure to natural forms of estrogen. Those who began menstruating at an early age (before age 11) or had a late onset of menopause (after age 55) will naturally have greater estrogen exposure—and should be sure to get regular Pap smears, mammograms and other screening tests.

The use of HRT is controversial. The drugs clearly are beneficial for reducing menopausal symptoms. However, long-standing claims that HRT helps reduce heart disease have not been borne out by research. Furthermore, HRT may increase the risk for blood clots, strokes and other serious problems.

The FDA requires that estrogen drug labels, including those on birth control pills, warn about possible cancer risks.

It is not yet clear if estrogen-like compounds found in soy increase cancer risk. More research is under way.

To protect yourself: Every woman should talk to her doctor about the risks and benefits of taking supplemental estrogen.

IQ

IQ, the abbreviation for *2-amino-3-methyl-imidazo [4,5-f] quinoline,* belongs to the chemical family called *heterocyclic amines,* which are produced by high-heat cooking. Cooked foods with the highest IQ levels include grilled, broiled or fried beef or fish.

Animal studies suggest that exposure to IQ may bring on cancers of the mammary gland, liver and small intestine. Some human studies suggest that people who eat the most grilled, broiled or fried foods have a higher risk for breast and colorectal cancers.

To protect yourself: Cook your foods more slowly at lower heats. Avoid or reduce the frequency of high-heat grilling and broiling. Do not blacken or char food.

METHYLEUGENOL

Methyleugenol is a naturally occurring substance found in many essential oils, including those in basil, nutmeg and cinnamon. It is used as a flavoring agent in many packaged foods. The words "natural flavoring" on a label may mean the product contains methyleugenol.

Other sources: Insect strips or traps…and baked goods, such as gingersnaps.

Animal studies suggest that long-term exposure to methyleugenol triggers DNA damage that increases the risk for liver cancer. We aren't sure if humans face the same risk—but nearly everyone is exposed to the chemical on a daily basis.

To protect yourself: Research is under way to determine the carcinogenic levels of methyleugenol. It is still unknown whether dangerous levels of methyleugenol are emitted from insect traps. Using less basil, cinnamon and nutmeg when preparing food may be helpful.

RADON

Radon—a colorless, odorless gas that is produced by the breakdown of uranium in soil and water—is one of the most dangerous carcinogens to which the American public is regularly exposed. The US Environmental Protection Agency (EPA) estimates that one in 15 American homes has elevated radon levels. As many as 22,000 lung cancer deaths are believed to be caused by radon each year.

Radon seeps into homes through cracks or other foundation openings. Since it's nine times denser than air, it tends to accumulate in basements or first-floor areas.

To protect yourself: Test your indoor radon levels. Levels for an average home should not exceed 4 picocuries per liter (pCi/L), according to the EPA. Radon testing kits are available at home-improvement and hardware stores for less than $20. The most common type is a small charcoal canister that's placed in the lowest part of the house for at least 48 hours, then mailed to a laboratory for analysis.

When radon levels are high, radon mitigation should be performed by a professional.

ULTRAVIOLET LIGHT

Scientists have known for a long time that different types of ultraviolet light—mainly the ultraviolet A (UVA) and ultraviolet B (UVB) radiation produced by the sun and indoor tanning beds—are likely carcinogens.

Exposure to UV light causes cell damage that will increase the risk for skin cancer, including melanoma, as well as non-Hodgkin's lymphoma. The more exposure, the greater the risk.

In 1994, the American Medical Association passed a resolution calling for a ban on tanning equipment—and yet up to 28 million Americans still use tanning beds. What's more, approximately one-third of Americans spend excessive amounts of time in the sun.

To protect yourself: Avoid the use of any tanning equipment, as well as excessive sun exposure. I drive a convertible, but I always wear a hat or other protective clothing…and I apply SPF 15 or higher sunscreen before going outdoors for extended periods.

WOOD DUST

Each year, approximately 600,000 Americans—mainly furniture makers, carpenters and mill workers—are exposed to hazardous levels of wood dust. Also at risk are people who work with wood in their spare time or who compost bark and other wood-containing organic material in the yard or garden.

Exposure to wood dust has been shown to increase lung cancer risk. It also increases the risk for Hodgkin's disease and cancers of the nasal cavities and paranasal sinuses.

To protect yourself: Wear a paper mask whenever you're cutting or sanding wood. The masks, available at hardware stores and home centers, cost about 10 cents each and can dramatically reduce the amount of dust that gets into the lungs or nasal cavities.

Acrylamide: A Tasty Risk

George M. Gray, PhD, executive director of the Harvard Center for Risk Analysis, Harvard School of Public Health, Boston.

When Swedish scientists reported that french fries, potato chips and other starchy foods contained extremely high levels of *acrylamide,* a potential carcinogen, the findings made headlines throughout the world. Some of the foods that were analyzed had up to *600 times* more acrylamide than the US Environmental Protection Agency (EPA) permits in a glass of water.

Nearly all foods contain some acrylamide, but starchy foods contain the most. This compound is also formed by chemical reactions that are produced during high-heat cooking, such as roasting and deep frying.

Although the initial reports were alarming, researchers have now put the risk into context. Acrylamide does increase cancer risk in laboratory animals—but only when it's consumed in extremely large doses. You would have to eat *tens of thousands* of french fries or other cooked starchy foods to get a hazardous amount.

Bottom line: Eat a varied diet rich in fruits, vegetables and other healthful foods. Reduce your intake of chips and other snack foods, which, of course, will decrease your intake of acrylamide—as well as salt, fat and other ingredients that we know are unhealthy.

Take a Nutritional Approach to Cancer Prevention

Mitchell L. Gaynor, MD, founder, Gaynor Integrative Oncology (*www.gaynoroncology.com*), senior medical oncology consultant, Strang Cancer Prevention Center, and assistant clinical professor of medicine, Weill Medical College of Cornell University, all in New York City. He is author of *Healing Essence* and *Dr. Gaynor's Cancer Prevention Program* (both from Kensington Health).

Statistics show that one in three Americans will be diagnosed with cancer. While this is scary to contemplate, most of us already have a pretty good idea of what we need to do to minimize our risk. *For example…*

- **Don't smoke.**
- **Stay out of the sun.**
- **Avoid consumption of saturated fat.**
- **Eat lots of fresh fruits and vegetables.**
- **Exercise regularly.**
- **Get regular cancer screening tests.***

In recent years, nutrition researchers have gone far beyond these basic strategies. They've shown that certain naturally occurring compounds have potent anticancer properties.

By boosting your consumption of the foods that contain these *phytochemicals,* you can drive your risk for cancer even lower…

- **Carotenoids,** including beta-carotene and lycopene. Found in fruits and orange, red and leafy, green vegetables. These powerful antioxidants fight cancer by neutralizing free radicals.

- **Isoflavones.** Found in tofu, soy milk, veggie burgers and other soy products. Among other effects, isoflavones block *angiogenesis.* That's the process by which new blood vessels form to bring nutrients to cancerous growths.

- **Sulforaphane.** Found in broccoli, kale, brussels sprouts and cabbage. It activates anticancer enzymes in the body.

- **Epigallocatechin gallate.** Found in green tea. This potent antioxidant—200 times more powerful than vitamin C—helps block the effects of nitrosamines and other carcinogens. Green tea should be drunk *without milk,* which reduces antioxidant activity.

- **Omega-3 fatty acids.** Found in salmon, haddock, cod, tuna, halibut, mackerel and sardines. These acids block the synthesis of *prostaglandins,* natural body compounds that promote tumor growth.

Other sources of omega-3 fatty acids include flaxseed oil (two tablespoons a day) or fish oil capsules (700 to 1,000 milligrams [mg], three times a day).

*Women: Mammogram for breast cancer (age 40 to 49, every one to two years…age 50 or over, every year). Pap test for cervical cancer (18 or over, every year). *Men:* PSA blood test for prostate cancer (50 or over, every year). *Colon cancer screening for men and women:* Digital rectal exam (40 or over, every year)…fecal occult blood testing (50 or over, every year)…flexible sigmoidoscopy (50 or over, every three years).

●**Ginger.** It contains gingerol and 13 other antioxidant compounds, each more potent than vitamin E. Recent studies involving mice showed that the consumption of ginger can prevent skin tumors.

Each day, drink two or three cups of ginger tea...or take one 550-mg ginger capsule.

●**Rosemary.** This popular herb contains *carnosol,* which is a compound that deactivates carcinogens and helps curb the effect of prostaglandins in the body. In recent tests, tumors shrank by 85% in mice that were fed large quantities of rosemary.

Human studies have yet to be done. However, given the fact that rosemary is safe, there is no downside to eating it on a regular basis. It's sold in tea form or as an extract, which can be added to green tea.

FITTING IT ALL IN

Nutritionists often say that five servings of fruits and vegetables each day are enough to maintain good health. But for maximum anticancer benefit, it's better to have six to eight daily servings (including at least one cruciferous vegetable and one tomato).

One serving equals one-half cup of vegetables...or one piece of fruit.

Problem: Even conscientious eaters often find that they have trouble fitting in all of these fruits and vegetables.

If you're having trouble getting your daily quota, consider juicing. Buy a quality juicing machine, such as those sold by Omega and Juiceman. Spend time experimenting with fruit and vegetable combinations.

Two tasty combinations...

●**Juice #1**—One head of cabbage, two carrots and one beet.

●**Juice #2**—One-third cup broccoli, two carrots, one apple and one cucumber.

Even with juicing, it's hard to get adequate amounts of certain anticancer nutrients from foods alone. *It's a good idea to take supplements containing...*

●**Alpha-lipoic acid.** This antioxidant helps replenish stores of vitamin E in the body and may prevent activation of certain cancer genes. Take 60 to 200 mg a day.

●**Vitamin E.** This antioxidant has been shown to reduce prostate cancer by up to one-third. Take 200 to 400 international units (IU) a day. (Amounts higher than 200 IU may be dangerous, so check with your doctor first.)

●**Selenium.** This mineral has been shown to reduce the risk for colon cancer by roughly 60%. Take 100 to 200 micrograms (mcg) daily.

THE IMPORTANCE OF RELAXATION

Stress, depression and pessimism depress the immune response, leaving the body vulnerable to cancer. To reduce your cancer risk, learn to relax.

Forget watching television. Focus on practicing meditation, yoga, tai chi or another relaxation technique.

One easy and highly effective tool for relaxation is toning.

What to do: Inhale through your nose, then release the breath through your mouth while making one sustained sound.

Toning can be done as often as you like—anytime, anywhere.

Warning for Women Smokers

Women who smoke cigarettes are three times more likely to develop lung cancer than men who smoke.

Theory: A woman's cells are less able to repair DNA damage.

If you smoke or once smoked: Ask your doctor about having an annual spiral CT scan. It is better than a chest X-ray at detecting lung cancer when it's still most treatable. Few insurance companies pay for the test. But it's worth the cost, generally $300 to $1,000.

Signs of lung cancer include persistent cough, shortness of breath, hoarseness, bloody phlegm, recurrent respiratory infections, chest pain, unexplained weight loss and/or loss of appetite.

Claudia Henschke, MD, PhD, professor of radiology, Weill Medical College of Cornell University, New York City.

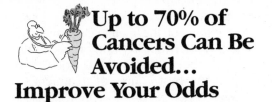

Up to 70% of Cancers Can Be Avoided... Improve Your Odds

Melanie Polk, MMSc, RD, director, nutrition education, American Institute for Cancer Research, 1759 R St. NW, Washington, DC 20009.

People often assume that cancer is out of their hands because it is "genetic." In fact, lifestyle decisions are much more important in determining who gets cancer—and who doesn't.

Even if your genes place you at risk for cancer, 60% to 70% of all malignancies can be avoided by paying attention to four lifestyle factors—diet, weight control, physical activity and not smoking.

IF YOU MAKE JUST ONE CHANGE...

Eating a plant-based diet is the single most important thing you can do to help lower your cancer risk.

Foods should be minimally processed and eaten as close to their natural state as possible. Processed foods may have lost some of their nutritional value.

Example: Eat a potato rather than potato chips or french fries.

Also limit intake of foods with added sugar, such as soft drinks and sweetened cereals.

If you eat red meat, have no more than three ounces per day.

Eating at least five servings—about one-half cup each—of fruits or vegetables every day can decrease your risk of cancer by 20%.

OTHER IMPORTANT STEPS

● **Maintain a healthful weight,** and be physically active. Try not to gain too much weight after reaching your full height (at about age 18 for women...24 for men).

Start by walking every day—working your way up to a brisk, one-hour walk daily. In addition, work up a sweat by engaging in some form of vigorous physical activity for at least one hour each week.

● **Drink alcohol in moderation**—if at all. There is no evidence that alcohol reduces cancer risk, though some evidence suggests that moderate alcohol consumption helps prevent coronary artery disease in men and possibly women. If you do drink, limit your consumption to one drink a day for women...two drinks a day for men.

Avoid alcohol entirely if you are a woman with an increased risk of breast cancer.

● **Select foods that are low in fat and salt.** Limit your intake of fatty foods. Use a moderate amount of monounsaturated oils, such as olive and canola.

Avoid animal fat and hydrogenated fat, which is commonly found in shortening, margarine and bakery items.

Watch those snack foods, salty condiments and pickles.

● **Prepare and store foods safely.** Keep cold foods cold and hot foods hot.

If you eat meat, avoid charring it. Limit your intake of cured or smoked meat. Take precautions when grilling—trim fat from meat, marinate it, then microwave it for half the cooking time before grilling.

● **Avoid tobacco in any form.**

CANCER RISK FACTORS

Anticancer precautions are particularly important for individuals at increased risk for cancer. *These risk factors include*...*

● **Family history of genetically linked types of cancer,** such as breast, ovarian and colon cancers.

● **Inflammatory bowel disease.**

● **Human papillomavirus (HPV) infection.**

● **Alcoholism.**

● **Hepatitis B or C virus (HBV/HCV).**

Additional risk factors for women...

● **First menstrual period before the age of 12.**

● **First child born after age 30.**

● **Childless and over age 50.**

● **Postmenopausal and on hormone-replacement therapy.**

---

*This information is based on a major study by the American Institute for Cancer Research that reviewed more than 4,500 studies to determine the relationships among diet, lifestyle and cancer risk.

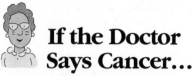

If the Doctor Says Cancer...

C. Norman Coleman, MD, director of the radiation oncology sciences program and deputy director of the center for cancer research, National Cancer Institute, Bethesda, MD. He is author of *Understanding Cancer: A Patient's Guide to Diagnosis, Prognosis and Treatment* (Johns Hopkins University Press).

Being given a diagnosis of cancer is inevitably an extremely stressful experience. But daily life—and treatment—should go more smoothly if the patient takes an active, informed approach to battling the disease.

Good news: Cancer rarely requires an immediate response. In most cases, it's okay to take several days or even a few weeks to learn about the specific type of cancer and various treatment options.

Helpful resource: The National Cancer Institute hotline. Call 800-422-6237.

OBTAINING A DIAGNOSIS

The patient's primary-care doctor should coordinate the steps necessary to confirm the initial diagnosis. That includes making plans for a biopsy and/or other necessary tests.

CONSULTING AN ONCOLOGIST

If tests confirm a malignancy, the primary-care doctor should refer the patient to a cancer specialist (oncologist).

There are three main kinds of oncologist...

● **Surgical oncologists** specialize in surgical removal of tumors.

● **Medical oncologists** specialize in chemotherapy treatment.

● **Radiation oncologists** specialize in radiation therapy.

Several oncologists may eventually be involved in treating the cancer. To prepare for that possibility, it's best to select one primary oncologist to coordinate all tests and treatments.

It's also a good idea to ask the primary-care physician to weigh in on key decisions. Given his/her knowledge of the patient's medical history, he may be able to offer guidance that specialists are unable to offer.

STAGING STUDIES

Before treatment can be initiated, the exact nature and extent of the malignancy must be determined. This process—known as "staging"—enables the patient and his doctors to decide upon the best course of treatment. It also provides a benchmark that indicates just how effective any treatment is.

Staging studies include physical exams, biopsies, blood tests and diagnostic imaging procedures.

Oncologists use different scales to indicate cancer stage. Some use the numerals 1, 2, 3 and 4—or the Roman numeral equivalents. Others use the letters A, B, C and D. In each case, the higher the number or letter, the more severe the cancer.

Example: Stage 1 breast cancer is a small tumor, no bigger than 2 centimeters (cm) in diameter. Stage 2 is a tumor between 2 cm and 5 cm. Stage 3 is a tumor larger than 5 cm. Stage 4 means the cancer has spread (metastasized) to other sites in the body.

Some oncologists further describe cancers using the *TNM* system. The T grade indicates the size of the primary tumor. The N grade indicates the degree to which cancerous cells have been found in the lymph nodes. The M grade indicates whether the cancer has metastasized.

Example: A 3-cm breast tumor that involves one lymph node—but which hasn't spread to other sites in the body—would be designated T2N1M0.

EVALUATING TREATMENT OPTIONS

Once the cancer is staged, the patient should spend a few days or weeks amassing information about his/her treatment options.

Helpful: A checklist should be prepared. It should be taken along each time the patient meets with any of his doctors. *The checklist should include...*

● **Patient's name,** address, phone number and medical record identification numbers.

● **Primary oncologist's name,** address and phone number, along with his speciality.

● **Names of all other doctors** involved in the treatment.

● **Type of cancer/tumor site.**

•**The cancer's stage,** along with results of staging studies.

•**Treatments being considered.** With each, list the duration of treatment, whether hospitalization is necessary and whether the patient will be able to pursue his normal activities.

•**Potential benefits** and side effects of each treatment.

•**Clinical trials** of experimental treatments in which the patient might want to enroll.

As the patient gathers information, he should touch base periodically with his primary-care physician and primary oncologist—to review the pros and cons of each treatment option.

If participation in a clinical trial of an experimental cancer treatment is being considered, the patient should find out exactly what is involved.

GETTING A SECOND OPINION

Since cancer is such a complex disease, it's usually best to consult several specialists before picking a treatment.

Second opinions are especially valuable when more than one type of treatment is available—for instance, if radiation therapy is being weighed against surgery or chemotherapy.

SELECTING A TREATMENT

Once all the information has been amassed, the patient should review his checklist with family and friends, then discuss each treatment with the primary oncologist to review the choice and formulate a specific plan.

Cancer Survival Secrets

The late Richard Bloch, philanthropist and cofounder of the tax-preparation firm H&R Block, Inc. In 1978, Bloch was diagnosed with terminal lung cancer and given three months to live...he died in 2004.

Almost from the very minute a diagnosis of cancer is confirmed, advice begins to pour in—from your doctor...your parents...your spouse...your friends.

But perhaps no one is better equipped to tell you how to beat the disease than cancer survivors themselves. *Here, several survivors suggest some strategies for making it through the difficult times...*

•**Get a second opinion as soon as possible after your initial diagnosis.** Ideally, you will get opinions from several specialists, including a medical oncologist, a radiation oncologist and a surgeon.

Long-term lung cancer survivor Richard Bloch was such a believer in this approach that he founded a free, multidisciplinary second-opinion panel staffed by more than 100 physicians in his native Kansas City, Missouri. "I believe that one out of every four patients the panel saw had his or her life saved because of the panel," Bloch said.

•**Commit yourself to doing everything in your power to beat the disease.** "This might sound silly," said Bloch, "but some people just turn everything over to their doctors and expect them to fix it."

You must become intimately involved in all aspects of your cancer treatment. It's tempting, of course, to leave the details to the doctors. But to maximize your chances of survival, you have to muster all of your resources and exhaust every option open to you.

•**Expect the first three months after the diagnosis to be awful.** That advice comes from Daniel Kohn, a therapist who was diagnosed with a brain tumor several years ago.

"You're going to be in shock and in denial, no matter how well-equipped you are," he says. "Just ride it through. It gets better."

•**Pick doctors who are affiliated with a major hospital.** Fight for your right to have the doctor you choose, no matter what your insurance company says.

•**Look beyond your family for emotional support.** When Bloch was diagnosed, the few cancer survivors he knew didn't seem interested in talking with him. So he launched the Bloch Cancer Hot Line (800-433-0464), a volunteer group of cancer patients who take phone calls from newly diagnosed cancer patients.

Many cancer patients find support groups very helpful. It certainly doesn't hurt to meet people who were given death sentences 10 years ago...and are still alive.

•**Have an advocate.** This is someone who accompanies you to doctor appointments, takes notes, keeps track of paperwork and argues for you when you're hospitalized.

A good advocate can also research the particular cancer and filter his/her findings to you so you aren't overwhelmed by all the information.

•**Get a fax machine.** Having one at home will make it much easier to send, receive and make copies of all your medical records (many fax machines do double duty as a copier).

If you have access to a fax machine at work or someplace else outside your home, think twice before using it. You may not want others to see all your medical records.

•**Make use of the Internet.** You're going to need information and explanations. But trying to get that from numerous sites can just add to the confusion.

If you don't have a home computer, make use of a friend's or one at a nearby library, copy shop or "cybercafé."

Especially helpful: National Cancer Institute, *www.cancer.gov/newscenter.*

•**Make friends with your doctor's staff.** That way, when you call with a question or problem, they'll treat you as an individual— and make sure you get what you need.

Drop off cookies, flowers or even gift certificates to thank them.

•**Ask your doctor's office to schedule the appointments** when you are referred to specialists. They can line up an appointment sooner than you can.

•**Buy a wig *before* undergoing chemotherapy**—if the drugs to be used are likely to cause hair loss. Your doctor can probably prescribe a wig for you. That's a good idea because it means that part or even all of the cost might be covered by health insurance.

•**Indulge yourself.** When Kohn took steroids as part of his treatment, he craved fatty foods like chicken wings and french fries. That's not unusual.

Kohn's wife was horrified. She thought he wasn't taking proper care of himself. But the junk food provided one of his few sources of pleasure during this time.

•**If you don't have cable television, get it.** You'll often be too sick to read or write. A funny movie or TV show can do wonders for your mood—and it's critical that you keep up your mood.

•**Plan for depression.** Bloch noted that "everything about cancer is depressing. Expect down days and plan things that cheer you up at those times."

Ask your doctor about antidepressant therapy to ease the feelings of hopelessness that often accompany cancer.

 # Surprising Strategies for Coping With Cancer

Joanna Bull, psychotherapist and founder, Gilda's Club Worldwide, a social and emotional support community for people with cancer and their families. To find out more about Gilda's Club Worldwide, call 888-445-3248 or visit *www.gildasclub.org.*

Living with cancer takes an emotional as well as physical toll. For more than 23,000 people with cancer and their families, Gilda's Club Worldwide has been the place to find—in each other—the emotional and social support they need.

Gilda's Club was founded more than a decade ago by Joanna Bull, cancer psychotherapist to the comedian Gilda Radner, who died of ovarian cancer in 1989. Gilda's Club has grown to 17 clubhouses in the US and Canada. Ms. Bull, who has been counseling people with cancer for more than 25 years, shared her advice on the things that make a difference in living well with this feared disease. *Suggestions...*

DISPEL MYTHS

You are the expert. It's your life and your disease. Your way is the right way, even if books, articles and well-meaning friends and relatives have different ideas. Unfortunately, myths have developed that may make you question yourself. *For example...*

Myth #1: **A positive outlook increases your chances of survival.** According to the conventional wisdom, having an optimistic, upbeat attitude strengthens your immune system and enhances your body's ability to fight cancer. The truth is that there is no scientific evidence that your outlook has a significant impact on recovery.

If you can maintain an attitude of hope and a conviction that everything will turn out well, that's great—and that works for some people.

But if you ordinarily see the world through a darker lens and tend to worry rather than stride ahead with confidence, it's unrealistic to expect that a cancer diagnosis will turn you into an optimist. Don't be tyrannized by the mistaken belief that being yourself puts your recovery in jeopardy.

Myth #2: **You must face facts.** There's a widespread belief that it's necessary to accept the seriousness of the disease, and that anyone who doesn't achieve this level of absolute honesty with themselves is "in denial."

For some people, minimizing the threat and even the imminence of death allows them to enjoy every day to the fullest. Since cancer is often full of surprises, no one truly knows the facts—the refusal to face them may be the wisest move of all for some.

Myth #3: **You must be a full partner in your health-care team.** Many people insist that it's crucial to take an active role in your own medical care. They say patients are obligated to educate themselves thoroughly about their disease, come to doctor visits with lists of questions and seek other medical opinions.

This approach isn't for everyone. If you feel more comfortable simply putting yourself in the hands of a health-care team you trust and doing what they think is best, go ahead.

Myth #4: **This is not the time to make big changes.** People living with cancer often are told not to make any significant decisions until they have the disease under control. But a direct look at your personal values and mortality may convince you to take steps that are difficult for others to accept.

Example: One woman came to the full realization that her marriage, which everyone thought was so wonderful, was actually stifling and even abusive. Face to face with the finitude of life, she left her husband. It made no sense to her friends who argued that now more than ever she needed caring support— but the decision was right for her.

Myth #5: **Depression is normal and does not need to be treated.** If your distress or anxiety makes it hard for you to function, don't just assume that this is a normal, inevitable reaction to the seriousness of your illness.

Counseling or medication can help you get back on your feet, particularly if you become severely depressed. It's absolutely essential if you have thoughts of suicide. Cancer is not a death sentence.

GET EMOTIONAL SUPPORT

Emotional support is a great source of strength. Plan for it. This may mean gathering your close friends and telling them what you need from them or leaning more on your spouse, who also will need support.

What's been helpful for many people is getting together with others who are going through the same thing. These support groups relieve the tremendous sense of isolation that serious illness can bring. Also, getting to know people who are willing to share the wisdom of their experience is the best antidote to the myths that surround cancer.

Even though you've found your own way of living with cancer, hearing about what works for others can give you fresh ideas and make you more confident in your own choices.

Example: You get anxious when you undergo medical treatment, such as radiation or chemotherapy. A fellow support-group member suggests relaxation techniques he found helpful. Following his example makes the experience much less of an ordeal.

To find a group in your area, check with hospitals or social service agencies. Internet chat rooms, including those offered by the American Cancer Society, provide alternatives for people who live in isolated areas or who are more comfortable communicating on-line than face-to-face.

A New Way to Look at Cancer Statistics

Cancer-survival statistics are better than they have been reported.

Reason: Cancer data in the traditional statistical method include patients who received advanced treatment and patients who received treatment as many as 20 years in the past.

A new statistical method separates the groups. When this new method is used, survival rates for the group receiving current treatments improve significantly.

Example: Breast cancer patients have a 71% chance of surviving for 15 years after diagnosis under the new method, versus only 58% under the old one.

Hermann Brenner, MD, MPH, epidemiologist, German Centre for Research on Aging, Heidelberg, and developer of the new statistical method, published in *The Lancet.*

Cancer Fighter on A Sandwich

Broccoli sprouts are rich in a compound that provides significant protection against breast and colon cancers. Sprouts grown from certain broccoli seeds contain up to 50 times more of this compound—*sulforaphane glucosinolate* (SGS)—than mature broccoli.

Caution: The amount of SGS in broccoli sprouts varies widely.

BroccoSprouts, a brand developed at Johns Hopkins University, is guaranteed to have 20 times the amount of SGS of mature broccoli on an ounce-for-ounce basis.

Visit the Web site *www.broccosprouts.com* for more information.

Paul Talalay, MD, pharmacologist, Johns Hopkins University, Brassica Chemoprotection Laboratory, 2400 Boston St., Suite 358, Baltimore 21224.

Cancer Cure?

Experimental vaccines made from patients' own tumors can stimulate the immune system to destroy deadly cancers.

Finding: In 18 of the 22 lung cancer patients who were studied, the vaccine stimulated immune response and caused fewer side effects than conventional cancer treatments.

Journal of Clinical Oncology, 330 John Carlyle St., Suite 300, Alexandria, VA 22314.

Coping with Chemo

Martin Groder, MD, psychiatrist and business consultant, Chapel Hill, NC.

Chemotherapy is a powerful weapon in the life-and-death battle against cancer. Unfortunately, its potent drugs can't kill bad cells without wreaking damage on the body. The toxic side effects of chemo are well-known and feared.

Martin Groder, MD, an eminent psychiatrist, discussed his three-year struggle with colon cancer and provided advice on how to cope with the effects of chemo...

STAY INVOLVED

Undergoing chemotherapy treatment can take the fight out of you. Nevertheless, you need to keep it from getting you down. You deserve to enjoy a satisfying life despite the tribulations. With a positive attitude, you can fight harder against the disease.

Many oncologists agree that those patients who are actively engaged in the struggle do best. Often, I would have to convince my doctors that a drug or procedure I had learned about was worth a try.

You can't fully use the resources of your medical team when you're weighed down by fatigue, anxiety and depression. For chemotherapy, it helps to be a fully involved member of the team.

BATTLE SIDE EFFECTS

Chemotherapy's side effects often are undertreated, so insist that your medical team take them as seriously as you do. Be sure to describe any difficulties you're having to your oncologist. Be clear about how disabling they are and insist on his/her help in finding ways to alleviate them.

● **Nausea and vomiting.** Physicians usually take some steps to quell these side effects, which are common yet distressing, but doctors may not go after them aggressively enough. If nausea and vomiting aren't controlled, you can develop a conditioned response that brings them on as soon as you enter the treatment room or even on the way there.

You may need to take multiple drugs. The medical arsenal has added powerful new antinausea medications, such as *ondansetron* (Zofran), to older and still-valuable agents like *prochlorperazine* (Compazine). Just one may not be enough. These medications combat nausea and vomiting by different mechanisms, so they complement each other.

I take Compazine in the morning before a nausea-inducing treatment, then Zofran at the time of the treatment and every eight hours for one day after.

● **Fatigue.** Few doctors take fatigue as seriously as nausea and vomiting, but it's nearly as common, and the toll on your spirit can be every bit as devastating. Here, too, the right medications can make all the difference.

Modafinil (Provigil) is effective against excessive sleepiness, when you feel like you can't keep your eyes open.

Overall general fatigue is best treated with the kinds of stimulants that are given to children for attention deficit disorder. One of the best is Concerta, a form of *methylphenidate* (Ritalin) that releases gradually over a 12-hour period. It needs to be taken only once a day and has a mild effect—you won't feel "speedy." Another drug, *dexmethylphenidate* (Focalin), works similarly.

I tailor my drug to the symptom. On the mornings of the days that I receive the kind of chemotherapy that makes me fatigued, I take Concerta, which I had to convince my doctor would work for me—and it has. When daytime sleepiness is a problem, I take Provigil.

DETOXIFY

Because chemotherapy is unavoidably toxic, do what you can to reduce your body's overall toxic load. Eliminate whatever adds unnecessarily to daily wear and tear.

While you want to eat a normal diet, don't foolishly indulge in foods that will tax your vulnerable digestive system. Avoid heavy, fatty dishes, such as barbecued spareribs and fried chicken. Emphasize foods that are light, nutritious and easy to digest. I have chicken soup, crackers, applesauce and banana-soy-yogurt shakes.

Alcohol also is toxic and should be avoided.

Expunge emotional toxicity from your life as well. In fact, make this the occasion for a good housecleaning. We all have activities, relationships and routines that no longer give us much satisfaction but that we hold on to from habit or a sense of obligation. This is the time to recognize that your real obligation is to yourself. I am not a morning person, for example, so I decided not to see patients before 2 pm.

Surround yourself with nurturing, supportive people. Don't let one person, such as your spouse, carry the whole burden of caring for you during difficult periods. Recruit a "social support network" of five or six close friends and family members to share the responsibility. It's not hard to garner support. Just ask. People want to help but often don't know how.

If some family members or longtime friends are draining your energy, ask a member of your support network to explain to them what you need.

BE OPEN

Secrecy is stressful. It's draining to cover up the things that you contend with every day, such as the effects of chemotherapy.

People who are honest about their health problems do best. This is particularly important when chemotherapy forces you to curtail your normal activities. You'll get a surprising amount of spontaneous assistance from employers, colleagues and others who know you're in a struggle for your life.

While I'm undergoing chemotherapy, I often ask friends, relatives and patients if they would like a thumbnail sketch of my medical status. Almost all say "yes," so I supply a two-minute summary of how the treatment is affecting me and how long I expect the chemo to last. This answers questions and helps dispel worry and fear.

GO WITH THE FLOW

Chemotherapy usually is given in cycles. There are periods between treatments when you feel relatively fine. Adapt your life to this rhythm, but do it sensibly. Use the interval between treatments to take care of business that accumulated while you were indisposed. Try to reduce the burdens so that you'll be ready for the next round. Schedule a vacation, or get back in touch with relaxing hobbies.

Don't get into a destructive cycle of trying to catch up on everything you've missed. You will end up overextending yourself. One night before an urgent surgery, I worked until 9 pm seeing patients. I made it through the operation, but I taxed my physical resources unnecessarily.

BE IN IT FOR THE LONG HAUL

Successive rounds of chemotherapy may lead to discouragement at what seems like an endless struggle.

These words, attributed to tennis great Bjorn Borg, are a source of inspiration for me—"I'm not a great player. I'm only better at hitting the ball one more time than my opponent."

That's the way it is with cancer, too. Ongoing research in chemotherapy promises to develop more powerful, less toxic treatments —some in the near future. If you hang in there and hit the ball one more time than your adversary, you'll stay ahead of the game.

Out-of-Body Cancer Therapy

Doctors have treated cancer for the very first time by removing a patient's liver, bombarding it with a high dose of radiation, then re-implanting it in the body. This experimental technique is meant to protect nearby healthy organs from the damaging effects of radiation.

New Scientist, Reed Business Information Limited, 151 Wardour St., London.

What You Must Know About Lymphoma

Andrew D. Zelenetz, MD, chief of the Lymphoma Service, Memorial Sloan-Kettering Cancer Center, New York City. He is board-certified in internal medicine and medical oncology, with research interests in Hodgkin's and non-Hodgkin's diseases and chronic lymphocytic leukemia.

In the last 30 years, the annual incidence of lymphoma has doubled in the US. Adults age 65 or older account for most of this increase.

Unfortunately, lymphoma can be missed for months—or even years. That's because many of the symptoms, such as swollen lymph nodes, night sweats and fever, appear to be minor. In some cases, lymphoma is discovered accidentally when doctors perform routine physical examinations.

Although some forms of lymphoma can be lethal, more than half of men and women diagnosed with the disease will survive five years or more. In fact, the five-year survival (cure) rate for some lymphomas now approaches 90%.

WHAT ARE LYMPHOMAS?

White blood cells called *lymphocytes* help fight infections. Although the exact cause of lymphoma is unknown, researchers believe that damage to lymphocytes—from environmental factors, such as pesticide exposure—causes the cells to become cancerous. The cancerous tumors, or lymphomas, may involve a single lymph node or cause widespread disease that affects the bone marrow, spleen or other organs.

More than 40 types of lymphomas have been identified, and they fall into two main categories...

•**Hodgkin's disease.** This condition is rare, with about 8,000 new cases occurring annually in the US. This form of lymphoma strikes men more often than women.

Early symptoms: Painless swelling of lymph nodes in the neck, armpits or groin…fatigue… fever and chills…weight loss…itching…and night sweats. Although the reason is unknown, enlarged lymph nodes may become painful if the sufferer drinks alcohol. Cough or shortness of breath may occur if swollen lymph nodes in the chest irritate airways. In many cases, there are *no* visible symptoms.

The cure rate for Hodgkin's disease ranges from 50% to 85%, depending on how advanced it is at the time of treatment.

•**Non-Hodgkin's disease.** This condition is eight times more common than Hodgkin's. About 65,000 cases are diagnosed annually in the US, most of them in older adults. Men and women are affected equally.

Early symptoms: Typically, the same as Hodgkin's disease.

Overall, the cure rate for non-Hodgkin's is about 50%, depending on the specific cancer and how advanced it is at the time of treatment.

POSSIBLE CAUSES

No one knows why the incidence of lymphoma is on the rise. The Epstein-Barr virus has been linked to some types of lymphoma, such as Burkitt's lymphoma and Hodgkin's disease. In addition, there's evidence that the common *H. pylori bacterium,* responsible for most ulcers, increases the risk for lymphomas in the stomach.

It's also believed that pesticide and herbicide exposure increases the risk for lymphomas. The typical American diet, high in saturated fat and processed foods and low in fruits, vegetables, whole grains and legumes, may play a role as well.

Aging is the most likely cause of most lymphomas. With fewer deaths from heart disease, high blood pressure and other chronic diseases, people are living longer. The older you are, the more time cells have to divide, which increases the risk for lymphoma.

DIAGNOSTIC TESTS

Your doctor may suspect you have lymphoma if you notice *painless* lymph node swelling…persistent bronchitis or flu-like symptoms…and/or weight loss or night sweats that last several weeks or longer.

Important: It's common for lymph nodes to swell and feel tender when you have a cold, flu or other infection. Nodes that hurt and swell rapidly are unlikely to be a sign of lymphoma.

A common early sign of lymphoma is an enlarged lymph node in the chest cavity. Your doctor may recommend you undergo a chest X ray or a *computer tomography* (CT) scan to look for swelling or masses.

If an enlarged lymph node is discovered, your doctor should obtain a tissue sample via biopsy to determine if the lymph node is cancerous.

Best: An *excisional biopsy,* in which an incision is made to remove all or part of a lymph node. Surgery may be needed to obtain tissue samples from enlarged lymph nodes in the abdomen or chest cavity.

If you have been diagnosed with lymphoma, you'll need a CT scan of the chest, abdomen and pelvis to determine the extent of the disease.

The size and number of the enlarged lymph nodes, along with pathology reports, determine the stage of lymphoma. The disease is classified into four stages—I, II, III and IV. The higher the number, the more the disease has spread.

A bone marrow biopsy is also used to stage the lymphoma. Bone marrow disease cannot be seen on a CT scan.

In some circumstances, the oncologist may recommend additional testing, including *positron emission tomography* (PET), *magnetic resonance imaging* (MRI) or *endoscopy,* in which a fiber-optic viewing tube is used to examine the stomach, small intestine or esophagus.

TREATMENTS

Lymphomas are generally treated with chemotherapy, radiation and/or monoclonal antibodies, such as *rituximab* (Rituxan). In more advanced cases, a combination of these therapies may be advisable.

In some circumstances, *autologous* (from the patient) or *allogeneic* (from a donor) stem cell transplantation may be necessary. The use of these treatments generally depends on the specifics of the disease.

PREVENTING LYMPHOMA

Until more is known about the cause of lymphoma, strategies to prevent the disease remain somewhat speculative.

The pesticide link is strong enough that I advise people to wear long pants and long-sleeved shirts when working with lawn or garden chemicals. If a lengthy amount of exposure is anticipated, then disposable coveralls are recommended.

Because many cancers—as well as heart attack and stroke—are strongly influenced by what we eat, diet is also a consideration. Eating meals that are low in fat and processed foods and high in nutritious vegetables, fruits, legumes, etc. may lower lymphoma risk as well.

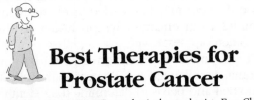

Best Therapies for Prostate Cancer

Robert G. Uzzo, MD, urological oncologist, Fox Chase Cancer Center, and assistant professor of medicine, Temple University School of Medicine, both in Philadelphia.

Prostate cancer is the second most common cancer in men (after skin cancer). Even so, there's still controversy over how aggressively to treat a prostate malignancy—or even *whether* to treat it.

Unlike most cancers, prostate cancer tends to grow gradually, often over decades. Older men with prostate cancer that's confined to the gland are statistically more likely to die from other causes than from the cancer itself.

Yet some prostate cancers do grow quickly. Even cancers that are initially slow growing can progress and become fatal. In fact, prostate cancer is the second leading cause of cancer death in men. The challenge is knowing when treatment is necessary—and choosing a treatment that is most likely to be effective.

KEY DIAGNOSTIC TESTS

Once a biopsy of the prostate is performed and cancer cells are discovered, the appropriate treatment depends on how aggressive the cells are likely to act. *Three main factors to consider prior to treatment...*

●**Prostate-specific antigen (PSA).** It's a protein produced by the prostate gland and detected in the blood. Elevated levels suggest that cancer cells are present. A normal PSA is below 4 nanograms per milliliter (ng/ml) of blood. A level between 5 and 10 suggests that prostate cancer cells *may* be present...a level above 10 is a strong warning sign. The higher the PSA, the higher the probability that cancer cells have spread outside of the gland.

Important: An elevated PSA reading can also be caused by an enlarged or infected prostate. In addition, there is evidence to suggest that a recent ejaculation may temporarily elevate a PSA reading. Also, a small percentage of men with a normal PSA will still have cancer. Therefore, all men should have a *digital rectal exam* (DRE) in addition to a PSA test to detect the presence of prostate cancer.

●**Gleason score.** If your PSA is abnormal (typically above 4 ng/ml), your doctor should perform a needle biopsy of the prostate to look for cancer. Multiple biopsies (typically six to 12) are taken from the prostate. Cancer cells are graded based on a system called the Gleason score, which ranges from 2 (least aggressive) to 10 (most aggressive).

Gleason scores ranging from 2 to 4 typically indicate the cancer is growing slowly and may not need immediate treatment. Scores from 8 to 10 indicate a fast-growing tumor that requires immediate attention. Scores in the middle range can indicate either slow- or fast-growing tumors.

●**Staging.** Prostate cancer is staged by digital rectal exam as well as a CT scan and/or a bone scan when appropriate. This determines where the cancer is located—and whether it has spread beyond the prostate gland.

A prostate malignancy is assigned one of four stages, with stage 1 being a very early cancer and stage 4 being the most advanced.

TREATMENT OPTIONS

Controversy exists regarding the best treatment for localized prostate cancer. There have been no head-to-head, randomized trials comparing the two main treatment options—surgery or radiation—for prostate cancer. Each of these treatments appear to have roughly equal survival rates for early-stage cancers over the short term, but no long-term data comparing the two are available.

"Watchful waiting" is also a reasonable strategy for older men with cancers that are unlikely to grow or spread quickly.

•**Surgery.** Surgically removing the prostate gland—a procedure called *radical prostatectomy*—is often recommended for men who have been diagnosed with localized prostate cancer. Many physicians, including myself, feel it's the best choice overall.

During this procedure, the surgeon makes a small incision below the navel. The entire gland and some of the tissue surrounding it are removed. Nearby lymph nodes will also be removed and checked for cancer.

"Nerve-sparing" radical prostatectomy is recommended for most patients. If the bundles of nerves on either side of the prostate gland are cancer free, the surgeon will attempt to leave them intact while removing the gland. This decreases a man's chances of suffering from impotence after surgery.

Some men who have surgery, even if it is nerve-sparing, become impotent. Erectile dysfunction drugs, such as *sildenafil* (Viagra), *tadalafil* (Cialis), and *vardenafil* (Levitra), may help in some cases, but not all. The surgery may also cause urinary dribbling for several weeks following surgery. While most men don't have a long-term problem, 5% to 10% of men may never regain total urinary control.

Important: Choose a surgeon who performs at least 50 nerve-sparing surgeries a year.

•**Radiation therapy.** Men who are too frail to have surgery for prostate cancer—or who do not want to undergo the discomfort and lengthy recovery time—may be candidates for radiation treatments. *Two radiation options...*

•*External beam radiation* is delivered from outside the body and targeted at the prostate. This treatment is generally well-tolerated. However, like surgery, it can cause complications, including impotence and diarrhea, which typically clear up in the long term.

Outpatient treatments are usually given five days a week for five to seven weeks.

It is important to look for a hospital that offers the *intensity-modulated radiation therapy* (IMRT), which gives higher doses of radiation to the prostate gland while minimizing the amount given to nearby healthy tissues.

•*Radioactive seeds* are inserted into the prostate gland with fine needles. The rice-sized seeds, which are made with iodine-125 or palladium-103, are implanted into the prostate gland to deliver high doses of radiation directly to the prostate. What's the advantage of using seeds rather than external radiation? Patients only have to come to the hospital once, when the radioactive seeds are inserted.

Current data suggest that the seeds tend to work only when there's a relatively low volume of cancer cells and the PSA and Gleason scores are in the low to moderate ranges. If these numbers are high, external beam radiation may be a better choice. The long-term risk for impotence is about the same as with surgery.

•**Hormone therapy.** Hormone treatment includes oral or injected medications or surgical removal of the testicles (orchiectomy). These therapies lower the production of testosterone and/or block the effects of testosterone and other male hormones (androgens). Lowering androgen levels can slow the growth of cancer—but it isn't a cure.

Hormone therapy is mainly used when the cancer has spread beyond the prostate gland. It may also be used in combination with radiation in men who have aggressive tumors with a high Gleason score. The hormone treatments can frequently cause cancers to go into remission for several years.

•**Watchful waiting.** Most prostate cancers progress over years, not months. Men who are in their 70s and older—whose life expectancy is generally less than 10 years because of other medical conditions—may be advised by their physicians to defer medical treatment if the cancer is expected to grow slowly and isn't causing symptoms.

A man will typically be advised to have PSA tests twice annually to determine if the volume of cancer cells is increasing. He should also have regular physical exams.

Better Prostate Cancer Detection

During the course of a typical prostate biopsy, six samples of suspicious cells are taken. However, this technique misses up to one in seven prostate malignancies.

Some research suggests that taking 10 to 12 cell samples uncovers 14% more cancers. Additional samples mean higher lab fees, but the new technique could save money and worry by eliminating the need for follow-up biopsies.

If scheduled for a prostate biopsy: Ask your doctor about testing more samples.

Robert Bahnson, MD, professor and director, division of urology, Ohio State University Medical Center, Columbus.

When a High PSA Reading Is Not a Problem

The blood levels of *prostate-specific antigen* (PSA) may increase temporarily because of inflammation in the prostate or because of recent ejaculation.

Study: Nearly 50% of men with high PSA readings—above 4 nanograms per milliliter—on one test had normal levels on subsequent tests.

If your PSA level is elevated: Wait at least six weeks before being retested. If the second reading is normal, you will have been spared an unnecessary biopsy. If not, the slight delay in further testing should not matter because prostate cancer typically progresses at a very slow rate.

James A. Eastham, MD, urologic surgeon, Memorial Sloan-Kettering Cancer Center, New York City. His study of PSA levels in 972 men was published in the *Journal of the American Medical Association*.

Prostate Biopsy Self-Defense

Make sure that two pathologists—one of whom is an expert in the field—study your biopsy results. Up to 2% of biopsies are misread, which could mean that signs of cancer are missed. Having two doctors read the biopsy reduces the chance of error.

Patrick C. Walsh, MD, urologist-in-chief, Johns Hopkins Medical Institutions, Baltimore.

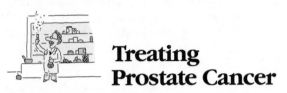

Treating Prostate Cancer

Sheldon Marks, MD, urologic oncologist in private practice, Tucson, AZ. He is author of *Prostate & Cancer: A Family Guide to Diagnosis, Treatment and Survival* (Perseus).

In years past, 30% of men diagnosed with prostate cancer already had an advanced form of the disease. Last year, of 179,000 men who were diagnosed, only 5% had advanced prostate cancer.

Reason: More men now routinely get a blood test for levels of *prostate-specific antigen* (PSA). Prostate cells produce this enzyme in high quantities when the gland is irritated or damaged. A normal PSA level is less than 4 nanograms per milliliter. A higher level suggests cancer.

It's clear that PSA tests help detect early-stage tumors. Yet physicians keep debating whether men should have a yearly PSA test.

Case against: Prostate cancer often grows so slowly that it poses little threat. Treating it early with surgery or radiation—which can cause impotence and incontinence—could create worse effects than the disease.

Case for: Each year, 37,000 men die of prostate cancer, making it the second-leading killer of men (after skin cancer). Getting treatment before the disease spreads can save thousands of lives.

Who should get a yearly PSA test? Men over the age of 40 who have a family history of the disease…and all men over age 50.

The yearly checkup should include a *digital rectal exam* (DRE). By inserting a gloved finger into the rectum, the doctor can detect prostate abnormalities.

If the PSA and/or DRE are abnormal, the next step is an ultrasound test with a prostate biopsy. If this confirms cancer, the goal is to find treatment that maximizes survival time while minimizing side effects.

STAGES AND GRADES

Prostate cancer severity is categorized by stage and grade. The four stages—A, B, C and D—indicate a tumor's size and the likelihood that it is still confined to the prostate or the extent to which it may have spread.

Low-grade prostate cancers tend to be slow-growing…high-grade cancers are fast-growing.

"STAGE A" TUMORS

Most of these tumors are discovered during surgery to relieve urinary problems caused by *benign prostatic hyperplasia* (BPH)—noncancerous, age-related prostate enlargement.

●**A1.** Small, low-grade tumor. An excellent option—especially for men over age 65—is "watchful waiting." Every six months, a PSA test, DRE and urinalysis are done to see if the cancer is growing. If so, it's time for treatment.

Men under age 65 should consider treatment sooner. Surgical removal of the prostate (radical prostatectomy) is often the best option.

Downside I: Surgery can damage nerves that control erections and blood vessels that supply the penis. After surgery, men tend to experience impotence. Potency often takes six to 12 months to return. But in 50% of cases, impotence is permanent.

Good news: Prescription impotence drugs, such as *sildenafil* (Viagra), *tadalafil* (Cialis) and *vardenafil* (Levitra), are helpful for two-thirds of these men. Other treatments for impotence include the intraurethral medication *alprostadil* (Muse), vacuum erection devices, penile self-injections of *alprostadil* (Caverject) and penile implants.

Downside II: Many men experience weeks or months of incontinence after surgery. For a few, the problem is permanent.

Kegel exercises before and after surgery can help control incontinence. To do them, repeatedly squeeze your pelvic muscles, as if trying to stop urine flow, for five minutes every waking hour until you stop experiencing incontinence.

Two radiation methods are also possible alternatives to surgery…

●**External beam.** Radiation is directed at the prostate in one 10- to 15-minute treatment daily. Typically, there are five sessions a week over seven weeks.

●**Interstitial seed therapy.** Tiny radioactive seeds are implanted in the prostate.

Up to 50% of men who undergo external beam radiation become impotent. The rate can be much lower with seed therapy.

●**A2.** High-grade, aggressive cancer. Patients under age 70 should consider radical prostatectomy…men over 70, radiation.

Men age 75 or older and who are in poor health should skip this type of treatment or opt for hormone therapy.

Male hormones (androgens)—which can spur cancer growth—are eliminated by removal of the testicles…or by injections of hormone-blocking drugs.

In the majority of men, hormone therapy causes permanent impotence. But one hormone medicine—*bicalutamide* (Casodex)—blocks the body's ability to use androgen while preserving potency.

●**A3.** Tumor discovered through a high PSA. Surgery or radiation is often best if the patient is expected to live 10 years or longer.

"STAGE B" TUMORS

These cancers, discovered by DRE, are confined to the prostate.

●**B1.** Cancer on one side of the prostate. For those who have a life expectancy of more than seven years, radical prostatectomy is often the best choice.

Second choice: Radiation. But men in their 80s and in poor health may prefer watchful waiting or hormone therapy.

●**B2.** Cancer on both sides of the prostate, with no evident spread outside the gland.

Best treatment: For men under age 70—surgery tends to be the best option. For men over 70, radiation is usually better.

If you choose radiation, ask your oncologist about pretreatment with hormone shots. Eight or nine months of these shots followed by radiation is more effective than radiation alone.

"STAGE C" TUMORS

The cancer is growing outside the gland, in surrounding fat or other nearby areas. It has not spread to lymph nodes or bone.

Men under age 65: Surgery is often best because it may remove almost all the cancer. "Step therapy"—surgery, followed by radiation if cancer returns—is also an option.

Men age 65 or older: Radiation is often best. It can stop cancer in both the prostate and surrounding tissue. Hormone therapy is an alternative for men who are predicted to live five years or less.

"STAGE D" TUMORS

The cancer has spread to lymph nodes or bones. In D1, cancer is still within the pelvis. In D2, it has moved beyond.

In Stage D, the goal is to control the spread of disease.

Best way: Hormone therapy. For men who are under age 65, it should be accompanied by "debulking"—surgically removing as much tumor as possible.

For men 65 or older, hormone therapy alone is usually better.

NUTRITIONAL STRATEGIES

•**Avoid beef and other fatty meats,** as well as whole-fat dairy products. These foods can stimulate cancer growth. Beef can also increase pain in advanced cancer.

•**Consume tomatoes,** red grapes, red grape juice, red wine (one glass a day), red bell peppers, watermelon and strawberries. They contain *lycopene,* a red pigment that can slow cancer growth.

•**Emphasize soy foods.** They contain *phytoestrogens,* compounds that may slow cancer.

•**Drink green tea.** It contains several cancer-fighting antioxidants. Drink four or five cups per day...or take the equivalent in green tea extract capsules.

•**Ask your doctor about taking a daily supplement** containing 200 micrograms (mcg) of selenium. This may slow the cancer.

You can also get selenium from grain products (such as bread, pasta and fortified cereal), organ meats (such as liver), fish and brazil nuts. A 3-ounce portion of fish, for example, contains 40 to 70 mcg of selenium.

Be sure to talk to your physician before taking any nutritional supplements.

USEFUL RESOURCES

Prostate Forum is the most accurate, up-to-date newsletter on nutrition and prostate cancer. 800-305-2432.

Cost: $55 for 12 issues.

In addition, visit these helpful Web sites...

•***www.auafoundation.org.*** The site of the American Urological Association Foundation contains comprehensive information on prostate cancer and updated research.

•***www.prostatepointers.org.*** Prostate Pointers is a thorough resource for newly diagnosed patients.

The Very Latest Thinking On Hormone Therapy

JoAnn E. Manson, MD, DrPH, professor of medicine and women's health at Harvard Medical School, chief of preventive medicine at Brigham and Women's Hospital, both in Boston, and one of the lead investigators for two highly influential studies on women's health—the Women's Health Initiative and the Harvard Nurses' Health Study. She is author with Shari Bassuk, ScD, of *Hot Flashes, Hormones & Your Health* (McGraw-Hill).

Hot flashes can strike at the most inconvenient moments, soaking your clothes ...night sweats can steal slumber...and vaginal dryness can make sex a pain. What's a menopausal woman to do?

Surprise: Hormone therapy (HT), nearly a pariah in the field of medicine, may be the best answer for some women. Five years after major studies indicated that HT increased the risk for cardiovascular problems and breast cancer—causing women across the US to toss their HT prescriptions in the trash—HT is on the rise again.

New findings: The latest studies along with reevaluations of earlier research have helped to clarify the benefits and the risks. HT remains the most effective treatment for symptoms like hot flashes and night sweats.

About 80% of women in the US experience hot flashes during menopause. The typical episode lasts one to five minutes, though hour-long "heat waves" can occur. During a major hot flash, a woman feels as if she's being consumed by an inner fire…her skin turns red and may drip with perspiration…her heart may pound…she may feel confused and/or light-headed…and she may experience a vague sense of dread. Menopausal women can have several hot flashes per day, and some have 10 or more. Episodes can persist for about four years—for a total of up to 15,000 hot flashes. I find that, for about one in four women, symptoms are severe enough to merit treatment.

BUT IS IT SAFE?

The term *hormone therapy* often is used to refer either to estrogen replacement alone or a combination of estrogen and a progesterone-like drug. Many refer to all progesterone-replacement drugs as *progestins,* though the accurate all-inclusive term is *progestogens* (which covers natural and synthetic forms). Women who have had a hysterectomy can take estrogen alone. Otherwise, estrogen is given with a progestogen to protect against uterine cancer.

Timing is key to the safety of HT. The risks for heart attack, stroke and blood clots related to HT use are low in recently menopausal women who are in good cardiovascular health. Also, the risk for breast cancer does not increase much until a woman has taken hormones for four to five years. Most women don't need HT for that long—menopausal symptoms often abate by then.

Essential factor: The amount of time since your final menstrual period. You reach menopause when you go 12 consecutive months without a period. The farther you are past menopause and the more risk factors you have for heart disease and breast cancer, the riskier HT is.

Here's the latest thinking…

●**Heart Disease.** Women who began HT up to 10 years after menopause and took it for seven years tended to have a lower risk for heart disease than women taking a placebo. Women who started more than 10 years after menopause tended to have an increased risk. The older a woman was, the greater the risk.

●**Stroke.** At all ages studied, HT increased the risk for stroke, but for younger women, overall risk remained low—it increased by about two cases per year for every 10,000 women.

●**Breast Cancer.** Women of all ages who took estrogen with progestin had an increased risk for breast cancer after four years of use. Longer use increased their risk. Women on estrogen alone for seven years did not have an increased risk for breast cancer (estrogen-only therapy is appropriate only for women who have had a hysterectomy).

●**Bone Fractures.** Estrogen clearly reduces bone fracture risk. However, this benefit requires long-term HT, so experts no longer recommend it to treat osteoporosis.

TODAY'S OPTIONS

If you and your doctor decide HT is right for you, consider the specific options.

●**Estrogen.** For relief from hot flashes, products include daily pills…or transdermal skin patches worn on the body…or a transdermal cream, gel or spray applied once or twice daily. Transdermal estrogen may be less likely to increase the risk for blood clots. Most doctors agree that with estrogen, a progestogen also is needed unless a woman has had a hysterectomy.

●**Progestogen.** May be taken orally. Topical creams and vaginal gels also are available.

●**Vaginal options.** For women whose symptoms are limited to vaginal dryness and discomfort during sex, options include vaginal creams, rings or suppositories. In my view, it is prudent either to halt vaginal estrogen use for a few weeks every three to six months or to add a progestogen intermittently.

●**Bioidentical hormones.** These are laboratory-made hormones with the exact same molecular structure as hormones produced by the human body. Some people believe them to be safer than the more widely used conventional hormones—but no large-scale trials have yet been done to test this belief.

Usage guidelines: Start with the lowest recommended dose. If symptoms do not diminish within four weeks, talk to your doctor. You may need to increase your dose incrementally until you find the dosage that works for you. I recommend that the total time spent taking HT be less than five years.

Better Breast Cancer Detection

Mammography plus ultrasound helps detect small cancers in dense breast tissue, which occurs in almost half of women. In the densest breast tissue, mammograms alone detect less than half of all invasive tumors. Adding ultrasound raises the detection rate to 97%.

Thomas M. Kolb, MD, radiologist in private practice, New York City, and leader of a study of breast cancer detection in 11,220 women, published in *Radiology*.

Foods that Prevent Breast Cancer

Sweet potatoes, carrots, apricots, spinach and other foods rich in beta-carotene help prevent breast cancer. In one study, breast cancer risk was 68% lower in women who consumed the highest quantities of beta-carotene than in those who consumed the least.

Prevention, 33 E. Minor St., Emmaus, PA 18098.

Carrots Combat Ovarian Cancer

One study showed that women who ate just four carrot sticks at least five times a week halved their risk for developing ovarian cancer.

Theory: Beta-carotene, the nutrient found in carrots that gives them their orange color,

helps prevent cancer with its potent antioxidant properties.

Good news: Other orange-colored foods, including apricots, sweet potatoes, cantaloupe, butternut squash and pumpkin, are also high in beta-carotene.

Daniel W. Cramer, MD, professor of obstetrics and gynecology, Harvard Medical School and Brigham and Women's Hospital, both in Boston. His study was published in the *International Journal of Cancer*.

New Pap Smear Testing

Pap smears are sometimes misread. Each year, 500,000 American women are told that their Pap smears are normal when they're really abnormal.

Result: These women fail to get proper diagnosis and treatment for cervical cancer in its earliest, most treatable stages.

Good news: The US Food and Drug Administration has approved *Papnet,* a computerized retesting method that identifies at least 7.1 times as many "false negatives" as manual rescreening.

Klaus Schreiber, MD, professor of pathology, Montefiore Medical Center, Albert Einstein College of Medicine, Bronx, NY.

Proper Screening For Colon Cancer

Samuel Meyers, MD, clinical professor of medicine, Mount Sinai School of Medicine, New York City. He is co-author of the medical textbook *Bockus Gastroenterology* (W.B. Saunders).

If someone told you that a 20-minute medical test literally could save your life, wouldn't it be foolish to refuse it? Unfortunately, millions of Americans are doing just that when they fail to receive a periodic colon cancer screening.

Result: Each year, up to 57,000 Americans die unnecessarily from the disease. Nine out of ten deaths from colon cancer could be avoided.

Here's what you must know to protect yourself against colon cancer...

SCREENING WORKS

Almost all malignancies of the large intestine and rectum start out as *premalignant polyps,* flat or mushroom-shaped growths that are harmless but may become cancerous. If a polyp is detected and removed, cancer will *not* develop. That's why screening—getting regular exams to detect polyps or cancer in its earliest stages—is crucial.

The most recent screening guidelines, published by the US Multisociety Task Force on Colorectal Cancer, recommend screening for *all* men and women beginning at age 50. If you have already had surgery for polyps or colon cancer—or if you have inflammatory bowel disease, such as ulcerative colitis or Crohn's disease—your risk for colon cancer is increased and you should have colonoscopy on a schedule determined by your doctor.*

Screening options...

●**Colonoscopy every 10 years.** This screening test is the most accurate and has been shown to prevent 85% to 90% of colon malignancies. Many health insurance plans now pay for screening colonoscopy, as does Medicare. Without health insurance, the procedure costs about $3,000.

Colonoscopy has a reputation for being both embarrassing and painful. However these criticisms are overblown and misleading. In fact, many patients say colonoscopy is not nearly as bad as they had expected.

What's involved: While you are sedated, a flexible, one-half-inch diameter tube that employs digital video optics is threaded through the anus and passed through the large intestine, enabling the doctor to see your entire

*People with a close relative (parent, sibling or child) who has had colon cancer or polyps should start regular screening with colonoscopy at age 40 (or five years earlier than the youngest diagnosis in the family). If you have two close relatives with the disease, have a colonoscopy every five years. If three relatives, you should have genetic counseling and possibly start colonoscopy screening at age 25 or younger.

colon lining on a video monitor. The procedure itself usually takes no more than 20 minutes.

Many people find the preparation, which involves laxatives to empty out the bowel, much more unpleasant than the colonoscopy itself.

Until recently, the standard bowel preparation method involved drinking four liters of a bad-tasting colon-cleansing solution, such as *Golytely,* the night before. *Newer products now make the process less unpleasant...*

●*Phospho-soda* also tastes bad, but you only take several tablespoons dissolved in liquid the night before and the morning of the procedure.

Helpful: While you can mix it with any clear liquid, most patients prefer to mix it in ginger ale to make it more palatable.

●*Visicol* contains the same ingredient but is in tablet form. Instead of downing a liquid solution, you'll need to swallow a total of 40 tablets in multiple doses.

Helpful: Whatever bowel prep method you use, consume at least three eight-ounce glasses of fluid the night before to help prevent dehydration. You can drink any liquid, but Gatorade, which contains electrolytes, is preferred.

●**Sigmoidoscopy every five years.** This test is less invasive than colonoscopy and requires less preparation (such as an enema the night before and the morning of the procedure) and no sedation. But because the procedure is less thorough than colonoscopy, it identifies only 50% of colon malignancies.

What's involved: The same flexible tube that is used in a colonoscopy is passed through the lowest third of the large intestine (sigmoid colon), where half of all tumors occur.

Sigmoidoscopy may appeal to people who don't want to be sedated. This procedure, which costs about $400, is also less expensive than colonoscopy.

Important: On a subsequent day, you should return to take a barium enema, followed by an X-ray, to allow the doctor to view the remaining two-thirds of the colon. A barium X-ray costs about $500.

Although sigmoidoscopy combined with a barium X-ray screens the entire colon, it is still less accurate than colonoscopy.

●**Fecal occult blood test once a year.** People who don't want to undergo colonoscopy or sigmoidoscopy can opt for this test. It is the least accurate screening option and only reduces colon cancer rates by one-third.

Typical cost: $5.

What's involved: A chemical applied to stool samples detects traces of blood, which would suggest the presence of polyps or tumors. No preparation is required, but you must avoid certain foods (such as red meats and broccoli) for three days and medications (such as aspirin) for a week before the test to ensure accuracy. Since the test detects blood, taking aspirin, which can cause internal bleeding, could trigger a false positive.

Some people find the procedure unpleasant because it involves smearing small bits of your own stool on specially treated cardboard. And if blood is detected, you'll need to have a colonoscopy.

ANOTHER ALTERNATIVE

Virtual colonoscopy uses *computed tomography* (CT) to provide detailed radiographic pictures of the colon. It is relatively noninvasive, requires no sedation and can be done at your radiologist's office. It does require the same kind of preparation as colonoscopy.

This test is less accurate than conventional colonoscopy—it detects 75% to 80% of polyps larger than one centimeter, but just 40% to 50% of smaller ones. Health insurers generally will not pay for it.

Typical cost: $900.

It may be a good option for people who suffer from heart or lung disease, for whom sedation can be risky.

Dietary Iron Increases Colon Cancer Risk

If you are among the 15% of Americans who are genetically predisposed to colon cancer (a condition determined by genetic testing), getting too much iron increases colon cancer risk by up to 40%.

Theory: Large amounts of iron can harm DNA, possibly triggering colon cancer. Iron-rich foods include liver, seafood and enriched flour.

More study is needed to determine the appropriate iron intake for people predisposed to colon cancer.

Nicholas J. Shaheen, MD, MPH, associate professor of medicine and epidemiology, University of North Carolina School of Public Health, Chapel Hill.

Skin Cancer: Debunking The Myths

Barney J. Kenet, MD, dermatologic surgeon specializing in skin cancer, NewYork-Presbyterian Hospital/Weill Medical College of Cornell University, New York City, and coauthor (with Patricia Lawler) of *Saving Your Skin—Prevention, Early Detection, and Treatment of Melanoma and Other Skin Cancers* (Four Walls Eight Windows).

Everyone knows that excessive sun exposure is dangerous, yet up to 50% of people over the age of 65 are diagnosed with melanoma or some other type of skin cancer.

Why? Even health-savvy individuals remain confused about the best ways to adequately protect their skin.

Most dangerous myths…

Myth #1: **A beach umbrella keeps you safe from the sun.**

Reality: When you're at the beach, a large percentage of ultraviolet (UV) light bounces off the sand onto your skin, even when you're beneath an umbrella. Water and snow have the same reflective effect.

When boating or sitting beneath a beach umbrella, apply a sunscreen to all the exposed areas of skin, including your face and neck—even if you're wearing a brimmed hat. When skiing, apply sunscreen to your face and neck.

Myth #2: **Sunscreen that has a sun-protection factor (SPF) of 45 is three times more effective than SPF 15.**

Reality: Most doctors recommend using a sunscreen with an SPF of at least 15. A higher

SPF will not give you much additional protection. A sunscreen with an SPF of 45 is only about 5% more protective than an SPF 15 sunscreen. The higher-rated sunscreen doesn't last any longer, either.

All sunscreens need to be reapplied every two hours—and whenever you're exposed to water. This includes "waterproof" sunscreens, which provide some protection while swimming but still must be reapplied.

Make sure your sunscreen is labeled "broad spectrum"—meaning it blocks both ultraviolet A (UVA) and ultraviolet B (UVB) rays. Look for titanium dioxide or Parsol 1789 in the listing of ingredients.

Myth #3: Sunscreen provides complete sun protection.

Reality: While sunscreen is essential, there are other steps you also should take. The most important is to minimize sun exposure between 10 am and 4 pm, when the sun's rays are most intense. Hit the beach in the early morning or late afternoon instead.

To protect the commonly neglected areas, be sure to wear...

• **UV-protective lip balm** with an SPF of 15 or higher.

• **A hat with a three-inch brim.** Baseball caps don't protect the ears or the back of the neck—common skin cancer sites, especially for golf and tennis players.

• **UV-protective sunglasses.** UV exposure can cause cataracts.

• **Sun-protective clothing.** UV rays can pass through many fabrics, including cotton. If you hold a garment up to a light and can see the shape of the bulb shining through, it's not providing adequate sun protection.

Many companies now offer lightweight, tightly woven garments that are designed for comfort and maximum protection.

Example: Solumbra 30+ SPF sun protective clothing (800-882-7860, *www.sunprecautions.com*).

If you will be outdoors and don't have special clothing, be sure to wear sunscreen under your shirt.

Myth #4: Family history is the best indication of skin cancer risk.

Reality: A family history of skin cancer *is* a major risk factor—but the most important factor is your own skin type. People who have light-colored skin and eyes (blue or green) and freckles are at highest risk for all types of skin cancer and sun-related skin damage, such as wrinkles.

People with many moles, freckles and spots have the next-highest cancer risk, followed by individuals with a family history of skin cancer. If you have any of these risk factors, you need to carefully monitor your sun exposure.

When skin is exposed to sunlight, it increases the body's production of *melanin,* the main skin pigment. This results in tanning, in which a brown color is imparted to the skin. The more difficult it is for you to tan, the more vulnerable you are to skin cancer.

If you're dark-skinned, tan easily, don't have many moles and have no family history of skin cancer, your risk is low but you should still protect yourself from the sun.

Myth #5: Building a "base" tan protects against sunburn.

Reality: There is no such thing as a "safe" tan. UV exposure increases lifetime risk of skin cancer and other skin damage. Rather than expose yourself to those pre-vacation rays, protect yourself by following the rules described in this article.

Myth #6: "Self-tanning" products help protect against sunburn.

Reality: Self-tanning products are perfectly safe and are a good way to appear tan without any sun exposure. However, the dyes in these products do not offer UV protection. Some of these products do contain sunblock—but they generally provide only two hours of protection following application.

Myth #7: Melanoma occurs only where the skin has been exposed to the sun.

Reality: Sun exposure is just one of the potential causes of melanoma. For unknown reasons, cancerous moles can also develop under the arm, between the buttocks or toes or on the bottom of the foot. If you have a mole, spot or freckle *anywhere* on your body that shows a sudden change in size, shape or color, get it checked by a dermatologist.

Myth #8: Melanoma is always deadly.

Reality: When it's limited to the top layers of the skin, melanoma has a cure rate of 100%. That's why it's important to do a monthly self-exam of all skin surfaces, using a full-length and a handheld mirror.

You should also get screened annually by a dermatologist (twice a year, if you have skin cancer risk factors). During the screening, the doctor should use *epiluminescence microscopy* (ELM). This technique, which involves examining moles with a handheld microscope, detects melanoma earlier than ever.

Melanoma Is on the Rise

Catherine Poole, journalist and melanoma survivor who lives in Glenmoore, PA. She and DuPont Guerry IV, MD, director of the melanoma program, University of Pennsylvania Comprehensive Cancer Center, Philadelphia, are the authors of *Melanoma: Prevention, Detection & Treatment* (Yale University Press).

Most forms of cancer are now on the decline, but the incidence of melanoma is rising. Researchers theorize that the continuing depletion of the atmosphere's ozone layer—which blocks cancer-causing ultraviolet light—plays a role in this rise.

I was age 38 when I learned I had melanoma. I happened to glance at the back of my right leg and saw what looked like tiny black bubbles coming out of a mark that I had assumed to be a harmless mole.

Aware that an obvious change in a mole can be a sign of skin cancer, I consulted a dermatologist. She ordered a biopsy, which confirmed our suspicions.

I was lucky—my melanoma hadn't yet spread to my lymph nodes or to any organs. I underwent surgery to remove the cancerous cells. Today, several years later—I'm cancer-free.

PREVENTING MELANOMA

Melanoma is rarer than the other two forms of skin cancer, *basal cell carcinoma* and *squamous cell carcinoma*.

These cancers—characterized by pink bumps or raised, scaly patches—can usually be eradicated via outpatient surgery.

Because it tends to spread (metastasize), melanoma is far deadlier. Fifteen percent of those who get it ultimately succumb to it—despite recent advances in treatment.

To reduce your risk: Minimize your exposure to the sun. Whenever you head outdoors, wear a broad-brimmed hat and sunscreen with a sun protection factor (SPF) of at least 15... and seek shade when sunlight is brightest (between 11 am and 3 pm).

CALCULATING YOUR RISK

Melanoma affects Caucasians almost exclusively. The more likely you are to freckle and/or burn, the greater your risk.

Other risk factors...

●**Excessive sun exposure**—especially before age 10.

●**A personal or family history of any type of skin cancer.**

●**A large number of moles...**or the presence of big, flat moles. Many people think moles are present at birth. In fact, they appear in childhood—in reaction to sun exposure.

Odds are slim that any given mole will turn cancerous, but every mole on your body should be monitored.

DANGER SIGNS

Consult a doctor at the first sign that you might have a melanoma. *Here are the ABCDs of what to look for...*

●**Asymmetry.** With a typical melanoma, half of the spot looks different than the other half.

●**Border irregularities.** Melanomas tend to have notched rather than round or oval borders.

•**Color variation.** Normal moles are usually of one color. Melanomas are often blends of tan, brown, dark brown, pink, black, white—even blue.

•**Diameter in excess of one-quarter inch.** Ordinary moles seldom grow larger than that. If the spot is three-eighths of an inch or larger, have a doctor evaluate it.

Since some melanomas are raised, melanoma specialists recently added an *"E"* (for elevation) to the melanoma alphabet. Any mole that develops a bump or becomes elevated should be checked out right away.

EARLY DETECTION IS KEY

As part of *every* routine examination, your doctor should perform a comprehensive visual exam of your skin. If your doctor skips this exam—many do—remind him/her to do it.

If your melanoma risk is very high, you may need to have skin exams four times per year—preferably by a dermatologist.

To find a good dermatologist in your area, contact the American Academy of Dermatology, 888-462-3376, *www.aad.org*.

Also essential: Skin self-exams *between* doctor visits. For most people, occasional self-exams are adequate. If you're at high risk, the self-exams should be done monthly.

Do the exams in a brightly lit room, using a full-length mirror, a handheld mirror and a flashlight.

Examine every inch of your body, including your shoulders, underarms, the back of your neck and the soles of your feet.

If you have a partner, ask him/her to help you check hard-to-see areas of your body.

If a self-exam turns up a suspicious spot, see a doctor at once.

DIAGNOSIS AND TREATMENT

The best way to check suspicious tissue is via an *excision* biopsy, in which the entire lesion is removed and examined.

If the lesion is on the face or another cosmetically sensitive area, a less extensive punch or *incisional* biopsy will suffice.

If you do have melanoma, treatment depends on how advanced it is...

•**Stage I and II melanomas** haven't yet spread. They can usually be cured via surgical removal of the affected tissue.

The five-year survival rate for early melanoma is 95%.

•**Stage III melanoma** has spread to nearby lymph nodes. Treatment involves surgical removal of the melanoma and the affected lymph node or nodes, often followed by chemotherapy.

The five-year survival rate for stage III melanoma is about 50%.

•**Stage IV melanoma** has spread to distant organs. Treatment involves surgical removal of all metastases in the region, combined with chemotherapy that uses a drug called *alpha interferon*.

The five-year survival rate for stage IV melanoma is about 5%.

For information on state-of-the-art melanoma care, contact the National Cancer Institute at 800-422-6237 or *www.cancer.gov/newscenter*.

More Effective Melanoma Screening

The *positron emission tomography* (PET) scan helps to identify aggressive cancers, such as melanoma, that are not easily detected by conventional screening methods.

How it works: PET scans detect tumor sites by identifying high quantities of blood sugar (glucose). Malignant cells use glucose to drive cell division.

Self-defense: Melanoma patients should ask their doctors about PET scanning to screen for recurrence of their disease.

Mary S. Brady, MD, attending surgeon, Memorial Sloan-Kettering Cancer Center, New York City.

Most Common Sites For Melanoma

Don't forget the backs of your legs and your back when applying sunscreen. These are the most common sites for melanoma—the deadliest form of skin cancer.

Other often overlooked spots: Hair part and the tops of ears.

Use a waterproof, broad-spectrum sunscreen —meaning it blocks out UVA and UVB rays— with an SPF of at least 15. Apply it 20 minutes before going outside. Reapply every two hours —more often if swimming or exercising.

Andrew Kaufman, MD, assistant clinical professor of medicine, University of California, Los Angeles, School of Medicine, and dermatologist in private practice, Thousand Oaks, CA.

Aspirin May Reduce Pancreatic Cancer Risk

In the largest study yet to examine the link between aspirin and cancer of the pancreas, it was found that female subjects who took aspirin just once a week had a 43% lower chance of developing pancreatic cancer than those women who did not take any aspirin.

Researchers have yet to identify the mechanism for this beneficial effect. Other studies have indicated that aspirin may curb pancreatic cancer risk in men as well.

Kristin E. Anderson, PhD, MPH, associate professor, division of epidemiology, School of Public Health, University of Minnesota, Minneapolis.

11

Surgery & Hospitals

Medical Mistakes Can Be Very, Very Costly

Medical mistakes can be physically, financially and emotionally devastating—and they can happen in even the best hospitals. How can you minimize your risk of something going wrong? *By taking an active role...*

• **When you're given a new medication,** ask what it is—and why you are getting it. Have the nurse check your chart to make sure that the doctor ordered it.

• **Know which tests and procedures you'll be getting...**and ask about their purpose, risks and discomfort. If you expect you'll be in no condition to monitor your hospital care after surgery, arrange to have a friend or relative act on your behalf.

MOST COMMON MISTAKES

Mistake: **Failure to investigate nonsurgical alternatives.** All surgery is inherently dangerous, so safer, *nonsurgical* treatments should always be considered before you schedule time in the operating room.

If your primary-care doctor recommends surgery, don't take his/her word for it. Ask the surgeon about other options.

Reason: A surgeon who specializes in gallbladder surgery, for example, probably knows more about gallbladder disease—including many *nonsurgical* treatment options—than a general internist.

Mistake: **Failure to get a second opinion.** Insurance industry surveys indicate that despite what many people think, very little unnecessary surgery is being performed in this country. For this reason, many insurance companies no longer require their customers to get second opinions before scheduling surgery. However, any time a recommendation for surgery seems to come right out of the blue, a second opinion is always worth the effort.

Edward L. Bradley III, MD, professor and education director for surgery and emergency medicine, Florida State University, Tallahassee. He is author of *The Patient's Guide to Surgery* (University of Pennsylvania Press).

323

***Mistake:* Having unrealistic expectations.** Before surgery, find out precisely what the surgeon plans to do, the reason for it and what the outcome is likely to be.

Example: If you assume that surgery intended only to *reduce* back pain will *eliminate* your back pain, you'll be disappointed even if the operation is an unqualified success.

Medical science has come to appreciate the biological connections between mind and body. People who approach surgery with an informed, positive attitude generally do better during the operation. They also heal faster.

***Mistake:* Failure to ask about laparoscopy.** Many operations can now be performed with a *laparoscope,* a telescope-like instrument. Laparoscopic surgery requires smaller incisions than conventional "open" surgery. As a result, less tissue is destroyed…and recovery time is dramatically shortened.

Laparoscopy is now the method of choice for gallbladder removal and repair of esophageal hernias. It's an option for other procedures, including fibroid removal and inguinal hernia repair. Ask your surgeon to explain the pros and cons.

***Mistake:* Failure to ask about the surgeon's credentials.** If you're having a hernia repaired or another simple operation, almost any decent surgeon can do it safely. But for complex orthopedic, abdominal or brain surgery—or if you have additional health problems that might cause complications—look for a surgeon who belongs to the main certifying organization. *They are…*

●**American College of Surgeons.** Election to this group by colleagues attests to a surgeon's professional and ethical reputation.

●**American Surgical Association or a surgical specialty society** (such as the American Academy of Neurological Surgery and the American Board of Thoracic Surgery). This identifies a surgeon with special expertise and experience.

***Mistake:* Failure to use a competent anesthesiologist.** Although the skill of the surgeon determines how successful the operation will be, the anesthesiologist truly holds your life in his/her hands.

That's why it's vital to scrutinize your anesthesiologist as well as your surgeon. When I had an operation recently, I chose the anesthesiologist first—then I picked the surgeon.

Strategy: Ask your surgeon for the name of the best board-certified anesthesiologist on the hospital staff. Have him/her arrange for that person to administer your anesthetics.

***Mistake:* Picking the wrong kind of anesthetic.** In many cases, the patient has at least some choice regarding anesthetics. If you do, discuss with the anesthesiologist the pros and cons of each option.

If you have a choice between a general anesthetic (which completely knocks you out) and a regional or local anesthetic, it's safer to choose one of the latter.

Reason: Being awake during surgery may be unpleasant, but you'll be less likely to suffer potentially fatal respiratory problems…and you should recover faster.

***Mistake:* Failure to check the hospital's track record.** Especially when complicated operations are involved, hospitals tend to specialize. You don't want a heart valve fixed in a hospital that specializes in eye surgery. *Ask the hospital representative…*

●**How often is this procedure performed at this hospital?**

●**What is the hospital's track record with this procedure?** In some states, figures are readily available. In New York, for example, you can find out how many patients died and how many had complications after cardiac surgery simply by contacting the state's department of health. But you have to ask.

***Mistake:* Eating, drinking or taking aspirin before surgery.** If you're scheduled for morning surgery, nothing—no solid food, no water—should pass your lips after midnight.

Also: Refrain from taking aspirin for at least four days before surgery. Aspirin can interfere with blood clotting…and that can have disastrous consequences for surgical patients.

***Mistake:* Scheduling surgery for a weekend.** Never schedule elective surgery for Saturday or Sunday. On those days, many hospitals run on reduced staff…and equipment and consultations are hard to obtain.

***Mistake:* Failure to inquire in advance about postoperative pain relief.** Today, more and more hospitals are offering their patients *patient-controlled analgesia* (PCA). This system lets you push a button on your IV to give yourself as much or as little painkilling medication as you'd like—within safe limits.

Patients who use PCA are generally much more comfortable than those who must wait for a nurse to administer the next dose.

Ask your surgeon and the anesthesiologist about PCA…and be sure to make your preference known immediately upon checking into the hospital.

How to Get Much Better Hospital Care

Marie Savard, MD, an internationally-recognized internal medicine physician, expert on wellness and champion for patient rights. She is author of *How to Save Your Own Life* (Warner Books) and *The Savard Health Record* (Time-Life).

Managed care and rampant cost-cutting have left many hospitals understaffed. Doctors are constantly rushed. Fewer nurses must care for more patients.

Result: Patients buzz for help and get no response…get diagnostic tests by mistake… receive medication with no explanation.

You can still get superb care in the hospital —if you become your own health-care "manager." *Seven things you must do…*

1. Have a friend or relative stay with you. A caring companion can get you water when you need it…help you to the bathroom…and command the attention of doctors and nurses when necessary.

Your companion can also look after your interests at a time when you may be too weak to protect them yourself. Your advocate can ask questions, take notes and clarify exactly what's being done—and why.

If possible, call on more than one person for help. That's because round-the-clock company is best. Posted visiting hours are only guidelines—and they are meant for visitors, not health advocates. In fact, nurses often appreciate having an extra set of hands when they're too busy to help you.

Exception: Space is always tight in intensive care units. Having an extra person in the ICU may prevent other patients from getting the care they need.

2. Identify a point person. On an average day, a hospital patient might talk with his/her primary-care doctor…surgeon and/or anesthesiologist…and an ever-changing cast of interns and residents.

It's not uncommon for patients to get conflicting information from all these professionals. You need a point person who can sort out everything and answer your questions.

Typically, that will be the attending physician. He's the doctor on record at the hospital as being in charge of your case.

The attending physician coordinates your care. Depending on your medical problem, he might be your surgeon, cardiologist or internist.

As soon as you've settled in your room, ask the nurse assigned to your case to identify your point person. Get his/her name, telephone number and pager number.

3. Obtain your daily schedule. Each day, the nurses on your floor receive a "plan of care" listing tests you're scheduled for…meals ordered…and special instructions from your doctor. They also receive a separate list of all medications that have been ordered for you.

Each morning, ask the nurse in charge of your care to let you see both lists. Take notes on all important entries. It's the best way to ensure that mistakes don't occur, such as undergoing the wrong test or getting the wrong medication.

4. Get to know the staff. You want the nurses, technicians and other staff members to see you as a real person—not just another face on the ward.

Make small talk when staff members come into your room. Ask about their weekends… families…interests. Introduce your friends and family to them. Above all, let them know that you appreciate their care.

5. Get the sleep you need. Sleeping in the hospital is hard. The environment is noisy and unfamiliar. Even worse, staff members from different teams and services usually awaken patients every few hours for medication… blood pressure checks…IV adjustments.

Ask your assigned nurse if all these tasks can be combined in one visit. Making arrangements ahead of time permits better coordination of your care and less interruption of your sleep.

6. Don't put up with pain. Adequate post-surgical pain management speeds healing and helps prevent stress and depression. Yet doctors often skimp on pain medication because they fear the possibility of side effects and addiction.

The concern about addiction is misplaced. Adequate pain medication during hospitalization does not lead to subsequent abuse of painkillers.

If you're in pain, alert the medical staff. Otherwise, they'll assume that the medicine you're receiving is effective. If your doctor or the nurses decline to help, request a consultation with the hospital's pain specialist if available.

7. Make sure to get a copy of your discharge summary. When you leave, the hospital will provide a summary of your treatment to your attending physician and any other doctors he designates. You should receive a copy of this summary, too.

The report will provide important information for any physician who treats you in the future. It lists the reason for your hospital admission, important test results and surgical findings, all medications prescribed and the recommended future plan of care.

The summary is usually sent to your physicians two to three weeks after your discharge. Before you leave the hospital, give your primary-care physician a self-addressed, stamped envelope. Ask him to send you a copy of the report when it arrives at his office.

In the meantime: Before you leave the hospital, get copies of the results of all tests specifically related to your condition.

If you were hospitalized for a heart attack, for example, this would include a copy of your final electrocardiogram (EKG).

How to Make Your Hospital Stay Briefer, Safer and Less Expensive

Sheldon Blau, MD, physician in private practice, Massapequa, NY. He is author of *How to Get Out of the Hospital Alive* (John Wiley & Sons).

S pending time in a hospital can be hazardous to your health. Tens of thousands of Americans die each year from hospital-related errors. One out of every 10 patients receiving treatment in a hospital acquires a hospital-transmitted infection.

Problem: Hospitals are run by people who may be overworked and stressed out.

To make a hospital stay briefer—and safer…

●**Ask the nurse when checking in if any other patients on your floor have a similar last name.** If so, ask to be moved. It's not uncommon for hospital personnel to confuse you with another patient.

If this is impossible: Write your name and allergies clearly on a piece of paper. Post the paper prominently above your bed. A list of your allergies will at least prevent confusion over medication or treatment.

●**Avoid sharing a room with a patient who has a draining infection or a persistent cough.** Most infections are spread through the air, so you want your room as germ-free as possible. Pay out of your own pocket for a private room if possible.

●**Be wary of combining medications with the wrong foods.** Certain drugs become ineffective, less effective or downright dangerous when mixed with the wrong foods—or when taken at the wrong time.

Examples: Certain types of penicillin aren't effective when taken immediately after eating specific foods…some antidepressants can trigger dangerously high blood pressure when taken with yogurt, chocolate, bananas or some cheeses.

Helpful: Asking your doctor or nurse to review your medications and your menu. Also ask for a list of foods that should never be taken with your medication.

•**Keep a chart by your bed of what medication you're supposed to receive—*and when.*** Nurses often get called away on emergencies and forget to bring you your pills. Or they can give you the same medicine twice. Keep careful track of the drugs yourself to prevent dangerous errors.

•**Know who is qualified to help you.** The woman in the white uniform who brings you medication might not be a nurse, and the guy with the stethoscope examining your chart might not be a physician.

Before you complain about pain or let someone examine you, ask who he/she is, and make sure he has the credentials to assess your condition or the authority to perform the procedure.

Hospitals have rules about who can do what, but the rules are not always followed.

•**Prevent falls.** This seems like a no-brainer, but hundreds of perfectly coordinated people who never hurt themselves at home wind up with broken bones because they forget they are sick and in an unusual environment. *Helpful...*

> •Lower the bed before trying to get out.
> •Don't try to climb over the side rails of a hospital bed.

•**Follow doctors' orders**—but not blindly. If your doctor tells you not to eat after midnight in preparation for a test or procedure, refuse breakfast if a tray arrives in the morning. Somebody at the hospital probably forgot to discontinue your meals.

However, if someone comes in to perform a procedure that you weren't told about, don't submit to it without seeing the orders and understanding why they were given. Take charge. It's your health, and you have a responsibility to protect it.

IF YOU'RE HAVING SURGERY

•**Mark with a pen the part of your body where your surgeon is supposed to cut.** Although this step might seem silly, it can help avoid a disastrous mistake.

•**Make sure that any surgeon operating on you has been vaccinated against hepatitis B.** Most patients worry about HIV infection, but hepatitis B is more common and more easily transmitted.

An estimated 1,900 surgeons are infected with it, so don't be shy about your surgeon's feelings. All surgeons should be vaccinated.

What Hospitals Don't Want You to Know

Timothy McCall, MD, internist, medical editor of *Yoga Journal* and author of *Examining Your Doctor: A Patient's Guide to Avoiding Harmful Medical Care* (Citadel Press) and *Yoga as Medicine* (Bantam). *www.drmccall.com.*

Hospitals are fighting for their survival. Cutbacks from the federal government and from managed-care plans have reduced their revenue streams. Throughout the US, hospitals are closing, merging or implementing draconian cost-cutting measures.

But it's not just hospitals that are at risk. Corner-cutting also threatens the well-being of patients. *Here's what hospitals don't want to tell you—and what you can do about it...*

•**They're discharging patients "quicker and sicker."** To save money, hospitals are routinely discharging patients much earlier than they used to. If they plan to send you home, be sure you'll have the support services you may need, such as visiting nurses and physical therapists, and that family members will be able to perform any duties expected of them. If you do not feel your condition or home circumstances make discharge safe, alert your doctor. If necessary, file an appeal with your insurer.

•**They've cut their nursing staffs.** Even though doctors get most of the glory, it's the nurses who run hospitals. They monitor your condition, administer medications and make sure medical equipment functions properly. But maintaining a skilled nursing staff is expensive, so hospitals have found it cheaper to substitute "aides"—many of whom have very little bedside training.

You have the right to inquire about the qualifications of anyone who will treat you. Ideally, your primary nurse will be a registered nurse (RN). It's best if each nurse working on a typical medical or surgical ward is caring for no more than five patients or no more than two in an intensive-care unit.

If the nurse-to-patient ratio is much higher than that, consider having family members stay with you at all times while you're hospitalized or, if you can afford it, hire a private-duty nurse.

●**They reuse disposable medical equipment.** Some equipment, such as the dialysis catheters—intended for single-use only—are routinely cleaned and reused, which raises some concerns about infection and product failure. While reusing equipment is not illegal, I recommend you request that only new equipment be used each time.

●**They do not report inferior doctors.** Although the law mandates that incompetence or any misconduct among physicians must be reported to the federal government, 60% of hospitals have never filed even a single disciplinary report in the last decade. Part of the reason is that doctors are hospitals' "cash cows." They have the power to direct their patients to competing hospitals, so there's an incentive to not make waves.

Your best bet: Avoid potentially dangerous doctors by learning as much as you can about your condition and medications. The more you know, the better your ability to spot a bad apple.

●**They overwork residents and interns.** Although new regulations cap the work hours of doctors-in-training at 80 hours a week, in the past similar regulations have been routinely violated. If you are admitted to a teaching hospital, ask your resident or intern how many consecutive hours he/she has been working. Thirty-six-hour shifts are still routine. If you're concerned, it's your right to refuse care from anyone who looks too exhausted to provide it.

If you believe a hospital is doing anything that imperils patients, I recommend reporting it

to your state's regulatory authority or contacting the not-for-profit Joint Commission on Accreditation of Healthcare Organizations at 800-994-6610 or *www.jcaho.org*.

More from Timothy McCall...

How to Choose the Right Surgeon

Besides the severity of your medical condition, most likely the biggest factor in determining the success of any operation is the surgeon. Obviously, good ones have better technical skills. But they are also more likely to be affiliated with the hospitals and other professionals—such as topflight registered nurses and anesthesiologists—who will increase your odds of a positive outcome.

Even so, numerous people simply use whatever surgeon they are assigned by the hospital, their primary-care provider or HMO.

It's not necessary to find the absolute best surgeon—usually, that isn't even possible. Your job is to make a reasonable choice in the time available and—most importantly—to avoid a bad surgeon.

Here's what I suggest...

●**Get a few names to begin your search.** If you have a primary-care doctor you know and trust, ask which surgeon he/she would choose for a loved one—and why. Also ask which surgeons are held in particularly high esteem by their colleagues. The answers may differ.

Remember, doctors sometimes make referrals based on friendship, reciprocal business relationships (you refer to me, I'll refer to you) or institutional affiliations, so it's wise to cast a wider net. If you have friends who work in local hospitals or clinics or who are otherwise in the know, ask them for the scuttlebutt on top surgeons.

●**Check credentials.** If the surgeon is on the faculty of a local medical school or on staff at a respected hospital—which are both good signs—chances are, he is board-certified. This means the doctor has completed a residency at an accredited hospital and passed a rigorous certifying exam.

To find out if a doctor is board-certified, consult the American Board of Medical Specialties' Web site at *www.abms.org* or call 866-275-2267. Also check the fields in which the doctor is certified. For example, a doctor who performs liposuction should be certified in plastic surgery, not just in general surgery or family practice.

•**Ask about the surgeon's experience.** How many times has the doctor performed the operation in question? How many of those procedures were done, say, this year?

There's no magic cutoff, but the more operations a doctor has done, the better. For heart surgery, I'd want a surgeon who does at least 100 a year.

Experience is particularly important for complicated operations, such as heart or brain surgery, and for newer procedures, including some "minimally invasive" laparoscopic operations, with which most doctors may have only limited experience. Ask the doctor what specific training he has had in the procedure you may undergo.

•**Ask about the surgeon's track record.** You want to find out not only how many operations a surgeon has done, but also how his patients have fared. Did they experience any wound infections or need to have the procedure repeated? Which complications have been most common? If a surgeon you're considering bristles at these questions or even declines to answer, look elsewhere.

•**Ask where the operation will be performed.** For heart surgery, you want to be at an institution that does at least 200 a year, according to recent studies. Community hospitals may be fine for routine procedures, such as hernia repair or gallbladder removal. But for complex or rare procedures, you are generally better off at a major teaching hospital.

•**Be suspicious of surgeons who are too "gung-ho."** The surgeons who always want to operate make me nervous. Surgery may not be the best option. One of the best orthopedic surgeons I've ever met routinely tries to talk patients out of having any operation he is not convinced will help them. When he recommends surgery, you know you need it.

Better Nursing Care

To ensure good nursing care when going to the hospital, ask your doctor which hospitals have the best nursing staffs. Call the nursing administrator and ask if nurses are part of a stable staff or brought in from agencies. Be sure family members are at the hospital to ensure that your needs are known. Know your own medications—when you take them and why.

Mary O'Neil Mundinger, RN, DrPH, dean, Centennial Professor in Health Policy, Columbia University School of Nursing, New York City.

How to Pick A Hospital

Charles B. Inlander, a consumer advocate and healthcare consultant based in Fogelsville, PA. He was founding president of People's Medical Society, a consumer health advocacy group. He is author of more than 20 books, including Take This Book to the Hospital with You *(St. Martin's).*

Some on-line hospital rating sites have limited coverage...rely on unofficial information...or don't adjust ratings for the severity of cases treated at each hospital.

Some hospital quality reports covering certain procedures can be found at the Centers for Medicare & Medicaid Services Web site, *www.cms.gov*. Check the National Voluntary Hospital Reporting Initiative, which lists hospital success rates for treating heart attack, congestive heart failure and pneumonia. Also, call and ask how many times a year the hospital has performed the procedure that you need. Compare three or four hospitals within 100 miles of your home. Both your doctor and the hospital should have performed the procedure often—higher volume tends to improve outcomes.

Find out the ratio of registered nurses (RNs) to patients—ideally, there should be at least one RN for every four patients. In intensive care units, there should be at least one RN for every two patients.

More from Charles B. Inlander...

Hospital Overcharge Self-Defense...Keep Records... Keep Track...Keep at It

Ninety percent of hospital bills include mistakes—three-fourths of which favor the hospital. These aren't small errors, either. One study found that the average overcharge totals $1,400.

Overcharges affect your wallet even if your HMO or insurance company pays most of the bill. Your copayments mount up...and future premiums may rise as a result of the hospital costs you incur.

Here's how to avoid paying the hospital more than you owe...

●**Keep a treatment log.** During your hospital stay, list every doctor's visit, procedure and medication in a notepad kept within easy reach of your bed. This will give you a clear record to check later against your itemized bill.

If you're too ill to maintain the log—or too groggy from anesthesia or medication—ask a family member or friend to keep it for you.

●**Question any service you suspect isn't okayed by your attending physician.** While you're in the hospital, your attending physician—the doctor who admitted you or the specialist assigned to your case—is the only person authorized to approve consultations, procedures and medications.

Nonetheless, the hospital may initiate services on its own to boost revenues or reward affiliated doctors.

Examples: A quick "drop-by" visit from a staff psychiatrist...an "assistant surgeon" drawn from the hospital's roster...a visit from your own family doctor, who may bring the hospital many referrals.

Patients are legally entitled to refuse to pay for any such unauthorized services. But it's usually easier to take preemptive action to prevent them in the first place.

While hospitalized, insist that your attending physician outline his/her treatment plan so you know what to expect.

If a nurse or another doctor announces an unexpected visit or procedure, ask to see the hospital record indicating the attending physician's approval. If you have any doubts at all, politely decline the service and insist on talking with the attending physician.

●**Insist on a fully itemized bill.** Don't settle for bills that list broad categories like "pharmacy" or "surgical charges." Hospitals are required to provide a detailed account of all charges. *The bill should list each...*

●Procedure you underwent.

●Doctor's visit to your hospital room.

●Dose of medicine that was given to you.

●Facility used, such as an X-ray suite, operating room, etc.

●Supplies provided for your care—bandages, IV lines, etc.

If you're hospitalized for two or more days, ask for a new itemized bill daily. That makes it easier to keep track of your charges and to start questioning any suspect items right away.

The hospital's operator can give you the number of the billing office. Call and request the update directly from the department head.

If he/she balks, talk with the hospital's patient representative (ombudsman). If this doesn't work—or if there's no patient rep—calling the hospital's chief administrator almost always brings a fast response.

●**Scrutinize your bill.** Even with the help of your detailed log, the abbreviations on the bill may be difficult to decipher. If any items on it confuse you, call the billing department for clarification.

Also check with your attending physician if any charges on the bill seem suspect.

The most common overcharges are for services and/or procedures that you didn't actually receive. The second most common overcharges are for duplications of service.

Examples: A charge for use of the radiology suite for an X-ray taken at your bedside ...a charge for six blood tests when you actually had only three.

●**Have your bill audited.** If any of the listed charges seem erroneous to you, ask the billing department to check your bill against hospital records to make sure all itemized services really were performed.

The department should conduct this audit willingly and at no charge...and promptly correct all mistakes.

•**Alert your insurer.** If you dispute the billing department's finding, and the dispute can't be resolved, contact your insurance company or HMO.

Taking this action doesn't mean you're accusing anyone of a crime. But it is the surest way to get prompt action.

Your best bet is to contact the insurance company's fraud division directly. Bypass the customer service department.

If you are covered by Medicare, contact the Inspector General of the Federal Health and Human Services Department at 800-447-8477.

For greatest efficiency when you call your insurer...

•**Have all pertinent documents on hand when you call.**

•**Be prepared to detail exactly which charges you feel are fraudulent,** and why.

If the insurance company agrees with you, it will generally take over and resolve the case. That might even involve going to court.

The bill typically goes on hold while matters are disputed.

Also from Charles B. Inlander...

Don't Be Afraid to Visit a Hospital Patient

Hospital visitors need not worry about picking up a bug from patients. Visitors are more likely to bring in germs that would affect patients—whose immune systems are weakened—than to get sick themselves. Most visitors do not stay in the hospital long enough to be exposed to anything infectious. And patients who are highly infectious often can't have visitors at all.

Use common sense when visiting so you do not bring in a minor infection, such as a cold, that could be dangerous to hospital patients. Be particularly careful when visiting the maternity ward.

Simple Way to Avoid Infectious Diseases

Each year, bacteria and viruses spread through hospitals and infect 2 million Americans. About 90,000 of these people die as a result of hospital-borne infections. Lax hand-washing practices among health care workers are largely to blame.

The US Centers for Disease Control and Prevention has issued guidelines advising doctors and nurses to replace soap and water with fast-drying alcohol gels. Gels are much more convenient—and they kill more germs than just soap and water. Regular use of alcohol gels could halve the rate of hospital-acquired infections, new studies indicate.

Outside the hospital setting, alcohol gels are a convenient way to "wash up" at restaurants, picnics, portable toilets and on airplanes. At home, the gels may be a good idea if someone in the family has a cold or has a severely compromised immune system, which makes him/her vulnerable to infections.

If everyone in the household is healthy, plain old soap and water suffices. Just be sure to wash your entire hand, including the back and between the fingers.

David Gilbert, MD, past president, Infectious Diseases Society of America, Alexandria, VA.

Take Aspirin in The Hospital

Aspirin may reduce infection risk in hospital patients. The *salicylic acid* that's in aspirin seems to inhibit reproduction of the *Staphylococcus aureus* bacterium, one of the most common causes of hospital-related infections, a new animal study has found.

Self-defense: Ask your doctor about taking one or two regular-strength (325-milligram) aspirin tablets two times a day while in the hospital. This may cut in half your risk of contracting a staph infection.

Ambrose Cheung, MD, professor of microbiology, Dartmouth Medical School, Hanover, NH.

How to Survive a Trip to the ER

Joel Cohen, MD, physician practicing in Mesa, AZ. He has practiced emergency and urgent-care medicine for many years and is author of ER: Enter at Your Own Risk *(New Horizon).*

Each year, millions of Americans visit hospital emergency rooms (ERs).* It's not news that overburdened hospital personnel are often rushed and tired, and the environment is noisy and chaotic. And because new doctors often train in emergency rooms, the person caring for you may have little or no experience treating your complaint.

To get the best possible care…

●**Speak up.** You must be as assertive in the ER as you are in all other health care situations.

Few people realize that they can request a specialist or more senior ER physician. If he/she practices in that hospital and is available, you have a good chance of being seen by the physician of your choice.

Smart idea: If you have a chronic condition, such as heart disease or emphysema, keep a list in your wallet of specialists recommended by your physician to request in case of an emergency.

At the very least, call your family doctor from the waiting room or while en route to the hospital. He may be able to meet you there—

*In the event of a life-threatening emergency, call 911. These emergencies include uncontrolled bleeding, chest pain, shortness of breath, fainting, a sudden unexplained weakness or paralysis, falling for no apparent reason, seizure, severe abdominal pain, a worst-ever headache or change in mental function.

or at least make a telephone call—to expedite your treatment.

●**When you are evaluated by a doctor,** focus on your main complaint. Stick to the one or two most important and distressing symptoms. Listing multiple symptoms may make diagnosis more difficult.

●**Check credentials.** You also have the right to ask about the experience levels of the doctors who treat you in the ER. Before you agree to any risky test, procedure or operation, ask how long the doctor has been practicing.

There is no single "correct" answer. But if you feel uncomfortable with the experience level of your ER doctor, ask to see the physician in charge or get a specialist consultation for a second opinion.

Helpful: If possible, bring a friend or family member with you to act as your advocate. This is especially important if you are too sick or weak to be assertive.

●**Avoid unnecessary tests and treatments.** Do *not* agree to any test unless you know the risks involved…what the test will show…and how the results will change your course of treatment.

Before allowing yourself to be treated, find out if the treatment is necessary or just a precaution…and whether treatment can wait until you've had a chance to talk with your primary-care physician. Your goal is to participate fully in the decision-making process.

Caution: Do *not* leave the hospital if you don't feel better or if you feel worse than when you first arrived. Tell the doctor that you feel just as sick…and that you would like a second opinion.

THE RIGHT DIAGNOSIS

If you're experiencing unexplained symptoms, here are the emergency tests you will need to ensure a proper diagnosis…

●**Chest pain or indigestion.** An *electrocardiogram* (ECG) to rule out heart disease.

●**Abdominal pain.** A *complete blood count* (CBC) and urinalysis to check for infection. A sonogram may be given if a physical problem, such as gallstones, is suspected. Follow up with your physician within 24 hours.

●**Shortness of breath.** An ECG, chest X-ray and simple blood oxygen test to determine if there is enough oxygen in your system and to rule out a collapsed lung or heart problem.

●**Numbness or paralysis of the face or limbs,** unexplained dizziness or falling. Each of these symptoms may signal a stroke. A *magnetic resonance imaging* (MRI) scan provides the most detailed picture of the brain. At a minimum, a *computed tomography* (CT) scan should be performed to determine if a stroke has occurred. If so, these tests will identify the type of stroke, so doctors can prescribe appropriate treatment.

Emergency Room Self-Defense

Ted Christopher, MD, chief of the division of emergency medicine, Thomas Jefferson University Hospital, Philadelphia.

Hospital emergency departments (EDs) are busier than ever. There are more than 100 million ED visits in the US annually, according to a study by the US Centers for Disease Control and Prevention. That is up from 90 million in 1992—an increase of about 35,000 patients a day.

Because of decreasing health-care budgets, examining rooms and equipment are in short supply. Doctors, nurses and technicians are overworked. No wonder the average wait to see a doctor is 49 minutes—with many ED patients waiting hours.

For better emergency care…

●**Call 911 or an ambulance if you suspect heart attack or stroke,** two "time-dependent" conditions that can quickly worsen. Ambulance technicians will begin your care on the way…and you'll be seen by a doctor as soon as you arrive at the hospital.

If your condition isn't truly an emergency, arriving by ambulance won't make a difference, and you could get stuck with the bill. The sickest patients always get taken care of first.

●**Go to the closest hospital if you think you have an emergency.** The majority of all hospital EDs are now being staffed with board-certified emergency physicians. Teaching hospitals are staffed with attending emergency physicians and many residents and interns. In nonteaching hospitals, there will be only one or two doctors on staff. You may spend time waiting in either setting.

●**Don't wait for a referral from your doctor.** It is no longer necessary to bring a referral or get prior approval from your doctor before going to the ED.

Everyone who comes to the ED undergoes *triage.* That's the process by which each patient is evaluated by a nurse to determine how serious his/her condition is and who is to be seen first by a doctor.

●**Know the names and phone numbers of all your doctors**—especially your primary-care physician, but also any specialists you may have seen. Your private doctors often possess medical information that can assist the emergency physician in treating you.

●**Bring all of your medications.** ED staff will learn a lot about your health history simply by reading the labels. If you're going to need drugs, it's vital that the doctors know what medications you're taking.

Helpful: Keep a list of all your medications, along with the details of other health information (serious allergies, for example), on the refrigerator door. If you're unable to talk, the ambulance crew can take the list to the ED.

Even better: Bring the actual bottles—the printed labels are easiest to read.

●**Report changes in symptoms immediately.** Don't suffer in silence in the waiting room. You'll see a doctor more quickly if you inform the staff that your symptoms are getting worse. You should be given medication, if necessary, even before you see a doctor.

Don't Have Surgery Until You Read This

Jerome Groopman, MD, Recanati Professor of Medicine, Harvard Medical School, chief of experimental medicine, Beth Israel Deaconess Medical Center, both in Boston, and a leading cancer and AIDS researcher. He is author of *Second Opinions: Stories of Intuition and Choice in the Changing World of Medicine* (Penguin).

I had spinal fusion surgery for back pain many years ago. The surgeon insisted it was the best treatment. I didn't get a second opinion from another doctor—and I'm still in pain. I later learned that only one in six patients has a good outcome from the procedure. Those are terrible odds. Had I gotten a second opinion, I might have known that physical therapy can work as well as or better than surgery, with none of the risks.

Less than one in four Americans gets a second opinion from another doctor, even though it often is covered by insurance. That can be a very dangerous mistake.

Getting a second opinion is a way to protect yourself if a doctor makes an error…test results are inconclusive…or treatment options for your problem aren't clear cut.

The initial diagnosis is *wrong* in a significant number of cases. A Johns Hopkins study found an error rate of 5.1% in pathology reports of female reproductive tract cancers…and Emory University pathologists found major errors in nearly 14% of the reports on tissue samples submitted for review.

WHEN TO GET A SECOND OPINION

Consult another physician if…

●**The initial diagnosis is unclear.** Your doctor uses conditional language, such as, "You *seem* to have an immune disorder" or "We're *not sure* if it's arthritis."

●**You have a rare or life-threatening disease** that doesn't require immediate emergency care.

●**The proposed treatment is one of several options.** Ask your doctor if the treatment he/she is recommending is standard for your condition. Some diseases, including many cancers, don't have established treatment protocols. There may be better options than those proposed by your doctor.

WHAT TO DO

●**Be honest with your doctor.** Let him know that you must defer a final decision until you have seen another physician. This often is the hardest part for patients because they're afraid the doctor will be offended. *Not true.* Doctors are accustomed to patients getting second opinions. Many encourage this for their own peace of mind, to catch errors and to ensure that the patient is satisfied with the treatment plan.

Raise the issue in a nonconfrontational way. You might say something like, "I'd like to find out about different ways to approach this problem. I think it would be useful to get a second opinion. What do you think?" If the doctor acts insulted, consider that a red flag—you don't want a doctor like that.

It may be tempting to get a second opinion behind your doctor's back. But if you do, you won't be able to have records and tests forwarded. Plus, you'll feel like you're sneaking around. When you're dealing with important health issues, you want to feel empowered.

●**Seek a second opinion from a doctor in a different practice or hospital than your primary physician.** Doctors who work together often share the same biases and style of practice. You want someone who has a fresh perspective.

Ask friends to recommend physicians—or to ask their own physicians for recommendations. Research your illness on the Internet to see if there are doctors who specialize in your condition.

If you find a specialist far from your home, just forwarding your records may not be enough. It may be worth the expense to visit in person. First call, or have your doctor call, the specialist to make sure he/she feels he can help.

●**Get a third opinion if the first two disagree.** Don't go along with any treatment until there is a clear consensus that it is the best approach for you. This might mean seeing three, four or even five doctors. Don't feel rushed. Most conditions allow time to look into all options.

I have ganglion cysts in my right wrist that make typing painful. I have gotten four opinions—two doctors want to operate, a third wants to explore it further and the fourth isn't sure what to do. Since the experts can't agree, I decided to take the safest route and work with a physical therapist. My wrist is getting better slowly.

●**Check your insurance plan.** Medicare covers second opinions when major treatments, such as surgery or chemotherapy, are recommended. If the second opinion does not agree with the first, Medicare covers a third opinion.

HMOs usually pay for second opinions, but only from doctors in the plan's network. You might have to convince the plan administrator —by writing a letter explaining your case, for example—to approve a second opinion from an out-of-network provider. Some plans cover three or more opinions. Others do not.

A second opinion usually costs the same amount as an office visit—more if additional tests are necessary.

●**Trust your instincts when sorting through conflicting opinions.** No one knows your body, personality and lifestyle better than you. A treatment that is right for one patient could be wrong for another. Your doctors' opinions should *guide* your decision, not determine it.

●**Bring a friend or family member to all appointments.** It's almost impossible to fully understand what your doctor is saying when you're in pain or frightened. Conditions that require second opinions invariably are complex. You should have someone with you who is clear-headed.

●**Avoid on-line medical services.** These Web sites provide second opinions for a small fee. You send in your X-rays, biopsy readings or other test results, and specialists review them and send you an opinion via e-mail. The doctor at the other end, however, doesn't know you or your lifestyle. And without that information, he/she can't make good decisions about what's best for you.

Important Presurgery Test

Before undergoing surgery, ask your doctor to check your albumin levels. A deficiency of this blood protein increases your chances of suffering postoperative bleeding or an infection by 50% or more. Few hospital patients are screened for low albumin prior to surgery.

Albumin deficiency, which can be detected by an inexpensive blood test, may indicate malnutrition, and can generally be corrected with a more nutritious diet prescribed by a registered dietitian.

James Gibbs, PhD, research assistant professor, Institute for Health Services Research and Policy Studies, Northwestern University, Evanston, IL.

Should You Forgo Surgery?

Sandra A. McLanahan, MD, executive medical director, Integral Health Center, Buckingham, VA. She is coauthor of Surgery and Its Alternatives: How to Make the Right Choices for Your Health *(Twin Streams).*

Each year, major surgery is performed 25 million times in the US. Surgery is sometimes the only solution to a health problem—but alternatives are often possible.

In some cases, diet, herbal treatment, acupuncture, yoga and other alternative treatments can eliminate the need for an operation.

Here are some common surgeries for which an alternative is often possible*...

CATARACT REMOVAL

A cataract is cloudiness in the eye's lens. By age 70, up to 70% of Americans suffer from decreased vision because of this condition.

Until recently, alternative medicine has primarily focused on measures to prevent cataracts or to slow their growth. But now, the evidence shows that these same measures may actually reverse cataracts, eliminating the need for surgery altogether.

Nonsurgical program for cataracts...

*Check with your doctor before trying any of these regimens.

●**Eat a low-fat, high-fiber diet.** Avoid refined sugar and flour. These foods elevate blood sugar levels, which increases risk for cataracts and accelerates their growth.

●**Take daily vitamin and mineral supplements.** This should include 25,000 international units (IU) of beta-carotene…400 IU of vitamin E (mixed tocopherols)*…200 micrograms (mcg) of selenium…50 milligrams (mg) of zinc…and 1,000 mg, three times daily, of vitamin C.

●**Make lifestyle changes.** Wear sunglasses outdoors (if you're often exposed to bright fluorescent light, try lightly tinted glasses indoors)…maintain a healthy weight…avoid tobacco smoke. Sunlight and tobacco smoke can damage eye tissues. Excess body weight increases levels of the stress hormone cortisol, which accelerates cataract growth.

●**Try herbs.** Da Wei Di Huang Wan (also known as Eight Flavor Rehmannia) is a combination of eight Chinese herbs. It has been reported in the *Journal of the Society for Oriental Medicine* in Japan to be effective in reversing early cataracts. Double-blind studies are still needed to confirm these findings.

This regimen should begin to improve cataracts within six weeks.

CORONARY BYPASS

Coronary heart disease (CHD) blocks blood flow through the arteries that feed the heart. This can cause chest pain (angina), which is frequently severe. But the bigger danger is heart attack.

When CHD is sufficiently advanced (based on the location and severity of blockage), surgery may be recommended to "bypass" the blocked arteries with grafts of blood vessels from elsewhere in the body. However, studies pioneered by renowned heart specialist Dean Ornish, MD, have shown that simple lifestyle changes are 90% effective at reversing coronary artery blockage.

Important: If your heart disease is unstable or has suddenly worsened—or if the risk for heart attack is high—then surgery may be your only option.

*Check with your doctor for proper amount—taking more than 200 IU may be dangerous.

Consider this nonsurgical treatment for coronary heart disease…

●**Cut dietary fat.** Fats in your diet should constitute no more than 10% of daily caloric intake. Consume monounsaturated, rather than saturated, fat. Eating less fat reduces the risk for fatty plaque buildup in the arteries (atherosclerosis) and helps prevent clots from forming.

Limit cholesterol intake to 5 grams per day. Avoid refined sugar and salt.

●**Take vitamin supplements every day.** The most effective supplements include folate (400 mcg) and vitamin B-6 (3 mg). These vitamins improve circulation and reduce levels of homocysteine, an amino acid that appears to promote atherosclerosis.

●**Exercise for one full hour,** at least three times a week. Choose aerobic activities, such as vigorous walking, swimming or biking. Exercise will reduce blood pressure and improve circulation.

●**Practice meditation,** deep breathing and/or yoga. Stress-reduction techniques work to lower blood pressure and balance out stress hormone levels, enabling the heart to repair damaged tissues.

●**Socialize more often.** Membership in religious groups, support groups and even in bowling leagues has been shown to reduce heart attack risk.

●**Get treatment for related health conditions.** If you have high blood pressure or diabetes, be sure they are being treated effectively. Both conditions promote atherosclerosis.

This type of regimen should help coronary heart disease improve within a few weeks. Significant changes can usually be seen within a few months.

HIP REPLACEMENT

Proper diet and exercise can often prevent or arrest hip problems.

Try this nonsurgical program for hip pain and disability…

●**Avoid red meat,** dairy products, refined sugar, salt and caffeine. Eliminating vegetables in the nightshade family (tomatoes, potatoes, eggplant and peppers) may also be helpful. These foods promote inflammation, which can contribute to arthritis.

●**Take daily vitamin and mineral supplements.** To help relieve pain and inflammation, take 1,000 mg of calcium...500 mg of magnesium...and 400 IU of vitamin E with mixed tocopherols (check with your doctor for proper amount). To promote cartilage repair, take 1,000 mg of vitamin C.

●**Try glucosamine sulfate.** This dietary supplement helps maintain and rebuild the cartilage that lines the joint.

Typical dosage: 500 mg, three times daily.

●**Take evening primrose oil.** This herb reduces inflammation and improves circulation.

Typical dosage: 500 mg, three times daily.

●**Lose weight.** This reduces the load borne by the joints.

●**Practice yoga.** This improves circulation and promotes healing.

●**Consider acupuncture,** massage or chiropractic treatment. These therapies reduce pain by increasing the body's natural painkilling endorphins.

This regimen should alleviate hip pain and disability within three months.

For a referral to a physician who is familiar with alternatives to surgery, contact the American Association of Naturopathic Physicians at 866-538-2267 or *www.naturopathic.org.*

Secrets of Successful Surgery

Peggy Huddleston, MTS (master of theological studies), researcher and psychotherapist in private practice, Cambridge, MA. She is author of *Prepare for Surgery, Heal Faster* (Angel River Press).

Even minor surgery can be very stressful. And no wonder, given the anxiety elicited by the idea of being "put under"... the risk of complications...and the fear of postoperative pain.

Stress does more than just make things unpleasant. It boosts the risk for infection and slows the healing of incisions.

Whether you are facing bunion removal or coronary bypass, the surgery itself and your recovery will go more smoothly if you follow this program. *Here's what to do...*

DEEP RELAXATION

Stress causes your body to produce cortisol. Chronic high levels of this stress hormone can torpedo your immune system just when you need it most.

To lower cortisol levels: Starting at least two weeks before the surgery, do the following exercise for 20 minutes or more, once or twice every day.

●**Sit comfortably or lie down.** Relax and close your eyes.

●**Focus on the muscles in your neck.** If they're tense, let them relax.

●**Now focus on other muscle groups—** shoulders, arms, chest, abdomen, back, pelvis, right leg and left leg. Feel the tension, then allow the muscle to relax.

●**Think of a loved one.** Recall a time when you most strongly felt love for him/her. Imagine receiving love in return.

Master all this, and you'll be able to have deep, healing relaxation all day—while driving, preparing meals, etc.

POSITIVE VISUALIZATION

During periods of deep relaxation, your mind is highly "suggestible." It treats *wishes* almost as if they were *reality.*

Use this time to "seed" your mind with images of fast-healing incisions, pain-free recovery and other desired outcomes pertaining to surgery.

Research conducted at the University of Texas at Austin showed that surgical patients who visualized a fast-healing incision healed faster than patients who did not perform visualizations.

What to do: Twice a day for five minutes, imagine chatting happily with your best friend just after surgery. "I feel fine," you might say. "Things went well."

Next, see yourself leaving the hospital. You might say, "My _____ [whatever body part was operated on] feels great. I'm healing just as fast as I'd hoped."

Now imagine yourself fully healed and doing something you love. If you're facing hip replacement surgery, you might see yourself dancing at an upcoming wedding reception.

SUPPORT FROM OTHERS

In the days leading up to surgery, friends and/or family members may ask, "How can I help?" That's terrific. Recent studies indicate that the emotional support of loved ones promotes fast, smooth recovery from surgery.

Tell those who want to help that you need their *love*. Ask them to think of you for the 30 minutes leading up to your surgery...and to "send" you their best wishes for comfort.

How does one send these wishes? Tell the person, "Think back to a time when you felt great love for me. When you feel truly connected to me—as if I were right next to you—imagine wrapping me in a blanket of love."

Specify the color of this imaginary blanket—whatever hue seems most reassuring to you.

This strategy is not as farfetched as it might sound. A growing body of scientific research confirms the power of such "distance healing."

For more direct support, have your partner or a close friend stay with you just before you head to the operating room. Skin-to-skin contact with a loved one—and his/her soothing words—are remarkably effective at helping control stress.

HEALING STATEMENTS

As you go under anesthesia—and throughout the operation—many patients are powerfully influenced by what they hear.

In a study conducted at the Royal Infirmary in Glasgow, Scotland, 30 women undergoing hysterectomy listened to a taped message during surgery that said, "You'll feel warm and comfortable. Any pain you feel after surgery will not concern you."

Result: After surgery, these women needed 23% less morphine than a control group who heard no comforting words.

To put healing statements to work for you, jot the following statements on a note card and ask your anesthesiologist to recite each five times...

As you go under: "Following this operation, you will feel comfortable. You will recover and heal well."

As the procedure ends: "The operation went well. You will wake up hungry for _____ [your favorite food]. You'll be thirsty and able to urinate easily."

Some patients are too embarrassed to ask for these recitations. Don't be. These days, most anesthesiologists are happy to cooperate, admitting that they talk to their patients during surgery anyway. In fact, much of the research on suggestibility during surgery was done by anesthesiologists.

Important: Talk to the anesthesiologist no later than the night before surgery—and preferably several days before surgery. If you cannot arrange a face-to-face meeting, talk by phone.

Ask about the anesthetic he'll use...and about the painkillers you'll use after surgery.

Just talking helps to establish a supportive doctor–patient relationship. A Harvard study of 218 surgical patients found that a five-minute talk with the anesthesiologist before surgery was more calming than an injection of the sedative pentobarbital.

Goof-Proof Surgery

Before undergoing surgery, write "no"—or ask your surgeon to write it—on the leg, knee, arm, etc., that should *not* be operated on. Many patients are more comforted by writing "no" on a healthy body part than by the more standard practice of writing "yes" on the area requiring surgery. The word "yes" also runs the risk of being washed off when the site is prepared for surgery.

Saul N. Schreiber, MD, orthopedic surgeon in private practice, Phoenix.

Smoking and Surgery

Smokers should try to quit before elective surgery...and to avoid smoking for at least three weeks afterward.

Doing so before surgery helps clear the body of nicotine, which constricts blood vessels and slows the healing process.

David Netscher, MD, professor of plastic surgery, Baylor College of Medicine, Houston.

Children and Surgery

If your child needs surgery, tour the hospital before checking in. Many hospitals offer preoperative tours for kids up to age 18.

Aim: To familiarize children with the hospital environment and make it less impersonal and frightening.

Tours may include visits to the admitting area, preoperative section, waiting rooms and several spots in the pediatric unit.

Some parents fear their children may be scared during a tour, making it harder to bring them in for the operation.

Reality: Tours usually relax children—and parents, too.

Katie Crocco, certified child life specialist, pediatric department, Bridgeport Hospital, Bridgeport, CT.

Secrets of Safe, Pain-Free Surgery

Michael J. Murray, MD, PhD, professor and chair of anesthesiology, Mayo Medical School, Jacksonville, FL. He is coauthor of *Clinical Anesthesiology* (McGraw-Hill).

Most people who need an operation are interested in finding a good surgeon. Few of us focus very much attention on the anesthesiologist.

Anyone who is scheduled to undergo surgery has the right to select the anesthesiologist. But the reality is that the surgeon frequently makes the choice.

Either way, it is a good idea to schedule a talk with the anesthesiologist at least one day before the operation.

Here are several smart questions to ask...

●**Is the surgical facility equipped for emergencies?** If you're having surgery in a hospital or a hospital-based outpatient clinic, the answer is most likely "yes." Both must meet tough national safety standards established by the Joint Commission on Accreditation of Healthcare Organizations (JCAHO).

In such settings, your chances of anesthesia-related complications are only one in 200,000.

Freestanding outpatient clinics and private physicians' offices aren't scrutinized as closely, and some states don't regulate them at all. Mishaps, while still uncommon, are *four times* more likely to occur here than at a hospital.

●**Will you be in the operating room during the entire surgery?** Your best shot at glitch-free surgery is when a qualified professional is present throughout the procedure to administer the anesthetic and monitor your blood pressure, heart rate, breathing, body temperature and other vital signs.

This can be either an anesthesiologist (a medical doctor who has completed a three-year anesthesia residency) or a *certified registered nurse anesthetist* (CRNA) who is supervised by a surgeon, physician or an anesthesiologist. Hospitals require that an anesthesiologist or nurse anesthetist be present during all surgeries.

Independent clinics *are not* governed by the same rules. Nurse anesthetists frequently work without supervision. Another possibility is that no one, other than your surgeon, dentist or plastic surgeon, is there to keep tabs on your vital signs.

In such cases, you should be certain that a pulse oximeter is clipped to your finger or to an earlobe to measure the oxygen levels in your bloodstream.

●**Do I have a choice of anesthesia?** For some surgeries, you don't have a choice—you must be asleep. In most other cases, however, you usually can—and should—pick out your type of anesthesia. *Your choices include...*

● *General anesthesia* is given intravenously or as an inhaled gas. It causes complete unconsciousness. General anesthesia is best used for major surgery, such as open-heart procedures.

339

• *Regional anesthesia* includes spinal and epidural anesthesia. It numbs only a section of your body, allowing you to stay awake. Regional anesthesia is often used for childbirth, orthopedic surgery and prostate surgery.

• *Local anesthesia* is usually reserved for minor procedures that require a pain-block only at the site of surgery. It allows you to stay awake. Local anesthesia is best used for minor surgery, such as hand or foot procedures.

• *Monitored anesthesia care* (MAC) is often used to supplement local or regional anesthesia. Low doses of sedatives are given intravenously to induce light sleep, but patients remain responsive.

• **What do you need to know about my medical history before surgery?** Underlying medical problems, such as diabetes, asthma, heart problems or arthritis, as well as prescription medications, over-the-counter pain relievers, like aspirin, and herbal supplements can alter the effectiveness of the anesthetic.

Tell your anesthesiologist *everything*, no matter how trivial or embarrassing. This includes any health condition that has sent you to a doctor within the last two years or requires medication…any family or personal history of anesthesia complications…any bleeding tendencies from taking anticlotting medications, such as aspirin or *warfarin* (Coumadin)…and any allergies (including allergies to particular pain-killers—or even to surgical tape).

Smoking, alcohol use and illegal drug use should also be noted, even if you're uncomfortable discussing such things.

Remember, divulging this information could possibly save your life. By knowing your medical conditions, the anesthesiologist will be prepared to treat them should surgical complications arise.

This is also the time to sort through your after-surgery pain-relief options, which include everything from pills to a patient-controlled IV pump. Discuss your preferences with your doctor and anesthesiologist.

• **What if I wake up during surgery?** You are unlikely to regain full consciousness during your procedure, but occasionally people will become vaguely aware of what's going on around them. If this happens, you will still be anesthetized enough so you won't feel pain.

Chances are your anesthesiologist will notice signs of consciousness, such as rising blood pressure, before you do—and then adjust your anesthesia accordingly.

• **Can I take something before surgery to calm my nerves?** Absolutely. Your anesthesiologist can administer a mild tranquilizer, such as *diazepam* (Valium) or *alprazolam* (Xanax), if you request one.

Talk very openly with your anesthesiologist about your fears. Many people who are about to undergo surgery worry about not waking up again. No fear is too silly to mention.

• **Will I have side effects from anesthesia?** Other than feeling woozy and light-headed, side effects should be minor. If you're in pain after the procedure, ask your anesthesiologist immediately to boost your pain medication or switch to something else. Don't be afraid to speak up.

With general anesthesia, your throat may be mildly sore. That's because a breathing tube is inserted during surgery to assist breathing. The soreness should diminish within 24 hours. To avoid this discomfort, ask if you can use a breathing mask instead of a breathing tube.

Safer Surgery

Bloodless surgery eliminates the risk of contracting hepatitis or other viral infections from someone else's blood. Also, many patients go home sooner and experience less fatigue. Collecting, filtering and reusing the patient's own blood during an operation carries only a slight risk of bacterial contamination.

The greatest blood loss occurs in cardiovascular, gynecologic and orthopedic surgeries. Patients considering such procedures should ask their surgeons what steps will be taken to minimize blood loss and reduce the need for a transfusion.

Patricia A. Ford, MD, medical director of the Center for Bloodless Medicine & Surgery, Pennsylvania Hospital, and associate professor of medicine, University of Pennsylvania, both in Philadelphia.

How to Reduce the Hidden Risk of Any Surgery—Anesthesia

Frank Sweeny, MD, anesthesiologist and former medical director, St. Joseph Hospital and Children's Hospital of Orange County, both in Orange, CA. A fellow of the American Board of Anesthesiology, he is also author of *The Anesthesia Fact Book* (Perseus).

Every year, millions of Americans undergo surgery or other procedures that require anesthesia. Some 2,000 or more will die or suffer serious complications, such as organ failure, brain damage or heart attack—not from the procedures themselves, but from factors related to the anesthesia. *To reduce risks...*

•**Ask who will administer the anesthesia.** Ideally, it should be either an MD anesthesiologist or a *certified registered nurse anesthetist* (CRNA). Both have extensive specialized training in anesthesia. An anesthesia *team* with a CRNA under the supervision of an MD anesthesiologist has the best safety record.

If you are scheduled to have anesthesia given by anyone other than an anesthesia specialist, inquire about his/her training in administering anesthesia and treating the complications associated with it. If you are having heart surgery, or if a young child requires anesthesia, ask for an anesthesiologist who regularly anesthetizes high-risk patients.

•**Meet with your anesthesiologist or CRNA.** Most anesthesiologists spend less than five minutes with their patients—even though a study showed that more than half the deaths caused by anesthesia were due in part to inadequate evaluations of patients prior to surgery. It is even more important to meet with your anesthesiologist if you have medical problems or if you or a family member has had trouble associated with anesthesia in the past. Ask your surgeon to help you set up a meeting with the anesthesiologist or CRNA who is scheduled to be in the operating room when you are having your procedure.

The anesthesiologist or CRNA who will administer your anesthesia should review your medical history, including whether anyone in your family has had problems with anesthesia. He should also perform a physical exam.

Be sure to tell him what medications you're taking, including herbs or supplements. Many herbs may interact with anesthesia to increase bleeding tendency (ginkgo, ginseng), cause cardiac stimulation (ginseng) or prolong the effects of anesthesia (kava, valerian). Discontinue all herbs and supplements at least two weeks prior to surgery.

•**Control medical problems.** One study indicated that almost half of anesthesia-related deaths occurred in patients who had underlying conditions, such as diabetes, high blood pressure, angina, etc., that weren't adequately controlled prior to anesthesia and surgery.

If you have medical problems, visit your doctor well in advance of surgery to be sure you're in the best possible health. It usually is better to postpone surgery than to go forward when you aren't in the best shape.

•**Make sure the facility is JCAHO accredited.** That means that the Joint Commission on Accreditation of Healthcare Organizations surveys the facility at least every three years to make sure that operating standards, including the use of anesthesia, follow the latest guidelines and safety procedures.

If you're having complex surgery—such as heart, prostate, total joint replacement, etc.—find out how many of these operations are performed at the facility each year. Studies show that results are better in those facilities performing more of these procedures.

Be wary of in-office procedures. There have been increasing reports of problems associated with anesthesia and surgery performed in doctors' private offices.

Avoid the Risk of Surgical Infection

Dale W. Bratzler, DO, MPH, principal clinical coordinator, Oklahoma Foundation for Medical Quality, a group that coordinates the national Surgical Infection Prevention Project, sponsored in part by the US Centers for Disease Control and Prevention.

You probably already know that infection is among the biggest surgical risks. Doctors know it, too—but don't always do enough to prevent it. Overall, 2% to 5% of surgical incisions get infected.

Danger: Mortality rates for patients with an infection are two to three times higher than for those who recover without an infection.

Every major surgical society recommends giving antibiotics as a preventive (prophylactic) *before* making the first incision. Unfortunately, surgeons often prescribe them at the wrong time.

Ideally, antibiotic medication should be given within the hour before the first incision is made. Adequate antibiotic levels should be maintained throughout the operation, then stopped at the end of surgery.

In one study, 20% of the patients were given antibiotics too early...others got the drugs hours after surgery began. Giving an antibiotic late is no better than giving a placebo. If it's given too early, wound infection rates also are higher. *To protect yourself...*

●**Discuss the use of prophylactic antibiotics** with your surgeon ahead of time.

●**Insist on antibiotics if you're having a high-risk procedure,** such as cardiac, vascular or colon surgery, hysterectomy or hip or knee replacement.

These simple steps will go a long way toward ensuring your safety.

In-Office Surgery: Eight Questions that Could Save Your Life

Ervin Moss, MD, executive medical director, New Jersey State Society of Anesthesiologists, Princeton Junction, NJ.

Surgery has moved outside of the hospital surgical suite and into a doctor's office near you.

This year, approximately 20% of all surgical procedures will be done in doctors' private offices. That's almost 10 million operations a year. These include cataract surgery...biopsies...ear tube insertions...cosmetic and plastic surgery...and hernia repairs.

Office surgery costs less than similar procedures done in hospitals or outpatient surgical facilities. It can be more convenient and "patient friendly," too. But office surgery also poses potential risks.

Even the best-equipped doctor's office lacks the state-of-the-art surgical suites and extensive support staffs found in hospitals. Some in-office surgeons lack the training required of their hospital counterparts. And office surgery generally isn't regulated by state or national agencies.

That's not to say that surgical procedures can't be done safely in doctors' offices. *But before bypassing the hospital, patients should ask the surgeon...*

●**Do you have hospital privileges to perform this procedure?** Surgeons earn hospital privileges—the right to operate in the hospital—by undergoing intensive scrutiny.

Surgeons who work in office settings may not have those privileges. And if they have a high rate of poor outcomes, they normally aren't required to report it.

Also important: Ask your doctor if he/she is board-certified for the type of surgery to be done. Certification means that the surgeon has passed written tests and keeps up with developments in his specialty through continuing medical education courses.

●**How many similar procedures have you performed?** Surgeons get better with practice.

A surgeon who has done only a few dozen procedures is still learning, Patients should choose surgeons who have performed many operations similar to the one they will undergo.

●**Who will administer the anesthetic?** The person administering the anesthetic should be a board-certified anesthesiologist or a certified registered nurse anesthetist. That's a registered nurse (RN) who has had two years of specialized training in anesthesiology.

States have standards regarding the types of anesthetic that nurse-anesthetists can administer in the hospital and the circumstances under which they can do so. These standards vary among states. Ask your doctor which standards his hospital follows. His in-office surgical practice should follow the same standards.

●**Is your office prepared for emergencies?** Are resuscitation and life-support equipment and medicine on hand in case things go wrong during surgery?

At a minimum, this equipment should include a "crash cart" with a defibrillator and airway resuscitation equipment.

●**Do you have an ongoing relationship with an ambulance company?** The drivers should know exactly where the office is...the best routes to get there and from there to the hospital...and which entries and exits are large enough to accommodate a stretcher.

●**Who staffs your office?** The doctor's office should employ at least one nurse who, like the surgeon and anesthesiologist, has training in advanced cardiac life support. All nurses assisting during surgery should specialize in operating room procedures. And—all nurses caring for patients after surgery should be specialists in post-anesthesia recovery.

●**Has your facility been accredited?** Several agencies inspect physicians' offices, protocols and procedures to certify that they meet standards for quality in-office surgery.

The most demanding agency is the Joint Commission on Accreditation of Healthcare Organizations (JCAHO).

Facilities offering in-office surgery aren't required to be JCAHO-accredited, but some go through the procedure voluntarily. Ask to see the accreditation certificate. It assures you that the facility is well-run and up-to-date.

●**How long will my procedure take?** In-office surgery is safest when it does not exceed four hours. Any operation lasting longer should be done in a hospital.

Secrets of Speedy Rehabilitation After Stroke, Surgery or Injury

Kristjan T. Ragnarsson, MD, professor and chairman, department of rehabilitation medicine, Mount Sinai School of Medicine, New York City.

Nearly 70% of Americans will require some form of physical rehabilitation during their lifetimes.

For most people recovering from a serious illness or injury, a program of exercise and other physical therapies is just as important as the medical treatment they receive.

Here are steps that you can take to ensure the success of a rehabilitation program...

●**Ask the doctor who treated your illness or injury for a referral for physical therapy.** Rehabilitation can take place on an inpatient or outpatient basis, depending on your condition. Your doctor should recommend a treatment plan and prescribe a specific number of rehabilitation sessions.

●**Compare facilities.** First, find out which rehabilitation programs are covered by your medical insurance...check out the reputation of each institution you're considering...then pay each a visit.

Helpful: Ask a staff member if you can speak to some former patients. Visit at least three facilities before selecting one.

Whether inpatient or outpatient, the rehabilitation facility should...

●Provide appropriate therapy—whether it be physical, occupational* or speech.

*Occupational therapy helps patients resume activities at home and at work.

•Offer a broad range of treatments for your specific problem.

Example: Therapies to treat inflammation and pain often include massage, ultrasound, whirlpool baths, electrical stimulation devices as well as heat sources.

The standard strength-training and aerobic equipment includes free weights and weight-lifting machines, *Thera-Bands* (elastic bands used to train muscles), balance boards, tread-mills, exercise bikes and "water treadmills," which allow you to walk or run in a tank of waist-deep water.

•Be within easy commuting distance of your home or office.

•Be clean, well-maintained and have a bright and cheerful ambience.

Important: Inpatient programs should be accredited by the Commission on Accreditation of Rehabilitation Facilities (CARF). You can contact it at 888-281-6531 or *www.carf.org*.

•**Check staff credentials.** Licensing varies from state to state, but the supervising therapist should be a *registered physical therapist* (RPT) or an *occupational therapist* (OT) with a master's degree.

Helpful: Ask how many years of experience is typical for the facility's RPTs and OTs...and whether the therapists participate in continuing-education programs. Also find out how many patients each therapist is assigned per hour. For optimal care, it should be no more than three.

•**Make sure you have "good chemistry" with your therapy team.** Since physical and occupational therapy involve a great deal of repetition, success depends largely on staying motivated. That is why you should have a good rapport with your team.

Meet briefly with every member of your team before signing up with a facility, and find out each person's area of responsibility. All team members should be friendly, supportive and available.

If you feel the chemistry is not good with one or more members of your team, ask for another therapist or switch facilities.

•**Be sure that you can confidently perform your exercises before returning to home.** Your supervising therapist should be available to answer any questions that may come up later. You should also schedule a follow-up visit with your physician within one month to monitor your progress.

•**Enlist the support of family and friends.** Once your formal rehabilitation is completed, have a relative or friend assist—or "spot"—you during your exercises to keep you motivated ...and safe.

•**Address psychological needs.** A physical injury or lengthy illness can trigger a wide range of emotions, from frustration to clinical depression. These feelings can limit your ability to stick with your rehabilitation program.

If negative feelings persist, talk to your doctor about getting psychotherapy. Drug treatment may also be needed.

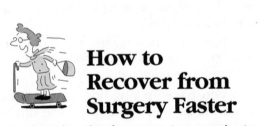

How to Recover from Surgery Faster

Stanley Fisher, PhD, former associate research scientist, Columbia University, and clinical psychologist and psychoanalyst in private practice, both in New York City. He is also author of *Discovering the Power of Self-Hypnosis: The Simple, Natural Mind-Body Approach to Change and Healing* (Newmarket).

Whether you are undergoing a coronary bypass operation or an emergency appendectomy, surgery is the rational decision to preserve or restore your health. You know this. *But your body doesn't.*

From the body's point of view, surgery is a knife attack, pure and simple. Because your body can't distinguish between a surgeon and a mugger, it responds with primitive mechanisms designed to protect itself from harm. Stress hormones pour out, tensing muscles and pumping blood so your muscles are fueled and ready to fight. This is the opposite of how you want your body to respond to surgery. You need to be relaxed.

Even when you're unconscious on the operating table, your body is far from shut down.

Surgeons maintain that no matter how well-anesthetized a patient may be, his/her body will perceptibly tense the moment the scalpel breaks the skin.

What you need is a way to communicate with your body to help it cooperate with the surgical process. Self-hypnosis allows you to do just that. Research indicates that 89% of patients who use this method recover faster than those who do not use it.

WHAT IS HYPNOSIS?

The word "hypnosis" may smack of mysticism or quackery. In fact, it's a legitimate way to tap the mind's own powers.

Normally, your mind is constantly aware of the outside world. In the trance state induced by self-hypnosis, your awareness of the outside world slowly drifts away, and your attention is concentrated inward. This inward focus allows you to use your imagination to create changes in the way your mind and body behave during surgery.

Hypnosis makes it possible to induce the trance state at will. Functions that are normally automatic—such as pulse rate and muscle tension—come under conscious control. Although it may be easier to achieve a trance state with the help of an expert, it is more convenient to learn to do it yourself.

PRACTICING SELF-HYPNOSIS

Self-hypnosis consists of two stages—entering the trance state…and, once you are there, delivering well-chosen messages to your mind and body.

People differ tremendously in the depth of the trance that they enter. A person who is very susceptible to hypnotism may feel completely removed from the outside world and virtually unaware of his surroundings. Others feel nothing special beyond a heightened sense of relaxation, comfort and ease.

Fortunately, people who aren't very hypnotizable can achieve the same benefits as those who are. This is possible because the depth of the trance is less important than the repetition of the message.

During the week before surgery, all patients should practice self-hypnosis every couple of waking hours—that's about eight times a day. The day before surgery, patients should do it every waking hour.

After the operation, be sure to keep up the same hourly schedule but concentrate entirely on helping your body heal. It is impossible to overdose on this treatment.

TRANCE-INDUCING PROCESS

Although there are many ways to induce a trance—and you can use any technique that works for you—many people get good results with this simple four-step process…

1. While sitting or lying comfortably, look up—with your eyes open—as if you're trying to see your eyebrows. Close your eyes, but keep looking up.

2. Take a deep breath. Hold it for the count of one…two…three.

3. Release your breath and allow your eyes to relax.

4. Imagine yourself floating down, as if on a soft, feathery couch or cloud, entering a safe, comfortable place, completely relaxed.

The entire process usually takes approximately 90 seconds.

After learning to induce the trance, you are ready to suggest to your body how you would like it to behave during and after surgery. Instruct your body to be limp, loose and very relaxed during surgery. Imagine how this will feel when you lie on the operating table.

Depending on the specific procedure, you may focus on relaxing the particular part of the body that will be operated on. Remind your body that the surgeon is there to help, not hurt. Imagine that you are working with the surgical team to bring health back to your body.

CONTROL YOUR EMOTIONS

It's only natural to feel anxious before an operation. You can't make the fear disappear, but you can *put it aside*. Imagine how the fear looks and what it feels like. See yourself putting it in a big box. The fear is still there, but it won't bother you as much.

Other messages are related to recovery. Tell your body to keep the wound dry, clean and free from infection. You might imagine your immune system as an army of soldiers fighting bacteria, or a cleanup squad removing debris. Choose an image that feels right for you.

Motivation is a key to success. Most importantly, remind yourself *why* you're having the surgery. Then focus on your post-operative goals—imagine yourself getting out of bed, feeling hungry, becoming more active and returning to your normal activities.

Use all of your senses. Think of how your muscles feel during a vigorous walk...savor the satisfaction of a gourmet meal...and the warm glow of a healthy and pain-free evening spent with those you love.

Protect Yourself from Hospital Staph

Arjun Srinivasan, MD, medical epidemiologist and infectious disease fellow, Johns Hopkins Hospital, Baltimore.

Drug-resistant forms of the bacterium *Staphylococcus aureus* (staph) are one of the most common causes of infection, found mainly in hospitals and other health-care settings.

Staph is normally present on the skin or in the noses of 20% to 30% of healthy Americans. Infection occurs when the bacterium gets beneath the skin—because of a cut or scrape or an invasive medical procedure—and multiplies. Most staph infections are minor. If you've ever had a pimple, boil or hair follicle infection (*folliculitis*), it likely was due to staph.

The bacterium can cause systemic (whole-body) infections in patients who have compromised immune systems. In hospitalized patients, staph is a common cause of wound infections, pneumonia, bone infections and life-threatening bloodstream infections (*bacteremia*).

Staph usually is spread by direct contact. It can be transmitted by sharing personal items, such as a towel or razor, which can carry the bacterium into small openings in the skin. In medical settings, staph is typically contracted after a health-care worker cleans a wound and then touches someone who also may have an open wound or even visibly healthy skin that has microscopic openings. Casual contact, such as hugging and kissing, is unlikely to spread a staph infection.

PREVENTION

Washing your hands with soap and water several times daily is the best way to prevent staph or avoid spreading it to others. Use waterless hand hygiene products when soap and water are not available.

It's especially important to wash your hands after cleaning or dressing wounds (your own or someone else's) or visiting someone who's been diagnosed with staph.

Other prevention strategies...

• **Wear latex gloves when cleaning skin infections.** Don't touch other parts of your body (or anyone else) while wearing the gloves and be sure to wash your hands after you remove them.

• **Keep cuts and scratches clean.** Wash them several times daily with soap and water. A doctor also may instruct you to apply an antibiotic ointment. Cover wounds with a bandage until completely healed.

• **Wash all linens, especially towels and washcloths, in hot water.** This is especially important if someone in your family has a staph infection. Adding bleach to the wash cycle will give added protection. Using high heat in clothes dryers also kills staph.

• **Only use towels once.** If you have a staph infection, using the towel repeatedly could spread the germs to other parts of your body—and threaten other people if they use the same towel.

• **Don't share personal items.** This includes razors, towels, toothbrushes, clothing, etc. Any of those items could harbor—and eventually spread—a staph infection.

• **Don't take antibiotics unnecessarily.** This occurs most often when people have a viral illness, such as a cold. The overuse of antibiotics can increase your risk of getting drug-resistant staph.

12

Health Insurance

How to Outsmart Your Managed Care Organization

Before the era of managed care, people who sought medical care were known as patients. Nowadays, they are called *customers* of a *health maintenance organization* (HMO), *preferred provider organization* (PPO) or another *managed care organization* (MCO).

Customers of MCOs don't always get what they are paying for...

●**Some MCOs won't cover key diagnostic tests for patients.**

●**Some MCOs refuse to pay for costly medications.**

●**Some MCOs push customers into surgery** with a surgeon who has substandard training—in a second-rate hospital.

There's really no need to become a victim of managed care. *Here's how to fight back...*

PLAIN FACTS ABOUT MCOs

It's important to keep in mind that managed care is big business. Your doctor may focus on easing symptoms and healing disease, but MCOs inevitably focus on the *bottom line*. Whatever its fancy brochure says, its allegiance is to its shareholders—not to you.

Like all businesses, MCOs try to maximize revenues while minimizing expenditures. Raising premiums is one way MCOs cut costs. They also reduce the *medical loss ratio*. In plain English, that means delivering as little health care as possible.

CHOOSING A DOCTOR

In most MCOs, customers must choose a primary care physician from a roster of participating doctors. These doctors are generally listed by their medical specialty.

Bruce A. Barron, MD, PhD, associate professor of obstetrics and gynecology, Columbia–Presbyterian Medical Center, and former senior medical director, Empire Blue Cross/Blue Shield, both in New York City. He is author of *Outsmarting Managed Care: A Doctor Shares His Insider's Secrets to Getting the Health Care You Want* (Three Rivers Press).

347

Trap: Just because a doctor is listed as an internist, cardiologist, etc., does not mean he/she has had the extra training and has passed the rigorous tests required for board certification.

It's common for MCOs to hire doctors who are not board-certified, even though board certification has long been considered a mark of medical expertise.

What to do: Call your MCO or the doctor's office to find out about board certification.

For a list of board-certified physicians in the US, consult the *Directory of Medical Specialists*. This book—available at most public libraries—also details doctors' training, experience, etc.

The American Medical Association offers similar information on its Web site, *www.ama-assn.org*. Or you can call the American Board of Medical Specialties at 866-275-2267.

Important: If a doctor you are considering practices as part of a group, check the credentials of his partners, too.

The doctor you select must be your ally. Will he help you fight to receive proper medical care? Will he help you get critical tests, treatments and referrals even if the MCO doesn't want to provide them? Ask at your first visit.

Although it is hard to know how a doctor will behave until a problem does arise, it is important to find out his general feelings on the subject.

GETTING FIRST-RATE CARE

Some doctors like to joke that managed care is fine—as long as you don't get sick.

Unfortunately, the joke contains a kernel of truth. And the more serious your illness, the harder it can be to get proper treatment and state-of-the-art medical care.

Example: An endoscopic examination of the stomach is often the best way to check for a peptic ulcer. But an MCO may refuse to cover endoscopy, arguing that this $1,200 procedure falls outside its "practice guidelines."

Each time you discuss treatment options with your doctor, ask whether his recommendations are constrained by rules set down by the MCO.

If so, ask what he *would* do—which tests, procedures, medications, etc., he would recommend—if there were no such constraints.

If this recommendation differs from his original one, ask that he explain his position in writing. That way, you'll have a record if you need to appeal an MCO decision.

If you need a specialist, do the ones affiliated with the MCO have the best qualifications? Or are there better specialists outside of the MCO's network?

If you need surgery, how do the surgical track records of hospitals affiliated with the MCO compare with the track records of hospitals unaffiliated with the MCO?

Death rates tend to be much lower in hospitals that do a high volume of a given procedure.

If you believe the MCO's rules will adversely affect your health, the MCO is required by law in some states to review your case. But you'll have a battle on your hands.

TAKING IT TO THE TOP

When you telephone the MCO to appeal a decision, you'll probably talk first to a "case manager." In many cases, this person is a nurse who simply explains the MCO's treatment guidelines.

If the case manager rejects your appeal, insist on speaking to a "medical director"—a doctor who works for the MCO.

Do not let yourself be intimidated. Non-physicians tend to be deferential around medical doctors. That's inappropriate here. You're dealing not with Marcus Welby, but with a representative of a giant corporation.

Find out the medical director's specialty. If he's a dermatologist and you have cancer, he may know less about your condition than you do. In such a case, ask to speak to a medical director who has training in oncology.

If this medical director rules against you, ask to speak with the MCO's "medical director for policy." This company official has greater power to help you.

Crucial: Each time you speak with a representative of the MCO, ask for a report of the conversation or ruling *in writing*. It's essential that you create a paper trail. That way, you'll have all the documentation needed if you choose to get an external review, in which an expert outside the MCO evaluates your case.

At some point as you make your way up the hierarchy, the MCO will probably give in to your demands.

If the MCO does not give in, file a complaint with the agency that regulates insurance companies. In most US states, it's the department of consumer affairs.

Another option: Contact the media. When television or newspaper reporters cover cases in which an MCO customer has been denied care, the MCO almost always capitulates.

How to Get the Most Out Of Managed Care

Charles B. Inlander, a consumer advocate and health-care consultant based in Fogelsville, PA. He was founding president of People's Medical Society, a consumer health advocacy group. He is author of more than 20 books, including *Take This Book to the Hospital with You* (St. Martin's).

Health care is big business. In fact, it is the country's number-one form of commerce. But patients face a stacked deck. Health care providers, such as doctors and hospitals, want to make money. Managed care organizations want to save money. And your personal health comes third.

The key to getting quality medical care is to be assertive. You cannot entrust this crucial issue to anyone else.

Here's how to get the most out of your managed care plan...

KNOW WHAT'S COVERED

Carefully read the plan documents provided by your employer or insurer to find out what is covered. Don't wait for a medical emergency to do this important fact-finding. Publications don't cover everything...and there may be gray areas that need clarification, such as care when traveling and some medications.

If you or someone in your family has a medical condition that doesn't seem to be covered, call the insurer's customer service number or their emergency hot line. Ask what treatment options are covered. Get the answer in writing before proceeding with any treatment. Otherwise, you may end up paying for it yourself.

Example: For mental illness, many plans will pay for a certain number of days of care in the hospital and a certain number of outpatient visits with a psychologist. But many people with mental illness are now being treated on a "partial hospitalization" basis, spending six hours a day in the hospital and going home at night.

CHALLENGE BAD RULINGS

Your physician may advise against a certain procedure simply because it isn't covered by your insurance plan. Don't automatically accept that. Your medical options should be determined by what is best for you—not by what your doctor thinks the plan will pay for.

Get a second opinion to determine which procedure is best.

If there is a conflict between two doctors about a serious condition, seek a third opinion.

Important: Never tell the physician from whom you are seeking a second opinion what the first physician said. That may prejudice his/her opinion...and he may not want to disagree with a peer for fear of losing future referral business.

USE SPECIAL PROGRAMS

If you have a chronic health condition—such as asthma, arthritis, high blood pressure, diabetes, etc.—participate in your plan's disease-management program.

This is a multidisciplinary team approach that includes physicians, nurses, social workers and pharmacists.

Aim: To prevent acute episodes that result in hospitalization.

Patients may receive special education about their conditions, frequent telephone monitoring and regular home visits by nurses.

Example: After one plan started a diabetes-management program, patients' emergency room visits dropped by 75%...hospitalizations dropped by 70%...and lost workdays declined by 63%. The annual savings amounted to about $1,500 per patient.

Ask if your plan has contracts with any *centers of excellence.* These are special facilities, such as the Mayo Clinic, the Cleveland Clinic and Memorial Sloan-Kettering Cancer Center, that are known for treating certain rare conditions, such as advanced heart disease or cancer.

Because they specialize in specific disorders, their staffs know better how to proceed without wasting time and money. They generally don't order unnecessary tests or perform procedures that are not needed.

CHOOSE YOUR HOSPITAL

Find the best hospital for your procedure. Don't automatically accept the facility that your plan routinely uses.

The medical support system at a specialized facility—nurses, technicians and other specialists—plays at least as big a role in your recovery as the surgeon.

MEDICAL CARE FOR CHILDREN

If your child has a serious illness, insist that he/she be seen by a pediatric specialist. Children have very different medical needs than adults. A doctor who sees only adults may not provide the best treatment for your child.

FOLLOW EMERGENCY RULES

Carefully follow the rules about emergency health care while traveling. Denials of such claims are frequently a source of consumer complaints, although many plans are relaxing their stance.

If you must go to an emergency room or be seen by a physician while away from home, get the following...

- **Detailed bill,** including the diagnosis and a list of services provided and charges.

- **Names, addresses and phone numbers of all health care providers,** as well as the medical license number of the primary doctor who treated you.

- **Copy of medical records of your care.**

- **Letter from the doctor or hospital** stating that the treatment could not have waited until you returned home and that transferring you to another facility would have adversely affected your health.

KEEP GOOD RECORDS

At the first sign of a problem regarding your medical treatment—say, your plan refuses to refer you to a specialist when you believe you need one—start keeping notes.

Document each interaction with your physician or plan employees, noting the names of those with whom you spoke, the date and time of each conversation, what was said and by whom. This documentation is crucial if you later challenge the plan's decisions.

APPEAL IF NOT SATISFIED

Many denials are later reversed, so file an immediate written appeal if you disagree with your plan's initial decision.

Contact the claims examiner for your case, and explain why you feel your benefits were wrongfully denied. Also state what action you want your plan to take.

If your appeal is denied, ask the claims examiner to explain in writing why the plan rejected your claim. Then move up the chain of command and speak with the examiner's supervisor. Again, ask for the plan's decision in writing.

If you're still not satisfied, ask to have your case reviewed by the plan's medical director. Sometimes it may be necessary to contact your state regulatory agency or a private attorney.

Best line of defense in appeal: Your health-care providers' opinions. Ask your doctor to write to the plan explaining why he/she feels certain tests or treatment are necessary. If medical research or second opinions support his view, be sure to include them as well.

More from Charles B. Inlander...

Get More from Your HMO

The one true benefit of *health maintenance organizations* (HMOs) to patients is their disease-management programs.

These increasingly popular programs provide coordinated team care to people who have such health conditions as asthma, diabetes or heart disease.

Teams usually include the patient's personal physician, a specialist, a pharmacist and other professionals, such as nurses and social workers.

Large HMOs and some smaller ones offer these programs, which patients can choose to join at no extra cost. If your HMO doesn't participate, urge it to consider doing so.

Also from Charles B. Inlander...

911 Danger?

Calling 911 can be very costly if you belong to an HMO. Some HMOs' membership materials purposely omit directing members to call 911 if they think they are having a heart attack or other major emergency. This may allow the HMO to refuse to pay for the cost of a 911 response—which can be as much as $1,000.

Troubling: Three-quarters of HMOs said they would deny a claim if a problem was determined not to be an emergency.

Self-defense: Know your HMO's policy on calling 911. If you are considering joining an HMO, find one that uses a *prudent layperson rule* for emergencies—meaning it will pay if a reasonable person would consider the situation an emergency.

How to Fight Your Insurer...and Win

Nancy Davenport-Ennis, founding executive director, Patient Advocate Foundation, 700 Thimble Shoals Blvd., Suite 200, Newport News, VA 23606, *www.patientadvo cate.org*. The foundation publishes *The Managed Care Answer Guide* and *Your Guide to the Appeals Process*.

William Shernoff, senior partner, Shernoff, Bidart & Darras, a law firm specializing in bad-faith insurance litigation on behalf of consumers, 600 S. Indian Hill Blvd., Claremont, CA 91711. He is author of *Fight Back & Win: How to Get Your HMO and Health Insurance to Pay Up* (Capital Books).

Don't throw up your hands in despair when your health, auto or home insurance company denies a claim. *There are ways to fight back...*

More than half of all Americans will have a disagreement with their medical insurers at some point. Problems often develop when you're not able to use a specific health care provider... or obtain approval for a specific treatment...or

when a bill is "kicked back"—unpaid—from the insurance company after treatment.

When a health claim is denied, the patient's health care provider normally handles the first stage of the appeals process. If the appeal is rejected, the patient needs to play an active role in further appeals.

●**Find out why your claim was rejected.** *It is usually because...*

●The treatment was not preauthorized, as required by the plan.

●The claim was not coded correctly by the insurance provider.

●The insurance company believes that your treatment was not medically necessary.

●The insurance company regards the treatment as experimental.

●The insurance policy specifically excludes that particular treatment.

●The health care provider who treated you is not included in the plan.

If you did not receive written notice of the denial, call the insurance company and request one. Without such documentation, you will have no foundation for an appeal.

●**Get a copy of your actual health insurance policy.** An estimated 40% of people facing rejected claims do not have this document. If you're insured through work, request a copy of the policy from your employer's human resources department.

●**Enlist help.** With the written denial and health-plan documents in hand, it is time to seek professional help. The Patient Advocate Foundation is a nonprofit organization that can provide references (800-532-5274)...or check the Web site for a list of resources in your region, *www.patientadvocate.org*.

●**Keep an eye on the calendar.** Every insurance policy has a limited window for filing appeals, generally 30 to 90 days from the date of rejection. After the deadline, it becomes substantially more difficult—or even impossible—to appeal.

●**Address the reason for the insurer's rejection in your appeal.**

● If the insurer says a procedure is medically unnecessary—find statistics showing the procedure may extend or improve quality of life. Also provide encouraging statistics from clinical trials.

● If the insurer claims that a medical procedure is experimental—you, your health care provider or your lawyer must prove otherwise, by citing studies on the subject published in well-regarded, peer-reviewed medical journals. Enlist the help of your health care provider.

● If the insurer excludes the procedure—file a compassionate appeal and cite facts to support exceptions.

Important: Doctors' appeals of rejected claims are most likely to fail when they focus on medical ethics and opinion and neglect what the insurance companies like—hard proof.

More from William Shernoff...

How to Get Your HMO to Pay Your Claims Fast

The larger the dollar amount of a claim filed with a *health maintenance organization* (HMO), the less likely the HMO is to pay for all—or even most—of it. No matter how frustrated you become with the HMO, don't give up. Managed-care companies count on most people to accept their decisions on claims, even if the companies are wrong.

Here are ways to get satisfaction on your medical claims...

● **Take an active role in the claims process.** Unlike conventional—or indemnity—insurance policies, in which you personally file your claims, HMOs handle your claims for you.

But if anything goes wrong—such as an HMO doctor's office neglecting to file the right forms or paperwork being improperly filled out—the HMO may deny the claim or delay payment for it. *Helpful...*

If your case is not routine: Ask the HMO to send you copies of all claims filed on your behalf. Review them, and promptly forward any missing information to the HMO's headquarters or home office.

Don't be afraid to contact the claims examiner who is assigned to your case. Ask him/her to explain any decision you believe is unfair. If you're not satisfied, move up the chain of command and contact the examiner's supervisor.

With a complex medical problem that will require ongoing treatment: Establish a personal relationship with the case manager (who oversees the examiner) in charge of your paperwork.

As a participant in the HMO, you have the right to see how the case manager has written up your problem—and what the HMO has recommended to your physician. When HMO employees know that you are taking an active role in your care, they are less likely to put up roadblocks.

● **Don't take the company's first "no" as the final answer.** File an immediate appeal in writing and be persistent.

Important: Carefully follow the complaint procedure outlined in your HMO handbook.

Explain why you believe your benefits were wrongfully denied...and clearly state what action you want your HMO to take.

To protect your future legal rights, include the following sentence in every letter that you write to the HMO...

"This appeal relates only to the denial of the benefits in question. It does not constitute and shall in no way be deemed an admission that I am limited in my right to pursue a 'bad faith' remedy in state court."

Send your complaint letter by registered mail, return receipt requested—even if you are not required to do so. It's amazing how often HMOs claim they never received communications from patients...so you should have proof to the contrary. Request a written response within 30 days.

Set up a folder for all the paperwork on the grievance, and track on a calendar each step of the complaint process and when the HMO's responses are due.

● **Go straight to arbitration if you feel you are not getting a fair hearing.** The internal appeal procedures set up by HMOs may not be as impartial as they seem.

Some are biased in favor of the health plan because decision makers in the appeals process are not likely to disagree with their fellow employees.

The HMO's appeals process is not your only remedy. You also have the right to *arbitration,* an independent process conducted by third parties who are not usually beholden to the HMO. The sooner you can get your appeal heard in this setting, the better. Your HMO handbook lists the arbitration entity.

●**Get another medical opinion from doctors outside your HMO.** If your HMO doctor is reluctant to order a costly or experimental test or procedure that you're convinced you need, get a second, or even a third, opinion— even if you must pay for it yourself.

If these outside doctors agree with you, ask them to write to the HMO on your behalf. The aim is to establish a written record that supports your case, should you later appeal.

●**Get documentation for using a nonaffiliated emergency room.** Most people who seek care in an emergency room that is not affiliated with their HMO network do so when they are away from home.

If you must visit a nonaffiliated emergency room, request a letter from the facility documenting that you had a real emergency, and it was medically necessary to admit you to that facility. The letter should also state that you could not be transferred to a facility in the HMO network without endangering your health.

●**Make as much noise as possible.** Start in your own company's human resources department with the person who is the official liaison with the HMO.

Then contact local consumer hot lines and consumer affairs reporters at television stations and newspapers.

Also complain to your local, state and federal elected officials—your mayor, state representatives and US senators. It's also wise to contact the Better Business Bureau and your state attorney general.

Complain to the regulators. Contact the appropriate state regulatory agency—usually the Department of Insurance or the Department of Corporations—and ask about the procedures for filing a complaint against the HMO. Many states have a waiting period, but in some emergency cases a complaint may be filed and heard within 72 hours. Be sure to let your HMO know that you are planning to contact the state regulator.

If you are covered by both an HMO and Medicare, you can appeal to the MAXIMUS CHDR, Center for Health Dispute Resolution (11419 Sunset Hills Rd., Reston, VA 20190. 800-629-4687, *www.healthappeal.com*).

If the CHDR rules in your favor, you can then have the HMO provide appropriate care and treatment or have the HMO pay for the care and treatment you received in the interim.

If you lose, file a complaint with the Administrative Law Justice division of Medicare.

●**Seek legal redress if necessary.** If your claim is modest, file a claim in small-claims court. You don't need a lawyer, and the odds of winning are good. Your case will probably be heard within six months.

If you have a major claim, look for a lawyer who specializes in "bad faith" cases against insurance companies and HMOs. You're best off hiring an attorney who works on a contingency basis. This means the attorney gets nothing if you lose but takes at least one-third of any amount you recover from the HMO.

When You Can't Resolve a Health Insurance Problem...

Vincent Riccardi, MD, founder, American Medical Consumers, a membership organization that provides information, advice and advocacy, 5415 Briggs Ave., La Crescenta, CA, 91214, *www.medconsumer.com*.

If your insurer has refused to cover an expensive treatment for a disabling or life-threatening condition, consider bringing in an independent "patient advocate."

Advocates work with insurers, physicians and health facilities to help patients get what they need from the health care system. Because of their familiarity with medical and insurance procedures and their ability to prove the medical necessity of care, they often succeed where patients fail.

Initial consultations—during which the advocate reviews the case and may recommend certain steps to the patient—usually cost less than $100. If an advocate is required to perform any additional work, patients pay an hourly fee or a percentage of the insurance reimbursement.

To find a patient advocate: Check with your employee benefits department—or search for "patient advocate" at *www.google.com* or another on-line search engine. Advocates usually work by mail and phone.

Questions to ask before hiring an advocate…

●**How long have you or your company been in business?**

●**What similar cases have you handled— and what were the outcomes?**

●**Are you the person who would work on my case?** What are your credentials? (A medical doctor or registered nurse is best.)

Advice About Appeals

You may be able to handle the early stages of a Medicare appeal yourself. But—if the claim is for what you consider to be a sizable amount, it's wise to retain a lawyer.

If Medicare loses, it has a right of appeal and you must continue to see things through.

There are several Medicare advocacy programs that provide free or low-cost counseling on the appeals process. *Among them…*

●**Center for Medicare Advocacy,** 860-456-7790, *www.medicareadvocacy.org.*

●**Medicare Rights Center,** 212-869-3850, *www.medicarerights.org.*

Peter J. Strauss, Esq., partner in the law firm Epstein Becker & Green, PC, 250 Park Ave., New York City 10177. He is a fellow of the National Academy of Elder Law Attorneys, and coauthor of *The Elder Law Handbook—A Legal and Financial Survival Guide for Caregivers and Seniors* (Facts on File).

Short-Term Health Insurance

Short-term coverage can help protect you between jobs. It may also be suitable for recent college graduates who are no longer covered by their parents' insurance…and for Medicare beneficiaries traveling abroad and not covered by other policies.

The cost of these policies depends on copays, deductibles and coverage limits. Renewal is not automatic—you must reapply at the end of each coverage period.

Limitations: Coverage may be limited to 180 days within a year…short-term policies do not cover maternity costs—except the cost of complications associated with birth…not all states allow the sale of short-term health insurance.

Roy Diliberto, CFP, chairman and chief executive officer, RTD Financial Advisors, Philadelphia.

If You Must Buy Your Own Health Insurance… Choose Wisely

Bruce Pyenson and Jim O'Connor, principals with Milliman, a consulting firm that works with insurance companies and health care providers, *www.milliman. com.* Mr. Pyenson is author of several books, including *J.K. Lasser's Employee Benefits for Small Business* (Prentice Hall).

Most health insurance is provided through group policies in the workplace. But there are millions of people who are self-employed or between jobs who have to find individual coverage on their own. Medicare also offers different coverage options.

While there are plenty of good policies out there, finding one that fits your needs takes some digging.

SIZE UP YOUR NEEDS

The health-care needs of families with young children are different from those of singles starting new jobs...couples without children... and empty nesters. Families with infants want a full range of preventive care that covers everything from routine vaccinations to ear infections. Healthy singles may only need bare-bones coverage for unexpected catastrophes.

In these days of managed care, there are four basic types of coverage...

HEALTH MAINTENANCE ORGANIZATIONS (HMOs)

A very prevalent type of group coverage, HMOs provide comprehensive medical care through networks of physicians. Typically, you pay $5 or $10 per in-network doctor visit and don't have to fill out forms after each appointment or worry about meeting a deductible requirement.

If you have a special health problem, you typically must first consult your primary care physician—who is also known as the *gatekeeper*. This physician may treat you him/herself or may refer you to a specialist. If you decide to use an out-of-network specialist or hospital, coverage—if any—is limited.

With limited choice about which doctors and hospitals to use and limited access to specialists, these plans are usually the most economical. Your out-of-pocket costs are fairly low for the wide range of coverage you get.

Best for: People with children who are new to a community—they have no relationships with physicians or hospitals. Also good for people with children whose current physician and hospital are part of the HMO network.

PREFERRED PROVIDER ORGANIZATIONS (PPOs)

These types of policies—which are more expensive than comparable HMOs—give you the ability to go outside the plan network for your medical care. Most PPO plans don't have a gatekeeper system, so you usually don't need approval to see specialists.

If you see a physician within the network, you get one level of benefits (usually 80% of a claim is covered). If you see a physician outside the network, you get another, lower level of benefits (only 60% to 70% of the claim might be covered).

Best for: People who want more choice about their health care providers...and whose doctors are part of the PPO network.

INDEMNITY POLICIES

These plans pay benefits no matter what doctor or hospital you go to. Such traditional policies appeal to people who have lived in the same community for a long time and have established ties to physicians and hospitals.

While they guarantee you the most latitude in terms of choosing your health-care providers, indemnity plans are also the most expensive. Sometimes, people who want the flexibility of an indemnity policy opt for high deductibles of as much as $10,000 to reduce monthly premiums.

"ANY DOCTOR" POLICIES

These hybrid plans use a PPO approach for hospitals but allow you to see any licensed physicians you wish. They are cheaper than indemnity policies but more expensive than full-fledged PPOs.

Best for: People who feel comfortable with the hospitals in the PPO network but want the flexibility of using any doctor they choose.

FINDING THE BEST PLAN

●**Research what is available in your state.** Because each state regulates insurance, choices will be limited. Not all insurance companies offer policies in all states. And a company's policies may be different in different states.

If your car and/or homeowner's insurance is with a company that sells through a network of agents, start by calling your agent.

If you belong to a professional or trade group or a college alumni association, find out if these organizations offer special health policies for their members. Such policies often cost less than individual policies but more than group policies.

If you have chronic health problems, these policies can be a good deal since you may not be able to get an affordable policy on your own.

●**Determine what different types of policies will cost you.** Call two major companies that write health insurance nationwide.

For HMOs: Aetna (800-872-3862)...United Health Group (860-702-5000).

For PPOs, "Any Doctor" and indemnity: Assurant Health (800-800-1212)...Mutual of Omaha (800-775-6000).

Simplify your search by using the Internet. Two sites that provide up to 20 different premium quotes are *www.insure.com* and *www.insweb.com*.

Be sure to get the answers to some crucial questions...

●**Does the plan cover maternity, mental health and substance abuse?**

●**What are the rules concerning pre-existing conditions (health problems you had before taking out the policy)?**

●**Ask the insurer about rate increases.** You want to know how often and by how much insurers boost their premiums each year. Ask what the increases have been for the past several years.

Some companies charge very low initial rates but then raise premiums by a large amount. Rate increases are currently running 10% to 15% a year. If your insurer is boosting rates by 30% or more annually, it's time to shop around.

●**Find out if customers are satisfied.** Get the names of current HMO members. Ask if they've experienced delays in obtaining membership cards, problems communicating with physicians, difficulty getting pharmacies to accept their coverage, trouble getting doctor's appointments quickly or trouble getting prompt referrals to specialists.

You can also call your state insurance or health department (they usually are listed in the state government pages of your telephone directory). Some states develop statistics that indicate complaint ratios of HMOs.

If you have established a relationship with a physician, you might also call him/her for feedback on the plan you are considering, particularly for HMOs.

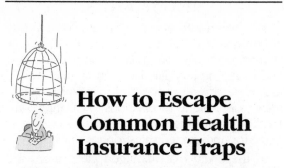

How to Escape Common Health Insurance Traps

Paul Lerner and Julie Lerner, brother-and-sister coauthors of *Lerner's Consumer Guide to Health Care: How to Get the Best Health Care for Less* (Lerner Communications). Paul is an AIDS activist. Julie is a long-term survivor of non-Hodgkin's lymphoma.

Health insurance does not cover every medical cost. In fact, the average American pays $1,200 out-of-pocket each year for medical expenses.

Here are seven of the most common traps that prevent consumers from getting the most from their health insurance...

Trap: **Failing to appeal a denial for coverage.** If your health insurer denies a claim for service, don't assume the battle is lost. Submit an immediate appeal in writing.

Get the name of the insurance company's medical director and send your appeal—by certified mail—directly to him/her.

Save copies of all written correspondence. For phone calls, keep a diary. Record the date and time of the call, the contact name and a conversation summary.

In your letter, stick to the specifics of your appeal. If possible, quote from the member contract section of your insurance plan information booklet to back up your appeal.

If your appeal is denied, don't give up. Most states guarantee an external appeal in which a third party objectively reviews your case. Contact your state insurance department for more information.

Trap: **Failing to inquire about "UCR" limits or fee schedules on out-of-network health services.** "UCR" stands for "usual, customary and reasonable" medical charges. These are defined as an average cost for a given medical service in your region.

A fee schedule typically assigns a reimbursement value to every service a physician provides. Most health plans use UCR limits or a fee schedule.

Unlike HMOs, which restrict your choice of doctors, preferred provider organizations (PPOs) and point-of-service plans allow users to consult out-of-network physicians. However, the user must pay a percentage of the cost.

Beware: The percentage paid by the health plan applies only to the UCR rate or fee schedule for that service.

Example: Let's say your plan covers 80% of the cost for a visit to an out-of-network specialist. Let's also say the specialist charges $200, but your health plan has determined that the service should cost $100. The insurer will reimburse 80% of $100—only $80. You must pay the remaining $120 yourself.

Before consulting with a doctor from outside your network, find out your insurance company's UCR limit or fee schedule for the service or procedure.

If there is a significant difference between the doctor's fee and the reimbursement rate, explain your situation to your doctor. He/she may be willing to negotiate a lower rate.

Trap: **Failing to keep track of your requests for referrals.** Because referrals to specialists are costly for managed-care companies, some may process them slowly. To prevent a long delay, be sure to monitor your requests closely.

Do not see a specialist until the referral has been approved. Once your doctor has agreed to the referral, make sure both your doctor and your plan follow through. If you don't hear back within one week, call your doctor's office manager to follow up.

Trap: **Failing to find out which prescription drugs are covered by your plan.** Health plans typically have a list of approved medications. If your doctor prescribes a drug that isn't on this "formulary," you may wind up paying for it—and some drugs are expensive.

Call your insurer's customer service department to make sure a drug prescribed for you is on your plan's formulary before you order it.

If the drug is not covered, talk to your doctor about substituting another drug. If your doctor still prefers the drug, request that he call and ask the insurer to make an exception.

Trap: **Failing to ensure that your treatment is "medically necessary."** Most insurers cover only procedures and services they deem "medically necessary."

Example: Rhinoplasty—nose reconstruction—that is performed for cosmetic reasons is typically not covered. But the procedure may be covered if it is medically necessary to correct a breathing problem.

If you consult a doctor for any health condition, be sure he indicates on your chart the necessity for the medical service or procedure. If your insurance plan denies reimbursement, ask your doctor to write a letter explaining the medical necessity.

Trap: **Failing to use preventive and wellness services covered by your health plan.** Many insurance companies offer preventive and wellness services at no cost. These may include flu shots...weight-loss and smoking-cessation programs...cancer screenings...and case management for diabetes, high blood pressure and several other chronic health conditions.

Read your member handbook carefully and discuss the policy with an employee-benefits person at your company.

Trap: **Failing to take advantage of your COBRA options.** Few people realize that they can maintain the health insurance they receive through an employer if they lose their job or become self-employed. This right is guaranteed for 18 months under a federal law known as the *Consolidated Omnibus Budget Reconciliation Act* (COBRA).

If you leave an employer that paid for your health insurance, ask the company's human resources department about COBRA coverage. You must pay the entire premium yourself, but the breadth of coverage and corporate rate almost always beat what you can purchase as an individual. You must sign up within 60 days of when your employer notifies you of your COBRA rights.

How to Get All the Medical Insurance You Are Due

To help you spot medical-claims errors and receive all the insurance payments to which you are entitled...

• **Get an itemized hospital bill,** and verify that you actually received all services listed.

• **If a claim is denied,** find out why—it may simply have been miscoded.

• **Ask for the surgeon's notes** on an operation if the insurer says charges are too high—they may show that your case was unusually complicated.

• **Get letters supporting your case** from all of your own doctors and from an outside physician verifying that the care you received was medically necessary.

Rhonda D. Orin, attorney, Anderson Kill & Olick, law firm specializing in representing policyholders against insurance companies, Washington, DC, and author of *Making Them Pay: How to Get the Most from Health Insurance and Managed Care* (Griffin).

Cutting Medication Costs

To save money on medications, speak to a pharmacist at your insurance company. Find out from him/her what medications your plan covers for your condition and at what payment levels.

Then take this information to your doctor. Doctors often think of medicines in terms of clinical effectiveness, not cost.

If your insurance doesn't offer a drug benefit or you are uninsured: Tell your doctor cost is important, and ask if there is a less expensive but equally effective drug available.

C. Daniel Mullins, PhD, professor of pharmacoeconomics, University of Maryland School of Pharmacy, Baltimore.

Patient and Doctor Confidentiality

Many doctors bend insurance rules so patients who need treatment can have their care covered. Almost 40% of doctors confided to researchers that they have manipulated insurance rules in some way.

Example: Some doctors exaggerate symptom severity so patients can spend extra time recovering in a hospital.

The study did not deal with deception to increase doctors' revenue—only to improve patient care.

Survey of 720 doctors by American Medical Association's Institute for Ethics, reported in the *Journal of the American Medical Association,* 515 N. State St., Chicago 60610. *www.jama.ama-assn.org.*

If Your Income Stopped Today...Would You Be Able to Pay Your Bills?

Ric Edelman, founder and chairman, Edelman Financial Services Inc., 4000 Legato Road, 9th Fl., Fairfax, VA 22033. He is author of *Discover the Wealth Within You* (HarperCollins) and *The Truth About Money* (Harper Resource).

An unexpected illness or injury could cause your income to drop, leaving you with an insufficient level of cash to pay your bills. Because of this possibility, you probably need to buy disability insurance.

SIGNS OF A GOOD POLICY

• **Consider supplementing employer insurance with individual insurance.** Many people are covered by an employer disability policy. But often employer disability coverage is taxable and limited to total disability. In such cases, it's advisable to buy your own policy that covers partial disability.

• **Look for a policy that covers 40% to 60% of your *take-home* pay.** The benefits received from disability policies are tax free.

Trying to find a policy that exactly matches your gross pay is a waste of money.

If your company insurance covers just 40% of pay, consider finding a policy that will provide another 20% of your take-home pay.

●**Consider policies that cover only your working life.** If you've already planned financially for your retirement, there's no need to spend more than necessary for additional disability coverage.

After you turn 65, you shouldn't have to worry about lost wages.

●**The policy should refer to your own occupation.** And make sure your policy says that your doctor—rather than the insurance carrier's doctor—decides whether or not you are disabled.

Example: Is a surgeon who breaks a finger disabled? He can still teach or practice medicine—but not perform his specialty.

Be sure the policy covers *partial disabilities*—defined as lost time or a reduction in pay from your current occupation due to disability. Maybe you can do some work, but if you're still suffering a loss of earning power, you need to be protected.

●**The waiting period before benefits kick in should be 90 to 120 days.** This will be much cheaper than a policy with a shorter waiting period.

FINDING A POLICY

Getting a good disability policy isn't as easy as it used to be. The best way is to hire an independent financial adviser who can comparison-shop a variety of disability contracts for you. Fake claims and other types of fraud have spurred the insurance industry to trim the benefits and charge much more for the most desirable provisions.

Important: Avoid paying extra for plans that return all premiums when the policy expires if you never filed a claim. You pay a big price for this privilege. The extra fees you pay over the years aren't worth it.

How to Know If Long-Term-Care Insurance Is for You

Joseph Matthews, San Francisco–based attorney. He is author of *Beat the Nursing Home Trap: A Consumer's Guide to Assisted Living and Long-Term Care* (Nolo Press).

Many insurance companies will now pay nursing home reimbursements for geriatric conditions. And home health care coverage is typically part of all good long-term-care policies.

But does it pay to buy a policy?

WHEN COVERAGE IS A WASTE

A good policy's premiums may run as high as $750 a year for people in good health who are 50 years old—and $2,000 a year for people age 70. Such a policy will pay a $100 maximum daily benefit for three years—with a 100-day deductible. If you can afford to pay 20 to 30 years of annual premiums, you probably don't need long-term-care insurance.

Reason: You can afford nursing home or home health care if it becomes necessary.

A person's odds of spending a long period in a nursing home are relatively low. So—most people who purchase this insurance collect few, if any, benefits because they simply don't need a long stay at a nursing facility.

Better: Consider investing the money you would spend each year on premiums in a separate investment account. This way, if you don't need long-term care, you will have the assets for other things or for inclusion in your estate.

THE IDEAL CANDIDATE

Even though the likelihood that you'll need a lot of long-term care is low, insurance coverage may make more sense for some people than for others.

Examples: People in their 60s and 70s who can't afford care...or have a small family that wouldn't be able to care for them...or have family members who live far away.

When considering coverage, remember that national health care costs rise faster than inflation, and your policy may not keep up with the cost.

Helpful: Be sure your policy includes inflation protection, although rapidly rising health costs may require you to pay more out of pocket when you need care.

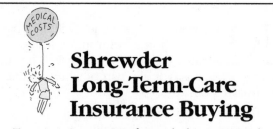

Shrewder Long-Term-Care Insurance Buying

Terry-Ann Orman, CFP, financial planning specialist, Wealth Management Group, Beers & Cutler PLLC, Washington, DC.

The best time to buy long-term-care insurance is in your early 60s. At that age, the premiums are relatively low and there is small chance of a health problem that could make it impossible to obtain coverage.

Waiting trap: Premiums may be twice as high if you wait until your 70s—if you can obtain coverage at all.

Note: The probability of needing long-term-care insurance is less than 10% for people under the age of 65…and rises to 40% for people in their 80s.

Comparison shop before you buy…make sure your package gives broad coverage and also includes protection against rising health-care costs.

When comparing insurers: Make sure that the insurance company is strong financially. Agencies such as Moody's Investors Service (*www.moodys.com*), A.M. Best Company (*www.ambest.com*) and Duff & Phelps (*www.duffllc.com*) make their ratings available to the public.

Ask questions until you thoroughly understand what the policy does—and does not—cover. Assuming good health, the basic policy premiums can range from $1,400 per year for a five-year benefit if the policy is purchased at age 60…to $2,900 per year if the policy is purchased at age 70.

What to Do If You Lose Your Health Insurance

Charles B. Inlander, a consumer advocate and health-care consultant based in Fogelsville, PA. He was founding president of People's Medical Society, a consumer health advocacy group. He is author of more than 20 books, including *Take This Book to the Hospital with You* (St. Martin's).

An average day in a hospital costs about $2,000. A typical cholesterol-lowering drug can cost about $100 a month. It's no wonder that we value our health insurance so highly.

However, losing your health insurance is a real possibility. Many people lose insurance because of a job layoff, their employer drops health benefits completely or they retire early. Others become uninsured when they cannot afford the insurance premiums their employer requires them to pay, or because of a divorce or the death of a spouse. *If you lose your health insurance and you do not qualify for Medicaid or are not yet 65 and eligible for Medicare, there are ways to get temporary insurance or needed medical services and prescriptions…*

•**COBRA.** In 1986, Congress passed the Consolidated Omnibus Budget Reconciliation Act (COBRA), allowing workers covered by an employer's group health insurance plan to continue to purchase that coverage for up to 18 months, at their own expense, if they have been laid off, taken voluntary leave or had their hours reduced to the point where they are no longer eligible for benefits. You may purchase that insurance for anyone in your family who was covered before you lost the insurance. Family members of an insured employee who dies also can purchase coverage under COBRA.

Important: COBRA only applies to companies with 20 or more employees. It does not apply if your former employer goes completely out of business. And it can be expensive. A typical employer-sponsored family health insurance plan, which includes hospital, doctor, dental and prescription drug coverage, can easily cost up to $12,000 annually.

•**Hospital care for the uninsured.** Under both state and federal laws, you cannot be turned away from a hospital emergency room if you are uninsured. And if you require more than just emergency room care, you cannot be denied admission to the hospital. Last year, hospitals provided more than $25 billion in care to people who were unable to pay their bills, whether they were insured or not. In addition, many hospitals run free or low-cost clinics that can be used to help monitor chronic conditions, such as diabetes, asthma or heart disease.

•**Free or low-cost prescription medications.** More than 475 public and private assistance programs, including those offered by more than 150 drug companies, provide free or low-cost prescription drugs to qualified patients who lack prescription medication coverage. To find out about these programs—and which you qualify for—consult the Partnership for Prescription Assistance, 888-477-2669 or *www.pparx.org.*

•**Negotiate with your doctor.** Losing your health insurance does not necessarily mean you cannot see the doctors you have always used. Most will work out reduced fees or extended payment arrangements for you and your family. But it's up to you to ask.

Latest Medicare Scam: Old Bills

Nora Johnson is a medical billing auditor with Medical Billing Advocates of America, a nationwide network of independent medical billing advocates, based in Salem, VA. *www.billadvocates.com.*

Recently, bill-collection agencies have been contacting some seniors saying that Medicare claims from years past have been denied, and these individuals must pay up. Some agencies have legitimately purchased lists of unpaid debts from hospitals—but others might be scams. Under no circumstances should you immediately pay any such bill.

Better: Send a certified letter to the collection agency stating that you're disputing the bill and that you want to see a copy of the Medicare denial. By law, you are entitled to receive this.

Many collection agencies will give up at this point, but if you are sent a copy of the Medicare form, try to determine the reason for the denial. Medicare claims are often denied because of coding mistakes or missed deadlines—these things are the fault of the hospital or health-care provider. If that's the case, contact the billing department at the hospital or the health-care provider, explain that the fault was theirs and ask to be sent a new bill showing a balance of zero.

Helpful: Medicare forms are difficult to interpret. If you can't figure out the reason for the denial, contact Medicare at 800-633-4227.

Even if the Medicare claim denial wasn't the hospital's fault, you can be billed only if the hospital can prove you signed an "Advanced Beneficiary Notice" form when you received treatment, establishing that you knew the procedure might not be covered.

Also, you might not have to pay the bill if the statute of limitations on debt collections has expired. That could be from three to eight years, depending on your state. Check with the office of your state's attorney general or visit the Web site *www.fair-debt-collection.com.*

Don't make even a small partial payment to the collection agency without confirming the charge is legitimate—doing so can reset the statute-of-limitations clock on the rest of the bill.

13

Alternative & Natural Solutions

Important Therapies That Are Too Often Overlooked

Even conservative, traditional doctors have started offering alternative therapies to their patients. They may recommend acupuncture to relieve pain and St. John's wort to curb mild depression.

But there are many effective alternative therapies that remain underused...

BLACK COHOSH

In Germany, a black cohosh extract called *Remifemin* is frequently prescribed as an alternative to *hormone replacement therapy* (HRT). Preliminary evidence suggests that black cohosh is effective at relieving premenstrual discomfort, menstrual pain and menopausal ailments.

This is good news given the evidence linking HRT to increased risk for heart attack.

Any menopausal or postmenopausal woman should ask her doctor about taking black cohosh supplements. They're sold at health food stores.

Caution: Do not take black cohosh longer than six months, since no studies have established whether sustained use is safe.

GUGGUL

An extract from the *mukul myrrh* tree, which is native to India, guggul is used in that country to lower cholesterol. Evidence is mounting that it is effective—and safe. In an Indian study, 40 patients with high cholesterol who took a 25-milligram (mg) supplement of guggul three times a day for 16 weeks cut their total cholesterol an average of 21%. Levels of HDL ("good") cholesterol rose by 35%.

If you have high cholesterol: Ask your doctor about taking guggul supplements.

MENTAL IMAGERY

Mental imagery begins with the patient entering a state of deep relaxation similar to

Kenneth R. Pelletier, MD, clinical professor of medicine, University of Arizona School of Medicine, Tucson. He is author of *The Best Alternative Medicine: What Works? What Does Not?* (Fireside).

362

that obtained via hypnosis. The physician or hypnotherapist then leads the patient through images in which treatments, recovery and desired outcomes are envisioned.

Mental imagery is of proven effectiveness against chronic pain and anxiety. It has also been used successfully to lower blood pressure and heart rate in heart patients and to improve cancer patients' production of cancer-killing lymphocytes, neutrophils and T-cells.

Writing down thoughts and feelings can be a powerful form of mental imagery. The *Journal of the American Medical Association* published a study of 112 people with asthma or rheumatoid arthritis who all received standard care. In one group, each patient wrote an essay on three consecutive days, describing his/her reaction to a traumatic experience.

Result: Four months later, those in the writing group had markedly improved health.

MIND–BODY RELAXATION

Meditation, hypnosis, stress management and biofeedback are all effective against anxiety and depression, asthma, high blood pressure, chronic pain and carpal tunnel syndrome.

Heart disease patients who are treated with stress-management classes and muscle tension biofeedback have fewer fatal heart attacks and require fewer heart operations than do similar patients on a standard aerobic exercise program.

Stress-management lessons focus on teaching better coping methods for stressful situations. Methods include visualization, meditative breathing and other relaxation techniques.

Muscle tension biofeedback involves placing electrodes on the skin to measure muscle tension. The patient learns to reduce tension by monitoring a dial or another feedback device.

Anyone who wants to reduce stress or anxiety can consider these techniques. Contact the National Center for Complementary and Alternative Medicine at the National Institutes of Health at 888-644-6226 or *http://nccam. nih.gov.*

PRAYER

Some studies suggest that prayer promotes healing—even when the patient is unaware of being prayed for. For example, in a study of 393 heart patients at San Francisco General Hospital, half the patients were prayed for, half were not. Neither patients nor doctors knew who had been prayed for.

After 10 months, the prayed-for group had required less medical care—and had lower mortality—than the group not prayed for.

REIKI

In this laying-on-of-hands technique, a practitioner sends "healing energy" through his hands into the patient's body. Reiki has proven effective in managing pain and healing wounds.

At the University of Michigan Medical School in Ann Arbor, researchers found that Reiki speeds healing of incisions.

People who have chronic pain or feel they are healing too slowly from a wound might want to try Reiki. Contact the International Center for Reiki Training at 800-332-8112 or *www.reiki.org.*

SOY FOODS

Soy foods are believed to slow menopause onset and prevent bone loss in menopausal women. Now a study at Stanford University School of Medicine suggests soy is effective when combined with daily supplements of vitamin D and calcium.

Soy derives its effectiveness from estrogen-like compounds known as *phytoestrogens*. Tofu, tempeh, soy milk, edamame (baby soybeans), soy cheese and miso are all rich in phytoestrogens.

Menopausal and postmenopausal women should ask their doctors about taking soy with calcium and vitamin D supplements.

Important: Consult your doctor before taking any herbal supplement. Women who are pregnant or nursing should not take herbs.

Powerful Herbal Medicines People Rarely Hear About

James A. Duke, PhD, leading authority on medicinal plants and former chief, US Department of Agriculture Plant Laboratory, Beltsville, MD. He is author of *Dr. Duke's Essential Herbs: 13 Vital Herbs You Need to Disease-Proof Your Body, Boost Your Energy, and Lengthen Your Life* (Rodale).

Many health consumers are familiar with the top-selling herbal medicines—the memory enhancer ginkgo biloba...the depression fighter St. John's wort...and the immunity booster echinacea. There are more than 10,000 medicinal herbs available, which are used to treat a variety of ailments, including flu, varicose veins, the bone-thinning condition known as osteoporosis and hemorrhoids.

Some herbs can work just as well as conventional drugs. Herbs often have fewer side effects, and they usually cost less, too.

ASTRAGALUS
STRAGALUS MEMBRANACEOUS

This herb has been used for centuries in traditional Chinese medicine in tea or soup, typically in root form.

Also called *huang qi* (pronounced "wahng chee"), astragalus is typically used to bolster the immune system to help the body fight off colds, influenza and harmful bacteria.

Typical daily dosage: At the first sign of cold or flu symptoms, prepare a tea of one teaspoon of liquid extract or one-half teaspoon of tincture in one cup of hot water, steeped and drained. Or you can use 2 grams (g) of the root.

Caution: Certain species of astragalus are toxic. Do not try to pick and use this herb on your own. Purchase it from a reliable source.

BUTCHER'S BROOM
RUSCUS ACULEATUS

This herb is often used in Europe for relief from varicose veins and hemorrhoids.

Typical daily dosage: Take one 300-milligram (mg) tablet...or 7 to 11 mg of total *ruscogenin,* the active ingredient.

CELERY SEED
APIUM GRAVEOLENS

The anti-inflammatory properties of celery seed help to ease arthritis and gout symptoms and lower blood pressure.

If you can eat celery without problems, you're unlikely to experience any side effects.

Caution: See your doctor before using celery seed for hypertension. It may augment the action of prescription antihypertensives.

Typical daily dosage: Take two 500-mg capsules of standardized extract or one-half teaspoon of tincture before meals. For seeds, one tablespoon of seeds in one cup of hot water or added as a spice to soups.

ELDERBERRY
SAMBUCUS NIGRA

This herb fights viral illnesses, including flu, cold and herpes.

In one study that was conducted during an outbreak of flu in Israel, 90% of people who took a standardized elderberry extract were better within three days.

Typical daily dosage: At the onset of flu, cold or herpes, one-half teaspoon of liquid elder flower extract before meals or two to three cups of elder flower tea (two teaspoons of dried elder flowers in one cup of hot water, steeped and drained).

FENUGREEK
TRIGONELLA FOENUM-GRAECUM

This herb is used to treat diabetes, diarrhea and constipation.

In studies conducted in India, fenugreek was shown to contain five compounds that cause significantly reduced blood sugar levels in people with type 1 or type 2 diabetes.

Fenugreek contains *mucilage*. This soluble fiber absorbs water and provides relief from diarrhea and constipation.

Mucilage also enhances the herb's ability to lower blood sugar levels and may reduce cholesterol and triglyceride levels.

Caution: Do not take fenugreek *instead of* prescription diabetes drugs. See your doctor if you want to try this herb to treat diabetes.

Typical daily dosage: 620 mg of standardized extract taken before meals, or one cup of fenugreek tea (one tablespoon of mashed seeds steeped in one cup of hot water).

KUDZU
PUERARIA MONTANA

This herb may help prevent osteoporosis and reduce cravings for alcohol.

Kudzu contains *genistein* and *daidzein*—phytoestrogens that protect against bone loss.

Typical daily dosage: Take three 100-mg capsules.

PUMPKIN SEED
CUCURBITA PEPO

In parts of Europe, pumpkin seeds are the standard treatment for benign prostate enlargement. The seeds are rich in zinc, selenium and other minerals that have been shown to reduce prostate cancer risk.

Typical daily dosage: Eat one-quarter cup of the seeds.

USING HERBS SAFELY

Plant medicines can sometimes intensify or block the effects of prescription drugs. Consult your doctor before taking any herb—especially if you are pregnant, nursing or take prescription medications.

If you're scheduled for surgery, tell your doctor about all the herbs you take…and stop taking them three weeks prior to the procedure. Some herbs reduce—or increase—blood pressure or diminish the effects of anesthesia.

The active ingredients in herbal medicines can vary, depending on the manufacturer. Choose "standardized" brands. These indicate the amount of the active ingredient—and give recommended dosages. You can buy them at health food stores.

Also, tell your pharmacist about any herbs you are taking, so he/she can monitor possible interactions with prescription drugs.

To find a physician familiar with herbal treatments, contact the American Association of Naturopathic Physicians at 866-538-2267 or *www.naturopathic.org.*

More from James A. Duke…

Supercharge Your Immunity With Herbs

Medicinal herbs are rich in antioxidants that help to maintain health and slow the aging process. They also can prevent or alleviate age-related problems, such as arthritis, high blood pressure and failing vision.

World-renowned botanist James A. Duke, PhD, knows which herbs are most essential to healthy aging. Dr. Duke, who is in his 70s, has a half-acre medicinal herb garden at his homestead in Fulton, MD. He discussed eight potent herbs that he uses himself.

Caution: While these herbs have no significant side effects and are far safer than most synthetic drugs, it is always smart to consult your doctor before taking supplements and/or treating a medical problem yourself.

Some herbs can interact with prescription and nonprescription drugs, either magnifying or weakening their effects. In addition, some people may be allergic to herbs. Be alert to symptoms, such as a rash, when taking any herb.

With your doctor's approval, you can take these herbs all at the same time, along with vitamins, if you wish. Follow the dosages suggested on the labels.

BILBERRY:
VISION DISORDERS

Bilberry is rich in *anthocyanins,* chemicals that keep the capillary walls strong and flexible. It also is loaded with antioxidants that defend delicate tissue against free radical damage.

In particular, bilberry protects the retina and its blood supply, preventing and improving vision disorders, such as macular degeneration.

Bilberry can ward off other eye problems, too, including cataracts, glaucoma and poor night vision.

CELERY SEED:
GOUT AND ARTHRITIS

I have a special fondness for this herb, which has protected me from agonizing attacks of gout for the last seven years. It lowers blood levels of uric acid as effectively as *allopurinol,* the drug commonly prescribed for gout.

Celery seed, available in capsule form, also contains 25 anti-inflammatory compounds that can reduce the pain and swelling of arthritis. It has chemicals that make blood vessels relax and open, helping to alleviate high blood pressure and angina (chest pain caused by deficient blood flow to the heart).

In folk medicine, celery seed is reputed to be a digestive aid. It is used to relieve gas and heartburn, though its effectiveness has yet to be clinically proven.

ECHINACEA:
COLDS AND FLU

This popular herbal medicine is a powerful ally against colds and flu. The purple coneflower from which it comes has been used medicinally by Native Americans for centuries.

At least three of the chemicals it contains—*caffeic acid, echinacoside* and *cichoric acid*—have known antiviral properties. In addition, echinacea also helps to boost the body's own infection-fighting powers.

Take echinacea at the first sign of an upper-respiratory infection or flu. I also take it when I know I'll be in crowds of people or around other sources of infection.

This is not an herb for everyday use—the immune system eventually could stop responding to it. I do not take it for more than eight weeks in a row.

GARLIC:
BLOOD PRESSURE AND CHOLESTEROL

This pungent bulb was prescribed by Hippocrates, the fifth-century BC Greek physician, and cited as a cure-all in an ancient Sanskrit manuscript. Today, we attribute the herb's medicinal effectiveness to its high concentration of sulfur compounds.

Garlic lowers blood pressure and cholesterol. There also is evidence that it can reduce the risk of cancer, particularly in the gastrointestinal tract.

Garlic contains at least 25 germ-killing compounds and fights off bacterial, viral and fungal infections.

Eat at least one raw clove or four cooked cloves daily…or take garlic capsules.

HAWTHORN:
POTENT HEART DRUG

An extract made from this flowering shrub can be useful against irregular heart rhythm, angina and shortness of breath. Hawthorn contains seven compounds known to prevent dangerous clotting and three that lower blood pressure. One study at the University of Madras in India suggests that hawthorn also may help reduce cholesterol.

MILK THISTLE:
LIVER PROTECTION

The liver, the organ vital to detoxifying the blood, is under constant assault by pollution. Alcohol, also, is bad for the liver. Milk thistle, a relative of the artichoke, appears to protect the liver. It contains *silymarin,* which strengthens cell membranes and boosts the organ's ability to repair itself. Milk thistle has even been used to treat hepatitis A and C.

I take milk thistle capsules when I'm traveling and will be exposed to smog. If I lived in a major city with pollution problems, I would take it every day.

I also take it before a celebration, when I may be drinking a bit more alcohol than usual.

You can take silymarin capsules or eat milk thistle seeds, available in health food stores, as you would sunflower seeds.

SAW PALMETTO:
PROSTATE PROBLEMS

At least half of men over age 50 have some trouble when urinating because benign prostate enlargement chokes off the flow. An extract of saw palmetto, a tropical shrub, has been used for years to treat this problem.

A review in the *Journal of the American Medical Association* concluded that saw palmetto facilitates urination in men who are suffering from prostate problems just about as well as medication. Natural chemicals in the herb appear to block a testosterone-type hormone that promotes prostate growth. Men without prostate problems may choose to take it as a preventive measure.

Saw palmetto also may slow down male pattern baldness.

TURMERIC:
HEART PROBLEMS AND ARTHRITIS

This spice, which is made from the root of the tropical plant *Curcuma longa,* is a common ingredient in mustard and Indian food—it's what makes curry bright yellow. Turmeric is packed with antioxidants and contains powerful anti-inflammatory compounds known as Cox-2 inhibitors.

Some research suggests that turmeric can stop inflammation about half as effectively as steroids such as cortisone—but without all the troubling side effects. This makes it a valuable ally against arthritis. In addition, turmeric protects the heart. It makes blood platelets less likely to clump and form dangerous clots. It also fights cholesterol buildup in the arteries.

Turmeric is available as an herbal preparation. You also can add turmeric to your diet when cooking. I like to use it to make a curried celery soup.

WHICH BRANDS TO BUY

Herbal products are sold by many manufacturers, but there is no federal regulation to ensure quality control.

To be safe, select a major brand, such as Nature's Herbs, Nature's Way or Solgar. These are available at most supermarkets, drugstores and health food stores. Buy preparations that clearly indicate on the labels the exact amounts of active ingredients.

Herbal Remedies: Secrets of Greater Effectiveness and Safer Use

Ethan Russo, MD, clinical assistant professor of medicine, University of Washington School of Medicine, Seattle. He is author of *The Handbook of Psychotropic Herbs* (Haworth Press).

People tend to assume that because herbs are "natural," they pose little risk to one's health. This is not true.

Some herbs are too toxic for medicinal use. Even some that are generally safe can cause liver or kidney damage.

And like drugs, herbal remedies can react dangerously with certain drugs or foods.

How can you use herbal remedies for maximum safety and effectiveness? Physician and herbalist Ethan Russo, MD, suggested several helpful guidelines. *They are...*

● **Avoid herbs known to be dangerous.** Given their inherent dangers, it's best to avoid chaparral, comfrey, life root, germander, coltsfoot, sassafras and ephedra (*Ma huang*).

● **Don't be misled by wild claims.** Federal law forbids herbal remedy manufacturers from saying their products offer outright cures.

But manufacturers often tout their products as providing relief from a ludicrously wide range of ailments.

Take manufacturers' claims with a grain of salt. The best manufacturers often make no health claims for their products.

● **Seek reliable information.** Most doctors know very little about herbs. The same is true for the average pharmacist.

Health food store clerks may sound knowledgeable, but their information often comes from herbal remedy manufacturers—hardly a source of unbiased information.

The most reliable source of information on herbs is *The Complete German Commission E Monographs: Therapeutic Guide to Herbal Medicines,* available from the American Botanical Council for $89.*

● **Work with a knowledgeable practitioner.** For a referral to an herb-savvy medical doctor in your area, contact the American Botanical Council at 800-373-7105 or 512-926-4900 or *http://abc.herbalgram.org.*

Alternative: Consult a naturopathic physician. In addition to basic medical training, naturopaths have extensive instruction in the safe use of herbs.

For referral to a naturopath in your area, contact the American Association of Naturopathic Physicians at 866-538-2267 or *www.naturopathic.org.*

● **Buy only standardized formulations of herbs.** Standardized herbal extracts have been

*Your library may have this book. If not, it can be ordered from the American Botanical Council (http://abc.herbalgram.org)...or via an on-line bookseller. Price may vary.

formulated to provide the active ingredient or ingredients at a specific concentration. That way, you're assured the product is both potent and safe to use.

Look for the word "standardized" or the words "German standards" on the label.

●**Follow label directions carefully.** Like drugs, herbs work best at specific dosages. Take only the recommended dosage, and be sure to take the herb with or without meals, water, etc.—as indicated.

●**Don't mix herbs and drugs.** Herbs can boost the potency of certain medications. If you're taking a prescription drug, don't begin taking any herbal extract until you've checked with your physician or naturopath.

If a doctor has prescribed a drug for you, let him/her know about any herbal remedies you're already taking. He may need to adjust the dosage.

Herb–drug interactions can include...

●St. John's wort and *fluoxetine* (Prozac). The combination can raise brain levels of the neurotransmitter serotonin. "Serotonin syndrome" can cause delirium and other dangerous symptoms.

●Ginkgo biloba and anticoagulants. Like aspirin, *warfarin* (Coumadin) and other anticoagulants, ginkgo thins the blood. Taken along with an anticoagulant, ginkgo can cause internal bleeding.

●**Watch out for allergic reactions.** Introduce herbs one at a time. Don't add a second herb until you've taken the first for an entire week without experiencing any symptoms of an allergic reaction—rash, upset stomach, dizziness or headache. If you experience any of these symptoms, stop taking the herb at once. Try taking it again one week later. If symptoms return, stop taking the herb for good.

Caution: If you become short of breath after taking an herb, call for an ambulance at once.

●**Don't take herbs during pregnancy.** Ginger, garlic and other herbs that are popular as foods are generally okay. But other herbs can cause serious problems for women who are pregnant or nursing.

It's also best to check with a doctor before giving any herbal remedy to a child under the age of 12.

Little-Known Risks from Popular Herbal Remedies

Joe Graedon, Durham, NC–based pharmacologist, and Teresa Graedon, PhD, authors of several books, including *The People's Pharmacy Guide to Home and Herbal Remedies* (St. Martin's Griffin).

Most people assume that herbal remedies are inherently safer than drugs because they're "natural"...and because they've been in use for thousands of years.

Herbs *are* less likely to cause dangerous side effects. But as the use of medicinal herbs increases, so does the risk of harm.

Here are the seven most commonly used medicinal herbs—in alphabetical order—and important precautions to take if you use them...

BLACK COHOSH

It is used to relieve symptoms of menopause —hot flashes, night sweats and mood changes. Women who are using hormone replacement therapy should not take black cohosh—it is an unnecessary duplication of effort.

CASCARA SAGRADA

Also known as *sacred bark,* this laxative works by stimulating intestinal contractions.

Risks: Cascara sagrada can cause severe diarrhea, which depletes essential minerals from the body. It can be dangerous when combined with other types of electrolyte-depleting drugs, such as diuretics.

Better choice: Bulk-forming laxatives that contain psyllium seed or methylcellulose.

Better still: Eat more foods that are high in bulk-forming fiber—such as fruits, vegetables and legumes (beans, peas, etc.).

GARLIC

Garlic is used to lower cholesterol...prevent blood clots...lower high blood pressure...and as an antifungal.

The effectiveness of garlic capsules versus fresh garlic remains an unresolved issue.

Risks: Garlic may increase the risk of internal bleeding in those taking anticoagulant medications, such as *warfarin* (Coumadin).

Bottom line: You would have to eat a lot of garlic before experiencing any problems. But if you already take a blood-thinner, garlic supplements could be dangerous.

GINKGO BILOBA

This herb is typically used to improve circulation…possibly delay mental declines that are associated with Alzheimer's disease…and reverse some of the sexual side effects associated with depression.

Risks: In people taking blood-thinning medications, ginkgo may increase the risk of internal bleeding because it inhibits blood clotting.

Ginkgo slows the body's ability to metabolize drugs. If you take *atorvastatin* (Lipitor) for lowering cholesterol or *nifedipine* (Procardia) for controlling high blood pressure, do not take ginkgo. Doing so could result in a dangerous buildup of the drugs in the bloodstream.

GREEN TEA

It has antioxidant and antibacterial properties that are believed to reduce cancer risk and may reduce the incidence of gum disease. Habitual drinkers may have lower cholesterol levels as well.

Risks: In theory, the vitamin K in green tea could reduce the effectiveness of anticoagulants, such as warfarin. But you would have to drink a lot of tea before this could happen.

The tannins in green tea can also block the absorption of iron—a problem for women with anemia.

Important: Supplements that contain concentrated green tea are more likely to cause problems than the beverage itself. It's best to *drink* green tea.

LICORICE

It speeds healing of ulcers, inflammatory bowel disease and other inflammatory conditions of the digestive tract.

Licorice inhibits the secretion of stomach acid and increases production of *prostaglandins,* which protect tissues in the digestive tract.

Risks: Regular use of licorice can deplete potassium from the body, especially when combined with diuretics such as *furosemide* (Lasix).

Low levels of potassium are particularly dangerous if you are taking the heart medication *digoxin* (Lanoxin), as this may result in dangerous heart-rhythm disturbances (*arrhythmias*).

Excessive black licorice use may also bring on increased blood pressure…fluid retention…reduced sex drive…and hormonal imbalances.

Safer: Deglycyrrhizinated licorice has been stripped of a harmful component to reduce the risk of side effects.

ST. JOHN'S WORT

St. John's wort appears to be as effective as prescription antidepressants for mild to moderate depression.

Risks: Combining St. John's wort with an antidepressant can cause irritability, muscle contractions, anxiety and/or panic. It may also cause photosensitivity, so do not spend a lot of time out in bright light. Sunglasses will not help.

St. John's wort may also reduce the effectiveness of oral contraceptives. Women who take St. John's wort while using birth-control pills may be more vulnerable to an unplanned pregnancy.

And St. John's wort can decrease the effectiveness of certain medications used to control the AIDS virus.

It is best to avoid combining St. John's wort with other medications unless you have discussed your specific situation with a naturopath, herbalist or knowledgeable physician.

Age-Old Remedies Are the Best Cures

Joan Wilen and Lydia Wilen, New York City–based experts on folk remedies and coauthors of *Bottom Line's Healing Remedies* (Bottom Line Books).

When we were growing up in Brooklyn, our mother had an old folk remedy for almost every ailment. And if she didn't know one, our grandmother did.

Folk remedies don't work for everyone, but they are worth a try. They are generally inexpensive, easy to follow, time-tested and safe (the hundreds of remedies in our book have all been doctor-approved). Only the effective remedies are passed down from generation to generation—the rest are left behind.

Everyone knows about prunes for constipation and cranberry juice for urinary-tract infections. *Here are some lesser-known favorites...*

ARTHRITIS

If you are plagued by morning stiffness, put a sleeping bag on your bed and zip yourself in for the night. Your own body heat will be trapped in the sleeping bag and will be evenly distributed.

This seems to be much safer than using an electric blanket or a heating pad and more effective in terms of ease of movement upon waking in the morning.

COMMON COLDS

Garlic, with its chemical compound *allicin,* is a natural antibiotic with antiviral, antifungal and antiseptic properties. It can also act as a decongestant and an expectorant.

So, when you have a bad cold, what is even better than chicken soup? Chicken soup with a minced clove of raw garlic.

GOUT

The classic folk remedy for gout is to eat four ounces of fresh Bing cherries daily. If cherries are not in season, drink bottled cherry juice or buy cherry-juice concentrate (at health food stores) and have one tablespoon three times a day. You can also eat frozen or canned cherries. While you're at it, add strawberries to your shopping list. They neutralize uric acid, a buildup of which causes this condition.

HANGOVER

To ease the symptoms of a hangover, cut a wedge of lemon and rub it on your armpits. As outrageous as this sounds, it works.

HAY FEVER

To relieve runny nose, sneezing and itchy, red eyes, chew a one-inch square of honeycomb. Swallow the honey and continue to chew the waxy gum for about 10 minutes, then spit it out.

Buy honeycomb that was collected in your local area so that it contains the same type of pollen that is causing your symptoms.

Most health food stores carry honeycomb. Check the packaging to be sure that it is from your part of the country.

To help immunize yourself, chew a one-inch square of honeycomb daily, starting a month or two before hay fever season.

Caution: Of course, if you are allergic to bee stings or honey, do not use this remedy.

HEADACHE

Peel a long, wide (one- to two-inch) strip of lemon rind. Rub the inside of the peel (pith) on your temples. Put the rind across your forehead, securing it in place with a bandage or a handkerchief.

While we were on a television show, the host told us he had a three-day-old headache. Nothing he tried had worked. We put the rind on his forehead and, 20 minutes later, his headache was gone.

INDIGESTION AND GAS

Prepare ginger tea by covering one tablespoon of fresh gingerroot with one cup of just-boiled water. Let it steep for 10 minutes. Strain and drink after a gassy and/or fatty meal. It helps digestion and helps get rid of the gas.

Keep gingerroot in the freezer to make it easier to grate. If the ginger is not frozen, simply cut three or four quarter-sized pieces of the fresh root for your tea.

If you don't have fresh ginger, mix one-half teaspoon of ginger powder in one cup of hot water. It is effective but doesn't taste as good.

INSOMNIA

For occasional sleeplessness, cut a yellow onion into chunks, and put them in a covered jar next to your bed.

When you are tossing and turning, uncover the jar and take a deep whiff. Close the jar, lie back and think lovely thoughts. You should be asleep within 15 minutes.

In the morning, discard the onion. Do not use the same one night after night.

LEG CRAMPS

Some people wake up in the middle of the night with leg cramps. Others get them after exercising. In either case, place a piece of silverware—a spoon is safest—right on the cramp. The spoon does not have to be sterling—stainless steel will do the trick.

Another cramp solution: Pinch your philtrum—the area between your nose and upper lip—until the cramp is gone. It usually takes just a few seconds. Use this remedy when you don't have a piece of silverware handy.

SORE THROAT

Mix two teaspoons of apple cider vinegar in one glass of warm water. Gargle a mouthful, spit it out, then swallow a mouthful. Keep doing this until you finish the glass.

Repeat the entire process every hour. Within three to four hours, the sore throat usually starts to feel much better.

Additional help: Drink pineapple juice. It contains healing enzymes that soothe irritated throat tissues and may help them heal faster.

STY

As soon as you feel a sty coming on, rub the area a few times with a gold ring. The gold may prevent it from becoming one of those atrocious, full-blown infections that can linger for a week or more.

A few years ago, Joan woke up with a sty on each eye. We were scheduled to do a TV show that day. She took a gold ring and rubbed her lids. By the time we arrived at the studio, both of her eyes were fine.

More from the Wilen sisters...

Remedies for Summer Ills

Try these home remedies for hot-weather health challenges. They work wonders— even if we don't always know why.

MOTION SICKNESS

●**Mix eight ounces of warm water with one-half teaspoon of ground ginger powder.** Drink this 20 minutes before traveling. It is more effective than popular motion sickness

medications. Taking two ginger pills, available at health food stores, also does the trick.

●**Suck on a lemon wedge** if you feel queasy while en route.

●**Inhale the smell of newsprint.** Make sure the newspaper was printed in the traditional method. To be effective, the newspaper's ink should have a distinct smell and come off on your fingers.

SUNBURN

Always apply sunscreen before going outdoors. *But if you do get a sunburn...*

●**Take a cool shower as soon as possible.**

●**Steep six regular tea bags in one quart of hot water.** When the tea is strong and cool, drench washcloths in it and apply them to the sunburned area. Repeat this process until you start to feel relief.

●**Burned your feet from walking on hot sand?** Apply tomato slices to the soles of your feet, and secure them in place with elastic bandages or handkerchiefs. Elevate your feet for 20 minutes.

SWIMMER'S EAR

●**To prevent swimmer's ear,** blow up a balloon three times after swimming. This dislodges trapped water that causes infection.

MOSQUITO BITES

To ward off mosquitoes...

●**Eat foods that are rich in vitamin B-1 (thiamine).** These include sunflower seeds, Brazil nuts and fish—or take a 25- to 50-milligram (mg) B-1 supplement three times a day starting two weeks before your expected exposure to mosquitoes.

●**Plant marigolds wherever possible...**or line your yard with potted geranium plants to keep mosquitoes away from your porch, patio, yard or pool.

●**Avoid consuming sugar or alcohol.**

●**Rub fresh aloe vera or parsley on skin.**

If you get bitten: Apply wet soap or a mixture of equal parts vinegar and lemon.

Proven Home Remedies for Common Aches And Pains

Thomas Rogers, ND, naturopathic physician in private practice, Whidbey Island Naturopathic, Oak Harbor, WA (*www.whidbeynaturopathic.com*), and adjunct faculty member who teaches medical procedures and orthopedics at Bastyr University, Kenmore, WA.

You don't need a doctor for headaches and heartburn and other minor health problems. Most ailments can be treated easily with remedies made from common household items or naturopathic products available at pharmacies and health food stores.

Caution: Any symptoms that seem unusual …come on suddenly…or don't go away within one week always should be checked by a physician. Also, if you are taking any medications, check with your doctor before taking any additional remedies.

Conditions you can treat yourself…

TENSION HEADACHE

A tension headache usually is triggered by physical or emotional stress. Aspirin and other nonsteroidal anti-inflammatory drugs may help, but they frequently cause stomach upset and, if overused, may trigger rebound headaches.

Remedies: Put a few drops of lavender oil on your index fingers, and rub it on your temples and the muscles at the back of your neck. Lavender penetrates the skin to slow activity in the limbic system, the part of the brain connected with emotions.

You also can try a combination supplement that contains *bromelain* (a pineapple enzyme) and *curcumin* (found in the spice turmeric). This combination suppresses the production of *prostaglandins,* pain-causing chemicals. Follow label directions.

HEARTBURN

This occurs when stomach acid surges into the esophagus.

Remedies: Add one-half teaspoon of baking soda to one cup of warm water and drink it. This mixture neutralizes acid. Or take capsules that contain *deglycyrrhizinated licorice* (DGL). Follow label directions. Licorice creates a gel-like barrier that protects the esophagus from stomach acid. Another option is a supplement called *Robert's Formula,* which contains soothing herbs, such as marshmallow and slippery elm (do not use this remedy if you are pregnant or nursing).

FLATULENCE

Gas is produced when bacteria in the colon ferment carbohydrates that aren't digested. The resulting buildup of hydrogen, methane and other gases causes discomfort and sometimes embarrassment.

Remedy: Have a cup of fennel tea, available in tea-bag form. Or pour eight ounces of boiling water over one-half teaspoon of crushed fennel seeds. Cover the cup, and let steep for 15 minutes. Drink the tea as often as needed.

SINUSITIS

Sinusitis is an infection of the sinus cavities behind the facial bones around the nose and eyes. It can cause difficulty breathing as well as facial tenderness and headaches.

Remedy: Add one-half teaspoon of salt to eight ounces of warm water. Cup some of the solution in your palm (wash your hands first), and sniff it deeply into each nostril. Or you can use a commercially prepared saline spray. Do this up to three times a day to reduce swelling of the sinus lining, promote better drainage and inhibit growth of harmful organisms.

Avoid milk, cheese and other dairy foods during sinusitis flare-ups. Dairy triggers the production of excess mucus.

COUGH

A cough results when nerves in the respiratory tract are irritated by a cold, flu or other type of illness.

Remedies: For a wet cough (one that produces phlegm)—boil water in a pot. Turn off the heat, and add three drops of eucalyptus oil. Lean over the pot with a towel draped over your head, and inhale the steam. This helps open nasal and bronchial passages and expel phlegm. Do this twice a day.

For a dry cough—make up a tea from wild cherry bark. Just measure one teaspoon of dried, chopped cherry bark into an eight-ounce cup, and pour boiling water over the bark. Cover up the cup, and let the bark steep for 15 minutes. Drink one cup three times a day.

PULLED MUSCLE

Soreness usually means that you have over-exerted a muscle, causing microscopic tears.

Remedies: Right after the injury occurs, wrap ice in a towel or T-shirt and apply to the sore area for up to 20 minutes at a time. Repeat every few hours. If possible, elevate the area above the level of your heart.

In addition, place three 30C pellets of homeo-pathic *Arnica* under your tongue every 15 minutes for one to two hours. This will reduce pain and inflammation.

Also take 500 to 750 milligrams (mg) of magnesium citrate daily until the pain subsides. To prevent diarrhea from the magnesium, divide the dose into several smaller ones and take them throughout the day.

SWIMMER'S EAR

This infection of the outer part of the ear usually is caused by fungi that thrive in moist environments.

Remedies: Warm half of an onion in a microwave for about 10 to 20 seconds and hold it very close to, but not touching, the affected ear for a minute or two. Warm onion releases sulfur-based gases that inhibit fungi, bacteria and viruses and ease pain. You can reheat and reuse the onion several times. Or moisten a cotton swab with citrus-seed extract, and apply it to the outer part of the ear and ear canal. Citrus kills fungi and bacteria.

To prevent the infection from recurring, just swab the outer part of the ear with rubbing alcohol after swimming or bathing. This makes it harder for fungi to survive.

INGROWN NAIL

This irritation where the nail enters the skin is painful and slow to heal but rarely serious.

Remedy: To ease pain and inflammation, mix one-half teaspoon of bentonite clay with one-half teaspoon of goldenseal powder and enough witch hazel to make a paste. Apply it

to the nail bed, and cover with a warm wash-cloth for 15 minutes. Do this twice a day until the area heals.

Simple Remedies That Really Work

Earl Mindell, PhD, RPh, professor of nutrition, Pacific Western University, Los Angeles, and an authority on nutrition, drugs, vitamins and herbal remedies. He is also author of *Dr. Earl Mindell's Natural Remedies for 150 Ailments* (Basic Health) and *Earl Mindell's Vitamin Bible for the 21st Century* (Grand Central).

Physicians often dismiss folk remedies as quaint, not effective or potentially unsafe. That's a mistake.

Research has now found that some traditional remedies work as well—or even better—than drugs. What's more, most of these traditional treatments are safer than drugs because they rarely cause side effects or interact with other medical treatments.

Best folk cures*...

COLDS

There is good reason that mothers have long advocated chicken soup as an effective cold remedy. Studies have confirmed that chicken soup increases the activity of antiviral immune cells and at the same time reduces throat and sinus inflammation.

What to do: Eat a bowl of chicken soup twice daily at the first sign of a cold.

Helpful: Add a pinch of cayenne to chicken soup. *Capsaicin,* the chemical that makes cayenne and other peppers taste hot, reduces congestion as effectively as over-the-counter (OTC) medications.

HEADACHES

Most headaches are caused by muscle tension and/or emotional stress. Millions of Americans cannot take aspirin or other painkillers because of allergies, drug interactions or side effects, such as stomach irritation.

*Check with your doctor before trying any natural remedy. Herbs can be dangerous for some people, including women who are pregnant or nursing.

What to do: Using your thumb and forefinger, squeeze the area between your upper lip and nose for five seconds. Repeat as needed. This technique helps to block the nerve signals and will significantly decrease headache pain in many sufferers.

INSOMNIA

Sleeping pills can be addictive and are notorious for side effects, such as dizziness, depression and headaches.

What to do: Drink a cup of valerian tea at bedtime. Valerian root, available in tea bags at health food stores, contains *valepotriates* and other sleep-inducing compounds. A traditional remedy for anxiety as well as sleeplessness, it's recommended by Commission E, the European equivalent of the US Food and Drug Administration.

Chamomile, hops and lavender teas will also help you rest, but they are not as potent.

NAUSEA

Ginger is the best treatment for all forms of nausea, including motion and morning sickness. The active ingredients, *gingerols,* are more effective than OTC antinausea drugs.

What to do: Each day you have nausea, drink two to three cups of ginger ale that contains natural ginger. This variety is available at health food stores. The ginger-flavored ingredients in commercial brands of ginger ale won't have the same effect.

As an alternative, make ginger tea. To prepare, chop one tablespoon of fresh gingerroot and steep it in hot water for about 10 minutes. Drink one to three cups daily.

SORE THROAT

Most people have heard that gargling with warm saltwater reduces sore throat pain. However, few prepare and use the mixture properly.

What to do: Add three teaspoons of table salt to one cup of warm water and stir. Gargle with a full one-cup mixture at least two to three times daily. Viruses, which cause colds, cannot survive in a high-salt environment.

TOOTHACHE

Conventional treatments range from OTC products, such as Orajel, to powerful prescription painkillers. But one of the best toothache treatments is a generations-old folk remedy.

What to do: Dip a toothpick in oil of clove, available at health food stores and some pharmacies, and apply it to the sore area. The pain will disappear almost instantly. Reapply as necessary. If pain persists for more than a few days, see your dentist.

Uncommon Cures for Asthma, Depression, Headaches and More

Larry Altshuler, MD, founder and medical director, Balanced Healing Medical Center, Oklahoma City (*www.bal ancedhealing.com*), and author of *Bottom Line's Balanced Healing* (Bottom Line Books).

Even though numerous major medical centers have begun combining alternative healing techniques with conventional medical therapies, most medical doctors in private practice still don't recommend these approaches to their patients. That's because most MDs aren't familiar enough with alternative medicine to know what works and what doesn't.

Here are four underused alternative therapies you may want to try*...

ACUPUNCTURE

In the US, acupuncture is used primarily to treat chronic pain and various addictions. The procedure is believed to stimulate the different types of nerves that activate parts of the brain involved in healing and in the transmission and perception of pain.

Each acupuncture session typically requires the insertion of eight to 12 needles, which usually penetrate the skin one to one-and-a-half inches. The procedure causes little to no pain. And, symptoms generally diminish within just six sessions.

*Before trying any of these treatments, consult your physician to ensure that they do not interfere with any other therapy you are receiving.

Conditions that often improve with acupuncture treatments...

•Asthma. Prescription inhalers and medication are the first-line treatment for asthma—but adding acupuncture treatments usually helps to reduce the severity and the frequency of future attacks. In some instances, the use of acupuncture enables patients to decrease their asthma medication.

•Depression. Acupuncture is believed to rebalance the brain neurotransmitters that are involved in depression.

In our clinic, we usually begin by prescribing acupuncture along with ongoing psychotherapy and natural antidepressants, such as St. John's wort—300 milligrams (mg) daily...ginkgo biloba—160 to 240 mg daily...and/or fish oil—4 grams (g) daily.

If there's still no improvement in the patient's depression, we then prescribe antidepressant medication.

•Hay fever. Acupuncture is the fastest and most effective way I have found to reduce or eliminate respiratory allergies. Most people can discontinue their medications following acupuncture treatment.

•Migraines. Acupuncture is one of the best treatments for an acute migraine attack, typically relieving pain within 30 minutes.

Each subsequent session also decreases the frequency and severity of attacks and may even cure them completely.

With their doctor's consent, most people can discontinue their medication, although some will still take it for occasional headaches or if they can't get in to see an acupuncturist.

•Smoking. Almost 80% of people can stop smoking with the help of acupuncture, according to studies.

If you try acupuncture, consult a practitioner trained in traditional Chinese acupuncture and certified by the National Certification Commission for Acupuncture and Oriental Medicine (904-598-1005, *www.nccaom.org*).

CRANIAL–SACRAL MANIPULATION

This technique, which is administered by a doctor of osteopathy (DO), involves manipulating the bones in the face and skull. It helps correct misalignments caused by obstructions, overloaded muscles and joints, and other structural problems in various parts of the spine.

Symptoms typically diminish with three to six treatments.

Conditions that often improve with cranial–sacral manipulation...

•Sinus problems. Sinusitis brought on by a structural obstruction responds well to this type of treatment.

•Temporomandibular joint (TMJ) syndrome. Manipulation can be useful to ease the headaches associated with this misalignment of the TMJ, which connects the jawbone to the skull—especially when the misalignment results from an accident.

•Tinnitus (ringing in the ears). Manipulation helps to correct structural abnormalities in the bones surrounding the ear, which can lead to tinnitus.

If you want to try cranial–sacral manipulation, consult an osteopathic physician certified by the American Osteopathic Association (800-621-1773, *www.osteopathic.org*).

HYPNOSIS

In this mind–body technique, the hypnotist places you in a deeply relaxed state and makes positive suggestions regarding your emotions, habits and bodily functions. Symptoms typically diminish with two to three sessions.

Conditions that often improve with hypnosis treatments...

•Anxiety and phobias. In the cases where psychotherapy brings no improvement, hypnosis is often effective.

•Chronic pain. Hypnosis can decrease ongoing pain by addressing emotional and psychological triggers.

•Irritable bowel syndrome (IBS). Persistent IBS frequently has underlying psychological causes, which quite often can be alleviated through hypnosis. One recent study discovered that hypnosis therapy alleviated the symptoms in 90% of IBS sufferers.

•Overeating. Hypnotic suggestion can help curb the urge to eat between meals and reduce the desire to eat unhealthy foods.

If you try hypnosis, consult with a hypnotist belonging to the American Society of Clinical Hypnosis (630-980-4740, *www.asch.net*) or to the National Guild of Hypnotists (603-429-9438, *www.ngh.net*).

MASSAGE

Massage boosts levels of the feel-good neurotransmitter known as *serotonin* while lowering levels of stress hormones.

Two commonly used types of massage are Swedish massage (which uses gentle pressure and broad stroking movements to help relax the muscles) or shiatsu massage (in which finger pressure is placed on key healing points along the body).

Symptoms typically begin to diminish after the first massage.

Conditions that frequently improve with massage therapy…

•**Anxiety.** Massage is an excellent treatment for reducing mild anxiety states. It has been shown to reduce or block the effects of *cortisol* and *epinephrine,* hormones that can damage body tissue when they are produced at excessive levels during anxiety-provoking or stressful conditions.

•**Back problems.** Massage will provide the most relief when it's used in conjunction with over-the-counter *nonsteroidal anti-inflammatory drugs* (NSAIDs), hot/cold compresses and/or ultrasound treatment, which incorporates high-frequency sound (20,000 Hz) and heat.

•**Tension headaches.** Pressure applied to trigger points in the neck, forehead and temples relieves most tension headaches.

Thirty-six states now license massage therapists. To find one, contact the American Massage Therapy Association at 877-905-2700 or *www.amtamassage.org.*

You also can ask your doctor for a referral.

All-Natural Ways to Help Arthritis, High Blood Pressure and More

Mark A. Stengler, ND, naturopathic physician in private practice, La Jolla, CA (*www.lajollawholehealth.com*). He is also associate clinical professor, National College of Naturopathic Medicine, Portland, OR, and author of several books on natural healing, including *The Natural Physician's Healing Therapies* (Bottom Line Books).

Among the significant advantages of most conventional prescription medications are their ability to work quickly and that they are standardized for predictable effects.

However, herbs, vitamins, minerals and other supplements can offer a safer approach because they are less likely to trigger side effects. Be patient—they may take as long as six to eight weeks to work.

Important: Never start a new treatment before consulting your doctor, especially if you currently are taking medication.

Here are six common health problems and the best natural treatments for each…

HYPERTENSION

About 50 million Americans have high blood pressure, the leading cause of stroke and cardiovascular disease. Conventional drugs work, but they often cause side effects such as fatigue, dizziness and anxiety.

Patients who have mild to moderate hypertension—a systolic (top) number of 140 to 179 and a diastolic (bottom) number of 90 to 109—often can achieve normal blood pressure with a low-sodium diet, exercise and weight loss. *These natural treatments also help…*

•**Hawthorn.** I recommend 300 milligrams (mg), three times daily.* This herb dilates arteries and improves coronary blood flow, reducing blood pressure. It also is a mild diuretic that reduces blood volume. Most patients who take hawthorn have a drop in blood pressure of 10 to 15 points over eight weeks. Once blood pressure is down, you may be able to reduce the

*Recommended dosages are for people who weigh 150 to 200 pounds. Adjust the dosage up or down according to your weight. Consult your doctor for more details.

dosage or stop taking the herb altogether. Be sure to ask your doctor.

●**Magnesium.** I recommend 250 mg, twice daily. You can take this with hawthorn to relax artery walls and increase blood flow.

INSOMNIA

The side effects of over-the-counter (OTC) and prescription insomnia drugs include daytime drowsiness and a high risk of addiction. Try out these natural treatments instead. Take each separately for two nights before making a decision about which works best for you.

●**Valerian.** I recommend 300 to 500 mg (or 60 drops of tincture), taken 30 to 60 minutes before bedtime and/or if you awaken during the night.

This herb appears to increase brain levels of serotonin, a neurotransmitter that's relaxing. Valerian is also thought to increase the amount of the neurotransmitter *gamma-aminobutyric acid* (GABA), which has a calming effect on the brain. Valerian is just as effective as the sleep drug *oxazepam* (Serax) but does not cause the "hangover" effect.

●**5-hydroxytryptophan (5-HTP).** I recommend 100 to 200 mg, taken 30 to 60 minutes before bedtime and/or if you awaken during the night. Levels of this amino acid, which helps elevate brain levels of serotonin, often are lower in people with insomnia.

●**Melatonin.** I recommend 0.3 mg, taken 30 to 60 minutes before bedtime. Levels of this sleep hormone rise during the hours of darkness—but many adults, especially those age 65 and older, have insufficient levels to achieve restful sleep.

SEASONAL ALLERGIES

It is best to avoid pollen as much as possible—by keeping windows closed and running an air purifier in the bedroom…staying inside during peak pollen times (usually mornings and evenings)…and washing bedding regularly. *The following natural treatments can be taken together and can help to prevent allergies…*

●**Nettle leaf.** I recommend 600 mg, three times daily. This herbal antihistamine is effective for mild to moderate allergies and causes none of the drowsiness of some antihistamines.

Helpful: After using nettle leaf for up to two weeks, cut the dose in half. The lower dose will be effective once the initial loads of histamine are reduced.

●**Quercetin.** I recommend 1,000 mg, three times daily. It belongs to a class of water-soluble plant pigments called *flavonoids*. Quercetin strengthens the immune system and inhibits the release of histamine in people with allergies.

PROSTATE ENLARGEMENT

About half of men age 50 and older suffer from benign prostatic hypertrophy, an enlargement of the prostate gland that can interfere with urination. The prescription drug *finasteride* (Proscar) will shrink this gland but may cause impotence. The following natural treatments don't bring on this side effect. *I often advise my patients to take all three for maximum effectiveness…*

●**Saw palmetto.** I recommend 320 mg daily. This herb inhibits an enzyme that converts *testosterone* to *dihydrotestosterone,* the form of the hormone that fuels prostate growth.

●**Nettle root (not leaf).** I recommend 240 mg daily. It reduces the hormonal stimulation of the prostate in a different way than saw palmetto and often is used in conjunction with saw palmetto.

●**Zinc.** I recommend 90 mg daily for two months, then 50 mg daily as a maintenance dose. Also, take 3 to 5 mg of copper daily. Long-term supplementation with zinc depletes copper from the body.

OSTEOARTHRITIS

This is the leading cause of joint pain and stiffness. Conventional treatments (aspirin, ibuprofen, etc.) reduce symptoms but often cause stomach bleeding. The following natural treatments don't have this side effect. *They can be taken together…*

●**Glucosamine.** I recommend 1,500 to 2,500 mg daily. Found naturally in the body, glucosamine promotes new cartilage growth and reduces inflammation. A four-week German study of patients with osteoarthritis of the knee reported that ibuprofen resulted in faster pain relief—but glucosamine supplements brought comparable pain relief after two weeks and were much less likely to cause side effects.

After a few months, you may be able to cut back to 500 mg daily. If you discontinue glucosamine completely, however, the benefits will wear off after a few months.

●**SAMe.** I recommend 400 to 800 mg daily. Pronounced "Sammy," this chemical compound (*S-adenosylmethionine*) is found in all living cells. It promotes flexibility of joint cartilage and cartilage repair.

One German study of 20,641 patients found that 71% of those people who took SAMe supplements for eight weeks reported good or very good results.

MENOPAUSAL DISCOMFORT

Hot flashes and night sweats are caused by declines in progesterone and estrogen. Conventional hormone replacement therapy reduces discomfort but may increase risk of heart disease, cancer and other ailments. *Natural treatments without these risks (use one or both)...*

●**Black cohosh.** I recommend that women take 80 mg daily for mild to moderate discomfort...160 mg daily for severe symptoms. This herb inhibits the release of *lutenizing hormone* (LH) by the pituitary gland. Elevated levels of LH after menopause is the primary cause of hot flashes, night sweats and other uncomfortable symptoms.

●**Natural progesterone.** I recommend 20 mg of cream (about one-quarter teaspoon), twice daily. Natural progesterone, derived from wild yams, is as effective as synthetic forms but less likely to cause side effects, such as water retention and weight gain. Apply the cream to breasts, forearms or cheeks for maximum absorption.

Important: Only use natural progesterone under a doctor's supervision. Blood levels have to be monitored very carefully, generally every six to 12 months.

Use Cold-Water Therapy For Relief

Alexa Fleckenstein, MD, board-certified internist who practices traditional and complementary medicine, Arlington, MA. Dr. Fleckenstein holds a German subspecialty degree in natural medicine.

For most Americans, a steaming hot bath or shower is a daily routine. But for more than 150 years, numerous Europeans have used invigorating *cold* showers and swims to promote good health.

Scientific evidence and numerous case histories support the use of "cold-water therapy" as an adjunct to standard treatments for frequent colds, insomnia, high blood pressure—even cancer and other serious disorders.

HOW IT BEGAN

Cold-water therapy was first popularized in Germany by the priest Sebastian Kneipp (1821–1897). In the winter of 1849, Kneipp successfully battled then-incurable tuberculosis by plunging several times weekly into the frigid Danube River. His 1886 book, *My Water Cure,* became an international best-seller.

THE MECHANISM

When practiced for at least four weeks, cold-water therapy...

●**Stabilizes blood pressure.** Cold water triggers the autonomic nervous system—which controls involuntary functions, such as heartbeat and breathing—to raise blood pressure, increase heart rate and constrict blood vessels.

The autonomic responses strengthen with each exposure. This stabilizes blood pressure, improves circulation and balances other bodily functions, such as the sleep/wake cycle.

●**Enhances immunity.** Cold water triggers the release of cytokines and other hormone-like substances that are key to improving immune function.

Recent finding: Breast cancer patients who underwent cold-water therapy for four weeks experienced significant gains in their levels of disease-fighting white blood cells, according to a German study.

●**Reduces pain.** Cold causes the body to release *endorphins,* hormones with proven pain-fighting properties.

●**Improves moods.** Cold water activates sensory nerves that lead to the brain. A cold, exhilarating shower can be emotionally uplifting and prime a person for new experiences.

THE REGIMEN

To gain the benefits of cold-water therapy at home, begin with your usual warm shower. When you're finished, step out of the water stream and turn off the hot water. Leave the cold water running.*

Start by wetting your feet first. Next, expose the hands and face.

Important: Jumping in all at once may hinder circulation.

Finally, step under the shower. Let the cold water run over your scalp, face, the front of your body and then down your back. You can begin by taking a cold shower that lasts only a couple of seconds.

After one month, the entire process should last no more than 40 seconds. Work up to whatever is comfortable for you.

If you can't tolerate the cold: Keep the water cold but expose only your feet, hands and face. Gradually increase the duration and area of exposure.

Caution: People who are very thin or frail may be unable to tolerate cold showers in the beginning. If you do not feel warm and invigorated after the shower, decrease the length of your next cold shower.

If you still don't feel warm within minutes, forgo cold showers. Instead, condition your body with cold sponge baths of the feet, hands, face—and then the rest of your body—after your warm shower.

*Water temperature should be about 60°F. In all but the hottest areas, water straight from the cold faucet will do. If your water is not cold enough to give you a good jolt, enhance the effect by air-drying—rather than towel-drying—your body.

Do not try cold-water therapy if you suffer from an acute illness, such as severe back pain...have hardening of the arteries (*atherosclerosis*)...Raynaud's disease...or have high blood pressure not controlled by medication.

Cold water causes a spike in blood pressure, which can be dangerous for those with conditions such as unmanaged hypertension.

The therapy can be safely used to reduce mildly elevated blood pressure (150/100 and below) or to raise low blood pressure.

If you have questions about your blood pressure: See your doctor for a blood pressure test before starting a cold-water regimen.

Oils that Improve Health

Eucalyptus is an antibacterial that soothes acne and relieves sinus congestion.

Geranium soaks up facial oiliness and also can tighten skin temporarily.

Lavender soothes tension headaches and migraines.

Rose hydrates and soothes sensitive, dry, itchy or inflamed skin.

Tea tree fights athlete's foot, dandruff, insect bites, cold sores and acne.

Caution: Except for lavender and tea tree, don't apply full-strength oils directly to skin. Dilute in a vegetable carrier oil such as almond oil or grape seed oil.

Victoria Edwards, founder, Aromatherapy Institute & Research, Fair Oaks, CA, quoted in *Self,* 4 Times Square, New York City 10036.

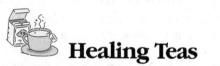

Healing Teas

Victoria Zak, award-winning researcher and writer in the health-care field, Holliston, MA. She is author of *20,000 Secrets of Tea* (Dell). In writing the book, Ms. Zak tested all of the herbs and consulted with herbalists and doctors of naturopathy about their use.

The right kind of teas can really work magic on a wide variety of common illnesses and ailments.

Rule of thumb: Drink a cup of tea one to three times a day until the problem subsides... then use intermittently to maintain health. Experiment to see which herbs or blends work best for you.

Important: Check with your physician before using any herbal treatment—particularly if you are taking prescription medications or are under a doctor's care.

And see your doctor if symptoms persist for more than one week.

Best way to brew: Steep one tea bag in six ounces of boiling water for three minutes. Steep dried herbs or loose tea in a tea infuser for three to five minutes. If you are making your own blend with dried or fresh herbs, use equal parts of the herbs to total one teaspoonful per cup of tea.

To enhance flavor: Add in some honey, lemon, cinnamon, real vanilla extract, a slice of orange or sweet anise...or blend with any fruit tea.

PREMENSTRUAL SYNDROME

Look for the following teas or a blend that contains one or more of these herbs—dandelion...hops...dong quai...feverfew...cramp bark. If you take cramp bark alone, make it a weaker tea and sip it slowly.

HEADACHE

My favorite blend for headaches is feverfew, parsley and milk thistle. Combine equal parts of each herb to total one teaspoonful for each cup of tea.

Also effective: Lavender...wood betony... and ginkgo.

COLDS AND FLU

Use a blend of *echinacea* and *elder* teas. You can make it yourself, or buy a premade mix. I like Traditional Medicinals products, available in most health food stores. Take for a maximum of one month...then take a one-month break before starting again.

SLEEP AID

Chamomile is a common sleep aid. Mix it with vervain for a stronger blend.

I drink deglycyrrhizinated licorice tea at bedtime—it calms the digestive tract.

UPSET STOMACH

For a digestive disorder: Papaya can work wonders...deglycyrrhizinated licorice also helps.

For motion sickness or nausea: Ginger or peppermint. Drink this tea iced to increase its soothing effects.

Use Vinegar to Treat Common Ailments

Jamison Starbuck, ND, naturopathic physician in family practice and lecturer, University of Montana, both in Missoula. She is past president of the American Association of Naturopathic Physicians and a contributing editor of *The Alternative Advisor: The Complete Guide to Natural Therapies and Alternative Treatments* (Time-Life).

Vinegar has been used to treat illness for thousands of years. The fifth-century BC Greek physician Hippocrates is said to have recommended a vinegar-and-honey mixture to his patients to clear up phlegm and ease breathing.

During the 10th century, vinegar was employed in hand-washing to prevent the spread of infection. Through World War I, vinegar was a staple in military medical kits—used as a wound disinfectant.

Recently, a colleague from the publishing world asked me to review a book touting the amazing powers of vinegar. Because I'm a longtime advocate of effective home remedies—and aware of vinegar's status as the most popular home remedy in America—I was happy to take a look.

Unfortunately, the book was filled with nonsense. *Here are the fallacies debunked...*

Vinegar cannot cure cancer, heart disease, high blood pressure or any other serious disease or illness.

Nor does it promote weight loss. There is simply no truth to the belief that vinegar is a natural fat-burner. Excessive vinegar consumption over several weeks or months can lead to heartburn.

Finally, vinegar does not prevent or treat arthritis. Arthritis has a variety of causes, including heredity, lifestyle and dietary choices. If you're having symptoms, consult your doctor.

Here's the truth about vinegar…

●**Vinegar can be used to treat itchy fungal infections of the skin**—Candida, athlete's foot, jock itch, etc. Painting white vinegar directly on the infected area helps curb the itch and eliminate the fungus.

I typically recommend starting with twice-daily applications of a 25% vinegar/75% water mixture and gradually increasing this to undiluted vinegar if your skin can tolerate it. You should see results within seven days.

●**Vinegar can help relieve sore throat pain.** Mix one or two teaspoons of apple cider vinegar in four ounces of warm water. Gargle with this solution four times daily for up to three days at the onset of a sore throat. It soothes pain and acts as a mild antiseptic, helping to kill viruses and/or bacteria on contact.

●**Vinegar makes a healthful—and tasty —addition to dark, leafy greens,** such as spinach, kale, chard, collard and beet greens. These vegetables contain lots of potassium, calcium and iron. But for proper digestion of these minerals, the body requires plenty of stomach acid. Studies show that many people over age 50 just don't produce enough acid. Vinegar is acidic, so it boosts the body's ability to draw essential minerals from food.

●**Vinegar offers soothing topical relief of sunburn pain.** While certainly it is best to avoid too much sun exposure, many people nonetheless end up with some sunburned skin at least once a year. If that is the case for you, try applying apple cider vinegar directly to your burn.

●**Vinegar is a good substitute for conventional household cleaners.** Folks with multiple chemical sensitivities or anyone who wants to lower his/her chemical exposure can substitute vinegar for harsh or strongly scented cleaning agents. Use vinegar on windows, floors and other household surfaces.

Caution: Do not consume vinegar if you have an ulcer, gastritis or an "acid stomach." It can exacerbate these conditions.

More from Jamison Starbuck…

How to Strengthen Your Immune System Easily

Strengthening the immune system is a popular concept these days. But if you're like many of my patients, you don't even know what comprises the immune system—much less if yours needs help.

In conventional medical parlance, the "immune system" consists of white blood cells, the lymphatic system, adenoids, thymus, spleen, tonsils and parts of the mucous membranes of the gastrointestinal and respiratory tract.

As your body's disease-fighting system, these organs and tissues are activated whenever you encounter microorganisms, foreign substances, such as soot, and/or allergens, such as pollen and animal dander. But your immune health is affected not only by blood cells and lymph tissue but also by emotional stress, physical activity, nutrition and liver function.

Symptoms of a flagging immune system can include chronic fatigue, frequent colds, flu or sinus infections. If you've had two or more of these symptoms for one week per month for three months or more, consider trying the following immune-boosting protocol. *Strategies…*

●**See your doctor to rule out disease.** Ask for a physical exam and lab tests, including a complete blood count…a blood chemistry panel, including cholesterol and glucose levels …a thyroid panel, which measures levels of *thyroid-stimulating hormone* (TSH) and the thyroid hormones T3 and T4…and an *erythrocyte sedimentation rate* (ESR) test—a marker of inflammation and illness.

●**Get enough vitamins.** The liver needs hefty supplies of vitamins A, C and E to give your immune system the energy it needs to keep you well. Dark-green veggies, such as spinach, kale and broccoli, as well as orange-colored fruit, such as mango, cantaloupe and apricots, are rich in vitamins A and C. Nuts and soy are high in vitamin E.

Nourish your immune system by consuming four vegetables, three fruits, two whole-grain or legume servings and 64 ounces of water daily. Sugar is an immune system depressant, so avoid cola, sweetened cereal, juice and desserts. Try to eat no more than one serving of sweetened food per day.

● **Choose gentle exercise.** If your immune system is fatigued, shun strenuous exercise, such as jogging, tennis and cycling. These activities stress the muscles and bones, which can just increase inflammation. Instead, walk or swim and/or perform yoga or tai chi.

● **Keep your mood balanced and upbeat.** Avoid disturbing situations whenever possible. Decline social invitations that are not enjoyable. Choose to watch comedies or romances instead of scary or violent films. Solve disputes or misunderstandings right away rather than letting them stew.

● **Take medicinal mushroom extracts.** In Asia, mushrooms have long been used as an immune-enhancing medicine. Modern studies confirm this benefit. My favorite mushrooms include cordyceps, maitake, reishi and shiitake. They are available in powdered or liquid form.

The mushroom extracts are safe to use for six months, but, if you suffer a chronic illness, check with your doctor first. For the appropriate dosage, follow the directions on the label.

Strengthen Your Body's Ability to Heal Itself

Leo Galland, MD, director, Foundation for Integrated Medicine, New York City. His latest book is *The Fat Resistance Diet* (Broadway). *www.fatresistancediet.com.* Dr. Galland is a recipient of the Linus Pauling award.

Unscientific as they were by our modern standards, the ancients can teach us a lot about health.

The Greeks and others focused less on specific diseases than on harmony between the mind and body. Maintaining mind–body balance, they knew, keeps us strong. When it is disrupted, we fall prey to illness.

Today, it's possible to have the best of both worlds—the insights of ancient wisdom bolstered by 21st-century science.

Power healing: The four key aspects of my concept of well-being are *relationships, diet, environment* and *detoxification.*

Strengthening these four pillars of healing will maintain the balance and harmony that protect against illness. If you're ill, these factors will work together with medical care to help you get better.

RELATIONSHIPS

In recent decades, evidence has grown that strong relationships are a potent force for maintaining good health.

Example: A California study found that marriage, close friendships and membership in church or community organizations lowered the overall death rate, as well as the risk of death from cancer, heart disease and stroke.

Good relationships strengthen your ability to deal with stress. The heart is under less strain and the immune system fights off disease and cancer better when you feel supported by friends and loved ones.

Social support makes you feel capable of doing positive things—for both yourself and your health.

The first step in strengthening this pillar of healing is to become aware of its importance. *Here's how…*

● **Take stock.** How much time and energy do you devote to others? What can you do to nurture more gratifying relationships?

● **Make an effort to help others.** Volunteering (at a soup kitchen, hospital, school, museum) reduces stress and eases health problems. By giving to others, you give to yourself.

DIET AND LIFESTYLE

It should come as no surprise that what you eat has great impact on your health, and that the standard American diet—high in fats, low in vegetables—is a recipe for serious illness.

You can strengthen this pillar of healing dramatically with one *simple step.* Eliminate—or at least *sharply reduce*—your consumption of the junk foods that make up 30% of the average American's calorie intake.

By avoiding processed foods—whose nutrients have been replaced by sugar, salt and shortening—you reduce the risk of heart disease and high blood pressure.

Healthful snacks: When you snack, choose raw vegetables, nuts and seeds rather than junk food.

Two nutrients deserve special attention…

•**Omega-3 fatty acids** have a positive impact on virtually every aspect of cell function. Their gradual disappearance from modern diets has been linked to diseases ranging from arthritis to depression.

Fish that are rich in omega-3s include salmon, albacore tuna and sardines. Flaxseed (oil and flour) is the best vegetable source.

•**Magnesium** regulates the enzyme reactions that support life in virtually every cell, but two-thirds of Americans don't get enough in their diets. Advancing age depletes the body of this mineral, as does stress. You probably need more magnesium if you suffer from irritability…palpitations…muscle tension or spasms.

Green vegetables (especially broccoli), beans, seeds and nuts are good sources of magnesium.

Lifestyle improvements should include regular physical activity. But you don't need to go to a gym. Just incorporate activity into your daily routine—by walking instead of driving the car, for instance.

ENVIRONMENT

Chemical and biological pollutants wreak havoc with the body, suppressing the immune system, damaging lungs and raising cancer risk, as well as causing minor health problems. Air pollution and toxic dumps are big culprits, but the risk of exposure is greatest indoors. *Here's what you can do…*

•**Don't permit anyone to smoke in your home.** Secondhand tobacco smoke increases cancer and heart disease risk and aggravates asthma. Carcinogenic tars cling to curtains and furniture.

•**Leave your shoes at the door.** Pesticides and other toxic wastes come in with you off the street, and are collected by carpets.

•**Fight mold.** It can cause severe allergy symptoms, eczema and asthma, as well as fatigue, joint pain and headache. Some types of mold secrete toxins that suppress the immune system. Use a dehumidifier to keep humidity below 50%…discard moldy food …ventilate your basement and attic.

•**Ventilate your stove, heater and dryer properly.** These appliances produce toxic gases, such as carbon monoxide, nitrogen dioxide and formaldehyde.

Helpful: Install a carbon monoxide detector. ***Cost:*** $50 to $80.

DETOXIFICATION

Your body has natural defenses against environmental pollutants as well as toxic substances produced by normal cell processes. The liver breaks these pollutants down, at which point they are excreted by the bowels and kidneys. *To enhance and support your body's detoxification efforts…*

•**Avoid over-the-counter medications when possible.** Many common drugs impair the liver's ability to break down toxic chemicals. Use natural substitutes.

Examples: *Acetaminophen* (Tylenol) depletes the body of *glutathione,* a key detoxification chemical that protects against cancer and boosts immune function. If you take Tylenol daily, work with your doctor to remedy the source of pain, rather than just treating the symptom. Avoid alcohol, which further depletes glutathione from the liver.

Cimetidine (Tagamet), *ranitidine* (Zantac) and similar drugs widely taken for heartburn impair liver function. Instead, learn strategies to avoid heartburn altogether—eat small, low-fat meals, at least three to four hours before lying down…take chewable calcium with each meal…avoid alcohol and coffee.

•**Actively boost your body's natural detoxification capability.** Do this by consuming foods that neutralize carcinogens and other chemicals that damage cells.

Helpful: *Cruciferous* vegetables (such as broccoli, cabbage, brussels sprouts, cauliflower) and those containing *carotenoids* (such as carrots, sweet potatoes, tomatoes).

The herb milk thistle protects and improves the liver's efficiency.

The most toxic environment in your body is the digestive tract. You can help your intestines expel toxins by eating more fiber (from fruits, vegetables and whole grains)…and add fermented foods (such as yogurt) to your diet. This will help maintain the healthy bowel bacteria that break down toxins.

How to Create Your Own Medical Miracle

Bernie Siegel, MD, founder, Exceptional Cancer Patients (ECaP), *www.ecap-online.org*. He is also retired professor of surgery, Yale University School of Medicine, New Haven, CT, and author of several books, including *Help Me to Heal: A Practical Guidebook for Patients, Visitors and Caregivers* (Hay House).

Bernie Siegel, MD, is one of the world's leading proponents of using the mind to help heal the body. As a practicing surgeon, he founded the organization Exceptional Cancer Patients (ECaP) in 1978 to promote the concept of self-healing. His best-selling 1986 book, *Love, Medicine & Miracles*, also addressed this subject.

Dr. Siegel answered some questions on how his ideas have evolved…

●**How has your notion of self-healing changed over the years?** My experiences with thousands of patients have made my convictions even stronger. My concept of self-healing involves the marshaling of all one's available physical and emotional resources in an effort to achieve good health. I work primarily with cancer patients, but the concept is the same with any illness.

The mind's healing power is always available to us—but many people don't make full use of this capacity until they experience a near-fatal accident, disease or illness. Ideally, we should all start unleashing our own healing powers well *before* we get sick.

●**How is that done?** By learning how to love yourself and life—while fully accepting that you're mortal and that life won't last forever. Unfortunately, many people are unable to love themselves because they felt unloved by others at some crucial point in their lives, usually during childhood.

The degree to which we feel loved and accepted as children has a huge impact on our health as adults. People who felt unloved tend to lead destructive lives—looking for the good feelings they didn't get from their parents in the form of food, cigarettes, alcohol or drugs.

In one long-term study, a group of Harvard students was asked to describe their parents. Of those who said their parents were loving and caring, 28% had a major illness over the next 35 years. Of those who said their parents weren't loving, 98% had a major illness over the same period.

In another study, monkeys who were separated from their parents for seven months in infancy and were later exposed to alcohol became alcoholics. Monkeys with a normal upbringing did not become alcoholics when exposed to alcohol.

●**How does someone overcome this lack of love in childhood?** By reparenting yourself or getting someone else to reparent you. This could be a teacher, grandparent or physician—any kind of "coach" who cares about you but can also be constructively critical.

Reparenting means dumping the old negative messages you've learned from parents and teachers and focusing on what's right about you. It also means giving yourself permission to live the life that *you* want to live. All too often, we give up our lives to make others happy. On a practical level, this may mean changing occupations, moving to another town and/or healing or ending relationships.

●**Does reparenting require a special technique?** No. It can take any form you want, including psychotherapy, imagery, meditation, journal writing—anything that helps you listen to the voice within, which tells you what you really want and need. But you have to be willing to work at it.

Reparenting is also an essential part of the doctor–patient relationship. If your doctor is not supportive, doesn't listen to you or doesn't treat you as a human being rather than a disease, you should get another doctor.

•**How does learning to love yourself influence the medical process?** People who love themselves tend to be what I call "exceptional" patients. An exceptional patient is a survivor—someone who refuses to participate in defeat and who chooses to take charge of the healing process. Everyone has the potential to be an exceptional patient, but most of us don't tap into this capacity. Some people have low self-esteem and are afraid to fail. Instead of taking responsibility for their health, they abdicate the responsibility to their doctor.

I've found that about 15% to 20% of all patients have an unconscious—sometimes even a conscious—wish to die. On some level, they welcome serious illness as a way out of their troubles.

Sixty percent to 70% of patients are, in a sense, simply performing for the doctor. They do what they're told, hoping the doctor will do all the work.

Finally, 15% to 20% of patients are what I term exceptional. They refuse to play the victim. They educate themselves about their disease, ask questions of the doctor and demand dignity and control.

In fact, because of their desire to know everything—why a particular test is being done, what the results mean and so on—these patients are often labeled "difficult" by physicians. But studies have found that many so-called "difficult" cancer patients have better survival rates than passive patients who never question the doctor.

•**Is there a scientific explanation for why exceptional patients do better?** Personality and psychology significantly affect the body's chemistry and healing ability. Researchers have found that aggressive, "difficult" patients tend to have more killer T cells (white cells that seek and destroy cancer cells) than submissive, "good" patients.

The validity of the placebo effect is also now widely accepted in the medical community. One-fourth to one-third of all patients will show improvement if they *believe* they are taking an effective medicine.

That's why I support and encourage all my patients who want to try alternative therapies, as long as they've chosen the therapy out of a belief that it will enhance their quality of life rather than from the fear of what will happen if they don't try it.

Hypnosis Heals

Hypnosis helps broken bones heal more quickly. A study of 12 people with broken ankles found that those who received hypnotherapy in addition to the normal treatment of casts and crutches healed more quickly, felt less pain and were better able to walk than those who were given only standard treatment.

Researchers advise people who want to benefit from hypnosis to consult a licensed psychologist or other professional with formal training in medical hypnosis.

Carol S. Ginandes, PhD, clinical instructor in psychology, department of psychiatry, Harvard Medical School, Boston, and principal investigator of the study.

Controlling Chronic Pain with Magnetic Therapy

Ronald M. Lawrence, MD, neurologist in private practice in Agoura Hills, CA. He is president of the North American Academy of Magnetic Therapy and coauthor of *Magnet Therapy* (Prima Health).

Do magnets have healing power? Alternative practitioners have long been convinced, and recent studies suggest that they may be right.

In a study published in the *Archives of Physical Medicine and Rehabilitation,* researchers at Baylor College of Medicine in Houston found magnets to be more effective than sham magnets at blocking pain caused by post-polio syndrome.*

In the controlled study, 76% of the patients who were treated with a magnet got some de-

*This syndrome, marked by leg pain, affects up to 20% of polio sufferers later in life.

gree of pain relief. Only 18% treated with a sham magnet got relief.

GROWING BODY OF EVIDENCE

In other studies, magnets have proven effective against...

•**Fibromyalgia.** Researchers at Tufts University School of Medicine in Boston showed that magnets help relieve muscle pain caused by this mysterious condition.

In the study, patients who slept on magnetic mattresses experienced greater pain relief than patients who slept on ordinary mattresses.

•**Diabetic neuropathy.** In research conducted at New York Medical College in Valhalla, magnetic foot pads were more effective than nonmagnetic foot pads at relieving numbness, tingling and pain associated with this diabetes-related problem.

Evidence suggests that roughly 80% of chronic pain sufferers could benefit from magnetic therapy. That's true for virtually any form of pain.

HOW MAGNETS RELIEVE PAIN

When held against the skin, magnets relax capillary walls, thereby boosting blood flow to the painful area.

They also help prevent the muscle spasms that underlie many forms of pain—apparently by interfering with muscle contractions. And—they interfere with the electrochemical reactions that take place within nerve cells, impeding their ability to transmit pain messages to the brain.

Of course, chronic pain *can* be controlled with aspirin and other over-the-counter and prescription painkillers. But unlike these pain medications, magnets do not carry any risk of side effects.

SELECTING MEDICAL MAGNETS

Medical magnets come in a dizzying range of shapes, sizes and strengths. They range in price from about $5 all the way to $900.

It's usually best to start with one or several coin-shaped magnets that are made from a rare earth metal called *neodymium-boron*. For most applications, these "neo" magnets work just as well as—and cost less than—other magnets.

Cost: About $10 each.

Magnetism is measured in *gauss*. A typical refrigerator magnet is about 10 gauss. That's too weak to penetrate the skin—and unlikely to be helpful in treating anything more than a minor bruise.

Medical magnets range in strength from 450 gauss to 10,000 gauss. The higher the gauss, the better the pain relief.

Since magnets aren't always helpful, it's best to purchase yours from a company that offers a money-back guarantee of at least 30 days.

PUTTING MAGNETS TO WORK

The magnet should be affixed to the skin directly over the painful area. Some people use ordinary adhesive bandages to affix the magnets. But *Transpore*—a paper tape made by 3M—works better. It holds well, and it doesn't pull the hairs from the skin when it's removed.

If the magnet fails to provide relief within a few days, reposition the magnet over the nearest acupuncture point. To locate these points on the body, consult a book on acupuncture.

If repositioning the magnet fails to bring relief within 30 days, odds are it's not going to work. Switch to another type of magnet... or speak with your doctor about using pain-killing medication or another conventional approach.

•**Aching feet.** Magnetic insoles can relieve foot pain and the achy feeling in the legs after you've been standing all day.

•**Arthritis.** If pain is limited to your fingers, a neo magnet taped to the affected joint should do the trick. Or—you can wear a magnetic wristband.

For fibromyalgia discomfort or for arthritis pain throughout the body, a magnetic mattress is usually best. If the $900 cost is too much for you, opt for a magnetic mattress pad.

Cost: $250 to $500.

•**Back pain.** Place four magnets about one-and-a-half inches on either side of the spine, two per side. If applying and removing several magnets proves troublesome, use a three- to four-inch ceramic strip magnet...or a magnetic back brace.

●**Headache.** Tape magnets to your temples…or to the back of your head, just above the neck. Or—use a magnetic headband.

●**Tennis elbow.** Use a magnetic band around the elbow. The same band also relieves hand and arm pain caused by repetitive strain injury.

Magnet Dangers

Magnets used to treat arthritis and other joint problems can cause implanted pacemakers and defibrillators to malfunction.

Placed in mattress pads by arthritis sufferers to ease joint pain during sleep, a magnet can change a pacemaker's settings so that it delivers a jolt that can cause cardiac arrest. A magnet can even turn off a defibrillator—with potentially deadly results.

If you have a pacemaker or defibrillator: Talk to your doctor before using magnets for any condition. Be careful around stereo speakers, too—some contain strong magnets.

Good news: Magnets that are worn around a person's lower arms, legs or waist—at least six inches from the pacemaker or defibrillator—are not close enough to the devices to cause cardiac problems.

Thomas A. Mattioni, MD, director, clinical cardiac electrophysiology laboratory, Arizona Heart Hospital, Phoenix.

 # Hand Reflexology

Bill Flocco, founder and director, American Academy of Reflexology, Burbank, CA, *www.americanacademy ofreflexology.com* and past president, International Council of Reflexologists. *www.icr-reflexology.org.* He is author of numerous teaching manuals on reflexology.

The devotees of hand reflexology maintain that there is a "map" of the human body on our hands. Every part of the body is matched by a corresponding "reflex point" on the fingers, palms and backs and edges of the hands.

Applying pressure to these reflex points stimulates nerve impulses that travel indirectly to the corresponding body areas. These impulses help muscles relax, open blood vessels, increase circulation and allow in more oxygen and nutrients—key facilitators of healing.

American physician William Fitzgerald, MD, introduced this therapy in his 1917 book, *Zone Therapy.* The technique soon expanded to include foot reflexology and is now used by thousands of "reflexologists."

For quick and effective relief of pain and muscle tension, the hands remain the primary area for reflexology.

Caution: Don't do hand reflexology if you have a hand injury. If you have any medical problem, consult a doctor first.

THE BASICS

Apply gentle pressure to the reflex points on your hand, using the *thumb roll* technique.

To work the reflex points on your left palm, place the fingers of your right hand on the back of your left.

Place the pad of your right thumb on your left palm.

Squeeze gently, pressing in with the thumb. As you press, bend the thumb so that the tip slowly rolls forward and downward. Maintaining contact between the right thumb and left palm, straighten the thumb so that it moves forward about one-eighth of an inch over the reflex area. Repeat this thumb rolling movement, gradually working the entire reflex area.

Use the same technique to work the palm or fingers. To work reflex points on your right hand, perform the thumb roll with your left. If your nails are long, use the sides of your thumb rather than the tip.

Reflex areas should be worked for at least five minutes. Work a broad area around the specified reflex points. Benefits should be felt in one or two sessions.

EYESTRAIN

The eye reflex points are at the base of the index, middle and ring fingers—the metatarsal phalangeal joints or "big knuckles." Thumb roll directly on these knuckles—as well as just above and below the knuckles—on both sides of both hands.

SORE SHOULDERS

The shoulder reflex points are on the backs of the hands in the grooves between the long bones. To work them, use your fingertips.

If your left shoulder is the problem, work the reflex points on your left hand. Put your right thumb flat on your left palm.

On the back of your left hand, place the tips of your right index, middle and ring fingers in the grooves. Gently apply and maintain even pressure, slowly and repeatedly moving your fingertips in the direction of the wrist.

If your right shoulder is the problem, work the reflex points on your right hand.

STOMACH UPSET

The soft portion of each palm—below the big knuckles—contains many reflex points for the digestive system. The stomach reflex points are mostly on the left palm. For stomach upset and heartburn, use the thumb roll to work the palm just beneath the large knuckles at the base of the index, middle and ring fingers.

Start by applying light pressure and gradually increase the pressure.

NECK PAIN

The neck's main reflex points are on the lower half of the thumbs. Thumb roll the area between the two knuckles of each thumb. The rolling thumb should roll from pad to tip, so that you apply sufficient pressure all the way around the area.

CARPAL TUNNEL SYNDROME

This painful, sometimes immobilizing hand and wrist condition often results from repetitive stress on the median nerve as it passes through the wrist. Working reflex points for the forearm can reduce pain. These reflex points are on the outer edges of the hands, midway between the base of the pinkie and wrist.

Thumb roll this area on whichever arm has the problem.

Caution: Although reflexology can help ease pain for carpal tunnel syndrome, the condition is potentially serious. If you have symptoms, see a doctor.

BACK PAIN

Reflex points for the spine are on the inner edge of the hand, from the bottom of the thumb to the wrist. Thumb roll this area on both hands. Reflex points for the lower back are toward the wrist.

FINDING A REFLEXOLOGIST

Self-care with hand reflexology provides many benefits, but for long-term results, certified practitioners are best.

Search the Internet, using the key word "reflexology" and the name of your state...or look in the Yellow Pages under "Reflexology." You can also call the American Reflexology Certification Board (ARCB) in Gulfport, FL, at 303-933-6921 for a referral to a certified reflexologist in your area or log on to *www.arcb.net.*

Ideally, your practitioner should be certified by the ARCB. It provides an independent testing and certification service.

Drug-Free Strategies for Irritable Bowel Problems

Geoffrey Turnbull, MD, associate professor of medicine, Dalhousie University and Queen Elizabeth II Health Sciences Center, both in Halifax, Nova Scotia. He is coauthor of *IBS Relief—A Complete Approach to Managing Irritable Bowel Syndrome* (John Wiley & Sons).

Are you frequently constipated? Do you suffer from abdominal pain, bloating and/or other digestive problems?

If so, you may be among the estimated 30 million Americans who suffer from *irritable bowel syndrome* (IBS).

IBS is not dangerous. However, the symptoms it causes can make life very unpleasant.

While there's no cure for IBS, nine out of 10 cases can be controlled via simple lifestyle strategies. Sadly, only half of all IBS sufferers ever consult a doctor.

TELLTALE SYMPTOMS

IBS typically strikes during one's twenties or thirties. The most common symptom is pain in the lower abdomen.

The pain often becomes intense during a bowel movement, then subsides...only to recur a few minutes later.

Caution: Abdominal pain that lingers after a bowel movement could be a sign of colitis, colon cancer or another serious ailment.

Other IBS symptoms include...

•**Constipation...**or episodes of loose bowel movements. These episodes typically occur every few weeks or so and last a few days.

A change in bowel habits that persists for weeks may indicate colitis, Crohn's disease or some other serious disorder.

•**Abdominal bloating or swelling.** This typically gets worse during the day, then disappears at night.

•**Sensation of incomplete emptying** after having a bowel movement.

•**Mucus in the stool.** Contrary to what many people think, mucus in the stool is not necessarily a sign of serious disease. Mucus mixed with blood, however, is often symptomatic of colitis.

If you're having any troublesome bowel symptoms, see a doctor right away. He/she should take a full history and conduct diagnostic tests to rule out more serious problems.

To augment any IBS treatments recommended by your doctor, consider trying the following self-help strategies...

DIET MODIFICATION

The first step in controlling IBS is to drink lots of water—at least eight eight-ounce glasses per day. *It's also essential to adopt a healthy diet that includes...*

•**Six to 11 daily servings of whole-grain bread,** whole wheat or bran cereal, brown rice or pasta.

•**Three to five daily servings of vegetables** (raw or cooked).

•**Two to four daily servings of fruit.**

•**Two or three daily servings of nonfat milk,** yogurt or cheese.

•**Two or three daily servings of meat,** poultry, fish, eggs, beans or nuts.

These dietary guidelines help ensure that you get all necessary nutrients and enough dietary fiber.

The body needs at least 20 grams (g) of fiber every day to regulate bowel function. The average American gets only eight to 10 g.

RETHINKING EATING HABITS

Irritable bowel syndrome often goes hand in hand with bad eating habits.

Examples: Skipping meals...eating too fast...overeating...and/or substituting burgers, fries, potato chips and other fatty foods for more wholesome foods.

To minimize IBS symptoms, plan sufficient time for meals...eat fast food no more than once a week...eat three meals a day...and eat only until you feel full.

Pay particular attention to how much you eat at parties and family gatherings. Overeating is often encouraged at these events.

Healthful snacks: Wheat bran muffins, whole wheat crackers, cereal, fresh or canned fruit, pretzels, baked potatoes, rice or pudding.

AVOIDING TRIGGER FOODS

IBS symptoms often arise following the consumption of certain foods. These "trigger" foods generally vary from person to person. *Common ones include...*

•**Raw vegetables.**

•**Cooked vegetables**—brussels sprouts, corn, broccoli, cauliflower, cabbage, onions and sauerkraut. (Cooked potatoes, beets, asparagus, green beans, peas, spinach, squash and zucchini are generally safe.)

•**Beans and lentils.**

•**Cantaloupe,** honeydew melon and unpeeled apples. (Peeled apples, oranges, nectarines, peaches, pears, ripe bananas, grapefruit and kiwi are generally safe.)

•**Beer.**

•**Coffee,** tea and other beverages that contain caffeine.

To pinpoint your trigger foods, keep a food/symptom diary for two weeks. After each meal, use blue ink to record all the foods and beverages you just consumed. Include the amounts and how each food was prepared. Use red ink to record any symptoms that occur during this time.

At the end of the two-week period, review your diary. Notice if any food or foods might be causing your symptoms.

Good news: In many cases, it's possible to continue eating a trigger food *without* experiencing IBS symptoms—if you eat smaller quantities...drink extra water...consume more fiber ...and/or avoid eating other trigger foods at the same time.

STRESS REDUCTION

Psychological stress causes muscles to tighten and raises heart rate and breathing rate. It also triggers the release of stress hormones.

Collectively, these physiological changes may disrupt the delicate rhythm of your body's digestive system.

Stress reduction is often highly effective at controlling IBS. In some instances, all that's required is regular exercise—perhaps just a 20-minute walk every day.

Other effective stress-reducing strategies...

• **Make a stress list.** Jot down all the sources of stress in your life. Rate each on a scale from 1 (not upsetting) to 10 (extremely upsetting).

Put an "A" beside *acute* stresses tied to specific events. Put a "C" beside *chronic* stresses, situations that have no foreseeable end.

Chronic stresses with high numerical ratings are the ones you should work hardest at alleviating in your life.

• **Keep a stress diary.** For two weeks, record any bowel symptoms, along with the stresses of the day and how they could have affected you.

• **Try deep breathing.** Sit up straight. Place one hand on your stomach, the other on your chest. Inhale through your nose as you press your stomach out. Then exhale through your mouth, pulling your stomach back in.

• **Be more assertive.** One of the most common sources of stress is a lack of assertiveness. Someone asks you to do something and you agree to do it—even though you lack the time or inclination to do it.

The next time someone tries to get you to do something you'd rather not do, become a "broken record." Restate your wishes, word for word, in response to each of the attempts at persuasion.

Natural Relief for Crohn's Disease and IBS

Peppermint oil relieves the painful cramping brought on by Crohn's disease and *irritable bowel syndrome* (IBS).

Helpful: Place one drop of the oil in a cup of warm water, add some sugar, if desired, and drink the mixture 15 to 30 minutes before eating—or when symptoms begin.

Warning: Don't take peppermint oil without water, and stop taking the mixture if it causes heartburn. Peppermint oil can be purchased at most health food stores.

Timothy Koch, MD, chief, section of gastroenterology, West Virginia University School of Medicine, Morgantown.

Natural Way to Treat Constipation

Corn syrup, long used as a folk remedy, will draw water into the bowels to soften stools, making them easier to pass.

Recipe: Drink one tablespoon of corn syrup stirred into a glass of warm water twice a day for one or two days.

Caution: Don't use this remedy if you're diabetic, dehydrated or taking diuretic medication, such as *furosemide* (Lasix) or *triamterene* and *triamterene hydrochlorothiazide* (Maxzide, Dyazide).

Victor S. Sierpina, MD, associate professor of family medicine, University of Texas Medical Branch, Galveston.

Anti-Diarrhea Root

Annemarie Colbin, PhD, certified health education specialist and founder, Natural Gourmet Institute for Health & Culinary Arts, New York City. She is author of several books, including *Food and Our Bones: The Natural Way to Prevent Osteoporosis* (Plume).

Most Southerners are only too familiar with kudzu. This hardy vine—which was imported from Japan a century ago to control soil erosion—has flourished in the South's warm climate, spreading relentlessly over gardens, lawns and houses.

It turns out that the root of this pesky plant has medicinal value. Cooked into a thick broth, it soothes and relaxes the gastrointestinal tract, providing relief from indigestion, heartburn and diarrhea.

Kudzu can also help relieve psychological stress. There's even some evidence that it relieves cravings for alcohol.

Unlike conventional drugs, kudzu provides relief without causing unpleasant side effects. Over-the-counter diarrhea remedies, for example, sometimes lead to constipation.

Kudzu starch is sold in health food stores as *kuzu*—its Japanese name. Pure kuzu is a lumpy white powder. If it's sold as a fine powder, it may be adulterated.

It generally costs $4 to $5 for 3½ ounces.

To prepare kuzu broth: Mix one tablespoon kuzu with one cup cold water until completely dissolved.

Cook on medium heat, stirring continuously. The mixture will thicken and then turn clear upon boiling.

Remove from heat, then add natural soy sauce (shoyu or tamari) to taste—about one tablespoon. Shoyu and tamari are available at health food stores and some supermarkets.

Eat up to one cup of kuzu broth a day until symptoms ease.

Important: If discomfort is severe—or lasts more than two days—consult your doctor.

How to Cure Stomach Ailments Naturally

Rob Pyke, MD, PhD, Ridgefield, CT–based internist and clinical pharmacologist. He is author of *Dr. Pyke's Natural Way to Complete Stomach Relief—Great Foods and Holistic Methods to Cure Your Upper Digestive Tract Forever* (Prentice Hall).

Whether it's heartburn, an ulcer or acid reflux disease, stomach distress is so common that many of us simply learn to live with it. Either that, or we take an over-the-counter (OTC) remedy and hope for the best. Only 10% of people who suffer from stomach problems consult a doctor.

As an internist and clinical pharmacologist, I'm well-versed in the conventional treatment of all gastrointestinal conditions. Prescription drugs are the primary defense. Some doctors may also counsel their patients to reduce stress, exercise regularly and lose weight to ease stomach problems.

But in 1994, my views on gastrointestinal ailments changed drastically—when I became the patient.

I was suffering from gastritis, an inflammation of the stomach lining. I also had heartburn and *gastroesophageal reflux disease* (GERD). That is a condition that results whenever the contents of the stomach "backwash" into the esophagus and cause irritation.

The gastroenterologist I consulted prescribed the medication *omeprazole* (Prilosec). But two weeks later, my condition still had not improved.

A review of the gastrointestinal tract showed hundreds of little holes in my stomach. That was the last straw. I decided to stop being a "passive patient," relying only on what my doctor told me. I researched conventional and alternative treatments and created a self-healing program that addresses the causes—not the symptoms—of stomach problems.

Caution: Before beginning self-treatment, consult a physician about your stomach problem. *This is especially true if you are experiencing symptoms such as...*

• **Stomach pain** that lasts more than one hour twice a week.

• **Loss of appetite** or unwanted weight loss.

• **Blood in your stool** or a darkening of the stool's color.

• **Vomiting episodes** that produce "coffee grounds" (dark matter that contains blood).

• **Difficulty swallowing.**

• **Pain that occurs when using *nonsteroidal anti-inflammatory drugs* (NSAIDs) or** while drinking alcohol or eating spicy foods.

SELF-CARE STRATEGIES

In addition to following your physician's advice, here's how to increase your chances of getting relief from stomach problems...

•**Avoid *all* offending foods.** Most people know the worst stomach offenders—hot peppers, peppermint, chocolate, soda, onions and nuts. But there are less obvious triggers, such as butter, milk, ice cream, coffee and tea. These offenders add or promote stomach acid or open the valve from the stomach to the esophagus, which can result in reflux.

•**Eat the right foods.** Artichokes (try out canned artichoke hearts in salad) and sauerkraut nourish friendly digestive-tract bacteria. Low-fat soy milk and yogurt buffer stomach acid. Papaya and pineapple contain helpful digestive enzymes.

•**Eat six small meals each day instead of three large ones.** You'll produce less stomach acid. Reducing meal size also helps to prevent reflux, the "burp up" sensation that occurs when food and stomach acid back up into the esophagus.

•**Drink no more than one cup of a beverage during each meal.** The more you drink, the more likely your food is to back up into the esophagus. Fluids also dilute digestive enzymes, which convert food into molecules that can be easily absorbed by the intestine.

Important: Drink at least eight eight-ounce glasses of water daily. Be sure to drink them between your meals. This helps dilute residual stomach acid.

•**Take 15 minutes or longer to eat each meal.** Most of us don't chew our food well enough. This means that large pieces of food enter the stomach, which can promote indigestion and cause the stomach to empty slowly. This results in excess acid and more opportunity for reflux to develop. Thoroughly chewing your food leads to better digestion.

•**Watch your body position.** To prevent indigestion and reflux, stay upright for at least two hours after eating.

To help stomach patients avoid nighttime reflux, many doctors suggest placing wooden blocks under the feet at the head of the bed.

This can work—but if you move around, you run the risk of knocking the bed off the blocks.

Better way: Get a five- or six-foot wedge of foam from a medical-supply store. The foam should be four inches thick at the head and gradually taper down. Wrap it in a small mattress cover.

Bonus: The wedge enables you to adjust only your side of the bed without disturbing your partner.

•**Ask your doctor about using vitamin supplements and herbs.** Taking certain vitamins and herbs helps prevent and treat stomach conditions.

To decrease stomach acid, consider taking 400 international units (IU) of vitamin E daily. Vitamin C (250 milligrams daily in buffered or ester form) helps heal stomach ulcers.

Important: Ask your doctor about taking these in addition to a regular multivitamin, especially because taking more than 200 IU of vitamin E may be dangerous.

Deglycyrrhizinated licorice, aloe vera and chamomile with catnip can also ease stomach upset. These are available at health food stores as capsules, gels, liquids or tea bags. Follow label instructions.

Quick Herbal Relief for Indigestion

Rosemary is often effective in treating indigestion, gas and bloating.

For best results: Take as a tea or tincture 15 minutes *before* eating. That helps maximize the effect of the herb's bitter compounds, which promotes the flow of digestive juices.

To prepare the tea: Add one teaspoon of dried rosemary to one cup of boiling water. Steep for 10 minutes, then strain. Or, add 10 to 20 drops of tincture to one cup of water.

Chanchal Cabrera, herbalist in private practice, Vancouver, BC, and member, American Herbalist Guild, Canton, GA.

Natural Treatment for Indigestion

More than 60% of people who drank a glass of carbonated water daily experienced a reduction in bloating, nausea, belching, pain and other symptoms of indigestion and constipation, according to a two-week study.

Theory: Carbonated water will stimulate the *proximal* (or upper part) of the stomach, which promotes more efficient digestion. Carbonated water may also increase the efficiency of gallbladder emptying.

If you suffer from indigestion and constipation: Ask your doctor if drinking carbonated water—in addition to other treatment strategies, such as a high-fiber diet—may be beneficial.

Rosario Cuomo, MD, professor, clinical and experimental medicine, University of Naples "Federico II," Naples, Italy.

Breathing Your Way to Better Health

Robert Fried, PhD, director, Stress and Biofeedback Clinic, Albert Ellis Institute, New York City. He is author of many books, including *Breathe Well, Be Well* (John Wiley & Sons).

Everyone knows that taking a deep breath is a great way to calm down and cool off when you're feeling angry.

And any woman who has used Lamaze breathing during childbirth is aware that focusing on one's breath provides a welcome distraction from severe pain.

But few people realize that how you breathe day in and day out plays a key role in triggering—or preventing—chronic conditions.

Among the conditions that are affected by breathing—high blood pressure...heart disease...migraines...and Raynaud's syndrome, a chronic circulatory disorder marked by uncomfortably cold hands and feet.

THE BREATH–BODY CONNECTION

The world is divided into two types of breathers...

•**Belly breathers** take slow, deep breaths, letting their abdomens rise with each inhalation and fall with each exhalation.

This form of breathing is ideal, but relatively few adults breathe this way.

•**Chest breathers** take rapid, shallow breaths. This form of breathing causes the body to expel too much carbon dioxide, adversely affecting how the blood carries oxygen to the organs and tissues.

To find out which kind of breather you are, sit comfortably and place your left hand on your chest, your right hand over your navel. Breathe normally for one minute. Note the movement of each hand as you inhale and as you exhale.

If your left hand is virtually motionless while your right hand moves out when you inhale and in when you exhale, you're a belly breather.

If your left hand rises noticeably—or if both hands move more or less simultaneously in a shallow motion—you're a chest breather.

Being a chest breather does *not* mean you're going to keel over anytime soon. But eventually, your health will suffer.

Reason: Chest breathing is less effective than belly breathing at introducing fresh, oxygenated air into the lower reaches of the lungs. That's where the tiny air sacs (*alveoli*) that absorb oxygen are most concentrated.

Less air reaching the alveoli means that less oxygen gets into the bloodstream with each breath. To get enough oxygen to meet the body's needs, these people must breathe more rapidly.

Rapid breathing upsets the blood's normal acid–base balance (pH), which is measured on a scale that runs from zero to 14.

Ordinarily, blood has a pH of 7.38 (slightly alkaline). When blood pH climbs above that level, arteries constrict, impairing blood flow to many parts of the body.

Results: Increased susceptibility to high blood pressure...insomnia...anxiety...phobias

...Raynaud's syndrome...migraines...and, for heart patients, angina.

HOW TO BREATHE RIGHT

No matter how poor your current breathing habits may be, it's reassuring to know that each of us was born knowing how to breathe properly. And—it's surprisingly easy to relearn correct breathing habits. *The keys...*

•**Stop sucking in your gut.** A flat stomach may be attractive, but clenching the abdominal muscles inhibits movement of the diaphragm. That's the sheetlike muscle that separates the abdomen from the chest cavity.

Since the movement of the diaphragm is what causes the lungs to fill and empty, proper breathing is possible only if it can move freely.

•**Avoid tight clothing.** Like clenching your abdominal muscles, wearing overly tight clothing can restrict movement of the diaphragm.

•**Breathe through your nose.** Doing so makes hyperventilation almost impossible. The only time you should breathe through your mouth is during vigorous exercise.

•**Practice belly breathing.** At least twice a day—for about four minutes each time—sit in a comfortable chair with your left hand on your chest, your right hand on your abdomen.

As you inhale, use your left hand to press lightly against your chest to help keep it from rising. Allow your right hand to move outward as air fills your belly.

With each exhalation, slowly pull your abdomen back in as far as it will go without raising your chest. With practice, your body will find its own natural rhythm.

Good idea: Practice belly breathing when you're stuck in traffic, waiting in line, etc.—whenever and wherever you can. It's a good use for time that would otherwise be wasted. Once you get the hang of it, practice belly breathing without using your hands.

You may want to augment the effects of these practice sessions by combining belly breathing with...

•Classical music. Stick with slow compositions, such as Pachelbel's *Canon* or Bach's *Jesu, Joy of Man's Desiring.* As you breathe, imagine that you are inhaling the music...and that it is filling every space in your body.

•Muscle relaxation. Imagine that the tension in the muscles in your forehead is flowing out of your body with each exhalation. Do the same thing, breath by breath, with your jaw, neck, shoulders, arms, hands, legs and feet.

•Imagery. Close your eyes, and imagine yourself standing on a sunny beach. Feel the warmth of the sun. As you inhale, imagine the surf rolling toward your feet. As you exhale, picture the surf rolling back out to sea.

•**Do on-the-spot breathing therapy.** Once you've mastered belly breathing, you're ready to start using breathing as an instant feel-better tool.

A few deep belly breaths can dissipate anxiety...ward off an impending panic attack or migraine...restore circulation to cold, numb fingers and toes...and help ease you to sleep if you're experiencing insomnia.

If you're diligent about practicing belly breathing, it should become second nature. For most people, the change takes about six weeks.

Caution: Breathing exercises are safe for most people. But if you've recently suffered an injury or had surgery, check with your doctor.

Certain disorders, such as heart disease, kidney disease and diabetes, lead to rapid breathing to compensate for chemical changes in the body. If you suffer from one of these ailments, slow breathing may be unsafe.

Aromatherapy... For Much More than Just Pleasant Smells

Jane Buckle, RN, PhD, director, RJ Buckle Associates LLC, Hunter, NY, a company that teaches aromatherapy and other complementary techniques to health care professionals. *www.rjbuckle.com.* She is author of *Clinical Aromatherapy in Nursing* (Arnold).

When you hear the word "aromatherapy," it probably makes you think of pouring a scented bath or lighting a fragrant candle.

But medical practitioners in the US and else-where around the world are using distilled oils of aromatic plants medicinally. Essential oils activate the parasympathetic nervous system, causing relaxation, which speeds healing.

AROMATHERAPY IN ACTION

Plant oils can be used in a warm bath…a "carrier oil"—such as almond or sesame oil—for massage…or a lotion.

The oil aromas can also be sniffed from a bottle…a cotton ball…or a *diffuser*—a machine that emits the aroma into the air.

Clinical and scientific studies support the use of aromatherapy as an adjunct to medical care for treating…

●**Anxiety.** Essential oils that were inhaled for three minutes relieved anxiety in men and women, according to research in the *International Journal of Neuroscience.* Use rosemary, Roman chamomile or patchouli.

Typical treatment: Sniff one to three drops when anxious.

Caution: Avoid using rosemary if you have high blood pressure.

●**Bronchitis.** Use spike lavender.

Typical treatment: One drop of spike lavender in a bowl of three cups of boiling water. Drape a towel over your head, close your eyes and inhale the steam. Do this for five minutes, four times a day.

●**Hair loss.** In people with patchy hair loss due to *alopecia areata,* essential oils helped restore hair growth, according to an *Archives of Dermatology* study that used a carrier oil containing a mixture of thyme (two drops), rosemary (three drops), lavender (three drops) and cedarwood (two drops).

Typical treatment: Massage the mixture into scalp for two minutes every day.

●**Headache.** Use peppermint. If pain isn't gone in five minutes, try Roman chamomile or true lavender.

Typical treatment: Five drops in one teaspoon of carrier oil. Apply to temples or sniff.

●**Hot flashes.** Use clary sage, fennel, geranium or rose.

Typical treatment: 10 drops in two cups of water in a spray bottle. Spray on your face during hot flashes.

●**Insomnia.** Use ylang ylang, neroli or rose.

Typical treatment: Five drops in a diffuser placed in the bedroom.

●**Low back pain.** Use lemongrass. If you get no relief in 20 minutes, try rosemary or spike lavender.

Typical treatment: Five drops in one teaspoon of carrier oil. Apply to the painful area every three hours.

●**Menstrual cramps.** Use geranium.

Typical treatment: Five drops added to one teaspoon of carrier oil. Rub on the lower abdomen and low back every three hours.

●**Muscle spasms.** Use clary sage, sage or lavender.

Typical treatment: Five drops added to one teaspoon of carrier oil. Apply to the affected muscles at least every three hours.

●**Osteoarthritis.** Use frankincense, rosemary or true lavender.

Typical treatment: Five drops added to one teaspoon of carrier oil. Apply to the painful area every three hours.

WHAT TO BUY

Aromatherapy is most effective when the essential oils are prepared with no extraneous ingredients.

Good brands include Northwest Essence (*www.rejuvthespa.com*) and Scents & Scentsibility (*www.scentsibility.com*). They are also available in health food stores.

USING AROMATHERAPY SAFELY

Some essential oils can irritate or burn skin if applied undiluted. Always dilute before using topically. If skin stings or becomes red, dilute with a plain carrier oil and wash with unperfumed soap.

Caution: The oils are flammable. Store away from candles, fires, cigarettes and stoves. Don't pour oil on lightbulbs to scent a room.

Essential oils can be lethal when ingested—even in tiny doses. Keep away from children and pets. Pregnant women and people with asthma or epilepsy should consult their doctor before using aromatherapy.

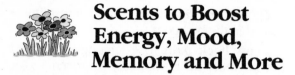

Scents to Boost Energy, Mood, Memory and More

Alan Hirsch, MD, founder and neurological director, Smell & Taste Treatment and Research Foundation, Chicago. He is a neurologist and psychiatrist, and author of *Life's a Smelling Success* (Authors of Unity) and *What Flavor Is Your Personality?* (Sourcebooks).

Scents stimulate important mental and physical functions. They trigger the release of neurotransmitters, chemicals that send signals to the brain. *What scents can do for you...*

CONTROL APPETITE

In a study of 105 people, we found that those who inhaled a chocolate-like aroma whenever they felt like eating lost nearly three pounds in two weeks. Another study of 3,193 volunteers found that sniffing banana, green apple or peppermint scents resulted in an average weight loss of 30 pounds in six months.

Sniff these scents often, and remember to smell every food before you eat it. Your brain will perceive that you're eating more, thus suppressing your appetite.

INCREASE ENERGY

These odors stimulate the part of the brain that promotes wakefulness...

●**Jasmine** causes an increase in beta waves in the brain, a sign of alertness. Jasmine tea is a great pick-me-up.

●**Strawberries and buttered popcorn** will cause exercisers to burn more calories.

●**Peppermint** works on sensory nerves and increases alertness. Try a peppermint candy or chewing gum.

●**Freshly brewed coffee** is very stimulating, probably because we associate the aroma with the energizing effects of caffeine.

BOOST ROMANCE

Both men and women are sexually stimulated by scents, but the odors that arouse them aren't the same.

For men: The smell of lavender or pumpkin pie increases blood flow to the penis by about 40%. The smell of doughnuts, black licorice, vanilla or women's perfume (any scent) also is sexually stimulating to men.

For women: The odors of cucumber and licorice are stimulating. Women are turned off by the smells of cherries, barbecued meat and men's cologne.

REDUCE ANXIETY

Fresh, natural scents generally induce calm. In one study we conducted, volunteers became extremely anxious when they were confined in coffin-like tubes, but then calmed down when the tubes were infused with the smells of green apple and cucumber. These odors seem to have an impact on the limbic system, the emotional center of the brain.

If you anticipate a situation in which you will feel anxious, wash your hair that morning with a green-apple–scented shampoo and/or put a dab of the shampoo in a cloth to take with you.

IMPROVE MEMORY

People who sniff floral scents increase retention of new material by 17%.

Sniff a floral odor when learning new material, then smell it again when you want to recall it. This is known as *state-dependent learning.* The material you learn in one state—while smelling roses—will be more accessible when you replicate that state in the future.

Natural Decongestant

To quickly unstuff your nose, sniff horseradish. It contains *allyl isothiocyanate,* a compound similar to the active ingredient in decongestants. Take a sniff two or three times daily. Keep your nose six inches from the jar, and don't spread your germs by breathing directly onto it. Better yet, keep a separate jar for decongestant purposes.

Caution: If sinus congestion lasts for more than a week, or is accompanied by green mucus, postnasal drip, pain or toothache, be sure to see your doctor.

Sanford M. Archer, MD, associate professor of otolaryngology, University of Kentucky Medical Center, Lexington.

14

Aging & Longevity

Secrets of Maximum Longevity

 **A** generation ago, extreme old age was rare. But today, more than 75,000 people in the US have reached age 100 or older. Antiaging researchers predict that humans may soon be living to age 120...or even 150.

What determines life span? Luck plays a role. So does heredity. But emerging research demonstrates the critical importance of three other factors—each of which lies completely within our control. *They are...*

•**Healthful lifestyle.** Keeping up a good diet and regular exercise, someone who has average "longevity genes" can expect to live to roughly the age of 75.

•**Nutritional supplements.** People who consume optimal levels of several key vitamins and minerals can generally expect to live an extra 10 to 15 years.

EATING FOR LONGEVITY

Nutritionists have long recommended minimizing the consumption of caffeine, sugar, fat and salt...while eating at least five servings per day of fresh fruits and vegetables.

That's good advice—as far as it goes. *But some foods are especially conducive to longevity...*

•**Soy foods.** Soybeans are rich in antioxidants. These compounds neutralize free radicals, substances that accelerate aging by causing cellular damage.

One antioxidant in soy, *genistein,* has been shown to prevent cancer. It also blocks formation of fatty deposits along artery walls.

This process, known as *atherosclerosis,* is the main cause of heart attack and stroke.

Optimal intake: 50 to 75 milligrams (mg) of soy protein per day. That's equal to one cup of soy milk or three servings of tofu.

Ronald Klatz, MD, DO, president, American Academy of Anti-Aging Medicine, 1510 W. Montana St., Chicago 60614. He is coauthor of *Stopping the Clock: Dramatic Breakthroughs in Anti-Aging and Age Reversal Techniques* (Keats).

●**Garlic.** In addition to boosting immune function and lowering LDL ("bad") cholesterol levels, garlic helps prevent cancer and acts as an antibiotic.

It's even a mild anticoagulant, so it helps reduce the risk for stroke and heart attack.

Optimal intake: Two or three cloves...a teaspoon of garlic powder...or four 300-mg garlic capsules three times a day.

●**Onions.** Red and yellow varieties contain *quercetin,* an antioxidant that deactivates carcinogens and prevents blood clots. It also boosts HDL ("good") cholesterol levels while lowering levels of both LDL cholesterol and triglycerides.

Optimal intake: One medium-sized red or yellow onion per day.

It's also essential to drink a lot of water—ideally eight eight-ounce glasses each day.

THE LONGEVITY LIFESTYLE

A nine-year study completed recently at Stanford University found that most people who live past age 100...

●**Sleep seven to eight hours a night.**

●**Always eat breakfast.**

●**Avoid smoking.**

●**Exercise regularly.**

●**Consume little or no alcohol.** Moderate drinking—no more than two drinks per day with meals—helps prevent heart disease in older people. But if you're younger than 45, the risk of alcohol-induced liver trouble or other illness outweighs the benefits to the heart.

Anyone who has a history of liver damage should avoid alcohol.

●**Avoid excessive weight gain or loss.** Men should weigh no more than 20% over their ideal weight, women no more than 10% over their ideal weight.

●**Eat sugary snacks infrequently,** if at all. They can cause blood sugar levels to fluctuate, and that can contribute to blood sugar abnormalities.

VITAL ANTIOXIDANTS

Many doctors maintain that vitamin and mineral supplements are unnecessary, as long as one eats a wholesome diet. Recent research suggests otherwise.

Finding I: In a Harvard Medical School study of 14,000 physicians, consuming high doses of vitamins C and E and beta-carotene were associated with a nearly 50% reduction in heart disease.

Finding II: In a study from Australia, the survival rate was 12 times higher among breast cancer patients who consumed high levels of beta-carotene than among breast cancer patients who consumed low levels of beta-carotene.

What level of supplementation is best? *Recent studies point to the following daily dosages...*

●**Vitamin C...**500 to 1,500 mg of *calcium ascorbate.*

●**Vitamin E...**100 to 400 international units (IU) of mixed tocopherols. Check with your doctor for the proper amount to take.

●**Beta-carotene...**10,000 IU.

●**Selenium...**100 to 200 micrograms (mcg). People who rarely eat cereal or nuts should also take a magnesium supplement—200 to 300 mg per day.

People age 50 or older should add 30 mg of *coenzyme Q-10* a day. This key nutrient helps prevent heart attack.

HORMONE THERAPY

The slow physical decline associated with aging is caused in part by falling levels of estrogen, testosterone and other key hormones.

Via hormone therapy, it's possible to raise these hormones to their youthful levels.

●**Testosterone replacement therapy (TRT)** boosts the sex drive and strengthens bones in men and women alike.

But TRT is suspected of raising the risk for prostate enlargement and prostate cancer.

●**Melatonin therapy** has been shown to extend the life span of mice by up to 25%.

Melatonin lowers LDL cholesterol levels and shows promise as a treatment for diabetes, cataracts and Alzheimer's disease.

●**DHEA therapy** boosts immune function and appears to fight cancer, heart disease, Alzheimer's disease, diabetes and osteoporosis.

Caution: Hormone therapy should be strictly supervised by a physician. For help in locating a qualified practitioner, visit the American Academy of Anti-Aging Medicine Web site at *www. worldhealth.net,* or fax your request to the Academy at 773-528-5390.

Are You Aging Too Fast?

The late Roy L. Walford, MD, former professor of pathology, University of California at Los Angeles School of Medicine. Dr. Walford was recognized internationally as one of the top experts in the field of gerontology. He published more than 350 scientific articles and six books, including *Beyond the 120-Year Diet* (Four Walls Eight Windows).

Self-tests are an easy way to determine your *functional age*—a measurement of how a person actually functions, rather than how many years he/she has been alive.

• **Elasticity test.** This measures the degree of deterioration of the connective tissue under the skin, a sign of aging.

Pinch the skin on the back of your hand between your thumb and forefinger for five seconds, then time how long it takes to flatten out completely.

Up to age 50, it will take about five seconds …by age 60, the average time is 10 to 15 seconds…by age 70, the typical time will be 35 to 55 seconds.

• **Static balance test.** How long can you stand on one leg with your eyes closed before falling over?

Perform this test either barefoot or wearing low-heeled shoes. Stand on a hard surface (not a rug) with both feet together and close your eyes. Lift your foot six inches off the ground, bending your knee at about a 45-degree angle. (If you're right-handed, stand on your left leg. Left-handers should stand on the right leg.) Have a partner close by to catch you in case you fall. Do the test three times, and calculate the average.

On average, a 100% decline occurs from age 20 to age 80. Most young people are able to stand for 30 seconds or more. Few older people will be able to hold the pose for longer than a few seconds.

If your self-test results do not fall within the normal range for your age, consult your doctor for specific advice on how to minimize the effects of aging.

Antiaging Strategies for Your Body and Mind

David W. Johnson, PhD, associate professor and department chair of physiology, University of New England College of Osteopathic Medicine, Biddeford, ME. He is author of *Feel 30 for the Next 50 Years* (Avon Books).

The aging process starts earlier than many people realize. Even if you're only 35 years old and have no symptoms of disease, microscopic damage is already occurring in the cells of your major organs.

But progressive damage to the body can be delayed. A multipronged program helps to reduce the risk for heart disease, cancer and other major ailments.

It may also slow the rate at which people develop "normal" problems of aging, such as hearing loss, vision loss, memory problems, etc.

ANTIOXIDANTS

As you may already know, antioxidants are compounds that deactivate *free radicals,* highly reactive molecules that attack cell membranes, proteins and even our DNA.

Free radicals have been implicated in heart disease, cancer and dementia.

Recent evidence suggests that free radicals are also responsible for the gradual decline of the immune system, which leaves older people increasingly vulnerable to infection. So far, four antioxidants seem to be especially beneficial…

• **Carotenoids.** These fat-soluble antioxidants help protect cell membranes.

To boost carotenoid levels in your body, eat more sweet potatoes and other red and yellow vegetables…and take a supplement containing 50 milligrams (mg) of mixed carotenoids every other day.

●**Vitamin E.** This fat-soluble antioxidant has been shown to protect the heart and brain... and to enhance the immune system.

It's hard to get enough vitamin E from grains and other food sources without also getting too much fat. For this reason, it's best to rely on a supplement. The usual dosage is 200 international units (IU) per day. Check with your doctor for the appropriate amount.

●**Vitamin C.** This water-soluble antioxidant —found primarily in citrus fruits—protects parts of cells that vitamin E and carotenoids can't reach. The usual dosage is 500 mg every other day.

●**Selenium.** This mineral, found primarily in seafood and liver, plays a pivotal role in neutralizing free radicals. Yet many Americans are deficient in selenium. The usual dosage is 200 micrograms (mcg) every other day.

In addition to these antioxidants, it's often a good idea to take supplements of folic acid (1 mg per day)...coenzyme Q-10 (50 mg per day)...and zinc (20 mg per day). Discuss the matter with your doctor.

A STRONG BODY

Why do people tend to get weaker and more easily fatigued as they grow older? For most of us, it's simply that our muscle mass has gotten smaller.

Aging-related muscle shrinkage is known as *sarcopenia*. Most cases of sarcopenia result not from the passage of time, but from disuse— lack of exercise, in other words.

In addition to maintaining strength and vigor, physical activity lowers the risk for heart disease, diabetes, osteoporosis, depression and certain types of cancer.

Exercise also helps prevent hip fracture, which can be debilitating for older people.

For decades now, doctors have been urging their patients to get regular aerobic exercise. That includes running, fast walking, bicycling, swimming and other activities that raise your pulse for an extended period of time.*

*Your goal in doing aerobic exercise should be to raise your heart rate to 50% to 80% of its maximum for at least 20 minutes a day, at least three days a week. To estimate your maximum heart rate, subtract your age in years from 220.

And, while aerobic exercise is essential, we now know that strength training (weight-lifting) is equally important.

Use free weights (dumbbells, barbells, etc.) or exercise machines to build muscle in your arms, legs and torso.

Start with a weight that you can lift eight times in a controlled movement. The last two repetitions should cause a burning sensation in your muscles. Rest for three minutes, then do another set. Gradually work your way up to three sets of 15 reps.

A SOUND MIND

The same antioxidants that help prevent heart disease and cancer—vitamin E in particular— also seem to prevent aging-related changes in the brain.

There's no indication that antioxidants improve thinking ability. But research on a family of cognition-enhancing compounds known as *nootropics* (Greek for "mind turning") has shown that these compounds can improve memory in certain individuals.

Two nootropics—each sold over-the-counter —seem especially beneficial...

●**Ginkgo biloba.** This herbal extract has been shown to improve memory and to shorten reaction times. It has also been shown to be effective in those diagnosed with early Alzheimer's disease, but this result is not definitive.

Typical dosage: 100 mg twice a day.

●**Phosphatidylserine.** This compound, derived from plants, helps stabilize cell membranes in the brain and facilitates communication between brain cells (neurons).

Researchers have noted improvements in attention, memory and concentration in individuals who take phosphatidylserine daily.

Typical dosage: 100 mg twice a day.

"Use it or lose it" applies to the brain as well as to the muscles. Solving complex problems, memorizing things and otherwise giving your brain a workout seem to stimulate neurons to form new connections. This process helps compensate for the neurons that die or become dysfunctional each day.

If your daily life involves few short-term memory skills, add some "memory games" to your routine.

Example: After watching a nightly news program on television, see how many of the stories you can recall. Have a family member keep track of how you do.

HOW ABOUT HORMONES?

As estrogen and testosterone levels dwindle, so does sex drive.

Falling levels of human growth hormone (hGH) cause muscle wasting.

Declines in the hormone DHEA have been linked to declining energy levels, memory loss and reduced immunity.

Hormone-replacement therapy can restore vitality for some people—particularly older people whose levels have dropped significantly. But it requires close medical supervision. Used unwisely, some types of hormone replacement may promote the growth of prostate cancer and breast cancer.

ANTIAGING HELP

If you'd like to find a physician who can tailor an aggressive antiaging program specifically for you, contact the American Academy of Anti-Aging Medicine at 773-528-1000.

Longevity Boosters From the World's Longest-Lived People

Bradley J. Willcox, MD, principal investigator of geriatrics, Pacific Health Research Institute, Honolulu, HI, and clinical assistant professor of geriatrics, University of Hawaii. He is also coauthor of *The Okinawa Program: How the World's Longest-Lived People Achieve Everlasting Health—and How You Can Too* (Three Rivers Press).

The residents of Okinawa, an island chain of Japan, are among the healthiest and longest-lived people in the world. Okinawa has more 100-year-olds than anywhere else—33.6 per 100,000 people, compared with approximately 10 per 100,000 in the United States.

The 25-year Okinawa Centenarian Study discovered that, compared with Americans, Okinawans have...

- **80% lower risk of breast and prostate cancers.**
- **50% lower risk of colon and ovarian cancers.**
- **40% fewer hip fractures.**
- **Minimal risk of heart disease.**

What's the secret to the Okinawans' longevity—and what can we do to achieve the same healthful vigor? *The following factors are especially important...*

ACCEPTING ATTITUDE

While many Americans have Type A personalities, Okinawans believe that life's travails will work themselves out. The average American might be said to suffer from *hurry sickness*. Okinawans prefer to work at their own pace, referred to locally as *Okinawa Time*. They don't ignore stress...but they rarely internalize it.

Stress signals your body to secrete large amounts of *cortisol* and other stress hormones. That damages the heart and blood vessels and accelerates bone loss.

To reduce stress: Don't take on more than you can handle...take advantage of flextime at work...don't get worked up about things you can't change, such as traffic jams or rude behavior...practice deep breathing and meditation.

LOW-CALORIE INTAKE

Okinawans consume an average of 1,900 calories a day, compared with 2,500 for Americans. Studies have shown that animals given a diet with 40% fewer calories than the diets of free-feeding animals live about 50% longer.

Reason: Harmful oxygen molecules (free radicals) are created every time the body metabolizes food for energy. Because the Okinawans take in fewer calories, their lifetime exposure to free radicals—which damage cells in the arteries, brain and other parts of the body—is reduced.

PLANT-BASED DIET

About 98% of the *traditional* Okinawan diet consists of sweet potatoes, soy-based foods, grains, fruits and vegetables. This is supplemented by a small amount of fish (and lean pork on special occasions). These plant foods contain *phytonutrients*—chemical compounds that reduce free radical damage. A plant-based diet is also high in fiber, which lowers cholesterol and reduces the risk of diabetes, breast cancer and heart disease. The *current* Okinawan diet is about 80% plant food.

Wok advantage: The Okinawans' style of cooking is high-heat stir-frying in a wok, which requires little oil. They typically stir-fry with canola oil, which is high in heart-healthy monounsaturated fat and omega-3 fatty acids. These fatty acids lower levels of LDL ("bad") cholesterol while increasing levels of HDL ("good") cholesterol.

SOY FOODS

Elderly Okinawans eat an average of two servings of soy foods daily—such as tofu, miso soup and soybean sprouts. Soy is rich in flavonoids, chemical compounds that reduce the tendency of LDL to stick to arteries, thereby reducing the risk of heart disease or stroke. Soy foods may also protect against cancer... menopausal discomfort (such as hot flashes) ...and osteoporosis. You don't have to eat a lot of soy foods to get similar benefits. One daily serving of tofu (about three ounces) or soy milk (eight ounces) may be protective.

FISH

Fish harvested from the waters surrounding Okinawa is an integral part of the daily diet. The omega-3 fatty acids in fish "thin" the blood and reduce the risk of clots—the main cause of heart attack.

Omega-3s also inhibit the body's production of inflammatory chemicals called *prostaglandins*. That may lower the risk of inflammatory conditions, such as arthritis and the bowel disorder Crohn's disease.

Americans can get similar benefits by eating fish at least three times a week. Cold-water fish —salmon, mackerel, tuna—contain the largest amounts of omega-3s. Fish oil supplements are a worthwhile alternative for people who are "fish phobic."

HEALTHY WEIGHT

The traditional Okinawan diet is low in fat and processed foods, as well as calories—so obesity is rare in elder Okinawans. This means their risk of weight-related health problems, such as diabetes, heart disease and cancer, is much lower than that of Americans. This is in stark contrast to younger Okinawans, who eat a more Westernized diet and have the highest obesity levels in Japan.

Postmenopausal bonus: After menopause, a woman's main source of estrogen is no longer the ovaries, but extraglandular tissues, mainly body fat. Women who maintain a healthful weight produce less estrogen, which reduces the risk for developing breast cancer.

JASMINE TEA

Okinawans drink about three cups of jasmine tea daily. It contains more antioxidant flavonoids than black tea. Those antioxidants may reduce risk for heart disease as well as some cancers.

NOT SMOKING

In the US, hundreds of thousands of people die from smoking-related diseases annually. Few elderly Okinawans have ever smoked... although one man who was interviewed for the study took up smoking when he was 100. But he got bored with it and quit the following year. About 60% of younger Okinawan men now smoke.

EXERCISE

People are healthiest when they combine aerobic, strengthening and flexibility exercises. Okinawans often get all three by practicing martial arts or a traditional style of dance that resembles tai chi. *Smart regimen...*

●**Swimming, biking, jogging, etc.** for at least 30 minutes, three times weekly.

●**Lifting weights** for at least 20 minutes, twice a week.

●**Flexibility exercises**—yoga or stretching —whenever you can and certainly after each aerobic or strength-training session.

SOCIAL LINKS

Moai is the Okinawan word that means "meeting for a common purpose." Groups of friends, colleagues or relatives get together at least once a month to talk...share gossip...and provide emotional or even financial support.

People who maintain active social networks live longer and are less likely to get sick. When they do get sick, they recover more quickly if they have the support of friends.

SPIRITUALITY AND RELIGION

People who have spiritual or religious beliefs live longer than those who don't. Spirituality and religion are a part of daily life in Okinawa. People pray daily for health and peace. They look out for one another in a "help thy neighbor" ethic called *Yuimaru*. Moderation is a key cultural value.

Women are the religious leaders in Okinawa. They also tend to have very high levels of life satisfaction and respect as they age.

Exercise at Any Age

In one study, sedentary women age 65 and older who started exercising had a 48% lower death rate over the next 12 years than those who remained sedentary.

The best exercises for older women are the low-intensity ones, such as walking.

Edward W. Gregg, PhD, epidemiologist, US Centers for Disease Control and Prevention, Atlanta.

Self-Defense Strategies for Older Patients

Robert N. Butler, MD, president, International Longevity Center, New York City. He is former chairman of the department of geriatrics and adult development at Mount Sinai Medical Center, New York City, the first geriatrics department in an American medical school. He won the Pulitzer Prize for his book *Why Survive? Being Old in America* (Johns Hopkins University Press) and is coauthor of *The New Love and Sex After 60* (Ballantine).

As people grow older, they are more likely to develop health problems that require first-rate medical care. And, unfortunately, as many seniors have learned, it can be hard to find a doctor suited to care for their special needs.

How can older people be sure to get good medical care? Robert Butler, MD, a well-known crusader for elder rights, explained how important it is to watch out for mistakes doctors sometimes make when treating elderly patients. *Here are the most frequent errors...*

Mistake: **Failing to appreciate the physical changes that come with age.** A disease that causes one set of symptoms in a young person may manifest itself quite differently in an older person. Not all doctors realize that. And an unwary doctor can easily miss the diagnosis.

Example I: If a 30-year-old man suffers a heart attack, he is likely to experience severe chest pain. But chest pain affects fewer than 20% of older heart attack victims. Instead, older victims may simply seem weak or confused.

Example II: An older person suffering from an overactive thyroid may exhibit apathy instead of hyperactivity, the classic symptom.

Mistake: **Urging older people to "take it easy."** Even if you've been disabled by a stroke or another medical problem, leading an active lifestyle helps keep you healthy—and happy.

Even people in their 80s and 90s can develop powerful muscles with a program of weight lifting. Such a program can literally put a bedridden patient back on his/her feet.

Mistake: **Being too quick to blame health problems on old age.** Doctors often assume that health problems are inevitable in older people, exhibiting a defeatist "what-can-you-expect-at-your-age?" attitude.

They order fewer diagnostic tests and generally treat disease less aggressively in old people than in young people.

Example: An elderly woman seems confused and disoriented. Assuming that she has Alzheimer's disease, her doctor neglects to order tests that might show the real culprit to be an easily correctable drug reaction.

Mistake: **Not giving the patient enough time.** A good physician takes the time to ask about your work status and lifestyle as well as your medical problems...and, in general, makes you *feel* taken care of.

At each office visit, the doctor should ask about any symptoms you have reported in the past. He should also review your response to medications...and ask about new problems.

Your first visit to a new doctor should be devoted to giving a thorough medical history and undergoing a physical exam and lab tests. This can take more than an hour. Once this comprehensive exam is completed, you probably won't need another exam for a year—unless there's a health crisis.

Mistake: **Failing to advocate preventive measures.** Some doctors seem to think, "Why bother trying to lower an elderly patient's cholesterol level? He's just going to decline soon anyway."

We now know that heart patients of *any* age can benefit from a program of dietary modification, lifestyle change and—if necessary—medication or surgery.

Mistake: **Giving inappropriate prescriptions.** Doctors are too quick to order tranquilizers and antidepressants for their older patients, thinking—incorrectly—that psychotherapy is of no use. And they often fail to realize that older bodies respond differently to drugs.

Example: It can take an older person twice as long to "clear" *diazepam* (Valium) from his body as a young person. A dose that would be appropriate for a young person could make an older person drowsy.

If you're not sure that your doctor knows about all the drugs you're taking, put your medications (including nonprescription drugs, nutritional supplements and herbal remedies) in a paper bag and bring everything with you to your next office visit.

For referral to a certified geriatrician in your area, call the American Geriatrics Society at 800-247-4779.

More from Robert N. Butler...

What You Can Do Now to Stay Healthy and Keep Out of a Nursing Home

People of a certain age get lots of sales pitches for nursing home insurance. Insurance companies assume that nearly everyone will spend time in such a facility. It is a distressing thought. But, fortunately, it's a fate you can avoid.

Key: Don't wait. The sooner you start a no-nursing home plan, the better your chances of having it succeed.

GOOD NEWS ABOUT DEMENTIA

Dementia is common among nursing home residents. Not too long ago, we assumed that cognitive decline was simply a part of getting older. However, new research shows this isn't the case. *There are three specific factors that help maintain cognitive health...*

●**Daily physical activity.** This often surprises people, but the research is clear—we can actually measure that people who are active physically are stronger cognitively. When the Roman poet and satirist Juvenal said, "A healthy mind in a healthy body," he knew what he was talking about.

We advocate that most people walk 10,000 steps a day to be sure they are getting enough exercise. The average person walks just 4,000 steps, so you'll probably need to establish new habits (and buy a pedometer) to make 10,000 steps part of your everyday life.

●**Social interaction.** Being socially engaged doesn't mean that you have to maintain a full social calendar. What it does mean is that you remain involved with other people, whether through work or volunteering.

For those who are retired, there are many volunteer opportunities, from your local community to the Peace Corps. And don't forget the importance of being active as a grandparent. That benefits all three generations.

●**Intellectual stimulation.** This directly impacts the brain. Many older people enjoy studying academic subjects, from history to astronomy, but we have found that learning another language is particularly good for strong cognitive skills. The work that goes into mastering foreign words and any unfamiliar language structure keeps the brain's neurons firing and busy.

FITNESS FACTS

The next crucial part of a no-nursing home plan is to create and maintain very good health habits. *To start, you must practice all forms of fitness, such as...*

●**Aerobic exercise.** Aerobic exercise—the kind that gets your heart rate up and keeps it there—is a must. To maintain heart and lung stamina, perform aerobic exercise for at least 20 minutes, three or more times a week.

Examples: Fast walking, jogging, swimming laps.

●**Strength training.** This form of fitness is often overlooked by many older people and it's incredibly important as you age.

Being strong allows you to more easily perform what are called ADLs, *activities of daily living.* Without strong quads—the muscles in front of the thigh—you lose the ability to get out of a chair, go to the bathroom, sit down easily. Without strong arm muscles, you have trouble lifting bags or opening and closing windows. Strength training is crucial, and you must keep it up throughout your life.

Examples: Squats, getting out of a chair without using your arms, chest presses.

●**Balance exercises.** Among older people, there are some 250,000 fractures a year and many of these fractures land the elderly in nursing homes. This is especially sad because many of the falls that cause broken bones can be prevented by improving balance. The sense of balance is like a muscle—you must exercise it regularly or it will weaken and lose its usefulness to you.

The easiest way to practice balance is to stand on one leg and move the other, bent at the knee, through space. Do this several times a day. Or try standing on one leg while you brush your teeth.

Safety reminder: Be sure to have something sturdy nearby to grab hold of in case you need additional support.

●**Stretching exercises.** Finally, you must practice flexibility, which refers to the range of motion of your joints.

Range of motion becomes increasingly important as you age. If it is compromised, then it, too, will intrude on your ability to function in your everyday life. For example, your shoulders need range of motion to enable you to reach for things…your hips and knees need range of motion to bend properly.

Keep your joints flexible through regular stretching exercises. Try stretching your arms across your chest. Or stretch the backs of your legs by standing with the palms of your hands braced against a wall while you stretch one leg at a time behind you.

OTHER HEALTH POINTERS

●**Eat a nutritious diet.** In addition to plenty of fruits and vegetables, your diet should be low in fats and have no trans fatty acids at all. Processed baked foods virtually always contain unhealthy trans fatty acids, but you're more likely to see "partially hydrogenated fat" on the label. They are the same thing, and you should not eat them. Trans fats are created during the chemical process of hydrogenating oils and they increase "bad" LDL cholesterol, increasing your risk of stroke and heart disease.

●**Maintain a healthy weight.** This will help you avoid many diseases that frequently bring patients into a nursing home, such as type 2 diabetes and some cardiovascular disease, especially high blood pressure that leads to stroke.

●**Quit smoking.** I wish I had no need to say *quit smoking.* But there are still people who haven't kicked the habit, even though statistics show it cuts seven years off the normal life span.

MAKE FRIENDS WITH YOUR DOCTOR

While it is important to remain as disease-free as possible, there is now some controversy about the benefit of having an annual physical examination. Statistics don't back them up as resulting in longer lives, but you should still find a way to get to know your doctor so that he/she is familiar with your medical history if something does happen.

We suggest having abbreviated checkups. Get routine testing for the problems that older people are prone to, such as glaucoma, high blood pressure and gender-specific ailments. And if you do have any kind of medical condition, chronic or otherwise, be sure to take your medication as the doctor has prescribed. Always call the doctor to discuss any concern you might have about a drug rather than make decisions about medicine on your own.

Life expectancy is higher than ever—an average of about 78 years compared with about 48 years in 1900. By adhering to these few simple measures, you'll greatly increase your chances of enjoying all the years ahead.

Also from Robert N. Butler...

Sexual Problems of Older People And How to Solve Them

Even healthy people who are in good relationships can do certain things to improve their sex lives.

First step: Learn to ignore the signals sent by our society—that sex is only for the young. There's no reason that men and women can't have active, fulfilling sex lives into their 90s. In fact, some women become *more* orgasmic during their later years. While men typically take longer to get erections as they get older, their erections also tend to last longer, which can increase enjoyment for both partners.

Of course, getting older does bring certain physical changes, which can cause problems. Fortunately, these problems can almost always be treated.

CHANGES WOMEN CAN EXPECT

When women enter menopause, one of the most prevalent complaints is vaginal dryness during sex, which can make intercourse feel scratchy or even painful. *Hormone replacement therapy* (HRT) with an estrogen–progestin drug is often effective in restoring lubrication.

In light of warnings about long-term use of HRT, you may want to talk with your doctor about other treatments. Vaginal estrogen cream, applied directly to the vagina an hour before intercourse...a vaginal ring (inserted every three months)...and Vagifem (available by prescription only), an estrogen tablet that is inserted into the vagina twice a week, are all effective at counteracting vaginal dryness, while exposing the user to much lower doses of estrogen than HRT.

Another effective solution, already practiced by one out of three women in the US, is simply to apply a lubricant before sex. Make sure to use a non-oil–based lubricant, such as K-Y Jelly, Astroglide, Slip Lubricant Gel or HR Lubricating Jelly. The oil-based lubricants, like petroleum jelly, or baby oil, may cause vaginal infection.

Another option is a moisturizing gel in tampon form, such as Replens or Lubrin. Unlike the lubricants, these gels are simply inserted

three times a week, and, therefore, do not interfere with sexual spontaneity.

CHANGES MEN CAN EXPECT

As I mentioned earlier, men take longer to get an erection as they grow older. They also usually require physical stimulation to become erect. It's important for their partners to realize that because a man may need to be *touched* to have an erection doesn't mean he's not attracted to his partner. It's just a natural part of aging.

But if a man has a consistent problem getting or maintaining an erection during intercourse, he may need to seek out treatment for *erectile dysfunction* (ED). The vast majority of ED cases have a physiological cause. If you're experiencing ED, have a physical, because ED may be symptomatic of an underlying medical problem.

The preferred treatments for ED include *sildenafil* (Viagra), *tadalafil* (Cialis) and *vardenafil* (Levitra). Cialis and Levitra are newer drugs, but they have been used safely in Europe for years. Tens of millions of prescriptions have been written for Viagra in the US, and the data show that it is a very safe drug.

Viagra works by dilating blood vessels in the penis. It is not an aphrodisiac—but if you are stimulated erotically, Viagra will let you achieve an erection for several hours after it takes effect.

Viagra is safe and effective for men with diabetes, heart disease, hypertension, anxiety and depression, and men who have been treated for prostate cancer.

Caution: If you are taking nitroglycerin or any other nitrate heart medicine, you should not use Viagra under any circumstances.

Take Viagra about an hour before you plan to have sex. Viagra works best on a relatively empty stomach, and you should avoid smoking or heavy alcohol use while taking it. Once you've used it successfully for several months, try sex *without* Viagra—you may find you no longer need it.

Problem: Viagra can occasionally cause headaches or give a bluish tinge to your vision.

TESTOSTERONE SUPPLEMENTS

Testosterone is the hormone responsible for physical desire in men and women. In Europe, it has been widely used to treat low libido, and there has also been a surge in sales of testosterone in the US in the past few years. But the long-term benefits and risks of testosterone supplements still aren't clear.

If a man (or woman, for that matter) is deficient in testosterone, a testosterone patch or cream may be helpful in restoring sexual drive and function. But less than 4% of ED cases are related to testosterone deficiency. If you have either prostate cancer or benign prostate enlargement, testosterone supplements can exacerbate your condition.

What we really need is a long-term study of testosterone therapy to establish exactly what the pros and cons are.

Also from Robert N. Butler on Hormone Replacement...

Can Testosterone Make You Younger?

Everybody wants to be young and sexy—but as men age and their bodies produce less testosterone, they often start to feel weak, have trouble with memory and become less interested in sex. Wouldn't it be great if they could reverse the aging process?

Millions of American men are trying to do just that by replacing the testosterone that their bodies no longer supply. Close to 2 million prescriptions for testosterone were written in the past five years. Sales were boosted by the availability of AndroGel, a prescription topical testosterone that is absorbed by the skin. Previously, testosterone could be delivered only by an injection.

DANGEROUS EXPERIMENT

Those men taking testosterone replacement therapy on their own are essentially participating in an uncontrolled and possibly life-threatening experiment. In the first place, nobody really is certain if male hormone replacement therapy works. Just because testosterone levels aren't as high as they were at age 30 doesn't mean that bringing them back to those levels restores virility.

Several studies have reported that older men (average age 52) who took testosterone developed big muscles but didn't get the strength that usually goes along with muscle buildup. These

men may have looked stronger, but they weren't any more robust than before they started taking the hormone—and nobody knows exactly why.

More troubling is that doctors don't know how a person's biochemical system responds to artificially introducing hormones that the body has stopped producing naturally. They don't know if testosterone replacement promotes prostate cancer or has other negative effects on the body.

Red flags were raised when the Women's Health Initiative study released its disturbing findings. Women who had received hormone replacement therapy had a higher incidence of breast cancer, heart attacks and strokes. Another study reported that women who began hormone replacement therapy at age 65 or older were twice as likely to develop dementia, including Alzheimer's disease.

WHAT TO DO

Long-term studies are required to examine what happens over time to men who take testosterone replacement therapy.

Until there are answers, the best advice for a man who believes that he is suffering from low testosterone is to go see an endocrinologist—a physician who specializes in treating hormone imbalance. He can measure testosterone levels. If a man has total testosterone levels that are very low (200 nanograms per deciliter or lower), a trial of testosterone replacement may be considered.

The physician also will ask what medications the man is taking. Some drugs, including the blood pressure drug *spironolactone* (Aldactone) and the heartburn drug *cimetidine* (Tagamet), may cause testosterone levels to decline.

In many cases, lifestyle changes will be recommended. Men experiencing sexual dysfunction usually are advised to restrict their alcohol consumption since even small amounts of alcohol have been linked to a diminished capacity for achieving or maintaining an erection.

Men who are concerned about their mental function often are told to exercise more. Exercising three times a week for 30 minutes at a time fosters mental alertness. A study reported in *The New England Journal of Medicine* showed that social dancing four to five days a week is good for older brains as well as bodies. Similar benefits come from a variety of activities, including jogging, hiking, racquet sports, swimming, bicycling and use of exercise machines.

To fight off weakness, eat a well-balanced diet. Choose from the various food groups—include protein-rich plants (beans, nuts) and animal foods (lean meat, poultry, fish and eggs) …whole-grain foods…vegetables…fruits…and dairy products.

Although we can fantasize about a magic pill, sensible lifestyle changes are the best answer right now—and they can be remarkably effective.

Don't Believe the Hype About hGH

Despite the hype, *human growth hormone* (hGH) does *not* slow aging. This is true whether hGH is taken orally or injected. Taken orally, hGH is inactivated by stomach acid, making it valueless. And, the same is true for *growth hormone releasing factor,* which also is being advertised.

By injection, hGH is only for patients with hGH deficiency caused by a disease of the pituitary gland, which produces hGH.

Caution: Taking hGH may cause tumors to grow. Side effects include diabetes and arthritis.

Paul S. Jellinger, MD, clinical professor of medicine, University of Miami, FL, and past president of American Association of Clinical Endocrinologists.

How to Age-Proof Your Body…Naturally

Norman D. Ford, writer, fitness enthusiast and anti-aging expert. He is a dedicated long-distance cyclist, and author of many health books, including *18 Natural Ways to Look & Feel Half Your Age* (Keats Publishing).

The human body is designed by nature to age at a very slow pace. We should be able to stay strong and healthy well into

our 80s and beyond. *But three aspects of our modern lifestyle speed up the process…*

- **Sedentary living.**
- **A high-fat, low-fiber diet.**
- **Worry, anxiety and stress.**

If you can address these three core areas, you can maintain a biological age that's many years younger than your chronological age.

In fact, researchers at the Human Nutrition Research Center (HNRC) at Tufts University in Boston established a number of "biomarkers" to measure aging, and they concluded that declines in every biomarker were caused primarily by a high-fat diet and lack of aerobic and strength-training exercise.

Fortunately, they also found these declines could be easily reversed in a fairly short time, simply by changing diet and lifestyle.

AEROBIC EXERCISE

Many people think it's "natural" to lose strength and fitness as they get older. But this decline has nothing to do with age…it starts the minute we put our feet up and start to take life easy.

Only about 10% of Americans exercise enough to improve their health. The rest have abandoned all strenuous exercise, and a slow, inexorable decline is under way.

But this decline isn't inevitable. At any age, a program of regular exercise will lower your biological age in a few short months—even if you haven't exercised for years.

Example: The human cardiovascular system has evolved to the point where it can function in top condition for at least 100 years. Studies have shown that a healthy 90-year-old heart can pump blood just as effectively as a 20-year-old heart. Yet without exercise, the average 65-year-old has lost 30% to 40% of his/her aerobic capacity.

To begin restoring the health of your heart, lungs and arteries—and maintaining it—I recommend doing some aerobic exercise every other day. This could be walking, swimming, bicycling or other brisk, rhythmic movement.

Start by doing 20 minutes, and build up until you're doing four to five miles of walking, or an hour of swimming or cycling. This will take a few weeks to a few months.

When you exercise, move briskly, but don't push yourself so hard that you feel fatigued.

You can begin this age-proofing technique —and start reaping benefits—immediately.

Hundreds of studies have shown that regular aerobic exercise reduces the risk of developing type 2 diabetes, raises your HDL ("good") cholesterol while lowering dangerous LDL cholesterol, reduces brain neuron loss, increases bone density and lowers the risk of breast and prostate cancer. It also creates tremendous increases in energy, stamina and endurance. And the more out of shape you are, the more rapid your progress.

STRENGTH TRAINING

Until the early 1990s, most exercise physiologists focused on aerobics as the principal anti-aging exercise. But they now believe that strength training may be even more important than aerobics because strength training builds more muscle mass in a way that aerobics can't.

Above everything else, muscle mass is the key to youthfulness. After scores of tests and surveys, the HNRC concluded that loss of muscle mass and strength is the underlying cause of almost every sign of aging. Muscle mass is also the key to shedding fat, since large, strong muscles burn more calories—24 hours a day, even when you're not exercising.

A thrice-weekly schedule of strength training—done on the days between your aerobic workouts—should be at the core of your anti-aging program.

Join a health and fitness club that has weight machines and instructors who can show you the right exercises.

I recommend doing nine exercises, to specifically focus on the following muscle groups: Pectorals, triceps, upper back, lower back, biceps, shoulders, abdominals, quadriceps and hamstrings.

For each exercise, find the maximum amount you can lift one time, then use 80% of that weight and lift it smoothly, up to eight or nine times in a row. It's OK if you can only do three or four repetitions at first. Once you can lift a weight 10 times or more, you'll need to increase the weight.

Begin with one exercise per muscle group, then gradually add an additional set or two as you gain strength and stamina.

LOW-FAT DIET

Scientists now believe that most premature aging is caused by disease, partly due to free radicals—electrically charged particles that wreak havoc on our cells by causing toxic chain reactions. Wrinkled skin, clogged arteries and weak immune response have all been linked to free-radical damage.

One of the main causes of free-radical buildup is a high-fat diet. Fat molecules produce free radicals as they're oxidized. If you eat too many fat molecules, these free radicals can cause plaque to build up in your arteries, which leads to heart disease, cancer and other diseases.

Fortunately, there's a natural antidote. Fruits and vegetables contain hundreds of compounds called *phytochemicals,* which work to prevent free-radical formation (which is why they're often called *antioxidants*).

The Framingham Heart Study found that increasing the amount of fruit and vegetables you eat greatly reduces your risk of heart attack.

These foods also tend to be high in fiber, which speeds digestion and may have anti-cancer benefits.

On the other hand, animal products—such as beef, eggs, fish, poultry, dairy products, etc. —contain no fiber and few antioxidants or cancer-preventing chemicals. To age-proof your body against disease, cut down on these foods and increase your intake of fruits and vegetables.

FREE YOUR MIND

Whatever you can do to eliminate stress will also help stop the aging process. One way is to practice forgiveness. Being unable to forgive is a major cause of stress. *Other stress-busters…*

• **Progressive muscle relaxation.** Lie on a rug in semidarkness with a pillow under your head. Tense each muscle group in turn for about six seconds, then relax. You can cover your whole body in about 90 seconds with this method. Next, concentrate on mentally warming your hands. With practice, you can increase the blood flow to your body in just a few minutes.

●**Watch TV as little as possible.** Television is the most passive, useless activity in which you can engage—yet half the US population sits hypnotized by the tube for up to four hours a day.

●**Use your mind actively and creatively.** The more you exercise your mind, the healthier and more alert you will be. Mental activity can even help speed up your physical reflexes!

New Rules for Living Longer

Edward L. Schneider, MD, dean emeritus, Leonard Davis School of Gerontology, University of Southern California, Los Angeles. He is author of *AgeLess: Take Control of Your Age and Stay Youthful for Life* (Rodale).

For years, many people have believed that you can extend your life span by practicing common health strategies, such as staying thin and reducing stress. But research has shown that many of the long-standing recommendations are *wrong*.

Sound hard to believe? The previous advice for healthful living was mostly based on observational studies. Researchers examined large populations and attempted to link lifestyle habits with specific diseases. But when some of these so-called "breakthroughs" were tested in placebo-controlled, randomized trials—the gold standard for scientific research—they failed.

Exercise and proper nutrition are the backbone of any antiaging prescription. *But the new rules for longevity dispel some common misconceptions about living longer…*

Misconception #1: **Thin people are healthiest.** Obesity is a killer—no one should be seriously overweight. But that doesn't mean that thin people will live longer or stay healthier throughout their lives.

The truth: People who are five to 10 pounds over their so-called "ideal" weights after age 55 tend to live longer and have fewer chronic diseases than those who are thin. After age 70, people who are 5% to 10% overweight are more likely to live longer.

Bottom line: Yo-yo dieting—the cycle of losing weight, gaining it back, then losing it again—is worse for your health than carrying around a few extra pounds. People who are slightly heavy tend to have a lower risk for suffering a hip fracture, which can be deadly.

Important: If your *body mass index* (BMI) is 25 or above, you may need to lose weight. If it's 27 or above, you're at increased risk for heart disease, high blood pressure and diabetes.

To determine your BMI: Multiply your weight in pounds by 703, and divide the result by your height (in inches) squared.

Misconception #2: **Stress is bad for your health.** Doctors always recommend avoiding stress, and for good reason. People who feel overwhelmed by stress have an elevated risk for stroke, heart disease, high blood pressure and other chronic diseases. But stress isn't really the issue.

The truth: A certain amount of stress is inevitable if you hope to have a rich and fulfilling life. What matters is *how* you handle it. Controlling your reaction to stressful events is far more important than attempting to avoid them.

Example: My teenage son is going to do things that make me angry. Since I can't prevent this, I try to react in ways that won't send my stress hormones off the charts. I can walk away from minor quarrels and give myself time to cool down.

Bottom line: Instead of dodging stress, develop effective methods for dealing with it—daily exercise, meditation, yoga, etc.

Misconception #3: **Older people need less sleep.** Americans average less than seven hours' sleep a night. Older adults tend to sleep less because of natural changes in their *circadian rhythms,* or biological clocks. They have trouble falling asleep and/or wake up early, possibly due to a change in the regulation of melatonin, a hormone that is critical to the sleep–wake cycle. But that doesn't mean they *need* less sleep.

The truth: Everyone should get seven to nine hours' sleep, regardless of age. Sleeping less weakens immunity and increases the risk for depression, falls and accidents.

Bottom line: If you need an alarm clock to wake up, you're probably sleep-deprived. Improve nighttime sleep with exercise…regular bedtimes…and reduced light in the bedroom. Do not drink caffeinated beverages or alcohol within two hours of bedtime.

Caution: Most people should not nap for more than 20 minutes. Doing so will disrupt your body's biological clock and make it harder to get refreshing sleep at night.

Think Positively and Live Longer

People who view aging as a positive experience live an average of seven-and-a-half years longer than those who look at it negatively, according to one study.

In any given year, other studies indicate pessimists have a risk of death 19% greater than average. The power of optimism is even greater than that of lower blood pressure or reduced cholesterol—each of which lengthens a life by about four years, according to some studies.

Becca R. Levy, PhD, associate professor of epidemiology, Yale School of Public Health, New Haven, CT, and leader of a study of 660 people over age 50, published in the *Journal of Personality and Social Psychology.*

Age-Proof Your Brain

The late Lawrence C. Katz, PhD, professor of neurobiology, Duke University Medical Center, and investigator, Howard Hughes Medical Institute, both in Durham, NC. He was coauthor of *Keep Your Brain Alive: 83 Neurobic Exercises* (Workman) and published more than 50 scientific articles on brain development and function.

Doctors used to think that brain development occurred only during a person's youth and that, as we age, our brain cells (*neurons*) inevitably die off.

But recent research confirms that humans add new neurons throughout life. This means that we can continue learning new ideas and mastering new skills.

Each neuron has branch-like appendages called *dendrites* that extend in different directions. Whenever a person's brain is stimulated by an experience—even in old age—new dendrites are created.

Neurons communicate with each other via electrochemical impulses sent through dendrites. More dendrites mean greater brain power. As we age, some dendrites naturally wither and die. The more we have left, the better our cognitive abilities remain.

Key: Building as many dendrites as possible.

Here are eight ways to stimulate dendrite growth and keep energizing your brain…

●**Switch hands.** Most of us rely on a dominant hand for daily activities. Switch to your nondominant hand. Research has shown that this type of exercise can substantially increase the number of circuits in the cerebral cortex.

If you brush your teeth with your right hand, use your left for a few weeks.

Switch to your nondominant hand as frequently as possible—when eating…styling your hair…writing…painting.

●**"Lose" a sense.** An abundance of new neural pathways form when you exercise your senses in ways you normally don't. It's well known, for example, that blind people end up developing other senses to a much higher level than those who have their sight.

Brain-imaging experiments involving blind braille readers show that extensive practice using the fingers to make fine distinctions between objects or textures causes "rewiring" of the brain.

Most of us rely on sight above all. Substitute the sense of touch for daily tasks and activities, as blind people must.

●Learn to distinguish different keys (house, car, etc.) by touch.

●Get dressed without looking…then try it with one hand.

●Close your eyes and explore a familiar room, such as your bedroom, with your hands.

Then "lose" other senses…

●Turn off the sound on the TV, and try to follow the plot.

•See if you can tell what's for dinner by the aromas you smell.

•Taste foods while holding your nose. This forces you to use different neural pathways to experience the food.

•**Use *all* your senses.** Something as simple as grocery shopping can stimulate the brain if you consciously use all your senses.

Smell the tomatoes…thump the melons…feel the plums…taste food samples offered. Buy foods for a theme meal—say a meal made up of only red foods.

The same can be done on a grander scale outdoors. *Whether you're fishing, hiking or just taking a stroll…*

•Feel changes in wind direction on your face and arms.

•Smell the air…and try to identify natural odors. Extensive research shows that linking places or things to the olfactory sense (smell) enhances memory.

•Listen intently to water splashing or a bird's song.

•**Be adventurous.** The less familiar an activity is to you, the more it stimulates your brain. Try things you've wanted to do, even if they initially feel uncomfortable.

Brain-imaging studies show that new experiences activate large areas of the cerebral cortex, indicating brain stimulation.

•Sign up for an acting camp.

•Travel by train across the US or by ship across the ocean.

•Vacation on a dude ranch.

•**Make small changes.** Even minor changes in your routine activate the cortex and hippocampus (a part of the brain crucial for memory formation). This stimulation will create new neural pathways.

•If you always watch TV from the same chair, switch.

•Dine in a different room.

•Reorganize your desk.

•Rearrange furniture.

•Take a different route to work or the gym.

Or simply do the same things—but *in a different order.* Eat breakfast for dinner and dinner for breakfast…or shower after drinking your coffee instead of before. Travel around the grocery store in the opposite direction.

•**Take up a challenging hobby.** Devote yourself to a new pastime that calls for complex skills. Artistic pursuits, for example, activate nonverbal and emotional centers in the cortex.

•Learn a musical instrument.

•Study a foreign language.

•Take up a sport, such as tennis or golf, that requires mastering multiple techniques.

•Take up photography.

•**Go low-tech.** Although technology has made our lives easier, it also has removed us from many experiences.

Example: Television, movies and the Internet may be entertaining, but they often pacify rather than actively engage the mind.

Take technology breaks. Do things the way people did them decades ago.

•Bake homemade bread or make spaghetti sauce from scratch.

•Run or walk outdoors, instead of on a treadmill inside.

•Go camping. Bring a sleeping bag, tent, simple food and a small gas stove. Leave the radio home.

•**Become more social.** Interacting with other people is the best single brain exercise. It brings all the senses into play, forces you to think quickly and hones your speaking skills.

Social contact is also important for psychological health. People with good social networks have fewer physical and psychological problems as they age than those who are socially deprived. Seek out social interactions of every sort.

•Go to the bank teller instead of the automatic teller machine.

•Make small talk with the cashier at your local supermarket.

•Telephone friends daily.

Also strive for more ambitious interactions. Arrange social gatherings that involve a variety of brain-boosting strategies.

•Join a book club.

•Hold a wine-tasting party to learn about tastes and bouquets of different vintages.

•Organize a potluck picnic in a nature preserve or park.

•Set up a musical jam session or an informal chorus group.

•Arrange a weekly game night for poker, bridge or Monopoly—anything that involves complex thought and social contact.

Brain-Boosting Pills: What Really Works...and What Doesn't

Jay Schneider, PhD, professor of neurology, pathology, anatomy and cell biology, Thomas Jefferson University, Philadelphia. He is coauthor of *Brain Candy: Boost Your Brain Power with Vitamins, Supplements, Drugs and Other Substances* (Fireside).

Do you sometimes lose track of where you parked the car? Or need a little extra time to program the VCR?

As we age, these and other lapses can make us feel like we're losing our mental edge.

That's why brain-boosting supplements, herbs and drugs are so popular. But do the top sellers *really* work? Are they safe?*

Here's the opinion of one leading expert...

•**Acetyl-L-carnitine.** This over-the-counter (OTC) amino acid is believed to jump-start the brain by helping to produce chemicals that power brain cell activity. Initial studies suggest that taking the supplement may improve memory and attention, even in healthy, young adults.

Acetyl-L-carnitine also may stave off the protein deposits that develop in the brains of early-stage Alzheimer's patients.

Typical daily dosage: 1 to 3 grams (g).

Caution: Do not confuse acetyl-L-carnitine with DL-carnitine, which can produce severe loss of muscle strength.

*The US Food and Drug Administration does not approve herbs or supplements. Always consult your physician before taking any of these products.

•**B vitamins.** Clinical studies show that thiamine (B-1), niacin (B-3) and pyridoxine (B-6) may improve memory and thinking. How do they work? Thiamine enables the body to metabolize carbohydrates, the primary source of energy for brain cells. Niacin appears to improve short-term memory and comprehension. Pyridoxine plays a role in forming several of the brain's neurotransmitters. Taking 20 to 50 milligrams (mg) daily of vitamin B-6 has been found to improve mood and memory.

Typical daily dosage: Follow dosage recommendations on the labels of B-complex and individual B vitamins.

Caution: In addition to being potentially toxic to the liver, more than 2 g daily of niacin can cause peptic ulcers and may exacerbate cardiac arrhythmia. More than 200 mg daily of B-6 can be toxic to nerve cells and may interfere with Parkinson's disease drugs.

If you eat plenty of foods that are rich in B-vitamins—organ meats, pork, legumes and nuts—you might not need to take supplements.

•**Fipexide.** This OTC stimulant is said to enhance thinking and learning by increasing levels of the neurotransmitter dopamine in the brain. In a single clinical trial, fipexide did improve mental functioning in a group of older patients with brain disease. However, this stimulant has been known to cause severe liver damage.

•**Gerovital.** This OTC supplement—marketed as an antiaging formula for body and brain—is nothing more than the local anesthetic *procaine,* combined with an antioxidant and a preservative. There is no scientific evidence that Gerovital rejuvenates the mind.

But excessive use can cause tremors, unconsciousness, convulsions, low or high blood pressure and respiratory or cardiac arrest.

•**Ginkgo biloba.** This Chinese herb has become a favorite alternative remedy to combat memory impairment.

Ginkgo has been shown to improve memory in Alzheimer's patients, but the evidence is not as strong in healthy people. Researchers attribute the benefit to the herb's antioxidant and anti-inflammatory properties.

Typical daily dosage: 120 to 240 mg.

Caution: Ginkgo inhibits blood clotting. So it should not be taken by people on aspirin or blood thinners, such as *warfarin* (Coumadin). Ginkgo should also be avoided by patients facing surgery or anyone with a clotting disorder, such as hemophilia or vitamin K deficiency.

●**Growth hormone.** This protein, secreted by the pituitary gland, promotes cell growth. Sold as a prescription drug, growth hormone is said to prevent physical *and* mental deterioration in adults who have acquired growth hormone deficiency.

However, its effectiveness as an "antiaging" drug is unsubstantiated. The risks are considerable. Growth hormone can cause fluid retention, hypertension and hyperglycemia. This, in turn, can lead to diabetes, high blood pressure and heart disease. It may also stimulate growth of existing tumors, such as colon malignancies.

●**Phenytoin (Dilantin).** Commonly prescribed to treat epilepsy, this anticonvulsant is sometimes falsely promoted as an "IQ-booster." However, there are no convincing studies to support this claim.

But there are plenty of data detailing the drug's potential side effects—everything from slurred speech and insomnia to potentially fatal disorders of the liver, blood and thyroid.

●**Phosphatidylserine.** This fat-like substance is one of the several OTC dietary supplements clinically tested on healthy and cognitively impaired adults. It has been shown consistently to improve memory and attention, without causing serious side effects.

Phosphatidylserine seems to enhance communication between the chemical messengers (neurotransmitters) in the brain. It also appears to inhibit synthesis of *cortisol,* a stress hormone that may interfere with thinking and memory.

Typical daily dosage: 100 mg taken three times a day.

Caution: Phosphatidylserine may slow blood clotting. For this reason, it should be avoided by the same people who are cautioned against taking ginkgo.

●**Piracetam.** This OTC supplement was the first "nootropic" (a drug designed specifically to improve brain function) marketed in Europe.

In the US, piracetam can be purchased only from mail-order or Internet retailers.

Piracetam has been widely tested on healthy and cognitively impaired adults.

When combined with memory exercises, it has been shown to lessen age-associated memory loss significantly. To date, there have been no serious side effects reported.

Typical daily dosage: 2,400 to 4,800 mg, divided in three doses.

●**Vincamine.** This herbal supplement, which is derived from the periwinkle plant, is said to enhance concentration in healthy adults, and boost memory and attention in patients with impaired brain circulation caused by cerebrovascular disease.

Vincamine does increase the cerebral blood flow, so it may be of some benefit if promptly administered after a stroke. But long-term use can cause life-threatening cardiac arrhythmias, as well as severe sleep disturbances.

Simple Strategies to Improve Your Memory

Betty Fielding, Lafayette, CA–based lecturer on the psychology of aging, and author of *The Memory Manual: 10 Simple Things You Can Do to Improve Your Memory After 50* (Quill Driver).

Occasional memory lapses often grow more frequent as we age, making many of us worry about what they portend for the future. But a little thought—combined with modest lifestyle modifications—can prevent most memory lapses.

MEMORY TRACES

Each of our senses leaves a different memory trace of a specific event. So can our thoughts, feelings and actions as we experience an event. Any of these traces can trigger our memory of that event.

The more senses, thoughts, feelings and actions we employ to experience something, the more likely we are to remember it later…

●**Tune in to your senses.** The more conscious you are of what your senses are detecting, the more memory traces you collect.

Example: When you are introduced to a stranger, *look* at his/her eye color, facial features, etc....*listen* to his name...*smell* his shaving lotion...and *feel* his handshake.

●**Develop mental images.** Mental images of events are easier to recall than are abstractions.

Example I: If you are given directions to an unfamiliar destination, use them to construct a mental map of the route.

Example II: If you have misplaced a certain object, mentally retrace your actions from the time you last remember holding it.

●**Use words to create additional memory traces.** For instance, to ensure that you will be able to find important papers, verbalize your action as you put them away.

●**Increase your focus.** You won't remember something if you didn't pay attention to it in the first place.

Helpful: Make notes of what you need to remember. Ask yourself—"What am I doing now?...Why am I here?...What is next on my list?" Be aware of your feelings so you can consciously respond in a way that helps you keep focused.

●**Organize your learning and your life.** The brain is organized so that fleeting thoughts and unexamined pieces of information never enter your long-term memory. *A vital step in improving your memory is putting your mind in order...*

•Develop a mind-set of curiosity and enthusiasm for research. To prime yourself to remember a lecture, for example, ask yourself—"Who was speaking?...What was his message?...Why does it matter to me?...Where—and when—was the lecture held?...How did the speaker present his material?"

•Utilize your calendar. Keep it in the same place...review your schedule twice daily...enter all family holidays, birthdays and annually recurring commitments before the new year begins... enter all appointments and due dates immediately.

•Organize your surroundings so you can find whatever you need with minimal effort. Have a place for everything, and put it there as soon as you finish using it.

●**Take care of your health.** Always eat a nutritious, balanced diet that follows the guidelines in the USDA food pyramid (*www. nal.usda.gov/*).

Particularly important for memory: Adequate amounts of vitamins B-6, B-12 and folic acid, as well as the antioxidant vitamins C and E and beta-carotene.

Also: Have regular medical checkups. Memory problems can be caused by cardiovascular conditions, thyroid dysfunction, diabetes, lung, liver and kidney problems or drug side effects.

●**Exercise.** Healthy people in their 70s who engage in regular physical activity demonstrate better thinking and memory skills than their equally healthy peers who are sedentary.

Exercise expands breathing capacity and increases the supply of oxygen to the brain. It also lowers blood pressure, which may reduce the likelihood of memory problems...and supports brain cell growth.

●**Challenge your mind.** Mental challenges exercise and expand thinking skills and memory capacity. Study a foreign language, play bridge and chess, do crosswords, etc.

●**Acknowledge aging-related sensory changes.** Changes in sight or vision can contribute to memory problems.

Example: David N. enrolled in a memory class, saying that he had lost his memory 40 years earlier. But during the class his memory seemed fine. At the end of the course, David confessed, "I have learned that I did not lose my memory 40 years ago. I developed a hearing problem then, and I was too embarrassed to ask people to repeat things. I didn't forget things...I just didn't learn them in the first place."

The central nervous system slows gradually with aging. You will think and act a bit more slowly. So take the time you need to focus on what is important to you, such as a person's name or a creative idea.

Force yourself to pay attention. Watch out for distracting thoughts. Refocus on what you are involved in at the moment.

How to Keep Your Brain Strong and Memory Working

Cynthia R. Green, PhD, president, Memory Arts, LLC, Upper Montclair, NJ, a company that provides memory fitness training to corporations and nonprofit organizations, and assistant clinical professor, Mount Sinai School of Medicine, New York City. She is author of *Total Memory Workout: Eight Easy Steps to Maximum Memory Fitness* (Bantam).

It is undeniable that aging will bring with it some changes in memory. These include the "tip of the tongue" phenomenon, the word that is achingly familiar but won't pop into your consciousness. This might happen because a delay in the way the brain processes information may be associated with age, so that you cannot retrieve information as quickly as you could when you were younger.

But there is no reason to give up. While you cannot reverse any physiological changes in the brain, there are ways to work around them. By creating healthy memory habits—memory fitness—you'll be remembering names, even to-do lists, in no time. *Here's how...*

BASICS

Underlying all memory techniques is the A.M. principle. Putting this principle to work will help you sharpen your memory immediately.

●**"A" stands for attention.** Often the reason people can't pull a word or name out of their consciousness is that they just didn't pay enough attention to it in the first place. If you want to remember something, you must pay close attention so that you really absorb it. You will need to develop two basic habits to accomplish this. *They are...*

●Be aware. Rather than mindlessly parking your car at the mall or meeting a new neighbor, remind yourself that you need to pay attention.

●Make the effort. You've reminded yourself to pay attention, now focus and do it. Take in the information on the spot that you'll need to recall.

Everyday example: You need to retrieve something from the other room. Instead of wandering in and forgetting what it was you wanted, say to yourself what it is as you get up to get it.

●**"M" stands for meaning.** Giving information meaning will help to make it memorable. Assigning meaning also helps your memory bank store the information, making it easier to find when you need it. *Three ways to help give information meaning...*

●Organize it. The best example of this is a way to learn a series of numbers. Rather than try to remember nine numbers in a row—intimidating for anyone—"chunk" them into groupings. Seem familiar? This is what you do anytime you learn someone's phone number with area code —you chunk it into three parts.

●See it. You can make many things memorable just by picturing them, be it visualizing the errands you must run, someone's e-mail address or even certain names. For some information, visual memory is stronger than verbal recall.

●Connect it. Think of this as cross-referencing in your brain—connect something you want to remember with something you already know.

Example: If you meet someone named Eloise, think of the now-closed New York City landmark, the Plaza Hotel—and the precocious young girl of fiction who roamed its halls in search of adventure.

TECHNIQUES

Below, you'll find six techniques for encoding information to memory. What they all have in common is that they get you to pay attention and give meaning to what you want to learn. These aren't all meant to work for everyone— what some people find useful, others will view as cumbersome. Choose only the ones that appeal to you and put them to work.

●**The repetition technique.** This is exactly what it says—if you need to remember something, give it your complete focus and then repeat it to yourself several times.

●**The link technique.** This technique is perfect for remembering any list. Think of it as dominoes—one word links up the next to the next. Although most of us generally write out our grocery lists, it's a good way to practice the link technique. Start with, say, potatoes (for mashing)—that links to butter to milk to steaks to salad greens. Once you get the hang of it, this technique is useful for just about any list.

• **The storytelling technique.** Making up a story connects bits of information and gives them meaning.

Say you have just met someone named Rose Cinder. You might come up with a quick story about a rose growing from the ashes. Although this one is more involved than most of the other techniques, many people favor it, in part because it's fun.

• **The connection technique.** Attach what you need to learn to something you already know. Say that you meet someone with the unusual last name "Sertage." While there is virtually no visual prompt in that name, it links nicely with a word you know well—"certain," but with a soft "g" ending.

• **First-letter association technique.** You know this one already, the surefire trick of creating acronyms to remember a word grouping —"TGIF" says something to everyone.

Use that same idea to remember the birth order of your niece's five kids. This approach doesn't work for everything, in particular if the words you need to remember all start with consonants. But for certain needs, it can be a great deal of fun as well as effective.

• **The snapshot technique.** While the visual memory is a powerful tool for remembering information, people tend to overlook it. For this technique, create a mental image of what you are trying to learn.

Example: To remember a recipe someone is giving you, get a picture of each item in your mind's eye as the person tells you. It's an easy technique to learn. And, as a bonus, it's a good way to boost your brainpower.

PRACTICE PERFECTS

Keep in mind that just as you need to work out regularly to keep your body healthy and your muscles strong, you'll need to practice memory techniques regularly.

Take advantage of your spare minutes by practicing these techniques with whatever is handy—license plate numbers, telephone numbers, to-do lists and even e-mail addresses. In no time, you should notice a big improvement in your memory skills.

Memory-Boosting Marvel

Dharma Singh Khalsa, MD, founding medical director, Alzheimer's Prevention Foundation, Tucson. He is author of *Brain Longevity: The Breakthrough Medical Program That Improves Mood and Memory* (Grand Central).

If you've begun to experience problems with your memory, ask your doctor about taking *phosphatidylserine*. This compound occurs naturally in the outer membranes of brain cells...and in certain plants as well.

In studies sponsored by the National Institutes of Health, phosphatidylserine improved memory and concentration in people suffering from age-related memory loss and even early stage Alzheimer's disease.

Phosphatidylserine seems to work just as well as two prescription medications used to treat Alzheimer's—*tacrine* (Cognex) and *donepezil* (Aricept). Tacrine can cause liver damage. Phosphatidylserine is free of harmful side effects.

For otherwise healthy individuals who simply want to hone their mental skills, I often recommend one 100-milligram (mg) capsule of phosphatidylserine per day.

For mild to severe memory impairment, two or three capsules a day often work better. There is no additional benefit to taking more than 300 mg a day.

Phosphatidylserine can also be taken in conjunction with ginkgo biloba, an herb that is believed to enhance memory. It's usually best to take 40 mg of ginkgo biloba for every 100 mg of phosphatidylserine.

Phosphatidylserine and ginkgo biloba are sold in health food stores.

Caution: Consult your doctor before taking ginkgo if you're taking aspirin, *warfarin* (Coumadin) or another blood-thinning drug. Women who are pregnant or nursing should avoid both phosphatidylserine and ginkgo.

Protect Yourself From Dementia

Jeff Victoroff, MD, associate professor of clinical neurology and psychiatry, Keck School of Medicine, University of Southern California, Los Angeles. He is also author of *Saving Your Brain: The Revolutionary Plan to Boost Brain Power, Improve Memory, and Protect Yourself Against Aging and Alzheimer's* (Bantam).

Of all the illnesses that threaten us as we grow older, very few are more frightening than dementia. Science hasn't yet devised a foolproof shield against the ravages of dementia, but you can take steps to put the odds in your favor.

AGING AND THE BRAIN

Scientific evidence suggests that the brain damage of dementia is largely an exaggerated form of what happens to normal brains over time. *For example...*

•**Neurodegeneration.** Brain cells are damaged by unstable molecules called free radicals. During aging, brain cells are less able to repair their own DNA. In addition, deposits of a protein known as *amyloid* form plaques that impede the workings of neurons. Increasing numbers of brain cells die. This process can lead to dementia and Alzheimer's disease.

•**Vascular factors.** A narrowing and stiffening of small arteries may decrease the delivery of blood to certain areas of the brain, resulting in ministrokes—blockages that kill small pockets of cells in the brain. This process may impair brain function.

What will determine how fast these changes occur? Some brains are genetically programmed to degenerate more rapidly than others. But up to 50% of the changes can be attributed to environmental factors, which include a person's lifestyle choices.

FORTIFY WITH FISH

In one study involving 5,500 men and women, eating fish at least once a week led to a 70% reduction in Alzheimer's risk.

Why? Omega-3s, fatty acids found in certain fish, facilitate the transmission of messages between brain cells—the foundation of all mental activity. These same fats help maintain cardiovascular health and slow the circulation decline that plays a significant role in brain damage.

What's new: Findings from a study conducted in the Netherlands indicate that something in the fish other than the omega-3 content may play a role in its benefits. This means that fish oil supplements might *not* be as effective as the whole fish.

Helpful: Eat four ounces of fish at least four times a week, particularly fatty fish, such as salmon, sardines, herring, trout and mackerel. Canned tuna is also good. To avoid potentially dangerous levels of mercury, pregnant women should talk to their doctor before eating fish.

GET YOUR ANTIOXIDANT ARMOR

The body produces its own antioxidants to neutralize brain-damaging free radicals. They work much more effectively with the help of antioxidant nutrients—vitamins C and E and beta-carotene.

What's new: Two studies, conducted by Martha C. Morris, ScD, at Rush-Presbyterian–St. Luke's Medical Center in Chicago, suggest that vitamin E—either from food or supplements—may reduce the risk for Alzheimer's disease.

Helpful: Ask your doctor about taking 400 international units (IU) of *natural* vitamin E (d-alpha-tocopherol) every day. The natural form crosses into the brain more readily than the synthetic vitamin. Also be sure to include vitamin E–rich foods, such as vegetable oils, wheat germ, almonds and other nuts and seeds, in your diet.

DRINK FOR BRAIN HEALTH

Moderate drinking—one or two glasses of wine, beer or liquor a day, for example—has been shown to protect the heart. This includes reducing the risk for brain-destroying strokes.

What's new: Alcohol consumption appears to be beneficial for brain function as well. Researchers at the University of Bordeaux in France followed 3,777 people age 65 or older and found that those who drank one or two glasses of wine per day were 45% less likely to develop Alzheimer's than were nondrinkers.

Helpful: Drink one glass of white wine a day. Other forms of alcohol may work too, but they are more likely to cause headaches, weight gain and other unpleasant effects. Beyond two drinks daily, the damaging effects of alcohol on brain cells may outweigh the benefits. Women should not exceed one alcoholic drink per day, because it may increase their risk for developing breast cancer, according to some studies.

Important: If you have had trouble controlling your alcohol intake in the past, do *not* start drinking to protect your brain.

EXERCISE FOR BRAIN HEALTH

Aerobic exercise helps to maintain healthy blood circulation and protects the brain from slow deterioration.

What's new: A Canadian study of 4,615 men and women age 65 or older found that brisk walking at least *three times* weekly cut the incidence of Alzheimer's by one-third. Jogging reduced the risk by 52%.

Helpful: Exercise enough to get your heart rate up and break a sweat—jogging, biking, walking faster than three miles per hour—for 30 minutes at least five times weekly.

MENTAL FITNESS

Studies have indicated that higher education and mentally challenging work can reduce Alzheimer's risk and slow memory loss.

What's new: Research conducted at Columbia University in New York City suggests that even people with low-level educations will have a reduced risk for Alzheimer's if they work at mentally challenging jobs.

Examples: Writer, teacher, researcher, designer or any job that requires creativity and learning new skills.

Helpful: Make learning a lifelong pursuit. Take up chess…learn new languages…develop computer skills.

Early Sign of Dementia

Abnormal walking may be an early sign of dementia. In a 21-year study of people over the age of 75, 43% of participants who had an abnormal gait, such as short-step shuffling or unsteady walking, developed non-Alzheimer's dementia over an average period of seven years. Only 26% of those with a normal gait developed dementia.

Theory: Vascular lesions, loss of nerve cells and other brain changes that alter movement patterns can also cause damage that may lead to dementia.

If you develop an abnormal gait: See your doctor for a thorough medical examination. He/she may suggest strategies that will help reduce your risk for developing dementia.

Joe Verghese, MD, associate professor of neurology, Albert Einstein College of Medicine, Bronx, NY.

Olive Oil Helps Keep Your Brain Healthy, Too

Eat to fight cognitive decline by including monounsaturated fats, such as olive oil, in your diet—instead of saturated fats, such as butter and other animal fats.

Recent study: Elderly Southern Italians consuming a typical Mediterranean diet were less likely to develop age-related cognitive problems if they consumed large amounts of olive oil—the oil with the most monounsaturated fat per ounce.

Also: Unsaturated fats work to lower LDL ("bad") cholesterol levels in the blood while helping to raise HDL ("good") cholesterol. This is important to people who are at risk for heart disease and stroke.

Vincenzo Solfrizzi, MD, PhD, specialist in geriatric medicine, department of geriatrics, Center for Aging Brain, University of Bari-Policlinico, Bari, Italy.

What You Can Do to Keep Your Brain Healthy

Gary Small, MD, director, Memory Clinic and Center on Aging, University of California, Los Angeles. He is author of *The Memory Bible: An Innovative Strategy for Keeping Your Brain Young* (Hyperion).

By the time we reach middle age, most people will occasionally forget names, and important dates may start to slip our minds. We'll miss an appointment or misplace our keys from time to time. As the years pass, the forgetfulness will get worse.

Beyond the simple nuisance, the worry persists—are these the first signs of Alzheimer's? Can anything be done?

Actually, there's a good deal you can do to sharpen your memory *and* reduce the risk that you'll fall victim to dementia.

UNDERSTANDING BRAIN AGING

As the brain ages, the synapses (connections between brain cells) function less efficiently. Brain cells die, leaving behind bits of abnormal protein—plaques and tangles—that accumulate in damaged cells. The brain actually shrinks.

Loss of brain cell function is most marked in the areas responsible for memory—near the forehead (frontal lobe) and near and above the temples (temporal and parietal regions). But while some people have significant memory loss by age 60, other people remain sharp well into their 90s.

What makes the difference? Some factors, such as our genes, we *cannot* control. But we *can* have an influence on the lifestyle factors, including exercise, diet and stress levels.

BRAIN-FRIENDLY LIFESTYLE

Memory loss can be triggered by heart disease, anemia, thyroid disorders and dehydration. High blood pressure and diabetes can also accelerate aging of the brain, but proper treatment of these conditions will help reverse much of your memory trouble.

Many medications can also impair memory. These include blood pressure drugs, sleeping pills, tranquilizers, stomach acid reducers and corticosteroids.

If your memory has worsened since you started taking a new medication, ask your doctor if it could be affecting your memory.

In addition to checking for medical conditions that may trigger memory loss, you should adopt a lifestyle that promotes cardiovascular health. This will improve blood circulation to the brain and reduce the risk for small strokes (*transient ischemic attacks,* or TIAs) that hasten its deterioration.

To promote brain health, pay attention to...

•**Exercise.** Regular aerobic exercise has been shown to protect against heart attack and stroke. Some studies suggest that it even lowers the likelihood of developing Alzheimer's disease. Walking for 30 minutes three times a week may be enough to gain this benefit.

Physical exertion also results in *immediate* brain gains. Immediately following any exercise, people are better at problem-solving and complex reasoning.

•**Diet.** Eat a low-calorie, low-fat diet that is rich in the omega-3 fats found in fish, flaxseed and olive oil. An Italian study found that a diet that includes three tablespoons of olive oil daily reduces memory loss.

Antioxidants, particularly vitamins E and C, protect the brain against damage by free radicals. Get these nutrients in your diet—almonds and leafy, green vegetables for vitamin E... citrus fruits for vitamin C. In addition, take daily supplements—400 international units (IU) of natural vitamin E (check first with your doctor for the appropriate amount)...and 500 milligrams (mg) of vitamin C.

•**Stress.** Research has shown that the stress hormone *cortisol* reduces a person's ability to retrieve information and memory. Even worse, this same stress hormone is linked to progressive shrinking of the *hippocampus*—an important memory center in the temporal region. High levels of stress also promote depression, which severely impairs memory and increases the risk for dementia.

To reduce stress, try relaxation exercises. Sit quietly, and breathe deeply and slowly. Relax each part of your body, starting with the top of your head and finishing with your toes. In addition, look for humor in tense situations... and talk about your feelings with family members, friends or a therapist, if necessary.

More from Gary Small...

Common Drugs Fight Alzheimer's

Nonsteroidal anti-inflammatory drugs (NSAIDs), such as *ibuprofen* and *naproxen,* seem to help clear the brain lesions caused by plaque buildup in Alzheimer's patients. These drugs bond to and help to break up the plaque, which also prevents new lesions from forming. All this suggests that anti-inflammatories may be useful in lowering a person's chance of developing Alzheimer's, but more research is needed.

Possible Cause of Alzheimer's

Alzheimer's disease may be linked to excess copper. A defect in the mechanism that balances copper in the body may raise blood levels of the mineral, creating toxic amounts in the brain.

Self-defense: Limit your intake of copper to 1.5 to 3 milligrams (mg) a day.

Examples: Two ounces of liver or four medium oysters contain about 2.5 mg of copper. And, three ounces of lobster contains 1.6 mg of copper.

The defect that permits excess copper to accumulate in the brain can be detected with a blood test.

Rosanna Squitti, PhD, researcher, department of neuroscience, AFaR-Fatebenefratelli Hospital, Rome.

Natural Helper For Alzheimer's

Aromatherapy may decrease agitation from Alzheimer's disease. In one study, applying lemon balm to the face and arms helped ease agitation in up to 60% of patients treated, compared with only 14% who received the placebo cream. The lemon balm group was also more sociable with others and better able to perform constructive activities.

Elaine K. Perry, PhD, senior scientist, Newcastle General Hospital, Newcastle upon Tyne, England. Her study was published in *The Journal of Clinical Psychiatry.*

Surprising Reasons Why People Fall

David M. Buchner, MD, MPH, chief, Physical Activity and Health Branch, US Centers for Disease Control and Prevention, Atlanta. He is a world-renowned expert in falls and injury prevention, and chairman of the steering committee for large-scale Frailty and Injuries: Cooperative Studies of Intervention Techniques (FICSIT) trials.

In 2004, two prominent Americans—diet guru Robert Atkins, MD, age 72, and veteran news broadcaster David Brinkley, 82—died of complications resulting from falls. These are *not* isolated cases. Each year, 12 million older Americans fall, resulting in about 10,000 deaths. In adults age 65 or older, falls are the main cause of accidental death.

Most people assume that they know how to prevent a fall. *But the truth is that many commonly held beliefs about falls are wrong...*

***Myth #1:* Most falls are just bad luck.**

Fact: Falls don't happen at random. They occur much more frequently in people who have muscle weakness, poor vision, problems with the inner ear, arthritis and poor sensation in the legs. Certain medications—particularly those that cause sedation—also increase the risk for falling.

421

Some older adults fall because of a drop in blood pressure that causes them to lose consciousness. These falls can be caused by an irregular heart rhythm or a drop in blood pressure that occurs upon standing (*orthostatic hypotension*).

Helpful: Anyone who falls more than once in a year or suffers an injury or temporarily loses consciousness from a fall should see his/her health care provider. Even if you have fallen only once, see your doctor for a thorough evaluation if you're concerned about problems with your balance or gait.

Myth #2: Physical activity increases the risk for falling.

Fact: Nearly 75% of older adults are sedentary or insufficiently active—and they lose up to 2% of muscle strength every year between ages 65 and 85.

A loss of strength combined with other problems, such as changes in the body's balancing center (vestibular system), greatly increases the risk for falling.

Older adults who fall frequently also lose physical confidence. To avoid having accidents, they become more sedentary. But this decreases muscle strength, making them even more likely to fall.

Helpful: Exercise for 30 minutes at least three days a week. This can reduce your risk for falling by up to 50%. Walking at a moderate pace for 30 minutes most days of the week provides many of the same health benefits as more vigorous exercise, such as jogging—and is less likely to cause injury.

Myth #3: Older adults don't gain much benefit from weight training.

Fact: Research shows 20% to 100% increases in muscle strength when older adults adopt regular strength training using exercise machines.

Helpful: Weight lifting or other forms of strength training should be performed two or three days each week.

Myth #4: Balance exercises aren't that effective in preventing fall risk.

Fact: Existing research suggests that balance exercises are the most effective type of exercise in a fall-prevention program.

There are several types of exercises and programs. *Consider one or more of the following to improve balance...*

• **Tai chi.** This ancient Chinese practice consists of a series of slow, flowing self-guided movements originally used in martial arts. It's taught at most health clubs and used at many rehabilitation centers.

• **Physical therapy.** Physical therapists can provide information and training about balance exercises. They can assess your balance abilities and recommend exercises.

Examples: Slowly walking backward, heel-to-toe, while holding a table for support...walking with arms outstretched or folded across the chest.

To locate a physical therapist in your area, consult the American Physical Therapy Association's Web site, *www.apta.org,* or ask your health care provider for a referral.

• **Fall-prevention exercise class.** Some community exercise classes include strength and balance exercises and are appropriate for older adults who may be at increased risk for falling. To find such a class, check with your health care provider or consult a local phone directory to locate community fitness centers in your area.

Myth #5: Blood pressure–lowering drugs are more likely than other medications to trigger falls.

Fact: Blood pressure–lowering drugs do increase the risk for falls when blood pressure is low or orthostatic hypotension develops. But fall risk actually is greatest in people who take four or more different drugs.

The use of multiple drugs (known as *polypharmacy*) commonly causes dizziness, inhibits muscle and nerve action and/or triggers orthostatic hypotension.

Problem drugs: In general, many antidepressants, antihistamines, sedatives, as well as blood pressure–lowering drugs.

Helpful: Make a list of the medications you take, and share it with all of your doctors.

Don't assume they know what you're taking from reviewing your medical records—omissions are common. It's almost always possible to reduce the risk for drug-related falls by changing or eliminating medications or lowering doses.

Caution: Never discontinue a drug without consulting your doctor.

Myth #6: **You can prevent most falls just by watching your step.**

Fact: Many falls occur when older adults attempt the same activities that they performed effortlessly when they were younger—going quickly up and down stairs, for example. Not being aware of age-related changes in balance and strength leads to risky behavior.

Helpful: Appraise your strengths and weaknesses. Be honest with yourself about your physical limitations. Consider safer ways of doing things—and be more careful.

Examples: Hold onto the rail when using the stairs...and use a "grabber" instead of climbing on a step stool to reach high shelves.

Myth #7: **Tripping hazards are the main home danger.***

Fact: People do trip on obvious hazards, such as throw rugs and electrical cords. But the bathroom is probably the most dangerous room in the house—not only because of slippery floors, but because rising from the bathtub or toilet can trigger dangerous drops in blood pressure.

Helpful: Install no-slip strips in the tub and "grab bars" next to the toilet and tub. Most older adults need brighter light to see clearly and avoid fall hazards, so be sure that all areas of your home are well-lighted.

More from David M. Buchner...

Test Your Mobility

To assess your mobility—and to learn more about your risk for falling—try a simple test. *Here's what to do...*

*If you're concerned about your risk for falling, schedule a home visit from an occupational therapist, who can inspect your house for potential trouble spots. To find an occupational therapist in your area, contact the American Occupational Therapy Association at 301-652-2682 or *www.aota.org*.

Sit in an armchair and check the second hand on your wristwatch. Get up and walk 10 feet at your normal pace. Turn around, return to the chair and sit down. How long did it take?

Use the guide below to determine your level of balance. If your rating is less than "good," see your doctor for a health evaluation and advice on improving mobility.

Good mobility: Less than 10 seconds.

Fair mobility: 10 to 20 seconds.

Poor mobility: 21 to 30 seconds.

Impaired mobility: More than 30 seconds.

Protect Your Bones Against Fracture

Felicia Cosman, MD, clinical director, National Osteoporosis Foundation, Washington, DC (*www.nof.org*), and medical director, clinical research center, Helen Hayes Hospital, West Haverstraw, NY.

Contrary to popular belief, osteoporosis is *not* just a women's problem. More than half of all Americans over age 50 have lost enough bone mass to put them at risk for osteoporosis.

All told, 8 million American women and 2 million men have osteoporosis. This means their bones have become porous and fragile enough to make them susceptible to fractures, particularly of the hip, spine and wrist.

BONE—THE HARD FACTS

Bones may seem rock-solid, but they're actually living tissue in which old bone is constantly being removed (a process called *resorption*) and replaced by new bone. While you're young, more bone is added than lost, so your bones grow thicker and stronger, reaching a peak in your early 20s.

After that, the balance shifts and your bones start thinning. The change is barely perceptible until the mid-40s...then it accelerates.

For women, the drop in bone density is most dramatic around the time of menopause. That's when production of the hormone estrogen, which keeps a brake on the resorption process, grinds to a halt. For men, the decline is more gradual, with the dwindling of the hormones, testosterone and estrogen, which men also produce.

RISK FACTORS

Lifestyle factors also play a role in osteoporosis. Many people consume less calcium as they grow older, and most are less physically active. *Other risk factors…*

●**Family history.** If a parent or sibling has suffered osteoporosis or a fracture, you are at greater risk.

●**Body type.** Thin, small-framed women and men are especially vulnerable.

●**Medical history.** Increased osteoporosis risk is associated with rheumatoid arthritis, lupus and other autoimmune conditions…chronic lung disease…an overactive thyroid…and malabsorption syndromes, such as celiac disease.

●**Medications.** Corticosteroids, epilepsy drugs and thyroid hormones can weaken bone.

SLOWING BONE LOSS

Calcium is vital for bone strength. But *all* cells in the body need the mineral to function properly. If you're not getting enough, your body will leach calcium from your bones.

The recommended daily intake for calcium is 1,000 milligrams (mg) daily. But for maximum bone health, you need at least 1,200 mg daily after age 49. It's hard to get that much calcium in the diet alone. Many Americans get less than *half* the calcium they need.

If you don't get at least three daily servings of high-calcium foods, such as yogurt, cheese or calcium-fortified juices, consider taking a supplement that contains at least 600 mg of the mineral to reach your total daily goal.

Calcium carbonate is the most economical, because it contains 40% calcium per supplement. *Calcium citrate* contains 25% calcium per pill. To make sure calcium carbonate is absorbed properly, take it with food. Calcium citrate can be taken without food.

Caution: Drugs that block stomach acid production (Prilosec and Prevacid, for example) interfere with calcium carbonate absorption. If you use them, take a calcium citrate supplement, which doesn't require acid for absorption.

Vitamin D enables your bones to absorb and utilize calcium. Milk is fortified with vitamin D, and your body produces it naturally when exposed to sunlight. To ensure you're getting enough vitamin D, take 400 international units (IU) daily…800 IU daily if you're over age 65.

Warning: High intake of protein and salt increases the rate at which you lose calcium via urine. To compensate for this, be sure to get at least 1,200 mg of calcium daily.

Exercise stimulates bone to replenish itself. To benefit *all* your bones, a full exercise program should include on-your-feet aerobic activity and resistance training.

Get 30 minutes of exercise—jogging, stair-climbing, dancing, aerobic calisthenics, racket sports or brisk walking—at least three times a week. Use weights or exercise machines that work the major muscle groups for 30 minutes, two or three times a week.

BONE-PRESERVING DRUGS

Medication to reduce the rate of bone loss is indicated *only* if you are at high risk for fracture because of osteoporosis or low bone mass or if you have one or more additional factors (such as corticosteroid use, prior fracture or family history of fractures).

Selective estrogen receptor modulators, such as *raloxifene* (Evista), act like estrogen, but only in some parts of the body, including bone. For use only by women, raloxifene reduces bone loss and may also lower the risk for breast cancer.

Bisphosphonates bind to bone and slow bone loss. These drugs, *alendronate* (Fosamax) and *risedronate* (Actonel), can be used by men and women and are highly effective at reducing fractures. *Teriparatide* (Forteo) is another bone-building medication for people with severe osteoporosis. It is given daily by injection for up to two years.

SHOULD YOU BE TESTED?

A bone mineral density test, a painless, 10-minute scan that uses minimal radiation, should be considered if your family history, unexplained fractures or loss of height suggests bone loss. Testing is also recommended for all women over age 65 and all men over age 75.

Home Remedies For Common Conditions

Doug Dollemore, who has written on the subject of aging for many years. Mr. Dollemore is author of several books, including *The Doctor's Book of Home Remedies for Seniors* (Rodale Press).

There's much we can do to maintain our own health and manage our own care as we age. *Here are some home remedies for common conditions...*

CLUMSINESS

If you're constantly tripping over your own feet, or can't wash the dishes without breaking one, you might try changing the way you do things. *Strategies...*

●**Stay physically fit.** Fitness will help you maintain your balance, especially when you reach out to grab something.

●**Get regular eye checkups**—to keep your corrected vision at its best.

●**Don't rush.** It's better to take a little extra time on a task than to have an accident—and possibly be injured.

●**Sit while doing chores that you can just as easily do seated.** This way, you can concentrate on the task without worrying about your balance.

●**Get a better handle on things.** Buy coffee mugs and other handheld items with thick handles. Wrap cork tape (used on bicycle handles and available in most bicycle shops) around the handles of spoons, knives, tools, etc., for a better grip.

●**Wear rubber gloves when washing the dishes.** You'll be better able to handle slippery glasses and plates.

MEMORY LOSS

As you age, you may find your memory is not as good as it used to be. But—there are a number of simple strategies that may help keep your mind sharp and your memory working to capacity. *For example...*

●**To-do lists** are a valuable way to remind yourself of things you have a tendency to forget. But don't rely on written lists exclusively.

At least once a week, exercise your memory skills by relying on a mental list.

●**Aerobic exercises,** such as brisk walking, biking and swimming can improve memory by 20% to 30%.

●**Get enough sleep** to keep your brain in top shape.

●**Keep your things organized.** If you always put everything in its place, you will know where to find it.

●**Talk to yourself** as you do a task to focus your attention on what you are doing and make it easier to remember later.

DESIRE

Sex should be enjoyed throughout life. (If you're having physical problems, see a doctor. They are generally correctable.) *To help rekindle your desire...*

●**Treat sex as play.** Use hugs, kisses and gentle caresses to show tenderness—emotional rewards are as fulfilling as physical ones.

●**Be romantic.** A moonlit walk...a single blossom left on your spouse's pillow...bathing together by candlelight.

●**Be creative.** Planting a garden, baking bread, building a piece of furniture—or any creative activity—can rev up your sex drive.

FOOT PAIN

For quick, temporary relief of most types of foot pain, take ibuprofen or other over-the-counter nonsteroidal anti-inflammatory drugs (NSAIDs)...but not for more than a few weeks at a time.

For longer-lasting relief, wear sneakers or running shoes, or put heel cups and/or other cushioned inserts in your shoes. And lose weight to reduce the pressure on your feet.

There are also two ways you can relieve foot pain by stretching your Achilles tendon. Do these stretches before going to bed and before getting up in the morning.

●**Sit or lie down,** bend your leg until you can reach your toes and use both hands to pull your toes toward your shin. Hold this pose for 20 seconds.

●**Place your hands on the wall and lean forward** with your feet flat on the ground, keeping your back straight and knees straight.

Repeat 10 times, holding each stretch for about 30 seconds.

You can also relieve foot pain by rubbing your feet with capsaicin cream...and reduce swelling by soaking them in warm water with Epsom salts (one tablespoon per quart).

Eating a half teaspoon of ground fresh ginger daily also reduces swelling.

OSTEOPOROSIS

A healthy diet and lifestyle are the keys to avoiding the bone loss that can lead to fragility. *Most important...*

●**Get enough calcium.** 1,000 milligrams (mg) per day for people under age 65, and 1,200 mg per day for those age 65 and older and all postmenopausal women not taking the hormone estrogen.

Sources: Two-and-a-half to three glasses of fat-free milk daily...or two-and-a-half cups of fat-free yogurt...or five ounces of no-fat cheese.

Non-dairy sources: Sardines with bones... tofu...collard greens...calcium-fortified orange juice. Calcium is absorbed most effectively when taken with vitamin D.

Sources of vitamin D: Milk, certain breakfast cereals and exposure to sunlight.

●**Protein** should make up 30% to 40% of your diet.

●**Strengthen bones** with weight-bearing exercises, but avoid those that require bending and twisting motions that strain joints and risk breaking bones. The recommended 20 to 30 minutes a day of aerobic exercises—like walking and weight lifting—three times a week can be made up from smaller chunks of time.

Helpful exercise: Stand up straight against a wall with your spine as straight as possible... squeeze your shoulder blades.

Also: Don't smoke tobacco...or consume more than one-and-a-half ounces of hard liquor ...or more than 12 ounces of beer...or more than five ounces of wine...or more than three caffeinated drinks...or more than 2,400 mg of sodium per day.

HIGH BLOOD PRESSURE

To minimize your risk of heart disease or stroke, aim to keep your blood pressure reading at or below 115/75. It may be possible for you to accomplish this without medication by making two simple changes—losing weight (even just a few pounds will help) and keeping your sodium intake below 2,400 mg a day.

Reduce sodium intake by eating low-sodium foods...adding spices instead of salt.

Also—eat enough fruits and vegetables to bring your potassium intake up to 3,500 mg per day (for example, a medium-sized banana has 467 mg of potassium and a four-ounce baked potato without skin has 607 mg)...take a brisk 30-minute walk every day...get 1,200 mg of calcium and 400 international units (IU) of vitamin D per day. And if you don't have any heart or kidney problems, get 400 mg of magnesium daily.

SNORING

Snoring occurs while inhaling during sleep. The soft tissues of the throat vibrate against your tongue or the back of your throat. *To help quiet snoring...*

●**Sleep on your side or stomach,** not flat on your back.

Helpful: Sew a tennis ball into the back of your pajamas.

●**Spray your nose with Nasalcrom spray** before going to sleep. This will help clear your nasal passages and improve breathing if you have allergies.

●**If your nostrils get sucked in as you breathe,** tape a Breathe Right nasal strip over your nose before going to bed.

●**Avoid alcohol and sleeping pills.** And don't smoke.

●**Humidify the bedroom.**

Severe snoring may be caused by *sleep apnea.* It occurs if the passage of air is completely blocked many times each night during sleep. This condition causes a dangerous increase in blood pressure and can result in heart failure, depression and mental clouding.

If loud snoring persists despite all your prevention techniques, consult a physician specializing in sleep disorders.

Hidden Threat to Older Adults

Carol Colleran, internationally certified alcohol and drug counselor (ICADC), and national director, older adult services, Hanley Center, West Palm Beach, FL, which provides abstinence-based recovery services for those with substance abuse problems. She is coauthor of *Aging & Addiction* (Hazelden).

M ost people don't think a silver-haired retiree could be a substance abuser, but it happens all too often. And unfortunately, many warning signs may be dismissed as part of normal aging.

According to a recent report of the Substance Abuse and Mental Health Services Administration, a federal agency, one in six American adults ages 60 or older is believed to use alcohol or prescription drugs in destructive, uncontrolled ways.

When addiction takes hold, considerable health hazards accompany it, such as hypertension, brain damage, liver ailments, secondary diabetes, memory loss and stroke.

WHY IT HAPPENS

Although many older alcohol and drug abusers have had substance abuse problems all their lives, for a rising proportion—about one-third—difficulties start *after* age 50.

Perhaps the single most common contributing factor in so-called "late-onset" substance abuse is a loss of sense of purpose, which frequently occurs when an older adult enters retirement, finishes raising a family, etc.

This is a real danger for people who may have given considerable thought to financial planning, but little to the "emotional retirement" that occurs when working life is left behind.

In one's personal life, the death of a spouse brings not only the ache of bereavement, but also a terrible sense that the survivor is no longer needed.

ACCIDENTAL ADDICTION

Drug or alcohol problems can sneak up on people who have no idea they're engaging in risky behavior. *Here's how...*

•**Alcohol.** As we age, the changes that occur in our bodies dramatically affect how we respond to substances like alcohol.

For example, the water content of the body decreases and fat content increases, which slows the rate at which some substances are metabolized. This can result in quicker intoxication and greater damage to the liver, kidneys and other organs.

A slowdown in the liver, stomach and kidneys also reduces the rate at which alcohol is broken down and processed.

Result: Even when you consume small amounts, it builds up and the effects last longer.

Women become intoxicated faster than men from small amounts of alcohol. In general, women have less body water than men of similar body weight, so that women will achieve higher concentrations of alcohol in the blood after drinking equivalent amounts.

Result: Many people who continue drinking the same modest quantities that they have for years—or even less than they used to—start running into difficulties.

To protect yourself: Limit your alcohol intake to no more than two drinks a day for older men, and one drink a day for women. (One drink equals one five-ounce glass of wine, one 12-ounce wine cooler, 1.5 ounces of hard liquor or one 12-ounce glass of beer.)

•**Drugs.** Most older adults don't intend to get high. They become dependent on medications that were prescribed for medical reasons.

Most common offenders: Opiate painkillers, including *codeine, oxycodone* (OxyContin), *acetaminophen* and *oxycodone* (Percocet)...and anxiety-quelling benzodiazepines, such as *diazepam* (Valium) and *alprazolam* (Xanax).

Caution: Do not discontinue any medication without consulting your doctor.

Problem: Most drugs are tested only on younger people, and doctors fail to adjust the dose to take into account the slowed-down metabolism of older adults.

Most of these drugs are stored in body fat. Because the aging body has a higher proportion of fatty tissue, more of the drug remains in the fat, lessening its effect on the body. This often causes the person to take more of the drug.

427

Also: Doctors frequently fail to follow guidelines advising that these medications be used only for limited periods. It's not unusual, for example, to see older adults who have been taking Valium regularly for 20 years.

To protect yourself: Whenever you are prescribed a drug, ask your doctor why you are taking it...how long it should be used... and whether it's known to commonly cause addiction.

TREATING A HIDDEN EPIDEMIC

Substance abuse in older adults often goes undetected. That's partially because many red flags that would arouse attention in a younger person are dismissed as the effects of aging. These warning signs often include shaky hands ...balance problems...erratic driving...and loss of memory.

If a problem is identified, treatment typically includes a medical evaluation, nutritional plan and counseling. Studies have found that, whenever possible, older adults should undergo treatment with people of the same age.

Twelve-step programs, such as Alcoholics Anonymous or Narcotics Anonymous, are excellent resources for older adults.

To find additional help, contact the Substance Abuse and Mental Health Services Administration's Referral Routing Service at 800-662-4357 or visit its Web site, *www.findtreatment.samhsa.gov.*

More from Carol Colleran...

Do You Have an Alcohol or Drug Problem?

If you answer "yes" to any of the following questions, ask your doctor for a referral to a professional substance abuse counselor...

● **In the last year,** have you ever drunk alcohol or used a drug more than you meant to?

● **Have you wanted to cut down on drinking or taking drugs?**

● **Have people criticized you for your drinking or drug use?**

● **Have you felt bad or guilty about it?**

● **Do you ever have a drink first thing in the morning** to steady your nerves?

● **If you take a drink or two,** does it relieve shakiness?

● **Do you find it hard to remember parts of the day** or night after drinking?

Also: Be alert for symptoms of substance abuse in older friends and relatives. These include sleep problems...mental confusion... poor nutrition or loss of appetite...incontinence ...repeated falls...unexplained burns and bruises ...isolation...and depression. If you are concerned, consult a doctor.

The Fountain of Youth Is in the Foods You Eat

Laurie Deutsch Mozian, MS, RD, Woodstock, NY–based author of *Foods That Fight Disease* (Avery). She is a nutrition consultant who lectures extensively on phytochemicals in foods.

The research is overwhelming. You may dramatically reduce your risk of developing chronic diseases—from cataracts and cancer to heart disease and stroke—by eating more fruits, vegetables, legumes and other plant-based foods.

These foods are loaded with protective compounds called *phytochemicals.* Unlike vitamins and minerals, which are essential for preserving health, phytochemicals actually stop changes in the body that can lead to disease.

Nearly all plant foods contain phytochemicals, but these few really stand out...

CRUCIFEROUS VEGETABLES

Broccoli, cabbage, cauliflower and other crucifers—such as arugula, bok choy, collards and watercress—contain a variety of cancer-fighting compounds.

Example: Broccoli contains *sulforaphane,* which boosts the body's ability to produce cancer-stopping enzymes. It also contains *indole-3-carbinol,* which lowers levels of harmful estrogens in the body and may reduce the risk of breast cancer.

BRIGHTLY COLORED VEGETABLES

The same plant pigments that give vegetables their bright color also provide impressive health benefits.

Examples: The orange or yellow flesh of winter squash comes from *beta-carotene,* a phytochemical that is a precursor to vitamin A. It blocks the effects of harmful oxygen molecules called free radicals in the body. Free-radical damage is thought to contribute to many conditions associated with aging—memory loss, heart disease, cancer, cataracts, etc.

Other top choices: Sweet potatoes, spinach, kale and carrots.

TOMATOES

Tomatoes deserve special mention because they contain the exceptionally powerful phytochemical *lycopene.* Lycopene may reduce risk of cancer. It also may protect against cancers of the breast, lung and endometrium.

For the most benefit: Lightly cook tomatoes in a little oil, which enhances the body's absorption of lycopene. If you don't eat a lot of whole tomatoes, take advantage of tomato sauce. Unlike some phytochemicals, lycopene isn't damaged by the high heats used in food processing.

PEAS AND BEANS

Legumes, in addition to being excellent sources of protein and dietary fiber, contain a rich array of phytochemicals.

Examples: Soy beans and most other beans contain *genistein,* which may reduce the risk of breast cancer as well as reduce hot flashes and other types of menopausal discomfort. Legumes also contain *saponins,* compounds that help lower cholesterol and may prevent DNA in cells from undergoing cancerous changes.

Take advantage of canned beans: They contain nearly the same phytochemical payload as dried beans, without the long cooking time. Rinse to remove salt before using.

FRUITS

Let color be your guide. Pink fruits, such as watermelon and guava, contain lycopene, which is twice as effective as beta-carotene at blocking free radicals.

Bluish fruits, such as red grapes and blueberries, contain *anthrocyanins,* which reduce the amount of cholesterol produced by the liver.

Few foods are better for your health than apples. Like many fruits, apples contain quercetin, which helps prevent buildup of cholesterol in arteries. Most of the quercetin is found in the apple's skin.

GARLIC AND ONIONS

These foods are members of the *allium* family, which also includes leeks, chives and shallots. Allium vegetables are incredibly rich in phytochemicals.

Examples: Garlic is loaded with allicin, which has been shown to lower cholesterol and high blood pressure. The active ingredient in garlic isn't released until the cloves are minced or crushed.

If raw garlic is too overpowering for your taste, sauté or bake the cloves until they're soft. This sweetens the flavor and reduces the "bite"—but it might also reduce the effectiveness of the phytochemicals. Raw garlic also contains *ajoene,* a phytochemical that makes blood platelets less sticky. Ajoene is not found in garlic capsules.

Onions contain *diallyl sulfide,* which may protect against cancer. In Vidalia, Georgia, the "onion capital of the world," the rate of stomach cancer is about half the national average.

GINGER

The phytochemicals found in ginger can help prevent nausea better than over-the-counter drugs. Some compounds in this herb also have anti-inflammatory effects, which may help joint swelling caused by arthritis.

FLAXSEED

Grains are rich in phytochemicals, but flaxseed is unique because it is a rich source of *lignans.* These compounds help prevent free radicals from damaging healthy cells and increasing risk of cancer. Lignans help lower cholesterol.

Important: Crush seeds or grind them in a small coffee grinder. Whole flaxseed has a tough coating that isn't broken down in the digestive tract. Ground flaxseed has a nutty taste that is good when sprinkled over cereal or added to soups or salads. Or use about one tablespoon in an eight-ounce yogurt.

Since flaxseed is high in fiber, you might want to start with a smaller dosage and gradually work your way up.

TEA

Tea, either hot or iced, is rich in *polyphenols,* which help prevent free radicals from oxidizing cholesterol in the blood. Cholesterol that is oxidized is more likely to stick to artery walls, increasing the risk of heart disease or stroke. Tea also contains the phytochemical *EGCG,* which appears to interfere with all stages of cancer. As few as four cups of tea a day have protective benefits.

Both ordinary black and green teas contain polyphenols. Green tea undergoes less processing than black tea, so it is a better source of polyphenols.

The Ultimate Antiaging Diet

Elizabeth Somer, MA, RD, Salem, OR–based registered dietitian, and a frequent guest on NBC's *Today Show.* She is author of several books, including *Age-Proof Your Body: Your Complete Guide to Lifelong Vitality* (McGraw-Hill).

Americans spend billions of dollars each year trying to eliminate wrinkles, gray hair and other signs that they are getting older. But *true* aging happens *inside* the body.

The best way to combat it is to eat a healthful diet—one that supplies nutrients without exposing cells to harmful substances that promote aging. *Here are the eight critical elements of an antiaging diet…*

●**Eat eight to 10 servings of fruits and vegetables daily.** One serving equals one piece of fruit…one cup of berries, cut fruit or cooked vegetables…or one cup of raw or leafy vegetables.

Most fruits and vegetables are fat free, fiber dense and the best source of antioxidants, which help prevent disease and may slow the aging process.

The more fruits and vegetables you eat, the lower your risk for weight gain, heart disease, cancer, diabetes and high blood pressure…and the better your chances of living a long life.

Eat fruits and veggies throughout the day. Try to include two servings of fruit or vegetables at every meal or snack.

Examples: Add a banana and a glass of orange juice to breakfast…snack on fruit or carrot sticks…have vegetable soup, V-8 juice, a salad or fruit for lunch…and aim for two servings of steamed vegetables for dinner.

Prepackaged or frozen vegetables are fine as long as they don't contain added sauces, butter or cheese.

Whenever possible, add vegetables to foods you ordinarily prepare without vegetables.

Examples: Grate carrots or zucchini and toss into spaghetti sauce or chili…add corn or green chili peppers to muffins…add frozen vegetables to canned soup.

●**Have beans five times a week.** One serving equals three-quarters of a cup.

All beans are a good source of *saponins.* That's a family of compounds that lower cholesterol levels, thereby lowering heart attack risk.

Canned beans are fine as long as you rinse away the high-sodium liquid.

Soybeans are loaded with *phytoestrogens,* estrogen-like compounds that may lower the risk for breast and prostate cancer.

Many people find they like soybean-based products—soy milk, soy burgers and other "fake meat" products.

●**Concentrate on minimally processed foods.** Select foods that are as close as possible to their original state. These foods tend to be low in fat, calories and sugar…and high in vitamins, minerals and fiber.

Examples: Choose a baked potato over potato chips…oatmeal over a granola bar…whole-wheat bread rather than white. For vegetables, fresh is often best—then frozen and then canned.

●**Drink eight eight-ounce glasses of water each day.** At least this much is needed to keep our bodies functioning properly.

Since we tend to neglect water consumption, it's a good idea to set up a reminder system.

At home: Each morning, line up eight glasses of water on the kitchen counter. Keep drinking all day long until they're gone.

At the office: Keep a container of water on your desk...or swallow 10 gulps of water each time you pass a drinking fountain.

While traveling: Keep a bottle of water in your car and refill it often.

Water and green tea are the only beverages that count toward your daily quota. Not juices, not milk and definitely not soda, coffee or black tea.

• **Steer clear of excess calories.** In studies involving lab animals, drastic reductions in caloric intake increase life span. If this finding holds true for humans, the typical human life span might rise to 180 years.

The best way to cut back on calories is to limit fat, sugar and alcohol—empty calories that don't supply any nutrients.

Also helpful: Substitute prune purée or applesauce for fats in baking...cut the amount of sugar specified in recipes by 25% to 50%... instead of eating a candy bar, drizzle fat-free chocolate sauce on fruit slices.

• **Eat little meals and snacks.** People who eat mini-meals and snacks throughout the day tend to have low cholesterol levels and low blood pressure. They're also unlikely to suffer from insulin resistance, which can lead to type 2 diabetes.

The trick is to distribute your caloric intake evenly throughout the day. Go no more than four hours between meals or snacks.

• **Enjoy food.** Don't become obsessed with fat grams or calorie counts. Food is a joyful thing and should remain that way. It shouldn't only be good for you. It should also look good, taste good and make you feel good.

• **Take supplements wisely.** Many people could benefit from nutritional supplements. But there's no need for megadoses or handfuls of pills—the aim is balance. Ask your doctor about taking a daily "moderate-dose" multivitamin.

Since no single pill can contain a day's supply of calcium and magnesium, it's often a good idea to take a combination supplement that contains 500 milligrams (mg) of calcium with 250 mg of magnesium.

STICKING WITH IT

When people adjust their diets too rapidly, the changes become an unpleasant chore. Plus, brain chemistry can work against you. Your taste buds are still "expecting" eggs and bacon or sausage, but you're feeding them shredded wheat instead.

Helpful: Set long-term goals. Where do you want to be by the end of the year? In a couple of years? Outline the steps you'll take to get there. Plan each change and slowly progress to your goal.

Chocolate Boosts Longevity

M en who eat just a few pieces of chocolate each month live nearly a year longer than those men who don't.

Antioxidant compounds in chocolate—similar to those found in red wine—get the credit, according to researchers.

British Medical Journal.

Eating Fish May Lower Risk of Blindness

A ge-related macular degeneration (AMD) is a leading cause of blindness. The *neovascular*—or wet—form represents 10% of AMD cases but causes 90% of AMD-related severe vision loss.

Elderly people who eat more than one serving a week of broiled or baked fish are 36% less likely to have neovascular AMD as people who don't...people who eat more than two servings per week are half as likely to have neovascular AMD.

Likely reason: Long-chain omega-3 fatty acids—fish is the only significant food source.

John Paul SanGiovanni, ScD, researcher, National Eye Institute, National Institutes of Health, Bethesda, MD, and leader of a study of 4,513 people, ages 60 to 80, presented at a conference of the Association for Research in Vision and Ophthalmology.

The Wrinkle-Cure Diet— What to Eat to Look Much Younger

Nicholas Perricone, MD, dermatologist and adjunct professor of medicine, College of Human Medicine, Michigan State University, East Lansing. He is author of *The Perricone Prescription* (HarperResource) and *The Wrinkle Cure* (Simon & Schuster).

Most people think that wrinkles are an inevitable part of getting older. *This is not necessarily so.*

Wrinkles happen when low-grade cellular inflammation—caused by pollution, too much sun, poor nutrition and by-products of the body's metabolism—triggers the release of *activator protein 1* (AP-1) and other chemicals that destroy collagen, the connective tissue that makes skin supple and elastic.

Improving your diet can prevent wrinkles and minimize the ones you have already. The key is to avoid inflammatory foods and to eat foods that block the inflammatory process. Most of these good foods also boost general health and help prevent cancer, heart disease and other illnesses.

PROTEIN

Protein is an essential component for repairing cells, including the collagen cells. Without enough protein, people quickly lose skin tone. The optimal amount is 65 grams (g) each day for women and 80 g for men. I recommend that people have three meals and two snacks every day—each of which should include a serving of protein.

Examples: Just four ounces of roasted chicken breast delivers about 31 g of protein

...one-half cup of navy beans has 7 g...four ounces of baked salmon has 22 g.

Animal protein—from chicken, eggs, pork, lean beef, fish, etc.—provides more amino acids, a component of protein essential for cell repair, and is more readily absorbed than plant protein. Vegetarians should supplement their diets with protein powders and soy foods, such as tempeh and tofu.

SALMON

In addition to high-quality protein that aids in skin repair, fish contains *essential fatty acids* (EFAs) that block inflammation. Fish is also the best dietary source of *dimethylaminoethanol* (DMAE), a substance that prevents metabolic by-products (free radicals) from damaging skin cells.

Recommended: Eat fish at least three times a week. Salmon—either canned or fresh—contains the most protective compounds. Eating salmon twice a day can make skin look more radiant in just three days.

If you don't like fish: You can take capsules of fish oil or flaxseed oil two or three times a day. Or you can have four teaspoons of flaxseed oil daily. You also can grind up one tablespoon of flaxseed, and sprinkle it on food. After fish, it's the best dietary source of EFAs.

DARK GREEN VEGETABLES

The dark, leafy greens—such as arugula, romaine and spinach—and broccoli contain EFAs, carotenoids and other antioxidants that block inflammation.

Recommended: Eat green vegetables at least twice a day.

OLIVE OIL

Olive oil is rich in *polyphenols,* another type of antioxidant that blocks inflammation. It also contains a monounsaturated fat called oleic acid, which makes it easier for the EFAs in fish and other foods to penetrate cell membranes. You can cook with olive oil or use it to make salad dressings.

Recommended: Two tablespoons of olive oil daily. Extra virgin Spanish olive oil contains the largest amount of skin-protecting polyphenols. We don't know why Spanish oil is the most protective—it might be the soil or the particular type of olive tree.

LOW-GLYCEMIC FOODS

An important consideration in a skin-healthy diet is a food's glycemic index (GI). The index rates a variety of foods on a scale of 1 to 100, depending on their effects on blood-sugar (glucose) levels. Blood-sugar control is important because sudden surges trigger an inflammatory response in the skin.

White bread, for example, has a very high glycemic index of 95, which means that it is quickly absorbed and floods the bloodstream with glucose, the form of sugar used by cells to produce energy.

Other high-glycemic foods: White rice, pasta, pretzels, candy, cake and other kinds of low-fiber starch.

Low-glycemic choices: Lentils, oatmeal (instant or regular), peanuts, nuts and most fruits and vegetables.

BERRIES

Fresh or frozen strawberries, raspberries, blueberries and blackberries are among the best sources of *anthocyanins,* compounds that block enzymes that degrade collagen as well as other connective tissue.

Recommended: Eat one-quarter cup of berries every day.

ANTIOXIDANT SUPPLEMENTS

I advise most people to supplement their diets with 1,000 milligrams (mg) of vitamin C in divided doses and 400 international units (IU) of vitamin E daily (check with your doctor—taking more than 200 IU of vitamin E may be dangerous for some people).

Vitamin C capsules and powders are absorbed more readily than hard tablets. For vitamin E, take a capsule combination supplement that includes *tocotrienols* and *tocopherols.* Take vitamin E with meals for better absorption.

LOTS OF WATER

Water plumps up skin cells…reduces the concentration of inflammatory chemicals…and improves the body's absorption of vitamins and minerals.

I avoid tap water, which is usually chlorinated and may contain unhealthy compounds like heavy metals. Treat yourself to spring water.

Recommended: Drink at least eight eight-ounce glasses of water every day.

Acne Medication for Facial Wrinkles

When used daily for 24 weeks by people with sun damage, *tazarotene* (Tazorac), a prescription acne and psoriasis medication, reduced the appearance of fine wrinkles by 22% and improved irregular pigmentation by 45%. The appearance of other types of sun damage, including liver spots, enlarged pores and roughness, was also improved.

Warning: Tazarotene can cause redness and peeling. Women who are pregnant or nursing should not take this drug.

Tania J. Phillips, MD, professor of dermatology, Boston University School of Medicine.

"Senior" Vitamins Are Not Worth the Cost

Special "senior" formula vitamins offer little more than regular multivitamin/mineral supplements—even for those age 65 or older.

Formulas, including *Centrum Silver* and *Geritol Extend,* may provide more of the B vitamins but hardly any additional amounts of other important vitamins and minerals, such as vitamin E and calcium.

Seniors require more nutritional supplementation because of their decreased ability to absorb nutrients and their generally less nutritious diets. However, most basic all-purpose multivitamins from a reputable manufacturer should be sufficient. They may be less expensive, too.

Michael Hirt, MD, founder and medical director, the Center for Integrative Medicine, Tarzana, CA.

How to Keep Your Bladder Very Healthy

Jerry G. Blaivas, MD, clinical professor of urology at Cornell University College of Medicine and a urologist in private practice, both in New York City. He is author of *Conquering Bladder and Prostate Problems* (Harper Collins) and several professional books on urology-related topics.

Bladder trouble affects one out of every three people over the age of 50. While we can't stop the aging process, there are ways to reduce the risk for urinary pain, bladder cancer, infections, etc.

FLUID INTAKE

Many health-conscious people make it a point to drink at least eight eight-ounce glasses of water each day. That's the level recommended by many doctors.

Reality: If you eat a wholesome diet and have no obvious bladder problems, drinking that much brings no real health benefits. And—that level of fluid intake can lead to the inconvenience of having to go to the bathroom a dozen or more times a day.

Bottom line: Most people can safely let their thirst determine how much they drink. *However, boosting fluid intake is often beneficial to people suffering from any of three conditions…*

1. Dark or discolored urine. Dark, concentrated urine can be a sign of dehydration or kidney infection. If boosting your fluid intake does not lighten your urine, consult a doctor.

Warning sign: Red or bloody urine. Unless you've recently eaten beets—which can tint your urine red—see a doctor at once. You may have an infection…or even cancer.

Some vitamin supplements and certain oral medications can give the urine an orange or bluish hue.

2. Urinary tract infections (UTIs). Although they're usually thought of as a women's problem, UTIs are also a problem for men. They're caused by *E. coli* and other infectious bacteria.

3. Kidney stones. Fluids help prevent kidney stones from recurring by lowering the concentration of the stone-forming minerals calcium and oxalates in urine.

In each of these three cases, it's prudent to boost your daily fluid intake to eight eight-ounce glasses of water, juice or other nonalcoholic beverages. That's 64 ounces daily.

Boosting your fluid intake will help prevent UTIs by flushing infection-causing bacteria from the bladder. Doing so will also reduce your risk for kidney stone recurrence.

LIFESTYLE STRATEGIES

Certain lifestyle habits can also play a role in the prevention and treatment of bladder problems. *For example…*

●**Bladder cancer.** Smoking is now thought to cause half of all cases of bladder cancer. The best way to avoid bladder cancer is to avoid smoking.

Blood in your urine or a burning sensation upon urination can be the first symptoms of bladder cancer. See a doctor at once.

●**Urinary tract infections.** Like some cases of bladder cancer, UTIs are characterized by a burning sensation upon urination…and an almost constant need to urinate. Sometimes the urine turns bloody.

Even without treatment, UTIs generally clear up within a couple of weeks. Yet the symptoms they cause can be extremely unpleasant.

To reduce your risk: Have a large glass of water, cranberry juice or another beverage *before and after* sex. That promotes urination, which helps rid your urinary tract of bacteria.

Cranberry juice's high acidity inhibits growth of bacteria that cause UTIs.

Cranberry juice also triggers the formation of a mucus-like barrier along the bladder wall. This slick surface keeps bacteria from adhering.

Since warm water is a perfect breeding ground for bacteria, take showers instead of baths whenever possible.

Tampons and diaphragms can also put you at risk. Any woman who is infection-prone should consider switching to feminine napkins and/or another form of birth control.

Some people find that vitamin C supplements seem to reduce the frequency of UTIs.

Too much vitamin C, however, can cause kidney stones. If you take vitamin C, do not exceed 1,000 milligrams per day.

Caution: Although UTIs are rarely serious for women, in men they often indicate urinary blockage, nerve damage or a sexually transmitted disease. Each of these possibilities requires a doctor's care.

•**Incontinence.** Most cases of urine leakage are caused by spasmodic contractions of the bladder or problems with the urinary sphincter. That's the muscular ring surrounding the base of the bladder, where it connects with the urethra (the tube that carries urine out of the body).

In many cases, it's possible to prevent incontinence via regular use of specialized pelvic muscle exercises called *Kegels*. Kegels work for both men and women.

What to do: Several times a day, squeeze your pelvic muscles as though you were trying to stop a bowel movement…and then squeeze the muscles it takes to stop urine in midstream.

A urologist can recommend medication and many other nonsurgical approaches to incontinence. If these fail, surgery is usually effective.

THE STRESS CONNECTION

Aging men have a nearly universal complaint—a weak urine stream. What causes the problem? In men, two of three cases stem from muscle tension in the prostate, which narrows the urethra and inhibits the flow of urine.

To strengthen the urine stream: Use yoga or another stress-reduction technique to help reduce muscle tension.

Reducing psychological stress may help relax these prostate and urethra muscles that can cause blockages that weaken urine flow. If these measures fail, a urologist can offer other ways to correct prostate problems.

15

Emotional Health

How to Get Unstuck In Work, Life and Relationships

You know that you need to make a change. Your job, a relationship with a friend or loved one or the way you live is no longer satisfying. Yet you feel powerless to make anything happen. Your life seems like a problem that you can't solve. You're stuck. *Here's how to get unstuck...*

ASK YOURSELF, "WHAT'S THE QUESTION?"

When you're stuck, you focus on general problem areas—"I hate my job" or "My wife and I fight all the time." Making changes becomes much more feasible once you can formulate a specific question, a variation on "What can I do?"

Examples: "What steps can I take to get a better job?"..."How can I get my wife to listen to me and communicate better?"

FOCUS ON THE PRESENT

It's easy to be stuck in the past, dwelling on things that happened to you. Your parents never loved you...you didn't go to the "right" college...your former spouse's abuse left you wary of getting close to anyone.

Living in the past keeps you fixated on what was done to you rather than on what you can do. Instead, put your energy into active problem solving.

Example: Peter was repeatedly passed over for a promotion. He knew it was because he had trouble getting along with his vain and overbearing boss. He could have remained resentful about losing the promotion, but he realized that wasn't going to get him anywhere. What he needed to do was get along better with his boss. Peter found that a bit of well-timed flattery and a sense of humor improved their relationship.

Joy Browne, PhD, licensed clinical psychologist and host of a daily syndicated radio show, based in New York City. She is author of several books, including *Getting Unstuck: 8 Simple Steps to Solving Any Problem* (Hay House).

436

BE YOUR NEIGHBOR

Ask yourself, "What if this were happening to my next-door neighbor? What advice would I offer?" You may be able to see your options more clearly when you consider them for someone else.

BE SPECIFIC

Susan had broken up with three desirable men in the past two years. She realized that she sabotaged relationships, but she wouldn't be able to stop doing so until she understood what she did specifically. She needed to think about how and when problems developed… and what role she played. Only then could she change the pattern.

Susan realized that she often started to feel resentful after a few months in a new relationship. She felt that the men she dated didn't take her needs into account. Susan thought about it and realized that she was partly to blame because she didn't express her needs. In her next relationship, she focused on thinking about what she wanted and letting her companion know.

DO WHAT WORKS

Each of us has strengths. Identify what works for you in business, friendship, etc., and import it into the problem area.

Example: A man who wanted to start dating after his divorce was paralyzed by fear of rejection. At work, he was a very effective salesman. When he thought of potential dates as "leads" and himself as the "product," he was able to promote himself with ease and be aware that not every call would make a "sale."

EXAMINE ASSUMPTIONS

What we believe about others determines how we treat them and how they act toward us. Be aware of your negative assumptions, then change them.

Example: Mark assumed that no one could be trusted. He looked for the con behind every potential deal and the selfish motive hidden in any act of friendship. Because he was so guarded and negative, people had a difficult time getting close to Mark, further isolating him.

Mark felt that he couldn't resolve the problem on his own and decided to see a therapist.

The therapist suggested that Mark select one person with whom to share a small confidence and carefully trade information over time.

Mark learned to tell himself, "Some people are good, some are bad. I'm smart enough to tell the difference and strong enough to take care of myself. I shouldn't jump to conclusions. I should give a relationship time."

CLARIFY WHAT REALLY MATTERS

The answers to two questions can bring the big picture into focus…

•**What if you had only one day to live?** This question cuts through the fog of daily life to quicken your sense of what really is important. It can startle you out of inaction.

•**What would you like inscribed on your tombstone?** Do you want to be remembered as a business dynamo…a talented athlete…a great parent…a generous friend?

When choosing between courses of action —accepting an important promotion at work that requires long periods away from home or agreeing to coach your son's soccer team— ask yourself which will make you worthy of your "epitaph."

Controlling Anxiety Without Drugs

Harold H. Bloomfield, MD, psychiatrist in private practice, San Diego, CA. He is author of numerous books, including *Healing Anxiety Naturally* (HarperCollins).

Each year, millions of Americans reach for a prescription medication to curb feelings of anxiety. Unfortunately, the *benzodiazepine* tranquilizers doctors often prescribe can cause foggy thinking, memory loss and sleep disturbance…and are highly addictive.

Putting up with the long-term consequences of stress involves its own risks. Each period of anxiety triggers the release of stress hormones, such as *adrenaline* and *cortisol*. *Chronically high levels of these hormones...*

●**Damage artery walls,** creating crevices where fatty deposits adhere. These deposits can trigger heart attack.

●**Raise levels of clotting factors,** thereby raising the risk for blood clots that can cause stroke or heart attack.

●**Constrict arteries,** which increases blood pressure levels.

●**Suppress immunity,** raising the risk for infection and cancer.

●**Cause premature aging of brain cells.**

Daily exercise and eating a low-fat, nutrient-dense diet help fortify the body against the effects of stress. So do getting plenty of sleep and practicing a relaxation technique, such as yoga or meditation.

If these measures fail to keep anxiety in check, ask your doctor about herbal remedies. Often, they're a better choice than prescription antianxiety drugs.

ST. JOHN'S WORT

For individuals whose emotional state alternates between anxiety and depression, St. John's wort (*Hypericum perforatum*) is often a good choice.

A common perennial plant with yellow flowers, this herb has proven to be just as effective as prescription antidepressants against mild to moderate depression. Since depression and anxiety often go hand in hand, the herb is widely recommended for anxiety—and for sleep disorders, too.

St. John's wort lowers levels of cortisol and enhances the activity of *gamma-aminobutyric acid* (GABA), a naturally occurring tranquilizer in the brain.

But you must be patient when trying St. John's wort. The antianxiety effect can take four to six weeks to kick in.

Caution: Do not take St. John's wort within four weeks of taking a monoamine oxidase (MAO) inhibitor antidepressant, such as *phenelzine* (Nardil) or *tranylcypromine* (Parnate). This combination can trigger a dangerous rise in blood pressure, along with severe anxiety, fever, muscle tension and confusion.

Most studies of St. John's wort extract have involved subjects taking dosages of 300 milligrams (mg), three times per day. At this level, side effects are generally mild.

St. John's wort seems to make the skin more sensitive to sunlight. People who have fair skin should apply extra sun protection, and people who are prone to cataracts should wear wraparound sunglasses.

VALERIAN

Valerian—derived from a large perennial plant native to India—is often helpful when chronic anxiety interferes with the ability to fall asleep or sleep through the night.

Like *triazolam* (Halcion) and other popular sleeping pills, valerian reduces the length of time it takes to fall asleep. Unlike these drugs, valerian produces an entirely "natural" sleep …and is nonaddictive.

The typical dosage of valerian is 900 mg taken one hour before bedtime. If you have chronic insomnia, valerian can take up to two weeks to provide relief.

SHOPPING FOR HERBS

Herbal remedies are sold over-the-counter in many drugstores and health food stores. For optimum benefit, check labels carefully, and choose only standardized herbal extracts.

●**St. John's wort.** Look for a product standardized to 0.3% *hypericin*.

●**Valerian.** Look for a product standardized to 0.8% *valerenic acid*.

Stick with reputable brands. These include Enzymatic Therapy, Murdock Madaus Schwabe and Sunsource.

Caution: Check with your doctor and/or pharmacist before taking any herbal remedy. Ask about potential side effects…and about any precautions that should be taken.

If you are pregnant, over age 75, in frail health or taking multiple prescription drugs, take herbal remedies only under close medical supervision.

Drug-Free Ways To Fight Depression

Hyla Cass, MD, assistant clinical professor of psychiatry, University of California, Los Angeles, School of Medicine. She is author of *St. John's Wort: Nature's Blues Buster* (Avery). *www.cassmd.com.*

Symptoms of depression—sadness, hopelessness, suicidal feelings, etc.—are usually caused by reduced levels of neurotransmitters, such as *dopamine, serotonin* and *norepinephrine*. These are the mood-controlling molecules that mediate thoughts and emotions in the brain.

Prescription antidepressants—such as *fluoxetine* (Prozac), *amitriptyline* (Elavil) and *phenelzine* (Nardil)—elevate one or more of these messenger molecules.

But the drugs are no panacea. Three out of 10 people don't respond to antidepressants. When the drugs do work, they often become less effective over time. They can also cause unpleasant side effects such as nausea...fatigue ...and sexual dysfunction.

Antidepressants certainly are not a cure when depression is symptomatic of any kind of medical condition, such as hypothyroidism, diabetes or anemia.

In one study, most people hospitalized for depression were found to have an undiagnosed physical illness that was causing their symptoms.

If you have symptoms of depression, it's essential to see your doctor. If the diagnosis is depression, together you may decide to explore alternatives to prescription antidepressants.

Some options...

●**See a psychotherapist.** Therapy allows depressed individuals to confront painful issues of self-esteem, anger and troubled relationships. Resolving these issues directly affects the levels of neurotransmitters within the brain.

●**Rethink your diet.** Depression is often caused by a deficiency of amino acids, vitamins or other nutrients the body needs to make neurotransmitters. Although slight, the deficiencies may be enough to alter brain chemistry and affect mood.

To restore the balance...

●**Eat adequate amounts of protein.** Fish, chicken, turkey, meat, tofu and dairy products provide the raw materials for neurotransmitter production.

Bonus: Salmon, mackerel and other fatty fish are also rich sources of the omega-3 fatty acids known to improve nerve signaling in the brain—enhancing mood and memory.

●**Eat more complex carbohydrates.** Complex carbohydrates are long chains of sugar molecules strung together. Because complex carbohydrates are digested slowly, they help prevent fluctuations in blood sugar levels that can cause depression. Whole grains, beans, peas and vegetables are all good sources of complex carbohydrates.

Bonus: Complex carbs help to elevate serotonin levels.

Foods to avoid: Donuts, cookies and other sugary snacks that trigger insulin release. This lowers blood sugar levels and makes mood and energy plummet.

●**Limit alcohol intake.** Like sugary foods, alcohol temporarily raises blood sugar, then makes it plunge.

Limit intake to one glass of wine or beer or one cocktail daily. Drink it only with meals to slow its absorption.

●**Take supplements.** *To boost mood without prescription drugs, you might take...*

●A high-potency multivitamin/mineral complex that contains about 50 milligrams (mg) of each of the B vitamins. This type of supplement will supply "co-factors" needed to manufacture neurotransmitters.

●*S-adenosylmethionine* (SAM-e). This bioactive form of the amino acid methionine enhances neurotransmitter activity. More than 100 double-blind, placebo-controlled studies have suggested that SAM-e is effective in alleviating depression.

Typical dosage: One 200-mg capsule once a day. After a week, it may be necessary to increase to two daily capsules.

Trap: SAM-e supplements are unstable in high temperatures. It's also important to buy supplements that are enteric-coated. And be sure to choose supplements that have been refrigerated at the store…and refrigerate them at home.

● **Try herbs.** *There are several natural mood-enhancers, including…*

● St. John's wort. Dozens of studies, involving more than 5,000 patients, have been conducted on this herb. The research shows that, on average, 70% of depressed people who take it report a significant decrease in symptoms and an increase in feelings of well-being.

St. John's wort appears to reduce the rate at which brain cells take up serotonin. That means more of it stays in *synapses*—the tiny gaps between brain cells—where it's needed to ferry mood-enhancing nerve impulses.

Dosage: The average dose is 300 mg three times a day, but some people get results with 300 mg only twice a day. However, others may require 300 mg up to four times daily.

In almost all people, full effects may not be felt for up to three weeks.

Warning: Do not take St. John's wort within four weeks of taking a *monoamine oxidase inhibitor* (MAOI) antidepressant such as *phenelzine* (Nardil) or *tranylcypromine* (Parnate). This drug combination can raise your blood pressure dangerously.

Some studies also indicate that St. John's wort can reduce the effectiveness of drugs used for AIDS and organ transplantation.

St. John's wort also increases a person's sensitivity to sunlight. If you're fair-skinned, take precautions to get extra sun protection. If you're at risk for cataracts, wear protective wraparound sunglasses.

● Ginkgo biloba. Reduced blood flow is a common cause of depression, especially in older people. A vasodilator, ginkgo improves blood flow to the brain. Ginkgo may also boost production of serotonin.

Consult your doctor before taking ginkgo if you're taking aspirin, *warfarin* (Coumadin) or another blood-thinning drug.

Typical dosage: 40 mg three times daily. Some people respond within four weeks. Others take several months. If you don't see a difference in four weeks, increase the dosage to 80 mg three times daily.

● **Get more sunshine.** Sunlight stimulates the brain's pineal gland to produce melatonin, a hormone that helps regulate sleep cycles and emotional mood.

Exposure to light is especially vital for people who suffer from *seasonal affective disorder* (SAD). This form of depression is triggered by the lack of sunlight in fall and winter.

The treatment is sunlight. Thirty minutes each day often does the trick.

If you can't get out in daylight—or live in a dark, northern climate—consider buying special lights that mimic sunlight's effects.

Good source for the lights: Tools for Wellness, *www.toolsforwellness.com* or 800-456-9887.

● **Get aerobic exercise.** Physical activities—such as walking, running, biking and swimming—all reduce stress hormones and increase the level of *endorphins* in your body. Endorphins are the mood-boosting, painkilling brain compounds which are famous for the feel-good "runner's high."

Exercising aerobically as little as 20 minutes several times a week suffices.

Let the Sun In

For many people, exposure to sunlight has an exhilarating effect and combats depression and lethargy. There is no exact prescription, however, for how much is necessary to achieve these effects.

Up to one-half hour each day exposed to sunlight should be enough to improve your mood and energy level.

Apply sunscreen before going into the sun to protect against harmful UV radiation without reducing the psychological benefits of sunlight.

Note: Indirect sunlight—through windows or under shelter with sun bouncing off surfaces—also produces these benefits.

Norman E. Rosenthal, MD, medical director of Capitol Clinical Research Associates, psychiatrist in private practice in Maryland, and author of Winter Blues *(Guilford).*

If Your Antidepressant Causes Impotence...

In a recent study, about 37% of men taking antidepressants reported some type of sexual dysfunction. However, when the pill was taken in the early morning, a significant number of men suffered no signs of erectile dysfunction during sex in the evening.

If changing the time of day doesn't help, *bupropion* (Wellbutrin) and *nefazodone* (Serzone) are two antidepressants that generally cause few sexual side effects.

If you're unable to switch antidepressants, other drugs can help counteract the side effects. These include *buspirone* (BuSpar), an antianxiety drug, and the impotence drugs *sildenafil* (Viagra), *tadalafil* (Cialis) and *vardenafil* (Levitra).

Eric Hollander, MD, professor of psychiatry, director of clinical psychopharmacology, Mount Sinai School of Medicine, New York City.

Alternative Treatment For Depression

Taking supplemental thyroid hormone can help many people manage their symptoms of depression—even if tests show normal hormone levels.

In some patients, the body can't convert the inactive thyroid hormone T4 to the *active* hormone T3. This leads to various symptoms, some of which resemble depression.

Supplemental thyroid hormone can be given in addition to antidepressants. Doses must be kept low to avoid heart arrhythmias, nervousness and other side effects. Ask your doctor for more information.

Richard N. Podell, MD, chronic fatigue expert and clinical professor, department of family medicine, Robert Wood Johnson Medical School, Springfield, NJ.

Feeling Fatigued Or Depressed?

If you feel unusually fatigued or depressed, get your blood calcium levels checked. About 100,000 Americans—primarily women—have *hyperparathyroidism,* a condition which leaves too much calcium in the blood and not enough in the bones. It is caused by overactive parathyroid glands in the neck.

Other symptoms include nausea, headaches, muscle weakness and constipation. Treatment may involve removing the parathyroid glands, medication to strengthen bones and/or working with your doctor to determine optimal calcium intake.

Sundeep Khosla, MD, professor of medicine, Mayo Medical School in Rochester, MN.

Cures for Common Phobias

Edmund Bourne, PhD, therapist in private practice, Kona, HI, who has specialized in anxiety disorders for two decades. He is author of The Anxiety & Phobia Workbook (New Harbinger).

Fifteen percent of the adult population suffers from a phobia severe enough that it restricts their behavior.

Fear of public speaking is the most common phobia, followed by fear of flying. Other types include fear of enclosed spaces...public places ...fire...heights...water...and social situations, such as dating or using public rest rooms.

Symptoms range from mild anxiety to full-fledged panic, including rapid heartbeat and breathing...lightheadedness...nausea...chills... tingling or numbness...trembling...sweating... and feelings of unreality, detachment, terror or lack of control.

CAUSES OF PHOBIAS

Phobias may have been started by a specific event, often during childhood—a bumpy plane ride might trigger a fear of flying, for example.

But phobias sometimes develop over time. If you see enough plane crashes on the evening news, you might develop the fear of air travel even if you have never been afraid to fly before.

Phobias may run in families. Certain ones have a genetic component—a person may be born with the tendency to panic. Other fears are learned.

Example: If a child repeatedly sees that his/her parent is afraid of water, he might develop this phobia as well.

FACE YOUR FEAR...SLOWLY

Exposure therapy is often the best way to curb a phobia. The person with the phobia confronts the fear incrementally with the help of a supportive friend or relative or a therapist. *Let's say you're afraid of elevators...*

●**Step 1.** Stand with a support person in front of an elevator, and watch other people get on and off. To relax, take slow abdominal breaths and focus on reassuring thoughts.

Examples: I've handled this before...this is an opportunity for me to confront my fears ...or it's just anxiety—it will pass.

Keep a list of these affirmations with you to pull out in difficult situations. Your support person should remind you to breathe slowly from the abdomen and focus on your affirmation statements.

●**Step 2.** Once the sight of an elevator no longer causes anxiety, you and your support person might practice stepping on an elevator when it has stopped. When that is no longer anxiety producing, you could then try riding it together for just one floor, then two, etc. until you feel relaxed.

●**Step 3.** Take a ride all by yourself—with the support person waiting there when the doors open. When you are comfortable with that, take a ride in the elevator without having your support person nearby.

This entire process could take weeks, months or, in some cases, longer.

Some phobias are harder to address. If you are afraid to fly, you can't beat the phobia just by walking on and off a plane several times. Instead, sit in a quiet room and visualize every aspect of taking a flight. Imagine what you would see, hear, smell and feel. Next, go to the airport and watch planes take off and land. Picture yourself in the plane. Finally, take a flight with a support person.

COPING WITH PANIC

What if a panic attack hits during exposure therapy? Some experts recommend *flooding*—pushing on despite the attack. Flooding works for some people, but in most cases, it just exacerbates the phobia.

I encourage my phobic patients to temporarily retreat. When you think you are about to lose control, pull back, take some abdominal breaths, wait a few minutes until the panic has passed and then try again.

DRUG THERAPY

When phobias are so severe that they significantly affect daily life, taking an antidepressant, such as *fluvoxamine* (Luvox), *paroxetine* (Paxil) or *sertraline* (Zoloft), often can be helpful.

Usually, the patient also meets regularly with a therapist who specializes in anxiety disorders. After 12 to 18 months, about half the people on antidepressants are able to taper off. The other half may need to go back on the medication intermittently or take a lower dose long-term to maintain quality of life.

Another group of drugs known as the beta-blockers, including *propranolol* (Inderal) and *metoprolol* (Lopressor), are helpful for cases of severe performance anxiety. These typically are taken 20 minutes before performing in public to control heart palpitations, shakiness, sweating, blushing and stomach upset. A pianist I treat takes Inderal for the shaky hands she suffers before performances.

Tranquilizers, such as *alprazolam* (Xanax) and *clonazepam* (Klonopin), can be appropriate for phobias that do not need to be confronted very often, such as fear of flying or heights. But tranquilizers can be addictive if taken more than twice a week.

Note: Klonopin is less addictive than Xanax.

DO HERBAL REMEDIES WORK?

Herbs may help control mild to moderate anxiety. But generally, I recommend exposure therapy for that level of anxiety.

If a patient still wants to try herbs, valerian is a mild tranquilizer. But it is important not to exceed the recommended dosage. In rare cases, valerian may cause depression or even, paradoxically, anxiety. Check with your doctor before taking valerian.

To find a therapist who specializes in anxiety, contact the Anxiety Disorders Association of America at 240-485-1001 or *www.adaa.org.*

How to Keep Upbeat and Stay Healthy

Gregg D. Jacobs, PhD, assistant professor of psychiatry, Harvard Medical School, Boston. He is author of *The Ancestral Mind: Reclaim the Power* (Viking).

Everyone has internal monologues that conjure up worst-case scenarios, but our initial reactions to stressful events often are out of proportion to the actual facts. Your check bounces, so you worry that your credit is ruined. You arrive at work late one day, and you're afraid your boss will be angry.

Negative automatic thoughts (NATs) like these can impair our physical and emotional health. Mental negativity stimulates the *amygdala,* the part of the brain that assesses threats, to unleash anxiety and anger. This is a valuable defense mechanism when threats are real—but destructive when we concoct scenarios in our minds that emphasize the negative and exaggerate potential harm.

Multiplied over the course of a lifetime, NATs can contribute to high blood pressure… headaches and digestive complaints…a weak immune system…depression…and other common health problems.

MANAGE MENTAL MONOLOGUES

A technique called *cognitive restructuring* (CR) can turn off some of the negative chatter. Studies of patients who recover from depression have shown that only 30% who practice CR suffer relapses, compared with 60% of those given pharmacological treatments. CR also is successful at treating anxiety, panic disorder and eating disorders.

To tame toxic thoughts…

●**Be aware of your stress reactions.** When you're under stress, monitor your thoughts. It's very easy to get caught in a cycle of negativity without really being aware that you are.

●**Say "stop" when you catch yourself churning out negative thoughts.** You can say it out loud or in your mind. It's a mentally decisive step that breaks the cycle of escalating NATs and negative emotions.

●**Breathe.** After you say *stop,* take a deep breath. Hold it for a few seconds, then let it go. Just one or two deep breaths can help you relax and divert your attention from the negative mental cascade.

●**Reframe the internal monologue.** NATs represent a distorted view of reality. Once you realize that you're seeing things in the worst possible light, you can try to reframe negative thoughts in a more realistic—and usually more positive—way.

Three ways to help you see things more positively…

●**Ask yourself key questions.** *Is this thought literally true? Am I "awfulizing" and assuming a negative outcome? Is there another way to look at the situation?* The answers to these questions can lead you toward a more realistic analysis.

●**Weigh the situation against past experiences.** Suppose you're stuck in heavy rush-hour traffic on the way to a doctor's appointment and you find yourself thinking the worst.

The doctor *could* be angry—but you've probably been late getting to appointments before and nothing negative has happened (assuming that you don't have a reputation for tardiness). NATs naturally deflate when you remember that similar situations in the past turned out fine despite your concerns.

●**Be a friend to yourself.** Most of us are much harder on ourselves than we are on our friends. We encourage our friends to find the positive in negative events…show them empathy and warmth…and help them put things in perspective. You should do the same for yourself. Ask yourself, *What would I say to a friend with a similar problem?* Then follow that advice.

The "stop-breathe-reframe" technique takes time to master because NATs are so automatic and habitual. With practice, nearly everyone learns to turn off, or at least turn down, negative mental chatter.

Self-Hypnosis... The Edge You Need To Overcome Bad Habits

C. Roy Hunter, certified hypnotherapy instructor, Tacoma, WA. He is author of *Master the Power of Self-Hypnosis* (Sterling) and *Hypnosis for Inner Conflict Resolution* (Crown).

Finding it hard to quit overeating? Smoking? Drinking? You're not alone. As we all know, the vast majority of people who try to break a bad habit fail at first. And many of them fail repeatedly.

You can remind yourself a hundred times a day that your habit is bad for you. Unfortunately, it's the *unconscious* mind that fuels bad habits. It doesn't care about logic. All it wants is the physical and emotional satisfactions your habit supplies.

Hypnosis helps you let go of the negative unconscious desires...and replace them with positive, habit-breaking emotions.

Hypnosis isn't magic. You will still have to work hard at breaking your bad habit. But hypnosis can give you the important edge you need to succeed.

MYTH vs. REALITY

Hollywood has given hypnosis an unrealistic image. The hypnotic trance is not a mystical state in which you lose all self-control. You cannot be forced to quack like a duck or do other humiliating things when you're under hypnosis. In fact, you won't do anything you don't want to do.

The hypnotic trance is nothing more than a state of very deep relaxation.

This relaxed state is similar to the one that exists just before you fall asleep, when the beta brain waves that predominate during consciousness are replaced by alpha waves.

You're still fully conscious, but your rational mind is less active than it usually is when you are "awake"...yet your imagination is more active. This shift is critical because imagination is the language of the unconscious.

With practice, the emotions you generate during each hypnosis session become permanently embedded in your unconscious. That gives your willpower a much-needed boost.

DO IT YOURSELF

Many psychologists practice hypnosis, but it's also effective when done on your own. *Here's how to do it...*

●**Carefully consider the emotional benefits associated with breaking your habit.** Odds are you've already given a great deal of thought to the physiological benefits—reduced risk for heart attack, stroke, cancer, etc.

But you must also consider all the emotional reasons you have for changing. These might include feeling more in control...pleasing your family...having more energy...looking better.

●**Put yourself in a trance.** Find a comfortable and quiet place to lie down or sit. Unplug the phone and turn off the lights.

Take several deep breaths as you imagine your cares slipping away. Then imagine a beach at sunset, a mountain meadow or some other relaxing scene.

Start thinking to yourself, "My toes are relaxed...my breathing is relaxed...I'm getting more and more relaxed."

You've entered a trance when you feel totally relaxed and your mind starts to wander. For most people, this takes about five minutes.

●**Imagine the pleasure you will feel upon successfully breaking your habit.** Once you've entered the trance, imagine that you have already reached your goal. Savor the emotions that thought triggers.

You might think, "My family is so proud of me"..."I look great"..."I feel so much better."

Over time, these feelings will become part of your unconscious...and will stay with you even when you're fully awake and going about your business.

●**Replace old "triggers" with new ones.** While still in the trance, imagine healthy new ways of behaving.

Perhaps you tend to have a cigarette each time you relax with a cup of coffee. During the trance, imagine that having the coffee triggers a *different* response from you.

You might say, "I don't *really* want a cigarette with my coffee. I'd rather focus on reading that novel I just started."

Repeat this scenario again and again.

●**Come out of your trance.** Count slowly from one to five. When you reach five, say, "Fully awake."

Most people notice a diminution in their cravings after just a few sessions of self-hypnosis.

For the first three weeks, it's best to do self-hypnosis for about 20 minutes each day. After that, you can cut back to 20 minutes once or twice a month.

Of course, you can always intensify your self-hypnosis schedule if you find your resolve weakening.

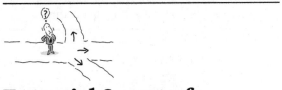

Essential Secret of Kicking Addictions

Jamison Starbuck, ND, naturopathic physician in family practice and lecturer at the University of Montana, both in Missoula. She is past president, American Association of Naturopathic Physicians, and contributing editor of *The Alternative Advisor: The Complete Guide to Natural Therapies and Alternative Treatments* (Time-Life).

Addiction to alcohol, tobacco or drugs destroys lives—those of the addicts and those of their friends and family. Short of incarceration, the only way to stop addictive behavior is to *decide* to stop. Typically, this decision comes after months or years of internal debate. *If you've reached this point, I offer several suggestions that might prove helpful...*

●**Make a commitment**—in writing. Pick a quit date. Write that date on a piece of paper, along with a written vow to quit, and post it somewhere highly visible. Your written vow will be a guidepost, especially in the midst of your journey, when the going gets tough—as it inevitably does.

●**Line up people who will support your decision to quit.** Choose individuals you respect but with whom you have no strong emotional ties. For most people, that means a doctor, clergyman, therapist...and/or maybe an ex-smoker or ex-drinker. Explain your plan, and meet with your support "team" regularly during the withdrawal period. Spend recreational time with people who encourage your decision to quit—which may mean you'll have to make new friends.

Books can be a big help. One book that my patients find particularly valuable is Doug Althauser's *You Can Free Yourself from Alcohol & Drugs* (New Harbinger).

●**Eat according to a schedule.** Eating on a regular basis helps curb your cravings—by keeping blood sugar levels relatively constant. Large swings in blood sugar levels are known to trigger intense cravings—for tobacco and alcohol as well as for food.

I usually advise my patients fighting addictions to eat three meals a day. Each meal should include a small amount of lentils, peas, soybeans or another source of protein. Fresh vegetables and fiber-rich foods like rice, barley, baked potatoes and whole grains are also important during withdrawal. These foods are digested at a slow, steady pace, so they help keep blood sugar levels constant.

●**Consider taking vitamin supplements and herbal remedies.** Vitamin pills don't make quitting easier. But certain vitamins do reduce withdrawal symptoms. I typically recommend 100 milligrams (mg) each of vitamins B-3, B-5 and B-6...400 micrograms (mcg) of vitamin B-12...800 mcg of folic acid...400 international units (IU) of vitamin E...and 1,000 mg of vitamin C. But consult with your doctor. These supplements should be taken with food on a daily basis.

Herbs, too, can be helpful—especially for people trying to give up smoking. Giving up cigarettes often causes a transient, but aggravating, cough and/or lung congestion. A tea made of mullein, marshmallow root, coltsfoot and peppermint helps keep the lungs clear.

Buy an ounce or two of each herb at a health food store. Mix them in a jar, and use two teaspoons of the herb mix per eight ounces of boiling water. Three cups daily during the first two weeks of quitting should help keep your lungs healthy.

People addicted to alcohol or drugs often benefit from taking milk thistle capsules. This herb helps curb the achy, flu-like symptoms that often strike during withdrawal.

I generally recommend 200 to 400 mg of milk thistle to be taken on a daily basis for the first month after the quit date.

Caution: People with a history of liver disease or who are taking a medication that affects the liver should consult a doctor before taking milk thistle.

You Know the Dangers of Smoking...Here's How To Quit!

David W. Wetter, PhD, professor and chair, Health Disparities Research, University of Texas MD Anderson Cancer Center, Houston. Research-based strategies and information on quitting smoking can be found at *www.surgeongeneral.gov/tobacco/default.htm.*

Despite all of the known health risks, 47 million Americans still choose to smoke cigarettes. *The big reasons...*

●**Cultural norms.** Caucasian teens smoke more than African-American and Asian teens. This may be because the latters' families are more disapproving of smoking.

●**Smoking beliefs.** Having positive beliefs about smoking can make a person more inclined to try smoking.

Examples: Thinking smoking reduces stress or keeps weight down.

●**Genes.** Scientists believe there is no single smoking gene...but there may be thousands of gene alterations that increase your risk for becoming a smoker.

BEST WAYS TO QUIT

●**Nicotine replacement.** Patches and gum curb withdrawal symptoms. In conjunction with behavioral changes, they can double the likelihood you'll quit. If patches and gum don't work, your doctor can prescribe a nicotine-replacement inhaler or spray...or *bupropion* (Zyban), which reduces cravings for cigarettes and limits weight gain.

●**Counseling.** It can be as effective as drug therapy. Costs are often covered by insurance. *Useful resources...*

●American Cancer Society, 800-227-2345.

●American Lung Association, 800-586-4872.

●**Identify times you are inclined to smoke** and find smoke-free alternatives.

Example: If you like a cigarette with coffee, take a walk instead of drinking coffee.

●**Once you quit,** vow never to have another cigarette. Ninety percent of smokers who have just one go back to smoking.

●**Don't be discouraged by failures.** Most people quit five times before succeeding.

How to Overcome Addictions You May Not Even Know You Have

Judith Wright, cofounder (with her husband, Bob), The Wright Leadership Institute, Chicago, which helps people fulfill their potential in all areas of life. She is author of *There Must Be More Than This: Finding More Life, Love and Meaning by Overcoming Your Soft Addictions* (Broadway). *www.theremustbemore.com.*

You've finished your day, and a long evening spreads out before you. What will you do with the time? Will you, like millions of others, spend the hours mindlessly surfing TV channels...browsing through Internet sites...reading the latest bestseller?

There's nothing wrong with these time killers, but sometimes they turn into what I call "soft addictions."

Soft addictions are seemingly harmless pastimes that encroach on your life. They eat up big chunks of your time and energy. Pursuing them numbs you to your feelings and possibly to other people, and robs you of a more creative and satisfying life.

Example: Watching TV. Knowing what's going on in the world is a worthy goal. But for some, watching TV becomes a way of life. The hours in the evening merge into the long hours of night. This TV time distracts you from building in-depth relationships or confronting personal problems.

A soft addiction, then, is any activity that you use regularly to fulfill needs other than what they are meant to fill—for example, eating for amusement or distraction rather than for nourishment...or shopping simply to while away the time.

FOUR CATEGORIES

•**Activities.** Anything that you do obsessively, from checking your investments or the weather, to bargain hunting, dieting or overeating, even cleaning your house.

•**Moods and ways of being.** Attitude modes that cut you off from others—blaming, being sarcastic, critical, cranky or constantly "on," complaining or being a know-it-all.

•**Avoidances.** Behaviors you use to escape real accomplishment, such as procrastinating, being late, playing helpless or the victim, hypochondria and stonewalling.

•**Things.** What you put in your mouth—chocolate, fast foods, cigarettes, carbs and coffee—as well as what fills your closet and your house, the latest fashions, trends, gadgets, wines and collections.

You might have several soft addictions—perhaps even a cluster of behaviors that you do regularly that consume your time and energy.

MAKING THE "ONE DECISION"

To start overcoming your soft addictions, you must first determine what you want to achieve in their place. Do you want to nurture your creative abilities? Get to know yourself better? Connect more with your family and friends?

When you decide the greater purpose of your life, write it down in a statement that will be your *One Decision*. This overarching statement will help guide you in the smaller decisions you make daily. With greater clarity of thinking, you'll opt for better choices about how to spend your leisure time.

TACKLING THE ADDICTIONS

"Know your enemy" is the first rule for overcoming soft addictions. What are yours? Make a list outlining how you fill your time, your general moods and attitudes, what you "must" eat or have and your avoidance strategies.

Strategy: If you don't like others to know how much time you spend engaged in an activity or feel guilty for indulging in it so often, it's a sure-thing soft addiction.

Under this plan, you don't go cold turkey. Instead, you *replace the addiction* with activities that nourish you. If you make plans to see friends for dinner, you won't be watching mindless TV shows. If you take an art course, you won't be leafing through catalogs. If you're studying photography, you won't be running off to the mall.

You do not have to completely give up your soft addiction activities. In moderation, most activities are fine. You will probably discover, however, that your attraction to soft addictions will wane as you bring more creative and fulfilling activities into your life.

To help you stay the course, make an *action plan* about how you are going to put your new approach to work. Include in it what you will add to your days—and what you will reduce from them.

Example: To increase my intellectual stimulation, I will read at least one quality book a month. To do this I will subtract up to two hours of TV watching a day.

You can sometimes give yourself a push by altering your environment. If you're frittering away hours playing solitaire or other computer games, take them off of your computer. Should cable-channel movies suck you in again and again, cancel the service.

Outline your action plan in three-week segments. Don't set unrealistic goals—change takes time. Get support by telling people whom you trust what you are doing.

Insight: Soft addictions protect the status quo—they are safe, proven and predictable, which is why we cling to them. They also repress uncomfortable feelings.

Let's say that as a child, you watched TV to block out fear when your parents argued. Now that you are an adult, you still quell anxiety by turning on the TV.

Once you stop doing this, be prepared for new feelings to emerge. Instead of running from them, stop to experience and investigate them. You can learn quickly about repressed feelings this way. Anytime you crave a soft addiction, ask yourself what you felt just before that desire hit.

Strategy: Spend at least a few minutes every day being still. Gaze out the window, meditate or just sit—this is a great way to become more comfortable with yourself. Take care of yourself as well—get enough sleep, treat yourself to a massage, go for walks someplace beautiful, such as at the park or beach.

Be Happy with Your Body Image At Any Age

Thomas F. Cash, PhD, professor of clinical psychology, Old Dominion University, Norfolk, VA, and psychologist in private practice, Virginia Beach. He is author of several books on body image, including *Body Image Workbook: An 8-Step Program for Learning to Like Your Looks* (New Harbinger).

The physical changes that accompany aging don't have to make you feel bad about your looks—but often they do.

Negative feelings about your body can lower your self-esteem, causing you to experience social anxiety and, as a result of your feeling unattractive, jeopardize sexual fulfillment.

The good news: It's never too late to transform the relationship you have with your body from a self-defeating, time-consuming struggle to self-acceptance and even enjoyment. *Here's how to do it...*

●**Assess how you currently see yourself.** Set goals for changing the way you feel about your looks. *Ask yourself...*

●How satisfied am I with my face, torso, hair, muscle tone and other aspects of my body?

●What is my ideal vision of myself? How close am I now to that vision?

●How often do I have negative feelings about my appearance? Negative thoughts?

●To what extent do these feelings and thoughts limit my life? Social opportunities?

●**Understand the causes of your negative body image.** Being good-looking doesn't guarantee a positive body image, just as being obese or homely doesn't guarantee self-loathing.

Body image is a state of mind. It is shaped over time in response to cultural influences, experiences with family and friends, and your own physical development.

Helpful exercise: Identify your body image ABCs. *They are...*

●*Activators* are the specific events and situations that trigger your thoughts and feelings about your body.

●*Beliefs* include the thoughts, perceptions and interpretations that typically occur in your mind in response to the activators.

●*Consequences* are how you tend to react emotionally as well as behaviorally.

Also helpful: Keep a body-image diary to record present-day ABC episodes that perpetuate your negative body image. By recording these episodes, you'll gain insight that will help you change the way you think about your body.

●**Manage body image through relaxation exercises.** Any negative thoughts and feelings about your appearance can lead to anxiety and stress. But, if you practice your relaxation and deep-breathing exercises every day, you will soon be able to relax before anxiety takes hold.

Helpful: Audiotapes can guide you through muscular relaxation and deep-breathing exercises. You can find suitable tapes at music and some natural foods stores.

●**Challenge your assumptions about appearance.** We all have these "appearance assumptions."

Example: *The only way I could ever like the way I look is if I change it.*

Record the appearance assumptions you hold to be true and then ask yourself, *What's wrong with this belief? What facts contradict my assumptions?*

Consider the assumption that physically attractive people have it all. Remind yourself of the following realities—beauty can breed envy and jealousy...it raises people's expectations about a person, and those lofty expectations may be impossible to meet...physical beauty is a weak foundation for self-esteem.

●**Correct your private "body talk."** Discover, dissect and dispute the negative messages your inner voice repeats about your body.

Examples: *Sophia Loren and I were born the same year, yet she's aging gracefully and I'm not.* Or, *I wasn't asked to attend my grandchild's school play because he's ashamed of my weight.*

Talk back to that voice with a new, more positive message...

●Remind yourself that not seeing yourself as a "10" on a 10-point scale of attractiveness does not necessarily make you a "1."

●Consider how you think about other people's looks. Is it fair to compare yourself to them?

●Replace the emotionally-charged language of your thoughts with more objective descriptions. Instead of referring to yourself as having *hippo hips,* see yourself with rounded hips... instead of *chrome dome,* see yourself as having experienced hair loss.

●**Don't overscrutinize your appearance.** Appearance-preoccupied rituals are often time-consuming and reinforce discontent with your body image. *To work on changing them...*

●Obstruct them. If you repeatedly pull a mirror out of your purse or pocket to check on your appearance, leave the mirror at home until you feel you have broken the habit.

●Delay them. Whenever you feel the urge to fix your hair or makeup, put off acting on it for a while—and make it a little longer each time. Soon, it will no longer be an urge, but instead a normal activity you engage in a few times a day.

●Restrict them. Allow yourself to perform the ritual once or twice a day, or allow yourself to perform it only at certain times of the day— morning and evening, for instance.

●**Treat your body right.** Think of your body as your friend. Nurture it by keeping it fit and eating healthful foods. The better you feel, the better your body image will be. *Other ways to befriend your body...*

●Write a letter in which you apologize to your body for prior mistreatment. Assure it you want to change the relationship, and thank your body for the good things it has given you.

●Accept compliments on your appearance graciously and without negative self-talk.

●Offer compliments to your reflection in a mirror at least once a day. Notice your smile, your energetic stance, the sparkle in your eyes.

●Remind yourself daily that you are in the process of developing a satisfying body image and living a fuller, more satisfying life.

Lower Stress in Five Minutes or Less

Dawn Groves, Bellingham, WA–based author of *Stress Reduction for Busy People, Massage for Busy People* and *Yoga for Busy People* (all from New World Library).

No time to relax? Don't be so sure. It can take only five minutes to unwind and refresh your mind. *Here's what to do...*

●**Move around.** Take a quick trip through the halls of your workplace—or around the block. Walk up and down a flight of stairs. Do 15 jumping jacks.

●**Stretch while seated.** Lace your fingers under your knee, and draw it to your chest. Repeat with the other knee. This stretches the leg and lower back.

Next, stretch your arms above your head, palms up and fingers interlaced.

Drop your hands to your sides, then raise your right shoulder to your right ear, keeping your head vertical. Repeat this stretch with the left shoulder.

Finally, bend back the fingers of each hand. This is especially important if you use a computer for long periods.

● **Take 10 long, deep breaths.** Your belly should expand as you inhale and contract as you exhale.

● **Massage your eyes and ears.** Place your palms over your eyes. Slowly spiral your palms while applying gentle pressure. Do the same for your ears.

Blocking out all sights and sounds, even for just a few seconds, is a psychologically refreshing experience.

● **Try aromatherapy.** Put a drop of lemon-lime or orange essential oil in a saucer. These gentle scents relax you without making your home or office smell like an incense store.

Great resource: *www.aromaweb.com.*

Quick and Easy Stress-Busters

Mina Hamilton, author of *Serenity to Go: Calming Techniques for Your Hectic Life* (New Harbinger). She has taught yoga and stress reduction for many years in New York City.

A hot bath is a proven stress reliever. So is a soothing massage. But sometimes you need to relax *right now*—while you're stuck in traffic or trapped at the end of a slow checkout line.

After years of teaching yoga and stress reduction, I have discovered how to integrate relaxation techniques into the rough and tumble of daily life. Remember—no matter what situation you're in, you can always choose how to respond.

Here are four real-life situations that allow you to put simple stress-busting techniques into action...

PLACED ON HOLD

Next time you're on hold with a customer-service line, use your nondominant hand to hold the receiver a few inches from your ear (far enough to soften the canned music, but close enough to hear when a human being answers). Loosen your grip on the receiver. If you're slouching, lengthen your spine. You may keep your eyes open or gently close them.

Mentally scan your body, from your head to your toes. Relax tense muscles, and breathe deeply and slowly from the gut.

While the music drones on in the background, use your second and third fingers to massage your forehead. Place the fingertips between your eyebrows, and press down gently for two seconds. Then move the fingers toward your hairline in a single, slow motion.

Once you reach the hairline, lift the fingers off the skin and bring them back to the spot between your eyebrows. Imagine your forehead becoming as placid as a mountain lake.

Move on to your cheeks. Place the second and third fingers on the skin, and make small circular motions. Massage one cheek at a time.

Now focus on your jaw muscle. Massage it along the jawline in a circular motion. Let your mouth fall slightly open as you perform these mini-massages. When someone finally answers the phone, you may feel disappointed!

TRAPPED IN TRAFFIC

It's only too easy to develop hostile attitudes toward other drivers. We think of them as anonymous faces inside massive chunks of metal. We forget what we have in common with our fellow human beings.

Take a look at the people around you. *What kind of lives do they lead? Where is that white-haired man going? Was that young business-woman up all night with a sick child?*

Instead of thinking of rude drivers as jerks, think about how much you share with each of them. Everybody trapped in this jam wants a loving spouse, a good job, the best education for their kids—just like you do.

STUCK AT YOUR COMPUTER

Those of us stuck at a desk, staring at a computer screen for hours, need to rest our eyes for at least two minutes every hour.

To do this, turn your chair away from the computer. If you wear glasses, take them off. Focus on an object 10 feet away from your desk for a moment. Next, shift your eyes to look at something close, such as a plant or a nearby desk. Without straining, shift your eyes back and forth between these two places. Take long easy breaths as you do this.

NO PLACE TO SIT

So you couldn't get a seat on the bus. If you've been sitting in a chair all day long, here's a chance to lengthen and stretch your spine.

Stand straight, with your knees gently bent and your feet slightly separated. Relax your neck and jaw. Allow your shoulders to drop. Elongate your spine by imagining that it is growing taller as you feel the muscles in your back stretching upward. Breathe deeply. Now slowly turn your torso, shoulders and head to the left. Then slowly turn to the right. You will feel better and calmer.

Better Breathing for a Much Healthier You

Michael White, founder and executive director, Optimal Breathing, a company that teaches breathing techniques to singers, athletes and people with breathing problems, Charlotte, NC. *www.breathing.com.*

You can increase stamina and overall health by breathing properly. The key is in the exhale. *Try this…*

Exercise: Stand facing straight ahead. Raise arms directly overhead. Force an exhale by squeezing the belly toward the spine until it hurts a little. Let the breath come in naturally and effortlessly.

When the breath is as big as it can get without forcing it, bend from the chest side to side like a metronome while simultaneously counting as fast as you can (like an auctioneer), clearly and softly but out loud, from one up to a maximum of 20.

Let the remainder of any exhale occur as you lower your arms. Repeat this exercise up to 10 times, several times a day.

When you are in stressful situations: Force out your belly breath, extending the exhale to at least four times the length of your inhale. Then let the deeper, longer inhale occur on its own.

This controls your stress response…lets you take in extra oxygen…and facilitates deeper relaxation for work, play and sleep.

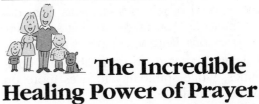

The Incredible Healing Power of Prayer

Dale A. Matthews, MD, internist in private practice, Washington, DC. He is also coauthor, with Connie Clark, of *The Faith Factor: Proof of the Healing Power of Prayer* (Penguin).

Many doctors and patients have learned from personal experience that religious faith is good medicine. In recent years, hundreds of clinical studies have demonstrated that this statement is not just a matter of faith, but rather of science.

THE FAITH FACTOR

People who regularly attend worship services enjoy better health than their counterparts with fewer religious ties. *Peer-reviewed studies have found that their advantages include…*

●**Lower rates of cancer,** heart disease and other serious conditions.

●**Speedier recovery from serious illness,** with fewer complications.

●**Longer life expectancy.**

●**Lower rates of depression,** anxiety and other mental illnesses.

●**Enhanced ability to cope with life-threatening and terminal illnesses** with greater tranquillity and less pain.

●**Decreased risk of addiction to alcohol,** drugs or tobacco.

●**Happier marriage and family life.**

These findings can be partly explained by the generally healthier lifestyle of religiously involved people.

Example: They are generally less likely to smoke, drink or take drugs, all of which have negative health effects.

But that isn't the whole story. Even after the statistics are adjusted to take account of these factors, religious involvement is associated with better health.

RELIGION AND SPIRITUALITY

Many people dislike religious institutions and create their own personal forms of belief, often a smorgasbord of religious elements from different traditions. You might say that spirituality poses questions. Religion composes answers.

Religion focuses more on establishing communities, while spirituality focuses more on individual growth.

Religion is more objective and measurable to outside observers. Spirituality is more subjective.

Religion is based more on behavior and outward practices. But, spirituality is based more on emotion and inner experience.

Religion prescribes certain kinds of behavior and proscribes others. Spirituality has few prescriptions and proscriptions.

Religion is particular, as it distinguishes one group from another. Spirituality, however emphasizes commonality.

Studies suggest that many health benefits are associated with specific forms of religious behavior—in particular, more frequent attendance at organized religious services. The effects of spirituality without religious practice have not been well-studied.

Among members of religious groups, those who have stronger internal religious and spiritual beliefs enjoy greater benefits than those who are motivated primarily by peer pressure.

BENEFITS OF ORGANIZED PRAYER

Worship services provide congregants with a break from their stressful day-to-day schedules. If congregants permit time for silent prayer or meditation, they also encourage the *relaxation response*. That's the health-boosting phenomenon first described by Harvard University's Herbert Benson, MD.

Worship is performed in an atmosphere of beauty, encompassing the building, furnishings, prayers and music—all of which produce a sense of peace and meaning.

People sing and pray with their whole being, moving their bodies and enlisting their souls, producing a deep sense of harmony.

During worship, people confess their sins and request forgiveness, unburdening themselves of guilt and refreshing themselves.

Participating in communal worship and familiar rituals and gaining strength through shared beliefs makes connections between worshippers and builds a community of people who will help each other and give emotional support in dealing with health problems and other challenges of life. Attendance at worship reinforces the belief that life has a meaning, which makes a positive contribution to health.

PRAYING FOR HEALTH

No one suggests that prayers for health—or anything else—will always be answered, but some studies have shown that they often help.

Here are a few suggestions based on my experience of ways to use prayer positively…

● **If you are sick, ask others to pray for you.** Family members and friends will probably be happy to help you, and many churches and synagogues maintain lists of people for whom they pray regularly.

● **Pray for your own healing.** Do not feel this is presumptuous. The Bible tells people to "ask, seek and knock…"—meaning, to pray for their own needs.

● **Pray consistently.** Continuing to pray regardless of immediate results is an expression of faith and hope. This is good both for our souls and our morale.

● **Pray for others who are suffering.** No matter how busy you are, you can find time to say brief prayers that express your good wishes for the comfort and healing of others. It will bring comfort and healing to you as well.

Proof that Prayer Heals

A total of 466 heart patients who were the object of other people's prayers during their hospital stay had 11% fewer complications than did 524 patients who were not prayed for.

Patients did not know prayers were being said for them. Those who did the praying knew only the patients' first names...and prayed only for "a speedy recovery with no complications."

The researchers note that, statistically, such a difference between the groups would occur by chance only one in 25 times.

William S. Harris, PhD, heart researcher, Lipids and Diabetes Research Center, Saint Luke's Hospital, Kansas City, MO. His study of 990 coronary care unit patients was published in the *Archives of Internal Medicine*.

Cultivate the Power of Patience

M.J. Ryan, coauthor of the *Random Acts of Kindness* books and founder of Conari Press. She is a consultant with Professional Thinking Partners, Park City, UT, *www.ptpinc.org*, a group specializing in coaching executives and entrepreneurs on life purpose, leadership and collaborative thinking. She is also author of *The Power of Patience: How to Slow the Rush and Enjoy More Happiness, Success, and Peace of Mind Every Day* (Bantam).

In this fast-paced world, patience has never been needed more—or perhaps been in such short supply.

Patience is not something a person either has or doesn't have. Patience is a choice we make again and again, day after day. The more we recognize that patience is a *decision,* the freer we are to make it.

Patience keeps us calm inside, no matter what is happening outside. Patience goes hand in hand with self-possession—the ability to choose a response, instead of being hijacked by our emotions and getting angry. Flipping over into the anger cycle floods the body with stress hormones, which intensify the anger.

REWARDS OF PATIENCE

Through patience, we earn the fruits of maturity and wisdom—healthier relationships, higher-quality work and peace of mind.

Patience engenders self-control—the ability to stop and be in the moment.

Advantages: Patience allows us to make wiser choices...become more loving, more at ease with the circumstances of our lives, more able to get what we want.

The key to patience is not always willpower. Often, it's *wait* power. If something isn't working out, give it time.

Example: With the kids out of college, Mark and Betty decided to sell their large suburban home and move to the city. Betty found the ideal condominium. They placed a bid, but lost out when their house failed to sell. Betty was heartbroken, but her intuition told her to be patient. A year later, the condo went on sale again. This time they sold their house quickly and bought the place of their dreams.

BANISH BOREDOM

Feeling bored is a common trigger of impatience. When we call something boring, we're saying we lack the patience for it. But during long stretches of parenting, partnering and working, nothing seems to be happening. We can consider those moments boring...or opportunities to tap into our patience.

Exercise: For a week, refuse to consider anything "boring." Whether in traffic or on hold, challenge yourself to find something of interest in what's occurring, either in yourself or in the world around you. How does the warm, soapy water feel on your hands as you wash dishes? When you weed the garden, how does it feel to bend and stretch in the sunlight?

What tests my own patience is waiting in line or in traffic.

Solution: I learned to distract myself.

Good distractions: Carry a paperback to read in line at the supermarket or read a magazine displayed there...listen to good music or books on tape in the car.

IMPATIENCE TRIGGERS

Becoming aware of what makes you lose your patience increases your options for responding in those situations.

Examples: My mother hates visual chaos, such as piles of toys...unmade beds...clothes on the floor. And I dislike working with my hands. Even junior high sewing class challenged me.

Can you eliminate what's hardest for you? If not, can you offer yourself compassion for how hard it is to be patient in those circumstances? Perhaps you get cranky when your blood sugar is low. Maybe you just need to have a small snack. Carry something with protein, such as peanut butter crackers, at all times.

My own solution is unabashedly to reassign mechanical tasks to my husband or daughter. When this isn't an option, I remind myself that these tasks are difficult for me, and I just have to try to do the best I can.

PATIENCE POINTS

By determining the circumstances that foster your patience, you will learn ways to control it.

Exercise 1: List situations in which you are naturally patient.

Examples: With small children…with animals…when making things with your hands.

Study your pattern of success. What keeps you calm at such times? Can you apply that to other situations?

Example: My client Bob was patient with system breakdowns at work but tended to yell at his kids. He realized that what kept him calm at the office was a mental picture of himself fixing problems in the past. Therefore, at home, as soon as his blood began to boil, he brought to mind the image of a happy outcome. By doing this, he lost his cool less often and communicated better with his family.

Exercise 2: Reflect on a situation that really tried your patience. What inner resources helped you through?

Examples: A capacity to understand others' perspectives…a belief in fundamental human goodness.

The next time you encounter a challenge, call upon these inner resources—which will be with you for the rest of your life—to make the hardship easier to bear.

PATIENCE WITH AGING

As we grow older, we just can't do everything we did before…and if we try, it often hurts. Developing patience with our own mortality may make it less frustrating. Be patient with your own vulnerability.

Advantages: Your body will be less stressed when you are not in a constant fight-or-flight reaction…and you will be happier.

Many older people attend readings from my book *The Power of Patience*. Since older people tend to have more patience than younger ones, I ask them what brought them. Many say they fear they are losing their patience—they remember when people were more courteous and had more time—and want to regain their former sense of peace.

PATIENCE WITH BUSY CHILDREN

Have compassion for younger adults who take life at a breakneck pace. Recognize that today's middle-income lifestyles tend to require that both spouses work outside the home. Most of these couples (especially those with kids) barely have time to breathe, much less to be highly attentive to their parents.

Fact: The average couple works 100 more hours per year now than 20 years ago.

So, if your kids take a while to call you back or can't visit very often, be compassionate—and patient!

PATIENCE WITH THE WORLD

Patience is at the heart of diplomacy, civility and lawfulness. Without patience, people can't work together and society can't function smoothly. With patience, we create the possibility of peace within and among ourselves.

More from M.J. Ryan…

Proven Patience Boosters

In today's world, maintaining patience is key. *Try these simple strategies to help you increase your patience quotient…*

●**Drop a pebble in your pocket.** When irritation rises, move the pebble to another pocket, which interrupts the anger cycle and creates a moment to think the situation through.

●**Reduce your caffeine intake.** Caffeine, a stimulant, can cause jitters and irritability.

●**Seek practical solutions** to frustrations with your mate.

Examples: Driven nuts when she hasn't replaced the toothpaste cap? Buy toothpaste in a pump. In a meltdown when he forgets to fill the ice cube trays? Your next refrigerator should have an automatic ice cube maker.

●**Take a walk.** When you reach your tolerance limit, go for a vigorous walk. You'll burn off accumulated stress hormones...and make it easier to reengage patience when you return.

●**Count to 10—or 20.** In a heated discussion, do this before responding. As you count, decide which matters more—finding an effective solution or blowing off steam.

●**Thank others for their patience.** Do this when you're the one holding things up, such as while fumbling for the right change. You'll defuse the tension while encouraging others to be patient as well.

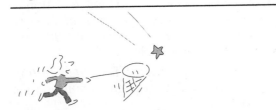

Forgive Your Way To Better Health

Fred Luskin, PhD, director and cofounder, Stanford University Forgiveness Project, Stanford, CA. He is author of *Forgive for Good: A Proven Prescription for Health and Happiness* (HarperSanFrancisco).

We all know that hostility increases the risk for developing heart disease. But research shows that forgiveness can moderate these dangerous effects on the heart. People who blame others for their problems appear to have a higher incidence of chronic pain, cardiovascular disease and other serious ailments.

Focusing on past grievances with your spouse, your friends, your relatives or even your neighbors can make you sick.

Why is forgiveness good for you? *There are two primary reasons...*

●**Forgiveness reduces chronic stress.** Self-generated, chronic stress triggers negative physical changes, including increased blood pressure and heart rate and decreased immune function, all of which eventually lead to disease.

●**Forgiveness increases one's sense of control.** Feeling in control is crucial to health. It moderates the stress response because one is less likely to panic and overreact to situations.

Feeling helpless can make you ill. When you learn how to forgive, you develop the emotional confidence to "get over" any difficulty.

DEFINING FORGIVENESS

Being forgiving does *not* require you to be an emotional doormat. You don't have to condone an unkindness...forget that something painful happened...excuse poor behavior...and/or deny or minimize your hurt.

Nor does forgiveness mean that you must reconcile with an offender. Forgiveness is for you, not the offender. It prevents you from wasting energy by being trapped in anger.

What then is forgiveness? It is the feeling of peace that you experience when you understand and accept that life doesn't always give you what you want...that you don't have to take a hurt so personally...that bad things need not ruin your present, even if they spoiled a part of your past.

HOW TO FORGIVE

Forgiveness is a skill. As with any skill, it requires practice to learn. *Use these techniques to master forgiving...*

●**Change the channel.** First, take responsibility for how you feel. Even though you are hurt, try to appreciate the good in your life. Rather than rehashing your grievances, focus on gratitude, love and appreciation of beauty.

Imagine that what you see in your mind is being viewed on a TV screen. Perhaps you are stuck on the Grievance Channel. *Reprogram your remote control to...*

●Gratitude Channel. As you wake up in the morning, give thanks for your breath and the gift of your life.

●Love Channel. Look for people who are in love, and smile at their happiness. Call a few close friends, and tell them you care about them.

●Beauty Channel. Find a favorite spot in nature. In times of stress, remember what that spot looks and feels like.

●**Calm down.** Learn to maintain your sense of peace in any situation, no matter how upsetting. A 45-second technique called Positive Emotion Refocusing Technique can calm you whenever you feel angry, hurt, depressed or bitter about an unresolved grievance or a relationship problem. *Here's how to do it...*

•Bring your attention to your stomach as you slowly inhale and exhale—each for two deep breaths. As you inhale, allow the air to gently push your belly out. As you exhale, consciously try to relax your belly so that it feels soft.

•On the third deep inhalation, bring to your mind's eye an image of someone you love or a beautiful nature scene that fills you with peace, awe or wonder.

•Focus on the image and the resulting warm feelings, and notice that your belly is still slowly moving in and out.

•When you feel relaxed, see if the part of you that is calm can allow you to see the situation differently.

•**Challenge your unenforceable rules.** An "unenforceable rule" is a desire that you think must come true, but that you don't have control over. This combination can make you feel helpless, mad, hurt and frustrated. You can eventually become bitter and hopeless.

Common unenforceable rules include: People must not lie to me...life should be fair ...people have to treat me with kindness...my life has to be easy...my parents and family should have treated me better.

If an unenforceable rule is "broken," there are six steps to follow...

1. Recognize that you may feel hurt, angry, alienated, depressed or hopeless. Acknowledge that your feelings may stem from memories of the past but that you are experiencing them in the present.

2. Remind yourself that you feel bad only because you are trying to enforce an unenforceable rule.

3. Assert your willingness to challenge your unenforceable rule.

4. Ask yourself the following question— *What experience in my life am I thinking of right now that I am demanding to be different?* This is your unenforceable rule.

5. Change your attitude from *demanding* things go your way to strongly *hoping* you get what you want.

6. Use that hope to motivate yourself toward finding practical solutions. When you temper your unenforceable rules, you will think more clearly and feel more peaceful. This is the essence of forgiveness.

16

Healthy Travel

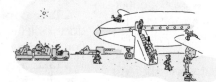

Medical Emergencies Overseas—It Pays to Be Prepared

Just imagine for a moment that you're on your much anticipated dream vacation to Paris, France. You're at the end of a long, enjoyable day of sightseeing and visiting museums—then suddenly, you fall on the steps of the Métro and break your leg. What do you do? *You realize...*

- **You don't speak French.**

- **You don't know how the French hospital system works.**

- **You don't know how you're going to pay for all the medical expenses.**

- **You worry about the quality of care you will receive.**

- **You find out it can cost $10,000 or more** to be evacuated back to the US.

Such a serious emergency is not likely to happen, of course. But what if you *did* have to deal with a medical emergency overseas?

GETTING HELP

Contact the US embassy or consulate. *A consular officer will...*

- **Find English-speaking doctors or dentists,** who can direct you to the other medical services you need.

- **Contact your family and/or friends back home.**

- **Arrange for the transfer of funds** from the US to cover your medical costs.

If you have an American Express card, use its free Global Assist Hotline to find emergency medical referrals. MasterCard Gold and Platinum cards offer a Travel Services Medical Assistance Program, which provides similar travel services.

Louise Weiss, award-winning travel writer based in New York City. She is a contributor to many travel books and publications and author of *Access to the World: A Travel Guide for the Handicapped* (Henry Holt).

WHO PAYS?

Don't assume that your health insurance will cover medical expenses abroad. Ditto for the US government. Medicare provides no coverage for hospitalizations or other medical costs outside the US.

Self-defense: Check your existing coverage—*before* you travel. Your health insurance may provide reimbursement for "customary and reasonable" medical claims abroad. But generally, you must pay the bills and seek reimbursement after you return home.

Supplemental Medicare (Medigap) policies—policies C through J—provide some foreign travel emergency coverage. This insurance—which you can buy from an insurance company—will pay 80% of medically necessary foreign emergency care above a $250 deductible. If you're age 65 or older and travel a lot, you may want to carry a Medigap policy just for this coverage.

Health insurance policies that cover the cost of medical evacuation are few and far between.

If your insurance doesn't cover all medical costs on overseas trips, consider buying a special travel medical insurance policy. For a few extra dollars a day—usually about $3 to $5—you can carry short-term coverage (typically 15 days to 12 months) for overseas hospital costs and other medical charges.

Important: Emergency evacuation insurance has to be obtained separately. If your own insurance covers foreign medical costs but not evacuation costs, buy a policy for this type of emergency medical assistance.

Ask your travel agent about short-term medical coverage and medical assistance insurance. *Also check out the following...*

- **US State Department** at *http://travel.state.gov/travel.*

- **WorldTravelCenter.com.**

PREVENTIVE MEASURES

- **Be fully immunized for your destinations.** Learn about suggested immunizations at the US Centers for Disease Control and Prevention international travel hotline (800-311-3435...*www.cdc.gov*).

Do not assume immunization information from embassies of the countries you will travel to is accurate or complete.

Not all vaccines or necessary medications are available from your family doctor. You may have to call a travel medicine clinic. Look in your local phone book under "Travel Medicine" or call a local medical center.

- **Take all your medications and medical devices with you when you travel.** Keep them in your carry-on bag. Make sure you have *more than enough* of each type of medication for the scheduled length of the trip in case of travel delays.

Helpful: Keep pills, especially narcotics, in their original containers. That helps you to avoid questions about whether or not they are legal drugs.

- **Take copies of prescriptions.** Also take a doctor's letter explaining any special treatment you require if you become ill.

- **Take a list of English-speaking doctors and dentists.** To obtain a list for your destination, contact the Office of Overseas Citizens Services, Bureau of Consular Affairs, Rm. 4811, Washington, DC 20520, *www.travel.state.gov/travel/about/about_1247.html,* or the International Association for Medical Assistance to Travellers at *www.iamat.org.*

You can sign up on-line for free (a donation is requested) and obtain a booklet listing English-speaking doctors as well as charts detailing climate and food sanitation conditions in 1,400 cities worldwide.

If you have a chronic medical condition, consider getting a MedicAlert tag that contains all your relevant medical information. Call 888-633-4298 or go to *www.medicalert.org. Cost:* About $35.

- **Drink only bottled water.** Do this even if you are told the local water is safe to drink. Avoid ice cubes...and, depending on where you are traveling, peel fresh fruits and vegetables that may have been washed in local water.

- **Carry medical emergency phone numbers** in your wallet. These numbers should include your doctor's and travel agent's.

Also carry the telephone number of the local US consulate...just in case.

When in Europe...

Europe's emergency phone number is 112. Emergency service operators at call centers usually speak English, French and German.

For nonemergencies, travelers should call the local police, ambulance services and fire departments.

The Wall Street Journal.

Basic Travel-Medicine Kit

For a basic travel-medicine kit, include cold remedy...insect repellent containing DEET ...sunblock with at least SPF 15...lip balm... foot-care products, such as blister pads and athlete's foot treatment...diarrhea remedy, such as *loperamide* (Imodium AD)...pain reliever, such as *acetaminophen* (Tylenol) or *ibuprofen* (Advil)...an antibiotic ointment, such as Neosporin...bandages, gauze and adhesive tape... tweezers...scissors...laxatives...thermometer.

Women should carry tampons or sanitary napkins...and medication for yeast infections. Keep everything—prescription and over-the-counter—in their original containers. Pack in carry-on luggage so there is no risk of loss.

If you must carry needles, syringes or other prescription medications: Get a letter from your doctor describing your diagnosis and the reasons you are using these products.

Mary Nettleman, MD, chairperson, department of medicine, Michigan State University College of Human Medicine, East Lansing.

Protect Your Health While Traveling

Mark Wise, MD, Toronto–based family practitioner who specializes in travel and tropical medicine. Dr. Wise is author of *The Travel Doctor: Your Guide to Staying Healthy While You Travel* (Firefly). His Web site is *www. drwisetravel.com.*

Few things are more frightening than suffering a medical problem while you are away from home. Fortunately, good planning can prevent most health mishaps.

When overseas travelers become ill, it's usually because of an infection or disease that is contracted in a foreign country. But both international and domestic travelers are vulnerable to unexpected complications arising from pre-existing medical conditions.

ARE YOU AT RISK?

Not everyone planning to board an airplane needs to visit his/her doctor. However, it may be important if you have a current medical problem. *Check with your doctor before flying if you have...*

●**Anemia.** If your hemoglobin level (measurement of a protein in red blood cells) is less than 8.5 grams per 100 milliliters, you may need supplemental oxygen during the flight because of the cabin's reduced oxygen level. You must arrange this with the airline at least 48 hours in advance.

●**Heart disease.** If you suffer from unstable angina, serious arrhythmias or congestive heart failure, you may not be fit to fly. If you've had a heart attack, wait at least two weeks before flying. All heart disease patients should consult their doctors before flying.

If you have recently had abdominal surgery, such as laparoscopic gall bladder removal, you should avoid flying for a few weeks. Any air that might have been introduced into your abdominal cavity during surgery will expand at higher altitudes, where cabin pressure is lower.

By the same token, a recently applied cast, which contains air bubbles, may become dangerously tight during flight as those bubbles expand and impede blood circulation to that area. Wait at least 48 hours after being fitted with a cast before flying.

DANGER ZONES

Some travel destinations can also cause medical problems. A high-altitude location—whether it is a Colorado ski resort, or the mountains of Nepal or Peru—may be dangerous for those patients with heart or lung disease. The air is thinner at high altitudes, which means there is less oxygen available to breathe.

Asthmatics should check with their doctors before visiting heavily polluted cities, such as Bangkok, Beijing and Mumbai.

Even healthy people are at increased risk for illness while traveling. Nearly 30% of those visiting Mexico, the Caribbean and other popular tropical destinations experience "traveler's diarrhea"—even when staying at top resorts.

Self-defense: Avoid local water (including ice cubes) as well as uncooked or undercooked food, which can cause gastrointestinal distress. *Loperamide* (Imodium) will help decrease your symptoms if you do become sick.

If you're traveling outside of North America, find out if there are any required or recommended inoculations. For more information, contact the US Centers for Disease Control and Prevention at 877-394-8747 or go to its Web site at *www.cdc.gov/travel.*

For more information on inoculations and medications for traveling, contact The International Society of Travel Medicine (770-736-7060 or *www.istm.org*) to locate a travel clinic in your area. Or see your doctor at least two months before your departure if possible.

Important: Pack all of your medical supplies in your *carry-on* baggage, rather than in checked luggage. Many medications and batteries can freeze when exposed to cold air in the plane's baggage compartment.

If you are carrying syringes, make sure you have a signed, stamped note from your doctor explaining why you need the syringes.

If you have a chronic disease, such as diabetes, emphysema or cancer, consider bringing a copy of your pertinent medical records.

If you have heart disease, bring a copy of your latest electrocardiogram.

Stock Up Before You Go

Buy extra medicine before you go on a trip, and ask your doctor for duplicate prescriptions in case your medication is lost or stolen.

Also, carry prescription medicines with you—not in your suitcase. And bring medicines in their original bottles.

If you use sedatives, tranquilizers or other narcotic drugs, take along a letter from your doctor that explains why you need them—this will help prevent any possible problems at border crossings.

Donald Sullivan, RPh, PhD, travel-medicine specialist, Columbus, OH, and author of *A Senior's Guide to Healthy Travel* (Career Press).

Don't Get Sick on Your Vacation

People often get sick while on a vacation. That's because when stress levels rapidly subside, resulting biochemical changes lower the body's immunity.

To prevent this effect: Relax slowly by exercising lightly, even while on vacation.

Helpful: Short bursts of exercise—a quick jog or brisk walk, for 10 minutes two to three times each day during the first and second days of vacation—can activate the body and boost immune response.

Marc Schoen, PhD, licensed clinical psychologist and assistant clinical professor, UCLA School of Medicine, Los Angeles.

Stay Away from These Cities If You Have Health Problems

Stuart R. Rose, MD, president, Travel Medicine, Inc., a company that provides information and products for safe travel, 369 Pleasant St., Northampton, MA 01060, *www.travmed.com*; 800-872-8633.

Try to avoid traveling to the three smoggiest cities—Mexico City, São Paulo and Cairo—if you have cardiac or pulmonary diseases, such as congestive heart failure, asthma, bronchitis or emphysema. The poor air quality may exacerbate symptoms.

Also avoid: Large cities in Southeast Asia and the major cities of China.

If you must spend time in any heavily polluted cities, minimize activities on the smoggiest days—stay indoors in an air-conditioned room. Have your medical condition evaluated before travel, and bring enough medicine to last you through the trip.

More from Stuart Rose...

Tropical Travel Ahead?

Before traveling to the tropics, consult with your physician about preventive measures you should take for several conditions, including...

●**Malaria.** Prevalent in rural areas of Asia, Central and South America, and especially dangerous in sub-Saharan Africa, even in cities.

Self-defense: Pre-exposure drugs, such as *chloroquine*...DEET repellent on skin...permethrin insecticide on clothing.

●**Dengue fever.** Caribbean, Latin America, Southeast Asia, India, Africa. The disease has flu-like symptoms with a high fever and rash.

Self-defense: Protect against mosquito bites—there is no vaccine.

●**Hepatitis A.** Risk in all underdeveloped countries.

Self-defense: Get your hepatitis vaccine at least two weeks before travel.

●**Travelers' diarrhea.** High risk in all underdeveloped countries.

Self-defense: Eat only well-cooked foods and drink only bottled water. Take along a standby antibiotic such as *ofloxacin* (Floxin).

Other precautions: Make sure all your routine shots are up-to-date...buy a travel insurance policy to cover emergency air ambulance evacuation.

Cost: $3 to $5 a day.

How to Stay Healthy While Traveling by Air

Thomas N. Bettes, MD, MPH, medical director, American Airlines, AMR Corporation, and occupational toxicology faculty, University of Texas Southwestern Medical Center, Dallas. He has written about medical advice for commercial air travelers in *American Family Physician*.

Despite several air disasters of the past, your risk of being killed in a plane crash is remarkably small. But the time spent on-board can leave you tired, stiff and dehydrated...and, if you have a chronic health condition, raise your risk of serious complications. *Here are the leading threats to airline passengers' health—and how to manage each...*

●**Dehydration.** During flight, cold, dry air inside the cabin can dry the skin, throat, eyes and nostrils.

To protect yourself, drink noncaffeinated beverages—six to eight ounces per hour while aloft. Pass up the coffee and alcohol. They're diuretics and will make you more dehydrated. Use moisturizer to keep your skin from drying out. Over-the-counter saline eye drops can help prevent dry eyes.

If you're flying overseas: Ask if you can be booked on a nonsmoking flight. If no such flights are available, ask to be seated well away from the smoking section.

All domestic airlines are now smoke-free.

●**Altitude sickness.** Airline cabins are typically kept at a pressure equivalent to 8,000 feet above sea level. This reduced pressure can cause mild *altitude sickness*—headache, fatigue and trouble concentrating.

There's no way to prevent altitude sickness, but being aware of it can ease any anxiety you might feel as a result of the symptoms.

If altitude sickness doesn't cause you to have headaches, engine noise might.

Self-defense: Ask for a seat far away from the engines. Bring along earplugs and *acetaminophen* (Tylenol) or another nonprescription pain medication.

●**Blood clots.** Stiffness isn't the only problem that can result from spending long hours in a cramped airplane seat. If blood pools in the legs, dangerous blood clots can form.

If your flight is longer than three hours, try to get up once an hour to stretch and walk around. While seated, periodically extend and flex your feet.

Caution: If you're already at risk for blood clots—because of smoking, obesity, oral contraceptive use or if you have a history of *deep venous thrombosis* (DVT)—ask your doctor about taking aspirin and wearing support stockings during the flight.

If possible, get a bulkhead seat. It will provide more legroom. Prolonged sitting can also cause swelling of the feet and ankles, especially in pregnant women and people with kidney trouble or heart failure.

To minimize swelling: Elevate your legs… walk around the cabin…and avoid nuts, pretzels and other salty foods.

AVOIDING COMPLICATIONS

If you've had recent surgery or have a chronic health problem, ask your doctor if you're stable enough to fly…

●**Recent surgery.** Postpone flying at least one week after major surgery—two weeks after coronary bypass surgery.

The danger is that air that might have been trapped inside the body during surgery could expand under reduced air pressure. This could cause torn sutures and other problems.

●**Special oxygen needs.** If your doctor recommends that you have supplemental oxygen during the flight, you'll need to call the airline to order it at least 48 hours in advance.

You'll also need to provide the airline with a medical certificate that spells out the proper flow rate and other important points.

●**Heart disease.** Anyone who has had a heart attack should wait at least two weeks before flying. Wait at least six weeks if there were complicating factors, such as arrhythmia or left ventricle dysfunction.

If there's any doubt as to your ability to fly safely following a heart attack, your doctor should give you a treadmill stress test.

If you take an antihypertensive drug or another heart medication, be sure to bring enough to last the entire trip. Keep it in your carry-on luggage.

It's also a good idea to bring along a copy of your most recent electrocardiogram.

Caution: Flying is off-limits to individuals with unstable angina, severe heart failure, uncontrolled hypertension and certain heart arrhythmias.

●**Diabetes.** Be vigilant about monitoring your blood glucose levels while flying…and about scheduling meals and medication dosing—especially if you'll be traveling across time zones.

Pack *twice* as much medication and supplies as you think you'll need. Bring half the supply on board with you in your carry-on luggage. Bring *all* of your insulin on board with you to avoid exposure to freezing temperatures in the cargo hold.

Important: Bring a "diabetes alert card" and a doctor's note specifying your dosages and explaining why you're carrying syringes. To obtain a free card, contact the American Diabetes Association at 800-342-2383.

●**Pregnancy.** To avoid premature delivery, pregnant women should avoid flying for at least a week before their due date (four weeks for overseas travel).

Women at risk for premature delivery should avoid flying entirely in the third trimester.

IN-FLIGHT EMERGENCIES

Domestic airlines are required to carry basic medical equipment, and crew members are trained in basic first aid.

Unfortunately, the first-aid kit can be used only by a physician or another trained medical professional, such as a nurse or paramedic. Whether there'll be one on your flight is a matter of luck.

Good news: Many airlines have upgraded their medical kits. A wider range of medical problems can be treated on-board, including heart attacks, asthma attacks and seizures.

In addition, some airliners are now equipped with automatic defibrillators, which can shock an erratically beating heart back into a normal rhythm. These devices can be operated by flight attendants.

Avoid Stomach Trouble When You Fly

Stay away from gum and carbonated drinks. Both increase the production of gas in the digestive tract. Drink plain water or juice. Eat only well-cooked foods. Avoid ones that can produce gas, such as broccoli, cabbage, cauliflower and beans. Eat slowly and chew thoroughly. Walk around to speed digestion.

Maria T. Abreu, MD, gastroenterologist and director, Inflammatory Bowel Disease Center, Cedars-Sinai Medical Center, Los Angeles.

What's Even Worse than Airline Food?

Aircraft water tanks often contain *salmonella* and other disease-causing organisms at levels that may be hundreds of times above government limits.

If you drink water—or even if you brush your teeth—during a flight, ask the flight attendant for bottled water.

The Wall Street Journal, 200 Liberty St., New York City 10281.

When You Shouldn't Get on a Plane

Edward R. Rensimer, MD, director, International Medicine Center, travel-health specialists, Houston, *www.traveldoc.com.*

There are certain medical conditions with which you should be careful not to fly. *Travel-health expert and physician Edward Rensimer, MD, explained...*

•**If you have poorly controlled asthma,** sinusitis, pneumonia, intense allergies or an ear infection—changes in air pressure on ascent and descent can cause severe pain or breathing problems.

•**For at least 24 hours after abdominal, eye, ear or facial surgery** or extensive dental work—the swelling and bleeding can be amplified, causing sutures to rip and severe pain.

•**For one day after sustaining a concussion**—brain irritability could cause seizures when oxygen levels decline at high altitudes. Any brain swelling can cause acute neurological events in-flight.

•**For several days after undergoing a colonoscopy**—bowels may be sluggish and gas infused into body cavities may rupture or perforate intestines at high altitudes.

•**If you have a serious communicable illness,** such as measles, tuberculosis or a viral respiratory illness.

Special concerns for children: Kids with active chicken pox should not fly—the disease can be fatal to adults and is spread easily in contained-air ventilation space. Do not fly with an infant who has diarrhea—frequent diaper changes may spread germs, resulting in dysentery, especially in other children.

First Aid for Air Travelers

Air travelers should pack a bottle of baby aspirin in their carry-on baggage. Aspirin isn't always included in the medical kits aboard commercial airliners—even though its clot-busting effect can be lifesaving in case of a heart attack.

If you think you're having a heart attack—aboard an airliner or anyplace else—chew one of the 81-milligram tablets while seeking emergency medical assistance.

Victor S. Sloan, MD, clinical associate professor of medicine, University of Medicine and Dentistry of New Jersey, New Brunswick. His suggestion was published in the Annals of Internal Medicine.

How to Avoid Jet Lag

Charles B. Inlander, a consumer advocate and health-care consultant based in Fogelsville, PA. He was founding president of People's Medical Society, a consumer health advocacy group. He is author of more than 20 books, including Take This Book to the Hospital with You (St. Martin's).

J et lag is rarely a problem following a short flight. But anyone who flies across three or more time zones is likely to experience a few days of fatigue, fuzzy thinking and mild stomach upset.

Jet lag is caused by the sudden disruption of the body's internal clock. The key to minimizing this disruption is to begin shifting over to the "new" time zone—and it helps to do so well in advance of your departure.

USING A TRAVEL WATCH

As soon as your travel plans are finalized, consult an atlas to determine the number of time zones you'll be crossing. That's how many days prior to departure you should begin your jet lag avoidance program.

Example: If you plan to fly from New York City to Mumbai, India (across 10 time zones), you should begin your program 10 days before takeoff.

During this period, bedtime, wake-up time, meals, etc., should be scheduled not according to your regular watch...but according to a second "travel" watch. On this watch, time must be adjusted each day until your departure.

Eastbound travel: On the first day of your jet lag prevention program, your travel watch should be set to the same time as your regular watch. Each day until your departure, advance the travel watch one hour. On the day of your departure, your travel watch should be on the same time zone as your destination.

Westbound travel: Start your program with your travel watch at the same time as your regular watch. Then, as you are traveling, set your travel watch back one hour a day until you reach the time zone of your destination.

For distant destinations, of course, your jet lag program will put you significantly out of sync with your home time.

Solution: Begin by setting your travel watch ahead or behind by just 15 minutes every day. Switch to the full one hour per day when you're halfway to your departure date.

LIGHT AND DARKNESS

To shift your body clock while you are still in your home time zone, you will need to manipulate your light exposure, activity patterns and diet. *Here's how...*

Eastbound travel: Expose yourself to bright light in the early morning hours—before sunrise, if necessary. After sunrise, spend a few hours outdoors. If that's impossible, sit near a bright lamp...or go to a brightly lighted building.

After mid-afternoon, you should avoid sunlight and other bright light. Once it's bedtime according to your travel watch, you should avoid all sources of light.

Westbound travel: Avoid bright light in the morning. You may need to wear a light-blocking eye mask until it's wake-up time according to your travel watch.

Wear wraparound sunglasses until midday. Try to get as much exposure to late-afternoon light as possible, then use artificial light to "extend" your day.

WHAT TO EAT—AND WHEN

Keep mealtimes consistent, using the times on your travel watch. If you vary your mealtimes, you'll throw your digestive system out of whack...and that sets you up for an even worse case of jet lag.

Eastbound travel: You'll be eating one hour earlier each day. At breakfast and lunch, have mostly protein-rich foods—beans, fish and low-fat meats and dairy products. Proteins are energizing.

For dinner, focus on vegetables, grains and other carbohydrates. Carbohydrates are calming.

Westbound travel: You'll be delaying meals by an hour a day. Eat carbohydrates for breakfast, proteins for lunch and dinner.

ACTIVITY LEVELS

Whenever your jet lag plan calls for exposure to light, try to engage in physical activity. If you cannot be active at that time, read...or do a crossword puzzle.

When you're supposed to avoid light, be sure to rest or sleep.

DURING THE FLIGHT

If you've followed your jet lag plan carefully, your body clock will be in sync with the new time zone when you take off.

Once airborne, continue to follow your light/darkness schedule. If you're supposed to be getting light exposure, keep the window shade up and use the reading light.

If you're supposed to be avoiding light, keep the window shade pulled down and wear your eye mask as much as possible.

Also important: Rest or sleep according to the time at your destination.

What about eating? Try to eat more protein when you need to be alert...and carbohydrates when you need to wind down.

FOLLOWING YOUR ARRIVAL

Schedule all of your meals and activities according to the new time zone—even if your body hasn't yet fully adjusted.

Avoid the urge to nap, even on your first day. Drinking caffeinated beverages can be helpful. If you absolutely cannot stay awake, nap for one hour or less.

Go to bed when the locals do. If you wake up too early the next morning, try to stay in bed until the clock says it's a more appropriate time to get up.

MELATONIN

Jet lag medication should be unnecessary if you followed your pretrip jet lag program. But if you failed to follow the program, ask your doctor about using melatonin.

The usual protocol calls for three doses—one the day before travel, a second on your travel day and a third dose on arrival day.

Caution: Melatonin is off-limits to pregnant or breastfeeding women...children...and many others who have medical problems.

New Treatment for Traveler's Diarrhea

The recently approved antibiotic *rifaximin* (Xifaxan) targets *E. coli* bacteria, which most commonly cause the infection. This action differs from that of antimotility agents, such as *loperamide* (Imodium) and *diphenoxylate* (Lomotil), which reduce diarrhea by slowing down transit time in the gut and may keep bacteria inside the intestine. Rifaximin is as effective as other antibiotics but does not cause the upset stomach and restlessness associated with *ciprofloxacin* (Cipro) and *norfloxacin* (Noroxin), other antimicrobials used to treat traveler's diarrhea. Rifaximin is taken three times a day for three days at the onset of symptoms.

Herbert DuPont, MD, professor of infectious disease, University of Texas School of Public Health, Houston.

Natural Relief for Traveler's Diarrhea

In a study, volunteers who drank three cups of milk a day for 10 days and were then infected with the bacterium *E. coli* had diarrhea for just one day. Those subjects who drank low-calcium milk had diarrhea for three days.

Theory: Taking calcium increases growth of the diarrhea-fighting bacterium *lactobacillius* in the gut.

Good news: Calcium supplements (1,000 milligrams daily in divided doses) may also do the trick for people who don't drink milk.

Ingeborg M.J. Bovee-Oudenhoven, MD, scientist, Wageningen Center for Food Sciences/Nizo Food Research, Ede, the Netherlands.

Cayenne Prevents Dysentery

Cayenne pepper increases the intestine's resistance to *enterococci* and other microbes that cause the severe abdominal pain, fever and diarrhea. If you're traveling in tropical climates or anywhere with poor sanitation, sprinkle enough pepper on one meal a day to make it very spicy.

Andrew L. Rubman, ND, director, Southbury Clinic for Traditional Medicines, Southbury, CT.

Self-Defense Against Viral Illness on Cruises

Outbreaks of gastrointestinal illnesses on cruise ships have actually diminished since 1990. But exposure to illness-causing viruses and bacteria is a reality of travel. On recent cruises, the Norwalk virus infected hundreds of passengers, causing diarrhea, nausea, stomach pain and/or vomiting. The biggest risk—especially among older people—is dehydration.

Self-defense: Wash your hands frequently and thoroughly both onboard *and* onshore.

Information on cruise-related health issues is available from the US Centers for Disease Control and Prevention, *www.cdc.gov/nceh/vsp/default.htm.*

Dave Forney, communicable disease specialist and chief, vessel sanitation program, US Centers for Disease Control and Prevention, Atlanta.

How to Handle Illness After a Trip

When illness strikes after an overseas trip, get immediate medical attention. Be sure to see a doctor if you have been to a region in which malaria is present and you develop a fever above 100°F, even if you took antimalaria pills—they do not always work …if you experience intestinal problems that last longer than one week or are accompanied by severe pain, fever or dizziness…or if you develop skin lesions.

Brian Terry, MD, travel-medicine specialist, Healthy Traveler Clinic, Pasadena, CA, *www.healthytraveler.com.*

17

Very, Very Personal

Why We Love—The Science Of Sexual Attraction

If you have ever been a "fool for love," blame it on evolution. The phenomena of love, lust and the desire for attachment aren't just emotions. They are basic drives—as powerful as hunger—and essential to our survival as a species.

Helen Fisher, PhD, one of the country's top experts on love, administered a series of experiments to look into the brains of people who are deeply in love and those who were just recently rejected. *Here's what she discovered...*

●**Does the brain actually change when we fall in love?** There is a complex interplay of chemicals involved. My colleagues and I performed brain scans (functional magnetic resonance imaging) on 20 men and women in love. The people in our research had increased activity in the *caudate nucleus,* part of the brain's reward system that produces the focus and motivation to achieve goals. The subjects also

showed activity in the *ventral tegmental* area, which is responsible for the intense energy and concentration that people in love experience. Increased blood flow in these areas explains the all-night talk sessions and endless letters and e-mails between lovers, as well as the outpouring of love-related poetry and art.

●**How does lust differ from love?** Humans have three basic mating drives—lust, romantic love and attachment. They happen in different regions of the brain and involve different hormones and neurochemicals—but they work in harmony to ensure reproduction and survival of the species.

●Lust is associated primarily with *testosterone,* the hormone that motivates men and women to have sex. People with higher levels of testosterone tend to have sex more often than those with lower levels.

Helen Fisher, PhD, research professor of anthropology, Rutgers University, New Brunswick, NJ, and former research associate, American Museum of Natural History, New York City. She is author of many books on human sexual and social behavior, including *Why We Love* (Holt). Her Web site is *www.helenfisher.com.*

●Romantic love is linked to *dopamine* and also most likely to *serotonin* and *norepinephrine,* brain chemicals that can produce feelings of ecstasy. In specific combinations, these chemicals motivate a person to focus his/her attention on a preferred individual and think obsessively about that person.

●Attachment, the desire of couples to stay together, is linked to elevated activities of *vasopressin* and *oxytocin,* neurohormones that promote the urge to bond and cuddle as well as to care for offspring.

Romantic love is metabolically expensive because people will lavish so much energy and attention on their beloved. But it pays off in evolutionary terms because romantic love leads to attachment and the desire to nurture and raise a family.

●**Can lust lead to love?** Love is far more likely to lead to lust than lust is to love. We find our new partners sexually attractive in part because increases in dopamine enhance the activity of testosterone.

●**Is "love at first sight" possible?** I think that love at first sight comes out of nature. With animals, brain circuitry must be triggered rapidly because they don't have much time to mate. We inherited this ability to prefer certain partners almost instantly.

●**Do men and women experience love differently?** Both exhibit similar elation and obsessive behavior—but men show more activity in a brain region associated with the integration of visual stimuli. Women have more activity in brain areas associated with memory recall.

Why this difference? Men are more visual than women, probably because for millions of years they sized up women by looking for signs of youth and fertility, such as clear skin, bright eyes, a big smile, etc. These and other visual cues caused men to become aroused and initiate the mating process.

On the other hand, a woman can't tell just from looking at a man if he would protect and provide for her and her future offspring. As we evolved, women probably depended more on memory—remembering if a man kept promises, was truthful, etc.

●**Why is rejection so difficult?** There are two stages, and each is associated with different chemical changes. *They are...*

●The *protest* stage is very painful. You love even more deeply after you've been dumped. This is the time when you call constantly, write pleading e-mails, show up unannounced and generally make a fool of yourself.

Dopamine activity most likely spikes during the protest stage because the brain's reward system keeps churning it out in an attempt to recapture the beloved.

The behavior of jilted lovers often alienates the ones they love. This seems counterproductive from an evolutionary point of view, but it might be a way of conserving energy in the long run. The rejected one behaves in ways that sever the ties and allow both partners to move on and find new mates.

●The *resignation* stage is accompanied by a drop in dopamine. People experience lethargy, depression and a lack of motivation. The resignation stage may allow the body to rest and recover. It also sends out signals to others in the community that you need support, which can attract potential mates.

●**How can we diminish the pain?** It can take several months, or even years, to recover from rejection. Treat it as you would an addiction. Remove cards, letters and photos of the beloved. Don't call or write. Stay busy and get more exercise—physical activity increases dopamine activity. Sunlight also improves mood.

Seriously depressed people usually benefit from psychotherapy and/or antidepressants.

●**Is falling in love just a matter of brain chemistry?** Chemical factors clearly are involved, but many environmental elements also are at work. For example, you must be interested in meeting someone in the first place. If the timing is not right, you won't trigger the brain chemistry for romantic love.

●**How can long-married couples keep their love alive?** Novelty drives up the activity of dopamine. Couples who are spontaneous and try new things are aroused mentally as well as physically. Just going on vacation can spark your sex life and rejuvenate a relationship that has become routine.

Sex Makes You Look Younger

People who engage in loving sex at least three times per week look more than 10 years younger than the average adult.

Possible reasons: Sex is pleasurable and produces feel-good chemicals...and loving couples like to look their best for each other.

David J. Weeks, PhD, clinical neuropsychologist, Royal Edinburgh Hospital, Scotland, and leader of a 10-year study of 3,500 people ages 18 to 102, published in *Sexual and Relationship Therapy.*

Best Ways to Boost Your Sexual Fitness

Robert N. Butler, MD, president and CEO, International Longevity Center, New York City. He is former chairman of the department of geriatrics and adult development at Mount Sinai Medical Center, New York City, the first geriatrics department in an American medical school. He won the Pulitzer Prize for his book *Why Survive? Being Old in America* (Johns Hopkins University Press) and is coauthor of *The New Love and Sex After 60* (Ballantine).

Don't allow advancing age to interfere with your sex life. Many sexual problems can be eliminated with a simple program that emphasizes a healthy diet and physical fitness.

Everyone knows that some medical conditions, including diabetes and hormone deficiency, can cause sexual difficulties ranging from impotence to lack of desire. It is also well known that many drugs, including antidepressants and blood pressure drugs, often produce unwanted sexual side effects.

If you experience sexual difficulties, see your doctor for a thorough exam and evaluation to rule out a treatable medical condition. But you should also be aware that a significant number of sexual difficulties are not linked to a medical condition or medication. For these cases, keeping your body fit—with proper diet, exercise and rest—is the best solution. *Here's what to do...*

EAT SMART

Excessive dietary fat and cholesterol produce artery-clogging plaque that not only increases your risk for heart attack and stroke but also restricts blood flow to the genitalia. This can hinder a man's ability to achieve or maintain an erection and may also reduce vaginal and clitoral sensitivity in women.

Self-defense: Consume no more than 30% of your daily calories as fat. Avoid saturated fat and trans-fats (abundant in fried foods and commercially baked goods). Choose unsaturated fats, found in olive and flaxseed oils, nuts and fish.

Avoid sugary snacks and high-fat fast food. Opt instead for whole-grain breads and pastas, fresh vegetables and fruits and proteins, including beans, lean beef, fish, skim milk and low-fat cheese.

A multivitamin can help to offset nutritional deficiencies. Most older adults should choose one without iron, since a reasonably balanced diet provides adequate amounts of iron. Excess iron levels have been shown to contribute to heart disease.

Important: Overindulging in alcohol can dampen sexual appetite and diminish sexual performance. Although alcohol lowers inhibitions, it's known to depress physical arousal.

Eating until you're uncomfortably full can leave you feeling too bloated and sluggish for sex. To avoid unnecessarily straining the heart, it's advisable to postpone sex for a few hours following a heavy meal.

A heart attack during sex is extremely uncommon. According to a study conducted at Harvard University, the risk for heart attack during sex among people who have coronary disease is 20 in 1 million.

A Japanese study found that when heart attacks do occur, the victims are usually men engaged in illicit sex following an eating or drinking binge.

GET MORE EXERCISE

For the stamina and flexibility required to enjoy sex, you need to exercise. Brisk walking usually provides the best overall workout for people age 60 or older. Aim for 10,000 steps each day, five to six days every week (2,000 steps equals roughly one mile).

If that sounds daunting, consider that even relatively inactive adults average 3,500 steps a day. Simple changes—taking the stairs instead of the elevator or walking rather than driving to a store, for example—can add to that number substantially. That means a two- or three-mile walk may be all that's required to reach your overall daily goal.

To stay motivated: Recruit a walking partner or join a walking club...and keep track of your miles with an electronic pedometer.

Supplement daily walks with strengthening and stretching exercises. If back pain prevents you from enjoying sex, toning the back and stomach muscles can help. Try crunches to strengthen the upper abdominal muscles...leg lifts to work the lower abs...and swimming to strengthen the back and shoulders.

GET MORE SLEEP

At least half of all adults over age 50 suffer from sleep disturbances. Insomnia, illness, pain or frequent nighttime trips to the bathroom can interfere with sleep cycles, depriving you of sufficient *rapid eye movement* (REM) sleep—the kind associated with dreaming. Chronic sleep deprivation can leave you too exhausted for sex and may also lead to a deficiency of important hormones, including human growth hormone, which helps keep your body lean, fit and energized.

Self-defense: Limit or eliminate naps and caffeine, particularly after the late afternoon. If you exercise in the evening, do so at least two hours before bedtime. Retire to a dark, quiet room at the same time each evening.

Ease yourself into slumber with a proven relaxation technique, such as deep breathing, meditation or a massage from your partner. If arthritis or muscle pain keeps you awake, ask your doctor about taking *acetaminophen* or aspirin before bed.

Caution: Overuse of acetaminophen may cause liver damage. Aspirin can cause stomach irritation. To minimize these risks, always take these drugs with a full glass of water.

Avoid sedative-hypnotics, such as *zolpidem* (Ambien) and *zaleplon* (Sonata), except to treat short-term sleeplessness caused by jet lag, for example, or grief over the passing of a loved one. If used for more than four consecutive nights, these sleep aids can trigger "rebound insomnia." Rather than inducing sleep, they heighten restlessness, leaving you more awake than ever.

Important: After age 60, it's common to experience a sleep pattern that occurs when you fall asleep at dusk and awaken before dawn. This can disrupt your sex life, particularly if your partner maintains a traditional sleep schedule.

Fortunately, this problem can usually be reversed with regular exposure to the late-afternoon sun. Aim to get about 30 minutes of sun *without sunscreen* between 4 pm and 6 pm. This will not only correct sleep patterns, but also help prevent osteoporosis by triggering the production of vitamin D in your body.

Warning: Avoid unprotected sun exposure between 10 am and 2 pm, when harmful ultraviolet rays are most intense.

ADDITIONAL STRATEGIES

Improved nutrition, exercise and rest typically lead to more satisfying sex within a matter of weeks. *For more immediate results...*

● **Use visual, tactile stimulation.** Men, especially, are aroused by sexual images and touch. Dim the lights and watch a steamy movie. Women may want to put on sexy lingerie. Share a gentle massage or engage in mutual stimulation.

● **Fantasize.** Imagining sexy scenarios can heighten arousal for both partners. Interestingly, however, one study showed that men's ability to fantasize tends to diminish with age. This may explain why many men rely on sexy pictures, videos and other visual aids.

● **Use lubricants.** Postmenopausal women, especially, may find their enjoyment of sex hampered by vaginal dryness. Water-based lubricants, such as Astroglide, can help. Oil-based lubricants may lead to vaginal infections.

● **Plan around arthritis pain.** Taking a hot shower before sex can help reduce joint pain and stiffness. So can taking your pain medication 30 minutes before sex. If you suffer from osteoarthritis, try to have sex in the morning, before joints have a chance to stiffen or become inflamed. If you have rheumatoid arthritis, sex in the late afternoon or evening may be preferable, since symptoms often subside with physical activity.

●**Vary times and positions.** Don't get stuck in the rut of always having sex at night, in the missionary position. If you or your partner are too tired for sex at night, plan a morning or afternoon sex date. If one of you has a heart condition, hip or back pain, let that person take the bottom position, which requires less vigorous movement.

●**Practice seduction.** Good sex starts in the brain, which means it should begin hours before you actually arrive in the bedroom. Throughout the day, shower your partner with caresses, kisses and other outward signs of affection. Genuine intimacy is really the most effective aphrodisiac.

When Was the Last Time You Had Sex?

Michele Weiner-Davis, MSW, internationally renowned seminar leader and marriage therapist, Woodstock, IL. She is author of several books on relationships, including *The Sex-Starved Marriage: A Couple's Guide to Boosting Their Marriage Libido* (Simon & Schuster). Her Web site is *www.sexstarvedmarriage.com.*

One in five couples has sex fewer than 10 times a year. A lack of frequent sex isn't a problem if both spouses are content with their sexual relationship. Conflicts develop when marital partners have significantly different sexual appetites. One in three married couples struggles with a gap in sexual desire. In fact, mismatched sexual desire is the number-one problem discussed in sex therapists' offices.

When couples have mismatched desire, one spouse yearns for more touching and physical closeness while the other doesn't understand why sex is such a big deal.

To the more sexual spouse, sex is important because it is about feeling wanted, attractive, loved and emotionally connected. Frequent rejection leads to resentment and hurt feelings, causing a rift in the marriage. That could result in infidelity and divorce.

CAUSES

The reasons why a spouse might lose interest in sex vary greatly. There might be a medical explanation, such as a hormone imbalance …a problem with the liver, kidneys or pituitary gland…undiagnosed diabetes…or a side effect of medication.

Stress, fatigue, depression, grief, a negative body image or unresolved issues from childhood, such as sexual abuse, also can sap your sexual desire. Other major libido busters are continuing arguments and feelings of anger between spouses.

IF YOU'RE THE SPOUSE WITH LOWER SEX DRIVE

In most marriages, low-desire spouses control the sexual relationship. They determine the frequency of sex. Too often, the low-desire spouse has the unspoken expectation, *I don't have to satisfy your sexual needs, but I expect you to remain faithful to our marriage.* This is an unfair arrangement. *Instead…*

●**Just do it.** Countless people in my practice have told me that they often weren't in the mood before they started making love, but once they got into it, they really started to enjoy themselves.

Research suggests that for more than half the population, sexual desire doesn't just happen. Most people have to be physically stimulated to feel desire for their partner. Ironically, this means that people who think they need to be in the mood to have sex might in fact need to have sex to get in the mood.

Example: A low-sex-drive wife conceded that while she frequently resisted her husband's advances, she usually enjoyed sex when she let her husband talk her into it. Her husband joked that she should write *I like sex* on her hand, so that she would remember it the next time he approached her.

●**Dispense with the checklist.** Some low-desire spouses convince themselves that they can't enjoy sex unless a list of conditions is met.

Example: A man feels he can't make love unless the bills are paid, after-hours business calls are completed and the next day's appointments are reviewed.

Unless attending to an obligation is absolutely essential, make your marriage the priority.

●**Give your spouse a gift.** Although sex might not be very important to you, it probably is to your spouse. In good marriages, people give their spouses what they want, even if they don't always want the same thing.

●**Find solutions to unresolved problems.** If relationship issues, such as anger or hurt feelings, or personal issues, such as depression or poor body image, are interfering with your desire for sexual intimacy, you may need professional help.

If you're a man whose interest in sex has dwindled, you may be a bit ashamed to ask for help. Don't be. Low desire in men is America's best-kept secret. Millions of men just aren't in the mood.

●**Schedule a complete physical** to rule out any underlying medical conditions.

IF YOU'RE THE SPOUSE WITH HIGHER DESIRE

The spouse with the greater sex drive often responds to sexual rejection by withdrawing emotionally or developing a short fuse. Both reactions tend to push the lower-desire spouse away further. *Instead...*

●**Search for the nonsexual triggers that will arouse your spouse.** Many highly sexed spouses try to boost a partner's libido with sex toys, X-rated videos or lingerie. People with low desire frequently feel more turned on by gestures of love outside the bedroom.

Example: A woman with low desire told me her biggest turn-on was when her husband went out on cold days to warm up her car for her. A low-desire man felt more passion for his wife when she acknowledged his hard work and financial contribution to the family.

Ask yourself, *What has my spouse been asking me for or complaining about?* Make a concerted effort to satisfy that request. Being responsive to your spouse's emotional needs is great foreplay.

●**Talk about your feelings.** Sharing feelings can be difficult, especially for men. It helps to discuss feelings of rejection openly and honestly. When you truly allow yourself to be vulnerable, your spouse is then more likely to feel sympathetic.

Example: A husband told his wife of 15 years that when she consistently said "no" to sex, he felt incredibly hurt and lonely in their marriage. He wondered why she didn't want him. For the very first time, she understood that her refusals had been hurting her husband emotionally, not merely denying him physical pleasure. She promised she would be more sensitive to his needs.

●**Steer clear of common turnoffs.** Blaming your spouse for the problems between you is one surefire way to keep him/her at arm's length. Mismatched sexual desire is the *couple's* problem, not just one spouse's problem.

Another turnoff to a low-desire spouse is when every touch, hug or kiss turns sexual. Make time for intimate touching without sex. It is also off-putting when a spouse is brusque all day and suddenly becomes loving in the bedroom at night.

●**Don't confuse denial of sex with intent to punish.** When a spouse continually refuses a mate's sexual advances, it is easy to perceive it as a punishment or personal rejection. That's unlikely to be the case.

●**Understand the ebb and flow of testosterone.** Both men and women are more turned on when their testosterone levels are high. Your sexual advances are more likely to be well received at those times.

Male testosterone levels typically peak early in the morning. Female testosterone is more likely to peak in the evening and mid to late in the menstrual cycle. Levels in postmenopausal women tend to be relatively constant throughout the day.

●**Spend more time together.** Schedule a relaxing day as a couple. Take time away from work. Turn off your cell phones. Hire a babysitter. Nonsexual time together without the kids can turn on a low-drive spouse.

●**Watch out for the sex substitutes that deepen the problem.** High-desire spouses will sometimes try to satisfy their unfulfilled sexual needs with behaviors that make their partners even less interested in making love, such as flirting, drinking or visiting pornographic Web sites.

The good news: A loving, pleasurable sexual relationship can be a tie that binds a marriage.

There is no reason why anyone who wants a more robust love life can't have one.

Make Time For Sex

Dagmar O'Connor, PhD, sex therapist in private practice, New York City. She is author of the *Do It Yourself Sex Therapy Video Packet* (Dag Media Corp.) and *How to Put the Love Back into Making Love* (Bantam Books).

Many couples schedule sex out of their busy lives, making ample time instead for work, kids, community activities, exercise, watching TV and seeing friends.

If you want to have a satisfying sex life, you must set aside "sensuality time" for yourself and your partner...

●**Cut back on TV viewing...**wake up earlier...and limit social engagements.

●**Plan one evening a week together at home**—and make the date unbreakable. Turn off the phone. Spend three hours talking... giving each other backrubs...enjoying your senses and being together. You don't have to have sex, but private, relaxed sensuality often leads to sex. Don't rush.

●**Practice turning yourself "on" by opening yourself up to sexual stimuli.** Let yourself be aroused by fleeting fantasies. Many couples enjoy sharing fantasies with each other. Wear sexy underwear to work...and call your partner and talk privately about making love later that day.

Once you start to relax and enjoy yourself, you will find that spontaneously sexy feelings come to you more easily.

More from Dagmar O'Connor...

How to Make Sex Exciting...Again

Passion is a powerful force in the beginning stages of most intimate relationships. Unfortunately, our hectic work schedules, child-care responsibilities—even Web surfing—can prevent couples from really nurturing their sexual relationship.

Good news: You *can* restore the sexual excitement of your relationship. The key is to make time for sensual contact. Remember, arousal is just as important as orgasm.

In my 30 years as a therapist, I have found that the best way to become a passionate lover is to stop blaming your partner...and to start identifying—and communicating—your own needs in a constructive way. *Here's how...*

●**Express your emotions and clear up any resentment.** Sexual feelings are intimately linked to emotional expression. Many of us were raised to repress basic emotions—particularly anger or sadness. This can inhibit sexual response.

People who have sexual difficulties often grew up in families with parents who never raised their voices. Those who don't argue usually consider anger "unacceptable."

If you have difficulty expressing anger constructively, practice venting this emotion on your own. For example, when driving alone in the car or showering, yell as loud as you can. After the initial embarrassment subsides, you may feel great. But you may feel sad later on. Anger often masks hurt or sadness.

●**Tell your partner *exactly* what you want—and need.** Many people are much better at expressing disappointment and anger than they are at communicating their desires.

Practice asserting your needs in all areas of your life. Being "nice" all the time prevents you from knowing what you are actually feeling.

Self-defense: If you typically say "yes" to all requests, try saying "no" 10 times each week. Also practice making requests of others. Learn to be more "selfish."

●**Become comfortable with your body.** If you are very self-conscious about your physical appearance, you probably won't get much pleasure out of sex.

Helpful: Relax in a bath a few times each week. Use the opportunity to look at and touch your body in a nonsexual way.

Stand nude in front of the mirror for a few minutes every day. Don't criticize your body. See it as an artist would. Appreciate what you have—don't dwell on your perceived imperfections.

When privacy permits: Lounge around in the nude with your partner. If you feel like it, touch each other in nonsexual ways. Once you've established this sort of physical intimacy, taking the next step to sex becomes much easier.

●**Put yourself in a sensual mood.** Fantasy is one of the best ways to do this.

Helpful: For women who feel inhibited about being sexy, consider going into a store to try on provocative dresses or lingerie. You do not have to buy this stuff—just use the clothes to see yourself in a different way.

Share your sexual fantasies with your partner. It's not necessary for you to act out these fantasies—although you may choose to. Your goal is to simply create your own sexy movies in your head.

●**Concentrate on *your* sexual pleasure.** Sex is not only an expression of love. It's also an opportunity to experience pleasure. Good lovemaking involves two partners "using" each other for their own pleasure.

Don't expect your partner to take care of everything. And don't be afraid to tell your partner exactly what you like and want from sex. You'll both benefit if each of you is willing to behave a bit selfishly.

●**Develop a nonverbal language with your partner.** Showing is inherently less critical than telling. Make a pact to communicate in a nonverbal way—by moving your partner's hand, for instance—if you find something unpleasant or pleasant during sex.

Helpful: Set aside 45 minutes to let your partner explore your body. Then reverse roles for 45 minutes.

●**Touch each other often when not in bed** to create a sense of closeness all the time.

●**Take turns initiating sex.** When to have sex is a big issue for most couples. One person might prefer to be intimate in the morning...the other at night.

If you started things last time, your partner should initiate the next sexual encounter.

Important: For this to work, the noninitiating partner should not say "no."

●**Schedule a weekly "date" with your partner.** Set aside one night a week to be intimate. Do whatever you want—sensual touching, talking together or just reading the paper.

If you have children: Hire a baby-sitter to take the kids out while the two of you stay at home. Take the phone off the hook and spend a few hours in bed.

To nurture your sex life at home, make your bedroom a place for rest and sensuality. Lock the bedroom door, banish the television from the room and avoid arguing or discussing problems while in bed—it should be a place for rest and pleasure.

Ten Foods that Boost Sex Drive

Foods that are rich in vitamin E, magnesium, niacin, potassium, zinc and the amino acid L-arginine all increase libido, boost sexual stamina and improve performance.

Top 10 "sexiest" foods...

1. Celery
2. Asparagus and artichokes
3. Avocados
4. Onions and tomatoes
5. Almonds
6. Pumpkin and sunflower seeds
7. Romaine lettuce
8. Whole-grain breads
9. Fruits and nuts
10. Chilies, herbs and spices, such as mustard, fennel, saffron and vanilla

Barnet Meltzer, MD, physician in private practice, Del Mar, CA, and author of Food Swings *(Marlowe and Company).*

Sex Boost from Soy

Soy can be sexy for women who are going through menopause. Soy foods are full of natural plant estrogens. Eating three to four ounces of tofu daily—or drinking one cup of soy milk—can provide an estrogen boost that makes sex more pleasurable.

Julian Whitaker, MD, director, Whitaker Wellness Institute, Newport Beach, CA, *www.whitakerwellness.com,* and author of *Shed Ten Years in Ten Weeks* (Fireside).

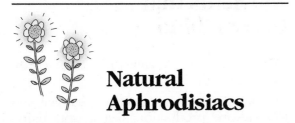

Natural Aphrodisiacs

Chris D. Meletis, ND, executive director, the Institute for Healthy Aging (*www.theiha.org*). He is author of several books, including *Better Sex Naturally* (HarperResource), *Complete Guide to Safe Herbs* (DK Publishing) and *Instant Guide to Drug–Herb Interactions* (DK Publishing).

Men who are troubled by erectile dysfunction (impotence) often assume that drugs—such as *sildenafil* (Viagra), *tadalafil* (Cialis) and *vardenafil* (Levitra)—are the answer. A woman who suffers from low libido may think that testosterone cream is the most effective way to boost her flagging desire.

While both of these approaches may offer a temporary solution, they will not remedy the underlying causes of these problems. Discovering and curing the cause of a sexual problem can be the key to long-term enjoyment of sex.

To identify the cause, I perform a detailed medical history and then order diagnostic tests, including a *prostate-specific antigen* (PSA) test for men and a Pap test for women.

In addition to low levels of testosterone, the hormone that fuels sex drive in both men *and* women, there are a number of possible scenarios. These include circulation problems that inhibit blood flow to the genitals…psychological stress, which diminishes interest in sex …and insomnia, which steals the vitality necessary to pursue sexual activity.

After unraveling the clues, I suggest safe, natural medications, such as herbs* to trigger the healing process.

ERECTILE DYSFUNCTION

More than half of men over age 40 have some degree of erectile failure, according to one recent study. The condition can be caused by a variety of health problems, such as poor circulation or nerve damage. For this reason, it's important to see your primary-care physician for a diagnosis. *The most effective herbal treatment for optimal erectile function…*

•**Ginkgo biloba.** An erection depends on healthy blood flow to the penis. Clogged arteries reduce circulation, which compromises a man's ability to achieve an erection. The herb *ginkgo biloba* dilates blood vessels, improving circulation and helping restore erections.

In a recent study, 78% of men with erectile dysfunction who took the herb regained their ability to have erections.

Good news for women: Women who use ginkgo biloba may experience longer, more intense orgasms.

People most likely to benefit from ginkgo biloba have circulatory symptoms, such as dizziness, varicose veins, cold hands or feet and/or high blood pressure.

Typical use: 40 milligrams (mg), three times daily. Look for a formula containing 24% *flavonglycosides,* the active ingredient.

Warning: Ginkgo should not be taken by anyone who uses blood-thinning medication, such as aspirin, antidepressants known as MAO inhibitors or anyone who has had a stroke or has a tendency to bleed or bruise easily.

INHIBITED SEXUAL DESIRE

A flagging libido can plague both men and women. *Fortunately, both sexes can benefit from the following…*

•**Ginseng.** This herb energizes the body, helping it respond better to almost any health problem. It also boosts the production of sex hormones, such as testosterone in men and women, to enhance sexual response.

*The US Food and Drug Administration does not regulate herbal supplements. Check with your physician before taking any of these products. Some may interact with prescription medications.

People likely to get the most benefit from ginseng have anxiety, blood sugar problems, fatigue, high levels of stress, menopausal symptoms or frequent infections like colds.

Typical use: Look for a product that contains *ginsenoside Rg1,* the active ingredient. Take 10 mg, twice daily.

Warning: Ginseng is a stimulant, and it is not recommended for people with high blood pressure or anyone taking medication for diabetes, bipolar disorder or heart disease.

FOR WOMEN ONLY

Hormone levels play an important role in a woman's sexual health and emotional involvement during sex. Too little estrogen can thin the vaginal walls, causing painful intercourse. Too little testosterone reduces sex drive. Too little progesterone or too much prolactin can lead to anxiety and depression.

The following herbs* can help to regulate female hormones...

•**Black cohosh.** This herb helps regulate hormones by controlling the secretions of the pituitary gland, which help balance estrogen and progesterone production. This can enhance a woman's interest in sex and help with vaginal lubrication.

Typical use: 500 mg, twice daily. Or, if you use a standardized tablet, take 2 mg of *27-deoxyacteine,* the active ingredient.

•**Dong quai.** The herb *angelica sinensis* is most commonly known by its Chinese name, *dong quai.* It balances estrogen levels and can enhance sexual pleasure.

Typical use: 500 mg, twice daily.

Helpful: Consider taking a formula that combines black cohosh and dong quai—particularly if you have symptoms of premenstrual syndrome (PMS) or are menopausal. Dong quai can increase energy and improve mood, while black cohosh helps reduce PMS symptoms, such as bloating, and menopausal problems, such as hot flashes.

DANGEROUS NATURAL REMEDIES

Stay away from...

•**Damiana.** Derived from the leaves of a shrub found in the Southwest US and Mexico,

*Women who are pregnant or nursing should not use these supplements.

this herb has many possible side effects, including diarrhea, vomiting, heart palpitations and anxiety. Use it *only* under the supervision of a doctor or naturopathic physician.**

•**Spanish Fly.** This beetle is pulverized and eaten. It contains the chemical *cantharidin,* which can damage your heart, kidneys, stomach and intestines—or even kill you.

Nutrients that Boost Libido

There are some vitamins that can increase your sex drive...

•**Vitamin A** is important for estrogen and testosterone production. Get it from dairy, eggs, leafy green vegetables and meat.

•**Vitamin B complex** produces energy—sexual and otherwise. Good sources of this vitamin are whole grains, meat, fish, dairy, fruits, nuts and vegetables.

•**Vitamin C** can boost drive and strengthen sex organs. Berries, citrus fruits, potatoes, green peppers and broccoli contain it.

•**Vitamin E** is needed for the manufacture of sex hormones, which boost sex drive. Find it in wheat germ, liver and eggs.

Ian Marber and Vicki Edgson, both clinical nutritionists in London, *www.thefooddoctor.com,* and authors of *In Bed with the Food Doctor* (Collins & Brown).

Sex Too Soon After Childbirth Can Be Deadly

It was reported recently that two English women died after having sex a few days after giving birth. The problem, say doctors, is that pregnancy-related changes make pelvic blood vessels vulnerable to fatal air embolisms.

The Medical Post.

**To locate a naturopathic physician in your area, contact the American Association of Naturopathic Physicians at 866-538-2267 or *www.naturopathic.org.*

Nature's Rx for Women's Health Problems

Jamison Starbuck, ND, naturopathic physician in family practice and lecturer, University of Montana, both in Missoula. She is past president of the American Association of Naturopathic Physicians and a contributing editor to *The Alternative Advisor: The Complete Guide to Natural Therapies and Alternative Treatments* (Time-Life).

Women often resort to quick drugstore fixes when they experience "female complaints." I advise women to consider their alternatives. Many women's health problems respond to gentle, natural medicines …and to lifestyle changes that help to improve your overall health. *My recommendations…*

•**Bacterial vaginosis (BV)** causes a gray-white discharge, mild burning and vaginal itching. Gynecologists often prescribe antibiotics to treat this condition.

But antibiotics can create problems. Like the digestive tract, the vagina is filled with bacteria that keep mucous membranes in good health. Antibiotics disrupt the vaginal "ecosystem" by eliminating not only the offending bacteria, but also the beneficial ones, like *lactobacillus.*

This can bring on another type of vaginal infection—*Candida vaginitis.* Also known as yeast infection, this causes vaginal itching and burning and a thick, white discharge.

For this condition, doctors typically prescribe antifungals—again upsetting the vaginal ecosystem and increasing the likelihood of BV. *Many women get stuck in this cycle. I tell my patients with these conditions to…*

•Avoid refined foods, sweets and alcohol. Each can weaken the immune system. Stick to these restrictions for at least one month after the infection clears up.

•Use capsules to encourage growth of beneficial bacteria. During the acute infection, insert one capsule of Oregon grape root (*Berberis aquifolium*) powder into the vagina each evening. Each morning, insert one lactobacillus acidophilus capsule. The capsules are available at most health food stores.

•Abstain from sex during treatment. It can irritate vaginal tissue.

An infection that's acute should clear up in one week. For stubborn cases, repeat the capsule protocol on alternating weeks for a total of four treatments.

•**Urinary tract infections (UTIs)** often occur when bacteria migrate from the vagina through the urethra into the bladder. Sexual intercourse, vaginal infection and chronic vaginal dryness increase your risk.

If you suffer from recurrent UTIs, see your family doctor for antibiotic treatment for the acute infection. *Then follow these steps to prevent relapse…*

•Drink 64 ounces of water daily to rid your bladder of pesky bacteria.

•Take an acidophilus/bifidis supplement that contains three billion of these live organisms every night at bedtime.

•Drink 12 ounces of unsweetened cranberry juice each day. It acidifies your urine, preventing bacteria from adhering to the bladder wall. If you don't like cranberry juice—or don't want the extra calories—take a daily capsule containing 900 milligrams (mg) of cranberry extract.

•**Fibrocystic breasts and premenstrual syndrome (PMS)** can both be caused by poor dietary habits. If you have fibrocystic breasts, avoid caffeine and sugar…and cut back on fat and refined food. Eat more whole grains, beans, peas, fruits and veggies.

In addition, take 50 mg of vitamin B-6, 400 international units (IU) of vitamin E and 3,000 mg of flaxseed oil or 1,500 mg evening primrose oil daily to reduce inflammation.

Low progesterone levels may contribute to PMS. For this condition, follow the fibrocystic breast protocol and try chaste tree berry (*Vitex agnus-castus*) to boost production of the hormone progesterone. Two weeks before your menstrual period starts, take 60 drops of Vitex tincture daily. Discontinue for two weeks following menstruation, then repeat.

Note: Women who are pregnant or breast-feeding should check with their doctors before taking any herb.

Hysterectomy Is Rarely the Only Solution

Brian W. Walsh, MD, assistant professor of obstetrics and gynecology, Harvard Medical School, and chief of surgical gynecology, Brigham and Women's Hospital, both in Boston.

Each year, half a million American women undergo *hysterectomy*—surgical removal of the uterus. This drastic procedure requires three to five days in the hospital, followed by up to six weeks of recovery at home.

Hysterectomy can be life-saving in cases of cancer of the uterus, cervix or ovaries. But nine out of 10 hysterectomies are done simply to control excessive menstrual bleeding or other less serious gynecologic problems.

These problems can almost always be controlled with treatments that are safer and less damaging to a woman's self-image than hysterectomy...and which preserve the woman's ability to bear children.

Here are five conditions that often lead to hysterectomy...and ways how each can be controlled in other ways...

ENDOMETRIOSIS

This condition occurs when cells from the uterine lining begin to grow *outside* the uterus —typically in the ovaries or behind the uterus. With each menstrual period, a woman with endometriosis experiences slight internal bleeding. This causes inflammation and irritates nerve endings, resulting in severe pain.

Alternative to hysterectomy: Laparoscopic surgery. The doctor inserts a flexible, lighted telescope (*laparoscope*) into the abdomen through a small incision in the navel. He/she then uses the laparoscope to remove endometrial deposits.

Because endometriosis usually recurs in time, the surgery may have to be repeated. But only in severe cases of endometriosis is hysterectomy required.

Hysterectomy—plus removal of both ovaries (*bilateral oophorectomy*)—stops the growth of endometrial deposits and causes existing deposits to shrink.

ADENOMYOSIS

This endometriosis-like condition is common in women who have had several children. It occurs when pregnancy-related changes in the uterine lining cause it to "invade" the walls of the uterus, thereby weakening it.

The uterine walls ultimately lose their ability to contract. It's this ability that lets a healthy uterus stanch the flow of blood at the end of each menstrual period.

Alternative to hysterectomy: Endometrial ablation. In this 30-minute outpatient procedure, a balloon inserted through the vagina and into the uterus is filled with water and then heated. The blood vessels collapse and fuse together, sealing them shut and stopping the bleeding.

FIBROID TUMORS

These benign uterine growths can be microscopic—or as large as a cantaloupe. Many fibroids—even some that are big—cause no symptoms. But if one presses against the uterine lining, menstrual bleeding can be profuse.

Alternative to hysterectomy: Hysteroscopic surgery. Fibroids that measure less than five centimeters (about two inches) in diameter can usually be removed without making any incision at all.

In this procedure, the surgeon inserts a laparoscope-like device (*hysteroscope*) through the vagina and uses an attached wire loop to slice away the fibroid bit by bit.

Hysteroscopic surgery can usually be done under local or spinal anesthesia.

Larger fibroids often require a more invasive procedure known as *myomectomy*. This involves removing the fibroids through an abdominal incision similar to that made in a cesarean section.

About 30% of women who undergo hysteroscopic surgery or myomectomy wind up needing a second operation, since fibroids can recur.

Fibroids tend to shrink after menopause—but never go away entirely.

Caution: Hysterectomy may be required for a fibroid that develops or enlarges following menopause. Such fibroids may be an indication of a malignant growth.

LACK OF OVULATION

Ordinarily, the ovaries secrete hormones that trigger ovulation. If the ovaries fail to secrete the necessary hormones, the lining of the uterus becomes thicker as cells accumulate there.

This process continues until the destabilized lining begins releasing a torrent of blood.

Alternative to hysterectomy: Hormone therapy. The hormones found in birth control pills are often enough to stop the bleeding.

Caution: If you have high blood pressure or are prone to blood clots, progesterone-only therapy may be safer than the Pill.

UTERINE PROLAPSE

Uterine prolapse is a condition in which the uterus drops out of its ordinary position. Most cases do require hysterectomy, but not all.

The ligaments and connective tissue that hold the uterus in place are stretched and weakened by pregnancy.

Over time, gravity stretches the ligaments further, dropping the uterus lower. In extreme cases, the uterus droops through the vagina.

Alternative to hysterectomy: Wearing a *pessary*. This donut-shaped device—which is roughly the size of a diaphragm—is inserted into the vagina and wedged against the pubic bone to hold the uterus in place.

Pessaries can be an especially good idea for frail women who want to avoid surgery.

Most Uterine Fibroids Can Be Left Alone

Nothing can be done to prevent fibroids, but since they are not linked to cancer, it rarely is necessary to remove them.

However, the location is important—a small fibroid in the central uterine cavity can cause bleeding and require surgery, while a larger

one elsewhere may produce no symptoms and be left alone to shrink after menopause.

If surgery, known as *myomectomy,* is needed, it sometimes can be done laparoscopically.

Steven R. Goldstein, MD, professor of obstetrics and gynecology, New York University School of Medicine, New York City.

Beware of Diagnosing Your Own Yeast Infection

In a recent finding, only about half the women treating themselves with over-the-counter remedies actually had vaginal yeast infections. The rest of the women had either another type of infection or no infection at all.

Problem: If left untreated, certain types of vaginal infections, such as *trichomonas* and *bacterial vaginosis,* can lead to infertility and make women more susceptible to AIDS.

Women experiencing vaginal itching, burning or irritation should consult their physicians.

Daron Ferris, MD, professor of obstetrics/gynecology and family medicine, Medical College of Georgia, Augusta. His study of 95 women was published in *Obstetrics & Gynecology.*

Oral Sex Trap

Research shows that yeast infections are far more common among women who receive cunnilingus.

Theory: Infection-causing yeast are found in the mouths of up to half of all adults…so oral sex may be an effective means of transmitting it to the vagina.

Brushing and flossing can help reduce yeast levels in the mouth…as well as rinsing with antiseptic mouthwash.

Judith Seifer, PhD, RN, past president, American Association of Sex Educators, Counselors and Therapists, Box 238, Mount Vernon, IA 52314. She is cocreator of the *Better Sex* video series.

New Treatment for Incontinence

Urinary urge incontinence, a condition that results in urine loss before being able to get to the toilet, can be greatly eased by taking medicine normally used for stomach upset, like Milk of Magnesia.

Recent finding: Women who took one teaspoon of *magnesium hydroxide*—the active ingredient in Milk of Magnesia, Mylanta and Maalox—twice a day had significantly fewer episodes than those taking a placebo.

Theory: Magnesium hydroxide minimizes contractions of the bladder muscle that is responsible for an overactive bladder.

Farnaz Alams Ganj, MD, assistant professor, obstetrics and gynecology, Akbarabadi Hospital, Iran University of Medical Sciences, Tehran.

Try Kegel Exercises For Incontinence

Urinary incontinence affects 38% of women and 19% of men over age 60. A study of almost 200 older women found that practicing simple exercises known as *Kegels,* together with some behavioral strategies, were significantly better at reducing accidents than drug treatment.

Kegel exercises involve repeatedly squeezing and relaxing the pelvic floor muscles that hold the bladder in place—and are the same muscles that are used to slow or stop the flow of urine.

It usually takes eight to 10 weeks of exercise to produce results. Then they should be continued as part of the daily routine.

Note: Kegel exercises also help men.

Kathryn Burgio, PhD, professor of medicine, University of Alabama, Birmingham.

 # Managing Menopause Without Drugs

Toni M. Cutson, MD, associate professor of community and family medicine and associate professor of medicine, both at Duke University Medical Center, Durham, NC. She is coauthor of "Managing Menopause," a report published in *American Family Physician.*

Hot flashes, mood swings, vaginal dryness, sleep disturbances and other annoying symptoms affect about 75% of menopausal women.

Even more troublesome is the increased risk for heart disease and osteoporosis associated with menopause.

To help control these common problems, doctors often prescribe *hormone replacement therapy* (HRT). HRT may also protect against stroke and Alzheimer's disease.

Hormone therapy can cause side effects, including breast tenderness, bloating and headaches. It has also been linked to a slightly higher risk for breast cancer, especially in women with a family history of the disease.

To avoid the possible drawbacks of HRT, many women treat their symptoms with a variety of nondrug alternatives—eating a low-fat, high-fiber diet...exercising regularly...and quitting smoking.

These are a good start. But there are additional ways to relieve the symptoms. Whether a woman takes hormones or not, she can benefit from eight commonly overlooked strategies. *Women should...*

●**Eat at least eight servings of fruits and vegetables each day.** These high-fiber, low-fat foods are typically rich in folic acid and other B vitamins, which reduce the risk for heart disease by helping to prevent arterial blood clots.

One serving equals one piece of fruit, one-half cup of cooked vegetables or one cup of raw vegetables.

Other osteoporosis-fighting foods: Calcium-rich products, such as dairy products (milk and yogurt) and fortified orange juice.

• Eat whole soy foods. They contain *iso-flavones,* estrogen-like compounds that reduce hot flashes, bone loss and LDL ("bad") cholesterol. Good sources include soy nuts, soy milk and tofu.

Caution: Avoid nutritional supplements and powders that claim to have the same active ingredients as soy foods. These products may contain unknown chemicals that could be harmful.

Worse, they may contain excessive levels of isoflavones, which increase breast cancer risk. Limit your soy intake to about 60 grams of isoflavones a day.

• Take a daily multivitamin. Choose a name brand, such as One-a-Day or Centrum, to get the recommended requirements for most vitamins and minerals. Do *not* take individual vitamin megadoses, however. They can be harmful.

Too much vitamin A, for example, can damage the eyes and skin. Megadoses of vitamin D can cause excess calcium in the bloodstream.

To prevent liver damage, avoid pills that provide more than 18 milligrams (mg) of iron. Because menopausal women no longer lose iron through menstruation, iron supplements make sense only if you've been diagnosed with an iron deficiency.

• Take a calcium supplement. A daily 1,500-mg dose helps prevent osteoporosis.

The calcium carbonate found in Tums is cheap and readily absorbed. Each Tums tablet provides 200 mg of calcium. But if you want a higher dose, try Tums E-X with 300 mg or Tums 500 with 500 mg.

• Try proven herbal remedies. Some menopausal women now take chasteberry to prevent hot flashes. But little research exists to support its effectiveness.

Similarly, avoid dong quai and licorice root. Dong quai can cause excessive blood thinning. Licorice root may precipitate headaches or high blood pressure.

Better: Black cohosh. This herb suppresses *luteinizing hormone* (LH), which triggers hot flashes. Some women claim it also improves their sex drive and eases night sweats and sleep disturbances.

Black cohosh is sold as Remifemin at health food stores.

• Limit alcohol consumption. Have no more than three glasses of wine—or three ounces of hard liquor—a week. Drinking wine in moderation may be beneficial to the heart, but too much alcohol exacerbates hot flashes.

• Relax. Many menopausal women blame hormone fluctuations for mood and memory problems. But psychological stress is often the real cause. While they're going through menopause, they may also be caring for elderly parents, sending children off to college or dealing with job stress.

To combat stress: Seek help for difficult situations. Turn down extra projects at work …ask siblings to help care for an elderly parent…or find a day program that caters to the social needs of seniors.

Get plenty of sleep and give yourself 30 minutes of quiet time each day. If your schedule doesn't permit it, even just five minutes is better than nothing.

• Rethink your sex life. The physical and psychological aspects of menopause often put a damper on a woman's sex life. But abstinence is not the answer.

Frequent sexual activity decreases vaginal dryness, improves sleep, reduces stress and helps alleviate moodiness.

Bonus: Having regular sex also helps to increase your libido.

Alternatives to Hormone Replacement

Menopausal women who are concerned about *hormone replacement therapy* (HRT) should consider these alternatives…

• Traditional remedies for hot flashes and night sweats, such as black cohosh, licorice, red clover and chasteberry.

• Estradiol and progesterone (best administered in a cream base)—these are prescription medicines that are identical to the female hormones produced in the body.

•**Soy-rich foods or ground flaxseed**—sprinkle over cereal, mix in a smoothie, etc.

Also helpful: Avoid alcohol and spicy foods, which can trigger hot flashes...dress in layers that you can take off during a hot flash.

Andrew L. Rubman, ND, director, Southbury Clinic for Traditional Medicines, Southbury, CT.

Natural Alternative to HRT

Postmenopausal women may be able to cut their risk for heart disease without *hormone replacement therapy* (HRT).

A recent study found that a nonprescription red clover extract (Promensil) boosted the elasticity of artery walls as effectively as HRT. Researchers believe *isoflavone* compounds in red clover are responsible for this effect. The loss of arterial elasticity—which often occurs in menopause—raises a woman's risk for heart disease.

Paul J. Nestel, MD, head, cardiovascular nutrition, Baker Medical Research Institute, Melbourne, Australia.

Fighting Hot Flashes in Women...and Men

Hot flashes in menopausal women—and in men who are being treated for prostate cancer with hormone therapy—can be effectively quenched with antidepressants.

In one study, menopausal breast cancer patients who took about half the standard dose of *venlafaxine* (Effexor) had a 61% reduction in hot flashes.

Preliminary results suggest a similar effect with other antidepressants, such as *fluoxetine* (Prozac) and *paroxetine* (Paxil).

That's great news because breast cancer chemotherapy often triggers early menopause, bringing on hot flashes as well as night sweats, disrupted sleep and mood swings.

Hormone treatments for menopausal women help—but may stimulate tumor growth. So antidepressants are a safer option.

Charles L. Loprinzi, MD, professor and chair of medical oncology, Mayo Clinic, Rochester, MN. His study was presented at a meeting of the American Society of Clinical Oncology.

Latest Ways to Prevent And Treat Impotence

Irwin Goldstein, MD, founding director, Institute for Sexual Medicine, Boston University. He is currently director of San Diego Sexual Medicine at Alvarado Hospital, CA and clinical professor of surgery at University of California at San Diego. He is also editor-in-chief of the *Journal of Sexual Medicine*.

The majority of men who have difficulty initiating or maintaining erections have underlying physical problems. Many of the same conditions that increase the risk of heart disease and stroke also increase the risk of erectile dysfunction by inhibiting blood flow to the penis.

When a man is sexually aroused, blood flows into spongelike structures in the penis and produces an erection. The main artery in the penis is only about one-half millimeter in diameter. Even small accumulations of fatty deposits (plaques) can inhibit blood flow.

Other common causes of erection problems include low testosterone...nerve damage from diabetes...and use of medications that interfere with nerve signals and/or blood flow.

Warning: Because erectile dysfunction may be an early sign of cardiovascular disease, men experiencing impotence should get a complete cardiovascular workup. This is particularly important if they have risk factors for heart disease, such as smoking, hypertension, diabetes or family history.

LIFESTYLE CHANGES

For most men, impotence can be prevented—and in some cases reversed—by making the same lifestyle changes that promote cardiovascular health. *Best strategies...*

•**Control cholesterol.** Men whose total cholesterol level is 200 or higher are more likely to suffer from impotence than men whose levels are lower.

According to new government guidelines, the optimal level of LDL ("bad") cholesterol is 100 to 129. HDL ("good") cholesterol should be 60 or above. Some patients can achieve these levels through dietary changes, such as eating less saturated fat and increasing fiber consumption.

Many patients, however, may need cholesterol-lowering drugs called statins. A starting dose of 10 mg of *atorvastatin* (Lipitor) or *pravastatin* (Pravachol) can lower LDL by as much as 40%. If a man already is experiencing erectile dysfunction, taking a statin may restore his ability to achieve erections.

•**Get checked for diabetes and hypertension.** Diabetes, which can damage nerves and blood vessels, is thought to contribute to almost half of impotence cases. More than 40% of men with hypertension (high blood pressure) also suffer from impotence.

•**Ask about drug side effects.** Virtually all blood pressure–lowering drugs and many drugs for treating diabetes can cause impotence as a side effect. So can some antihistamines (such as Benadryl and Banophen) and potentially hundreds of prescription drugs, including sedatives (such as Valium), antipsychotics, antidepressants and pain medications (particularly narcotic analgesics, such as codeine).

Drug side effects are highly individual. Switching to a different drug, even one in the same class, may reverse the problem. Ask your doctor to review all the medications you currently are taking.

•**Prevent cycling injuries.** Men who regularly bike may experience arterial trauma that impairs blood flow and causes erectile dysfunction. Consider replacing a narrow bicycle seat with a wider one that has a prominent "nose." This distributes weight over a wider area and can reduce damage to blood vessels.

•**Test testosterone.** Levels of this hormone naturally decline with age. Men who have very low levels may experience declines in libido and difficulty getting erections. Every man who suffers from erectile dysfunction should have a blood test that measures levels of testosterone. Restoring normal testosterone levels with skin patches or other treatments can be effective.

•**Stop smoking.** Smoking damages the inner lining of blood vessels in the penis and elsewhere and increases risk of plaque buildup. Studies show that men who smoke one pack of cigarettes or more daily have a 60% higher risk of erectile dysfunction than those who never smoked.

TREATMENTS

Men have many options for treating erectile dysfunction. If it is the result of a medical condition, the cost of treatment may be covered by insurance. Check with your insurer.

•**Oral drugs** relax blood vessels in the penis and promote better circulation. Almost 70% of patients are able to achieve erections with oral medications. The three drugs below share many similarities but have differences as well. Talk to your doctor about the best option for you. Side effects may include headache, facial flushing and/or nasal congestion.

•Viagra (*sildenafil*) takes about one hour to work. The ability to achieve an erection lasts about four hours. High-fat meals interfere with Viagra's effectiveness (unlike with the other two drugs).

•Levitra (*vardenafil*) is the fastest-acting oral drug. An erection can occur within 10 minutes in 30% to 40% of men or within 30 minutes in 60% of men. The ability to achieve an erection lasts 10 to 14 hours.

•Cialis (*tadalafil*) is the longest-acting drug. Men who take it have the ability to get erections for up to 36 hours. An erection can occur 30 to 60 minutes after taking it.

•**Vacuum devices** can be a good choice when oral drugs aren't effective. A hollow plastic tube is placed over the penis. The man uses a pump to create a vacuum in the tube, which pulls blood into the penis. The blood is held in place by slipping a rubber tension ring around the base of the penis. After orgasm, the ring is removed and the erection subsides.

Cost: $300 to $500.

Caution: Devices sold over the Internet may cause damage to the penis.

●**Injections.** The drug *alprostadil* (Caverject, Edex) is injected into the penis with a very fine needle and usually causes an erection in five to 20 minutes. Doctors often recommend injections when oral drugs or vacuum devices aren't effective.

Alternative: A combination of drugs—*prostaglandin E, papaverine* and *phentolamine*—can be compounded by a pharmacist. It can be injected in place of the single-drug injection. The combination isn't yet approved by the FDA, but it is much more effective—and can forestall surgery in men who suffer severe impotence. Talk to your doctor.

●**Penile implants.** In an outpatient procedure, a surgeon implants either inflatable tubes or semirigid rods into the penis (implants do not interfere with ejaculation). The inflatable tubes are more expensive than the rods, but they are the best choice for most men because they can be inflated or deflated as needed. Recovery takes two to four weeks, and the tubes or rods can last more than a decade.

More from Irwin Goldstein, MD...

Top Doctor Answers Tough Questions About Viagra

*S*ildenafil (Viagra) has helped millions of men improve their sex lives. Now there are two other drugs, *vardenafil* (Levitra) and *tadalafil* (Cialis), that can help, too. *Here, straight answers to the most commonly asked questions about these drugs...*

●**Some people believe that Viagra gives men an erection that lasts for hours. Is that true?** No. Viagra doesn't cause an erection, it *facilitates* one. It enhances the physiological processes that allow the penis to fill with blood and stay rigid in response to a signal from the brain. That signal is sparked by desire. Without the desire, nothing is likely to happen. After orgasm, a man loses the erection, as he would if he weren't taking the drug.

Viagra doesn't kick in for at least an hour. It can facilitate an erection for up to 12 hours.

●**Does that mean that men can make love several times in one night?** Yes—although surveys indicate that only 10% of men choose to have a second interaction.

●**There are ads for Viagra on the Internet. Do men really need to see a doctor first?** Most emphatically yes. Erectile dysfunction is a medical problem and deserves a medical—and psychological—evaluation. It could be a symptom of a life-threatening illness, such as prostate cancer, heart disease or diabetes.

●**If a man tried Viagra once, and it didn't work, would a stronger dose help?** I suggest trying Viagra at least five different times. If the drug still doesn't work, you may need a higher dose, or you can try one of the other drugs—Levitra or Cialis. Ask your doctor. If your testosterone levels are low, normalizing them might make the Viagra even more effective. Bringing down high cholesterol levels through diet and/or medication also might help.

●**If a man takes an antidepressant that causes erection problems, can Viagra help that?** Viagra is extremely effective when the problem is a side effect of medication, as can be the case with certain antidepressants, as well as antihypertensives, diabetes and heart medications, etc.

In fact, Viagra is very effective for a wide range of physical and psychological causes of erectile dysfunction. When erection problems are the consequence of radical prostatectomy, nerve damage or severe scarring to the penis, however, Viagra may not work well or at all.

●**Some men have died after taking Viagra. Is it dangerous?** Actually, Viagra is an amazingly safe drug—but the sex itself can be rather strenuous. As you near orgasm, blood pressure and heart rate rise. Some hearts cannot take this. It is not unusual to find men in the coronary care unit who have had heart attacks during sexual intercourse.

Important: Although Viagra is safe to take with most drugs, you shouldn't use it if you are taking nitrate medication, like *nitroglycerin,* for heart disease. This combination can cause fatal drops in blood pressure.

●**Does Viagra have side effects?** Viagra can cause headaches, stomach pain and/or intense facial flushing. A small percentage of men—maybe 2%—stops using it for these reasons.

•**Is it OK to have a few drinks before taking Viagra?** Alcohol may loosen up inhibitions, but it sabotages the ability to achieve an erection, whether or not you take Viagra. Consume alcohol only modestly.

•**Why is it a bad idea to take Viagra right after dinner?** Food interferes with absorption of Viagra, so take it at least 30 minutes before eating. I advise patients to take the medication in the late afternoon if they plan to have sex in the evening.

•**Can taking Viagra help women who have sexual problems?** It does benefit women with sexual problems caused by insufficient blood flow to their genitals. However, most female sexual problems are related to diminished libido or diminished or absent orgasm, which are unrelated to blood flow.

•**Will Viagra help a person's relationship?** Not necessarily. Some women believe that it makes men excessively goal-oriented—they think more about their erections and less about emotional intimacy. Some couples discover that even when sexual problems are resolved, relationship problems persist. They may need counseling as well.

•**Can taking Viagra now prevent erectile dysfunction in the future?** Possibly. Nothing is better for the health of the penis than an erection. A German study of 100 men found that those who took Viagra nightly for one year had better erections than those who took it only occasionally.

If you are at risk for erection problems—perhaps you have diabetes or high blood pressure or you smoke—ask your doctor about taking low-dose Viagra every night to prevent difficulties later on, just as you might take low-dose aspirin to prevent heart attack.

•**Are the other erectile dysfunction drugs, Levitra and Cialis, better?** Levitra is stronger—it works faster, lasts longer and the dose is smaller, so it may be of more benefit to some men. Cialis is effective for three days.

•**Should men be wary of Levitra and Cialis because they are newer than Viagra?** No. These drugs have been used in Europe for many years. Plus, they have all gone through rigorous testing by the US Food and Drug Administration.

Natural Treatment for Impotence

Natural alternatives to Viagra, Cialis and Levitra, for treating impotence include extracts of ginkgo leaves or ginseng root. Both are available at drugstores and health food stores. Consult your physician before trying either remedy. *These are the dosages I would consider...*

Ginkgo biloba: 40 milligram (mg) extract, taken three times a day. Don't use it if you take aspirin or blood thinners.

Ginseng: 100 mg to 200 mg extract daily. Men using ginseng should have their blood pressure monitored regularly. Don't use it if you drink caffeinated beverages regularly or take other stimulants. And be patient—it may take several months before you see results.

Adriane Fugh-Berman, MD, associate professor, department of physiology and biophysics, Georgetown University School of Medicine, Washington, DC, and author of *Alternative Medicine: What Works* (Williams & Wilkins).

Help for Premature Ejaculation

Premature—or rapid—ejaculation (ejaculation that occurs after less than one minute of intercourse) isn't usually a psychological disorder, but a biological one.

Recent research indicates that premature ejaculation may be genetic and caused by a hyperactivity of the sympathetic nervous system, which controls the involuntary activities of the glands, organs and other parts of the body.

Treatment with the *selective serotonin reuptake inhibitor* (SSRI) antidepressants, such as *paroxetine* (Paxil), may help to alleviate the problem by increasing serotonin levels in the brain. This neurotransmitter is believed to prolong ejaculation time. Talk to your doctor for more information.

Pierre Assalian, MD, director, human sexuality unit, McGill University Health Centre, Montréal.

Vasectomies Do Not Affect Sex

Semen contains less than 5% sperm—the rest is fluids from the seminal vesicles and prostate. Vasectomies stop only the flow of sperm. They should not affect sexual desire or performance.

Caution: Some sperm can remain in semen for up to 30 ejaculations after a vasectomy. It's advisable to continue using birth control until it is confirmed that there is zero sperm in the ejaculate. A simple lab test can determine when semen no longer contains sperm.

Vasectomy reversal is possible, with up to a 90% success rate.

Jonathan Jarow, MD, professor of urology, pathology, radiology and reproductive biology, Johns Hopkins Medical Institutions, Baltimore.

Natural Treatment for Prostate Enlargement

Prostate enlargement can be treated safely and effectively with *Pygeum africanum*.

An herbal remedy that is derived from a species of prune tree native to Africa, pygeum has been used for 30 years in Europe. But since the harvesting of pygeum is threatening the prune trees, it's sensible to take pygeum only if the usual treatments for prostate enlargement—the drug *finasteride* (Proscar), alpha-1 blocking agents like *terazosin* (Hytrin) and the herbal remedy saw palmetto—fail to work. Pygeum is sold in health food stores.

Russell H. Greenfield, MD, medical director and integrative physician, Carolinas HealthCare System, Charlotte, NC.

Getting Help for Embarrassing Medical Problems

Margaret Stearn, MD, general medicine practitioner, Oxford, England, with a special interest in diabetes and urologic medicine. Dr. Stearn is a Fellow of the Royal College of Physicians and author of *Embarrassing Medical Problems: Everything You Always Wanted to Know But Were Afraid to Ask Your Doctor* (Hatherleigh Press).

If you suffer from a backache or dizziness, it's easy to tell your doctor. But what about those nagging symptoms that you are too embarrassed to discuss?

Unfortunately, many patients deprive themselves of effective treatment and, in some cases, endanger their long-term health by failing to disclose certain medical problems. *How to get some help...*

BAD BREATH

Saliva production diminishes during sleep, allowing food debris to stagnate in the mouth. Bacteria break down these residues, producing an unpleasant smell. That's why almost everyone has bad breath (*halitosis*) upon waking. It usually disappears after you brush your teeth.

To determine if you have bad breath: Lick the inside of your wrist, wait four seconds, then smell.

Persistent halitosis is generally caused by gum disease (*gingivitis*). If your gums bleed when you brush your teeth, you most likely have gum disease and, as a result, bad breath. *What to do...*

• **See your dentist** for a checkup and thorough cleaning.

• **Brush your teeth at least twice daily.**

Best method: Clean teeth two at a time for six seconds, moving the brush in a small circular motion while angling it toward the gum.

Or consider buying a battery-powered toothbrush, which often controls gum disease better than manual brushing.

Cost: $20 to $120.

• **Clean the back of your tongue,** where bacteria accumulate. Use your toothbrush or a tongue scraper.

• **Use an antibacterial mouthwash,** such as Biotene Antibacterial, Cepacol Antiseptic or Listerine Antiseptic.

• **Floss nightly**—especially the molars.

If halitosis persists: See your doctor.

EXCESSIVE PERSPIRATION

Perspiration itself is not smelly, but it is a breeding ground for bacteria that will quickly break down into malodorous fatty acids.

Excessive perspiration (*hyperhidrosis*) could affect armpits, feet or palms. *What to do…*

• **Armpits.** Women and men should shave their armpits to reduce bacterial buildup.

Also switch to an antiperspirant with an active ingredient that is different from what you're currently using.

• **Feet.** Wear clean, loose-fitting socks made from wool or cotton and at least 30% man-made fiber, such as nylon or polyester. Wash socks in hot water to kill bacteria.

Avoid shoes made from synthetic materials. They trap moisture, which allows bacteria to multiply. This is also true for sneakers, so don't wear them for more than four hours a day.

Bathe your feet daily in warm water that contains about 10 drops of tea-tree oil per pint of water. It has antibacterial properties. Use a pumice stone to remove hardened, dead skin from your heels and soles.

• **Palms.** Rub your palms every few hours with an astringent oil, such as cypress or geranium. These essential oils, which are available at health food stores, can be added to almond oil or a lotion for easier application.

If self-treatment doesn't help: Discuss with your doctor. He/she may prescribe a 20% *aluminum chloride* solution or an anticholinergic drug, such as *propantheline* (Pro-Banthine), to reduce the perspiration.

Botulinum toxin (Botox) injections are also a treatment option for severe hyperhidrosis.

As a last resort, surgical division of the sympathetic nerves that cause sweating is almost 100% effective for feet and palms and about 40% effective for armpits.

FEMININE ITCHING

Severe itching of the vulva (*vulval pruritis*) is usually caused by a vaginal yeast infection. *What to do…*

• **Try an over-the-counter cream,** such as *clotrimazole* (Gyne-Lotrimin) or *miconazole* (Monistat 3). If this doesn't help within a few days, your doctor may recommend a prescription medication, such as *fluconazole* (Diflucan).

Other possible causes of the itching include eczema, psoriasis or an allergy.

To relieve the itch: Soak in warm water that contains two handfuls of Epsom salt or ordinary kitchen salt…or dip a washcloth into a salt-water solution and apply to the affected area.

• **Wash only with unscented cleansers,** such as Dove Unscented Beauty Bar or Neutrogena Transparent Dry Skin Formula Fragrance Free. When shampooing your hair, don't let the foam touch your vulva…and wash underwear with an enzyme-free, perfume-free detergent made for sensitive skin.

• **Don't use feminine deodorants** or apply deodorant or perfume to sanitary pads…don't use fabric softener…and don't swim in chlorinated water.

FLATULENCE

It's normal to have some gas. Air swallowed during eating typically collects in the stomach and is passed via belching.

Bacteria also cause certain foods, especially beans, to break down into hydrogen, methane and carbon dioxide.

Most people experience gas (*flatulence*) more than 10 times a day. *What to do…*

• **Avoid eating large quantities of gas-causing foods at one time.** These include beans, peas, broccoli, cauliflower, artichokes, cabbage, raisins, prunes and apples. They contain hard-to-digest carbohydrates that ferment in the bowels.

Foods that don't cause flatulence: Potatoes, rice, corn and wheat.

• **Avoid carbonated beverages** as well as hot drinks.

• **Take your time while eating.** Don't rush when you eat…put your fork down between bites…and be sure to chew food thoroughly.

●**Don't chew gum.**

There are over-the-counter antiflatulence aids—such as Beano, charcoal tablets, Gas-X or Phazyme—that can also relieve flatulence.

JOCK ITCH

Jock itch (*tinea cruris*) causes an itchy, red rash in the groin area. The rash is triggered by the same fungus that causes athlete's foot. In fact, it's often "caught" from your own feet. *What to do...*

●**Try an over-the-counter antifungal ointment,** such as *tolnaftate* (Tinactin). If this does not help, consult your doctor.

●**Wear loose, 100% cotton underwear.**

●**Wash with unscented soap,** and dry the groin area carefully after bathing.

●**Wash underwear with an enzyme-free, perfume-free detergent.**

Help for Those Persistent and Annoying Problems

Dean Edell, MD, host of the nationally syndicated radio talk program "The Dr. Dean Edell Show." A former assistant clinical professor of surgery, University of California, San Diego, he is also author of *Eat, Drink & Be Merry* (Quill).

Millions of Americans suffer needlessly from various niggling health problems that they assume are too minor to warrant professional help.

At the very least, these problems are just an annoyance. At worst, minor ailments are a sign of more serious, underlying conditions, such as infection. *The most common health problems that go untreated...*

ANAL ITCHING

The skin around the anus is always moist—a perfect breeding ground for fungi. Spicy foods or irritating chemicals in toilet paper also can cause anal itching. So can hemorrhoids or persistent diarrhea caused by some antibiotics.

What you may not know: Anal itching is *not* caused by poor hygiene. It's usually quite the opposite—vigorous scrubbing increases tissue damage and irritation.

What to do: Try daily applications of over-the-counter (OTC) 0.5% hydrocortisone cream. Also helpful...

●**Check your diet.** Some people are sensitive to acidic foods, such as tomatoes and citrus fruits. Avoiding these foods may reduce itching.

●**Wash very gently after having a bowel movement.** Moistening toilet paper with water will reduce irritation. Do not scrub the area, just pat gently. Dry the area thoroughly when you're done. OTC wipes, such as Tucks or disposable baby wipes, also can be used. Make sure that they don't contain alcohol, which can be irritating to the skin.

●**Avoid toilet paper with scents or dyes.**

●**Wear cotton underwear.** It "breathes" and reduces excess moisture.

●**Don't scratch.** It just irritates the skin and makes itching worse.

If the anal itching persists for more than a few days, ask your physician to test you for pinworms, fungal growth or other types of infections that may cause itching.

DANDRUFF

It's natural for dead skin cells to flake off and fall away—but people with dandruff can shed skin cells up to three times more quickly than normal.

Dandruff is linked to *Pityrosporum ovale,* a tiny fungus that lives on the skin. It's not clear if the fungus promotes rapid skin turnover or if it happens to thrive on people with an abundance of flaky skin.

What you may not know: Daily use of ordinary shampoo dries the skin and makes flaking worse.

What to do: Use a dandruff shampoo that contains *selenium sulfide,* such as Selsun Blue, or *ketoconazole,* such as Nizoral, every day for about a week. Then use it every few days, alternating with your regular shampoo, to keep dandruff under control. When shampooing, let the lather stand for about five minutes before rinsing it off.

EARWAX

The sticky, wax-like substance (*cerumen*) is produced by glands in the ear canal. It traps dust and other foreign particles and prevents them from damaging structures deeper in the ear. Earwax is unsightly and can potentially block the opening to the ear canal.

What you may not know: The amount and type of earwax (dry or oily) that you generate is genetic.

What to do: Use a wax-removal product that contains *carbamide peroxide* every few months.

Recommended brands: Murine Ear Drops and Debrox. Put a few drops in the ear, wait a few minutes, then flush out with a bulb syringe containing warm water.

Earwax that's interfering with normal hearing should always be treated by an ear, nose and throat specialist, who will use a curved instrument called a curette to remove it. The procedure is generally painless and quick.

SMELLY FEET

Exposure to air quickly dries perspiration on other parts of your body, but shoes and socks trap moisture. Bacteria that thrive in the moist environment produce very strong odors.

What you may not know: Wearing the same shoes every day can cause feet to smell more.

What to do: Wash your feet several times daily with soap and water to remove bacteria. Some people apply rubbing alcohol to their feet to kill off germs. It works temporarily but dries the skin.

Go barefoot for a few hours daily to help keep your feet dry and odor-free. Wear only cotton socks. They absorb moisture and make feet less hospitable to odor-causing germs.

URINARY LEAKAGE

About 13 million Americans suffer from accidental leakage of urine from the bladder.

In women, the most common cause of urinary leakage is a weakening of the urinary sphincter or pelvic floor muscles as a result of pregnancy. And, urinary leakage in men is most often the result of surgery to treat prostate enlargement or cancer. Obesity may also cause incontinence because it puts constant pressure on the bladder and surrounding muscles.

What you may not know: The majority of men and women who suffer from urinary leakage are too embarrassed to tell their doctors about the problem.

What to do: Both women and men often can regain bladder control with Kegel exercises that strengthen the pelvic floor muscles. These are the same muscles you tighten when you stop the flow of urine.

Several times every day, squeeze the muscles, hold for a few seconds, then relax. Repeat the sequence at least 10 times.

Also helpful for women and men…

•**For several weeks, go to the bathroom by the clock**—every half hour, for example, whether or not you need to go. Then slowly lengthen the time between bathroom visits as you achieve more control. With practice, you should be able to urinate every three to four hours, without "accidents" in between.

•**Antispasmodic drugs,** such as *tolterodine* (Detrol) and *dicyclomine* (Bentyl), work to calm an overactive bladder.

Index

A

Acetaminophen
  accidental overdose of, 141–142
  alcohol and, 142
  for aches and pain, 139, 143
  for arthritis, 237
  with antidepressants, 131
  for colds, 4
  liver damage and, 470
  side effects, 254
Acid reflux and migraines, 236
Acne. *See also* Pimples
  chocolate and, 100
  medication for sun damage, 433
Acupressure
  for adrenal fatigue, 17
  for allergies, 9
  for headaches, 230
  for hiccups, 30
Acupuncture, 374–375
  for chronic pain, 251, 374
  for headaches, 230, 375
Addictions
  in elderly, 427–428
  quitting, 445–446
Adenomyosis, alternative treatments for, 478
Adrenal glands
  fatigue and, 17
  fibromyalgia and, 254
  hypertension and, 60
Aging/antiaging. *See also* Dementia; Longevity; Memory
  antiaging diet, 397–398, 401–402, 405, 409, 430–431
  antiaging strategies, 399–401, 408–410
  brain development, 411–413, 413–414
  exercise, 400, 408–409, 422, 469–470
  falls, reasons for, 421–423
  functional age test, 399
  medical care for elderly, 403–404
  medications for the elderly, 24
  mobility, test for, 423
  range of motion exercises for elderly, 405

"senior" vitamins, 433
sex and older people, 406–407, 425
substance abuse, "late-onset," 427–428
supplements, 147–149, 399–400, 413–414, 469
AIDS
  screening test for HIV, 116
Alcohol
  acetaminophen and, 142
  addiction, in elderly, 427
  breast cancer and, 295, 301
  cirrhosis and, 78
  dangers of, 167
  depression and, 439
  diabetes and, 62
  fatigue and, 15
  gout and, 85
  hay fever and, 10
  as headache trigger, 227
  heart disease and, 286
  hepatitis and, 78
  hypertension and, 288
  inflammation and, 77
  insomnia and, 19, 180
  insulin resistance syndrome and, 66
  kudzu to reduce craving for, 365
  liver and, 77
  pancreatic diseases and, 80–82
  sex, effect on, 469
  sinusitis and, 6
  skin problems and, 32, 34
  stroke risk and, 290
  tinnitus and, 44
Allergies. *See also* Hay fever; Migraine headaches
  acupressure for, 9
  earwax and, 490
  food, 167–168, 248, 490
  food, and drugs, 147
  hearing loss and, 43
  to herbs, 368
  natural remedies for, 377
  shots for, 10
  sinus infections and, 5, 6, 8
  yogurt for, 181
Alpha hydroxy acid (AHA), 31–32

Alternative medicine. *See also* Homeopathic remedies; Supplements
  for adrenal fatigue, 17–18
Altitude sickness, 461
Alzheimer's disease. *See* Dementia; Memory
Amenorrhea. *See* Menstruation
Anal itching, 488
Anemia
  green tea and, 369
Aneurysm
  genetic history test for, 118
  screening test for, 91
Angina
  herbs for, 366
Antacids, 183
Antiaging. *See* Aging/antiaging
Antibiotics
  before dental procedures, 48
  before surgery, 342
  effect of calcium on, 145
  colds, effect on, 4, 100, 144
  immune system, effect on, 57
  for gum disease, 49
  for infections, 100
  myths about, 144–145
  ointments, 139
  for sinusitis, 7–8, 8
  for urinary tract infections, 83
  UV exposure and, 96
Antidepressants. *See also* Medications
  impotence and, 441
Antihistamines
  for colds, 4
  for coughs, 139
  for hay fever, 10
Antioxidants, 156–158, 174
  antiaging, role in, 399–400
  for longevity, 398
  for wrinkles, 433
Anxiety
  aromatherapy for, 396
  controlling without drugs, 437–438
  disorders (phobias), 441–443
  essentials oils for, 395
  hypnosis for, 375
Aromatherapy, 394–395, 396

effect on Alzheimer's, 421
for appetite control, 396
for sinusitis, 45
Arthritis. *See also* Chronic pain; Gout
cause of, 237
essentials oils for, 395
exercise for, 218, 238–239, 244–246, 246, 249
foods, effect of, 247, 248
ginger for, 240
heart attack, increased risk of, 249–250
folk remedy for, 370
joint replacement surgery, 242–244
magnetic therapy for, 386
massage, 247
medications, 248–249
mental imagery to control, 362–363
natural treatments for, 364, 365, 367, 377–378
pain remedies, 236–238, 248
relief, 236
sex and, 470–471
stretching exercises for, 244–245
supplements, 57, 74, 95, 150, 238, 239, 244, 246, 247
surgery, 237, 240, 242–244
tea, 246
therapeutic taping, 247–248
timing of medications, 137
treatment strategies, new, 248–249
water intake, 239

Aspirin
after transient ischemic attack (TIA), 290
for air travel, 463–464
with antidepressants, 131
before surgery, 324
as cause of tinnitus, 43
for colds, 4
dosage, 141
emergency treatment of heart attack, 267
heart attack/stroke risk, to decrease, 55, 140, 269
dementia, to prevent, 140
effect on blood pressure, 137, 141
effect on stool test, 116
for emergency treatment of heart attack, 94
for foot problems, 87
ginkgo biloba and, 440
for gout, 84
grape juice and, 175
in hospital, to reduce infection risk, 331
liver damage and, 470
for pain relief, 142
pancreatic cancer, reducing risk of, with, 322
Reye's syndrome and, 139
stroke risk, to lower, 290
vitamin C to protect stomach, 141

Asthma
acupuncture for, 375
breathing problems diagnosed as, 11
caffeine and, 100, 162
cleaning products and, 76
exercises for, 219
foods for, 162–163

medications for, 11
mental imagery to control, 362–363
mind–body relaxation for, 363
when not to fly, 463
when traveling, 460
Astragalus, 364
Atherosclerosis, 61
inflammation and, 75
medications for, 61
screening test for, 91–92
Athlete's foot, 25, 487–488
medications for, 87
Atkins diet, 194–195
Atrial fibrillation, 292

B

Back pain
chiropractic, 262–264
essentials oils for, 395
exercises, 257–259, 259–260
magnetic therapy for, 386
managing, 261–262
reflexology for, 388
when to see doctor, 260
yoga for, 259–260
Bacterial infections
antibiotics for, 100, 144
herbs for, 364, 366
Bad breath, 486
Baldness, and link to heart disease, 284
Belching, 28, 489–490
Belly fat, diet for losing, 191–193, 193–194
Binge eating disorder (BED), 200–202
Biofeedback, for headaches, 231
Biopsy results, accuracy of, 110–111
Bipolar disorder, omega-3 fatty acids for, 152
Birth-control pills. *See* Oral contraceptives
Black cohosh, 362, 476
risk of, 368
Bladder. *See also* Incontinence
healthy, 434–435
Bladder cancer
reducing risk of, 296
smoking and, 434
Bleeding, from rectum, 54
Bloating, 53–54
causes, 28
Blood clots
gum disease and, 47
during air travel, 462
Blood pressure. *See also* Hypertension
cold-water therapy and, 378
falling blood pressure, danger of, 289
as part of physical exam, 89–90
Blood sugar. *See* Diabetes
Blood tests. *See* Screening tests
Body image, acceptance of, 448–449
Body mass index, 42, 190, 273, 410
Body odor, 486–487
Bone density. *See also* Osteoporosis
building, 69–71
dairy products and, 69
errors in screening test, 111
exercise for bone growth, 72
foods for bone strength, 69–71, 72

supplements for, 59, 69, 72
tea for, 176, 177
Botox
for headaches, 234
for excessive perspiration, 487
Brain health
exercise for, 404–405, 419, 420
foods to boost brainpower, 165–166, 420
olive oil for, 419
importance of, in aging, 411–413, 420–421
supplements for, 413–414, 420
Breast cancer
foods that reduce risk of, 306, 316
hormone therapy and, 314–316
mammograms, 55, 97, 109, 112–113, 295, 316
Pap smear, 55, 113, 297, 316
reducing risk of, 295
risk factors, 315
soybeans and risk of breast cancer, 182
weight and, 402
Breast-feeding
herbs and, 368
melatonin and, 465
reduced risk of cancer from, 296
Breast and reproductive organs
exam, 90
Breathing for health, 393–394, 451
Breathing problems, exercise-related, 11
Bromelain
for inflammation, 255
for sinusitis, 9
Bronchitis, essentials oils for, 395
Bunions, causes and treatment, 25–26
Bursitis. *See* Knee injuries
Bypass surgery. *See* Heart disease

C

Caffeine
for asthma attacks, 162
benefits of, 172–173
bone density and, 70
to burn fat, 204
calcium excretion and, 72
during pregnancy, 172
fatigue and, 15, 166
ibuprofen, increased effectiveness with, 228
insomnia and, 19, 180
migraine relief, 231
myths about, 100
pills, 172
as preventive for diabetes, 65
skin blemishes and, 32
in tea, 177
tinnitus and, 44
as trigger for hunger, 189
weight loss, role in, 194
Calcium. *See also* Osteoporosis
absorption, and vitamin D, 154
caffeine and calcium excretion, 72
calcium diet, 196–197
hyperparathyroidism and, 441
men's need for, 159
nondairy sources of, 175

Calluses, causes and treatment, 26
Cancer. *See also* specific cancers
  aspirin to reduce risk of, 140
  chemotherapy, coping with, 304, 306–308
  clinical trials, as treatment option, 303
  cooking and cancer risk of high heat, 297–298
  coping strategies, 304–305
  diagnosis and treatment of, 302–303
  exercises for, 218
  family history, importance of, 97
  genetic history tests for, 118
  Gleason score, 310
  herbs for, 366
  hidden carcinogens, 297–298, 299
  hormone therapy, 311, 313
  mental imagery for, 362–363
  radiation therapy, 308, 311, 313
  reducing risk of, 294–297, 299–300, 301
  risk factors for, 301
  screening tests for, 55, 92, 111–113, 299
  staging of, 302, 310, 313–314
  supplements to prevent, 82
  survival secrets, 303–304
  tea to reduce risk of, 176, 299
  vaccines for, 306
  vitamin D and, 153
Candida, vinegar to treat, 381
Carbohydrates. *See also* Foods
  for depression, 439
  food cravings and, 199
  low-carb diet to reduce insulin resistance, 66
  triglyceride release and, 272–273
Carbon monoxide, 226
Cardiovascular disease. *See* Heart disease
Carpal tunnel syndrome. *See* Repetitive stress injuries
Cascara sagrada, risks of, 368
Cataracts
  alternatives to surgery, 335–336
  aspirin to reduce risk of, 140
  foods for, 39–40, 40, 163, 365
  obesity and, 42
  preventing, 39–40, 40
  St. John's wort and, 438
  supplements for, 39–40
  surgery for, 40
Cavities. *See also* Gum disease, protecting against
  fluoridated water, 49–50
  fluoride toothpaste, 50
Cellulite, 32
Cervical cancer, reducing risk of, 297
Chemicals
  cancer, risk of, from, 296
  in cleaning products, and inflammation, 76
  liver, effects on, 77
Chemotherapy. *See* Cancer
Children
  colds and, 4
  herbal remedies and, 368

melatonin and, 465
sun exposure, protecting from, 296
when not to fly, 463
Chiropractic, for chronic pain, 251, 262–264
Chlamydia infection, 281
Chlorine, sinusitis and, 6
Chocolate
  benefits for the heart, 286
  cravings for, 200
  effect on acne, 100
  longevity and, 431
Cholesterol. *See also* Fats; Medications; Screening tests
  alternatives to medications, 135, 276–277, 279–281
  cranberry juice to lower, 277
  DASH diet, 97–98, 271, 289
  exercises for, 218
  fiber and, 182, 266
  foods for lowering, 265–266, 275–276
  herbs for, 362, 366, 367
  levels in women, 59
  levels and impotence, 482
  medications for, 59, 64, 65, 130, 135, 278–279
  Mediterranean Diet, 290
  nuts, value of, 177
  orange juice to lower, 277
  screening test for, 91, 93, 112, 116
  statins for, 278–279
  stroke risk, 290
  supplements, 59, 266, 276–277, 280
  vaccine, 278
  vitamin E for, 95
Chondroitin. *See* Glucosamine
Chronic fatigue syndrome (CFS), 11–13. *See also* Fatigue
Chronic obstructive pulmonary disease (COPD), 58
Chronic pain. *See* Back pain; Fibromyalgia; Pain
Chronotherapy, 137–138
Cleaning products, vinegar as substitute for, 381. *See also* Chemicals
Clinical trials, participating in, 122–123, 133, 303
Cluster headaches. *See* Headaches
COBRA (Consolidated Omnibus Budget Reconciliation Act) health insurance, 357, 361
Cocoa, as disease fighter, 174
Cognitive-behavioral therapy, for chronic fatigue syndrome, 13
Cognitive development. *See* Brain health
Cognitive restructuring, 443–444
Colds and flu, 3–5
  antibiotics and, 100, 144
  boosting immunity to, 1–3, 364
  exercise and, 5, 218
  feeding/starving, 3
  flu shots, 57
  folk remedies for, 373
  herbs for, 364, 366, 370
  myths, 99
  supplements, effect on, 4

teas for, 177, 380
wine and effect on, 3
Cold sore remedy, 5
Cold-water therapy, 378–379
Colonoscopy, 59, 97, 112, 317
  virtual, 318
  when not to fly after, 463
Colon polyps, 158
Colorectal cancer, 59–60. *See also* Colonoscopy
  broccoli and, 306
  dietary iron and, 318
  fecal occult blood test, 116, 318
  foods to decrease colon cancer risk, 60
  reducing risk of, 295–296
  screening tests for, 316–318
  sigmoidoscopy, 59, 112, 317
Communicating with your doctor, 101–102
  contacting, 98–99
  medical errors, protecting against, 106, 106–107
  patient responsibilities, 107–108
Computed tomography (CT) scan. *See* Screening tests
Congestive heart failure, foods for, 163
Conjunctivitis, 41, 42
Constipation
  carbonated water for, 393
  causes, 28
  corn syrup for, 390
  fenugreek for, 364
  laxatives for, 139
Cornmeal, as cure for toenail fungus, 27
Corns, causes and treatment, 26
Coronary artery disease (CAD), in women, 59
Corticosteroids. *See* Steroids
Cortisone-based drugs. *See* Steroids
Cosmetic surgery savings, 121
Cough, 54
  with chronic obstructive pulmonary disease (COPD), 58
  folk remedies for, 372–373
  OTC medications for, 139
Cramps, stomach, 28, 53–54. *See also* Leg cramps, nighttime
Cranberry juice
  to lower cholesterol, 277
  for urinary tract infections, 434, 477
Cranial–sacral manipulation, 375
C-reactive protein (CRP), 46–47, 90, 283
Crohn's disease, 54
  colon cancer, risk for, 317
  natural remedies for, 184, 390
  omega-3 fatty acids for, 152
Cushing's syndrome, 198
Cuts
  antibiotic ointments, 139
  cleaners, 27
  emergency treatment of, 93
  Reiki for healing, 363

D

Dandruff, control of, 30, 32–33, 488, 491
DASH diet, 97–98, 271, 289

Decongestants
  for colds, 4
  for hay fever, 10
  natural, 396
  for sinusitis, 6, 8
Deep vein thrombosis
  genetic history test for, 117–118
  gum disease and, 47
  sitting as risk factor, 77, 462
DEET, for mosquitoes and ticks, 30
Dehydration. *See* Water
Dementia. *See also* Memory
  abnormal gait, as sign of, 419
  aromatherapy and effect on
    Alzheimer's, 421
  aspirin to prevent, 140
  brain health, maintaining, 404
  copper and, 421
  NSAIDs and, 421
  statins and, 279
  strategies for preventing, 418–419
Dengue fever, 461
Depression
  acupuncture for, 375
  after heart attack, 270
  as cause of fatigue, 12
  drug-free treatments, 439–440
  foods for, 166
  hyperparathyroidism and, 441
  medications for, 12, 23, 130, 131, 146
  mind–body relaxation for, 363
  as risk factor for heart disease, 281
  sunlight and, 440
  supplements for, 439–440
  thyroid hormone supplement for, 441
  treating, 97, 130
Dermatitis, allergic or contact, and
  makeup, 34
DHEA therapy, 398
Diabetes. *See also* Insulin resistance
  adult-onset (type 2), 61–63
  air travel and, 462
  anodyne therapy, 65
  carbohydrates, high intake of, and,
    175
  cholesterol-lowering drugs, 65
  cinnamon for, 173
  coffee as preventive, 65
  diabetic neuropathy, magnetic therapy
    for, 386
  diabetic retinopathy, 41, 140
  exercises for, 218
  fenugreek for, 364
  foods for diabetics, 62
  glycemic index of foods, 192, 433
  impotence and, 482
  indicators, 63
  inflammation and, 75–76
  medications for, 62, 63
  omega-3 fatty acids for, 152
  syndrome X, 273–275
  treatment, 63–65
Diagnostic tests. *See* Screening tests
Diarrhea
  causes, 28
  fenugreek for, 364

  kudzu for, 390–391
  OTC medications for, 139
  travelers' diarrhea, 461, 465, 465–466
Dieting. *See also* Foods; Obesity; Weight
  almonds and, 189
  Atkins diet, 194–195
  belly fat, losing, 191–193, 193–194
  body mass index, 42, 190
  caffeine and, 173, 204
  calcium diet, 196–197
  calories, role in weight loss, 194
  dangerous diets, recognizing, 197
  drugs, weight-loss, 67, 190, 197
  fat burning, increasing, 204, 204–205,
    206
  ketogenic diets, 190
  low-calorie diets, 190
  secrets for weight loss, 186–187,
    189–191, 191, 202
  surgery, weight-loss, 190
  weight-loss programs, 190
Digestive problems, 183–184
Dining out, 180, 184–185, 202–204
Disability policies, 358–359
Discount health care clubs, 121–122
Disease-management programs, 349,
  350–351
Disinfectant, making your own, 4
Diuretics
  effect on gout, 85
  for kidney stones, 83
  UV exposure and, 96
DNA testing, 117–119
Doctor, choosing a, 102–103, 124. *See also*
  Communicating with your doctor
  choosing an anesthesiologist, 324
  in a managed care organization,
    347–348
  choosing a surgeon, 328–329
Drugs. *See* Medications
Duct tape, as cure for warts, 27
Dysentery, 466

E

Ears. *See also* Hearing loss; Tinnitus
  ear infections, when not to fly with,
    463
  earwax, 488–489, 490
Echinacea, 366
Echocardiogram, 59
Eggs, health benefits of, 166
Elderly. *See* Aging/antiaging; Longevity
Electrocardiogram (ECG), 59
Emergency medical treatments, 93–94
  carrying medical history, 120, 133
  in-flight, 462–463
  overseas, 457–458
Emergency phone number, in Europe,
  459
Emergency room visits, 332–333, 333
  managed care plans and, 350, 351, 353
Emphysema
  exercises for, 219
  genetic history test for, 118
Endometrial cancer. *See* Uterine cancer,
  reducing risk of

Endometriosis, alternative treatments for, 478
Energy, increasing. *See* Fatigue
Environment in the home, healthy, 383
Ephedra, dangers of, 160
Epsom salts
  for corns, 26
  for insomnia, 18
Erectile dysfunction (ED), 406, 407,
  482–483
  antidepressants and, 441
  aphrodisiacs, natural, 475–476
  natural treatments for, 485
Essential oils, 379, 390
  for hot flashes, 395
Estrogen. *see* Hormones
Exercise, 55–56, 95–96, 207–209. *See also*
  Stretching exercises; specific conditions
  avoiding injury, 213–214
  best time to, 213
  body-shaping exercises, 206–207
  exercise-induced heartburn, 220
  guidelines, revised, 217
  heart rate, measuring, 208
  injuries, heat or cold for, 215
  Kegel exercises, 435
  opportunities for, 209, 209–211
  raisins before working out, 215
  to reduce inflammation, 76
  Slow Burn exercises, 215–217
  walking, 223, 223–225, 469–470
Exposure therapy, 442
Eye disorders. *See* Cataracts; Glaucoma;
  Macular degeneration; Vision
Eyes. *See also* Vision
  conjunctivitis, 41
  dry eyes, 41, 42
  eyestrain, reflexology for, 387
  floaters, 42
  foods for eye health, 96
  as part of physical exam, 90
  strategies for eye health, 96
  styes, 41
  supplements for eye health, 96

F

Fainting, prevention, 29
Falls, reasons for, 421–423
Familial disorders. *See* Genetic history
Familial Mediterranean fever, genetic
  history test for, 118
Family medical history. *See* Genetic
  history
Fatigue. *See also* Chronic fatigue
  syndrome (CFS); Sleep, insufficient
  adrenal glands and, 17
  aromatherapy for energy, 396
  causes, 11–12
  chemotherapy and, 307
  exercises for energy, 15, 16
  foods and, 15, 17
  foods for mental fatigue, 166
  hyperparathyroidism and, 441
  inflammation and, 76
  stretching exercises for, 16
  supplements for, 14, 15, 16, 17
  treating, 13–14, 14–16

Fats. *See also* Olive oil
  to boost immunity, 56–57
  exercise to burn, 205, 206
  food cravings and, 199
  food strategies for lowering, 265–266,
    280
  gallbladder, effect on, 77
  hidden fats, 169
  insulin resistance syndrome and, 66
  pancreas, effect on, 81
  polyunsaturated fats, to prevent ulcers,
    28
  reduced-fat foods and weight gain, 202
  trans fats, 164, 165, 169, 277, 280
Fecal occult blood test, 116, 318
Feet
  aching, magnetic therapy for, 386
  arches, fallen, 26
  athlete's foot, 25, 381
  bunions, 25–26, 87
  calluses, 26
  corns, 26
  exercises for foot problems, 26
  fungal infections, vinegar for, 381
  hammertoes, 88
  orthotics, 87
  pain relief, 425–426
  perspiration, excessive, 487, 488, 489
  plantar fasciitis, 86–87
  self-test for problems, 88
  smelly, 487, 488, 489
  stretching exercises for, 26, 86–87, 88
  toenail infection, 87
  toenails, ingrown, 26–27, 373
Fenugreek, 364
Fever
  acetaminophen for, 139
  feeding/starving, 3
Fiber
  beans as source of, 182
  hemorrhoids and, 490
  intestinal problems and, 28
  to lower cholesterol, 266
  to reduce cancer risk, 96
  weight loss, role in, 188
Fibrocystic breasts, natural remedies for,
  477
Fibroid tumors, alternative treatments for,
  478–479, 479
Fibromyalgia, 253, 253–254
  chronic fatigue syndrome and, 12
  magnetic therapy for, 386
  yoga for, 253
Fish
  Alzheimer's, role in preventing, 418
  for anti-inflammatory effect, 76–77
  for eye health, 96
  for immune system, 2
  for insulin resistance syndrome, 66
  for longevity, 402
  macular degeneration and, 431
  mercury levels in tuna, 178
  raw, dangers of, 167
  recipes, 70, 71
  sardines for bone strength, 70
  shellfish, health benefits of, 166

  for wrinkles, 432
Fish oil supplements, 170
  danger of, 161
Flatulence. *See* Gas, intestinal
Flaxseed, 429–430, 482
  for hemorrhoids, 490
  oil, 170, 432
Flu. *See* Colds and flu
Fluoride
  fluoridated water, 49–50
  thyroid function and, 68
Flying, and sinusitis, 7
Foods. *See also* Fish; Fruits; Vegetables;
    Water; specific conditions
  beans, 181–183
  bread, rye vs. whole wheat, 175
  breakfast, high-protein, 192–193
  cravings, 199–200, 201
  dining out, 180, 184–185
  disease fighters, 174–175, 182
  cooking to increase antioxidants, 174
  dangers of some, 167–168
  DASH diet, 97–98, 271, 289
  eggs, health benefits of, 166
  fiber-rich, 96, 182
  glycemic index of foods, 192
  greens, vinegar with, 381
  hepatitis and, 80
  hidden salt, sugar, and fat, 168–169
  inflammation and, 76–77
  junk foods, 382–383
  low-calorie snacks, 191
  low-glycemic foods, 433
  Mediterranean Diet, 290
  nuts, health benefits of, 166, 177
  organic, 98, 177
  peanut butter, healthier, 202
  protein, complete, 181
  recipes, 70–71, 180–181, 191
  refrigerating/freezing guidelines, 185
  to relax mind and body, 179–181
  serving size of, 164
  smart shopping, 164–165
  vegetarian meals, 55, 180, 276, 401–402,
    428–430
Forgiveness and health, 455–456
Fractures, emergency treatment of, 93
Fraud, medical, 123–125
Free radicals, 13–14, 40, 147, 148
  aging and, 401, 402, 409, 418, 430
  antioxidants and, 156–157, 399–400
  inhibiting effects of, 34
  skin damage, role in, 33, 432
Fruits
  to avoid chronic diseases, 428–430
  bloating and, 28
  dangers of some, 167–168
  disease fighters, 174
  energy levels and, 15
  ethylene gas, producers of, 178
  highest in phytochemicals, 1
  organic, 1–2
  for preventing cataracts, 39
  for sun protection, 34–35
  washing, 2, 80, 178
Fungal infections

  folk remedies for, 373
  herbs for, 366

G
Gallstones
  exercise and, 28
  foods for, 163
  for longevity, 398
Gamma globulin, 79, 80
Garlic, 366, 370, 429
  risks of, 368–369
Gas, intestinal
  to avoid, 487, 490
  beans and, 183
  causes, 28, 490
  herbs for, 370, 372
Gastroesophageal reflux disease (GERD),
    natural remedies for, 184
Gastrointestinal problems, 183–184
Gender-specific medicine, 58–60
Genetic history
  importance of, 97, 119–120
  testing, 117–119
Ginger, 370, 374, 429
Gingivitis. *See* Gum disease
Ginkgo biloba
  as aphrodisiac, 475
  for depression, 440
  for erectile dysfunction, 485
  risks of, 369
  for tinnitus, 44
Ginseng
  as aphrodisiac, 475–476
  energy levels and, 15
  for erectile dysfunction, 485
Glaucoma, 40–41, 365
Glucosamine
  for arthritis, 57, 95, 239, 244, 247,
    377–378
  for joints, 74, 95, 150, 241
Glucose tolerance test. *See* Diabetes
Glycemic index of foods, 192
Gout, 84–85, 85–86
  celery seed for, 364, 365–366
  cherries for, 370
  food triggers, 85, 86
Guggul, 362
Gum chewing, and gas, 28
Gum disease
  causes, 46–47
  treatment, 48–49, 50

H
Hair loss, essentials oils for, 395
Halitosis (bad breath), 486
Hawthorn, 366, 376
Hay fever
  acupuncture for, 375
  circadian rhythms of, 138
  food triggers, 181
  honeycomb for, 370
  strategies for relief, 9–10
Headaches, 54, 95. *See also* Migraine
    headaches
  anti-headache diet, 228
  Botox for, 234

caffeine for, 173
chiropractic for, 263
diets for, 228, 230
essentials oils for, 395
folk remedies for, 370, 372, 373–374
foods as cause of, 95, 228, 229
guided imagery for, 229
magnetic therapy for, 387
medications for, 229
natural remedies for, 229–231
reflexology for, 229
supplements for, 230
teas for, 380
triggers, 226–227, 229, 232
water for, 255
Health insurance. *See also* Managed care
    organizations (MCOs); Medicare and
    Medicaid
    appeals, 356, 358
    bending rules for improved patient
        care, 358
    buying your own, 354–356
    common traps to avoid, 356–357
    discount health care clubs, 121–122
    long-term-care insurance, 359–360,
        360, 361
    loss of, 360
    short-term, 354, 458
    when traveling, 458
Health maintenance organizations
    (HMOs). *See* Managed care
    organizations (MCOs)
Health scams, 125
Hearing loss
    earwax and, 43
    foods affecting hearing loss, 43
    hearing aid, 44
    reversing, 43
Heartburn
    avoiding when eating out, 184–185
    exercise-induced, 220
    natural remedies for, 184, 372
Heart disease. *See also* Cholesterol
    air travel and, 462
    alcohol, benefits of, 285, 286
    baldness, and link to, 284
    blood tests for risk factors, 281–282
    chocolate, benefits of, 286
    citrus fruits, benefits of, 286
    coronary bypass, alternatives to, 336
    coronary bypass-surgery side effects, 284
    coronary bypass surgery in women,
        283
    C-reactive protein (CRP) test, 283
    diabetics and higher risk for, 64
    emergency room misdiagnosis, 283
    emergency treatment of, 94, 267
    food triggers, 267
    gum disease and risk of, 47
    herbs for, 366, 367
    homocysteine levels and, 282, 282–283,
        285
    hormone therapy (HT) and, 315
    inflammation and, 75
    mental imagery to control, 362–363
    omega-3 fatty acids for, 151–152

prevention strategies, 265–266, 270–272
recovering from heart attack, 270
risk factors doctors overlook, 281–282
screening tests for, 75, 91–92, 113
sex and, 268–269
split peas, protective action of, 286
spouse/partner's needs, 267–268
steroid use and, 60
supplements for, 284–286
tea to reduce risk of, 176–177
therapeutic hypothermia, 267
timing of medications, 138
triglycerides and, 272–273, 279
waist size and risk of, 275
when traveling, 459–460
in women, 59
Heatstroke, emergency treatment of, 94
Hemochromatosis, test for, 117
Hemorrhagic stroke. *See* Stroke
Hemorrhoids, home remedies for, 364,
    488
Hepatitis, viral, 78, 78–80
    when traveling, 461
Herbal medicine, 364–365, 365–367. *See
    also* Folk remedies; Homeopathic
        remedies; Supplements
    antiaging herbs, 400–401
    risks of, 368–369
    safety and effectiveness of, 367–368
Heredity. *See* Genetic history
Herpes, elderberry for, 364
hGH (human growth hormone), 408
Hiccups, acupressure for, 29
High blood pressure. *See* Hypertension
Hip care, 73–75
    hip replacement, alternatives to,
        336–337
HIV, screening test for, 116
HMOs (health maintenance
    organizations). *See* Managed care
        organizations (MCOs)
Hodgkin's disease, 308–309
Home environment and health, 383
Homeopathic remedies. *See also*
    Alternative medicine; Supplements
    effect on colds, 4
    for insomnia, 18
    myths about, 100
Homocysteine, 282, 282–283, 285
Honey, benefits of, 171
Hormone therapy (HT). *See also*
    Hormones
    alternatives therapies, 481–482, 482
    antiaging, 401
    black cohosh as alternative to, 362, 368
    bone loss, minimizing with, 72–73
    to boost HDL cholesterol, 59
    breast cancer risk and, 314–316
    as carcinogens, 297
    colon cancer, decreased risk with, 60
    dangers of, 315
    for longevity, 398
    natural substitutes for, 480–481
    for sexual problems in older women,
        406
    testosterone with, 61

Hormones. *See also* Hormone therapy (HT)
    as cancer treatment, 311, 313
    bone fractures and, 315
    estrogen and bone density, 59
    estrogen as carcinogen, 297
    health problems and, 60–61
    insomnia and, 18
    for lack of ovulation, 479
    in patch form, 132
    progesterone, natural, 378
    stress hormones, 437–438
Hospital stays. *See also* Surgery
    aspirin to reduce infection risk, 331
    billing errors, avoiding, 330–331
    dangerous cost-cutting measures,
        327–328
    emergency room visits, 332–333, 333
    getting better care, 325–326
    hand-washing procedures, 331
    hospital rating sites, 329
    medical errors, avoiding, 323–325
    nursing care, better, 329
    patient-controlled analgesia (PCA), 325
    safety during, 326–327
    visits to patients, 331
Hot flashes. *See* Menopause
Human growth hormone (hGH), 408
Human papillomavirus (HPV), 297
Humid air
    and colds, 5
    for restful sleep, 21
    and sinusitis, 6
Humming, as treatment for sinusitis, 9
Hygiene, for avoiding colds, 3, 4
Hyperactivity, sugar and, 100
Hypertension, 426. *See also* Blood pressure
    ambulatory blood pressure
        monitoring, 137
    DASH diet for lowering blood
        pressure, 97–98, 271, 289
    diabetes and, 64–65
    exercises for, 218
    foods to lower, 288
    herbs for, 364, 366, 376–377
    hormones and, 60
    hostility and, 138
    impotence and, 483
    lowering with stress management, 95
    medications for, 64–65, 130, 146,
        422–423
    mental imagery to control, 362–363
    mind–body relaxation for, 363
    new strategies, 287–288
    prehypertension, 291
    "pulse pressure," 287
    salt and, 100, 287–288, 289
    stroke, risk of, 289
    weight loss and, 288, 289
Hyperuricemia, 86
Hypnosis, 375–376
    for chronic pain, 251–252
    to heal broken bones, 385
    to overcome bad habits, 444–445
Hypoglycemia, alcohol, effect of, on, 15
Hypothermia, emergency treatment of,
    93–94

Hypothyroidism. *See* Thyroid
Hysterectomy, alternatives to, 478–479

I

Ibuprofen. *See also* Nonsteroidal anti-inflammatory drugs (NSAIDs)
  increased effectiveness with caffeine, 228
Immune system
  boosters, 1–3, 56–58, 364, 381–382
  exercise and, 3, 57, 382
  foods for, 1–2, 56, 381–382
  herbs for, 364, 365–367
  licorice as tonic for, 16
  medicinal mushrooms for, 382
  omega-3 fatty acids for, 152
  supplements for, 2, 57
  tea for, 176
Immunizations
  for adults, 109
  when traveling, 458
Immunomodulators, 36–37
Impotence. *See* Erectile dysfunction
Incontinence, 435, 489
  Kegel exercises for, 480, 489
  magnesium hydroxide for, 480
Indigestion, 53–54
  carbonated water for, 393
  causes, 28
  herbs for, 370, 392
  reflexology for, 388
  teas for, 380
Infections
  antibiotics for, 100
  staph, 346
Inflammation, 75–77
Insect repellents, 29
Insomnia. *See also* Fatigue; Sleep, insufficient; Snoring
  caffeine and, 100
  causes, 18, 19
  essentials oils for, 395
  exercise for, 19
  folk remedies for, 370, 374
  foods for, 20, 22
  medications for, 18, 20, 22, 23
  natural remedies for, 18, 20–22, 377
  teas for, 380
  treatments, 19–20
Insulin resistance, 66–67, 285. *See also* Diabetes
  exercise for, 67
  foods for, 66
  syndrome X, 195, 273–275
  vinegar for, 65
Insurance, health. *See* Managed care organizations (MCOs)
  loss of, 360
Internet
  fraud, 125
  for gathering medical information, 101, 104, 304
  weight-loss programs, 190
Iodine and thyroid function, 68
Iron
  green tea and absorption of, 369
  elderly and, 469
  leaching from cookware, 160–161

Irritable bowel syndrome (IBS)
  drug-free strategies, 388–390
  foods for, 163, 389
  hypnosis for, 375
  natural remedies for, 184, 390
Ischemic stroke. *See* Stroke
Itching
  anal, 488
  feminine, 487

J

Jet lag, caffeine for, 173
Jock itch, 487–488
  vinegar to treat, 381
Joint pain. *See* Arthritis; Glucosamine
Joint-replacement surgery, 237, 242–244

K

Kegel exercises, 435
Kidney cancer, reducing risk of, 296
Kidney disease, polycystic, genetic history test for, 118
Kidney stones, 82–83
  risk of, on high-protein diet, 195, 196
Kissing and colds, 4
Knee injuries
  preventing, 241
  surgery, 240, 242
  treatment, 241–242
  types, 240–241

L

Lab tests. *See* Screening tests
Lactic acidosis, 85
Laser eye surgery (LASIK), 38–39
Laxatives, 139, 368
Leg cramps, nighttime, 24
  folk remedies for, 371
  tonic water for, 25
Leg pain as stroke risk, 292
Licorice
  for adrenal fatigue, 18–19
  antihypertensive drugs and, 146
  for digestive problems, 183
  risks of, 369
  as tonic for immune system, 16
Light therapy for insomnia, 20
Liver
  diseases of, 78, 78–80
  herbs for, 366
Longevity
  chocolate and, 431
  exercises for, 402
  factors in, 397–399
  low-calorie diet and, 401, 431
  Okinawans and, 401–403
  optimism and, 411
Long-term-care insurance, 359–360, 360, 361
Low-carb diets, to reduce insulin resistance, 66
Lung cancer
  reducing risk of, 295
  screening test for, 92
  women's risk of, 300
Lymph nodes, as part of physical exam, 90

Lymphoma, 308–310

M

Macular degeneration
  bilberry for, 41
  fish for, 431
  foods for, 41
Magnesium, 383
  for hypertension, 377
Magnetic resonance imaging (MRI). *See* Screening tests; Stroke
Magnetic therapy, 385–387
  dangers of, 387
Makeup, and skin care, 34
Malaria, 461
Mammograms, 55, 97, 109, 112–113, 295
  plus ultrasound, 316
Managed care organizations (MCOs). *See also* Health insurance; Medicare and Medicaid
  appealing decisions of, 348–349, 350, 351–352, 352–353, 358
  choosing coverage, 354–356
  dealing with, 347–349, 349–350
  emergency room visits, nonaffiliated, 353
  patient advocate, 353–354
  second opinions, on managed care decisions, 353
Massage
  for arthritis, 247
  for headache management, 95, 229, 231
Mattress
  discounts on, 122
  for restful sleep, 21
Medical bills, reducing, 121–123
Medical checkup, 89–91
Medical emergencies, treating. *See* Emergency medical treatments; Emergency room visits
Medical emergencies overseas, 457–458, 463–466
Medical errors, avoiding, 106, 128–129, 358
  during hospital stays, 323–325
  on prescriptions, 120, 126–127
  on screening tests, 111–113
Medical history, carrying for emergencies, 120, 133
Medical kit for emergencies, 94
Medical myths, 99–100
Medical privacy. *See* Confidentiality
Medical red flags, 53–55
Medical research, doing, 101–102, 104
Medicare and Medicaid
  advocacy programs for appeals, 354
  patients' access to medical records, 105
  scams, 361
  supplemental policies when traveling, 458
Medications. *See also* Nonsteroidal anti-inflammatory drugs (NSAIDs); Prescription drugs; Steroids; specific conditions
  accidental addiction, in elderly, 427–428
  chronotherapy, 137
  combining, dangers of, 135, 145–147, 422–423

combo drugs, 135–136
  coupons for, 122
  Cox-2 inhibitors, 143
  depletion of nutrients by, 136
  errors, avoiding, 106, 106–107
  fatigue and, 16
  foods, combining with, 326–327
  herbs, interactions with, 136, 145–147, 159, 368
  influence of drug companies, 134–135
  instructions for taking, 136
  liver, effects on, 77
  narcotics, 143
  side effects, 128, 129–131, 132, 135
  switching, by health insurers, 121
  timing of, 136–138
  tranquilizers, misprescription of, 131
  UV exposure and, 147
  weight gain from, 131, 190
  when traveling, 458
Medicinal herbs. *See* Herbal medicine
Medigap coverage, 361
  supplemental policies when traveling, 458
Mediterranean diet, 290, 419
Melanoma, 320–322
  myths about, 319–320
  positron emission tomography (PET), 321
  reducing risk of, 296
  ultraviolet light and, 298
Melatonin, 149
  for insomnia, 18, 22
  for jet lag, 465
  light, effect on, 24, 440
  therapy, for longevity, 398
Memory. *See also* Aging/antiaging; Dementia
  aromatherapy for retention, 396
  improvement, strategies for, 414–415, 416–417, 425
  lapses, 54
  phosphatidylserine for, 417
  stress and, 420–421
  supplements for, 415
Men
  calcium, need for, 159
  gender-specific medicine, 58–60
  sexual problems in older men, 406–407
  urinary tract infections in, 435
Ménière's disease, 44
Menopause. *See also* Hormones; Hormone replacement therapy (HRT)
  alcohol and, 481
  body fat and, 402
  cholesterol and, 112
  hot flashes, treatments for, 395
  hypothyroidism and, 67
  natural treatments for, 362, 368, 378, 476, 480–481
  psychological stress as factor, 481
  screening test for, 116
  sexual problems in older women, 406, 481
  soy foods for, 363, 481
  supplements for, 481

Menstruation. *See also* Premenstrual syndrome (PMS)
  cramps, essentials oils for, 395
  relation to osteoporosis, 69
  skin blemishes and, 32
Mental changes, 54
Mental fatigue, foods for, 165–166
Mental imagery for effective healing, 362–363
Mercury levels in tuna, 178
Metabolic syndrome. *See* Diabetes; Insulin resistance syndrome
Microdermabrasion, 26
Micronutrient starvation, 1
Microwaving in plastic, 185
Migraine headaches, 235
  acid reflux and, 236
  acupuncture for, 375
  caffeine for, 173, 231–232
  chiropractic for, 263
  counseling for, 234
  diets for, 228, 230
  exercise for, 235
  food triggers, 232, 235
  herbs as triggers, 233–234
  medications for, 229, 232–233, 235–236
  natural remedies for, 229–231, 231–233
  reflexology for, 229
  stroke risk and, 293
  supplements for, 230, 232, 235
Milk thistle, 366
Mind–body relaxation, 363
Mineral supplements. *See* Supplements
Mobility, test for, 423
Mold, eliminating in home, 383
Monosodium glutamate (MSG), as headache trigger, 227, 235
Mosquitoes and ticks
  avoiding, 29, 371
  for bites, 371
Motion sickness
  folk remedies for, 371
  teas for, 380
Multiple sclerosis, 255–257
Muscles
  loss of mass, prevention of, 220, 400, 409
  spasms, essentials oils for, 395

N

Narcotics for pain relief, 143
Nasal congestion, OTC medications for, 139
Nasal fungus, and sinusitis, 8
Nasal sprays
  for colds, 4–5
  for hay fever, 10
  for sinusitis, 8
Natural remedies. *See* Alternative medicine; Homeopathic remedies; Supplements
Nausea
  causes, 28
  folk remedies for, 374
  teas for, 380
Neck pain, reflexology for, 388. *See also* Back pain

Nicotine in patch form, 132
Noise, and insomnia, 21
Non-Hodgkin's disease, 309
Nonsteroidal anti-inflammatory drugs (NSAIDs). *See also* Aspirin
  Alzheimer's, effect on, 421
  with antidepressants, 131
  for arthritis, 237
  for colds, 4
  effect on stool test, 116
  effect of timing of medications, 137
  for foot problems, 87
  for pain relief, 143
  side effects, 254
Nursing home
  insurance, 359–360, 360
  staying out of, 404–405
Nutrition. *See* Foods; Supplements; Water
Nuts, health benefits of, 166, 177
  almonds for weight loss, 189

O

Obesity. *See also* Dieting; Weight
  among Okinawans, 402
  appetite control with aromatherapy, 396
  binge eating disorder (BED), 200–202
  body mass index, 42, 190
  cataract formation, role in, 40, 42
  elevated triglycerides, link to, 273
  exercises for, 218
  gallbladder disorders and, 77–78
  hypnosis for overeating, 375
  incontinence and, 489
  medical conditions causing, 198–199
  omega-3 fatty acids for, 152
  as risk factor for insulin resistance syndrome, 66
  sleep apnea and, 293
Olive oil. *See also* Essential oils; Fats
  for brain health, 419
  for wrinkles, 432–433
Omega-3 fatty acids, 148, 151–153, 271, 383
  Alzheimer's, role in preventing, 418
  longevity and, 402
Optimism, 443–444
  as factor in longevity, 411
Oral contraceptives
  caffeine and, 172
  cancer risk, reduction of, 296
  herbal supplements to avoid with, 146, 369
  risk of clotting and, 118
Orange juice to lower cholesterol, 277
Organic foods, 98
  pesticides in, 177
Organ transplantation and St. John's wort, 440
Osteoarthritis. *See* Arthritis
Osteomalacia, 153
Osteopath, for chronic pain, 251
Osteoporosis, 71–73, 423–424, 426
  dental problems and, 52
  exercise and, 74, 219
  foods for, 480
  hip fractures and, 73

kudzu for, 365
in men, 59
menstrual cycles and relation to, 69
prunes as preventive, 71
risk of, on Atkins diet, 195
screening test for, 69, 72, 73, 424
soy foods for, 363, 481
use of steroids and, 60
vitamin D for, 153
Ovarian cancer
foods that reduce risk of, 316
reducing risk of, 296
screening test for, 92
Overeating, hypnosis for, 375
Ovulation
lack of, alternative remedies, 479
test for, 116–117

P

Pain. *See also* Aspirin; Back pain;
Nonsteroidal anti-inflammatory drugs
(NSAIDs)
as cause of insomnia, 18
chiropractic for, 262–264
gender-specific, 58
hypnosis for, 251–252, 375
liquid pain relievers, 229
magnetic therapy for, 385–387
medications for, 130, 142–143
mental imagery to control, 362–363
mind–body relaxation for, 363
natural treatments, 250–251, 254–255
patient-controlled analgesia (PCA), 325
Reiki for, 363
therapy for diabetics, 65
Pancreas. *See also* Pancreatic cancer
pancreatitis, 80–81
screening test for pancreatitis, 81
Pancreatic cancer, 81–82
aspirin and reduced risk of, 322
reducing risk of, 296
Panic attack, 442
Pap smear, 55, 113, 297
new retesting method, 316
Patient advocate, 353–354
Patient rights
Patient Bill of Rights, 104
Peripheral artery disease (PAD), 292
Periodontal disease. *See* Gum disease
Perspiration, excessive, 486–487
Pesticides
foods with high and low levels of,
177–178
in organic foods, 177
Phobias
cures for, 441–443
hypnosis for, 375
Phosphatidylserine, 417
Phototherapy
as treatment for psoriasis, 36
using tanning beds, 37
Physical exam, 89–91
Phytochemicals, 1–2
Pimples. *See also* Acne
in adults, 32
foods and, 32

Pineapple enzymes. *See* Bromelain
Pneumonia, when not to fly, 463
Poison ivy
emergency treatment of, 93
preventing outbreaks, 35
Pollen. *See* Allergies; Hay fever
Polycystic kidney disease, genetic history
test for, 118
Polycystic ovary syndrome (PCOS), 198
Positive Emotion Refocusing Technique,
455–456
Post-polio syndrome, 385
Potassium, food sources of, 160
PPOs (preferred provider organizations).
See Managed care organizations (MCOs)
Prayer, healing power of, 363, 451–452,
452–453
Prednisone. *See* Steroids
Preferred provider organizations (PPOs).
See Managed care organizations
(MCOs)
Pregnancy
air travel and, 462
herbs, avoiding during, 368, 476
medications and, 10
melatonin and, 465
mercury in fish, avoiding during, 418
ovulation test, 116–117
Premenstrual syndrome (PMS)
black cohosh for, 476
B vitamins for, 155, 156
chronic fatigue syndrome and, 12
natural remedies for, 477
teas for, 380
Prescription drugs. *See also* Medications;
Steroids
as cause of weight gain, 198–199
coverage in health plans, 357
cutting costs of, 358
dosages, adjusting, 130
errors, avoiding, 120, 126–127
splitting tablets, 129
stocking up before traveling, 460
Privacy. *See* Confidentiality
Problems, solving, in work, life,
relationships, 436–437
Prostaglandins, 74, 142, 248, 251, 369, 402
Prostate. *See also* Prostate cancer natural
treatments for, 365, 366, 377, 486
testosterone replacement therapy and,
398
Prostate cancer
biopsy readings, 312, 312
digital rectal exam, 312–313
prostate-specific antigen (PSA) test
levels, 312, 312–313
reducing risk of, 294–295
supplements, to slow growth of, 314
surgery for, 311
testosterone replacement therapy and,
398
treatments for, 310–311, 312–314
zinc and, 160
Protein intake
bone strength and, 70, 72
kidney stones and, 83

Prunes, as bone-loss preventive, 71
Psoriasis
description, 36
tanning beds for, 37
treatment, 36–37
Psoriatric arthritis, 37
Pulmonary embolism
genetic history test for, 117–118
gum disease and, 47
Pulse points, as part of physical exam, 90
Pulse therapy, 87

Q

Quinine
as cause of tinnitus, 43
for nighttime leg cramps, 25

R

Radiation. *See* Cancer; Screening tests;
X-rays
Radon, 298
Ragweed. *See* Hay fever
Recipes
for bone strength, 70–71
as dessert alternative, 180–181
low-calorie snacks, 191
Rectal
bleeding, 54
exam, 90
Recycling codes on plastic, 185
Reflexology, 387–388
for headaches, 229
Reiki, 363
Relationships and good health. *See* Social
links and good health
Religion and spirituality, 452
Repetitive stress injuries, 219
magnetic therapy for, 387
mind–body relaxation for, 363
Research, doing medical, 101–102, 104
Restless legs syndrome (RLS), and sleep
problems, 24
Retinitis pigmentosa, 41
Retinoid creams, 32, 33–34
Reye's syndrome, aspirin and, 143
Rheumatoid arthritis. *See* Arthritis
Ringing in the ears. *See* Tinnitus
Risk factors for,
breast cancer, 315
cancer, 301
heart disease, 64, 281–282, 315
hepatitis, 79
hip problems, 74–75
kidney stones, 82
skin cancer, 319
stroke, 291–292, 315
Rosacea
alcohol consumption and, 34
treatments, 34

S

Sacred bark (cascara sagrada), risks of, 368
Salt
calcium excretion and, 72
cancer risk from, 297
cravings for, 199–200

DASH diet and, 97–98, 271, 289
hidden salt, 168
hypertension, relationship to, 100, 287–288, 289
kidney stones and, 82, 83
in treatment of fatigue, 14
in treatment of tinnitus, 43–44
as trigger for compulsive eating, 188
Saturated fat, and effect on cataract risk, 40
Saw palmetto, 366
Scams, medical, 123–125
Screening tests, 55, 108–109. *See also* specific conditions
blood tests, 90–91, 117, 281–282, 282–283
computed tomography (CT) scan, 8, 114, 115, 291, 318
digital rectal exam, 312–313
for drug use, suspected, 116
endoscopy, 309
home medical tests, 115–117
interpreting test results, 92–93
magnetic resonance imaging (MRI), 112, 114, 291
magnetic resonance arteriogram (MRA), 227
for menopause, 116
positron emission tomography (PET), 321
stool test, 112
stress test, 113
ultrasound, 316
X-rays, 115
Seasonal affective disorder (SAD)
depression and, 440
insomnia and, 18
Seborrheic dermatitis, 32
Self-healing, 384–385
Self-hypnosis. *See* Hypnosis
Senility. *See* Dementia
Seniors. *See* Aging/antiaging; Longevity
Sensitivity test for allergies, 10
Serotonin, 13, 20, 199, 200
depression and, 439, 440
"serotonin syndrome," 368
sex and, 468
Sex. *See also* Erectile dysfunction; Women
after childbirth, 476
after heart attack, 268–269
alcohol, effect on, 469, 484
aphrodisiacs, natural, 475–476
aromatherapy for stimulation, 396
dangerous natural remedies, 476
foods that boost sex drive, 474, 475, 476
frequency of, 471–473
headache during, 226
and looking younger, 469
making sex exciting, 473–474
making time for, 473
older people and, 406–407, 425, 481
oral sex and yeast infections, 479
premature ejaculation, 485
safe-sex practices and reduced cancer risk, 297
sexual attraction, science of, 467–468
sexual fitness, boosting, 469–471
Shoulders, sore, reflexology for, 388
Side effects of medications, 135

chemotherapy, 307
dangers of not recognizing, 128
effect of timing of medications, 137
eliminating, 129–131
in women, 132
Sigmoidoscopy, 59, 112, 317
Singing, and snoring, 11
Sinusitis
acute, 7–8
antibiotics for, 7–8, 9
causes of, 5–6, 12
chronic, 8
cranial–sacral manipulation for, 375
folk remedies for, 372
humming as treatment for, 9
medications for, 7–8
natural treatments for, 45–46, 396
prevention of, 6
treatment for, 6–7, 7–8, 9
surgery for, 7, 8
symptoms of, 6, 7, 44–45
when not to fly, 463
Skin cancer, 58–59. *See also* Sun exposure
in men, 58–59
myths, 318–320
reducing risk of, 296
risk factors, 319
ultraviolet light and, 298
Skin care. *See also* Skin cancer; Sun exposure
antiaging strategies, 31–32, 33–34
blemishes in adults, 32
cellulite, 32
face, washing, 32
foods for healthy, 32
moisturizing, 34
oily skin, 491
rosacea, 34
self-defense, 35
supplements for, 33
wrinkle-cure diet, 432–433
Skin examination, during physical, 90
Sleep, insufficient. *See also* Fatigue; Insomnia; Snoring
alcohol and, 15
bathroom visits and, 24
effect on calorie consumption, 189
effect on immune system, 1, 2–3, 56
jet lag, 464–465
migraines and, 232
naps and, 15
sex, effect on, 470
sleep apnea, 11, 12, 23, 293, 426
teas as sleep aid, 380
Sleep
best hours for, 22
to burn fat, 205
colors in bedroom, conducive to sleep, 21
sinusitis and, 6–7, 46
temperature for restful sleep, 21
Smoking
acupuncture for, 375
bladder cancer and, 434
caffeine and, 172
calcium excretion and, 72
cancer, risk for, 82, 295, 296, 297

effect on Vitamin C and cataract risk, 39, 40
free radicals and, 33
longevity, effect on, 402
nicotine in other forms, 132, 446
quitting, 446
second-hand, 98
sinusitis and, 6
surgery and, 338–339
as trigger for hunger, 189
Snoring, 426
as cause of fatigue, 12
effect of singing on, 11
Social links and good health, 382. *See also* Sex
in elderly, 402, 404, 412–413
solving problems, 436–437
Soft drinks
calcium excretion and, 72
diet soda and tooth damage, 52
Sore throat
folk remedies for, 371, 374
OTC medications for, 139
vinegar for, 381
Soy products
bone density and, 70, 72, 363
as cancer fighters, 314
for heart health, 271, 280
for longevity, 397, 402
menopause and, 363, 481, 482
sex drive and, 475
as source of calcium, 175
soybeans and risk of breast cancer, 182
Spine alignment exercises, 257–259
Spirituality and religion, 452
Sprains, emergency treatment of, 93
Statins. *See* Cholesterol
Steroids
for arthritis, 237
for asthma, 11
bone density test and, 111
for bunions, 87
dangers of long-term use, 60
effect of timing on side effects, 137–138
for gout, 85
for hay fever, 10
immune system and, 57
for multiple sclerosis, 256
natural alternative to, 150
for sinusitis, 8
St. John's wort
for anxiety, 438
cancer drugs and, 159
for depression, 440
risks of, 369
Stomach cancer, reducing risk of, 297
Stomach problems. *See also* Indigestion
curing naturally, 391–392
flying and, 463
Stomach upset. *See* Indigestion
Stress
antiaging stress busters, 409–410
as cause of acne, 100
as cause of colds, 4
as cause of fatigue, 12

as cause of insomnia, 18
chronic pain and, 250, 259, 260
depletion of B vitamins from, 155
gum disease and, 48
heart attack and, 271–272
immune system, effect on, 1, 57–58
irritable bowel syndrome and, 390
longevity and, 401, 410
management, 56, 363, 449–450, 450–451
memory loss and, 420–421
menopause, and effect of, 481
reduction, to burn fat, 205
skin blemishes and, 32
tests, 59, 64
vitamin C, effect of, on, 156
Stretching exercises, 212–213, 222–223.
    See also specific conditions for walking
    muscles, 224
    yoga poses, 220–221
Stroke
    avoiding, 289–290
    diagnosis test, 290–291
    fast MRI, 291
    gum disease and risk of, 47
    hemorrhagic, defined, 289
    homocysteine levels and, 282, 282–283
    hormone therapy (HT) and, 315
    inflammation and, 75
    ischemic, defined, 289
    migraine and, 293
    risk factors, 291–292
    stents as alternative to surgery, 293
    surgery, artery, 293
    transient ischemic attacks (TIAs), 140, 291
    treatment window, 290
Sty, folk remedy for, 371
Substance P, 242, 250, 253
Sugar. *See also* Foods
    addiction, breaking, 170–171
    alternatives to, 180
    hidden sugar, 168–169
    hyperactivity and, 100
    for mental fatigue, 166
    other names for, 164
Sun exposure. *See also* Skin cancer
    acne medication for sun damage, 433
    clothing, protective, 35, 319
    depression and, 440
    for the elderly, 470
    folk remedies for, 371
    foods for sun protection, 34–35
    St. John's wort and, 438
    sunglasses for eye health, 96
    sunscreen, 31, 33, 35, 296, 318–319
    vinegar for sunburn relief, 381
    for vitamin D, 153–154
Supplements, 55, 94–95, 149, 431. *See also*
    Alternative medicine; Calcium;
        Homeopathic remedies; Vitamin C;
        Vitamin D; Vitamin E
    B vitamins, 154–156
    checking quality of, 146–147
    chromium picolinate, dangers of, 161
    combining with drugs, 128–129, 145–147,
        159
    disintegration standards, 151

ephedra, dangers of, 160
fish oil supplements, dangers of, 161
glucomannan, 150
natural vs. synthetic, 100
overdosing, 156, 158–159, 159
performance-enhancing, 149–150
potassium, food sources of, 160
timing of, 150–151
Surgery. *See also* Hospital stays and
    specific condition
    albumin levels test, 335
    alternatives to, 335–337
    anesthesia, 339–340, 341
    antibiotics before, 342
    artery-clearing, 293
    blood, reusing patient's, 340
    children and, 339
    choosing a surgeon, 328–329
    deep relaxation, value of, 337
    hypnosis, 345
    infection from, 342
    in-office, 343
    laparoscopic, 324
    marking body parts, 338
    positive visualization, value of,
        337–338
    recent, and air travel, 462
    recovering faster, 344–346
    rehabilitation program, 343–344
    second opinions, importance of, 109–110,
        334–335
    self-hypnosis, before surgery, 345
    smoking and, 338–339
    waking up during, 340
    for weight-loss, 190–191
    what to ask, 323–325
Swimmer's ear, folk remedies for, 371, 373
Syndrome X. *See* Insulin resistance

T

Tanning beds, as treatment for psoriasis, 37
Tea
    for arthritis, 246
    for bone density, 176
    as disease fighter, 176–177, 430
    guarana, to burn fat, 204
    healing teas, 379–380
    for immune system, 176
    longevity and, 402
Teeth. *See also* Cavities; Gum disease;
    Water, fluoridated
    fillings, silver, 50
    osteoporosis and, 52
    relaxing at dentist's office, 51
    risks of, 369
    sensitive, 52
    sugar-free soda and, 52
    tea to prevent cavities, 177
    toothache, folk remedy for, 374
    whitening, 50–51
Temporomandibular joint (TMJ)
    syndrome, cranial–sacral manipulation
        for, 375
Tendinitis. *See* Knee injuries
Tennis elbow, magnetic therapy for, 387
Tension headaches. *See* Headaches

Testicle and rectal exam, 90
Testosterone
    bone maintenance and, 59
    cancer treatments and, 311
    as cause of acne, 100
    low levels of, 61, 483
    lust and, 467
    in patch form, 132
    supplements for erectile dysfunction,
        406–407
    testosterone replacement therapy, 398,
        407–408, 483
Test results, interpreting, 92–93
Tests. *See* Screening tests
Thyroid
    disease, 67–68, 198
    foods for, 68
    as part of physical exam, 90
    screening test for hypothyroidism, 67
Ticks and mosquitoes, avoiding, 29
Tinnitus
    causes, 43
    cranial–sacral manipulation for, 375
    natural treatment, 44
    treatment, 43–44
Toenails. *See* Feet
Toxins
    in the body, 13–14, 33
    chemotherapy, detoxifying during,
        307
    detoxifying, 383
Tranquilizers, misprescription of, 131
Trans fats, 164, 280
    hidden, 169
    labeling requirement, 165
Transient ischemic attacks (TIAs). *See*
    Stroke
Traveling. *See also* Medical emergencies
    overseas
    emergency phone number, in Europe,
        459
    illness after, 466
    pre-existing medical conditions, 459–460
    smoggiest cities, 461
    stocking up on prescription drugs, 460
    travel-medicine kit, 459
    in the tropics, 461
Tretinoin, 34–34
Trigger point injections, 253
Triglycerides
    heart disease and, 272–273, 279
    syndrome X and, 273–275
Turmeric, 367

U

UCR ("usual, customary and reasonable")
    charges, 356–357
Ulcers
    dosages of drugs for, 130
    exercises for, 219
    natural remedies for, 184
    to prevent, 28
Ultraviolet (UV) light
    cancer risk of, 298
    cataracts and, 39
    drugs and, 147

exposure, 31, 33, 318
sunglasses as protection, 96
as treatment for psoriasis, 36
Upset stomach. *See* Indigestion
Uric acid, 82
as cause of gout, 84
Urinary tract infections (UTIs), 434
natural remedies for, 477
risk of kidney stones and, 82, 83
screening test for, 117
Urinating during night, 24
Urine, dark or discolored, 434
Uterine cancer, reducing risk of, 296
Uterine prolapse, alternatives treatments, 479

V

Vacations. *See also* Medical emergencies
overseas; Traveling
cruises, viral illness on, 466
getting sick after, 466
getting sick during, 460
Vaginal infections, natural remedies for, 477
Varicose veins
butcher's broom for, 364
endovenous radio-frequency vein
closure, 25
Vasectomies, 485–486
Vegetables
to avoid chronic diseases, 428–430
for bone strength, 69–71
dangers of some, 167–168
disease fighters, 174–175
energy levels and, 15
ethylene gas, producers of, 178
highest in phytochemicals, 1
organic, 1–2
for preventing cataracts, 39
recipes, 70
for sun protection, 34–35
washing, 2, 80, 178
Vegetarian meals, 55, 180, 276
to avoid chronic diseases, 428–430
longevity and, 401–402
Veterans' Administration, patients' access
to medical records, 105
Vinegar for common ailments, 380–381
Viruses
antibiotics and, 100, 144
cruises, viral illness on, 466
herbs for, 364, 366
Vision. *See also* Cataracts
aspirin and, 140
bifocals, 37
bilberry for vision disorders, 41, 365
blindness, stem-cell transplants for, 42
disturbances, 54–55
eyestrain, reflexology for, 387
glaucoma, 40–41, 365
laser eye surgery (LASIK), 38–39
loss from osteoporosis drugs, 73
macular degeneration, 41, 365, 431
obesity and blindness, 42
retinitis pigmentosa (RP), 41
Vitamin A

for immune system, 57
overdosing danger, 159
for thyroid health, 68
Vitamin C
for antiaging, 400
as antioxidant, 157
for arthritis, 246
effect on cataract risk, 39, 40
effect on colds, 4
effect on stool test, 116
effect on stress, 156
for gum health, 48
for longevity, 398
to lower cholesterol, 276
for muscles and tendons, 74
omega-3 fatty acids and, 153
in orange juice, 156
for thyroid health, 68
for urinary tract infections, 434–435
Vitamin D, 153–154
for arthritis, 246
role in calcium absorption, 154
Vitamin E, 149
Alzheimer's, role in preventing, 418
for antiaging, 400
as antioxidant, 157
cataracts and, 39
effect on cholesterol deposits, 95, 276
heart attack recovery, role in, 270
for heart protection, 285
for immune system, 57
for longevity, 398
omega-3 fatty acids and, 153
to prevent cancer, 82
for thyroid health, 68
Vitamin supplements. *See* Supplements or
specific vitamins
Vocal cord dysfunction (VCD), 11
Vomiting
with abdominal distress, 53–54
with headache, 54

W

Waist size and relation to heart disease
risk, 275
Walking. *See* Exercise
Warts, duct tape as cure for, 27
Water
for arthritis pain, 239
bladder and, 434
to burn fat, 205
cataracts and, 40
dehydration when traveling, 461
dieting, role in, 186, 188–189
for eye health, 96
fluoridated, 49–50
for headaches, 255
immune system and, 2
importance of, in weight control, 195
kidney stones and, 82, 83
nighttime leg cramps and, 24, 25
to prevent gout, 85
purification systems, 179
reminder system, 430–431
safety of tap, 178–179

skin care and, 32
sinusitis and, 8
to treat fatigue, 13, 16
for wrinkles, 433
Weight. *See also* Dieting; Obesity
appetite control with aromatherapy, 396
body mass index, 42, 190
cancer risk and, 295, 296
control and hypothyroidism, 67–68
"fat but fit," 211
gain and fatigue, 16
hip problems and, 73
hypnosis for overeating, 375
longevity and, 402, 410
loss and arthritis, 239
loss and blood pressure, 98, 288, 289
loss, exercise for, 187
loss and gout, 85
loss, unexplained, 54
reduced-fat foods and weight gain, 202
weight gain, hidden causes, 189–190,
198–199
weight-gain triggers, 188–189
Wine
dangers of, 167
effect on colds of, 3
Women. *See also* Menopause;
Menstruation; Pregnancy; Premenstrual
syndrome (PMS)
accidental addiction in elderly, 427–428
alcohol and effect on breast cancer risk
in, 301
coronary bypass surgery in, 283
feminine itching, 487
gender-specific medicine, 58–60
health problems of, natural remedies
for, 477
hyperparathyroidism and, 441
hysterectomy, alternatives to, 478–479
lung cancer, risk of, in, 300
sexual problems in older women, 406,
476, 484–485
side effects of medications in, 132
Wood dust, as carcinogen, 298
Wounds
cleaners, 27
emergency treatment of, 93
Reiki for healing, 363
vinegar as disinfectant, 380
Wrinkles. *See* Skin care

X

X-rays. *See* Screening tests

Y

Yeast infections
dangers of self-diagnosis, 479
natural remedies for, 477, 487
oral sex and, 479
OTC medications for, 140, 487
Yoga poses, 220–221
Yogurt for allergies, 181